# Muslims of Medieval Latin Christendom, *c.* 1050–1614



In the face of crusades, conversions, and expulsions, Muslims and their communities survived to thrive for over 500 years in medieval Europe. This comprehensive new study explores how the presence of Islamic minorities transformed Europe in everything from architecture to cooking, literature to science, and served as a stimulus for Christian society to define itself. Combining a series of regional studies, Brian Catlos compares the varied experiences of Muslims across Iberia, Southern Italy, the Crusader Kingdoms, and Hungary to examine those ideologies that informed their experiences, their place in society, and their sense of themselves as Muslims and as members of multi-confessional societies. This is a pioneering new narrative of the history of medieval and early modern Europe from the perspective of Islamic minorities; one which is not, as we might first assume, driven by ideology, isolation, and decline, but instead one in which successful communities persisted because they remained actively integrated within the larger Christian and Jewish societies in which they lived.

BRIAN CATLOS is Associate Professor of Religious Studies at the University of Colorado at Boulder and Research Associate in Humanities at the University of California Santa Cruz.

# Muslims of Medieval Latin Christendom, *c.* 1050–1614

Brian A. Catlos

*University of Colorado at Boulder*
*University of California, Santa Cruz*

CAMBRIDGE
UNIVERSITY PRESS

**CAMBRIDGE**
**UNIVERSITY PRESS**

University Printing House, Cambridge CB2 8BS, United Kingdom

Cambridge University Press is part of the University of Cambridge.

It furthers the University's mission by disseminating knowledge in the pursuit of education, learning and research at the highest international levels of excellence.

www.cambridge.org
Information on this title: www.cambridge.org/9780521717908



First published 2014
First paperback edition 2015

*A catalogue record for this publication is available from the British Library*

*Library of Congress Cataloguing in Publication data*
Catlos, Brian A.
Muslims of Latin Christendom, ca. 1050–1614 / Brian Catlos, University of Colorado at Boulder, University of California, Santa Cruz.
pages cm.
ISBN 978-0-521-88939-1 (hardback)
1. Muslims – Europe – History – To 1500. 2. Arabs – Europe – History – To 1500. 3. Europe – Civilization – Arab influences. 4. Europe – Civilization – Middle Eastern influences. 5. Europe – Civilization – Islamic influences. I. Title.
BP65.A1C38 2014
940.0880297–dc23
2013021433

ISBN 978-0-521-88993-1 Hardback
ISBN 978-0-521-71790-8 Paperback

For Wadjih F. al-Hamwi

أستاذي،

صديقي،

أخي و...

أبي

# Contents

# Illustrations

# Maps



Links to related illustrations, documents, and maps can be found at www.muslimsofmedievallatinchristendom.info.

# Preface

In the popular imagination medieval Europe is a land defined by Christian religion and culture, inhabited also by a small, persecuted Jewish minority, but which was essentially uniform in terms of religious identity. Muslims, on the other hand, are typically imagined as having constituted a foreign "other," living in an Islamic world separated from what is often referred to as "the West" by a well-defined frontier marked by ideological opposition and political violence – Crusade and *jihād*. In this view, these worlds are seen as two self-contained and largely homogenous and incompatible components of an oppositional binary, as if they were two personalities, locked in what many would see as a timeless struggle – a "clash of civilizations" rooted in the fundamental, immutable, and irreconcilable differences believed to underlie their two cultures. On the other hand, relatively few outside of the Academy are aware that Islamic communities in fact comprised *part* of medieval European society, and that from the eleventh century through to the seventeenth century – beyond what is traditionally regarded as the end of the Middle Ages – populations of free Muslim subjects lived within the bounds of Western Christendom, or that Muslim slaves and travelers were a common fixture of European society long before the opening of the Atlantic world.

In fact, the Muslims of medieval Europe included substantial communities scattered right across the Latin-dominated Mediterranean, from the Atlantic coast to the Transjordan, as well as in Central and Eastern Europe. In some areas they survived only for a century or two, while in others they persevered for well over five hundred years. They did not live as isolated enclaves, they were not uniformly poor, and were not necessarily subject to systematic repression; rather, they comprised diverse communities and dynamic societies that played an important role in the formation of what would eventually emerge a modern European culture and society. This book sets out to survey the history of the Muslims of Latin Christendom, examining the experience of the various regional communities, and the circumstances that contributed both to their survival and to their demise. It aims also to investigate the relations of the

Muslims, Christians (and Jews) who lived in medieval Europe in terms of how they imagined each other, how they structured their relationships, how they interacted politically, economically, culturally, and socially, and the impact they had on the development of European culture and society.

What is revealed is a tremendous variety of experience, both in terms of the internal life of these communities, their integration with the Christians under whose domination they lived, and their capacity to survive and persist. It reflects a history rich in possibilities, and shows that their survival and demise cannot simply be ascribed to the ideological conditions or changing religious culture of pre-modern Europe. Over the course of this study it will become clear that a whole range of factors, both local and regional, pragmatic and idealistic, contributed to their experience – a fact that may carry valuable lessons for our understanding of religious and cultural diversity, both in the world of the Middle Ages and in the world of today.

"History," the saying goes, "is written by the winners." If so, then this is a book about "the losers." It is a book about the conquered, rather than the conquerors, about those who submitted, rather than those who triumphed. It is about communities and individuals who chose to stay in their ancestral lands and live under the regime of rulers and cultures whom they considered to be illegitimate, and who considered them, at best, to be infidels, and, at worst, agents of the devil; who chose to put their own salvation and the fate of their descendants in jeopardy; and who chose to live as a subjugated, second-class people, in a world in which it was most certainly not held to be self-evidently true that all men were equal or that they had certain unalienable rights. This is a book about the Muslims of Latin Christendom: an ethno-religious minority that comprised a significant proportion of the population of the Christian lands of the Mediterranean in the Middle Ages, and yet whose existence has been all but forgotten outside scholarly circles and the campaigns of local Spanish tourism boards.

Why is this case? It is not because there were few of them. In 1609, when the expulsion of the converted Christian descendants of the last Muslims of Spain was undertaken, over 300,000 were forced from their native lands into foreign exile – roughly twenty times the number of Spanish Jews who chose expulsion over conversion in 1492. A hundred and twenty years earlier Portugal's Muslims had been expelled. It is not because it was specifically a Spanish problem. Significant communities existed also in Southern Italy, the Holy Land, and Hungary, and Muslim captives and slaves were sold and sent to the corners of Christendom. It is hardly a question of impact. Contact with Muslims and the Islamic world was one of the essential forces that shaped the European culture that emerged out of Latin Christendom. The existence of significant Muslim minorities within this society was a powerful engine of acculturation, adaptation, and innovation – a challenge and a stimulus for the Christians under whom they lived.

The historical obscurity of these Muslim minorities is due to two factors. The first relates to sources. It is indeed the case, for the most part, that "the winners" – consciously or not – determine the material that remains for future historians to use. Leaving aside the vicissitudes of war, fire, and natural disasters, the records and artifacts that survive the passing of ages are – generally speaking – those that are regarded as having some value and use, or a continuing relevance. In the centuries that passed since the disappearance of these communities, relatively few of the documents relating to the Muslims of Latin Christendom passed those tests, and those that did tended to be concentrated in a few specific regions. The second issue is scholarly bias and concern. Until the 1970s and the explosion of research relating to groups that had hitherto been considered marginal to the grand historical narrative, such as peasants, women, heretics, few historians perceived the subject Muslim communities as being a worthy object of historical inquiry.

Since then, however, there has been an flurry of academic interest, and a tremendous volume of historical research has been carried out on Italy and the Spanish kingdoms (quite a bit less on the Muslim communities of the Frankish East and Hungary). Both in Italy, and Spain – where Islamic society persevered beyond the Middle Ages – the impact of the Muslim past was undeniable: it left its imprint on language, food, popular culture, literature, architecture, and in a rich historical record. This has provided material for North American, British, French, and – most of all – Spanish historians to produce countless monographs, journal articles, and papers, examining every imaginable aspect of subject Muslim (*mudéjar*) history. It is this great output of scholarly work that has made the present study both possible and necessary. The overwhelming majority of the studies that have been carried out focus on specific communities, towns, regions, or kingdoms, or on specific themes or perspectives, and most are restricted to a rather narrow period of time. This has provided us with a means for understanding *mudéjar* society in rich detail, but has made it difficult to rise above the particularities of concrete communities and to discern larger patterns in their history. No scholarly monograph has undertaken to analyze the subject Muslim communities of Latin Christendom as a phenomenon, or has taken a broadly inclusive, comparative approach to the subject.

This is altogether understandable, given the challenges such a project presents. These communities were scattered across the breadth of the

Latin lands, and followed distinct historical trajectories in each region. The availability and nature of sources vary dramatically from place to place and over time, making comparison difficult, and obscuring overarching narratives and common trends. Compounding this is the tendency for historical studies of these communities to be burdened by the agendas of the historians who have written them – agendas that reflect a whole range of modern ideological positions relating to the relationship of Christianity and Islam, the nature of ethno-religious culture and identity, and the place of Muslims in the national identities of European countries. Nevertheless, it is precisely the aim of the present study to provide such an analysis.

The first part of the book, "Static diasporas: Muslim communities of Latin Christendom," presents a historical narrative of the Muslim minorities from the mid eleventh century through to the beginning of the sixteenth – a political history of a people with no great heroic figures, no long-ruling dynasties, and no independent, sovereign territory. The second part, "Living in sin: Islamicate society under Latin dominion," adopts a thematic approach, and analyzes the ideological structures, administrative institutions, and quotidian relationships that gave shape to subject Muslim society and the *mudéjar* experience under Christian rule. The aim is to present a synthesis – an assessment of the history of the Muslim subjects of pre-modern Europe and of their relations with the Christian majority alongside whom they lived. It endeavors to propose a history of Christian domination of Islamic communities and the Muslim response to that domination, understood as much as possible from the perspective of those communities themselves. Hence, it is not a book about "European perceptions" of Islam, or Orientalism. It is not a book about Christian theological prejudices, or Crusade. It is not a book about the impact of Islam on the development of the West. And it is not a book about the brutality of Western colonial violence, or apparatuses of ethnic and religious oppression – although all of these matters necessarily enter into the discussion. Rather, it is a book about how subject communities persevered through centuries of domination, and the effect this had on them and on the societies in which they lived. Most significantly, perhaps, it presents a history that has not, up to this point, been accessible as a whole to scholars and students, and so constitutes a glimpse of a hitherto under-illuminated dimension of the complex world of the medieval past – a history of peoples who, while largely voiceless, were far from insignificant. It does not pretend to be exhaustive, and cannot aspire to be complete; its aim is to present the major trends and the most significant forces that shaped this encounter between the Islamic and Christian worlds, and to serve as a digest of present research and a starting point for further reading.

# Acknowledgements

To say that this is a book that owes an immense debt to countless scholars is no hollow conceit. Faced with the enormous work of my colleagues and those who have gone before us, the research and writing became at once a rich pleasure and an exercise in humility – the more I learned, the more I was reminded of how little I knew. I regret that the notes and bibliography appended to this volume give only a suggestion of the scholarship that has contributed to this study, but the practical exigencies of publication make it inevitable that much would go unacknowledged. Nevertheless, a number of institutions and individuals deserve to be thanked directly and by name; with the qualification that any shortcomings of this study are, of course, my own.

First I would like to thank Núria Silleras-Fernández, who not only endured the writing of this book at close quarters, but read drafts and provided critical advice throughout. My editors at Cambridge, Michael Watson and Elizabeth Friend-Smith, are to be credited for their support (and patience!). The University of California Santa Cruz supported this project with a series of faculty research grants, and a fellowship "top up" from the Humanities Division, as did the University of California Office of the President, indirectly, through the Mediterranean Studies Multi-Campus Research Project. My colleagues in the History and Literature departments at UCSC, notably Gail Hershatter and Sharon Kinoshita, also deserve thanks for their mentorship and advice. The National Endowment for the Humanities provided a Faculty Research Fellowship and funding for three Summer Institutes for College and University Professors that I co-directed, in which I had a chance to discuss my work with scholars from across the USA. Thanks are due especially to David Abulafia, David Nirenberg and Paul Freedman for the many letters of reference they have written me in support of this project. The Institució Milà i Fontanals (Consejo Superior de Investigaciones Científicas) in Barcelona has been my second academic home for some fifteen years. The director, Luís Calvo, and colleagues including Maria Teresa Ferrer i Mallol, Josefina Mutgé, and Roser Salicrú i Lluch, have been critical in my development as a scholar, and have provided me with a stimulating environment to work in during the summer months. It has been a pleasure to participate in a series of research projects at the IMF (currently, Dr. Salicrú's Consolidated Research Group 2009-SGR-1452). The archivists and staff at the Arxiu de la Corona d'Aragó have also been instrumental; special thanks are due to the Director, Carlos López, and to Albert Torra. I owe a debt also to many Spanish scholars, but I should specifically thank Jaume Riera i Sans, Carlos Laliena Corbera, Esteban Sarasa Sánchez, and Josep Torró i Abad. I had the privilege of studying under J. N. Hillgarth at Toronto; his rigor and generosity remain an inspiration.

Some of the many others whom I should credit either for their ongoing support, for assisting with specific queries and general advice, or for generously sharing their work, include: Filomena Barros, Simon Barton, Joshua Birk, Richard Cassidy, Pete Catlos (my brother), O. Remie Constable, Fred Denny, Ana Echevarría Arsuaga, Paul Cobb, Monica Green, Fabiana Guillén Diop, David Freidenreich, Ángel Galán Sánchez, Mercedes García-Arenal, Claire Gilbert, L. P. Harvey, Peregrine Horden, Paul Hyams, Benjamin Z. Kedar, József Laszlovszky, Karla Mallette, Mark Meyerson, Jean-Pierre Molénat, Lisa Nielson, Gabriel Rota, Flocell Sabaté i Currell, Belén Vicéns Sáiz, Stefan Stantchev, Miguel Torrens, Robin Vose, David Wacks, Gerard Wiegers, and especially, Andrew Watson, dissertation supervisor, friend, and careful reader. My graduate student, Aaron Stamper, assisted with the bibliography and index and with other assorted queries. I should also thank my colleagues, the Department of Religious Studies and the College of Arts and Sciences of the University of Colorado at Boulder (my new academic home), all of whom have been extremely welcoming and supportive, and have provided an ideal environment for finishing this project. The excellent work of the staff of the Inter-Library Loan Service at Norlin Library (University of Colorado at Boulder) was also instrumental. Finally, Bar Bona Sort, in carrer Carders, Barcelona, provided crucial support over the course of several summers in the form of dependable, highspeed wi-fi, and industrial-strength *mojitos*; Paul's Coffee Shop in Louisville, Colorado, fueled me with *americanos*. If I have left anyone out, please excuse the oversight.

# Abbreviations

| | |
|---|---|
| ACA | Arxiu de la Corona d'Aragó (Barcelona) |
| Ar. | Arabic |
| ARP | Arxiu del Reial Patrimoni |
| *C.* | *cancillería* |
| *carp.* | *carpeta* |
| Cat. | Catalan |
| Cast. | Castilian |
| CODOIN | P. de Bofarull y Mascaró, *et al.* (eds.), *Colección de documentos inéditos de la Corona de Aragón* (Barcelona: José Eusebio Montfort, 1847–1910). |
| CSIC | Consejo Superior de Investigaciones Científicas/Consell Superior d'Investigacions Científiques |
| Lat. | Latin |
| MR | Mestre Racional |
| PCG | Menéndez Pidal, Ramón (ed.), *Primera crònica general de España* (Madrid: Gredos, 1977). |
| *pergs.* | *pergamins* |
| Port. | Portuguese |
| Rom. | Romance |

# Note on usage

All dates provided within the book are Common Era (CE) unless otherwise noted. Place-names are given in the modern form used by their native inhabitants, with the exception of some for which the current English name is more recognizable (e.g. "Mecca," not "Makka"). For sites that were formerly under Islamic rule the Arabic name is also provided at the first instance of each. I have eschewed the use of "Spain" for the period prior to the Hapsburg era, for the "Iberian Peninsula," or simply "Iberia." "Spain" (*Hispania*) was imagined as a unity only in certain specific contexts, was of variable meaning, and tended, in any case, to be expressed as often as not in the plural as "the Spains," or "all the Spains" (as in *Imperator totius Hispaniae*).

The transliteration system used for Arabic conforms to standard academic use. Technical terms relating to Arabo-Islamic culture are normally given in Arabic and pluralized in Arabic, with exceptions made occasionally for words that have passed into the English lexicon, or for the sake of prose style (even sometimes at the cost of consistency). Definite articles are sometimes added even when technically unnecessary (e.g. "the *dār al-Islām*"). Terms in Latin and other languages are treated similarly. In excerpts from documents, the words *Sarracenus*, *Moro*, *Agarenus*, and the various other epithets are translated simply as "Muslim," except in rare cases where a pejorative sense was clearly intended, or the terminology itself is discussed.

Personal names occur in a number of forms. Normally, the names of individuals are given in the form in which they occur in the primary sources, with the exception of well-known personalities, whose names may appear in English or whatever language they are normally expressed in. The names of individual subject Muslims usually appear in a Latinate/Romance form, even if corrupted. The names of rulers and other major personalities are given in the form corresponding to the language of the principality they ruled over (e.g. "Alfonso" in Castile, "Afonso" in Portugal, "Alfons" in the Crown of Aragon). The rulers of Norman Sicily and the Crusader Levant are given in English (e.g. "William II," not “Guilelmus II”), for the sake of prose style, and because there was no singular contemporary vernacular tradition which determined their form. The names of emperors and popes are given in English. Regnal years are provided where appropriate. Locative surnames are sometimes translated, sometimes not (e.g. Bernard of Sahagún, but Sibila d’Acerra). Honorifics are usually given in English, except for Muslim rulers, who are better known by the Arabic versions.

# Introduction
# Islam and Latin Christendom to 1050

When the news reached Ṭāriq that Roderic was near, he rose up before his comrades, he praised and extolled God, and afterwards incited the people to the *jihād*, and made them crave martyrdom. Then, he said, "O People! To where will you flee with the sea behind you and the enemy before you? All that remains, by God, is resolve and perseverance. Verily, by truth, I shall be he who meets this tyrant myself, and will not waiver until I reach him or die first in the attempt!"
(ʿAbd al-Malik b. Ḥabīb, the pre-battle harangue of Ṭāriq b. Ziyād (790–852)[1])

Contemporaries might be forgiven for regarding the meteoric rise of Islam in the seventh century as either miraculous or diabolical. Within the space of less than a century a people regarded as uncivilized and illiterate raiders – *sarakenoi* or *agarenoi* – would bring down the Persian Empire, conquer some of Byzantium's richest provinces, and extend their rule across the southern shore of the Mediterranean and over the Tigris and Euphrates to the banks of the Indus.[2] This was a conquest borne in part out of opportunity – the two great empires were exhausted after decades of struggle and plague, and their subjects dissatisfied and

[1] From the *Kitāb al-Tāʾrikh* ("History Book"), O. Herrero Soto, "La arenga de Tariq b. Ziyad," p. 55. Ṭāriq led the invasion force that defeated Roderic, king of the Visigoths, at Wādī Lakku (Guadalete) in 711.

[2] "Hagarene" is not a reference to Hagar, the concubine of Abraham, as often presumed, but to *muhajirūn*, derived from *hijra*, meaning "a striving" or "going out." "Saracen" derives not from Abraham's wife, Sarah, another common assumption, but from either *sharqiyyin* ("Easterners"), or *saraqat* ("raiders"). By the fifth century Arabs were identified as "Ishmaelites" in Jewish writings, and in the early centuries of Islam the northern tribes of Arabia constructed geneaologies linking them to ʾAdnān, the son of Ishmael (Ismāʿil); for Christian writers "Hagarene" became a synonym of "Muslim." Christian chroniclers also referred to Muslims as "Moabites," "Chaldeans," and other Biblical peoples who were rivals of the Israelites. "Maurus" or "moro" was current in the Iberian Peninsula from the seventh century. Although some Christian writers associated certain of these names with specific ethnic groups (e.g. Berbers, or Persians), others used them interchangeably. The terms "Arab" and "Turk" were used somewhat more consistently, but they too were often simply generic synonyms for "Muslim." See F. Donner, *Muhammad and the Believers*, p. 86; I. Shahîd, *Rome and the Arabs*, pp. 130–38; I. Ephʾal, "'Ishmael' and 'Arab(s)'," pp. 233–34.

disillusioned. But it was also fruit of a religious revolution that had transformed Arabic society, galvanizing the divided nomadic tribes of the peninsula and aligning their ambitions with those of the local, sedentary, commercial elite. Islam was styled as the perfection of the faith of Abraham, the continuation of Judaism and Christianity revealed to the Prophet Muḥammad in Arabic. It embodied a moral certainty and universal mission typical of theologies of liberation, from Christianity to Capitalism, and its adherents imagined themselves as obliged by God not only to observe its precepts, but to extend the opportunity to all men to live in a just, divinely ordered world – whether by conviction or force. Like all successful revolutions it was one in which the higher moral good seamlessly coincided with the personal "goods" of those who led it.

Hence, when Ṭāriq b. Ziyād (if he ever existed) – the Berber client of Mūsā b. Nuṣayr, the Arab governor of Ifrīqiya – set out to topple Roderic (710–12), the weak Visigothic King of Spain, he did it with one eye towards Heaven and the other on the bottom line. The emergence of the Muslim Arabs and their irruption into the Romano-Persian world did not have the aim of destroying the old order, but of taking control of it. It was a movement for which the groundwork had been laid in centuries previous, as Arab kingdoms flowered along the peripheries of the two empires, warrior clans served as clients and proxies in the imperial wars, and settlers from the peninsula ranged northwards into Syria and Mesopotamia. The Arabs were in fact only the latest iteration of the "barbarian" peoples that had invaded and infiltrated the Persian and Roman worlds for centuries. What set them apart was not only their success, but the fact that they would not be subsumed religiously, linguistically, or culturally by the peoples they conquered.

In the West, *Hispania* was effectively the end of the line for the Muslims; even with the reinforcements provided by the pagan Berbers who converted to Islam (often merely nominally) and swelled the ranks of the victors, the Arab-led forces were overstretched. As they pushed forward, the obligation to leave even a skeleton garrison in conquered territories depleted the Muslims' numbers, and led to the risk of revolt. Still, once they had overrun the peninsula, they advanced over the Pyrenees and into the vacuum left in Septimania by the defeat of the Visigoths. But southern Gaul was not Egypt or Persia – it was a poor, depopulated land with little to offer the conquerors. As the Muslims raided further into the inhospitable Frankish north, the risks grew and the returns diminished. When in 732 a raiding party led by ʿAbd al-Raḥmān al-Ghāfiqī, the Governor of al-Andalus, set out to sack the cathedral of Tours, its defeat by the Merovingian palace mayor, Charles

Martel, claimed the lives of many Muslim warriors, including the governor himself. But this battle, inflated to epic proportions by Gibbon and his modern imitators, did not signal the salvation of "Europe" from the ambitions of a ravenous Islam; rather it heralded the subjugation of Aquitaine and the usurpation of the Frankish throne by Martel. There was not yet a "Europe" to covet or conquer, and what there was was too underdeveloped and poor to tempt the Muslims. The Oxford University that Gibbons fantasized might have fallen prey to that "circumcised people" did not yet exist, and London was, as of yet, nothing more than a huddle of shacks scattered among dilapidated Roman ruins.[3] Sporadic Muslim raids would continue on the continent through the 900s, but there was nothing of sufficient value in Frankish Europe to merit a campaign of conquest. Constantinople, by contrast, was a wealthy prize close at hand, but the last serious attempt by the Arabs to conquer it had taken place in 718.

Nor was the establishment of Islamic dominion over the Mediterranean the interruption of Western history that historians since Pirenne have often imagined it.[4] The collapse of the world of Antiquity provoked the expansion of the Muslim Arabs, not the reverse. Quite to the contrary, the establishment of *pax Islamica* re-established Mediterranean unity and trade, and set the course for the re-emergence of wealthy urbane societies here. It was not a unity derived from a functioning imperial authority, as had been the case with Rome; rather, Islamic unity was derived from the use of a common language, a common religio-intellectual framework, compatible institutions, and a moral and social consensus that emerged organically out of the overlapping economic and political relationships that held the *dār al-Islām* – the "abode" or "world of Islam" – together. Hence, when the Umayyad Caliphate was overthrown in the mid eighth century, and when in the early 900s two rival Caliphates challenged the authority of the ʿAbbāsids of Persia, Islamic civilization did not collapse – paradoxically, it was strengthened by its disunity and diversity.

[3] Gibbons summed up Martel's accomplishment as follows:

> A victorious line of march had been prolonged above a thousand miles from the rock of Gibraltar to the banks of the Loire; the repetition of an equal space would have carried the Saracens to the confines of Poland and the Highlands of Scotland; the Rhine is not more impassable than the Nile or the Euphrates, and the Arabian fleet might have sailed without a naval combat to the mouth of the Thames. Perhaps the interpretation of the Koran would be taught in the schools of Oxford, and her pulpits might demonstrate to a circumcised people the sanctity and truth of the revelation of Muhammed ... (E. Gibbon, *The Decline and Fall of the Roman Empire*, vol. v, p. 389)

[4] This was the thesis of H. Pirenne's *Mohammed and Charlemagne*.

## *Latin Christendom and Islam to 1000* CE

Having accomplished in [Gascony] whatever opportunity and usefulness dictated [Charlemagne] decided to contest the difficulty of the Pyrenees mountains, go to Spain, and with Christ's aid bring help to the Church, which was laboring under the extremely hard yoke of the Saracens. ("The Astronomer," *Vita Hludovici Imperatoris* (*c.* 840)[5])

Nor did "Christian Europe" conceive of Islam and the Muslims as constituting an existential threat. Indeed, neither the kings nor the Church of the Latin West gave much consideration at all to Islam prior to the mid eleventh century. Obviously, there was an awareness that Christian *Hispania* had been conquered, and that the Holy Land was under the rule of "pagans." The raiding of "Saracens" along the Mediterranean coasts and their occasional incursions deep into the Frankish hinterland were cause for alarm, but beyond the Iberian Peninsula, Muslims remained for the most part a vague and distant concern. In the 800s the storied ʿAbbāsid Caliph, Hārūn al-Rashīd (766–809), and the Emperor Charlemagne (768/800–14) would exchange embassies and gifts, and in the 900s the Umayyad Caliph of Cordoba (Qurṭuba), ʿAbd al-Raḥmān III (912/929–61), and the Emperor Otto the Great (936/62–73) could rattle sabers at each other – but all to little effect. For the rulers of Latin Christendom there were more pressing threats closer to home: the pagan Norsemen, the Magyars, and their own perennially rebellious aristocracies.

Even the Latin Church, localized, institutionally primitive, and dogmatically underdeveloped, had scarcely any sense of who these infidels were that had risen up in Arabia and had brought so much of Christendom under their dominion. The papacy – only tentatively emerging as a functioning authority in the western lands – was focused on the conversion of European pagans, the proprietary attitudes of the landed nobility, the worldly corruption of it own clergy, the specter of Judaism, and the establishment of its independence from the authority of the Byzantine emperors. Islam remained a distant and vague abstraction. Latin Christianity itself was only groping towards self-realization and self-definition.

Real engagement with the *dār al-Islām* was established gradually as the Christians of the northern shores of the Mediterranean intruded into and were drawn into the commercial, intellectual, and cultural milieux of a prosperous and populated Islamic world that stretched from the Pillars of Hercules to the remote passes of Bactria and beyond the Horn of Africa.

[5] "The Life of Emperor Louis," pp. 226–302, in T. Noble, *Charlemagne and Louis the Pious*, p. 229.

The export of slaves, timber, and salt, and the ingress of silk, spices, and gold introduced Latin Europeans to the wealth and possibilities that this world embodied precisely at the time that theirs was beginning to stabilize, consolidate, and to develop the infrastructure and markets that would create, from the year 1000 forward, both the potential for engagement with, and the conditions for expansion into, an increasingly fragmented and vulnerable Islamic Mediterranean.

While there was certainly a sense that the Islamic world was a distinct place from Christendom, and Islam a rival of Christianity, the closer one approached the supposed frontier, the more elusive it became. Local princes and potentates made alliances, fought against each other, and even intermarried, with little regard for their religious identity. Common folk innocently and intuitively mixed the religious and magical beliefs they were exposed to in ways that caused no small amount of consternation to the arbiters of orthodoxy among them. Even the clergy who served them were often woefully unfamiliar with their own religious dogma. On the other hand, by the 1050s Latin pilgrims, both clergy and lay, were journeying in increasing numbers either to the Holy Land, in the name of redemption, or to al-Andalus in search of knowledge, and were becoming aware in a personal sense of the tremendous wealth and complexity of the *dār al-Islām*. Through all of this the Latin approach to the Muslim world remained open, pragmatic, and largely unburdened by ideology. Even Charlemagne, whose ancestor, Charles Martel, has been risibly credited with stopping the Muslim conquest of "Europe," and whose own campaigns on his southern frontier were framed in terms of religious struggle, regarded Muslim princes as his legitimate counterparts. As Charlemagne's biographer, the "Astronomer," would relate:

> [Charlemagne] ordered his people to convene in a general assembly in the autumn, in the royal estate at Thionville. In that place there appeared three envoys of the Saracens beyond the sea, two of them Muslims and one a Christian, bearing vast gifts from their land, different kinds of perfumes and textiles. After they had sought and received peace, they departed.[6]

Hardly a proto-Crusader, the emperor's ill-fated mission to *Hispania* to overthrow the Umayyads in the 780s had been undertaken in collaboration with the Muslim ruler of Zaragoza (Saraqusṭa), and his defeat at Roncesvalles had not been at the hands of Marsilia's "panyims," as in the eleventh-century "Song of Roland," but at the hands of nominally Christian Basques.

[6] *Ibid.*, p. 278.

## Islam and Christian minorities

This is a written agreement from ʿAbd al-ʿAzīz b. Mūsā b. Nuṣayr to Tudmīr [Theodimir] son of Ghabdūsh, affirming that [the former] has entered into a peace whereby [the latter] shall be under the peace and protection of God, as well as under the protection of His Prophet, may God bless Him and grant Him peace! No evil shall be done to him or to his followers of any kind, nor shall he be removed from office. They shall not be killed or taken captive, nor shall they be separated from their children and their wives. They shall not be coerced in matters of religion; their churches shall not be burned down; and their objects of worship shall not be taken from his domain. This shall be done providing he acts in good faith and complies with the following conditions . . . (ʿAbd al-ʿAzīz b. Mūsā b. Nuṣayr, "Pact of Tudmīr" (April 713)[7])

For all of Ṭāriq b. Ziyād's fiery rhetoric, the Arabo-Islamic conquest of *Hispania* was neither unremittingly bloody nor overly idealized. After the initial rout of Roderic's forces and a few skirmishes, it was accomplished largely by intimidation and negotiation – along the same pattern as the Arab conquests from Syria to Khurāsān, and from Egypt to the Atlantic coast. It is striking how little ʿAbd al-ʿAzīz, the son of the conqueror of the Visigothic kingdom (and the new husband of King Roderic's widow, Egilona), demanded in return from Theodimir, lord of Auroriola, in exchange for his protection. The former lieutenant of the vanquished Visigothic King was not to shelter any rebels, nor succor any enemies of ʿAbd al-ʿAzīz, nor conceal any important information from his new lord. In addition, every freeman in his province was to yield an annual tribute of one *dīnār*, four bushels of wheat, four of barley, four measures of wine and of vinegar, and two of honey and oil. Slaves were to pay half.

As such, the treaty epitomizes the pragmatic approach Muslims had taken towards religious minorities since the time of the *hijra* and the establishment of the first Islamic community at Madīna under the authority of the Prophet. Legitimate non-believers (originally including only Christians and Jews) were to be fought into submission, but once they had yielded, were to be protected and respected in exchange for the payment of tribute, under the arrangement known as *dhimma*. Pagans and idolators were to be forced to convert. Later, as Islamic jurists articulated a formal and detailed legal position for *dhimmī*s they attributed the policy to the Caliph ʿUmar (634–44) and extrapolated the "Pact of ʿUmar" – a document they claimed he wrote for the Christians of Syria as a blueprint

[7] R. I. Burns and P. Chevedden, *Negotiating Cultures*, p. 231. This version of the pact appears in Aḥmad al-Dabbī's twelfth-century biographical dictionary, *Bughyat al-multamis fī ta'rīkh al-rijāl ahl al-Andalus*. The province of Tudmīr has been identified as Aurariola. The capital of the province appears to have been Orihuela.

for such arrangements. In reality, these agreements were made *ad hoc* at the discretion of field commanders, like ʿAbd al-ʿAzīz, in response to practical conditions. The "Pact of ʿUmar" was a *post factum* juridical fantasy.[8]

In the tradition of nomadic, pastoral warriors, the early Muslim Arabs regarded their subjects essentially as a form of livestock. Despite the universality of the message of Islam, there was little will to allow non-Arabs to enjoy its spiritual or material benefits; the conquerors lived quarantined in camp-cities they set up alongside existing settlements, and did not actively encourage conversion (indeed, sometimes they forbade it). Nevertheless through intermarriage, clientage, and slavery, significant numbers of native peoples soon became Muslims, and came to identify with Arabic culture. Historians debate the pace of this process, but by 1000, a substantial proportion of the population of Syria, Palestine, and Sicily, and the overwhelming majority of al-Andalus, were Arabic-speaking Muslims. This is remarkable because there were so few conquerors; for example, according to tradition, ʾAmr b. al-ʾĀṣ invaded and conquered Egypt with only one thousand men. Even when one takes into account the Berber converts and clients who soon comprised the bulk of the Muslim forces that moved westwards, the invaders were never more than a tiny minority.

In sum, the great majority of Muslims who lived in formerly Christian-ruled lands were not "foreigners," but indigenous. And doubly so; not only were they descended from the pre-conquest inhabitants of their regions, but through their conversion they had transformed local Islamic culture. This came about as the result both of passive acculturation, and active advocacy, notably the *shuʿūbiyya* movement – a reaction against Arabic socio-cultural hegemony that peaked in the ninth century, and staked a claim for local Islamicate cultures. In Hungary, on the other hand, the Muslims were certainly newcomers, but no less so than the pagan Magyars, who became Hungary's Christians and from whom they were largely indistinguishable prior to 1000. In other words, it is less appropriate to think of the Arabo-Islamic expansion merely in terms of invasion (although it certainly involved invasions) as much as a process of transformation.

Through all of this, numerous non-Muslim communities persisted in these lands: Mozarab Christians in the Iberian peninsula, Greek Orthodox in Sicily, Egypt and the East, Coptic Christians in Egypt, Syriac Monophysites and other Christian denominations in the Levant, and important communities of Jews (including Rabbinical Jews, Karaites, and Samaritans) throughout these lands. This was a consequence not so much

[8] See A. S. Tritton, *The Caliphs and Their Non-Muslim Subjects*, and M. Cohen, "What was the Pact of ʿUmar?"

of the "constitutional" rights *dhimmīs* enjoyed thanks to their status in the Qur›ān and Tradition, but because of the roles they played in Islamic polities and societies. Non-Muslim subjects were subject to special taxes and did not have the same rights as Muslims. Their services were provided and paid for by their own religious administrations, which were themselves under the control of the Muslim sovereign – a situation that the collaborationist *dhimmī* elite was quite comfortable with. Members of the non-Muslim elite were often placed in positions of great authority and power, in which they could not only assure the stability of their community, but their own prosperity. This was advantageous to Muslim rulers because, on the one hand, the minority officials had almost no capacity to rebel and were entirely dependent on their patron, and on the other, they provided a cover for unpopular policies that Muslim rulers might want to implement.

There may have been occasional bouts of persecution, and episodes of popular tension were sometimes expressed in the form of anti-Christian violence, but this was rare prior to the year 1000. If humor is any indication, even ordinary Muslims appreciated the advantages that diversity provided the societies they lived in. Hence, the thirteenth-century Persian joke: "In the month of Ramaḍān someone said to a shopkeeper, 'There's no business this month.' He answered, 'May God give long life to the Jews and the Christians!'"[9] True, the ethno-religious diversity of the Islamic world was not based on equality, and it should not be imagined nostalgically; but it functioned – at least until the second half of the eleventh century, when economic and social forces threatened the stability of the Islamic world, and when political control of the Caliphates and their successor states came increasingly into the hands of peoples from the peripheries of the Islamic world – the Saljūqs, Almoravids, Almohads and Franks – who had little patience for, or understanding of infidels, or the advantages of ethno-religious diversity.

## A new world, 1000–50

> And just as the our wise predecessors indicated to us, after seven hundred years having passed, the sect of Maomat, borne by the Saracens, would cease and be destroyed... (Anonymous, *Fuero* of Jaca (twelfth century)[10])

If in the 900s the three Caliphates of the Islamic world had reached their apogee, soon after the year 1000 they were all clearly in disarray. The ʿAbbāsid Caliphate, the oldest, most prestigious and venerable, had been

9 B. Lewis, *Islam*, p. 282; see also B. Lewis and B.E. Churchill, *Islam*, p. 28.
10 M. Molho, *Fuero de Jaca*, p. 174 {O: 19}.

drifting into decadence for some time, as its provinces, both far and near, gradually shook off the power of Baghdad, even if they maintained the pretense of its authority. Through this time the Caliphate presided over an incredible cultural, scientific, and technological *élan*, which drew together and transformed regions as diverse as Central and South Asia, the Mediterranean, and the southern fringes of the Sahara. By the late ninth century, however, the dynasty was in crisis, and the empire would only be saved by the ascent of the Būyid dynasty – Persian Shīʿī *condottieri* who seized power and ruled behind the façade of the now powerless caliphs. As it was transformed, the ʿAbbāsid Caliphate had effectively abandoned the relatively poor West, and reoriented itself towards Central and South Asia and beyond.

The Fāṭimids, the schismatic Ismāʿīlī dynasty that had seized Egypt in 969 and challenged ʿAbbāsic domination of the Arab heartlands, had built a prosperity based on its tremendous domestic output together with trade down the Nile corridor and into the Red Sea and Indian Ocean. However, Egypt too was in decline, having suffered under the misrule of the messianic al-Ḥākim (996–1021) and the incompetent al-Mustanṣir (1036–94), and was becoming increasingly dependent on foreign, slave soldiers. By the end of the century, both Ifrīqiya and Sicily had fallen away from Cairo.

In al-Andalus ("Islamic Spain"), the resolutely Sunnī Umayyad Caliphate of Córdoba, which had been declared in 929 as a response to that of the Fāṭimids twenty years earlier, enjoyed a primacy that would scarcely outlive its founder, ʿAbd al- Raḥmān III. Under this first Caliph of the revived Umayyad dynasty, Córdoba established its hegemony over the Maghrib and commanded the lucrative gold trade originating beyond the Sahel and the Niger Delta. This funded a military that became the unrivaled power of the Western Mediterranean and kept the Christian fringes of the Iberian Peninsula firmly under its sway. By 978, however, real power was in the hands of al-Manṣūr – Muḥammad b. Abī ʿĀmir – a brilliant and unprincipled *parvenu* who ruled as dictator under the title of *ḥājib* ("chamberlain"), and brought ever-greater numbers of Berber tribesmen into al-Andalus to strengthen the military and undermine the Arabo-Andalusī elite. However, the center of this increasingly polarized society could not hold, and in 1008, only six years after his death, al-Andalus was plunged into *fitna*, or ethno-political civil war. It would be a generation before al-Andalus would re-emerge, now shattered into a score of petty sectarian principalities, the *taifa* kingdoms, each at war with each other, and most enjoying only the most tenuous authority over their subjects.

The mid eleventh century would bring the next stage of decadence and decline to the Caliphal world, in which political and military power across the *dār al-Islām* would be seized by "barbarians" from the fringes of the

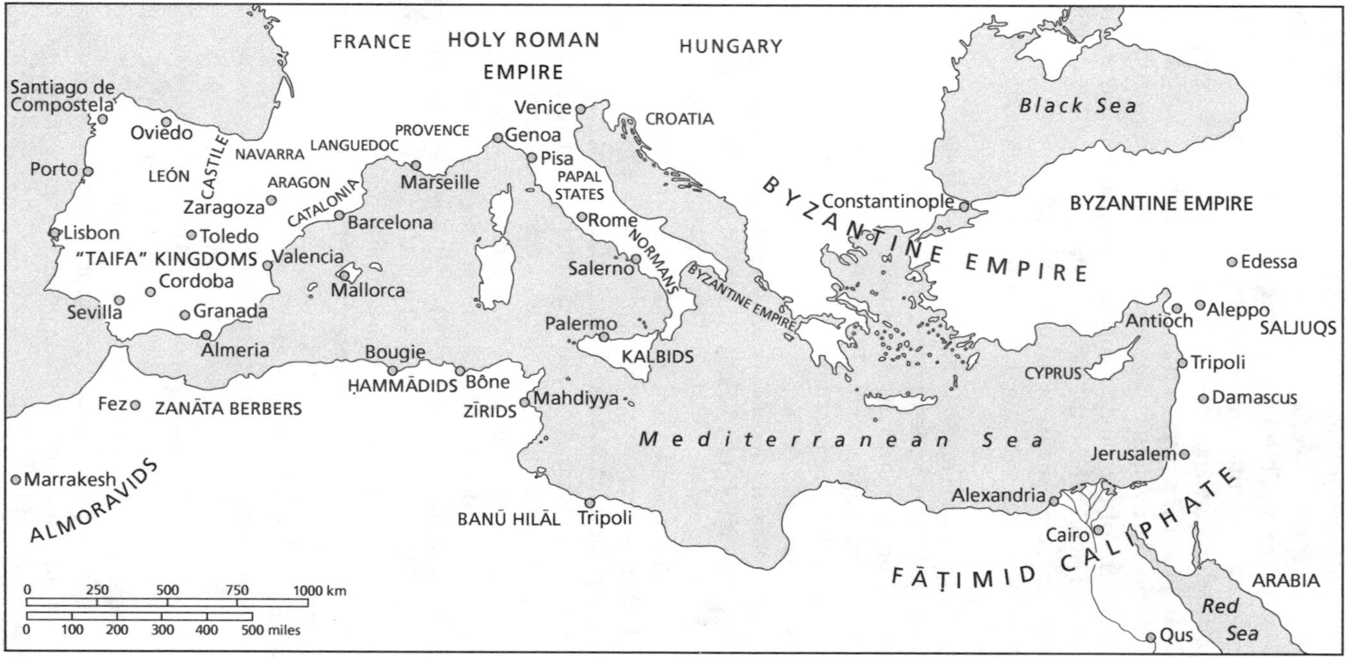


Map 1 The Mediterranean, *c.* 1050

imperia – peoples who had been exposed to the power and prosperity of the Arabo-Islamic civilization as warriors and traders, and having been drawn in to it, were now claiming control. In the ʿAbbāsid East this took the form of the Saljuqs – recently Islamicized Turkic nomads, who swept the Būyids from power and then pushed westwards towards the Fāṭimids in the name of re-establishing Sunnī unity in the Islamic world. The fall of Byzantine Anatolia (*Rūm*), on the heels of 1071's Battle of Manzikert, was collateral damage. In Egypt, this phase was marked by the ascent of an Armenian military dynasty in 1073 under the leadership of the converted slave and general, Badr al-Jamālī. In al-Andalus and the Maghrib it would be Lamtūna warriors, recent and rigorous converts to Sunnī Islam, who, having cut their teeth fighting pagans in the Sahel, would sweep through the Maghrib and obliterate the petty kingdoms of al-Andalus from 1090 or so. Each of these foreign, non-Arab and non-Persian peoples would transform and be transformed by Islam and the world it had established, and each would quite quickly be absorbed into the institutional, cultural, and religious fabric of the *dār al-Islām*.

But there was one group of tribal barbarians originating on the undeveloped fringe of the Islamic world that was distinct. The *Ifranj* or "Franks" – Latin Christians – had also been drawn increasingly to the prosperity and sophistication of the Islamic world from the middle of the tenth century. They too came as clients, merchants, and warriors, and they too would set out to construct their own dominion over the crumbling edifice of Islamic rule in the Mediterranean. But unlike the others, they did not convert to Islam and were not subsumed by Arabo-Islamic culture; by the 1060s they would be expanding into al-Andalus and southern Italy, striking at Ifrīqiya and the Maghrib, and soon after, invading Syria and Palestine. Their own religious culture derived from the same Abrahamic foundations as Islam, and therefore Islam offered them no advantage as a religious system; they already possessed an alphabet and a literary tradition of their own, so they had little impetus to take up Arabic, and they had their own institutional traditions, remote and tenuous as memory of Rome may have been at that time, on which they had founded their law and organized their societies. Therefore, they came as true conquerors, who set themselves above and apart from the Muslim populations that gradually, and often accidentally, slipped under their control. But their approach was pragmatic, rather than dogmatic, and like the Muslim conquerors centuries earlier, they would care for their infidel subjects precisely to the extent their own prosperity depended on it.

As for the Muslim subjects of the "polytheist" Franks, these would become tributaries, subject peoples, and subordinates – foreigners in their own lands. When faced with the choice between "rescue" by the puritanical Almoravids or an illusory autonomy under Alfonso VI of Castile, the last *taifa* King of Seville, the dissolute poet al-Muʿtamid b. ʿAbbād (1069–91), is said to have quipped, "Better [to] be a camel driver than a driver of pigs."[11] Evidently, not all of his fellow Muslims felt the same way, or had the same opportunity to choose, and for more than five centuries communities of Muslims survived, struggled, and throve under Christian rule in the Latin West. In that time, except for those instances when they were pushed into revolt by repression or inspired to resist out of hope, they remained remarkably quiescent under infidel rule; in the thousands of charters and royal orders that survive in the Iberian Peninsula alone, the Latin rulers addressed them and their communities as "all Our faithful Muslim subjects."[12]

[11] al-Maqqari, *The History of the Mohammedan Dynasties*, vol. II, p. 273.

[12] The salutation appears as "universis fidelibus nostris Sarracenis," or more commonly in the third person as "universis fidelibus suis."

*Part 1*

# Static diasporas

## Muslim communities of Latin Christendom

Although in Islam the entire collective of believers is conceived of as a single *umma*, the Muslims of medieval Latin Christendom were not "a people" and did not comprise a uniform or internally consistent group. This "imagined community" included men and women of diverse ethnic and geographic roots, ranging from indigenous peoples of European lands, to North Africans, and sub-Saharan Africans, to people of Arabic and Persian descent, and of Turkic and Slavic origin.[1] Although, as the language of divine revelation, Arabic enjoyed a great prestige and a near-universal currency among these peoples, they also spoke and wrote other locally current languages. In some communities, Arabic was either not spoken (or even read) or its use restricted to a narrow learned elite. Similarly, while Arabic and Persian social and cultural traditions came to strongly characterize Islamic societies in the early centuries, their values were not shared universally or consistently among the various Muslim communities from the shores of the Baltic to the Straits of Gibraltar, and even when their values were recognized, they were not always put into practice. This was the case even prior to Christian domination, after which local differences were not only entrenched, but intensified as a consequence of contact and integration with the societies of their new infidel overlords. And while many Muslims may have formally espoused a longing for a united *dār al-Islām* under the authority of a single Caliph or Imam, in reality this had been fiction almost from the time of the Prophet. By the eleventh century Islam had become so diverse and variegated, and so internally conflicted even in terms of religion, that it might seem that beyond the *shahāda* – the declaration of faith: "There is no god but God, and Muḥammad is the Messenger of God" – there was as much dissent as common ground as regards what constituted proper Islam.

[1] The *umma* corresponds, perhaps, to Anderson's characterization of the national community: "It is *imagined* because the members of even the smallest nation will never know most of their fellow-members, meet them, or even hear of them, yet in the minds of each lives the image of their communion." B. Anderson, *Imagined Communities*, p. 6.

Nevertheless, treating the Muslims of Latin Christendom as a coherent group should not be interpreted as a manifestation of a colonial or Orientalist academy nor a mere scholarly conceit. Whereas these communities' common condition as minorities in Latin lands may have been accidental – depending as it did on which lands were conquered – and temporary, it was a common condition that they themselves were aware of. Although Islam was predicated on the confident optimism that the entire world would soon be governed by God's principles – that the *dār al-Islām* ("the abode of Islam") would supersede the *dār al-ḥarb* ("the abode of struggle") – and the near-miraculous expansion of the first Islamic century seemed to bear that out, it soon became clear that this progression would be neither uniform nor swift. There would be lulls in the fighting, and some jurists would begrudgingly recognize a zone of truce with the Infidel (the *dār al-ʿahd*, "the abode of covenant"). And there would be setbacks.

As early as the *muwallad* rebellions of the ninth century, Islamic jurists in Iberia were confronted by the prospect that Muslims might be forced to live under the jurisdiction of infidels and apostates.[2] Although previously some Muslim-ruled areas had been lost to Christians, the mid eleventh century marked a watershed, in which within the space of a hundred years significant territories across the Mediterranean from the Iberian peninsula to the Holy Land were conquered by *al-Ifranj* ("the Franks") – contemporary Muslims' generic term for Christians of the Latin West. These conquests were marked on the one hand by massacres and displacements, but perhaps their most remarkable characteristic is that in many areas significant numbers, even the majority, of the Muslim inhabitants chose not to flee before the Christian advance, but to remain in their homes and become willing subjects of infidel kings.

Whether this was prompted by expediency or by the hope (vain in most cases) that they would eventually be liberated, in short order their status as subjects became normalized. From the perspective of both parties, the victors and the vanquished, Muslims' position in society, secondary as it may have been, was legitimate. These communities were not isolated, however, from the larger Islamic world. They continued to see themselves as "good Muslims" – although many jurists in Islamic lands might dispute this – and continued to inhabit a larger Islamic universe. Merchants, scholars, and pilgrims continued to crisscross the Mediterranean and journey to the Holy Places, and few were tempted to convert despite the pressures and marginalization they endured. They inhabited a world in

[2] *Muwalladūn* refers to formerly Christian converts to Islam and their descendants in the Iberian Peninsula. They typically entered a relationship of *mawlā* ("clientage") with Arabic families, often appropriating their genealogical lineage.

which social status, legal jurisdiction, fiscal category, and economic opportunity were determined largely by religious identity. Integration was impossible in societies that were consciously sectarian and deliberately exclusionary, and in which Muslims, however much they may have been accommodated (and however much they might accommodate), would always be considered, in some sense, as enemies. Likewise, despite their differences, Muslims across Latin Christendom continued to consider themselves – if not always first, and not always foremost – as part of the larger Islamic *umma*, and continued to be regarded as such by their free co-religionists.

The diversity of the Muslims under Christian rule becomes evident as one looks at the fates of the communities in the various kingdoms and regions. Hence, this first part of the book consists of a narrative history, or a series of narrative histories, each focusing on a particular region of Latin Christendom and particular subject Muslim communities at a particular time. The status, condition, and experience of Muslim subjects also changed dramatically over time, and several chronological phases can be discerned. The period to the mid to late twelfth century was characterized by early and dramatic Christian advances into the *dār al-Islām*: in Iberia, southern Italy, North Africa, and the Holy Land, and to a lesser extent, of voluntary Muslim immigration, particularly in eastern Europe. A long thirteenth century was characterized by what might be called "stabilization." In parts of Latin Christendom, such as southern Italy and Hungary, this took the form of the elimination of Muslim minorities. In other areas, such as Ifrīqiya and the Levant, it was Latin lordship that was eliminated. And finally, in Iberia, it represented a period of normalization and entrenchment of the Islamic minority, and the beginning of a period of détente. From the mid fourteenth century the situation of the communities of the Iberian peninsula – the only remaining region in the Latin West with a significant Muslim population – entered a new phase as a consequence of political, economic, and social transformations provoked by factors including the Black Death, the Hundred Years War, and internal developments of Roman Christendom. The history of the *mudéjares* (as Muslims of Christian Spain have come to be referred to) entered a final stage around the turn of the sixteenth century, marked not so much by the fall of Granada to Castile and Aragon's "Catholic Monarchs," but by the forced conversions which were mandated in the various peninsular kingdoms.[3] Continuing to live as a distinct ethnic community and in many cases

[3] *Ahl al-dajn*, "people who remain," refers to those Muslims who remained living in lands that passed under non-Muslim dominion; it may also imply domestication. For the latter, see R. Zorgati, *Pluralism in the Middle Ages*, p. 88. It is the root of the rare term *mudajjan*,

secretly practicing Islam, these so-called "Moriscos" were finally forcibly expelled from the kingdoms of Spain in the years between 1609 and 1615.[4] This marked the conclusion of nine hundred years of Islam in Iberia, the extinction, after five centuries, of the last Muslim communities of what had been the world of Latin Christendom, and the end of the "static diaspora" provoked by the expansion of the medieval Latin West.[5]

and of the Castilian *mudéjar*, a term that is not attested until the late Middle Ages. *Mudajjan* appears very occasionally in fourteenth-century treaties and memoirs. See, for example, A. Giménez Soler, "La Corona de Aragón y Granada", pp. 90, 149, and 151.

4 *Morisco*, from "moro" ("Muslim"), means "Islamicate," rather than "Moorish." "Moor" has been generally abandoned as a term for referring to Muslims of Christian Spain. It conveys a racial/ethnic dimension (in reference to "Mauritania" or Morocco, or the early modern English "Blackamoor") that supports the distorting and inaccurate idea that these people were of North African origin. Few were; in the late Middle Ages, the great majority of Muslims in the peninsula were the descendants of indigenous converts, or had ancestors who had been living there for centuries.

5 The expansion of Spain and Portugal into North Africa and South Asia from the sixteenth century onwards, a process which resulted in new Muslim populations being brought to the peninsula, falls beyond the scope of this book.

# 1 The tide turns

## The Christian Spains I (*c.* 1055–*c.* 1150)

I was told as much by Sisnando. He said to me face to face: "Al-Andalus originally belonged to the Christians. Then they were defeated by the Arabs . . . Now that they are strong and capable, the Christians desire to recover what they have lost by force. This can only be achieved by weakness and encroachment. In the long run, when [al-Andalus] has neither men nor money, we'll be able to recover it without any difficulty." (ʿAbd Allāh b. Bulughghīn, King of Granada, *Al-Tibyān* (*c.* 1090)[1])

In the Iberian Peninsula, dominated directly or indirectly by Muslim rulers since the early eighth century, the hundred-year span that began in the mid eleventh century saw a complete reversal of the political and economic situation in this extensive, populous, and economically dynamic territory. Whereas at the turn of the millennium the Christian principalities had been little more than clients of a seemingly invincible and ever more aggressive Umayyad caliphate, by the middle of the eleventh century they had clearly gained political and military initiative. At that point the North African-based Almoravids (al-Murābiṭūn), who had reunited what remained of al-Andalus after the spectacular advances of Christian princes over the previous hundred years, were certainly a force to be reckoned with, but were increasingly riven by their own divisions. In any event, theirs was a political-ideological project that was focused not on expanding northwards into the Christian world, but rather, eastwards, with the aim – like the other revolutionary/reforming regimes which had coalesced along the periphery of the Islamic world – of dominating and restoring order to their own house, the *dār al-Islām*. In the meanwhile, in the lands conquered by the princes of the Christian Spains, the fate of Muslim inhabitants varied greatly. In some areas it seems that the majority of the population must have been enslaved, expelled, or converted, while in others the shift to Christian lordship would have seemed hardly an interruption at all – at least at the beginning.

[1] Amin T. Tibi, *The Tibyan*, p. 90.

Likewise, what we know about the fate of the Muslims of the various regions also varies greatly. This was due to the simple fact that for many of these areas the surviving archival documentation is frustratingly thin, such as for Castile, or all but non-existent, as for Portugal. Much here is a mystery, and is likely to remain so. The Kingdom of Aragon marks the exception in this sense, as a substantial number of ecclesiastical and municipal records survive from this period – documents which for the most part record land exchanges, many from the time immediately following the conquest. These are complemented by a few surviving surrender treaties and settlement charters, local law codes, and royal decrees, and filled out by assorted chronicles, produced both by the conquerors and by Muslim observers, as well as by Arabic geographies and biographical works. Finally, archeological work and studies of ceramic and other material goods are helping us to understand the transformation of the landscape and economy that the conquest entailed. Little surprise that with the exception of concrete episodes, such as Alfonso VI of Castile's conquest of Toledo (1085), El Cid's rule over Valencia (1094–99), and Afonso Henriques's capture of Lisbon (1147) with the help of Anglo-Norman, Fleming, and German Crusaders, historians working on the experience of Spanish Muslims under Christian rule in this era have concentrated on Catalonia and the Kingdom of Aragon. Here, debate has revolved around the degree to which the Christian conquest represented a cataclysmic rupture with the pre-conquest Islamic past, and whether Islamic society can be said to have survived in any meaningful sense. In sum, this chapter follows the history of the first century of the conquest and subjugation of the Muslims of al-Andalus – a time during which the Christian powers enjoyed only a marginal advantage, when allegiances and alliances were not necessarily drawn along religious lines, and when it was far from evident that the Iberian peninsula would one day conquered by unbelievers.

### *The Muslims of al-Andalus*

Popular tradition, encouraged by political agendas some of which originate in the Middle Ages, has portrayed the Muslim conquest of Iberia as an invasion by Arabs and Berbers, who overran and displaced the native Christians, initiating a period of occupation that lasted until these territories could be "reconquered" by "the Spanish" and the "foreign" Muslims expelled. Whereas there certainly was a conquest of Iberia that began in the early eighth century and rapidly brought most of the peninsula under Islamic rule, the Muslims of al-Andalus (at least by the eleventh century) were hardly foreigners. The armies that crossed over the Straits of Gibraltar in 711 CE with their families and dependents numbered perhaps a few thousand. It was a force of troops and families, overwhelmingly North African of origin, many of whom were scarcely Islamicized, all under the leadership of a small cadre of Arab Muslims. After mid-century, there was no significant Arab immigration to the peninsula, and relatively little Berber settlement.

The ninth and tenth centuries saw a process in which the majority of the native populace converted to Islam.[2] The tremendous output of Andalusī scholars, poets, and cultural figures, many originating from the countryside and from the contested and heterodox frontier regions, confirms the thoroughness of the process of conversion. At the same time, descendants of early North African settlers were also absorbed in what emerged as a distinct Andalusī identity, characterized by Arabic language and social customs, but flavored, both consciously and not, by indigenous tendencies and customs. Remarkably, the significant Christian and Jewish minorities here were also culturally and linguistically integrated. By the tenth century, when the Umayyad Caliphate had established itself as the military, political, and cultural arbiter of the Western Mediterranean, Andalusī culture was recognized as a distinctive but orthodox Islamo-Arabic tradition. Resolutely Sunnī and clearly dominated by the Mālikī legal school, this was a society that produced scientists, artists, religious thinkers, and litterateurs whose fame was recognized across the Islamic world. It was a society whose cosmopolitanism was fed not only by the traders and students who traveled here, but by mercenaries and slaves who came or were brought to serve, from beyond the Sahara and Christendom, and from the pagan East. Nevertheless, apart from religion and language, it was their prosperity and sophistication that distinguished Andalusīs from their Spanish Christian neighbors. Through the caliphal period intermarriage and concubinage were frequent across all social strata, bilingualism and biculturalism were common, and the frontier between Christendom and Islam was fluid and often ephemeral. Conversely, Andalusīs displayed a marked antipathy towards North Africans, who were widely considered to be uncouth, barbaric foreigners. Indeed, the designation "Berber" (*barbar*), which collapsed the various,

[2] For the debate concerning the rate of conversion, see R. Zorgati, *Pluralism in the Middle Ages*, pp. 25–31, and B. Catlos, *The Victors and the Vanquished*, pp. 27–28. Regarding Bulliet's methodology Harrison rightly points out (as careful readers will have noted) that the "conversion curve" refers to the total population of converts to Islam, not the total population, but the latter's argument for late survival of numerous indigenous Christian communities in al-Andalus is not convincing. See A. Harrison, "Behind the Curve"; cf. R. Bulliet, *Conversion to Islam*.

distinct peoples of Muslim northwest Africa into a single unflattering category, was an Andalusī invention.[3]

## The fall of Toledo and the Muslims of Castile and León

[The tyrant Alfonso VI] entrusted the governing of Toledo to the aforesaid Sisnando. He endeavored to lighten the suffering of the Toledans and make bearable the base condition at which they had arrived, demanding little and comporting himself justly, thereby reconciling them to Alfonso's presence ... (Ibn Bassām, *Dhakhīra fī maḥāsin ahl al-Jazīra* (*c.* 1100)[4])

On May 25, 1085, after two months camped outside the city walls with his court and his army, Alfonso VI, King of Castile (r. 1072–1109), King of León (r. 1065–1109), and "Emperor of All Spain," rode in triumph through the Bāb al-Shagra gate of Muslim Ṭulayṭulah, reclaiming Toledo – once the *de facto* capital of the Visigothic kingdom Muslim armies had destroyed almost four hundred years earlier – for Christendom. Rather than representing a triumph of arms in battle, however, the conquest of this important Islamic city – the capital of one of the major independent *taifa* ("sectarian") kingdoms of al-Andalus – was the fruit of a combination of diplomacy and intimidation, and a symptom as much of Muslim disarray as of Christian determination. Alfonso had become the patron and protector of Yaḥyā b. Ismāʿīl b. Yaḥyā b. Dhi'l-Nūn (1075–85), the heir of a military dynasty of North African Hawwāra origin. In 1085 Alfonso took the city because

[3] There is an abundant and rich body of historical writing on the latter history of the *taifa* kingdoms, the taking of Toledo, and the expansion of Castile and León. See É. Lévi-Provençal, "Alphonse VI," and generally: H. Kennedy, *Muslim Spain and Portugal*; V. Lagardère, *Les Almoravides jusqu'au règne de Yūsuf b. Tāšfīn*, and *Les Almoravides. Le djihâd andalou*; D. Wasserstein, *The Rise and Fall*; the dated, but excellent, R. Menéndez Pidal, *La España del Cid*; and in English, R. Fletcher, *The Quest for El Cid.* For Castile and León and the other peninsular principalities (Portugal, Catalonia, Aragon, and Navarre) in this period, consult T. Bisson, *The Medieval Crown*; P. Linehan, *Spain, 1157–1300*; J. O'Callaghan, *History of Medieval Spain* and *Reconquest and Crusade*; T. Glick, *Islamic and Christian Spain*, and *From Muslim Fortress to Christian Castle*; C. Laliena Corbera, *Musulmanes et Chrétiens*; C. Bishko, "The Spanish and Portuguese Reconquest"; D. Lomax, *The Reconquest*; J. M. Lacarra, "La Reconquista y repoblación"; J-P. Molénat, *Campagnes et monts de Tolède*; and B. Reilly, *The Contest of Christian and Muslim Spain.* Primary sources for *mudéjares* and the Christian conquest include local, royal, and monastic chronicles from Castile, Navarre, and the Crown of Aragon; early municipal legal codes and royal proclamations from the same period; Muslim surrender treaties and population documents; administrative documents and land transfer documents from ecclesiastical and municipal archives; assorted royal privileges, grants, and decrees; *libros de repartimiento*; Andalusī histories, memoirs, and poetry; *cantares de gesta* (notably the various iterations of the Cid story).

[4] "Treasury of the Delights of the People of the Island (al-Andalus)," in R. Menéndez Pidal and E. García Gomez, "El conde mozárabe," pp. 31–32. Ibn Bassām was a Muslim from Santárem who witnessed the Christian conquest first-hand.

Yaḥyā, who ruled Toledo under the optimistic sobriquet, al-Qādir, "the Powerful," had agreed to cede it to him.[5]

Over the previous half-century the *taifa* kingdoms had been slowly buckling under pressure from the Christian kingdoms, particularly Castile and León. Struggling to control what remained of the former Umayyad Caliphate of Córdoba (Qurṭuba) and facing internal instability, the *taifa* kings turned to Christian princes as protectors and patrons, providing tributary payments in exchange for military support against their Muslim and Christian rivals. It was because of this, that the Dhi'l-Nūn dynasty of Toledo developed close links to Alfonso; in fact, Yaḥyā's grandfather, the powerful al-Ma'mūn, had welcomed a young Alfonso into his court as a refugee when the youthful future king had fled his own brothers' intrigues.

So much for gratitude: when al-Qādir came to power Alfonso sensed his weakness and made ever-increasing demands for tribute. As the territories under Toledo's control fell away, the Muslim King imposed ever-heavier extra-canonical taxes on the populace in order to satisfy his Castilian protector, aggravating the general atmosphere of discontent and fueling ethnic antipathy towards the Berber rulers, particularly among the mercantile and religious elite. Popular resistance was met with violent repression, until al-Qādir was ousted by rebels, who in 1077 handed the city over to 'Umar al-Mutawakkil, the King of Badajoz (1068/69–94/95), and scion of another Berber military dynasty, the Banū 'l- Afṭas. Soon after, Alfonso offered to retake the city for his deposed ally but only on the condition that the latter immediately surrender it in exchange for being installed by the Christian king as ruler of Muslim Valencia. A six-month siege was enough to drive the inhabitants of the city to accept Alfonso as their new lord and seek terms of surrender. It was a momentous event – the fall of the first Muslim kingdom in Iberia to a Christian conqueror. As 'Abd Allāh ibn Bulughghīn, the last *taifa* King of Granada (1073–90) recalled in his memoirs, "The fall of Toledo sent a great tremor through al-Andalus and filled the inhabitants with fear and despair of continuing to live there."[6]

### *Toledo under Christian rule*

Toledo was a cosmopolitan mix of Andalusī and North African Muslims, Jews, and Mozarabs (Arabized Christians), to which Alfonso's conquest

[5] For the conquest of Toledo, see B. Reilly, *The Kingdom of León-Castilla under King Alfonso VI*, ch. 9, "The Reconquest of Toledo (1082–1086)," pp. 161–84.

[6] See the contemporary memoirs of 'Abd Allāh ibn Bulughghīn, A. Tibi, *The Tibyan*, p. 113. 'Abd Allāh (1073–90) was the last Zīrid *amīr* of Granada. He was a tributary of Alfonso VI and was ultimately deposed by the Almoravids and sent into exile, where he wrote his memoir.

would add Castilian and non-Spanish European settlers ("Franks"). Each group would live under a separate legal regime, all under the King's authority.[7] For the Muslim population, their conversion from the dominant to a subject class must have been disconcerting; however, those who wished to leave the city were allowed to go in peace with whatever of their personal goods they could transport. The fears of the native population regarding Alfonso's intentions would have been allayed to no small degree by the king's deliberately conciliatory policies, notably a gift of 100,000 *danānīr* (sing.: *dīnār*) to the people of the city, who were exhausted after the long siege, so that they could buy victuals and sow their crops. The *fuero*, or legal code, he granted them included guarantees of safety of person, property, and cult, and not the least, a pledge to preserve the *masjid al- jāmiʿa* or congregational mosque for its Islamic inhabitants.[8] Such an impressive compromise, however, was not to last.

Moving on from the city, Alfonso left it under the control of Sisnando Davídez, a Mozarab warrior and diplomat and an Arabic-speaking native of Muslim al-Andalus.[9] Formerly having served the *taifa* King of Badajoz (Baṭalyaws), he would have been seen as a reassuring figure by the native populace; indeed, it was Sisnando who had negotiated the city's surrender. Soon after, however (possibly as early as 1086), Alfonso's pious and reform-minded Queen, Constance of Burgundy, became regent in the city, and either on her own initiative or that of her adviser and newly elected Bishop of Toledo, Bernard of Sahagún, the main mosque was appropriated and converted into a cathedral.[10] This act was as a catalyst for, if not a cause of, the rapid disappearance of the city's Muslim community, either as a consequence of emigration south to Islamic lands or conversion.

While one would expect the cultural and religious elite to abandon Toledo and seek to re-establish themselves in Islamic courts where they would find patronage and prestige – as most likely did – for the farmers and craftsmen who made up the bulk of the population, the prospect of emigration and the rupture and loss it entailed would have held little appeal.

Not really clear

[7] See the *fueros* issued by Alfonso VII in T. Muñoz y Romero, *Colección de fueros*, pp. 360–70. For post-conquest Toledo, see L. Cardaillac and J. L. Arántegui, eds., *Toledo, siglos* XII–XIII, and J.-P. Molénat, *Campagnes et monts*, and "Mudéjars et mozarabes."

[8] See Martin-Cleto Porres, *Historia de Ṭulayṭula*, p. 79. The *fuero* does not survive, but various contemporary and near-contemporary Christian and Arabic sources agree on these terms. See Alfonso García Gallo, "Los fueros de Toledo," pp. 408–09.

[9] For Sisnando, see R. Menéndez Pidal and E. García Gómez, "El conde mozárabe." One contemporary Christian chronicle claims he was by origin a captive; see S. Barton and R. Fletcher, *The World of El Cid*, p. 52.

[10] Tension ran high among native Mozarab clergy and noblemen and the newly arrived Franks; see, for example B. Reilly, *The Kingdom of Castilla-León under King Alfonso VI*, especially ch. 6, "King and Cult (1076–1080)," pp. 93–115.

And so, it seems – as contemporary Muslim writers attest – the bulk of the population stayed in Toledo and converted rather rapidly to Christianity, following the example of the *faqīh*, Abū'l-Qāsim b. Khayyāt, who clumsily rationalized his apostasy on the basis that both Christians and Muslims worship the same God.[11] And while it is likely that some sort of Islamic community remained in the city, there is in fact only one specific reference to a Toledan Muslim who remained in the city in the years immediately following the conquest – a chronicler named Ibn Muṭāhir. Moreover, there are few concrete documentary references to a residual Muslim population in the surrounding countryside and none to a general exodus. All of this suggests the rapid conversion of local Muslims to Christianity.

On the other hand, some historians have suggested that the populace departed *en masse*, betting that the Christian takeover would be temporary and that the restoration of Islamic rule would soon come at the hands of the Almoravids. This dynamic, tribally oriented religio-political movement had – on the principle of rigorous Sunnī reform – established a dynasty that ruled an expanse stretching north from the Sahel to the southern shores of the Mediterranean, and clearly had its eyes on stabilizing and recovering al-Andalus. Had this been the case, however, it is more likely that the native Muslims of Toledo would have stayed put and awaited liberation.

Conversion to Christianity in this area was undoubtedly encouraged by the presence of a substantial Mozarab population.[12] These "would-be Arabs" (from *must'arabīn*) were native Christians who had adopted Arabo-Islamic popular culture and, to some extent, social mores. Arabic was their language of choice, and they continued to use Arabic personal names (including Qur'ānic names, such as al-'Azīz and Ibn 'Uthmān) long after the Christian conquest.[13] As a group, Mozarabs would have provided a vector by which native Muslims could convert without abandoning their culture; indeed, they would be joining a group which valued and respected it. Further, whereas in many cases conversion would be discouraged by the prospect of the loss of property and the disintegration of family networks, these disincentives would be all but in eliminated in the case of a broad and generalized conversion movement. The apocryphal legends of local saints, Casilda de Briviesca and Pedro de Sopretán – reputedly

11 See Gregory VII's reflections on the commonalities of Islam and Christianity; below, p. 328. Ibn al-Kardabūs breaks with the consensus of chroniclers and claims that many Muslims left. See F. Maillo Salgado, *Historia*, p. 106.

12 For the Mozarabs, see C. Aillet, *Les Mozarabes*, and D. Olstein, *La era mozárabe*.

13 See for example, the signatures on Alfonso VII's 1118 *fuero* of Toledo, in T. Muñoz y Romero, *Colección de fueros*, pp. 367–69. In late twelfth-century Sicily, Greek Christians (likely converts and their descendants) sometimes continued to use Arabo-Islamic names. See J. Johns, "The Greek Church," p. 150.

an aunt and uncle of al-Qādir, who were said to have abandoned Islam – represent the assimilation of the general conversion in the folk-imagination.[14] Indeed, conversion seems to have been a not uncommon response to Christian occupation, at least in the lands conquered by Castile and León prior to the mid twelfth century.

### *Conquest and coercion: The campaigns of Fernando I and Alfonso VI*

The process of conquest had begun under Alfonso's father, Fernando the Great ("Emperor" from 1056 to 1065), who, having united the sliver of Christian-ruled territory stretching from the Ebro to the Atlantic by force and intrigue, turned his energies south towards the bitterly inimical *taifa* kingdoms. It was he who pioneered the tributary policy of the *paria* payments, exploiting competition among Muslim princes to encourage their dependence on him as a prelude to conquest.[15] His initial campaign was directed at the kingdom of Badajoz. In 1055 Fernando drove south of the Duero to capture Viseu, and ten years later, after a siege of several months, received the surrender of Coimbra (Qulumriya) – a fortified town 200 kilometers northwest of the *taifa*'s capital. The hinterland along the banks of the Duero had for centuries constituted a "frontier zone" – lightly settled by Mozarabs and Muslims, who had passed back and forth between Christian and Islamic suzerainty since the ninth century. Given their shared cultural affinities and long history of political embroilment, the area's Muslims would have been well acquainted with Christians and their mores, and may not have felt compelled to abandon their lands when Fernando took over. Indeed, later evidence suggests that some Muslims did remain here, and they came to constitute the kernel of what would later be the Islamic *comunas* of northern Portugal, but given the near silence of contemporary sources we can say little more.[16]

[14] See, for example, A. Butler, *et al.*, eds., *Butler's Lives of the Saints*, p. 66.

[15] See F. Maillo Salgado, *Historia* p. 77. Ibn al-Athīr, writing in the early 1200s, cites the same causes for the ultimate loss of the March in the mid twelfth century. See É. Fagnan, *Ibn el-Athir*, p. 567. *Parias* refers to the tribute that the *taifa* kings were forced to pay to Christian princes (at times, more than one at a time). Typically the payment of *parias* not only protected the tributary from attack by the payee, but also guaranteed the latter's protection against third-party aggression. In other words, it functioned like "protection money." See M. de Epalza, "El Cid," pp. 108–12. Contemporary Muslims used the word *jizya* – the word for the tribute paid by non-Muslim *dhimmis* living under Islamic rule. See E. Lapiedra Gutiérrez, "Los reyes taifas."

[16] The rather partisan *Historia silense* recounts with relish how Muslims were killed at Lamego, overlooking the south bank of the Viseu, 60 kilometers east of Porto, and pressed into labor to construct the local church. See R. Fletcher, *World of the Cid*, p. 49.

In the years leading up to and following 1085, Ferr
increased pressure on the *taifa* kingdoms, attacking
kingdom, Zaragoza, while demanding ever-highe
from the others. *Taifa* resistance was met by puniti
Christian raiders wreaked havoc across the central
nation of military threat and growing domestic unr
shock of the loss of Toledo – an event which reverb
*al-Islām* – prompted the warring *taifas* to set aside their differences and appeal for aid to the Almoravids. It was to be their end. These pious and hardened Berber warriors – self-declared saviours of Sunnī Islam – not only dealt a near-crippling defeat to Alfonso at Zallāqa in October 1086, but heralded the end of the *taifa* era.[17] Over the next eight years the Almoravids deposed almost all of the *taifa* kings, absorbing their lands into their own empire. Initially, the Muslim populace would have been relieved, but the cart-loads of severed Christian heads that the Commander of the Faithful, Yūsuf b. Tāshufīn, had ordered collected from the field of Zallāqa and sent through the major towns of al-Andalus, were as much a message for native Muslims as an expression of triumph over the Infidel, and foreshadowed tensions between the liberators and the liberated that would soon emerge. In the meanwhile, the Almoravids campaigned against Alfonso; and while they would not succeed in recapturing Toledo, they dealt a serious blow when they killed the King's only male son and heir-apparent, Sancho, in battle at Uclés in 1108.

### *El Cid and the rise and fall of a Christian* taifa *kingdom*

By this time, Zaragoza was the only remaining *taifa* kingdom not under Almoravid rule – the kingdom of Valencia (Balansiya), ruled from 1094 by the exiled Castilian soldier-of-fortune, Rodrigo Díaz de Vivar, having been taken in 1102. A renowned warrior, who had gained his famous sobriquet from the grateful soldiers of Muslim Seville whom he had led to victory over Granada in the 1070s, "the Cid" (from *sīdī*, "my lord") had also been a popular hero in Muslim Zaragoza, which he defended in the 1080s against both Christian and Muslim aggressors.[18] In 1089 he partnered with al-Qādir, the erstwhile King of Toledo, and worked to

[17] For the battle called Sagrajas by the Christians see B. Reilly, *The Kingdom of León-Castilla under King Alfonso VI*, pp. 187–206; for the Almoravids, see V. Lagardère, *Les Almoravides*.

[18] The best English-language study of the Cid and his times is R. Fletcher, *The Quest for El Cid*. Rodrigo was given his nickname by the grateful Muslim soldiers of Seville, whom he helped to defeat an army from Granada in battle. See *ibid.*, p. 129.

blish Valencia as a major peninsular power, a struggle that brought m into conflict with virtually every neighboring power, Christian and Muslim. While Rodrigo was away from the city in 1092 facing these challenges, the local *qāḍī*, Ibn Jaḥḥāf, captained a revolt in which al-Qādir was killed and he himself took power at the head of a popular government. The Cid retaliated with a brutal campaign of plunder, and forced the city to surrender to him on July 15, 1094. With this conquest, Rodrigo became, in effect, a Christian *taifa* king, ruling over an overwhelmingly Andalusī Muslim population – a position as fraught with ambiguities as had been his life as a warrior on the Christian–Muslim frontier.

Not long after the surrender, Ibn Jaḥḥāf was put on trial and burned alive, ostensibly for regicide, but also to force him to hand over the riches he had hidden in the kingdom.[19] Other wealthy inhabitants were also imprisoned and threatened by the Cid in order to force over their wealth; this despite a surrender agreement that guaranteed the possessions and freedom of worship of the inhabitants. One of Ibn Jaḥḥāf's kinsmen, ʻAbd Allāh, took over as *qāḍī*. In the aftermath of the Almoravids' aborted attempt to retake the city in 1094, Rodrigo, now secure in his rule, set about subjugating the major towns of the hinterland, sharing out land and booty with his companions and soldiers. Despite the surrender agreement in 1095/96 the Christians took over the main mosque of the city, which the Cid re-consecrated as the new cathedral and where he installed a bishop of Gallic origin.

But there was little possibility to resettle the city with Christians. Thus, the Castilian *Primera crónica general* describes the Cid as garrisoning the fortress, but making little other intervention into the life of the capital. In contrast to most Muslim accounts, it emphasizes his ginger treatment of the natives, as when he famously ordered his men to close off the fortress windows that overlooked the town, lest they offend local sensibilities by casting their glances on Muslim women inside their homes. The inhabitants were assured freedom of worship and the right to be judged according to Muslim law by their own magistrates, with Rodrigo functioning as overall authority.[20] Nevertheless, early in 1097 the *imām* Ḥamdūn b. Muʻallim decided to abandon the city, taking with him a group of followers disillusioned with the Cid's rule.[21] Thus, many of Rodrigo's policies foreshadowed what would become the standard *modus operandi* in Christian Valencia and the rest of the Crown of Aragon. This included the use of Jews as administrative and fiscal officials, a policy which provoked

[19] See *ibid.*, pp. 165–66. [20] See *PCG*, vol. II, pp. 591–92.
[21] M. Marín, "Des migrations," p. 48.

the indignation of the Muslim populace, but which also had precedents in several Muslim *taifa* kingdoms.[22]

With the death of the Cid of natural causes in 1099, the Almoravids tightened the noose on the kingdom. Xàtiva (Shāṭiba) had already fallen to them, and it was clear the capital would soon follow. When the siege began early in 1101, Alfonso VI saw that he would not be able to relieve the city and that Rodrigo's wife, Jimena, who had been left in charge, could not hold on to it either.[23] Therefore, on his advice, she abandoned the city in April 1102, ordering her men to set it on fire, and on May 5, 1102, the Almoravid forces regained a devastated Valencia; many of the families who had left during the occupation now returned.[24] In the countryside, the Cid's brief period of domination would have little effect, constituting only the latest episode in the gradual disintegration of the old Andalusī order. His greatest legacy would be his reincarnation as a proto-nationalist holy warrior and hero of the Castilian "Reconquest" – a process that began perhaps during his own lifetime. This has contributed to a sense that the Cid was somehow a singular figure; in fact, he was only the most successful of the many opportunistic *condottieri* who operated on the frontier of al-Andalus and Christian Spain, and who include, on the Christian side, figures such as the Mozarab, Sisnando Davidez; the Cid's "nephew," Minaya Álvar Háñez; and the Portuguese warrior, Giraldo Sem Pavor ("the Fearless"), to name only the most famous – figures who were lionized in the popular, contemporary Christian *romancero* (*chansons de geste*) and villainized by Muslim chroniclers.[25]

### *The death of Alfonso and the decline of the Almoravids*

Alfonso's son, Sancho, who died at Uclés in 1108, had been born to Sayyida ("Zaida"), the daughter-in-law of King al-Muʾtamid of Sevilla.[26] He was the fruit of a political marriage designed as a last-ditch effort by al-Muʾtamid

[22] In Valencia, the Cid's use of Jews as administrators provoked popular discontent, but both Granada and Almería had had Jewish *wuzarāʾ* (sing.: *wazīr*), and Jews were prominent in the political and cultural life of several *taifa* kingdoms, notably that of Sevilla and Zaragoza. See R. Fletcher, *The Quest for El Cid*, p. 181.

[23] *Ibid.*, p. 196, and B. Reilly, *The Kingdom of León-Castilla under King Alfonso VI*, pp. 309–12.

[24] See M. Marín, "Des migrations," p. 48.

[25] Compare Álvar Háñez as he appears in the *Primera crònica* and in Ibn Kardabūs; see *PCG*, vol. II, p. 549 (ch. 977) and 552 (ch. 881), and to his portrayal in F. Maillo Salgado, *Historia*, pp. 128–29. The Castilian warriors García Ordoñez de Nájera and Gonzalo Núñez de Lara y Osma also fought at the defense of Muslim Huesca. See, generally, J. Alemany, "Milicias cristianas"; E. Lapiedra Gutiérrez, "Christian Participation"; and S. Barton, "Traitors." For Sem Pavor, see E. Lapiedra Gutiérrez, "Giraldo Sem Pavor."

[26] See B. Reilly, *The Contest*, p. 92.

to secure Alfonso's help against the now-threatening Almoravids, and to reinforce, for the Castilian King, his image as a protector of Andalusī Muslims.[27] But the death of the heir paved the way for a serious crisis in Castile-León after Alfonso's death in 1106, wherein the king's eldest daughter, Urraca, took the throne in the name of her son, Alfonso, while his younger daughter, Teresa, set in motion the separation of Portugal. Urraca struggled to keep the "empire" together, setting herself against both Teresa, and her own son and heir.[28] However, the queen's ill-conceived marriage with Alfonso I of Aragon provoked a war between the two kingdoms, and her attempts to marginalize the young Alfonso VII (1111–57) as he came of age sparked a civil war at home. Naturally, the Almoravids took advantage of this situation, and many territories were returned to Muslim rule, including, for a few days in 1117, Coimbra. But stability returned to Castile-León in 1126 with the death of Urraca, when the now-mature Alfonso VII was able to secure his Aragonese flank and turn against the Almoravids. The race was now on between Castile-León, Aragon, the Catalan counts, and the emerging kingdom of Portugal to each grab as much Muslim-dominated territory as possible.[29]

Alfonso VII was aided in this by several factors. The Almoravids had never been successful at raising large armies, and this limited their capacity to mount offensive campaigns and take advantage of Castilian disarray. This weakness was exacerbated by rebellions they were facing in al-Andalus and the Maghrib from the 1120s, and which led them to turn increasingly to Christian mercenaries and captives to supplement their forces.[30] In 1121 the followers of the charismatic preacher, Ibn Tūmart, founder of the revolutionary Almohad (al-Muwaḥḥid) movement, proclaimed him *mahdi* – an apocalyptic, messianic figure who would restore peace and justice to the world. Soon after, he established a base at Tin Mal, in the Atlas Mountains above Marrākush, from where he would set in motion the overthrow of the Almoravids.[31] Meanwhile, in al-Andalus, the population had wearied of the proud and rigorous Almoravids, who had come to be seen as foreign occupiers. Legalistic puritans, they alienated the populace by suppressing the Mālikī school of

[27] See the discussion in R. Menéndez Pidal, *La España del Cid*, vol. II, pp. 760–64. Al-Mu'tamid was deposed in 1091, which must have been just after the relationship had been established. See also R. Fletcher, *World of the Cid*, p. 88.

[28] For Urraca, see B. Reilly, *The Kingdom of León-Castilla under Queen Urraca.*

[29] See, B. Reilly, *The Kingdom of León-Castilla under King Alfonso VII*, esp. chs. 1–4, pp. 1–133, and *The Contest*, esp. chs. 6–9, pp. 126–230, and P. Linehan, *Spain*, ch. 1, "1157–79," pp. 1–35.

[30] See, for example, F. Clément, "Reverter et son fils."

[31] For the Almohads, see A. Fromherz, *The Almohads*, and A. Huici Miranda, *Historia política*, esp. vol. I, pp. 9–157.

*fiqh* that had monopolized local jurisprudence, and rejecting both philosophy (*falsafa*) – a pillar of Andalusī intellectual culture – and the mysticism of the Sūfīs, which was then electrifying Iberian Muslims.[32] Disenfranchised members of the local elite, like Sayf al-Dawla, heir to the deposed Hūdid dynasty of Zaragoza, and Muḥammad b. Mardanīsh ("Rey Lobo" or "King Wolf" to the Christians), became Castilian vassals and fought the Almoravids and Almohads alongside Christian forces. Meanwhile, popular rebellions – notably, a Sūfī-inspired insurrection at Almería – set out to overthrow local Almoravid governors.[33] Ironically, in this atmosphere many Andalusīs now came to regard Christian princes like Alfonso as potential saviors from what they saw as "Berber" oppressors.[34]

### *Too much, too soon: the conquest of Almería*

In contrast to the Almoravids, Alfonso found himself with ever-greater military resources at his disposal. The expanding frontier of Iberian Christendom had encouraged the development of autonomous municipalities, ruled by councils and unbeholden to any lord but the king. One of the pillars of these councils' identity was townsmen's obligation and right to make war for their own profit and to serve the king. The lure of booty and the social privileges attached to military service in this "society organized for war" put sizeable, if not always dependable, armies of commoners at the Iberian kings' disposal.[35] And although the councils fought amongst themselves as much as against Muslim foes, they helped to ingrain a notion of religious warfare in society as a whole – a process that coincided with the early successes of the Crusades in the Holy Land. The Crusade movement provided a doctrine and spiritual rationale for campaigns to conquer Muslim territory across the Mediterranean, and gave Christian rulers access to financial resources, specifically tithes, which ordinarily would be claimed by the Church. As early as 1089 Urban II (1088–99) had granted Crusade-like status to the Catalan efforts to conquer Muslim Tarragona, and in 1145 Eugenius III

[32] For Sufism in al-Andalus, see G. López Anguita and A. González Costa, *Historia del sufismo*. The movement would reach its apogee in the late twelfth century with the Murcian shaykh, Abū ʿAbd Allāh Muḥammad b. al-ʿArabī; see Ibn al-ʿArabī, *The Sufis of Andalusia*, pp. 21–59. In the mid fourteenth century Ibn Baṭṭūṭa found Sūfīs in Granada, but they had been occasionally persecuted by the Naṣrid kings. See L. P. Harvey, *Ibn Battuta*, pp. 64–65 and *Islamic Spain, 1250 to 1500*, pp. 29–31.

[33] See L. Sánchez Belda, *Chronica*, p. 55 {196}. For example, Ibn Ḥamdīn, the *qāḍī*-ruler of Córdoba, overthrew and killed "rex Zafadola," but then was forced to flee and himself take refuge with Alfonso VI. See R. El Hour, "The Andalusian Qāḍī," p. 82.

[34] B. Catlos, *The Victors and the Vanquished*, p. 67. [35] See below, p. 356.

(1145–53) had called the Second Crusade, which attracted fighters from across Latin Christendom to the Holy Land, and – en route – to Iberia.[36] The Crusades had also inspired the establishment of a new type of martial organization, the Military Orders. These monastic brotherhoods of knights, loyal to the papacy and sworn to protect the Holy Land and its pilgrims (and by extension to combat Islam in general), would become key to the conquest and administration of the Iberian Muslims.[37]

As Almoravid central power dissolved in the 1130s and 1140s the race was on among the various Christian powers and the Almohads to succeed them. It was in this context that Alfonso VII drove southwards deep into Almoravid territory. Caught between the Castilians and the Almohads, who had landed in 1146 at Algeciras (al-Jazīra al-Khaḍra), Yaḥyā b. Ghāniya, the Almoravid governor of southern Spain, threw his lot in with Alfonso, as would Muḥammad b. Mardanīsh, governor of Valencia and the surrounding territory.[38] The Castilian King pushed on, his goal being the rich and thriving emporium of Almería (al-Mariyya). With some thirty thousand inhabitants sequestered behind its stout walls, and a major center for textile production and trade of all sorts, the city was a considerable prize both economically and strategically. On October 17, 1147 the city yielded to Alfonso after an eleven-week siege in which his own forces were joined by those of King García Ramírez of Navarre (1134–50), and of Count Ramon Berenguer IV of Barcelona (1131–62). Crucial to this success was the involvement of Genoan and Pisan naval forces, which completed the blockade.[39] However, when the Italians learned the natives were negotiating a separate peace with the Castilian King, they assaulted the city, breaching the walls, and – according to Caffaro, an eyewitness – massacred thousands of the populace, while those holed up in the fort were able to ransom themselves.[40]

When the dust had settled, Alfonso was confirmed as ruler of Almería, and Genoa was given control of the city and its inhabitants as per the agreement established beforehand, and the Italians left behind a garrison

[36] Some time between 1096 and 1099 Urban II granted a Crusade indulgence to those who would fight the Muslims in Tarragona. See "Urban's Letter to the Counts of Besalú, Empurias, Roussillon, and Cerdaña and Their Followers," in E. Peters, *The First Crusade*, pp. 45–46. For the Second Crusade, see J. Phillips and M. Hoch, *The Second Crusade*.

[37] For an overview, see C. de Ayala Martínez, *Las órdenes militares*; for a case study, see A. Forey, *The Templars*.

[38] Yaḥyā b. Ghāniya's nephew ruled over Almoravid Mallorca. Ibn Mardanīsh was apparently descended from Christians.

[39] For the campaign, see O'Callaghan, *Reconquest*, pp. 44–46.

[40] The *Chronica Adefonsis Imperator* claims there was a general massacre of Muslims. See, L. Sánchez Bleda, *Chronica*, p. 187, and compare to Caffaro, *De captione*, pp. 28–29.

of "one thousand" men under the authority of two consuls. The city had suffered greatly and immediately declined – many had been killed, the elite had fled, and whole neighborhoods lay in ruins. Ibn Mardanīsh arranged for the refugees who had fled north to his territory during the campaign to return, and these accepted Alfonso as their lord once he had granted them the rights of communal and judicial autonomy. Unlike Toledo, however, Almería would not remain in Christian hands. In 1156 the Almohads laid siege to the city, which had already apparently been abandoned by the Genoese. Alfonso and Ibn Mardanīsh marched to the garrison's relief, but were forced to break off in midsummer 1157, sparking a general withdrawal of his forces from southern Spain. The King died on the march northwards, and did not live to see the city return to Muslim rule in late August. As the Almohads took control of what remained of al-Andalus, Castile-León was in no position to respond. Following the traditions of his dynasty, Alfonso VIII had divided his realms among his sons, León for Fernando and Castile for Sancho, sparking fresh struggles between the Christian kingdoms that the Almohads were more than ready to exploit.[41]

## Alfonso "the Battler" and the Muslims of the "Crown of Aragon"

And Ibn Rudmīr [Alfonso I] laid siege to the land (that is to say, Zaragoza) for some months, and its people underwent distress and suffering until they made peace with him with the condition that they give the land to him, and they put it in his hands, and those of them who wished might pay the head-tax (*al-jizya*) . . . and those who wished might depart . . . with a complete safeguard (*amān*) until they arrived at Muslim lands . . . (Ibn Kardabūs, *Tārīkh al-Andalus* (mid thirteenth century)[42])

On December 18, 1118, Alfonso I (1104–34) of Aragon, known deservedly as "the Battler," accepted the surrender of the capital city of the last *taifa* kingdom, Zaragoza, a major economic and cultural center.[43] The city had lived through tumultuous times, typical of the last days of the *taifas*. Caught between predatory Christian princes and the Almoravids, the divided and fraught Banū Hūd dynasty had staved off destruction by making massive *paria* ("tribute") payments to its Christian neighbors

[41] The Almohads briefly recaptured territory that had been conquered in the early 1100s. See, for example, B. Catlos, *The Victors and the Vanquished*, p. 84, H. Kennedy, *Muslim Spain and Portugal*, pp. 202–16 (esp. for Ibn Mardanīsh); and generally, A. Huici Miranda, *Historia política*, vol. I, pp. 197–378.

[42] "The History of al-Andalus," in F. Maillo Salgado, *Historia*, pp. 117–18.

[43] See G. Beech, *The Brief Eminence*.

and invoking the protection that this implied to enlist the Christian kings in its defense against their co-religionists. With the fall of Toledo and a looming sense among the piously inclined that Islam in the peninsula was under threat, the populace of the city turned against their own rulers, demanding that they refrain from further alliances with Christians. This proved impossible, and ceding to popular pressure and the arrival of an Almoravid governor in 1110, the king, ʿAbd al-Mālik b. Hūd ʿImād al-Dawla, abandoned the city for his castle at Rueda, and threw his lot in with the Christians. His son, Aḥmad, known in Christian chronicles as "Zafadola" (a corruption of his honorific, Sayf al-Dawla – "Sword of the Dynasty") became a vassal of Alfonso VII of Castile, and a major figure in the native anti-Almoravid resistance. Under the Almoravid Governor Ibn Tīfalwīt, the situation in Zaragoza stabilized, but only until his death in 1117. In late spring 1118 Alfonso laid siege to the city, and when the newly appointed Almoravid Governor, ʿAbd Allāh b. Mazdalī, was killed on November 16, the inhabitants surrendered, despairing of further relief.[44]

The taking of Zaragoza was part of larger strategy that dated back at least half a century, to the time of the first Aragonese King, Ramiro I (1035–63). As the *taifa* kingdom weakened, the Aragonese encroached on its territory. Significant gains came under Pedro I (1094–1104; also King of Navarre), who took the major towns of Huesca (Washqa, 1096) and Barbastro (Barbashturu, 1100) and began to encircle the capital.[45] Alfonso, a tireless warrior, came to power when both Castile and the Almoravids were weak, and pressing his advantage, took over nearly all that remained of the Muslim kingdom: territory stretching far to the south and west of Zaragoza, including the mid Ebro, Jalón, and Jiloca valleys. Dealing a series of military defeats to the Almoravids, including Cutanda (1120), Cullera (1125/26) and Alcalá (1129), Alfonso neutralized Almoravid military capacity and was able to press local Muslims into negotiated settlements.[46]

### *Conquest by negotiation*

Functionally identical to the Muslims' mode of conquest four hundred years earlier, Alfonso's *modus operandi* consisted of approaching Muslim

[44] B. Catlos, *The Victors and the Vanquished*, p. 94.

[45] See C. Laliena Corbera and P. Sénac, *Musulmans et Chrétiens*.

[46] For an overview of Alfonso's campaigns, see C. Stalls, *Possessing the Land*. The Muslims of the region were in disarray, but they fought back with determination. See, for example, B. Catlos, *The Victors and the Vanquished*, p. 62, and C. de la Puente, "Vivre et mourir pour Dieu."

locales and offering the alternative of attack or protection. Unable to defend themselves, local leaders had little choice but to negotiate their submission, the terms of which were set down in formal treaties. Each of these followed the same basic pattern: the local Muslim elite would be confirmed in their position of power and, in exchange for paying tribute or tax, the populace were allowed religious freedom and political autonomy, and liberty of movement. For their part, Muslims were typically required to relocate to residences outside the town walls within a period of one year. The few surviving agreements resemble each other closely, and all provide for liberties that would have been considered indispensable for Muslim subjects and reasonable for the Christians to concede.[47]

This was a "carrot" strategy that Alfonso employed in campaigns against both Muslims and Christians, combined with the "stick" of occasionally brutal and indiscriminate violence.[48] The objective was to secure control of territory before rival Christian princes could, and to induce the native inhabitants to willingly accept him as their lord. Gaining the consent of native Muslims not only relieved him of the need to garrison conquered territory (which would reduce his own military capacity), but guaranteed that the land would remain populated and productive. Moreover, these Muslims became a source of revenue for the King that by-passed seigniorial intermediaries; Aragonese Muslims became direct royal subjects. It also freed up Alfonso to wage war against his wife, Urraca, as he pressed his claim by marriage to the thrones of Castile and León. Once Alfonso VII had secured these titles after 1126, the Aragonese king turned south in an effort to block the advances of the Catalans into Almoravid territory. In 1134 he laid siege to Muslim Fraga (Ifrāgha) and it was here, as he toured the town's defenses, that a sharp-eyed archer on the walls shot an arrow into the king's eye and killed him.

Alfonso's death, however, does not seem to have inspired his Muslim subjects to revolt, although it did provoke a resurgence under the Almoravids and the loss of much of southern Aragon. As for local Muslims, all evidence indicates that a working accommodation had been reached between the victors and the vanquished.[49] Staunchly pious Muslims and members of the *'ulamā'* would have felt compelled to leave Christian-ruled Zaragoza, and many evidently did, with most heading south to relocate in and around Valencia.[50] Of course, with their

[47] For the surrender treaties, see B. Catlos, "*Secundum suam zunam*," pp. 13–17; A. Echevarría Arsuaga, "La 'mayoria' mudéjar," pp. 14–27; and below, p. 380.
[48] See R. Fletcher and S. Barton, eds., *The World of El Cid*, p. 186.
[49] For the Almoravid campaigns, see J. Béraud-Villars, *Les Touareg*.
[50] M. Marín, "Des migrations," p. 50.

education and skills, many educated Muslims could find the patronage on which their livelihood depended only in Muslim courts; the identity of the ruler, however, made less difference to ordinary folk, the bulk of whom apparently stayed. Moreover, there is little or no evidence of conversion to Christianity here. One factor may have been the lack of a substantial Mozarab population in these parts. Although there was evidently a community in Zaragoza, and in his famous raid of 1125 deep into the Islamic south, Alfonso I was said to have brought back thousands of Christian refugees to settle in his lands, within a generation the Mozarab community seems to have been absorbed by the Latinate Aragonese Christians.[51]

The durability of Islam here is linked to the gradual nature of the conquest in these territories. For the first generation or two Christian domination may have been scarcely noticeable, and even as new settlers began to arrive there is no indication of friction or tensions. The law codes promulgated in the first half-century of Christian rule indicate that Muslims and Christians existed side-by-side but as separate communities. There was also a long history of cross-frontier interaction in this region and a high degree of mutual familiarity. As was the case in Castile, many Muslims were prepared to regard a Christian king as a viable, if not completely legitimate sovereign, and some Muslims fought as soldiers for Alfonso alongside his Christian troops both in his war against the Almoravids and his attacks on Castile.[52] And if the strategy of Aragonese Muslims was to wait out the Christian occupation, they were rewarded – if only temporarily – when after death of "the Battler" much of the territory he had gained reverted briefly to Muslim control.

### *A proto-Crusade?*

The willingness of local Muslims to negotiate is all the more surprising given the first significant experience they had with Christian conquerors. In 1064 a force of soldiers of fortune consisting of Normans, Burgundians, Aquitainians, and Catalans surrounded the town of Barbastro in the foothills of the Pyrenees. After a lengthy siege (the proverbial "forty days" according to the contemporary al-Bakrī) in which the inhabitants defended themselves spiritedly until their water

[51] For Alfonso's raid and Aragonese Mozarabs, see R. Hitchcock, *Mozarabs*, pp. 99–108. The collaboration of Andalusī Mozarabs with the Aragonese king was the grounds used by the Almoravids to justify the transportation of the remaining Christian community to the Maghrib. See D. Serrano, "Dos fetuas."

[52] According to a hostile Castilian source, when Alfonso I seized Burgos from Urraca, he turned his Muslims troops loose, allowing them to commit all manner of atrocities against the city, and, specifically, on the local nuns. See L. Torres Balbás, *Algunos aspectos*, p. 25.

supply was cut off, terms were reached.[53] Under the arrangement, the defenders would be able to leave the town with as many of their belongings as they could carry, under the safeguard of the attackers. No sooner had they set out, however, than the Christians swept down on them, massacring the men, carrying off the women and children, and taking the town. After some time, the main leaders of the force, notably the Norman, Robert Crispin, re-crossed the Pyrenees laden with loot and slaves, including a large contingent of young women.[54] According to a contemporary Andalusī chronicler, Ibn Hayyān, a Jew sent to ransom some of the town's women reported that those attackers who remained had set up household in the town in the style of its former inhabitants, wearing their clothes, enjoying their foods, and taking their daughters as concubines and musicians.[55] The taking of Barbastro and the betrayal of the truce scandalized and alarmed Andalusīs, and the following year al-Muqtadir of Zaragoza led a half-hearted Muslim coalition that retook the town and slaughtered the Christian occupiers.

This siege of Barbastro came on the heels of a letter by Pope Alexander II (1061–73) granting the remission of sins to the faithful who would fight the Muslims of Spain. In view of this, some historians have characterized this campaign as the earliest Crusade; however, it is not clear to whom the letter was addressed, or that it had been transmitted to those who took part in the attack. Whatever the case, raiding al-Andalus was increasingly seen by non-Iberian Christians as an opportunity for both enrichment and salvation.[56] This had been encouraged both by Alfonso VI's recruitment of Burgundian nobles to his court, and by the publicity offered by the route to Santiago de Compostela, which was becoming the most popular pilgrimage site in Latin Christendom.[57] Much as the Almoravids and Almohads viewed Christians as mere infidels and their native co-religionists as effete and untrustworthy, foreign Christian knights and clerics regarded the native elite with contempt and the Muslims almost as animals or devils. Hence, the early eleventh-century chronicler Adetmar de Chabannes recounts with relish the cruelties and tortures that the Norman adventurer Roger de Tosny inflicted on Muslim

[53] See B. Catlos, *The Victors and the Vanquished*, pp. 82–84.

[54] Guillem VIII, Duke of Aquitaine, was also at the siege and carried back many Muslim slaves to his court at Poitiers, undoubtedly including singers, musicians, and dancers. See p. 491, below; cf. p. 278.

[55] See R. Boase, "Arabic Influences," pp. 464–66.

[56] For an idea of the to and fro regarding whether the siege "counts" as a "Crusade," see, for example, A. Ferreiro, *The Siege of Barbastro*, and C. Laliena Corbera, "Guerra santa," pp. 190–94.

[57] See R. Fletcher, *St. James's Catapult*, esp. chs. 3–5, pp. 53–128.

oners with the specific aim of terrorizing the populace.[58] rrespondingly, Andalusī Muslims distinguished between more trust-.. orthy Iberian Christians and their oath-breaking foreign co-religionists. In this spirit, in 1069 al-Muqtadir concluded an alliance with "his friend" (*amicum suum*) Sancho IV Garcés, King of Pamplona (1054–76) against any and all extra-peninsular aggressors.[59]

### *Ramon Berenguer IV and the "Crown of Aragon"*

The death of Alfonso the Battler was further complicated by the fact that he had died childless. Foreseeing Castile's resurgence and the fractiousness of the Aragonese nobility, the wiley king willed his realm to the papacy and the nascent Military Orders, guaranteeing the succession would be mired in litigation in order to prevent Aragon's dismemberment.[60] As a compromise between the parties, his brother, Ramiro II (1134–37), a monk and bishop, was crowned King and allowed to rule just long enough to produce an heir, Petronila. She was immediately betrothed to the powerful Count of Barcelona, Ramon Berenguer IV, with the provision that Ramiro return to the Church and any offspring of the royal couple would inherit both realms.[61] This was the origin of the "Crown of Aragon," a dynastic aggregate that the couple's descendants would rule for over three and a half centuries.[62] With this union, the Counts of Barcelona – who had been endeavoring over the previous century to force the other Catalan counts to recognize their overlordship – gained the prestige of kingship and the military resources of Aragon, while the Aragonese gained an outlet to the sea and the security of their eastern flank.

With the crumbling of Almoravid power in al-Andalus and the Maghrib, Ramon Berenguer went on the attack. In 1147 he was at Alfonso VII's side at the unsuccessful siege of Mallorca, and in July 1148 he led a similar operation, again with Genoese naval support and the aid of the Templars and foreign crusaders, against Tortosa (Ṭurṭūsha), a strategically important sea and river port of approximately 12,000 inhabitants, located near the

[58] Adémari Chabannensis, *Chronicon*, ed. P. Bourgain (Turnhout, 1999), p. 174; English translation in: Adémar of Chabannes, "Chronicle (on Roger of Tosny)," in E. Van Houts, ed., *The Normans in European History*, p. 270

[59] J. M. Lacarra, "Dos tratados," p. 131. The latter is from a treaty of 1055; see J. M. Lacarra, *Documentos para el estudio*, vol. I, pp. 84–85 {69}.

[60] Lourie presents the most likely explanation of the puzzling testament. See E. Lourie, "The Will," and "The Will . . . A Reply."

[61] See B. Catlos, *The Victors and the Vanquished*, p. 74; T. Bisson, *The Medieval Crown*, pp. 16–17.

[62] See T. Bisson, *The Medieval Crown*, p. 31.

mouth of the Ebro.[63] Here, the townsfolk put up a vigorous defense in the face of the assaults, hoping to repeat their success of 1091, when they had repelled a joint Genoese–Pisan attack. But the tremendous destruction wrought by artillery wore them down, and in early November they made a pact with the attackers. They would send envoys to the Muslim princes of Spain urging them to come to their relief, and if no help were forthcoming within forty days they would surrender.

When the grace period expired with no sign of aid, the populace sued for peace, and on December 30, 1148 accepted a pact deliberately modeled on Zaragoza's treaty of submission with Alfonso I. This agreement took the form of a contract (*firmamentum*) between the Count and the Muslim town's officials and inhabitants, guaranteeing their legal rights and administrative autonomy. It defined the taxes to which they were to be subject, and allowed for a transitional year, at the end of which they were to move outside the town walls and hand over the main mosque. Matters such as jurisdictional disputes between Muslims, Christians, and Jews were covered in detail, indicating that the inhabitants were expecting and expected to remain as subjects of their Christian conquerors.[64] As per their own agreement, the victors divided up the city, with the Genoese taking their standard one-third share as the price for their support, and Ramon Berenguer taking two, one of which was given to the Templars. Christian settlers likely began arriving not long after the conquest, but for the first generation under infidel rule, life likely changed little for the Muslim inhabitants, except for their having to relocate to an extra-mural faubourg.

Ramon Berenguer followed his success at Tortosa by re-establishing control over the territories that had been taken by Alfonso I and by conquering the interior along the banks of the Ebro. Lleida (Lārida) fell on October 24, 1149, and the town's Muslims were granted terms on the Zaragoza–Tortosa model.[65] Sovereignty over the city was shared by Ramon Berenguer, his ally, Count Ermengol VI of Urgell, and the Templars. This same year Fraga and Mequinensa (Miknāsa) were taken, and in the following decade Tarragona and its interior were secured (both from independent Muslim collectives and Norman soldiers-of-fortune). In 1151 the Count of Barcelona signed the Treaty of Tudilén

[63] Twenty-seven years earlier, Ramon Berenguer III had planned to invade Mallorca, a campaign that the *wāli* of Muslim Lleida was obliged by treaty to assist. See B. Catlos, *The Victors and the Vanquished*, p. 73.

[64] For the treaty, see CODOIN, vol. IV, pp. 130–35 {56}.

[65] For Lleida, see J. Mutgé i Vives, *L'aljama sarraïna*, pp. 1–3. A privilege of Ramon Berenguer IV (1153–59) granted the surrendering Muslims of the towns of the lower Ebro "laws such as they have at Zaragoza and Tortosa." See J. Font i Rius, "La carta de seguridad," p. 283.

with León, dividing continental Iberia into two zones of conquest and influence; the Muslim *Sharq al-Andalus* as far as Murcia was to go to the Catalans and all lands west to León.

In general, the areas conquered by Ramon Berenguer and his son, Alfonso II, Count-King of Barcelona and Aragón (1164–96), were populated by Christian settlers fairly rapidly, thanks to the burgeoning population of the Pyrenean valleys and the deliberate policies of those rulers. Colonization was further entrenched by grants to monastic orders, particularly the Cistercians, and to Military Orders, notably the Templars and Hospitallers. At the same time, a pragmatic approach to the Muslim populace also yielded results. There is little evidence of a mass departure of Muslims from the region, and every indication that with the exception of the most important cities, both the towns and the countryside remained firmly, if not overwhelmingly, Islamic.[66] Nor is there any evidence of substantial conversion to Christianity. For the first generations the pre-conquest local elites stayed in power and Christian domination meant little more than the diversion of long-established tribute and taxes to the new overlords.

## Afonso Henriques and the Siege of Lisbon

The men of Cologne and the Flemings, when they saw in the city so many spurs to their greed, did not observe their oaths or their religious guarantees. They ran hither and yon. They plundered. They broke down doors. They rummaged through the interior of every house. They drove the citizens away and harassed them improperly and unjustly. They destroyed clothes and utensils. They treated virgins shamefully. They acted as if right and wrong were the same. They secretly took away everything that should have been common property. They even cut the throat of the elderly Bishop of the city, slaying him against all right and justice ... (Osbernus, *De expugnatione Lyxbonensi* (*c.* 1147)[67])

In the panic that followed the dramatic *entrée* of the Almoravids into the peninsula in 1086, ʿUmar b. al-Afṭas al-Mutawakkil, King of Badajoz, the first of the *taifa* rulers who had sent for help to Yūsuf b. Tāshufin, turned in desperation to Alfonso VI of Castile for rescue from the North African *mujāhidūn*. Like al-Qādir of Toledo, al-Mutawakkil was the scion of a Berber military dynasty that felt little affinity with its Andalusī subjects. In 1093 he agreed to hand Santarém (Shantarīn), Lisbon (al-Ushbūna), and Sintra (Shintara) over to the Castilian King in return for protection.[68] It

66 Again, the account of Ibn al-Kardabūs represents an exception. He claims that 50,000 Muslims left Zaragoza after the conquest. See Ibn al-Kardabūs, *Ṭārikh al-Andalus*, p. 119.

67 Text adapted from J. Brundage, *The Crusades*, p. 103.

68 See B. Reilly, *The Kingdom of León-Castilla under King Alfonso VI*, p. 235.

was a gambit that would fail; within a year the Almoravids retook Lisbon and Sintra, and despite Alfonso's promises of protection, arrested and executed al-Mutawakkil after they took Badajoz. Santarém would be recovered in 1111, and little evidence of its brief period under Castilian rule survives. Here, too, Christian intervention had likely been minimal and most of the natives evidently stayed put. For the elite, of course, emigration would seem to be a better option, although it was not without its risks. Hence, the chronicler Ibn Bassām, a refugee from the 1093 occupation, lamented: "In Santarém we were well-off and from a family of good standing, whereas now I have to move from place to place begging for a livelihood ... I stayed in Sevilla for several years ... resigned to solitude and poverty."[69]

The resurgence of the Almoravids coincided with the disarray in Castile-León that followed Alfonso VI's death. The County of Portugal had been inherited by the King's daughter, Teresa, and her husband, Henry of Burgundy, and after Henry's death in 1112, Teresa took power, holding off the Almoravids at Coimbra, and battling her sister, Urraca. Although her attempts to incorporate Galicia into her realm failed, Teresa, who styled herself as "Queen of Portugal," held on to power even as her son, Afonso, came of legal age. Leading rebellious nobles against his mother, Afonso defeated her in battle in 1128 and sent her into exile.[70] By this time the Almoravids themselves were faltering and in 1138 Afonso scored a signal victory over them at the Battle of Ourique. The south of al-Andalus now lay exposed to his raids, which reportedly brought Muslim (and Mozarab) prisoners north as slaves.[71] His most serious political rivals, however, remained the Christian kingdoms of León and Castile.[72]

### *The conquest of Lisbon*

The 1140s brought new opportunities for Afonso (1139–85) to push southwards. The Almoravid Commander of the Faithful, Yūsuf b. Tāshufīn, had died in 1143 and his son and successor Tāshufīn

[69] A. Tibi, "Ibn Bassām," p. 134.

[70] For Teresa, see S. Lay, *The Reconquest Kings*, pp. 55–70, and B. Reilly *The Kingdom of León-Castilla under Queen Urraca*, pp. 124–50.

[71] Some of these found were sold as far north as Galicia and the Basque Country. The monastery of San Salvador de Sobrado de Monxes (A Coruña) bought a number of Muslim captives to work the land. Most converted and married into local families. See C. González Paz, "Sarracenos." The Granadan poet al-Hijārī found himself laboring in isolation in "cold Vizkaya." See R. Fletcher, *The Quest for El Cid*, p. 178.

[72] For the conquest of Muslim Portugal, see H. Kennedy, *Muslim Spain and Portugal*; D. Wasserstein, *The Rise and Fall*; S. Lay, *The Reconquest Kings*.

b. Yūsuf was killed two years later. The Almohads would lay siege to the capital of Marrakesh in 1146, and when it capitulated the following year (thanks in part to the defection of the Almoravids' Christian troops), members of the ruling family were put to death. The anti-Almoravid revolts in al-Andalus saw governors and officials overthrown by popular "republican" movements, often led by the local *qāḍī*, or Islamic magistrate, and a counsel of leading citizens. Both Lisbon and Santarém became Portuguese tributaries, and in March 1147 with the aid of Arabic-speaking Mozarab troops, Afonso seized well-fortified Santarém in a stealthy night attack. A chronicle written by a monk later in the century had Afonso exhorting his troops to kill every Muslim inhabitant of the town, but while there may have indeed been a massacre, it is hardly conceivable that the King would have ordered it, as killing the population would have run completely counter to his own interests.[73]

At this time, while Castilian attention was focused on the Almería campaign, the Crusades were bringing large contingents of northern European knights down the Atlantic coast on their way to the Holy Land. Thus, in 1143 Afonso took advantage of a passing Crusader fleet to besiege Lisbon, but the blockade failed. Then, in summer 1147, a large fleet bearing warriors from Flanders, Germany, and Britain who had answered the call to the Second Crusade dropped anchor at Porto – perhaps at the King's instigation.[74] With this, Afonso prepared his second move against Lisbon. But before the siege was put in place he sent the Bishop of Porto to the city in an effort to negotiate its surrender. Although in the end Afonso's envoy demanded only that the inhabitants yield the castle, and gave assurances they would be permitted to live in the city according to their customs, and that their property, liberties, and religious freedom would be safeguarded, he was rebuffed.[75]

The Crusaders arrived in July 1147, the various contingents divided amongst themselves and largely suspicious of Afonso. While the bitter siege wore on, Christians endured the insults of the defenders, who taunted them for the infidelities they claimed the Crusaders' wives were committing in their absence.[76] As the situation inside the city worsened, some of the desperate defenders fled, only to be killed, forcibly baptized, or forced back by the Crusaders to face the wrath of their co-religionists.

[73] The taking of the city is described in the brief chronicle, *De expugnatione Scalabis*; see A. Herculano and J. José da Silva Mendes, *Portugaliae monumenta historica*, pp. 93–95.

[74] See J. O'Callaghan, *Reconquest and Crusade*, pp. 41–49.

[75] See the contemporary account in C. David, ed., *The Conquest of Lisbon*, and J. Philips, "Conquest of Lisbon," ch. 8 in J. Philips and M. Hoch, *The Second Crusade*, pp. 136–66.

[76] C. David, *The Conquest of Lisbon*, p. 131.

Envoys were sent to neighboring Muslim princes in an appeal for help, but few made it through. One did – to Abū Muḥammad b. Ṣidray b. Wazīr of Evora (Yabūra) – but he demurred, claiming he could not aid them by virtue of his own treaty with Afonso.[77] By the time the walls were breached and the Muslims agreed to surrender, Afonso had little control over the Christian army. The agreement the king had made with the inhabitants, which was to permit them to leave the city under safeguard, was ignored by the troops, who stormed into the city on October 24; they killed and looted both Muslims and Mozarabs indiscriminately, even murdering the city's sitting bishop.

In the aftermath, some of the survivors undoubtedly fled, while others may have converted, integrating with the Mozarab community that by some accounts made up half of the city's population. However, a significant number of Muslims remained, evidenced by the *fouro* (law code) Afonso would grant the community twenty-three years later.[78] Nor did the atrocities at Lisbon (and, perhaps, Santarém) foster a generic distrust of Christians among local Muslims. After Lisbon's fall the Muslims of other towns, such as Sintra, surrendered to Afonso and became his subjects. In any case, the Christians were not the only ones killing civilians. In 1154 when the Almohads suppressed the revolt of one of their own governors at Niebla (Labla, 50 kilometers west of Sevilla), this was accompanied by massacre of the local populace.[79]

### The beginnings of "*Mudejarismo*"

This is the charter that the King, Emperor Alfonso, son of King Sancho, whom God blessed, made with the *alcudi* of Tudela, and with his *algalifos*, and with the *alforques*, and with the good Muslims of Tudela, and with Alfalibi: and confirmed those *alcudes*, and those *alfaques*, in their *alfaquias*, and those *alguaziles* in their alguazilias ... (Alfonso I of Aragon, surrender agreement with the Muslims of Tudela (1115)[80])

The surviving surrender agreements confirm that, whereas the Islamic political and cultural elite of the *taifa* kingdoms may have fled the Christian advance, local authorities and their constituents more often

[77] M. F. Lopes de Barros, *Tempos e espaços*, p. 89.
[78] For the text of 1170's "Foral dos Mouros Forros de Lisboa, Almada, Palmela e Alcácer," see A. Herculano and J. José da Silva Mendes Leal, eds., *Portugaliae monumenta historica. Leges et Consuetudines*, pp. 396–97.
[79] F. Roldan Castro, *Niebla musulmana*, p. 55. For challenges to the Almohads, and the reprisals they took, see H. Kennedy, *Muslim Spain and Portugal*, pp. 204–06.
[80] T. Muñoz y Romero, *Colección de fueros*, pp. 415–17.

intended to stay in their lands. Had this not been the case, they would not have negotiated agreements that reaffirmed their own status as community leaders, established permanent rights for Muslims, and which – as at Tudela – described in detail how members of their community would interact with Christian and Jewish subjects.[81] Initially, the conquest amounted essentially to the displacement of a Muslim political and cultural elite by military and fiscal authorities, who were Christian. It was, in effect, a "static diaspora" – one in which the people were not dispersed, but the politico-confessional border shifted above them.

Those who chose to stay included not only farmers and members of the lower socio-economic strata, but also substantial numbers of craftsmen and artisans. In fact, Muslims in these lands continued to dominate certain economic sectors for centuries, notably construction, carpentry, and other decorative crafts, the manufacture of certain arms and armor, soap-making, and high-end tailoring, to name but a few. Most of the religious, cultural, and intellectual elite would have departed – the prospects for patronage under Christian rule would have been minimal, and such piously inclined individuals would have found life under infidel rule unpalatable. Hence, many of the *ᶜulamā* of Zaragoza headed south for Valencia and Sharq al-Andalus.[82] That said, some clearly stayed on, as evidenced by the survival of literary and scientific culture in centers like Toledo and Zaragoza.[83] And while the networks needed to sustain a vibrant Islamic culture were certainly put under strain, and knowledge probably became more local, in most areas they did not entirely disappear altogether – travel to and from the Islamic world remained possible. What survived, then, were socially and economically diverse, autonomous communities, living largely according to their pre-conquest organization under an often largely abstract Christian jurisdiction, alongside a small but steady stream of non-Muslim settlers who were establishing themselves in these newly conquered territories. Population estimates are impossible to make with any accuracy, but one can say with confidence that in some areas, such as the central *Meseta*, the Muslim population may have dropped to a negligible minority (less than, perhaps, 5 percent of the

81 For the role of local Islamic authorities in such negotations, see below, n. 86. Locally negotiated surrender treaties were completely consistent with Andalusī political practice.
82 See M. Marín, "Des migrations."
83 Clearly, Arabized Jews played a crucial role in the survival of Andalusī learning and its appropriation by Latins, but there is evidence also for the persistence of Arabic science and letters among Muslims. The northern Ebro Valley was a locus of translation, and a medical school (*madrasa*) functioned in Zaragoza into the fourteenth century. See C. Burnett, "A Group of Latin-Arabic Translators," and L. García Ballester, *Historia social de la medicina*, pp. 68–70.

total population). The minority was likely even smaller, al' concentrated, in Navarre, where Muslim settlement had . limited to the area around Tudela and the zone of the upper Ebr Ribera"). In the Kingdom of Aragon, Muslims would remain a numerica majority, although unevenly distributed, through this period.[84]

From the perspective of native Muslims, remaining in their lands under Christian rule was rendered possible by the concessions they were granted – most importantly communal administrative and judicial autonomy, and the right to their property and to practice their religion. Although in the twelfth century, with the construction of the image of "the Cid" as a religious warrior and the incarnation of St. James as "Matamoros" – "the Moor-killer" – the rhetoric of "the Reconquest" began to take shape under the influence of clergy and nobles inspired by the culture of Burgundy and the north of France, the aim of Christian rulers was control of the territory and its people, not the expulsion of native Muslims.[85] Quite the contrary, sovereigns such as Alfonso VI, who referred to himself in correspondence with the *taifa* kings as *al-Imbraṭūr dhū'l-Millatayn* ("Emperor of the Two Religions"), deliberately presented themselves as the legitimate rulers of their Muslim subjects – the corollary of which was that the Muslims were their legitimate subjects.[86] This was recognized formally, as in Aragon, where they acquired the status of *moros de paz* ("Muslims of the Peace"), or in Portugal, *mouros forros* ("free Muslims"). For these Muslims, whatever ideological repulsion the notion of Christian rule carried would have been mitigated both by the conciliatory policies of Christian rulers and the collaboration of Muslim leaders with Christian allies. Indeed, it is only historical hindsight that allows us to read the political history of Iberia in this period as a contest between Christendom and the Muslim world. It was, in fact, a battle for peninsular hegemony among a shifting array of Christian and

[84] It is virtually impossible to make concrete estimates regarding the Muslim population in these territories. Extrapolations from incomplete and idiosyncratic royal tax records – which do not appear until the thirteenth century in the Crown of Aragon, and the fourteenth or fifteenth century, elsewhere, are little better than guesses. The first formal census of the peninsula was not undertaken until early sixteenth century, and such evidence cannot be read backwards.

[85] The legend of Santiago, including his alleged appearance at the Battle of Clavijo in 844, was the late twelfth-century invention of the Frankish monastic chroniclers who became the ideologues of the Leonese monarchy. For the legends of Pelayo, St. James, and the development of the Reconquest ideology, see, for example, C. de Ayala Martínez, "Fernando I," and R. Fletcher, *Saint James's Catapult*, ch. 3, "The Early Cult of Saint James," pp. 53–77.

[86] See A. Mackay and M. Benaboud, "Yet Again," and "Alfonso VI of León and Castile."

Muslim powers, each of which pursued its own agendas and chose its allies and enemies with little regard to religious identity.

### *Religion and frontier*

The notion of "frontier" has also been overemphasized. From the time of the Islamic conquest, the divisions between Islamic and Christian Iberia had been subtle and imprecise. Christian and Muslim principalities were deeply entangled politically, and their elites intermarried. Christians and Muslims traded with as many as raided each other, fought alongside as well as against one another, and there was a wide range of contact across the social spectrum. Bilingualism and biculturalism, as well as polyglossia and diglossia, were common on both sides of the porous frontier, while the presence of Mozarabs in positions of authority in both Muslim and Christian principalities sustained a mutual familiarity and acted as a conduit for communication and collaboration. This peninsular *modus vivendi* came dramatically to light when outside actors came on the scene. With few exceptions, atrocities such as massacres, forced conversions, and mass deportations were carried out by recently arrived or transient non-natives: the Normans at Barbastro, the Crusaders at Lisbon, and the Almoravids in al-Andalus.

Most remarkable is the Andalusīs' reaction to Almoravid rule. Initially hailed as saviors from both the predatory Christians and the effete *taifa* kings, their foreign mores, heavy hand, and juridical and religious policies soon alienated the Andalusī populace. Within a generation, rebellions erupted across al-Andalus, in which North African governors were deposed, and replaced by popular governments under the leadership of local oligarchies or Islamic magistrates. At times these "republican" movements appointed new leaders, at times they negotiated with Christians, and at times they remained autonomous. There was a long tradition of popular political movements here; thus, the locally negotiated surrender treaties are completely consistent with Andalusī political practice.[87] The novelty was that, faced with their own disarray, the populace was prepared to appeal to and accept a Christian *ṣulṭān*. There was also a long tradition of disregard towards Berbers, and native hostility towards the Almoravids was palpable. Hence, Christian chroniclers distinguished between Berber "Moabites" and local "Hagarenes," and at least two

[87] The popular Islamic republics that sprouted up in the eleventh and twelfth centuries were often headed up by a *qāḍī*; see M. Fierro Bello, "The *Qāḍī* as Ruler." It was local Islamic magistrates who tended to negotiate with would-be conquerors, whether Almoravid, Almohad, or Christian. See R. El Hour, "The Andalusian Qāḍī," pp. 78–81.

surrender treaties (Tortosa and Tudela) specifically guaranteed that it would be forbidden for Christians to take reprisals against local Muslims for misdeeds committed by Almoravids.[88]

Under their new, infidel sovereigns, Muslims were faced with the choice of converting to Christianity or remaining in their faith. And while there seem to have been few if any instances of coercion, outcomes varied strikingly from region to region. In the west of the peninsula, the lands of Castile, León, and Portugal, most who stayed seem to have converted. There can be little doubt that the large and well-established Mozarab communities in these areas acted as a vector for conversion, providing a framework in which Christian religion could be adopted without rejecting Arabo-Andalusī culture.[89] For their part, the conquerors here would have been very familiar with the notion of Arabic-speaking, "Orientalized" Christians, thanks both to Mozarab emigration and the fact that Christians had begun to conquer Muslim territory as early as the tenth century.

On the contrary, in lands conquered by Aragon and Catalunya, there was virtually no conversion to Christianity. Here, the population seems to have been overwhelmingly Muslim, with small native Mozarab and Jewish populations. In the aftermath of the conquest, non-Muslims arrived as settlers, and while they did not necessarily displace or compete with the natives, the divisions between their communities were strictly maintained, at least on a formal level. Accommodation was further facilitated by the gradual pace of Christian settlement here, reflected by the often-lengthy interval – sometimes more than a decade – between the conquest of these Muslim towns and the consecration of what had been their congregational mosques as Christian churches.[90] Hence, the *fueros* granted to Christians here in this period tend to make no mention of their Muslim neighbors; the communities developed independently. This belies the quotidian reality of interaction that emerged in the first decades after the conquest. As Christian monasteries and noblemen were granted Muslim-occupied lands, and as Christian settlers plugged themselves into or settled alongside existing grids of agricultural and craft production, with native Muslims as neighbors, customers, and suppliers, interaction and integration would have been inevitable.[91] With the exception of occasional

[88] CODOIN, vol. IV, pp. 130–35 {56}. These terms were not used with any consistency. For "Hagarene," see below, p. 534.
[89] See, for example, M. J. Rubiera Mata, "Un insólito caso," p. 347.
[90] See B. Catlos, *The Victors and the Vanquished*, pp. 110–11.
[91] For the piecemeal nature of Christian colonization in much of Aragon, wherein Christian settlers moved into existing rural and urban land grids, see *ibid.*, pp. 112–16.

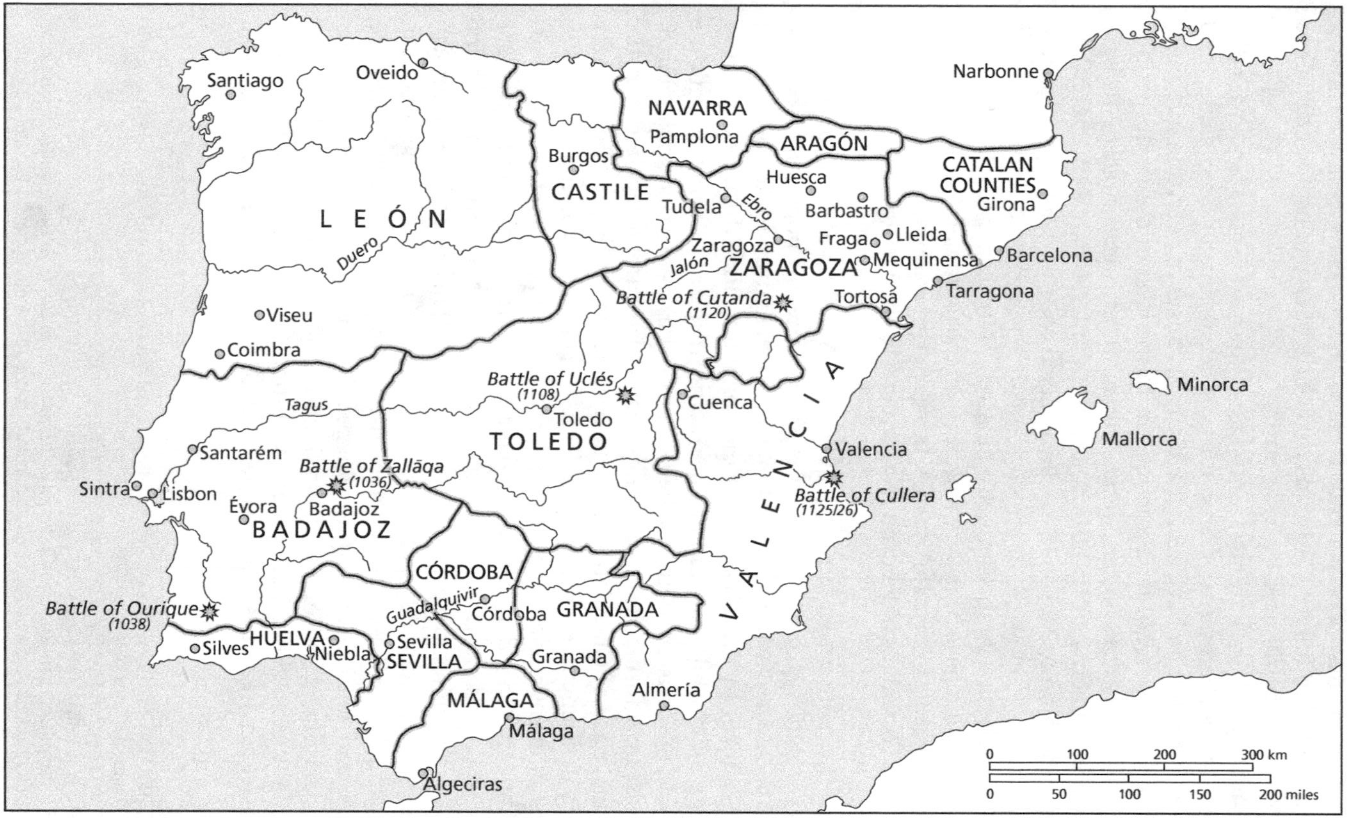


Map 2 The Iberian Peninsula, *c.* 1050

incidents, both groups were evidently confident enough to engage with each other on their own terms and with little, if any, apparent friction.

### *Society and culture*

Interestingly, the most durable and visible impact of Muslims' determination to remain in their ancestral lands, even at the price of their submission to Christian rule, are the churches that pepper the villages and towns of the territory of Castile-León, Aragon, and Catalunya conquered between 1080 and 1150. In a process that took up to thirty or forty years, depending on the locale, as Christian settlement reached "critical mass," the mosque-cum-churches were either wholly or partially demolished and replaced with purpose-built churches built in basilica-type style. Much of this building work, including the design and engineering, but most clearly the decoration, was carried out by Muslim workers and craftsmen. This "*mudéjar* style," characterized by intricate geometric brickwork relief interspersed with colored ceramic tiles, is the emblematic indigenous style of this broad swathe of the peninsula.[92] Whatever this meant for local Christians: whether it was a recognition of their admiration for Arabo-Islamic aesthetics or artisanal skill, or a manifestation of Christian domination over Islam and its culture, the fact remains that *mudéjares* were very directly implicated in the physical establishment and extension of Chrisianity in this region. Local Muslims built and decorated the churches their Christian lords and neighbors worshiped in. Whatever complex and perhaps self-contradictory reaction this may have elicited among both Christians and Muslims, church construction served as one of the motors of *mudéjar* prosperity and integration, and of the mutual confidence with which local Christian and Muslim communities interacted. Moreover, Muslims were not called on to do this because they were cheap and readily available labor. The accounts we have of the payment and employment of these artisans show that they were well paid and highly esteemed.[93]

The origin of *mudéjar* society – as free Muslims under Christian rule came later to be called – cannot be understood simply in terms of religious identity. Ethnicity, class, and local conditions were also powerful factors. Stunned at the surrender of Toledo, the poet and *faqīh* Abū Muḥammad b. al-ʿAzzāl called on his fellow Muslims to flee:

92 See below, p. 425.

93 For a survey of various aspects of mudéjar architecture and artistic production, see M. Lacarra Ducay, *Arte mudéjar*, *Actas del* I *Simposio Internacional de Mudejarismo (1975)*, and *Actas del* II *Simposio Internacional de Mudejarismo: Arte (1981)*.

Men of al-Andalus, to horse!
Mount your steeds and swiftly ride;
It were an erroneous course
Longer here to abide.
Garments ordinarily
By their fringes are divested;
Our imperial robe I see
From the middle wrested.[94]

But few apart from his fellow literati, savants, and courtiers seem to have paid him heed. Rather, they opted to stay, straddling the fine line between living as faithful subjects of a universal sovereign and as enemies of the True Faith. The anonymous chronicler of Sahagún captured this ambiguity when he recalled (or imagined) the paradoxical attitude of the Muslims mourning the death of Alfonso VI in Toledo:

With the king now dead, of such a sort and so great was the wailing and crying in the city, that it can't be set down in writing or told in words, since the Christians, their women, the Jews and the Muslims, with theirs, the old women and the old men, the young lads, with the maidens, and infants . . . made such a great racket and noise . . . that in all of the city there was no other sound but that of the crying, saying thus: "Today, on this day, the sun has risen over the Muslims and infidels, has darkened greatly over the Christians."[95]

[94] A. J. Arberry, *Moorish Poetry*, p. 76. [95] A. Ubieto Arteta, *Crónicas anónimas*, p. 33 {20}.

# 2 A triumph of pragmatism

## The Christian Spains II (*c.* 1150–*c.* 1320)

And in the morning, after We had heard Mass, We went up to the fortress, and the governor with Us, and five of the best Muslims of the city of Murcia. And they said that We should divide the town just as had been agreed between them and Us. And We said that from the mosque that was near the fortress down to the gate where the camp was should be of the Christian, and that the mosque should be included in our part. They said that that had not been agreed and their documents said that they would keep their mosques and that they would have them as they had had them in the time of the Saracens. And We said to them that it had been agreed in this manner but that they had not understood it. Because We wished that they should conserve the mosques but, "What would the Christians do without a church that they could go into? And that the church should be at the gate of the fortress. And that from there the sabaçala should call out near to My head when I am sleeping ... that, as you can well understand, is not fitting. Now, you have some ten mosques in the town. Make your prayers in those and leave this one to Us." (Jaume I, *Llibre dels feyts* (1276)[1])

The period from the 1150s to the 1350s marks a second phase in the experience of Muslims under Christian rule in the peninsula and the extension of Christian domination. It was during these two centuries that the bulk of the territory of the peninsula came under Christian control, and also the period in which relations between Muslim and Christian society were stabilized and regularized. This was a process involving the promulgation of detailed law codes, both secular and canonical, which delineated Muslims' status in Christian society, and in which the organization of their communities underwent a process of "Christianization" and formalization. Nevertheless, Muslim communities – in the many areas where these persisted – were not passive victims of Christian colonization, but participants in a process of social formation that they were able to influence thanks to their value to their royal, ecclesiastical, and seigniorial overlords, and their capacity to renegotiate the terms of their submission on an ongoing basis. Once the initial trauma of the conquest had passed, this was a period characterized by stable

[1] "Book of Deeds," adapted from Jaume I, *The Book of Deeds*, p. 319 {445}.

inter-confessional socio-economic relations with remarkably few episodes of repression and very little pressure, violent or passive, to convert to Christianity. It was an era marked by pragmatism and compromise among both Christian rulers and their Muslim subjects. *Mudéjares* in many regions throve as legitimate, if second-class, participants within larger Christian-dominated societies.

In contrast to the earlier period, there is a far greater quantity of sources for the study of *mudéjar* society at this time, although few records survive that were produced by subject Muslims themselves, and the abundance of material varies considerably from region to region. In addition to the law codes mentioned above, administrative documentation expanded dramatically, particularly in the Crown of Aragon, thanks to the organization of centralized chanceries and the ready availability of (Muslim-manufactured) paper. An important innovation was the *repartimiento* or *repartiment*, the detailed surveys composed at the moment that Muslim towns were captured, and that recorded the sharing out of land and structures among the conquerors and settlers. Municipal and ecclesiastical record-keeping also expanded in this period, as did notarial practice – together, the documentation produced provides important evidence for economic and social interaction among Christians, Muslims, and Jews. That said, the geographic distribution of extant sources is extremely uneven. Little remains from Castile and León, Navarre or Portugal, whereas the surviving documentation for the lands of the Crown of Aragon is voluminous and varied.[2]

[2] For the general narrative of the Almohad period and its aftermath, see H. Kennedy, *Muslim Spain and Portugal*; L. P. Harvey, *Islamic Spain*; P. Linehan, *Spain, 1157–1300*; J. O'Callaghan, *History of Medieval Spain*, and *Reconquest and Crusade*; T. Glick, *From Muslim Fortress to Christian Castle*; J. N. Hillgarth, *The Spanish Kingdoms*; A. Huici Miranda, *Historia política del imperio almohade*; and M. Á. Ladero Quesada, *La formación medieval de España*. For the period from 1220 to 1320, J. Torres Fontes, *Repartimiento de la huerta*; and J. Zabalo Zabalegui, *La administración*. See also the voluminous work of R. Burns, including, *The Crusader Kingdom of Valencia*, *Islam under the Crusaders*, *Diplomatarium of the Crusader Kingdom of Valencia*, *Society and Documentation in Crusader Valencia*, *The Worlds of Alfonso the Learned*, and his many articles. Key works on *mudéjares* for this time include (in addition to the above) R. Burns, "Muslims in the Thirteenth Century Realms of Aragon"; B. Catlos, *The Victors and the Vanquished*; M. L. Ledesma Rubio, *Estudios sobre los mudéjares*, and her many other works; A. Echevarría Arsuaga, "Los mudéjares de los reinos"; M. García-Arenal and B. Leroy, *Moros y judíos*; P. Guichard, *Les musulmans de Valence*, and "Le Šarq al-Andalus"; L. P. Harvey, *Islamic Spain*, esp. chs. 4–9, pp. 55–150; J. Hinojosa Montalvo, *Los mudéjares*; F. M. Lopes de Barros, *Tempos e espaços*; E. Lourie, "Free Moslems" and "Anatomy of Ambivalence"; D. Menjot, "Les mudéjares du Royaume de Murcie"; Á. L. Molina Molina and M. del C. Veas Arteseros, "Situación de los mudéjares en el Reino de Murcia"; O'Callaghan, "Mudejars of Castile and Portugal"; F. Soyer, "Muslim Freedmen"; S. de Tapia, "Los mudéjares de la Extremadura"; J. Torró Abad, *El naixement d'una colònia*, and "Pour en finir"; the *Actas* of the various editions of the *Simposio Internacional de Mudejarismo*; and the myriad of studies of local Muslim *aljamas* (see p. 165/n.4 below). Primary sources that refer to *mudéjares* of this period include population

## Andalusīs and the decline of the Almohads

... and rejecting the lordship of the Almohads, the Andalusīs followed Auehut (*Ibn Hūd*) as if king and lord, who ... pounced viciously on the Almohads, capturing men, cutting their throats, striking off the penises of some, cutting off the breasts of women, and wretchedly putting children to death. (Anonymous, *Crónica latina de los reyes de Castilla* (thirteenth century)[3])

Following the victories of the mid twelfth century that brought the northern cities of al-Andalus under Christian control, a new foreign Islamic power moved into the peninsula. The process of Almoravid disintegration that facilitated the Christian advance also marked the emergence of the Almohad movement in the High Atlas Mountains. This Fāṭimid-influenced Sunnī movement – consciously Maṣmūda Berber-oriented and millenarian-flavored – was characterized both by cold moral certainty and iron political will. As a natural part of their program to dominate the Islamic West, the Almohads aimed at taking control of al-Andalus and reversing the Christian advance, and by 1150 the south had submitted to or been conquered by them. In July 1195 the third Almohad Caliph, Abū Yūsuf Yaʿqūb Manṣūr (1184–99), decisively defeated Alfonso VIII of Castile (1158–1214) at Alarcos (al-Arak); however, no serious attempt was made to follow up this victory by capturing Toledo, less than 150 kilometers to the north. Seventeen years later, almost to the day, the Castilian king would take his revenge at Las Navas de Tolosa (ʿIqāb) where, with the support of Navarre and Aragon, and fortified by a Crusade bull from Innocent III, he crushed the army of Abū Yūsuf's intemperate young son and successor, al-Nāṣir (1198–1213).[4] This opened up the Muslim south

charters (*cartas pueblas*) and municipal law codes and the great royal legal compilations of Castile and the Crown of Aragon, land transfer and administrative documents of the Military Orders and the Church, the abundant chancery records of the Crown of Aragon, assorted royal privileges, *libros de repartimientos*, royally commissioned, local, and monastic chronicles, historical accounts and poetry written by Andalusī refugees, the early Catalan "Grand chronicles," and diplomatic treaties between Christian and Muslim powers. By 1300 notarial registers and municipal archives yield valuable data for the Crown of Aragon. Material culture and archaeology have also provided clues, particularly to rural life in the kingdoms of Valencia and Aragon, and Cataluña.

3 "The Latin Chronicle of the Kings of Castile," L. Charlo Brea, *Crónica latina*, p. 76.

4 Las Navas de Tolosa, a battle in which the Christian princes of the peninsula marched as Crusaders against the Almohads behind the banner (and shield) of that larger than life Archbishop of Toledo, Rodrigo Jiménez de Rada, has been portrayed in Spanish historiography as a watershed event that heralded the irrevocable decline and demise of al-Andalus, and marked an era of Christian solidarity and unity of purpose. Much of this, however, is a product of religious idealism, historical hindsight and modern nationalistic impulse. One only need recall that of the princely heroes of the battle, in the previous years Alfonso VIII of Castile had been chided by the papacy for his philo-Muslim ways (see below, n. 43), Sancho VII of Navarre had gone on a diplomatic mission to Morocco courting Almohad aid against Castile (see N. Barbour, "The Relations of King

to conquest and – although an Almohad presence would persist in al-Andalus until 1229 – the battle effectively marked the end of that era of Andalusī history. It also marked the beginning of a half-century in which virtually every Christian campaign in the peninsula up to the defeat of al-Azraq in the 1250s was formally qualified as a Crusade.[5]

Important as it was, historical hindsight has imbued the battle and the larger struggle between Castile and the Almohads with an exaggerated flavor of religious solidarity and political inevitability. In truth, throughout the twelfth and thirteenth centuries the Christian kingdoms remained rivals, and each was fractured by internal struggles. The series of treaties among Christian princes dividing their future conquests of al-Andalus: Tudilén (1151), Cazorla (1179), Almizra (1244), Torellas (1304), and Elche (1305), must be understood in the context of the near-continuous warfare, whether direct or by proxy, between those same Christian kingdoms, rather than as a symptom of confessional solidarity. Hence, as the declared enemy of Castile, León became a natural ally of the Almohads, aiding their defense, while in the late thirteenth century, Aragon and Castile would clash both directly and through the use of Muslim proxies and allies, such as the kingdom of Granada and the Valencian rebel al-Azraq. Among Castilians, noblemen bent on resisting Alfonso VIII, like Pedro Fernández de Castro, felt no compunction in fighting alongside Abū Yūsuf's troops.[6] Their Muslim counterparts were individuals like Ibn Mardānish – King of Valencia and the Levantine coast (the area known as Sharq al-Andalus, "the East of al-Andalus") – and the Banū Hūd, the descendants of Zaragoza's dispossessed *taifa* dynasty, each of whom formed alliances with Christian kings and used Christian mercenaries.[7]

Likewise, the Almohads became increasingly dependent on Christian military aid in North Africa in the form of captives and mercenaries. This policy, like their diplomacy, seems to fly in the face of their domestic program vis-à-vis non-Muslims, in which they formally dissolved the pact

Sancho"), Afonso II of Portugal would be excommunicated in 1219, and Pere the Catholic of Aragon would die in 1213 at Muret, defending his heretic-sheltering vassals of Languedoc against Crusading forces led by Simon de Montfort. As for the kingdom of León, it had been an ally of the Almohads for some time (see N. Barbour, "Two Christian Embassies," 190). Al-Andalus survived for nearly three centuries. For a reassessment of the battle and its significance see the essays in S. Doubleday, *et al.*, *Journal of Medieval Iberian Studies* 4 (1) (2012).

[5] See J. O'Callaghan, *Reconquest and Crusade*, pp. 78–123.

[6] See S. Barton, "Traitors of Faith?," pp. 29–30.

[7] For Ibn Mardānish, see I. González Cavero, "Una revisión de la figura de Ibn Mardanish." For the Banū Hūd, see above, p. 33. The family reappeared in the guise of Muḥammad b. Yūsuf b. Ḥūd al-Judhāmī, who led an uprising against the Almohads in the aftermath of Las Navas, and was briefly recognized as ruler of Andalucía until his assassination in 1237.

of *dhimma*, and put pressure on local Jews and Christians to convert.[8] But this was only one dimension of their rigorous approach to religiosity. It was one that targeted Andalusī Muslims as well, as when, for example, the Almohads ordered the Mālikī legal texts that enjoyed a near-monopoly on Andalusī legal thought to be burned. Such policies account for the visceral reaction of locals to their rule. As a consequence, the rebel Muḥammad b. Yūsuf b. Hūd could present himself as a "liberator of the people of al-Andalus," who after seizing towns they had held, set about to "purge the mosques polluted by Almohad superstition."[9] In sum, the Almohad period served as a catalyst for the integration and acculturation of Andalusī Muslims and northern Christians, as a consequence of the military alliances they embarked on and their shared perception of the Almohads as foreign occupiers. It was not only Jewish and Christian refugees who moved north from al-Andalus to settle in Christian lands, but also Muslims.[10]

## The Conquest of Seville and the Muslim south

Everything declines after reaching perfection . . .
The tap of the white ablution fount weeps in despair,
like a passionate lover weeping at the departure of the beloved,
over dwellings emptied of Islam, whose inhabitants now live in unbelief,
where the mosques have become churches in which only bells and crosses are found . . .
O who will redress the humiliation of a people who were once powerful,
a people whose condition injustice and tyrants have changed?
(Ṣāliḥ b. Sharīf al-Rundī (d. 1285), untitled poem (mid-thirteenth century)[11])

On December 22, 1248, Fernando III, King of Castile (1217–52) and León (1230–52) made his formal entrance into the city of Seville (Ishbīliya), the former Almohad capital in al-Andalus and the most important city of the wealthy Islamic south. One month earlier, the inhabitants, including the poet Ṣāliḥ b. Sharīf al-Rundī, had surrendered, agreeing to abandon the city under the watchful eye of the Christian garrison occupying the city's great *alcazar* (*al-qaṣr*), and taking only what they could carry.[12] In this instance, the

8 See, for example, D. Corcos, "The Nature of the Almohad Rulers."
9 M. Desamparados Cabanes, *Crónica latina de los reyes de Castilla*, p. 96.
10 The hostility of the Almohads towards the Mālikī legal orientation of the Andalusī *'ulamā'* fueled resentment and resistance. See B. Catlos, *The Victors and the Vanquished*, p. 67.
11 J. Monroe, *Hispano-Arabic Poetry*, p. 336.
12 Some did not make it; the most venerable *imām*, 'Alī b. Jabīr al-Dabbāj is described in the biographical dictionary, *Al-Takmīla*, as having dropped dead eight days after the surrender, unable to endure the fact that the call of the *mu'adhdhin* had been replaced by the

native Muslims were not merely required to relocate outside the city walls, but to move west to Islamic Jeréz (Sharīsh) or be transported across the Straits to Ceuta (Sabta). This uncompromising approach characterized the Castilian, Leonese, and Portuguese conquests of the peninsular south – campaigns marked by forced exiles and punctuated by massacres. Given the region's recent history of volatility, such an approach would have been seen as prudent. The Andalusīs had proven to be inveterately independent-minded and ungovernable. They had welcomed and rejected a series of Muslim overlords and Christian protectors, and flirted with popular government. Moreover, despite the decline of the Almohads, the region remained at risk from competing Christian sovereigns, semi-independent Muslim warlords, and foreign Islamic powers.

Once Fernando had entered the empty city and established a secular and ecclesiastical institutional framework, the task came to divide the spoils among the conquering army and the Christian settlers who had come to occupy it. A *Libro de repartimiento*, or "Book of Allocations," surveyed the town and its hinterland in minute detail, recording the distribution of property and testifying to the absolute rupture that the Christian conquest entailed.[13] Land, property, and installations were shared out among the various parties who contributed to the conquest, and in particular among Christian settlers who would form the demographic base of the new city – no indigenous Christian population had remained. Among the settlers were a substantial Jewish contingent who would come to constitute a wealthy and dynamic sector in the new city, settled behind the walls of their *judería* or ghetto, but with extensive landholdings elsewhere within and around the city. A small *morería*, or Muslim neighborhood, was established, inhabited by a few Muslims who may have been allowed to stay and others who came after the conquest, including ʿAbd al-Ḥājj al-Bayyāsī ("of Baeza"), the first *alcalde de moros* ("magistrate of the Muslims") appointed by Fernando. The city's mosques were either given over to the Church or distributed by the king for re-use as commercial buildings, churches, or synagogues. With the addition of a small royal chapel, the great congregational mosque was transformed into the cathedral. The Almohads' immense minaret, modeled on those of Marrakesh and Ribat, became the Christian bell-tower, La Giralda.[14]

clang of bells. M. Marín, "Des migrations," p. 43. The *ʿalim*, Ibn ʿAmïra, cited the same reason for departing Valencia after its conquest by Jaume I in 1238. See al-Himyarï, *La péninsule*, p. 63 (Arabic: p. 50).

13 J. González, *Repartimiento de Sevilla.*

14 For the narrative of the conquest and colonization of Seville, see M. González Jiménez, *La repoblación*; see also the maps in I. Montes Romero-Camacho and M. González Jiménez, "Los mudéjares andaluces," pp. 75 and 76.

## *The conquest of the Muslim south*

The taking of Seville marked the mid-point of the conquest of the Guadalquivir valley, which began soon after Alfonso VIII's victory at Las Navas and concluded with the taking of Cádiz (Qādis) by Alfonso X in 1264 – a series of campaigns characterized by forced relocations and the killing of Muslim inhabitants. The kings of Castile were struggling not only against the weakening but still-dangerous Almohads, but also against their Christian rivals, León and Portugal, as well as destabilizing elements within their own kingdom, most notably a willfully independent upper nobility. This, along with local Muslims' inveterate rebelliousness, as well as their propensity to resist both directly and by exploiting divisions among the would-be conquerors, encouraged a certain ruthlessness on the part of the Christians. Hence, Alfonso VIII's massacres of the Muslim inhabitants at Baeza (Bayyāsa) following his decisive victory in 1212, and the abandonment of other settlements, like Úbeda (Ubbadha), prior to the Christians' arrival.[15] Meanwhile, Alfonso IX of León (1188–1230), erstwhile ally of the Almohads, took control of the upper Guadiana valley in 1230, forcing the surrender of Mérida and taking Badajoz, which had vacillated between Portuguese, Almohad, and Leonese rule, and whose citizens, like those of Elvas (Yalbash) to the west, had previously repulsed Christian invaders.[16] But such gestures would be futile; the rout and capture by the Portuguese of a large militia from Seville in 1225 had made patent the incapacity of the Andalusīs to mount an effective defense. Elvas, like many other towns of the frontier, was simply deserted by its Muslim inhabitants. By this time, Alcácer do Sal (al-Qaṣr) – the strategic key to the Algarve, which had been captured by the Almohads in 1191 – had been retaken after a bitterly fought double siege. In 1217, in defiance of Afonso II's (1212–23) treaty with the Almohads, various bishops and the commanders of Military Orders enlisted foreign Crusaders en route to the Holy Land, and laid siege to the town. It was vigorously defended by the Almohads, together with the princes of the Muslim south, until the arrival of the Templar reinforcements (purportedly aided by an angelic host) sealed the Christian victory. Terms were harsh; thousands of captives were reportedly taken, and many converted, including the *qāʾid*, ʿAbd Allāh b. Wazīr.[17]

[15] See *PCG*, vol. II, pp. 704–5 {1021}.

[16] See H. Kennedy, *Muslim Spain*, pp. 256–72.

[17] J. O'Callaghan, *Reconquest and Crusade*, pp. 79–80. Apparently, Ibn Wazīr reconsidered his conversion, and escaped to Muslim lands a few days later. See H. Kennedy, *Muslim Spain*, p. 259.

In this period local Muslim warlords, like Ibn Hūd of Murcia, Abū Zayd of Valencia, and ʿAbd Allāh al-Bayyāsī of Baeza, were torn between their formal duty to defend Islam and the pragmatic necessity of becoming Christian allies and vassals. Ultimately each chose *realpolitik* over religious duty, becoming true-life versions of the *Poema de mio Cid*'s fictional Abengalvón, the loyal and noble Muslim Lord of Molina, who hosted and succored the fictionalized Campeador and Álvar Hañez as they headed south towards Valencia.[18] In real life, each paid the price for their collaboration in the form of popular rebellions led by religious figures or headed by rival strongmen. Muḥammad b. Hūd, the penectomizing ally of Castile, faced uprisings in Malaga and Granada, and was assassinated in Almería in 1238. Muḥammad b. Yūsuf b. al-Aḥmar, who had been acclaimed by the people of Arjona (Arjūna) and had led the revolt against Ibn Hūd, was forced in turn to recognize Fernando III's overlordship. Zayd Abū Zayd, the Almohad Governor of Valencia, who had become effectively independent with the dynasty's decline, pledged himself to Fernando III in 1224, only to be overthrown in a revolt led by Zayyān b. Mardanīsh – a grandson of Alfonso VI's former vassal, "El Rey Lobo" – five years later. Al-Bayyāsī, whose short-lived kingdom was essentially Fernando's creation, was killed in 1226, having lost the support of the populace as a consequence of his raiding of the Muslim Guadalquivir.[19] Even before its conquest, Seville, now an autonomous "republic," had become a tributary of Castile. All the while, as the Muslim south dissolved into chaos, disarray, and populism, the great aristocratic families – the Banū Maslīma, the Banū Al-Shad, the Banū Khaldūn, and others – pulled up stakes for Muslim North Africa, leaving the general populace to fend for themselves.[20]

This disarray was contrasted by the stability that Fernando III achieved once he had united León and Castile in 1230. By 1233 he had pushed south to the banks of the Guadalquivir. In 1236 Córdoba was taken. In 1244, Ibn Aḥmar rebelled against him, providing a pretext for the conquests of Arjona and Jaén (Jayyān). As the cities of the Muslim south fell, the smaller towns and hamlets of the countryside capitulated with little resistance or were taken by force, the fate of their inhabitants varying

[18] C. Smith, *Poema de mio Cid*, pp. 47–50 {II: 83–84} and 81–83 {III: 126–27}; in translation, R. Hamilton and J. Perry, *The Poem of the Cid*, pp. 101–05, and 161–63.

[19] See H. Kennedy, *Muslim Spain*, pp. 266–72.

[20] This self-exiled Andalusī elite became the avante-garde of literary culture in Ifrīqiya. See R. Rouighi, *The Making of a Mediterranean Emirate*, ch. 6, "Emirism and the Writing of History," pp. 148–72.

according to the caprices of the conquerors. Treaties of vassalage, or *pleitesías*, were granted to many communities as an inducement for Muslims to remain in their lands under Christian control. While on the one hand, it seems that the countryside did remain largely Muslim-inhabited, the *Primera crónica* reports many Muslims killed and many more taken prisoner in the course of the raids and clashes in and around the Guadalquivir valley.[21] During this period an important slave market was established in Córdoba, and as a consequence enslaved Muslims were sent northwards. That said, Christian losses both in battle and to captivity were also considerable.

By taking Seville in 1248, Fernando effectively contained rival Portugal, limiting its potential expansion to the area west of the Guadiana River. Here, Sancho II (1223–47) reduced what remained of the Andalusī al-Gharb ("the West"), which was in little position to offer resistance or to hope for relief. In 1247 a broad coalition supported by the Church and nobility overthrew Sancho and forced him into exile. It fell to his brother, Afonso III (1248–79), who had led the rebellion and now styled himself as King of Portugal and Algarve, to complete the conquest. In 1249, Ukshūniba (modern Faro) yielded after a long siege, and in 1250 the remaining towns of the Algarve recognized Portuguese lordship.[22] At Faro Afonso granted the Muslims the same terms he offered the other towns of the region: complete freedom and security of person, property, and religion, in exchange for their submission. Moreover, he proposed "that the Muslim knights become his vassals and ride with the king when he obliges and he will show them favor and grace" – a curious offer to make in a campaign that was officially sanctioned as a Crusade.[23]

As for the eastern limits of Castilian influence, these had been settled most recently by 1179's Treaty of Cazorla with the Crown of Aragon.[24] In 1243 Aḥmad b. Muḥammad b. Hūd of Murcia (Mursiya) recognized the suzerainty of the *infante* Alfonso (the future Alfonso X), and with the Pact of Alcaraz, became an autonomous tributary of Castile.[25] Of an independent al-Andalus only the new Naṣrid kingdom of Granada would remain. Here, Muḥammad b. Yūsuf b. Naṣr b. al-Aḥmar (d. 1273) established himself as king, over the resistance of his one-time allies, the Andalusī aristocratic family, the Banū Ashqīlūla. His son,

[21] See, for example, R. Menéndez Pidal, *Primera crónica*, vol. II, p. 753 for a battle at Huelves between Fernando's forces and Muslim refugees from Triana (in Sevilla), and p. 754 for the surrender of Carmona (Qarmūna) to Fernando III.

[22] S. Lay, *The Reconquest Kings*, p. 259.

[23] M. F. Lopes de Barros, *Tempos e espaços*, p. 83.

[24] See J. O'Callaghan, *Reconquest and Crusade*, p. 56.

[25] *Ibid.*, pp. 169–71.

Muḥammad II al-Faqīh (1273–1302), guaranteed the survival of the dynasty by defusing their rebellion and initiating the relationship of clientage vis-à-vis Castile that would characterize the kingdom of Granada for most of its history.

## The subjugation of the Balearics and Valencia

These [peasants] overflowed with mounting impetuousness, and the presumptions of Ibn ʿAbbād were fulfilled. They twisted in the name of God, all that had been eternally predestined for misfortune, and said:

No enmity exists between the two religions and accursed be any who denies this.

They arranged with the Christians (*al-Rūm*) to comply with all that was fitting as allies. (Ibn ʿAmīra al-Makhzūmī, *Kitāb ṭārikh Mayūrqa* (1231–51)[26])

As Fernando III was bringing southern Iberia under Castilian control, his kinsman, Jaume I of Catalonia and Aragon, embarked on a series of campaigns that would gain him the sobriquet "The Conqueror" and end Muslim rule in the northeast and the Balearics. Located between Iberia, North Africa, and Sicily, the islands were of obvious strategic and commercial value. As early as 1120 Jaume's predecessor, Ramon Berenguer III of Barcelona (1082–1131), had planned an invasion of Almoravid Mallorca, in which he had obliged his client, Ibn Hilāl, the Almoravid Governor of Lleida, to commit troops. From the twelfth century, Pisans and Genoans had been competing for a commercial presence and influence over the islands.[27] After the collapse of the Caliphate, Mallorca (Mayūrqa) throve under the rule first of Almoravid, then Almohad governors, each of whom became independent as their respective ruling dynasties collapsed. As Ibn ʿAmīra's account suggests, here as elsewhere, native divisions were key to Christian success.

In 1229, with the aid of a papal Crusade bull and the collaboration of Catalan, Pisan, and Genoan merchants, Jaume I (1213–76) conquered Mallorca by force of arms and pushed Menorca (Minūrqa) into vassalage. No sooner had Jaume finished with the Balearics, than he turned towards Valencia, which his privateering Aragonese vassals, like Blasco de Alagón, had been encroaching upon since the 1220s. The city would fall in 1238, and in the years that followed Jaume drove his forces south of the Xúquer River, obtaining the surrender of most of the region's towns in the mid 1240s. Jaume's career of conquest would end at Murcia in 1266, where he pacified the *mudéjar* uprising against his cousin (once removed), Alfonso

26 "Book of the History of Mallorca." Ibn ʿAmira, *et al.*, *Kitāb tāʾrīḫ Mayūrqa*, p. 96.

27 See, above, p. 538, n. 63; for the Norman attack on Mallorca, see below, p. 111.

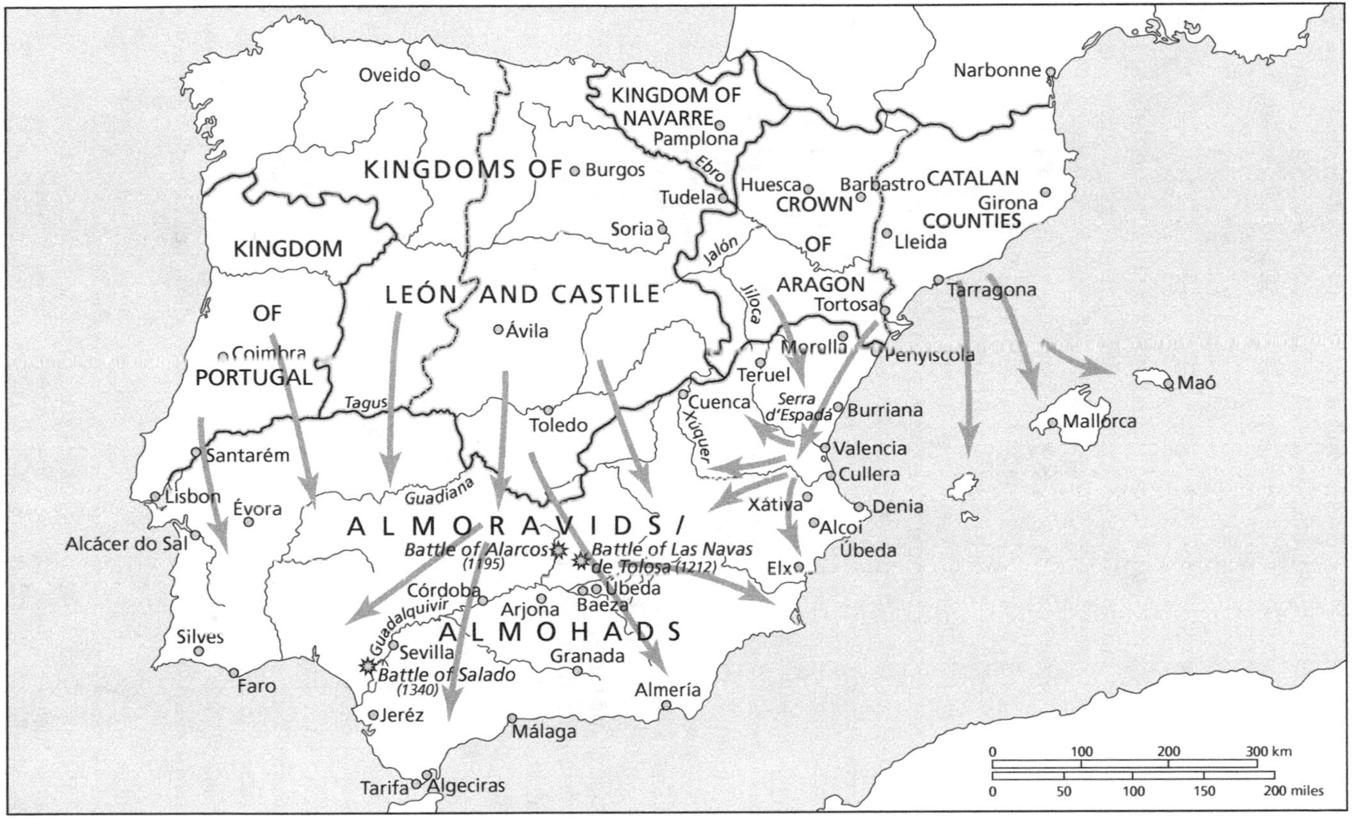


Map 3 Conquests of the Castilians, Aragonese, and Portuguese, 1150–1300

X of Castile (1252–84). These conquests and many other matters are recounted in detail by Jaume I himself in his *Llibre dels feyts* ("Book of Deeds"), a remarkable, if not wholly reliable, royal autobiography.[28]

### *The conquest of Mallorca*

Mallorca had not been conquered definitively by Muslims until the tenth century, but soon after the conversion to Islam of the native inhabitants began. In the late eleventh century the island emerged, alongside Pisa, Genoa, and Barcelona, as a centre of maritime trade and piracy.[29] In 1126 a Ṣanhāja grandee, Muḥammad b. Ghāniya, took the islands in the name of the Almoravids. Thus, as the dynasty declined, Mallorca became an Almoravid rallying point, and a launching pad for a series of devastating and destabilizing campaigns against the Almohad Maghrib. In 1202/1203 the islands fell to the Almohads, whose governors also ruled it as independent kings. Under Berber rule, the islands throve and their Islamicization was completed, while their ethno-cultural character became pronouncedly Maghribī, thanks to the significant numbers of North Africans who settled there at this time. Although separated from the mainland, the Islamic Balearics were not entirely insulated from the chaos, unrest, and vulnerability that characterized post-Caliphal al-Andalus. Thus, there were stirrings of discontent and division, particularly among the Andalusī refugees who arrived on the island and had little sympathy for the Almohad regime. In August 1229 these Andalusī elements mounted an unsuccessful coup that was brutally suppressed, aggravating the divisions among the island's Muslim populace, and inspiring some to collaborate with the Christians.

Nevertheless, when Jaume's invasion fleet arrived at the island the following month, it was clear the King would have a fight on his hands, and after establishing a beachhead, he headed straight for the capital of Madīna Mayūrqa (modern Palma de Mallorca). This city, of perhaps 25,000 inhabitants, represented roughly 75 percent of the island's population. After a series of skirmishes, a siege was laid and the undermining of the city's defenses began. The King decided early to accept no terms from the *wālī*, Abū Yaḥyā Muḥammad al-Tinmallī, who offered increasingly generous concessions first for the Christians to break off and, then, for the Muslims to abandon the island. For his part, Jaume capitalized on

[28] See Jaume I, *The Book of Deeds*, for a recent English translation; the most comprehensive Catalan edition is *El Llibre dels Fets de Jaume el Conqueridor*, ed. R. Vinas.

[29] See, generally, G. Rosselló Bordoy, *L'Islam a Les Illes Balears*.

the divisions among the Mallorcans; soon after his landing a local notable, Ibn ʿAbbād, who the King refers to in his memoirs as "an angel," joined his forces, while the people of the countryside began to support and supply the invaders. Muslim sources accuse these traitors of having "apostatized," but it is likely this was a characterization of their collaboration, rather than conversion to Christianity.[30]

The walls of Madīna Mayūrqa were breached on December 31, 1229 and the Christians took the city, overcoming fierce resistance and carrying out a brutal massacre of the inhabitants. The unpopular Abū Yaḥyā was captured and granted Jaume's protection, which in this case meant that he was tortured to death in an attempt to force him to reveal the location of his treasures. In order to encourage his cooperation, Jaume – according to one report – had the King's sixteen-year-old son killed before his own eyes.[31] The city's inhabitants were claimed as booty by the King, and they and their moveable property were auctioned off. Those who could fled to the hills around Pollensa, which remained a center of resistance under the leadership of ʿUmar b. Aḥmād b. al-ʿUmarī into the winter of 1231.[32] However, as the Christian forces pressed on, the resistors wavered, and either actively abetted Jaume, or offered to yield to his authority. In his memoir Jaume describes how he concluded a treaty with a resistance leader, Shuʿayb, promising:

> to him and four others of his lineage, I should give inheritances, and horses, and arms, to each of them a pack-horse or mule, good and fit for riding, and that the Saracens should be allowed to remain in the land; those who would might do so, and live free under my rule; as for those who would not submit and accept that capitulation, I should deal with them as I pleased.[33]

The contemporary chronicler Ibn ʿAmīra reports, however, that the surrendering Muslims were not only exiled from the island, but forced to pay the cost of the voyage. Jaume's *repartiment*, the survey of his new holdings on the island, was originally drafted in Arabic, indicating Muslims colluded or were conscripted to participate in the project, but not a single landholding is registered to a Muslim tenant.[34]

30 James I, *The Book of Deeds*, pp. 95–96 {71}, and M. Ben Ma'mar, *et al., Kitāb tā'rīḫ Mayūrqa*, p. 96.

31 In his autobiography Jaume presents his own behavior as rather more chivalrous. See Jaume I, *The Book of Deeds*, p. 109 {87}.

32 Al-ʿUmarī was a *qāḍī*, and served as magistrate and legal authority to the resisters; his death in 1230/31 may well have contributed to their collapse. See M. Marín, "Des migrations," pp. 54–55.

33 Jaume I, *The Book of Deeds*, p. 127 {113}.

34 For the *repartiment*, see P. de Bofarull Mascaró, *Repartimientos de los reinos*, pp. 1–142.

### *Menorca becomes a client*

As soon as Madīna Mayūrqa had fallen, Jaume dispatched his fleet to Menorca (Minūrqa), where the military Governor, Abū ʿUthmān b. Saʿīd b. al-Ḥakam, together with the local sheikhs and notables, offered their vassalage to the Count-King of Barcelona and his successors, including an annual tribute, or *jizya*, to be paid in kind. According to Jaume, he had tricked them into thinking he had brought a large army to the island, by landing at night and having scores of fires lit on the beach as to resemble an immense camp. The Count-King accepted the terms offered, with the further stipulation that the island's fortresses be turned over to his troops, and the treaty was put into writing, with the leading citizens swearing on the Qurʾān to respect it.[35] For the next fifty years Menorca would exist as an autonomous subject principality of the Crown of Aragon. The tribute was paid without complaint and in return the island-kingdom throve as a cultural and commercial center and as a transit point for Muslims leaving Iberia for the *dār al-Islām*.[36] Ibiza (Yābisa) remained Muslim only until 1235, when Guillem de Montgrí, Archbishop-elect of Tarragona, forced the island's surrender, having received the right from Jaume to conquer and exploit it.[37]

Whereas the submission of Menorca had little immediate effect on the island's Muslim inhabitants, Mallorca was completely transformed. While a significant population of slaves remained, free Muslim society seems to have all but ceased to exist in the half of the island that became the direct domain of the King, considering that the great majority of those who had managed to surrender to Jaume or obtain their freedom emigrated in the wake of the conquest. This is not surprising, perhaps, given the pronouncedly tribal and clanic character of Islamic society here and the fact that tribal connections between Mallorca and the southern mainland were quite strong. In the territories not controlled by the King, the new landlords made use of both free and enslaved Muslim workers, and in the late thirteenth century evidence of a vestigial Islamic population emerges. Indeed, as early as 1231 the island's Templars received permission from Jaume I to settle thirty households of Muslim peasants on their lands.[38] These settlers and all of their descendants were to enjoy royal protection of property and person; however, the Muslim population of the island was apparently never constituted into *aljamas*, and like other *mudéjares* who were scattered around the fringes of the peninsula as individual families or small groups, did not

[35] Jaume I, *The Book of Deeds*, pp. 130–31 {119}.
[36] See, generally, M.-À. Casasnovas, *Història de Menorca*.
[37] J. O'Callaghan, *Reconquest and Crusade*, pp. 35–36.
[38] Lourie, "Free Moslems," p. 625.

enjoy juridical autonomy or access to Islamic law.[39] By the 1240s the papacy was complaining of the Church's and Military Orders' use of Muslim colonists on the island.[40] By the 1270s it seems there were a considerable number of *mudéjares* on Mallorca, Ibiza, and Menorca (post-1287), including craftsmen and tradesmen, and most of whom would have been immigrants from the mainland Crown of Aragon.[41] They were apparently under the same fiscal regime as their Christian neighbors, with the difference that from the 1270s they were subject to an additional tax, the *morabetin*, which they paid for the privilege of living on the islands. As for Abū Yaḥyā's family, two of his surviving sons converted to Christianity. One took the name of Jaume, and was married into a family of powerful Aragonese magnates. In 1250 he was granted the castle of Gotor, in Aragon, with jurisdiction over its Christian and Muslim inhabitants. The *wālī*'s daughters were sold as slaves, with the notoriously lascivious Jaume apparently taking his pick of the most beautiful.[42]

### *The kingdom of Valencia*

Even before the final pacification of Mallorca, Jaume had determined to follow up by conquering the *Sharq al-Andalus*, "Eastern al-Andalus" or Islamic Valencia, capitalizing on the energy of his Aragonese vassals and the Military Orders, the inertia created by the Mallorcan Crusade, and the disarray of the Muslim kingdom.[43] Jaume had attempted this in the 1220s but local Muslims under the Almohad prince Zayd Abū Zayd had held him off with the support of Tunisian Ḥafṣids. Overthrown in 1229, Abū Zayd went over to Jaume, eventually converting to Christianity in 1236 under the name of Vincent (the patron saint of Valencia), and becoming the King's vassal and an adornment to his entourage.[44] By this time Jaume's Crusade was underway, and from 1232 his forces proceeded southwards along the Mediterranean coast, taking major towns such as Morella (Mawrala; 1232), Burriana (Madīnat al-Khaḍra; 1233) and Penyiscola (Banaskula; 1233), often in the face of fierce resistance.[45] At one point the King himself took a crossbow bolt to the face. It was as a

[39] *Ibid.*, p. 646. [40] *Ibid.*, pp. 628–29.
[41] Menorca was finally conquered in 1287; see below, p. 77.
[42] See Jaume I, *The Book of Deeds*, p. 109 {87}; A. Santamaría, *Ejecutoria*, pp. 67–69.
[43] Much has been written on the conquest of Valencia and its Muslim inhabitants. See the works of R. Burns, as well as P. Guichard, *Les musulmans de Valence*, and J. Torró Abad, *El naixement*.
[44] See R. Burns, "Almohad Prince," and "The Daughter of Abū Zayd."
[45] Morella had been taken earlier, in 1117, but reconquered during the Almohad resurgence following the death of Alfonso the Battler.

consequence of their resistance that the surrendering Muslim inhabitants of Burriana were forced into exile, given only five days to evacuate the town along with a guarantee of the king's protection as they moved south. On the other hand, the Muslims of Penyiscola petitioned directly to the king to surrender to him personally, offering to become his subjects if he would grant them rights and liberties that they had enjoyed under Muslim princes, in particular as pertained to religion. When Jaume arrived, they greeted him as lord, and sent him gifts of food; he responded by forbidding his men from despoiling the land, and setting down in writing the terms of their subjugation.[46] Once this treaty had been concluded the Muslim garrisons in the surrounding territory turned over their castles to representatives of the Military Orders.

Soon after, Jaume determined to take the kingdom by conquering the capital. By 1237 he had established a siege camp on a hillock (*puig*) just outside Valencia and blockaded the city by sea. After a counter-attack had been decisively defeated and it became clear the Ḥafṣids could not provide relief, Zayyān b. Mardanīsh sent his nephew to conduct secret negotiations with the Christian King. On September 29, 1238 an agreement was concluded, whereby within five days the Muslims would abandon the city with all that they could carry and would be escorted to Cullera or Denia (Muslim Dāniya), or take up residence elsewhere in Jaume's realms. Three days later, tens of thousands assembled on the fields south of the city and readied to depart; the King kept his word, going so far as to execute those members of his own forces who dared harass them.[47] On October 9 Jaume entered the city of Valencia. The congregational mosque was reconstituted as the cathedral, and the city was shared out amongst his vassals and allies, with the grants recorded in a *llibre de repartiment*. Thus, Valencia became the capital of new, separate kingdom under Jaume's rule, endowed in 1240 with a distinct set of laws (the *Furs*) established by royal authority.[48]

Having taken Valencia, Jaume's resources were stretched, but he was compelled to push on southwards both in order to exploit his advantage and forestall further Castilian advances. Morvedre and Segorb were taken in 1238 and their Muslim inhabitants allowed to remain, but in 1240 when Jaume reached Xàtiva – once a dynamic center of Islamic culture – he could to do no more than force the local rulers, the Banū Mardanīsh,

[46] See Jaume I, *The Book of Deeds*, p. 173 {184}. [47] *Ibid.*, p. 230 {283}.

[48] For the *repartiment*, see P. de Bofarull Mascaró, *Repartimientos de los reinos*, pp. 143–656, and M. D. Cabanes Pecourt and R. Ferrer Navarro, *Llibre del repartiment*. For an analysis of the *llibres de repartiment* of the kingdom, see E. Guinot Rodríguez and J. Torró Abad, *Repartiments a la Corona d'Aragó*.

into a truce. Similarly, the Banū Hudayr would manage to hold on to the small semi-autonomous principality at Crevillent (Qarbillan) under both Castilian and Aragonese suzerainty, holding the title of *larrayz* (*al-ra'īs*; "headman") until 1318.[49] In the meantime, the *infante* Alfonso of Castile was raiding territories that by right of the Treaty of Cazorla pertained to Aragon. As tensions between the two Christian kingdoms came to a head, they concluded the Treaty of Almizra on March 1244, re-partitioning the Muslim territories south of the Xúquer River.[50] With this dispute resolved, in short order most of the remaining towns of southern Valencia fell to Jaume, including Dénia, Alcira (Jazīrat Shuqr), and Bi'r.

However, local communities and their leaders capitalized on Jaume's dwindling military capacity and competition between Aragon and Castile to obtain favorable surrender settlements and establish relationships that were more tributary than subordinate in nature. Ever more short on Christian colonists, the King turned much of this territory over to the lordship of the Military Orders, whose commanders tended to establish accommodating relationships with native Muslims, in order to ensure the continuing productivity and prosperity of their lands.[51] Maintaining the existing economic infrastructure of the new kingdom of Valencia was important not only because of its production of high-yield and high-profit horticultural products, but because of local craft industries, which produced items such as high-quality ceramic and strategically important commodities, like paper. Royal preoccupation with establishing a Christian population can be seen in the clauses normally attached to land grants, which specified that if the grantee did not take up actual residence on the property that had been ceded to him, the gift would be voided. For this reason, Jaume also encouraged Jewish settlement, and colonies were established in most of the major towns of the kingdom in the aftermath of the conquest.[52] The kingdom remained, however, overwhelmingly Muslim in population; the tenuous nature of Christian dominion would soon encourage revolt amongst the Muslim subjects of both Castilian-controlled Murcia and southern Valencia, and this would lead in turn to a new phase of colonization.

49 P. Guichard, "Un seigneur musulman."

50 J. O'Callaghan, *Reconquest and Crusade*, p. 106.

51 See R. Burns, *The Crusader Kingdom of Valencia*, ch. 10 "The Military Orders as Frontier Institutions," pp. 173–96.

52 See J. Ray, *The Sephardic Frontier*, pp. 1–35, and specifically for the Kingdom of Valencia, M. Meyerson, *Jews in an Iberian Frontier Kingdom*, pp. 1–5. The Count-Kings of the Crown of Aragon had been using Jews as colonists since the mid twelfth century; see, for example, the charter granted by Ramon Berenguer IV for Arracina (a suburb of Tortosa) in 1149, in J. M. Font i Rius, *Cartas de población*, vol. I: 126–28 {76}.

*The Crown of Aragon, Castile, and the Islamic Mediterranean*

The conquest of Mallorca and Valencia, and the increasingly commercial orientation of the Catalan economy led the Crown of Aragon to engage in the broader Mediterranean world – one that remained very much defined by Islam. In effect, the Crown of Aragon, and to a lesser extent, the kingdom of Mallorca, which was severed temporarily from the Crown by the testament of Jaume I, were drawn into an environment of competition among Christian powers attempting to dominate the Islamic and Byzantine Mediterranean and each other.[53] This was driven by two priorities: territorial expansion and control of trade. In terms of territory, in the late thirteenth and fourteenth centuries the Crown of Aragon expanded almost exclusively at the expense of Christian principalities, acquiring for varying lengths of time Sicily (from 1285), territories in Greece (from 1303), Sardinia and Corsica (from 1325), and Naples and southern Italy (from 1442). In the 1280s Pere the Great (1276–85), Jaume's eldest son and principal heir, launched an invasion of Ḥafṣid Ifrīqiya, capitalizing on divisions within that dynasty, but abandoned this enterprise when Sicilian rebels, who had ousted their Angevin overlord in the episode known as "the Sicilian Vespers," invited Pere to rule over them as king. In response, to Pere's coup, Pope Martin IV (1281–85), a creature of Charles of Anjou, declared a Crusade against the Crown of Aragon. This was joined by Pere's brother, Jaume II, King of Mallorca (1276–1311), and supported by Ḥakam b. Saʿīd, Abū ʿUthmān's successor in Menorca. Pere repelled both the land and sea invasion in 1285, aided notably by troops drawn from *mudéjar* communities in Aragon and Valencia.[54]

In the recent past Sicily had been home to an important Muslim minority, but its remnants had been transported *en masse* to the Italian mainland over a half-century earlier. Otherwise, the only significant Islamic territories gained were islands along the coast of Ifrīqiya that had been contested through the twelfth century by the Normans and a succession of Muslim rulers. Jerba (Jarba), a large island rising out of the sand bars only 2 kilometers off the coast, was taken by force in 1284, as was the archipelago of Kerkennah (Qarqana), a cluster of islands off Sfax (Safāqis), in 1287 – both by the admiral Roger de Lauria (or Llúria, in Catalan), who was installed as seignior. In each case, the Muslim inhabitants were induced to remain under Christian rule and subjected to a harsh tributary regime, but lived

[53] See D. Abulafia, *The Western Mediterranean Kingdoms*, esp. chs. 2 and 5, "The Emergence of Aragon-Catalonia," and "The Mediterranean in the Age of James II of Aragon," pp. 28–56 and 107–32.

[54] See below, p. 78.

effectively as autonomous Islamic communities.[55] In each case they eventually succeeded in ousting their Aragonese overlords (in 1314 and 1325, respectively) with help from the North African mainland. In the following centuries the Aragonese dynasty made attempts to retake the islands, and carried off significant numbers of prisoners. Slavery was, in fact, the principle means by which Catalan maritime expansion affected the character and condition of the Muslim population of the Crown of Aragon.[56] For example, Pere the Great's invasion of Ifrīqiya, unsuccessful as it may have been, netted huge numbers of captives who were then distributed as slaves throughout his territories. The contemporary chronicler and soldier, Ramon Muntaner, described the scene as follows: "And when [King Pere] thus attacked, he scattered the Saracens, so that no two remained together, and so many were massacred that it would be horrible to relate; and so many were captured that a Saracen could be bought for one *dobla*. So that all the Christians were rich and joyful, and above all the Lord-King."[57]

On the whole, however, relations between the Crown and the Muslim princes of the littoral can be characterized as interdependent – aggression was mitigated by diplomacy, trade, and collaboration against rival co-religionist regimes. While raiding and privateering continued on both sides, bilateral trade agreements and military alliances were concluded as early as the 1250s. Trade consulates (*fondaci/fanādiq*) were established in North African and Egyptian ports, and as far east as Damascus. Muslim and Christian merchants and mercenaries moved back and forth across the confessional frontier, traveled on each others' ships, and engaged in collaborative commercial ventures.[58] When the late twelfth-century Valencian traveler and diarist, Muḥammad b. Jubayr, traveled east on the *ḥājj*, he did so on board Christian ships.[59] A similar situation held vis-à-vis the Naṣrid kingdom of Granada – a vassal-state of Castile-León that Aragon was occasionally able to pull into its political orbit. From the 1280s companies of Granadan *genets* (mercenaries) were used against both Castile and Navarre and became a common feature of the Aragonese countryside.[60]

As for Castile, the need to secure the coast of Andalucía, to complete the conquest of Granada, and to control the lucrative trade route through the Straits of Gibraltar, together with the allure of African gold, and the emerging threat of the Banū Marīn of Morocco, drew the kingdom southwards. In 1260 Alfonso X launched his "African project," the only result

[55] See L. Mott, *Sea Power*.

[56] See, for example, F. Marzal Palacios, "Solidaridad islámico"; R. Salicrú i Lluch, "L'esclau com a inversió?"; and M. T. Ferrer i Mallol and J. Mutgé, *De l'esclavitud a la llibertat*.

[57] R. Muntaner, *Chronicle*, p. 102 {51}. [58] See below, pp. 249–51 and pp. 256–60.

[59] See Ibn Jubayr, *The Travels*. [60] See B. Catlos, "Mahomet Abenadalill."

of which was a temporary seizure and sack of Salé (Salā) in which substantial loot and a great number of captives were carried off.[61] Between 1292 and 1294 Tarifa (Ṭarīfa) was conquered, and in 1309, Gibraltar (Jabal al-Ṭāriq). In the 1330s the Marīnids went on the offensive in concert with Granada, retaking Gibraltar and Algeciras (Jazīrat al-Khaḍrā), which they established as a beachhead. The threat from Morocco pushed the normally hostile Christian powers of the peninsula into alliance, and thus both the Christian and Islamic axes characterized their campaigns in religious terms (Crusade and *jihād*). After suffering a rout at the hands of the Moroccan navy in 1339, Castile and Aragon joined with Portugal and decisively defeated the allied Muslim forces at Salado in 1340.[62] In the event, Alfonso XI of Castile's (1312–50) attempts to follow up this victory were stopped short by the Black Death, which arrived at his siege-camp at Gibraltar in 1350 and struck the King dead.

The engagement of the Iberian Christian powers in the world of the Islamic Mediterranean had a profound impact on the situation of *mudéjares*. In a very direct sense, Christian military victories and piratical raiding boosted subject Muslim populations as a consequence of the substantial numbers who entered Christendom as slaves, and through their contact with free *mudéjares*, invigorated and modernized Islamic society in the peninsula.[63] The increasing role Christian powers took in Mediterranean trade allowed for Iberian Muslims to continue trading actively across the geo-religious divide, and bilateral treaties between Islamic and Christian powers typically contained provisions for the freedom of movement and protection of both foreign Muslim and *mudéjar* merchants.[64] Regular diplomatic missions arranged for the repatriation of Muslims and Christians who had been seized by pirates during time of truce, and Christian kings issued *guidatica* (letters of protection, singular: *guidaticum*) to Muslim merchants crossing their territories by land or sea.[65] But reciprocal relations were not confined to commerce; Muslim and Christian kingdoms remained politically entangled, and interdependent militarily – infidel mercenaries and allies were prominent, and Jewish, Muslim, and Christian diplomats were frequent (and honored) visitors in courts on both sides of the confessional frontier. The Almoravids and Almohads had come to rely increasingly on Christian soldiers of fortune,

[61] H. Salvador Martínez, *Alfonso X*, pp. 161–62; J. O'Callaghan, *Crusade and Reconquest*, p. 117, and *The Gibraltar Crusade*, ch. 2 "Alfonso X's African Crusade," pp. 11–33.

[62] See J. O'Callaghan, *Reconquest and Crusade*, pp. 211–12.

[63] B. Catlos, *The Victors and the Vanquished*, p. 238.

[64] See, for example, R. Salicrú i Lluch, "La diplomacia y las embajadas," and, generally, her *El sultanat de Granada*.

[65] See R. Burns, "The *Guidaticum* Safe-Conduct."

whereas in the Crown of Aragon, a Granadan nobleman commanded the kingdom's mercenary contingents and Almohad princes who had fled the Marīnid revolution took refuge in Valencia, serving a Christian king.[66] These varying registers of contact between these two religious worlds fed the paradox of Christian attitudes towards Islam and Muslims – Islamic culture continued to be regarded as sophisticated and prestigious through the fourteenth century, even as Muslims came to be thought of increasingly as enemies of God and Christendom. Hence, in 1364 King Pedro the Cruel of Castile (1350–66) attempted to recruit the diplomat, courtier, and scholar Walī al-Dīn ʿAbd al-Raḥmān b. Khaldūn (later famed as a universal historian), to his own court.[67] Simultaneously, in coastal areas, where the military struggle and the fear of raiding shaped daily realities, a tendency to perceive all Muslims as enemies of Christians and Christianity took root and grew.

## Revolts and resettlements

[It is further agreed] that the *Wazīr* shall give to the Exalted Prince [the *infant* Alfons] from the four castles, which he shall hand over to him when three years have elapsed, half the tithe [*al-'ushr*]; and whatever castles the *Wazīr* obtains [for] the ruler of Aragon, either by force or capitulation, the *Wazīr* shall have half of the revenue . . . (Abū ʿAbd Allāh b. Hudhayl "al-Azraq," Treaty with Aragon (1245)[68])

The sense that Muslims presented a danger to Christian society was not only provoked by the threat of foreign Islamic powers; the mid thirteenth century was marked by a series of *mudéjar* uprisings. Although occasionally these rebellions took on a confessional flavor and drew on the rhetoric of religious struggle, they were first and foremost local political events, and were restricted to specific areas of the south: the Valencian hinterland beyond the Xúquer River, Alfonso X's kingdom of Murcia, and parts of Andalucía. They found no echo in sparsely Muslim Castile and León or Portugal, nor among the substantial, long-established *mudéjar* communities of the Crown of Aragon and Navarre. In fact, rather than rebellions *per se*, these episodes represent the final phase in the process of Christian conquest. They took place in territories that had surrendered by negotiation, and in which pre-conquest authority and demographic structures remained essentially unchanged. Christian control here was at best tenuous and largely consensual, and there had been little colonization.

[66] See B. Catlos, "A Muslim Mercenary," p. 296; see also below, pp. 244–49.

[67] See Ibn Khaldūn, *The Muqaddimah*, vol. I, p. viii; J.-P. Molénat, "The Failed Encounter." For a recent biography, see A. Fromherz, *Ibn Khaldun*.

[68] R. Burns and P. Chevedden, *Negotiating Cultures*, p. 49.

Hence, the Arabic version of al-Azraq's treaty with the Crown of Aragon presents this local Muslim ruler, whose base was in the hills south of Valencia, not as a defeated supplicant, but as a local ruler pragmatically establishing a legitimate treaty (*'ahd*) with an infidel prince. Only a few years after it was signed, faced with intensifying Christian demands, and sensing an opportunity to capitalize on competition between Aragon and Castile, al-Azraq ("the Blue," so-named perhaps for the color of his eyes) launched a decade-long insurrection, one that presaged a second rebellion, "the Saracen wars" of the 1270s.

### *Al-Azraq's revolt*

Details of the rebellion remain obscure and all the more difficult to disentangle given that King Jaume's autobiography – hardly a model of objectivity – is our main source. The scattered revolt in southern Valencia got underway as early as 1247, and soon after Muslims under al-Azraq's leadership scored a significant military victory over a punitive force sent by the King. Jaume struggled to respond, but found himself hampered by his Christian subjects' divided loyalties.[69] The Military Orders, who had become the major seigniors in the south, as well as noblemen and townsfolk, frequently saw their best interests as served by defending their Muslim tenants and neighbors against their own King. Many Muslim communities, on the other hand, did not support the revolt, and offered extra tribute to the Christian King as compensation and as proof of their own loyalty. Jaume reacted to these two situations by lobbying Innocent IV to have his pacification campaign designated a Crusade and by pressuring his most important Muslim vassal, the *al-qā'id* (castellan) of Xàtiva, to withhold supplies from the rebels. Indeed, as the revolt faltered and Jaume's position improved, the uprising provided a means for the king to gradually wrest Xàtiva from Muslim control through the "combination of bullying and negotiation" that was his hallmark.[70] A series of treaties negotiated with the *al-qā'id* and the elders (*shuyūkh*) of the city beginning in 1248, had the inhabitants yield first the fortress, and then the town itself. Under a treaty of 1252 Xàtiva was re-founded as a Christian city with the remaining Muslims settled in an extramural suburb.[71] Here they enjoyed the liberties and autonomy typical of surrender treaties granted to Muslims, although the King had the prerogative of appointing the Islamic

[69] The revolt is the subject of R. Burns and P. Chevedden, *Negotiating Cultures*.
[70] *Ibid.*, *Negotiating Cultures*, p. 67.
[71] See I. O'Connor, *A Forgotten Community*, ch. 2, "The Christian Conquest of Xàtiva and its Aftermath, 1244–1252," pp. 28–54.

magistrate and tax official and held monopolies over key utilities, such as the local butcher shop and ovens. Statutes were established to keep the Christian and Muslim populations separate, and to protect the dignity and integrity of the religio-cultural communities of each.[72] As through much of conquered al-Andalus, the shift to Christian control prompted the departure of the local political and religious elite to Tunis, Granada, and Menorca, but a significant number of the population – particularly the artisanal or "industrial" class – remained.

In the meanwhile, al-Azraq's rebellion lost steam. And while Jaume's reports of a mass exodus of *mudéjares* is exaggerated, the war most certainly provoked the movement and resettlement of free Muslims within the kingdom – a process that undermined the socio-economic framework of what had been *Sharq al-Andalus* – and generated large numbers of slaves who would be sold within the Crown of Aragon and beyond. Brief respite for the rebels came in 1258 when they established a truce with Jaume's rival Alfonso X of Castile, but this only redoubled the Aragonese King's determination to crush the revolt. That year "a Saracen, a great confident of Alazarch" went over to Jaume, proposing in exchange for property and cash to trick al-Azraq into selling off his own supplies.[73] This was to be al-Azraq's end; his final gambit, which involved a feigned conversion to Christianity and a nocturnal ambush of the king, was foiled by Jaume's habitual good luck. Later that year the defeated rebel gave up his castles to the King in exchange for passage to Ifrīqiya.

### *Revolt in Andalucía*

No sooner had the uprising in Valencia been quelled than another flared up in Castilian-controlled territory, both in the Guadalquivir valley, which had been conquered, and in Murcia, which was ruled by Alfonso X's vassals, the Banū Hūd, and their rivals, the Banū Ashqīlūla. While the cities and major towns of the Guadalquivir had been all but purged of their free Muslim inhabitants (although there were undoubtedly significant numbers of slaves), a substantial Muslim population remained in the country, cultivating the land and practicing crafts as they had previously, but now living as tributaries of the Christian sovereign. They enjoyed broad communal autonomy and privileges, and some were granted the right to maintain fortified refuges for their own protection. Organization was local in nature, and the power of local warriors (*alcaldes*, from the Arabic, *al-qā'id*, pl.: *al-quwwād*) and the authority of councils of elders

[72] R. Burns and P. Chevedden, *Negotiating Cultures*, pp. 107 and 117.
[73] Jaume I, *The Book of Deeds*, p. 279 {373}.

(*sheikhs*, or *shuyūkh*) was officially recognized.[74] Decades of warfare had left the infrastructure of these areas devastated, however, contributing to a shift away from irrigated agriculture towards herding, and the weakening of the native socio-cultural fabric. The conquest itself was concluded in 1262, when Alfonso had reduced by force the last remaining focus of Andalusī resistance, the "kingdom of Niebla" (Labla), whose major center was Huelva (Walba).[75] In the meanwhile, Castilian determination to colonize and absorb the region of Murcia led to infringements of the terms of the Pact of Alcaraz, feeding popular and elite discontent.[76] As a consequence, the Banū Hūd joined with the Marīnids and Granada in planning a region-wide uprising, including a plot to kill the King in Seville.

In May 1264 *mudéjares* rose up across the south, taking control of most of the important towns, with the exception of major centers such as Seville, Córdoba, and Jaén. Castilian chronicles report the massacre of colonists in the towns that were seized, and Christian communities banded together for mutual defense.[77] Alfonso soon broke up the Muslim coalition, however, by exploiting the rivalry between the Banū Hūd and the Banū Ashqīlūla, and pushed Muḥammad b. al-Aḥmar to accept a truce by marching on Granada in early 1265. Later that year, Jaume I intervened from the north, obtaining the surrender of Elx (Alsh, Castilian: Elche), Murcia, and the rest of the region, which he returned to the power of his son-in-law, Alfonso. Local *mudéjares* accepted this arrangement because the remaining Muslims were prepared to live as subjects of Christendom under the broad concessions of autonomy Jaume was prepared to offer, and because of the divisions and rivalries that characterized their own society. The elders of Elx, for example, were brought over thanks to the King's bribery of the envoy they sent to negotiate.[78]

In each case, Muslims were required to remain loyal to Castile and little else as the price of peace. Broad religious freedom and juridical autonomy was guaranteed, and set down in formal charters by the King's secretary of Arabic, the Barcelonan Jew, Astruc Bonsenyor. According to the *Book of Deeds*, the Murcians grumbled when the King insisted on appropriating and consecrating as a church their congregational mosque, but could take comfort in the fact that the call to prayer would still echo through town and countryside. Jaume's sanitized nostalgia, however, does not square with contemporary Muslim sources, which recount the fleeing of refugees

74 See M. González Jiménez, *La repoblación*.
75 For Niebla, see F. Roldan Castro, *Niebla musulmana*.
76 See L. P. Harvey, *Islamic Spain 1250 to 1500*, pp. 48–51.
77 For the context and narrative of the revolt, see J. O'Callaghan, *The Gibraltar Crusade*, ch. 3, "The Crusade against the Mudéjars," pp. 34–59.
78 See Jaume I, *The Book of Deeds*, pp. 305–07 {416–21}.

and forced displacements, massacres, and the enslavement of women and children by the advancing Christian forces.[79]

### *"The war of the Muslims"*

In any event, this was not to be the last of the revolts in *Sharq al-Andalus*. Increasing fiscal demands by the Crown, seigniors, and municipalities aggravated *mudéjares* here and infringed on the liberties their treaties of submission had guaranteed. Christian *condottieri* and demobilized mercenaries raided with near-impunity, and took vulnerable *mudéjares* as their victims of choice. Further, Muslims had become the targets of popular Christian violence. A mixture of insecurity and opportunism, seasoned by a sense of religio-cultural conflict and confrontation bred by forty years of Crusade propaganda, encouraged attacks on Muslim communities.[80] These reached their apogee in 1275–76, with a series of assaults on the *morería* (Muslim neighborhood) of Valencia and other large towns, as well as many rural *aljamas*. Property was seized or destroyed and both free Muslims and converts to Christianity were killed or captured and sold as slaves. The king's reiteration of his Muslim subjects' legal rights offered them little protection, and embattled *mudéjares* sought refuge with the Military Orders or by holing up in fortifications. Jaime ordered judicial investigations into scores of cases of abuse, but demanded the Muslims cease to occupy his castles. This was a situation particular to that kingdom; in neighboring Aragon, for example, which also had a substantial Muslim population (perhaps one-third of the total population), there is only one recorded incident of popular violence against Muslims. In 1263 the *aljama* of the hamlet of Ambel was attacked; some were killed and others forcibly baptized. The King not only went after the culprits but declared the coercion conversion of these *mudéjares* to be void.[81]

The Valencian *mudéjares* themselves were emboldened by the ever more frequent cross-border incursions of Granadan and Moroccan raiders. As early as 1262 Muslims in the Sierra del Espadán, near Valencia revolted, and soon after the Muslim lord of the Sierra de Finestret rose up. In 1275 the Banū Marīn sacked Llutxent, and in the following year al-Azraq returned from Granada to lead a fresh insurrection and an invasion of Naṣrid and Marīnid troops – an uprising Christians referred to as "the war of the Muslims," *guerra Saracenorum*. Although al-Azraq was killed in

[79] H. Salvador Martínez, *Alfonso X*, pp. p. 171. For the mosque in Murcia, see above, p. 50.
[80] See B. Catlos, *The Victors and the Vanquished*, pp. 279–84.
[81] M. Ledesma Rubio, "Marginación y violencia," p. 206.

battle at Alcoi in that first year, the uprising was not suppressed until at least 1277, with serious resistance continuing into 1279 and isolated outbreaks until 1304. At the outset of the revolt King Jaume, embittered by what he saw as the disloyalty and ungratefulness of "his Muslims," abdicated in favor of his son, Pere. And although he urged his son to expel the Muslims from Valencia *en masse*, as he himself had once pledged to the papacy, both Jaume and Pere carefully distinguished between their loyal and rebellious Muslim subjects, protecting the former, and neutralizing the latter.[82] For his part, the new King martialed the resources of the entire Crown of Aragon to regain control of Valencia, including the Christian and Muslim communities of the kingdom of Aragon and Catalonia. As a consequence, Aragonese *mudéjares* contributed to the suppression of this Muslim revolt both through taxes they were forced to pay and, it seems, by military service also.

Although the *guerra Saracenorum* did not mark the end of the *mudéjar* Valencia, it was certainly a turning point. In the aftermath of the uprising, Muslim communities were reconstituted, refugees were summoned back to their lands, former rebels were rehabilitated, and even some new Muslim settlers entered the kingdom. However, while a few important urban centres, notably Xàtiva, would remain largely Muslim, the *mudéjar* population became overwhelmingly rural in orientation, and increasingly marginalized and servile in status. Moreover, *mudéjares* were pushed away from the coasts and into the hills – and into the most marginal lands in those hills – both as a deliberate policy to neutralize possible uprisings, and as a consequence of the imposition of a Christian economy that favored cereal production over the irrigated horticulture that Muslims had developed to such a high level.[83] Further, the war only exacerbated the Christians' sense of hostility and suspicion, and Muslims in the kingdom of Valencia came to be seen generally as infidels, foreigners, and potential slaves – in 1309 the *morería* was again attacked.[84] Thereafter, Christian settlers were required by royal policy to live within fortified enclaves, and many *mudéjar* communities demanded the right also to segregate for their own protection. At this point, the Muslims who enjoyed the greatest security and opportunity were those who lived as tenants of Military Orders and ecclesiastical foundations, organizations whose

[82] Jaume I, *The Book of Deeds*, pp. 379–80 {564}.

[83] For the agricultural reconfiguration of the kingdom and the concurrent displacement of Muslim farmers, see J. Torró i Abad, "Field and Canal Building."

[84] This attack coincided with a punitive expedition Jaume II undertook against the Muslims of Almería. The Valencian clergy were particularly reactionary, and as early as the 1240s, the Bishop of Valencia, Arnau de Peralta, had been calling for the expulsion of the kingdom's *mudéjares*. See P. Santonja, "Arnau de Vilanova," p. 243.

corporate interests lay in defending their Muslim subjects and nurturing their communities.

### *From vassals to subjects*

The situation in the Castilian-dominated south was very similar. Here, the ceaseless campaigns of the early thirteenth century had crippled the social and economic infrastructure. Population had declined even before the Christian conquest and pastoralism eclipsed agriculture in many regions. South of the Tajo, colonization was light, and much of the territory was ruled by Military Orders. Since husbandry was the foundation of their economy, the Orders had little interest in stimulating Christian settlement, or in retaining anything more than the vestigial Muslim population required for this sort of activity.[85] Although a scattering of Muslims remained in the Guadalquivir valley, major cities were left with almost no Islamic presence. If tax contributions can provide an index of the comparative size and wealth of communities, it is striking that in the late 1200s Seville's Jews generated twenty times more revenue than the city's *mudéjares*. The effect on Muslim society was most dramatic in the region of Murcia, which saw a general exodus towards Granada in the wake of the revolts of the 1260s. Only a handful of minor Muslim communities survived, and through a series of royally authorized *repartimientos* the countryside was transformed into a landscape of large estates, sparsely inhabited by Christians.[86] In Murcia itself, Alfonso quickly abrogated the most generous of Jaume's concessions – including the right to call the *ʾadhān* from the city's minarets – but maintained the political fiction of a Muslim protectorate under the rule of the Banū Hūd. These were now styled the "Kings of Arrixaca," after the extramural suburb into which the city's Muslims had been corralled. In 1295 Ibrāhīm b. Hūd, the last to hold this title, sold his properties in Murcia to Fernando IV. By this time not a few members of the royal family along with other remaining high-status Muslims had converted to Christianity and integrated themselves in the Castilian elite – the rest had departed.[87] Fernando, for his part, endeavored to put a brake on the *mudéjar* exodus by granting an extraordinarily generous series of privileges to Muslims who remained or settled in the kingdom.[88]

[85] See, for example, M. Á. Ladero Quesada, "Los mudéjares de Castilla," (1978), pp. 357–60.
[86] See J. Torres Fontes, *Repartimiento de Murcia.*
[87] See M. Rodrígues Llopis, *Alfonso X: aportaciones*, p. 84, for examples.
[88] See J. Torres Fontes, *Repartimiento de Murcia*, and *Repartimiento de la huerta.*

In Menorca, it was Christian opportunism rather than Muslim resistance that led to the destruction of Islamic society. In 1287 Pere's brother and successor, Alfons "the Liberal," determined to end the Aragonese protectorate over the island. His pretext was an incident in 1282. Allegedly, when a fleet en route to raid the port of Collo (al-Qulla, in Algeria) called in at Maó, the Menorcans sent warning of the attack to their co-religionists on the southern shore – an act of disloyalty which could be seen as abrogating their status as vassals. In 1286 a Crusade was duly authorized, and on the following January 17, Alfons's forces landed at Maó and fought a brief but hotly contested battle, while Ḥakam b. Saʿīd took refuge in a fortress in the island's interior. Four days later the beleaguered Muslim king sent a delegation of surrender.[89] Alfons's terms were uncomprising: with the exception of the *amīr* and two hundred of his dependents, who would be given passage to the *dār al-Islām*, the entire island and all property and persons on it were to become his personal chattels. Those who could afford to ransom themselves at the price of seven and a half *duplas* per person were given their freedom and allowed to settle where they wished, some choosing to move to the Aragonese mainland and others to Islamic kingdoms; the rest were auctioned off as slaves.[90] As coldly bureaucratic testament to this human tragedy, "On the Capture of Menorca" (Register 70 of the royal archive), records hundreds of *albarana* (warrants of sale; singular: *albaranum*) of men, women, and children – families torn apart and scattered across the Crown of Aragon. On the one hand this would have reinforced Christian stereotypes of Muslims as slaves, but on the other, the ingress of such a large number of free and recently free foreign Muslims into the Crown would have certainly had a stimulating and restorative effect on *mudéjar* society and culture there.

In the late thirteenth and early fourteenth centuries resistance to royal authority was not limited to Muslim subjects; this was a time of simmering Christian revolt as well, and in the Crown of Aragon in particular *mudéjares* were caught up in these upheavals as both victims and protagonists, as well as defenders of their infidel rulers. Noble banditry and feuding were endemic, and while Christian peasants and townsmen were certainly victimized, Muslims were regarded as easy targets by noblemen aiming to strike at their rivals' prosperity or merely to pillage and plunder. A steady stream of complaints arrived at the royal court lodged either by the seigniors of *mudéjares* or by Muslim subjects themselves; the King's

89 See C. Parpal y Marquès, *La conquesta de Menorca*.

90 The price for redemption was 7.5 *duplas*, or about thirty *sous*, which had the purchasing power of approximately twenty pounds of wax, thirty quarts of good wine, or five or six muttons.

agents investigated allegations, and restitution was ordered in cases of abuse.[91]

Muslims' relationship to municipalities was more complex, as they too participated in the municipal militias that served in royal armies and raided independently. Generally, when faced by an external threat, Muslim and Christian townsfolk would band together in mutual defense, as royal law, in fact, required them to do. Reports of communal violence aimed at Muslims in Aragon are rare. Even when the Shepherds' Crusade crossed the Pyrenees in 1320 and entered the Aragonese uplands, it was Jewish communities that they attacked. There were only two reports of assaults on Muslim communities and in neither case were deaths or injuries reported.[92]

As it was, *mudéjares* were far from defenseless. Free Muslims carried arms and could count on the active protection of their lords – ironically, the Military Orders, clerical organizations founded with the intention of fighting the Infidel were the staunchest defenders of their Muslims tenants' lives and property. *Mudéjares* were quite aware, however, that it was royal authority that provided the fundamental guarantees of security and survival. Hence, when the nobles and municipalities of the Kingdom of Aragon rose up in revolt against Pere "the Great" and Alfons "the Liberal" in the "Union" of the mid 1280s, their *mudéjar* subjects remained steadfastly loyal. When Pope Martin IV (1281–85) launched the Crusade against Aragon in response to Pere's taking of Sicily, levies of Aragonese and Valencian *mudéjares* were called up and fought with distinction against the French-led forces. An order was put out for 600 Muslim crossbowmen to defend Girona in 1285, armed with "heavy ("two-foot") crossbows."[93] The accuracy of Muslim crossbowmen was such that one of their number, perched atop the walls of the city, was said by the contemporary chronicler Bernat Desclot, to have fired a bolt through the window of a nearby church and killed a French "count" whom he had spied lying inside, convalescing on a cot.[94]

## Infidel subjects

We are given to understand by Our porter, Guillermus de Marsilia, that two of the Muslims who you arrested at his behest on account of the attacks they committed

[91] Examples abound in the chancery records; see, for example, B. Catlos, *The Victors and the Vanquished*, pp. 169–71 and 277.

[92] D. Nirenberg, *Communities*, pp. 8–34; J. Riera i Sans, *Fam i fe*; and M. Barber, "Lepers, Jews and Moslems."

[93] ACA, C., Pere II, *pergs.*, *carp.* 117, no. 485 (June 26, 1285).

[94] B. Desclot, "Llibre del rei en Pere," 571 {163}.

against the said *porter* of Ours entered and took refuge in one of the churches of the said town. Whereby . . . We order you . . . to remove the from the said church, since infidels should not enjoy the liberty of the Church . . . (James II of Aragon, letter to the bailiff of the town of Daroca, July 11, 1308[95])

In the period from 1150 to 1300CE what remained of al-Andalus came under Christian control, with the exception of the rump kingdom of Granada, which was established under the Banū 'l- 'Aḥmar, or Naṣrids, as a fickle tributary of Castile.[96] By this time the threat of invasion from North Africa had largely passed, but the capacity of the Christian kingdoms to colonize new territories had also reached its limit. Therefore, the slight risk of maintaining a *mudéjar* population needed to be measured against the economic loss that expulsion would entail, and consequently Muslim minorities were maintained, albeit unevenly, across the peninsula. In parts of southern Navarre, the area of Aragon formerly under Islamic rule, and in southern Catalonia, Muslims comprised a numerically significant minority, amounting, in 1300, to perhaps 30 percent of the population in those regions. Their communities here were economically diverse with a strong "urban" character; although most Muslims practiced some agriculture, many or most worked in trades, crafts, or commerce simultaneously. Over some two centuries under Christian rule, *mudéjares* here had acculturated and adapted to the Christian socio-cultural milieu, and yet maintained their religion, language, and identity. Relations with the Christian and Jewish communities among whom they lived were stable and characterized by symbiotic interdependence, marked by occasional friction. The situation was similar in Old Castile, León, and central Portugal, all of which had experienced an increase in the population of both slaves and free Muslims as a consequence of the hard-fought struggle for control of the south of the peninsula. Here, and in Mallorca at this time, Muslims were a numerically smaller minority and tended to be even more urban in orientation, although some seigniorial estates made use of Muslim agricultural labor. The kingdom of Valencia represents an exception – *mudéjares* continued to comprise the numerical majority of the population even at the end of the thirteenth century. And while an urban Muslim society remained, it was also the area where *mudéjares* figured most prominently as poor and marginalized farmers. Murcia, the Guadalquivir, and the Portuguese Algarve were home to a vestigial Muslim population grouped in a few

[95] ACA, C., reg. 140, f. 120r (July 11, 1308).

[96] See L. P. Harvey, *Islamic Spain, 1250 to 1500*, ch. 2, "The Rise of the Banū 'l-Aḥmar," pp. 20–40; B. Boloix Gallardo, *De la taifa de Arjona*; and M. J. Viguera Molins, *El reino Nazarí de Granada.*

towns and scattered across the countryside. There were Muslim slaves in "Upper Aragon," "Old Catalonia," northern Portugal, Menorca, and Roussillon, but very few free Muslims, and most of these were too isolated to be formally constituted as part of local communities.

By the mid thirteenth century each of the Iberian kingdoms had come to grips legally and conceptually with the fact that Muslims constituted an established and permanent element in Christian society, with a secondary but legitimate status. Muslims had become subjects by virtue of conquest but within the context of treaties, grants, and decrees that were, at bottom, bilateral in nature. The surrender treaties and local *fueros* (law codes), the Aragonese *cartas pueblas* ("settlement charters") and *convenienças*, and the Castilian *posturas* and *pletesías* were essentially personally negotiated contracts between the conqueror or ruler and specific Muslim communities. They varied considerably in content and tenor, and – although they were held to be subject to renewal upon royal succession – they were not "laws" in the permanent, anonymous legislative sense. Nevertheless – much as happened with the development of Christian municipal law – from the mid 1100s certain models came to be accepted as "standard" approaches to subjugation.[97] For example, the 1118 treaty of Zaragoza became a template in the Crown of Aragon. Late in the twelfth century, kings pushed to standardize and regularize their treaties, as in 1170 when Afonso Henriques and his heir, Sancho, conceded a "charter of loyalty and constancy" (*cartam fidelitas et firmitudinis*), also known as the "Law of the Muslims" (*foral dos mouros*), to Portugal's most important Muslim communities.[98] By the 1240s the pragmatic, *ad hoc* accommodations that had been made at the time of conquest were normalized as royal policy and accepted as legal principle. Although all Muslims, native or foreign, were referred to as *sarraceni* (or *moros*, *mouros*, or *sarrayns* in the various Romance vernaculars), *mudéjares* were distinguished by terms such as *moros forros* (from *ḥurr*, or "free"), *moros de paz* ("of peace"), and *moros de palio* ("of the [royal] mantle"), to distinguish them from both slaves and foreign Muslims.[99]

97 The same general observations can be made of laws granted to Christians and Christian communities in this era, including their personal and *ad hoc* qualities and the tendency for certain models to emerge as standard. See, for example, J. Lalinde Abadía, *Los fueros*. Indeed often, particularly in the twelfth century, the same legal promulgations applied to both Christians and Muslims of a locale, as well as Jews. See, for example, the population charter issued for Lleida in 1150 in J. M. Font i Rius, *Cartas de población*, vol. I, pp. 129–32 {79}.

98 For the 1170 *foral*, see M. F. Lopes de Barros, "Foral dos Mouros"; for the text, A. M. Flores and A. J. Nabais, *Os forais*, pp. 39–52.

99 Sometimes *moros de paz* referred to foreign Muslims travelling under the king's protection.

The principle of *mudéjar* juridical, fiscal, and administrative autonomy came to be entrenched in Iberian legal doctrine, although in practice the boundaries between Christian and Muslim communities were often fluid and contextual, and there was a steady encroachment of royal authority into Muslim affairs. The legal status of Muslims was at once reinforced and narrowed thanks to the introduction of the principles of Roman law in the Iberian kingdoms at this time, for example, with Alfonso X's promulgation of *Las Siete Partidas* (adopted soon after by Dinis of Portugal (1279–1325)), and with Jaume I's contemporary *fueros* of Aragon, Valencia, and Mallorca, as well as through the continuing elaboration of Canon Law.[100] Protecting Muslim (and Jewish) minority communities was very much in the kings' interests, as these populations were not subject to the customary laws that granted seigniorial authority and invited seigniorial interference. The minorities were, in principle, direct judicial and fiscal dependents of the kings. However, Muslims were also valuable to seigniorial, municipal, and ecclesiastical parties as tenants and vassals. The same "frontier towns" whose citizen militias provided a framework for the military-colonial enterprise of the "Reconquest" welcomed Muslims as settlers and townsmen soldiers.[101] Many town charters echoed that of Cuenca, welcoming "all settlers, whoever may come to Cuenca to settle, whatever may be their condition; that is, whether Christian, or Muslim, or Jew, or free, or slave . . ."[102] And while the military service of minority groups has been largely written out of the history of these medieval municipalities, Muslims served alongside Christians in many urban armies. For example, the Muslim cavalry of the militia of Ávila distinguished itself in Alfonso X's campaign to retake Soria from his rebelling nobles.[103] The competing interests of the various estates and corporations had the result that while royal (and Church) law granted Muslims significant and concrete protections, the agendas of their lords and of the kings ensured that the restrictive aspects of these same law codes were rarely enforced before the late thirteenth and early fourteenth centuries.

[100] See below, p. 351.
[101] See E. Lourie, "A Society Organized for War"; J. Powers, *A Society Organized for War*.
[102] J. Powers, *Code of Cuenca*, p. 31.
[103] A. Hernández Segura, *Crónica de la población de Ávila*, p. 49. When the troops arrived at Ayllón, a letter from Alfonso X arrived ordering the Muslims home with a stipend of 200 *maravedís* for their trouble, but two nobles journeyed to Vitoria and petitioned the King to let the *mudéjares* continue on campaign. In the fifteenth century the Muslims of Elvas are noted serving as cavalrymen in the municipal forces. See M. F. Lopes de Barros, *Tempos e espaços*, p. 418.

Christian and subject Islamic authorities agreed on the need to maintain separate organizational frameworks for local Muslim communities in order to facilitate tax collection and social control, on the one hand, and ensure the coherence, protection, and integrity of Islamic society on the other. Hence, across the peninsula *mudéjares* were organized into local collectives. These were known as *aljamas* (from the Arabic *al-jāmiʿ*, or "community") in Navarre, Castile, and the Crown of Aragon, and *comunas* in Portugal.[104] On occasion, when one or both communities were small, Jews and Muslims were incorporated into a single fiscal *aljama*, or even assessed along with local Christians, to facilitate tax collection. *Aljamas* were constituted both under royal and seigniorial authority, and authority within the *aljama* was based on elective representatives, royally or seigniorially appointed officials, or a combination of both.[105] From the late thirteenth century *mudéjar* communities tended to lose their autonomy and come under increasing Christian control both through the influence of the monarchy and the predatory agendas of Christian officials. Thus self-government, like true juridical independence, represented a principle and aspiration rather more than a reality. On the other hand, despite the centralizing efforts of the kings, *mudéjar* society remained local in orientation through the thirteenth century, consisting of autocephalous communities with no over-arching kingdom-wide officialdom or institutions.

The fragmentation of *mudéjar* society came about through the impact of the conquest on Islamic society in al-Andalus, the incremental nature of that conquest, and the resulting multiplicity of Christian interests and entanglements with local *aljamas*. Christian conquest and colonization signaled the abrupt disappearance of the Muslim social, political, military, religious, and cultural elites, who – with the exception of a few converts – emigrated to the *dār al-Islām*, where they could expect to re-establish their livelihoods with relative facility. Dramatically shorn of their leadership, these *mudéjar* communities were reconstituted under the control of a new, much more modest Muslim elite, comprised of tradesmen, craftsmen, and merchants, whose interests and influence were, with exceptions, local or provincial in scope.[106] This fragmented petty elite rarely had the power or potential to influence royal policy vis-à-vis Muslims (contrary to the case of the Jewish elite), and therefore, while they could be effective at protecting local interests, they generally could not forestall a gradual

[104] For communal organization and institutions, see below, pp. 390ff.
[105] See B. Catlos, *The Victors and the Vanquished*, pp. 126–28.
[106] For the *mudéjar* elite, see below, pp. 456ff.

decline of status and freedoms which characterized peninsular Islam from the late 1200s on.

The fourteenth century would see a general trend towards the increasing establishment and enforcement of sumptuary laws, restrictions of movement (both internal and external), increasingly discriminatory tax regimes, a growing spirit of Christian chauvinism, and the gradual encroachment of seigniorial authority.

### *Muslims in Iberian society to 1320*

This was also an era in which *mudéjar* society was drawn into the social, cultural, and economic environments of the Christian Spains. With the exception, perhaps, of Valencia, where *mudéjares* were more numerous, cohesive, and generally resistant to Christian domination, Muslims quickly acculturated, adopting "Christian" styles of dress, Latin and Romance vernaculars, Romance names and anthroponymic forms, pastimes and attitudes, both as a consequence of the inevitable attraction of a dominant culture and the need to relate to majority society, and also because of economic, institutional, and social integration.[107] This did not come at the cost of either Islam or Arabic; for the most part, *mudéjares* were able to maintain an impressively resilient, vibrant, and cohesive Arabo-Islamic culture simultaneous to their immersion in Hispano-Christian culture. Such conversion to Christianity as there was in this period seems to have been limited to the initial moments of conquest, when some Muslims, particularly in Valencia, made the decision to leave their faith rather than their homes. But this was not a mass movement in any sense, and through the mid fourteenth century episodes of apostasy are rare and anecdotal. At this time neither the apparently manifest destiny of Christianity, nor the efforts of mendicant preachers, nor the humiliation of subjugation and danger of enslavement were enough to turn significant numbers of *mudéjares* from their faith, even after emigration came to be forbidden or severely limited in the late thirteenth and early fourteenth centuries. Islam among the *mudéjares* was provincialized but was not quarantined; it continued to answer the spiritual and communal needs of its adherents, and continued to maintain links to the wider *dār al-Islām*.

That said, although change in many areas was gradual, Muslim society was dramatically and inevitably transformed under Christian rule, as the foundations of the Iberian economy shifted, new fiscal and administrative

[107] See below, chapter 10.

regimes were established, and commercial relations realigned. In town settings Iberian *mudéjares* came to concentrate on a broad but specific range of trades, many of which they dominated as a group. These included, for example, crafts associated with building and decoration, tailoring and shoemaking, soap-making, weapons manufacture, and husbandry, to name a few.[108] On the other hand, their participation in high-status professions, such as medicine and even translation from Arabic, declined. Muslims continued to be involved in commercial ventures, ranging from local and regional to "international." As movement became increasingly circumscribed and risky for Muslims, and trade came to be increasingly oriented towards the Christian lands and markets, they were edged out of regional commerce, although their religious orientation and culturo-linguistic facility gave them a competitive edge in trade with the Islamic world, in which they remained important players.[109] Under Christian rule, the countryside was transformed also. The "ḥiṣn/qarya" settlement model, so characteristic of rural al-Andalus, was rendered immediately obsolete and abandoned, and royal fiscal regimes which had developed in the context of cereal production hastened the demise of the diverse and complex irrigated horticultural systems that had been the hallmark of the Andalusī countryside.[110] Where these irrigation systems did persist they were infiltrated by Christian colonizers and came under the control of Christian lords. These may have maintained the form and function of pre-conquest irrigation systems, but no longer would these systems develop as the organic manifestations of segmentary, agnatic, tribal Islamic society. In sum, changes in economic, demographic, and fiscal structure were ultimately more powerful transformational factors than the imposition of an infidel religious culture on the Muslims of Christian Iberia.

### *A diversity of experience*

Despite the fact that these developments took place within a common framework of Iberian Christian culture, the experience of Muslims in the peninsula and the approach that the various kingdoms took to Islam and *mudéjares* varied. This came as a consequence of the size and constitution of the Muslim community in each kingdom and each kingdom's

[108] See below, pp. 425–31.
[109] See, for example, R. Salicrú i Lluch, "Mudéjares y cristianos en el comercio," J. L. Soler Milla, "Comercio musulmán," and below, pp. 256ff.
[110] See, for example, T. Glick, *From Muslim Fortress*, pp. 18–29; P. Sénac, "De ḥiṣn musulmán"; as well as the extensive archaeological work undertaken under the auspices of the Casa de Velázquez in Madrid.

economic and political orientation. In Navarre, for example, the *mudéjar* community was a small, town-oriented minority that was not crucial to the function of the kingdom's economy but made significant contributions to royal and seigniorial incomes. Tudela was the most important Muslim center here, with smaller communities dotting the Ebro, Alhama, Huecha, and Queiles rivers.[111] Navarre had been ruled by Alfonso I of Aragon during the crucial decades of the conquest of the *taifa* of Zaragoza which established a *mudéjar* presence, but became independent after his death, and from 1234 under the rule of the House of Champagne drifted into the orbit of France. Far from the *dār al-Islām*, Muslims here were not regarded as a threat, but rather as inoffensive and unobtrusive subjects, useful for their particular skills and specializations and their productive capacity. The situation in Portugal appears to have been similar, but surviving sources prior to the mid fourteenth century allow us to do little more than confirm the existence of discrete Muslim communities in the zone of the Tagus River and in the Algarve.[112] The inhabitants of the larger *comunas* paid a range of taxes and fees to the king, while the Military Orders collected rents and fees from their Muslim tenants. Once the dust of the conquest had settled, there is no evidence of communal violence or tension between Christians and Muslims here.

The Crown of Castile and the Crown of Aragon had the most substantial *mudéjar* populations and offer a most instructive contrast to one another. Although there were considerable numbers of Muslims living in both realms, Castile continued to relate to Islam and Muslims predominantly in the context of a rival religio-cultural system, whereas the Crown of Aragon's approach tended to be pragmatic and non-ideological. A number of factors were at play in each case. First of all, there were, both proportionately and absolutely fewer *mudéjares* in Castilian lands; they tended to be concentrated in a few particular areas. For example, in the last quarter of the thirteenth century, what had been a substantial *mudéjar* population in the Guadalquivír Valley all but disappeared, whereas the Muslim population in Old Castile increased.[113] Moreover, in Castile *mudéjares* occupied a rather narrow band in the economic spectrum – notably the craft professions noted above, and farmers and herders, although there was also a small literary-scientific elite. As a consequence of this lack of diversity, their integration in the Christian economy was limited and their visibility in Christian society low.

[111] See M. García-Arenal and B. Leroy, *Moros y judíos*, p. 18.
[112] See the map in M. F. Lopes de Barros, *Tempos e espaços*, p. 142.
[113] See M. González Jiménez, "El fracaso," pp. 133–35.

Islam, on the other hand, loomed large in the Castili consciousness. This was, in part, the result of a politic ported by monarchy and Church that presented Castilian po sion in terms of reconstitution of the Visigothic kingdom that ha conquered in 711 – a "Reconquest" sanctified as Crusade and personifie in the figure of St. James "the Moor-killer."[114] Further, Alfonso X's aspirations to the title of Holy Roman Emperor – sovereign of all Christendom – demanded he adopt a formal, ideologically orthodox position vis-à-vis Islam.[115] Hence, the detailed and exacting provisions regarding the segregation and marginalization of Muslim and Jews in his *Siete Partidas*, and his commitment to the project of translating Arabic letters and adapting Islamic high culture. At the same time, the Castilian nobility and monarchy were profoundly engaged with the foreign Muslim upper class. The Naṣrid kings were Castilian vassals, and the courts of the Christian kingdom and those of its Muslim neighbors were profoundly linked. Castilian nobles battled in the name of Saint James against Islamic foes, but they also served as mercenaries in Muslim armies and fought alongside Muslim knights and noblemen who served in their own armies. The common profession of arms and aspirations to universal authority inspired a sense of affinity among the Castilian and North African elites. Hence, the tendency of chivalric Castilian literature – from the anonymous *romances* dating back to the time of El Cid to the short stories of Don Juan Manuel, *El Conde Lucanor* – to apprehend (upper-class) Muslims on surprisingly equivocal terms, and the Castilian monarchy's increasing *maurophilia*, from the fourteenth century onwards.[116] In short, it may be said that Castile conceived of Islam as a civilization, extremely potent (albeit naturally inferior), and of *mudéjares* as manifestations of the lower order of that civilization.

By contrast, after the conquests of Valencia and the Balearics, the military–political expansion of the Crown of Aragon was oriented towards Christian lands (Italy and the Mediterranean islands, in particular), whereas its commercial expansion was oriented primarily towards the Islamic world – in other words, the reverse of the situation of Castile. The rulers of the Crown certainly made political use of the Crusade movement (as well as being targets of it), but it was not an essential feature of the monarchy's political discourse nor did it provide a basis for the legitimization of its authority. The Crown, therefore, apprehended Islam

114 See, generally, N. Cabrillana, *Santiago Matamoros*.

115 See H. Salvador Martínez, *Alfonso X*, ch. 4, "The Quest for the Imperial Crown," pp. 121–47.

116 See D. Wacks, "Reconquest Colonialism."

rather differently, with a pragmatic approach notable for its absence of religious and ideological posturing. The commercial class provided the main nexus of contact with the Islamic world, imbuing relations with a strong element of pragmatism. While the Crown was certainly embroiled politically with Granada and the principalities of the Maghrib, these contacts lacked the intimacy that characterized Castilian engagement. Few Muslim notables were to be found in the Catalano-Aragonese court, which displayed a general indifference to Arabo-Islamic culture.[117] Muslims, whether heroes or villains, are all but absent from the vernacular literature of the era and there was no officially sponsored project of translation or assimilation. Conversely, there was little sense that Muslims were seen as a threat, in spite of the fact that in much of Catalonia, most of Aragon, and practically all of Valencia, most towns had a Muslim *aljama* of some size, many nobles and ecclesiastical foundations had *mudéjar* tenants and vassals, and Muslim slaves, both foreigners and enslaved *mudéjares*, were common. Larger *aljamas* were powerful enough to be able to renegotiate their relationship with the monarchy on an ongoing basis, often from a position of surprising strength.[118] And while there may have been few high-status Muslims in the Crown of Aragon, *mudéjares* here were profoundly and broadly integrated in the larger economy and Christian society, and came under remarkably little ideological or legal pressure. Thus, as was the case in so many spheres, in terms of relations with Islam and the status of *mudéjares*, the Crown of Aragon and Navarre seems to represent a pragmatic and moderate counterpoint to Castile's epic and romanticism.

Here, as in the previous period, *mudéjares*' involvement in architecture is broadly indicative of the relative ease and confidence with which Muslims and Christians apprehended each other. In the areas conquered and subdued by force in the thirteenth century one finds none of the distinctively Muslim brickwork churches that characterize the Ebro, Duero, and Tajo valleys, that had been conquered with so little resistance in the late eleventh and twelfth centuries.[119] Valencia and Mallorca have little or no church architecture resembling that of Aragon; the undercurrents of hostility and mistrust with which Muslim and Christian society

[117] This was not a consequence of a generic distrust of Muslims on the part of the royal administration. The court of the Crown of Aragon was home to a powerful Jewish elite, which lobbied to ensure key positions, whether that of royal physician or royal scribe of Arabic, went to members of their families. See, for example, D. Romano, *Judíos al servicio*, and "Judíos escribanos y turjamanes."

[118] See, for example, below, pp. 174 and 385.

[119] For the origins of the "*mudéjar*" architectural style, see J. L. Corral Lafuente, *et al.*, *La cultura islámica*, pp. 45–53; and, below, p. 425.

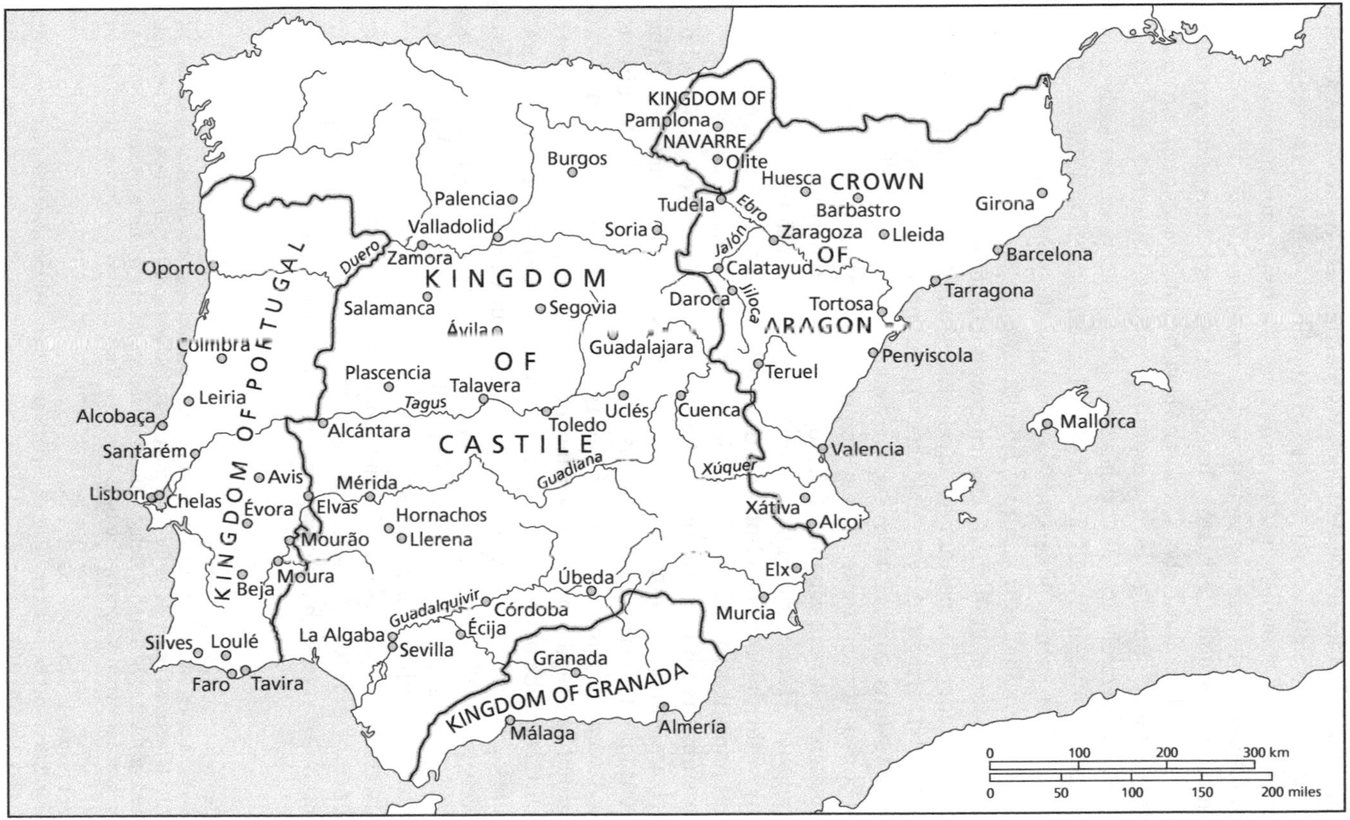


Map 4 Subject Muslim settlement in the Iberian Peninsula, *c.* 1320

regarded each other precluded such visible and easy borrowing and collaboration. In Valencia, but more so in Andalucía, many converted mosques were not demolished, and therefore Christian churches remained manifestations of Christian victory and domination – a potent symbol for both *mudéjares* and Christians. Indeed, in the mid fourteenth century, Castilian rulers (and the Castilian Jewish elite) displayed an overt "Maurophilia," building and decorating palaces, churches, and synagogues deliberately in "Moorish" style.[120] These were certainly constructed by *mudéjares* and foreign Muslim craftsmen brought in from Granada, but even in Valencia, Navarre, and the north, where building styles were gradually turning away from the twelfth-century *mudéjar* styles, Muslim workers, craftsmen, and engineers continued to dominate the building trade. The position of royal master builders and carpenters in Aragon, Navarre, and even Valencia were often held by *mudéjares*, and these Muslims enjoyed both prosperity and prestige.[121] The buildings they constructed in these areas were not "Muslim" in style – these were craftsmen who were capable of deploying a broad repertoire of styles and techniques. Hence, through this period Muslims continued to construct many of the palaces and churches that noblemen lived in and clergy and commoners worshiped in, whether in "mudéjar" or "Christian" styles.[122]

In sum, the mid twelfth to mid fourteenth centuries were a period in which a working relationship was established between the *mudéjares* of the various kingdoms and the Christians among whom they lived. Conditions varied according to locale, but in every case, the Muslim minority was regarded as a legitimate and permanent feature of these societies. There was little or none of what might be described as religious violence, marginalization, or oppression, except in areas and contexts where Muslims were actively involved in political and military resistance to Christian rule. The revolts that raged in Andalucia and Valencia in the second half of the century, incredibly, had almost no impact on local Christian–Muslim relations in Aragon, Navarre, Catalonia, and – we may presume, in the absence of sources – Castile and León.[123] This was a state of affairs the Church – or at least the papacy – regarded with a certain jaundice. In 1205

[120] See below, p. 425.

[121] For example, in the 1280s, Çalema Alatili, a master engineer (*magister geniorem*) of Lleida, worked on projects for Pere the Great, including his royal palace in Tarazona, and in the 1290s Abrafim Bellido of Zaragoza, entrepreneur and merchant, served as master builder in Valencia. See B. Catlos, *The Victors and the Vanquished*, pp. 196 and 217–18.

[122] See below, p. 425.

[123] For differences between *mudéjar* society in Valencia and Aragon, see Catlos, "The Ebro Valley and Valencia."

Innocent III would remark of Alfonso VIII, the future hero of Las Navas, that "by his conduct it would appear that he loved the mosque and the synagogue more than the Church."[124] Then years later, the same Pope convened the Council of Lateran IV, which established Muslims' and Jews' formal, marginal position under Canon Law.[125] In fact, this so-called *convivencia*, to use a flawed and nebulous term, was a delicate equilibrium which would be put to the test by the multiple crises of the fourteenth century, at time in which these Muslim communities' capacity to persevere would be conditioned by their ability to respond to the rapidly changing environment in which they lived.

[124] L. Torres Balbás, *Algunos aspectos*, p. 69. [125] For Lateran IV, see below, p. 372.

# 3 Pushing the boundaries
## Italy and North Africa (*c.* 1050–*c.* 1350)

The beginning of the establishment of the regime of the Franks ... and their departure to the lands of Islam and their conquest of some of them was the year 478 [1085]. They took the city of Toledo and other parts of al-Andalus as already mentioned. Then they attacked in the year 484 [1091] the island of Sicily and conquered it, and they turned to the coast of North Africa and conquered part of that ... (ʿIzz al-Dīn b. al-Athīr, *Al-Kāmil fī'l ṭārīkh* (*c.* 1231)[1])

With the benefit of historical hindsight, Ibn al-Athīr viewed the incursions of Latin Christians – the *Ifranj* ("Franks") – into the *dār al-Islām*, from Iberia to the Holy Land, as a coherent and coordinated campaign, beginning with al-Andalus and continuing in Sicily. In fact, the Norman attack on Sicily predated the fall of Toledo; while the last Muslim hold-out on the island was indeed subjugated in 1091, the capital, Palermo (Balarm), had fallen as early as 1072, a full decade after the invasion had begun.[2] But the similarities to the so-called "Spanish Reconquest" are, in fact, striking. This conquest was part of a process of political instability and disintegration in Islamic Sicily (Ṣiqilliya) into which the Norman d'Hauteville clan was opportunistically drawn, and in which local Muslim leaders were complicit and local Muslim communities acquiescent. If anything, Sicily presented an ethno-religious panorama even more complex than that of al-Andalus. Here, the Normans encountered a population consisting of indigenous converts to Islam, a large number of North African settlers, Arabized native Christians, Egyptian- and Syrian-identifying Jews, and a significant population of Greek-identifying Christians. As in al-Andalus, the dominant Islamic culture was Sunnī and Mālikī; however, Sicily had only been Muslim for a little over a century and a half. Further, Fāṭimid political domination and Berber immigration had led to significant Shīʿī and Ibāḍī (Khārajī) influence. Into this environment came the northern

[1] "The Complete History," excerpted in C. Hillenbrand, *The Crusades: Islamic Perspectives*, p. 52.

[2] To be fair, a contemporary Damascene, al-Sulamī, made the same observation, but got the chronology correct. See below, p. 129.

European Normans, and soon after, the Calabrese and Lombard colonists who transformed the island. Thus, post-conquest Sicily was characterized by a complex matrix of ethnic identities, several of which ran across confessional and cultural divides, and which the early Christian rulers were obliged to manage with delicacy and flexibility. By the early thirteenth century, Christian rule had consolidated and a rigorous approach to the increasingly restive Muslim population was adopted. That famous Arabophile and alleged atheist, the Emperor Frederick II Hohenstaufen (1220–1250; King of Sicily from 1198), would forcibly transport the island's Muslim population to mainland Lucera beginning in 1224, and under the rule of the Angevin, Charles II (1285–1309), that colony would be dismantled and its inhabitants sold into slavery beginning in 1300.

Our sources for the study of Muslims living under the rule of the Normans and their successors in the central Mediterranean are both abundant and sparse. On the one hand, there is a tremendous variety of material, including Arabic and Latin chronicles, Christian legal and administrative texts and Islamic *fatāwā*. Surviving records of the famously trilingual royal chancery include correspondence of the kings and their neighbors, as well as royal and ecclesiastical administrative records. Norman Sicily was heavily embroiled in the Islamic Mediterranean and figures prominently in the *diplomataria* of the Fāṭimid Caliphate and the chronicles of Ifrīqiya, and even surfaces in Geniza letters. Added to this is what survives of the considerable cultural output of what we might call *mudéjar* Sicily: the *dawāwīn* (singular: *dīwān*) of Siculo-Arabic poets and savants, and rich material remains, not the least the "Oriental" palaces and gardens of the Norman kings. Even with all of this material, however, the surviving records do not approach those found in Christian Iberia in volume or variety, and the history of the Muslim communities under Latin rule can only be apprehended as if a palimpsest – scraped almost clean, and overwritten by the Christian narrative.[3]

[3] For the later Islamic, Norman, Hohenstaufen, and Angevin periods of Sicily, and southern Italy, see, for example, D. Abulafia, *Frederick II*; "The Norman Kingdom of Africa"; "The End of Muslim Sicily"; M. Amari, *Storia dei Musulmani di Sicilia*; A. Aziz, *A History*; J. Birk, "Sicilian Counterpoint"; M. Brett, "Muslim Justice"; G. Brown, *The Norman Conquest*; F. Chalandon, *Histoire de la domination normande*; P. Chevedden, "A Crusade from the First"; H. Houben, "Religious Toleration"; J. Johns, *Arabic Administration* and "Malik Ifriqiya"; G. Loud, *The Age of Robert Guiscard*, and *The Latin Church*; K. Mallette, *Kingdom of Sicily*; D. Matthew, *The Norman Kingdom of Sicily*; A. Metcalfe, *Muslims and Christians in Norman Sicily*, and "Muslims of Sicily"; A. de Simone, "Ruggero II e l'Africa islamica"; H. Takayama, *The Administration*; J. Powell, "Frederick II and the Rebellion of the Muslims"; J. Taylor, *Muslims in Medieval Italy*; W. Tronzo, *The Cultures of His Kingdom*. Substantial published primary sources in European languages include M. Amari, *et al.*, *Biblioteca arabo-sicula*; Amatus of Montecassino, *The History of the Normans*; P. Egidi,

## Islamic Sicily and southern Italy

One day I was standing beside the house of Abū Muḥammad al-Qafṣī, the lawyer, a specialist in contracts. Looking out from his mosque at a distance of a shot of an arrow, I noticed about ten mosques, some of them facing each other, often separated by a road. Inquiring as to the excessive number of them, I was told that the people are extremely proud, each wanting his own private mosque to share with only his family and his small inner circle. (Ibn Ḥawqal, *Kitāb al-masālik wa 'l-mamālik* (*c.* 977)[4])

Even more than al-Andalus, Sicily had the reputation in the Islamic world as something of an earthly paradise: a fertile, bustling island, with an abundance of resources, an agreeable climate, and a dynamic society. But for Ibn Ḥawqal, the well-traveled geographer who visited Islamic Sicily at the height of its prosperity and power, the individualism – even atomization – that characterized Islamic society here was one if its most salient characteristics. As a consequence of its late absorption into the *dār al-Islām* – and, indeed, the conquest of Sicily was the final "classic" Islamic conquest – its political instability, and the diversity of both its indigenous and Islamic population, Ṣiqilliya was even more volatile than al-Andalus. In general, early medieval southern Italy was politically and culturally highly fragmented, contested by Byzantines, "Lombards," and other local Latinate groups, all in close proximity to Rome, the seat of a papacy grasping towards universal Christian authority, and under the long shadow of the Germano-Latin would-be Roman Emperors. The opportunities presented by this environment attracted Muslim raiders as early as the 650s, but it was not until the ninth century that interventions came in earnest.

According to the chronicles, in June 827 forces sent by the Aghlabids, the dynasty of governor-princes who ruled Ifrīqiya in the name of the ʿAbbāsids, landed at Mazara (Mazāraʿ) in western Sicily, at the invitation of a rebellious Byzantine general, Euphemius. This initiated a campaign of conquest that would not be completed until the fall of Taormina in 902. Meanwhile, privateers and Aghlabid clients raided up and down the Italian coasts as far as Tuscany and Veneto, sacking St. Peter's in Rome in 846, and establishing a short-lived but stable principality at Bari (Bāru; 847–71), as well as other footholds in Apulia and Calabria. Sardinia and Corsica were raided repeatedly and by 869 Malta had been conquered. For their part, the local Lombards saw the Muslims both as enemies and

*Codice diplomatico*; H. Falcandus, *The History of the Tyrants*; G. Loud, *Roger II and the Creation of the Kingdom of Sicily*; G. Malaterra, *The Deeds of Count Roger*; Ibn Jubayr, *Travels*; and Guillaume de Pouillem, *La geste de Robert Guiscard*.

4 "The Book of Roads and Kingdoms," in W. Granara, "Ibn Hawqal in Sicily," p. 97.

potential allies in their own rivalries; thus, as early as 835 Naples imported Muslim warriors and in later decades petty princes, like Radelgise of Benevento and Siconolfo of Salerno and Capua, enlisted companies of Muslim mercenaries in their campaigns against each other. Meanwhile, as the conquest of Sicily was concluding, the Aghlabid dynasty was faltering against the pressure of popular and regional dissatisfaction, Berber resistance couched in Kharajism, and finally, by a full-blown Shīʿī rebellion, which overthrew the regime and put the Fāṭimids in power in Ifrīqiya in 909. But Sicily proved hard to govern for the new rulers, thanks to tensions between Arab colonists in Palermo and the Berbers settled around Agrigento (Jirjant), Sunnī religious resistance, ʿAbbāsid loyalism, and the irrepressible rebelliousness of local leaders and communities. In 948 the Fāṭimids installed their clients, the Banū Kalb, as governors, and after the Shīʿī caliphate shifted its center of operations to Egypt in 973, these became increasingly independent.

Under Abū 'l-Futūḥ Yūsuf b. ʿAbd Allāh (989–98) Islamic Sicily reached its apogee; the Byzantines were kept at bay, raiding continued along the Italian mainland, and the capital, Palermo, became a dynamic center of Arabo-Islamic art, literature, and learning. Sicilian prosperity was driven by the island's abundant natural resources and tremendous productive capacity, the latter augmented by innovations from the East. It soon became a "bread basket" for gold-rich Ifrīqiya, then under the rule of another dynasty of erstwhile Fāṭimid governors, the Banū Zīrī (the same extended family of Ṣanhāja Berbers who would rule over the *taifa* kingdom of Granada). In the meantime, North African clans continued to migrate to Sicily, particularly the south and west, while a considerable Christian population – primarily Greco-Byzantine, but apparently including "Mozarab" elements, confessionally oriented towards Rome – remained on the island, along with communities of Jews with links to Egypt and Syria. The Muslim population of the north coast was Arab-identifying, and comprised both settlers and their descendants and indigenous converts from Christianity.[5]

Despite his cutting criticism of some Sicilians' piety and intelligence, Ibn Ḥawqal described the island as thoroughly Islamic. By his reckoning 7,000 faithful gathered in Palermo's congregational mosque for Friday

[5] There were also indigenous Arabic-speaking Christians in Sicily; see A. Metcalfe, "Muslims of Sicily", p. 313. For Houben the famous trilingual Grisandus tombstone inscription (a Greek–Latin–Arabic epigraph commissioned in 1163 by a cleric of William II in memory of his father, Drogo) is not proof of Muslim–Christian *convivencia*, but confirmation of Arabic speaking among Christians. See H. Houben, "Religious Toleration," p. 327. For a general critique of what has been at times an uncritically rosy perception of Muslim–Christian relations in Sicily, see C. Dalli, "Contriving Coexistence."

prayers, while the city boasted more than 300 private mosques.[6] The surrounding hamlets, he said, had more mosques that did most of the major cities of his time, with the possible exception of Córdoba. The island's various ethno-religious communities lived in a working accommodation, characterized by an impressive, if perhaps purely pragmatic degree of acculturation.

The Kalbid gilded age, however, would be brief, as a consequence of both internal instability and outside pressure. The weakness of Yūsuf's son, Ja'far (998–1019), prompted a civil war within the family, and encouraged the Zīrids to mount an invasion in support of the rebels, while the legitimate *amīr*, al-Akhtāl, called on Byzantium for help. Meanwhile, the Venetians and Pisans struck at Islamic territories on the Italian mainland. In short order, Sicily tilted into a chaos resembling that of the Andalusī *taifas*, if more acute. In 1053 the citizens of Palermo cast out al-Hasan (or "al-Ṣamṣām") the last *amīr* of the dynasty, and established a republic under the authority of a *qāḍī*. The Zīrids, for their part, fared little better. In punishment for their disloyalty, the Fāṭimids unleashed the Bedouin Banū Hilāl and Banū Sulaym tribes to plunder an already economically depressed Ifrīqiya. The Banū Zīrī were forced to withdraw to the coastal cities, which themselves became subject to Pisan and Genoan raiding and demands for tribute. In Sicily, where local warlords (*quwwād*; singular: *qā'id*) vied against each other, the struggle between Ibn al-Ḥawwās, lord of Agrigento, al-Maklātī, of Catania (Qaṭāniya) and Ibn al-Thumna of Syracuse (Siraqūsa) would prove decisive. Ibn al-Thumna killed al-Maklātī, but was defeated by Ibn al-Hawwās soon after, in 1060. Casting about for allies, Ibn al-Thumna turned to a new group of warriors who had been making a reputation as soldiers of fortune in Italy – the Normans – whom he invited to join him as allies in the taking of Sicily.

## Roger I and the Norman Conquest

It was in the year 453 of the Arabic reckoning (1061 of the Christian era), that the illustrious, wise, excellent and powerful ruler, Roger, son of Tancred, conquered most of this land, and with the help of his companions came to humiliate the pride of the rebels who opposed his domination and resisted with arms . . . Once the land was under his command and he had established his power on a firm foundation, he spread the benefits of his justice over the inhabitants, reassuring them in the practice of their religions and the observation of their laws; he assured them

[6] W. Granara, "Ibn Hawqal in Sicily," pp. 96–97.

Map 5 Subject Muslim communities of Sicily, Southern Italy, and Ifrīqiya, 1060–1350

the protection of their belongings, their lives, their women and their children.
(Muḥammad al-Idrīsī, "*Kitāb Rujjār*" (*c.* 1154)[7])

Contrary to Ibn al-Athīr's contentions, the Normans' *entrée* into Islamic Sicily was not the consequence of a premeditated Frankish campaign against Islam; rather, the d'Hautevilles were one of many Latin warrior clans who, like their Berber homologues, saw the opportunities offered by the wealthy and unstable eleventh-century Mediterranean. It was the chaos of Lombard Italy and the waning of Byzantine power that drew eight sons of a minor Norman nobleman, Tancred d'Hauteville, from misty Contentin to the sunny Mezzogiorno beginning in the 1030s. In 1038 the brothers William and Drogo, along with other soldiers of fortune, joined the Byzantine invasion of Sicily, which despite early successes, including a brief capture of Syracuse in 1040, was ultimately inconclusive.[8] In the succeeding decades a string of kinsmen followed them south from Normandy, and in short order the family had been subsumed in the politics of the peninsula. William (d. 1045) took the title of Count of Apulia, while brothers, cousins, and their clients fanned out, taking on all comers in their quest for patrimony and pillage – marrying into the local aristocracy, and attacking local lords, Byzantine functionaries, the papacy, Lombard and Muslim castellans, and each other with predatory indifference.[9] By 1059 William's half-brother Robert Guiscard ("the Cunning") had emerged as the family strongman, and succeeded in prizing from a vulnerable Pope Nicholas II (1058–61) investiture "by the grace of God and St. Peter [as] Duke of Apulia and Calabria, and in future, with the help of both, of Sicily."[10]

Whatever God and St. Peter's contributions to the enterprise may have been is an open question, but that of Robert's brother Roger Bosso ("the Great") is clear. Like his elder sibling, Roger was a consummate warrior, shrewd strategist, and ruthless leader.[11] Taking him as a formal

[7] "The Book of Roger" adapted from the French translation of *Kitāb nuzhat al-mushtāfi 'khtirāq al-āfāq*, in J. Amédée, *Géographie d'Édrisi*, vol. II, pp. 74–75.

[8] For the conquest period, in addition to the works cited above in n. 6, see G. Loud, *The Deeds of Robert Guiscard*; D. Matthew, *The Norman Kingdom*; G. Theotokis, "The Norman Invasion."

[9] "This was an inborn trait of the sons of Tancred: they were always avid for domination. Whenever they were in a position of power, they suffered no one to have lands or possessions near their own without being jealous of them, so that either they would take possession of everything for themselves or they would immediately make their neighbours serve them as subjects." G. Malaterra, *The Deeds of Count Roger*, p. 116 {2.38}.

[10] G. Loud, *The Age of Robert Guiscard*, p. 130.

[11] For the sake of style and in accordance with convention, the English versions of the d'Hauteville rulers' names have been used (as opposed to "Rogerius," "Rupertus," "Wilelmus," etc.).

partner in 1062, Robert pledged to share their conquests in Calabria and Sicily as co-rulers. Roger had already launched two raids on the east coast of the island in 1060 and 1061 – in which Calabrian Muslims took part – and it was Robert and Roger who answered the appeal of Ibn al-Thumna ("Betumen" in the Latin chronicles) in May 1061, crossing over to Sicily and eventually capturing Messina and Troina, and accepting the surrender of Rometta.[12] The allies proceeded to besiege Ibn al-Ḥawwās ("Belcamet") at Enna (Ḳaṣryānnih), but broke off when the city would not yield. Soon after, Ibn al-Thumna was killed by local Muslims who were resisting pressure to recognize his authority and that of the d'Hautevilles – an event which would provide a "diplomatic pretext" for the Norman conquest. Based in the northeast of the island, Roger's forces began to probe and raid the countryside. The local Christians at times supported the invaders, but also resisted, and a serious Greek uprising occurred at Troina. Nevertheless, the Normans defeated a substantial Muslim force led by Ibn al-Ḥawwās at Cerami in 1063, and followed this up with *chevauchées* that gained them loot and prisoners and sowed terror among the island's inhabitants. In 1064 Palermo was attacked, but without success.

For his part, Ibn al-Ḥawwās turned to the Zīrids for support in the face of the Christian invasion but was killed a few years after, when his troops and those of the North African relief force clashed. In consequence, the Zīrid commander, Ayyūb b. Tamīm, claimed the island and installed himself in Palermo. However, the combination of popular resistance and a decisive Norman victory in 1068 at Misilmeri (southeast of the city), led Ayyūb to abandon Sicily.[13] In effect, through the 1060s Muslim Sicily was saved only by determined grass-roots resistance and tributary payments turned over to the Normans, as well as the fact that Robert and Roger were faced with their own revolts on the mainland. It was clear that before they could commit to Sicily they needed to conquer Brindisi and Bari, Byzantium's last footholds on the peninsula. Each was put under siege.

The fall of Brindisi (1068) and Bari (1071) allowed Robert and Roger to move their forces to Palermo, which seems by that point to have been under the rule of some sort of popular assembly, apparently headed at least for a time by a merchant named Ibn al-Baʿbāʿ. The campaign began with a diversionary attack by Roger on Catania, which surrendered in a matter of days. In the meanwhile, Palermo had been blockaded by land and sea in late 1071, and as the months dragged on the inhabitants began

[12] J. Johns, *Arabic Administration*, p. 31. [13] See J. Johns, "Arabic Sources."

to feel the pressure of hunger and the desperation of realizing no relief force would come.[14] The Ifrīqiyan-supported Sicilian fleet had been destroyed in battle, and the Normans and Zīrids had clearly come to a temporary understanding as a result. The Norman assault on the city evidently took place in the first days of January 1072; the harbor was breached, while infantry stormed the walls. Amidst the massacre and looting that followed, the defenders took refuge in the city's fortress and began to parley. On January 9 or 10 representatives of the city's civil and military authorities appeared before Robert and Roger, saying "they were unwilling to violate or relinquish their law ... but that under the present circumstances, they had no choice but to surrender the city, to render faithful service to the duke, and to pay tribute. They promised to affirm this all with an oath according to their own law."[15]

In other words, the d'Hautevilles' *modus operandi* was effectively identical to that being developed by their counterparts in Iberia. Massacre and pillage were used to reward their own warriors with plunder and to terrorize the native population into acceptance of Norman overlordship in a tributary arrangement. The fall of Palermo, however, did not signal the fall of Islamic Sicily; it would be twenty years until the island was pacified. In the meanwhile, Roger – who had been left in control of the conquest by Robert in 1072 – had to contend with entrenched local resistance, challenging terrain, resurgent Zīrids, revolts and distractions on the mainland, and a shortage of manpower and resources.

Roger continued to exploit local divisions and to attempt to bully the local population into submission. At times these tactics succeeded, such as when with apparent Norman complicity an uprising overthrew "Bechus," the ruler of Castronuovo, in 1078. Through the 1070s the northeast of the island gradually fell under Latin control. Some Muslims chose to convert to Latin Christianity, such as Elias Cartomensis, who became – until his capture and execution by his erstwhile co-religionists – one of Roger's lieutenants, and the commander, Ibn Ḥammūd, who ceded Agrigento in 1087.[16] On the other hand, Roger's nephew, Serlo, was assassinated in 1072 by a certain "Ibrahīm" – an ostensible ally, with whom he had made "a pledge of brotherhood." Indeed, it was rumored that Roger's own illegitimate son, Jordan, had been contemplating converting to Islam in the course of the rebellion he was said to have launched against his father in the early 1080s.

[14] See G. Loud, *The Deeds of Robert Guiscard*, pp. 34–36.
[15] Malaterra, *The Deeds of Count Roger*, p. 125 {2.45}.
[16] Roger himself stood as Ibn Ḥammūd's godfather. See J. Johns, "The Greek Church," pp. 137–78.

The central highlands, particularly around Enna, remained difficult to take and control, forcing Roger to construct fortresses to overawe the local populace even once they had surrendered to him. Notable revolts took place at Iato in 1076, Pantalica in 1091, and the Val di Noto in 1092. Moreover, by the late 1070s the Zīrids were not only attacking Norman-held Sicily, but also Calabria. Meanwhile, Syracuse had emerged as the center of organized resistance under a certain Ibn ʿAbbād ("Benavert"), who had the resources and audacity to mount counter-attacks by both land and sea against Norman Sicily and the mainland. However, he was killed on board ship in May 1086 defending his city against the Norman fleet – a circumstance that prompted the surrender of Syracuse. This was followed in short order by the capitulation of much of the central island, including Agrigento. Roger's scorched-earth campaigns had provoked famine and hardship, demoralizing the populace and undoubtedly contributing to his successes. Having concluded a treaty with the Zīrid *amīr* of Ifrīqiya, Tamīm, in 1087, Roger was confident enough to launch an attack on nearby Malta in 1090, which resulted in the submission of the local *qāʾid*. Malta would become a Norman condominium for a century.[17] In the following year Noto, the last Muslim-ruled town in Sicily, surrendered to him.

### *Norman rule*

In the meanwhile, the reorganization of Islamic Sicily was under way. The conditions under which Sicilian Muslims recognized Christian lordship conformed to those established at Palermo and Romuetta, as well as contemporary Iberian models. Islamic law was to be preserved, and goods and persons to be protected; local authorities were co-opted, when possible. Muslims were to pay a tribute or taxes, which would have resonated conceptually with the *jizya*, or "head tax," that *dhimmī* communities paid in the Islamic world.[18] Military service, it seems, was also expected, given that Muslim troops were among those serving Roger in his campaigns on the mainland, notably at Salerno in 1076 and Capua in 1098.[19] If true, the Count's alleged insistence that these soldiers not be permitted to convert to Christianity likely reflected his awareness both that such conversions

17 As late as 1175 Malta was described as "inhabited by Muslims, but under the dominion of the King of Sicily"; A. Luttrell, "Malta nel periodo normanno," pp. 470–71.

18 The term *jizya* is apparently not used in connection with the Normans until the occupation of Ifrīqiya in the 1140s. See J. Johns, *Arabic Administration*, p. 37.

19 G. Loud, *Roger II*, p. 196. Roger II employed Muslim soldiers and engineers at the 1133 siege of Montepeloso during the uprising in Apulia. See R. Rogers, *Latin Siege Warfare*, pp. 100–02, 111 and 115.

could provoke unrest among his Muslim subjects in Sicily, and that having an army of infidels carried practical advantages.[20] As in Iberia, pragmatism was at the root of his accommodations – they were necessary because without some element of local collaboration and consent, maintaining control of the island with only a small band of knights would have been impossible.

The precariousness of the first decades of Norman rule may also account for the notable absence of religious posturing in connection with the occupation. Whereas there was certainly an awareness of confessional difference on the part of the conquerors, the chauvinistic rhetoric that characterizes the Norman Christian chronicles likely reflects the vocation of their clerical authors, rather than widely held sensibilities. Nor did they necessarily carry weight as propaganda. In contrast to the Leonese monarchs of Iberia, the Norman elite could not claim they were reconquering a Christian kingdom that had been taken from their ancestors by the Infidel – all the more so, given their campaigns against Christian rivals, the Lombards and Byzantines.[21] According to the contemporary chronicler, Malaterra, it was reported that St. George had appeared to lend a hand against the infidels at Cerami in 1063, but there is little to suggest that this solitary saintly appearance was anything more than a lone chronicler's embellishment. Nevertheless, the fact that this was a campaign carried out by Christians against Muslims invited the invocation of religious difference as a *post factum* moral justification for the war – one that appealed both to the papacy, which stood to increase its influence as a consequence, and to the Norman rulers and knights, for whom it provided political legitimacy and moral absolution.[22] And while the mosque in Palermo, itself formerly a Byzantine church, was converted to the Latin rite immediately after the conquest, this did not reflect a general policy of decommission and reconsecration of mosques. The indigenous Byzantine Christians had their own churches and converting

[20] According to Eadmer, the hagiographic biographer of Anselm, Archbishop of Canterbury, it was the saint who had convinced Roger's Muslim soldiers to convert, but the count refused to allow it. None other than Urban II was present, Roger's Muslim troops having defended him against the depredations of Henry IV. See Eadmer, *The Life of St. Anselm*, pp. 110–12. Thanks to Joshua Birk for this reference; Birk points out that the anecdote serves to bolster the case for Anselm's virtues (who would be canonized between 1163 and 1170), while sullying Roger Bosso and, therefore, must be read critically.

[21] The contemporary pro-Norman cleric did attempt to give Robert Guiscard the "Cid treatment," by composing a lengthy poem in honor of his campaigns, and emphasizing the religious aspects of his career. See G. Loud, *The Deeds of Robert Guiscard*.

[22] See P. Chevedden, "A Crusade from the First." That said, from the time of the Battle of Cerami onwards, those fighting to conquer Muslim Sicily apparently enjoyed a papal indulgence (or so claimed Malaterra). J. Johns, "The Greek Church," p. 134.

mosques to Latin churches in the absence of Latin settlers would have been counterproductive, except in larger towns, where it would have carried symbolic significance.

In practical terms, then, the conquest was hardly a "war against Islam." As in Iberia, there was no attempt at ethnic or religious "cleansing," and no effort was made to convert the Muslim populace to Latin Christianity; nor is there any evidence of large-scale conversion.[23] It amounted to, at least initially, a displacement of the Islamic upper class. The remaining Muslim military elite either converted to Christianity or went into exile. Most would have fled to Ifrīqiya, while others were settled in Calabria by Roger. As in Christian-occupied al-Andalus, the *'ulamā'* and cultural elite would also have had little inducement to stay. Many departed, a fact testified to by the currency of the *nisba* al-Ṣiqillī ("the Sicilian") in early twelfth-century Ifrīqiya and Fāṭimid Egypt. As the self-exiled poet-*qāḍī* Abū Mūṣā al-Ṣiqillī railed, "Oh, blond tribe, my blood is on your hands / among you is my killer and the one who shed my blood."[24] For the bulk of the population, however, emigration was neither practical nor necessarily desirable; for them, life may have continued much as before albeit under a veneer of Latin rule. Roger's division of the lands and his sharing out of spoils among his supporters entailed for the most part a redirection of tribute and taxes rather than a transformation of rural society; the actual amount of tax paid by Muslim subjects probably did not change significantly as an immediate consequence of the conquest. The illusion of continuity for his subject communities was undoubtedly something that Roger appreciated would work to his favor; tellingly, the title he bestowed on his own governor of Palermo in 1072 was *amīr*.[25] In any event, Roger's policies towards his new Muslim subjects were consistent with the positions he took vis-à-vis his Byzantine Christian subjects.

Roger Bosso died in 1101, four years after having been confirmed by Pope Urban II as apostolic legate and Count of Sicily. Urban had visited Roger in Sicily, and the Count's troops had supported the new Pope's first, abortive entry into Rome in 1088.[26] Bosso was survived by his third wife, Adelaide del Vasto. The young dowager was mother of his two sons,

[23] J. Johns, "The Greek Church," p. 133. It appears, on the other hand, at least in the countryside, conversion to the Greek rite did occur, but this took place over several generations. See *ibid.*, pp. 145–53.

[24] K. Mallette, *Kingdom of Sicily*, p. 138.

[25] For Roger's approach to presenting himself as a ruler on Muslim terms, see C. Stanton, "Roger de Hauteville."

[26] With the Investiture Controversy at full bore, Urban II's election was challenged by Henry IV's Pope, Guibert, who also had the support of the city of Rome. In the face of the

Simon and Roger, aged eight and six, and Simon's death in 1105 left Roger the sole heir. In the years of his minority, Adelaide served as regent, but the success and stability of the realm was due as much to the efforts of the *amīr*, Christodoulos, an enigmatic Greco-Sicilian courtier, who effectively ran the kingdom until Roger II was able to rule in his own name, beginning in 1112.

## The Norman Kings of Sicily and "Africa"

> O King! who stands firm
> hardy and rooted, on the rock of his roughness
> The spirits of his enemies provoked him, and he scattered them
> laughing as they received the blade-edge from his sheath . . .
>
> (Abū Ḥafṣ ʿUmar b. Ḥuṣn al-Naḥwī al-Ṣiqillī, ode in praise of Roger II (*c.* 1154))[27]

Eighteen years later, on Christmas Day 1130, Roger II (as Count: 1105–30; as King 1130–1154) was made King of Sicily in the cathedral of Palermo, crowned not by Christ, as in the famous mosaic of the Martorana Church, but anointed by a cardinal sent by the schismatic Pope Anacletus II (1130–38), a close ally and dependant.[28] At Roger's side would have stood Elvira, his beloved Queen, mother of his three young sons, and the daughter of Alfonso VI of Castile and Isabella (who may well herself have been Sayyida, the Castilian King's Muslim paramour). A contemporary chronicler evoked a city strewn with stunning carpets, glistening livery and banquet settings, with attendees, from dignitaries down to servants, decked out in silk.[29] The magnificence and exotica of the ceremony may have helped distract from the dubious air of novelty which hung over the occasion: Roger was the new King of a new kingdom, hastily acclaimed by a clutch of loyal barons on the strength of an anti-Pope's bull.

But Roger was undeniably rich and powerful: the uncontested leader of the Normans of southern Italy, ruler of the wealthy island domain of Sicily, Duke of Apulia and Count of Calabria. Hence, his coronation sparked an immediate reaction, and over the next decade two Emperors,

emperor's armies, the rightfully elected pontiff depended on Roger Bosso, Bohemond of Taranto, and Mathilda of Tuscany. Urban would not actually sit on the papal throne until 1094. For context, see U.-R. Blumenthal, *The Investiture Controversy*.

27 K. Mallette, *Kingdom of Sicily*, p. 145.

28 To be fair, Anacletus's claim to the throne of St. Peter was not much weaker than that of the other pope, Innocent II (1130–43), whose legitimacy was only universally acknowledged after his rival's death.

29 See Alexander of Telese's vivid account in his "History of King Roger," in Loud, *Roger II*, p. 79.

Lothar III (1125/1133–37) in Germany and Romanos III Argyros (1028–34) of Byzantium, along with Innocent II, the Kings of France and England, and Pisa and Genoa, launched invasions and supported rebellions of local Norman and Lombard princes. It was not until after nine years of hard-fought and brutal campaigns that Roger managed to triumph, after forcing Innocent II, who had been taken prisoner in a surprise attack led by his son, Roger (later Roger III; 1193), to recognize him as "King of Sicily, Duke of Apulia, and Prince of Calabria." In the final years, Roger treated his rebellious Christian subjects in Apulia with exemplary brutality, including blindings, executions, sackings, and symbolic disinterments. His relations with his Muslim subjects, on the other hand, were rather more favorable. Sicilian *mudéjares* were quiet at home and served him as soldiers on the mainland; for his part, Roger had begun to look beyond Sicily and to position himself as sovereign of the Muslims of what had once been Roman Africa.[30]

### *The conquest of Ifrīqiya*

Even before the matter of Italy was settled, Roger was pushing south towards the ever-more vulnerable coast of Ifrīqiya. As early as 1123 he had sent a fleet against Mahdia (al-Maḥdiyya) and massacred the inhabitants of Pantelleria (Qawṣara) in retaliation for their piratical raids on Sicily. In 1135 Jerba suffered a similar fate; the women and children were carried off to be sold as slaves, and the surviving population was put under the control of a Norman royal governor, under whom it seems they resumed their privateering. The Zīrids, in the meantime, faced increasing resistance from their own populace – due in part to their conciliatory policies towards Roger and in part to the declining economy – and from rival princes, whether local governors, or their own cousins, the Banū Ḥammād of Bougie (Bijāya). Eventually, ʿAlī b. Yaḥyā (1116–21) sought the protection of the Almoravids, who sent a fleet that sacked Nicotera in Calabria. Roger responded by raiding a Zīrid fortress and by sending ships to aid Barcelona's campaign against the Almoravids. The Fāṭimids, on the other hand, became close allies, as a consequence of their economic ties with Sicily, common enmities with Byzantium and the Almoravids, and thanks to the allure Cairo's wealth and sophistication held for the Normans.

[30] For Roger's use of Muslim troops on the peninsula, see D. Abulafia, "The Italian Other," p. 227; G. Loud, "The Deeds Done," p. 34 {Book II, p. 34} and 37–38 {Book II, p. 42}; R. Rogers, *Latin Siege Warfare*, pp. 102, 100, 101, and 115.

These Mediterranean campaigns were largely the initiative of the *amīr* Christodoulos, whose raiding and demands for tribute accelerated the Zīrids' disintegration.[31] He was assisted by George of Antioch, the son of Melkites (Byzantine Christians) who had settled in Ifrīqiya to serve the Zīrid King, Tamīm b. al-Muʿizz (1062–1108). In 1114 George had defected to Sicily, serving Roger as an envoy to the Fāṭimid court and as a naval commander, until in 1127 he was named *amiratus amiratorum* – "supreme commander."[32] Arabic sources refer to him as Roger's *wazīr*. Under George, the Norman navy became a force throughout the central and eastern Mediterranean, and the Zīrid kingdom was destroyed after decades of repeated attacks. Tripoli (Ṭarābulus al-Gharb) yielded in 1146, while Mahdia fell in 1148, followed by the other principal cities of the Tunisian coast, including Sfax and Sousse (Sūsa). Malta, which had functioned as a tributary, had been brought under direct rule in 1127. At George's death in 1151, only Bône (al-ʿAnnāba) remained free of Norman control. When it was conquered in 1153 by the admiral's successor, the enigmatic crypto-Muslim eunuch, Philip of Mahdia, Roger II became effectively, if briefly, *malik Ifrīqiya* – "King of Africa."

The conquest of Ifrīqiya was a chaotic affair. Gabès (Qābis) had already become a Norman protectorate, since some years earlier a local rebel had seized power and requested and obtained Roger's recognition and investiture. However, an outraged populace rose up in disgust and summoned the Zīrids to restore Muslim authority. Here, Roger's "conquest" of 1148 consisted in suppressing the uprising and installing a new prince, Muḥammad b. Rushayd. In Tripoli, Abū Yaḥyā b. Matrūḥ had been forced under Roger's protection and had to suffer the indignity of a Norman garrison in the citadel; nevertheless, he ruled as a sovereign, supported by the *qāḍī* Yūsuf b. Zīrī. Mahdia, the Zīrid capital – a city with a substantial Christian population – had been burdened by heavy Norman tribute since 1140, and in the face of George's army, Ḥasan b. ʿAlī withdrew, leaving the populace to seek shelter in the homes and churches of their infidel neighbors. It appears that this city came under direct Norman rule, and that the remaining Muslims paid the *jizya* and became effectively, *dhimmiyyūn*; however, its sister-city, Zawīla, the ceremonial capital,

[31] Historians have tended to accept (somewhat uncritically) the view of near-contemporary chroniclers, that the decline of Ifrīqiya was due to the irruption of the hordes of the Banū Hilāl and the Banū Sulaym on the region, a position reaffirmed by Abulafia (see D. Abulafia, "The Norman Kingdom of Africa"). Brett, however, sees the Banū Hilāl as a historiographical "fall guy," and argues that Norman policy was what undermined the Zīrī economy and rule (see M. Brett, "Ifriqiya as a Market"), and that the invasion of the Banū Hilāl and Sulaym was a symptom rather than a cause of decline.

[32] B. Catlos, "Who was Philip of Mahdia," p. 82.

may have remained under nominal Muslim rule. Sousse yielded without a fight, but there was serious resistance at Sfax, where – as at Mahdia – the local populace fiercely resisted Norman attacks.[33] At Tunis (Tūnis), the popularly installed Banū Khurāsān were able to resist conquest, but apparently became Roger's tributaries. Bône was conquered with the complicity of the local elite, who yielded once Philip of Mahdia allowed them to move their wealth out of the city to their estates in the countryside. This pragmatic concession, however, sparked Roger's suspicions, and his admiral and former favorite was put to a grisly death upon his return to Palermo, on charges of secret apostasy to Islam.

Whatever religious motives may have served as an ideological justification for these campaigns, *realpolitik* and economics made them inevitable.[34] The collapse of Zīrid power invited intervention by the Fāṭimids, Byzantines, Almoravids, and the Italian trading republics, thus threatening Roger's prosperity. Sicily was Ifrīqiya's bread basket, providing wheat and a range of other foodstuffs, precisely at a time when North Africa was plunging into a serious food crisis. This trade was particularly lucrative for the King, who controlled much of the agricultural production in Sicily, which was located on his extensive *demesne* lands. Other important exports included sugar, cotton, silk, indigo, henna, papyrus, and paper. In exchange, Sicily received products such as finished cloth; but most important was the gold that reached Ifrīqiya via trans-Saharan caravan routes and which Roger struck as the *ṭarī* (*tarí*, *tarenus*) – a coin that represented his continuation of the Aghlabid and Kalbid "*ṭarī*" *rubʿ* (or quarter-*dīnār*).[35] As a consequence of this trade, the city of Palermo alone generated as much revenue as the whole of that other contemporary Norman conquest, England. It is arguable, however, that this African adventure can be qualified either as a "conquest" or "Norman." With the exception of most of the warriors and some of the merchants involved, these campaigns were carried out by Byzanto-Islamic figures like Christodoulos, George of Antioch and Philip of Mahdia, and with the tacit cooperation of a Fāṭimid court, under the influence of a powerful Armenian contingent and managed by the Christian *wazīr*, Bahrām.

33 For the Norman presence in Ifrīqiya, in addition to works cited above, see K. Belkhodja, "Roger II en Ifriqiya"; M. Brett, "The City State" and "The Armies"; R. Brunschvig, *La Berberie orientale*; and H. Idris, *La Berbérie orientale*.

34 By contrast, in the famous account of Ibn al-Athīr, when Pisan agents suggested to Roger Bosso that he conquer Ifrīqiya he expressed his disdain by raising a leg and farting at them, remarking that conquering the territory would prejudice the very lucrative economic relationship he had with the Muslim southern shore. See B. Catlos, "Who was Philip of Mahdia," p. 77.

35 Robert Guiscard and Roger Bosso had also minted Arabic-style coins after the conquest of Palermo in 1072. See J. Birk, "Sicilan Counterpoint," pp. 179–82.

The domination of Ifrīqiya posed a distinct set of problems from that of Sicily: there was only a small indigenous Christian population (apparently confined to Mahdia and Zawīla), there were few settlers (aside from merchants) who could be tempted to colonize, it was on the edge of a vast Muslim hinterland, and its population was notoriously prone to self-assertive unrest.[36] Thus, the conquest of the various cities followed a general pattern. Norman attack, sometimes initially resisted, was met by the flight of the population to the countryside. After the city had been plundered, the citizenry would be tempted to return with a truce (*amān*), under the terms of which the Normans would receive taxes (such as the *jizya*) and a popularly approved *qāḍī* would be installed. Although Mahdia and Jerba were ruled directly by Norman governors – and it was here that churches were established or refitted by the new rulers – most other territories were nominally ruled by Muslim *quwwād*.[37] Remarkably, the consensus among Islamic chroniclers was that, on the material level, Roger's conquest was beneficial. While the Normans collected port dues and other commercial taxes, the economic stability they brought was welcome. And while undoubtedly Latin (and Greek) merchants and artisans came in some numbers, there was little colonization or displacement. If Roger II had envisioned a future "Africa" that was Christian, neither he nor his successor, William I (1154–66), pushed either a program of religio-cultural transformation or of political and administrative micro-management. Instead, each became – as the *dīnār* coins they minted at Mahdia proclaimed – *malik* ("king"). Moreover, each deployed an Islamicate *laqab* (honorific): *al-Muʿtazz bi-'llāh* ("powerful through God") and *al-Hādī bi-Amr Allāh* ("the Guide by the Command of God"), respectively.[38] In effect, Roger had established a Christian sultanate.

### *A "three-tongued people"*

This was a manifestation of what Johns designates as *populus trilinguis*, a "propaganda of syncretism and eclecticism which proclaimed that, under the unifying rule of the d'Hauteville monarchy, the various peoples of the kingdom should be fused together into a single Sicilian people."[39] Indeed, one of the most striking aspects of Roger's kingship was its performative quality vis-à-vis religio-cultural identity. He deployed distinct languages, imagery, and regalia to present himself as the legitimate

[36] For the persistence of an indigenous Christian community, see H. Bresc, "Le Royaume normand."
[37] See *ibid.*, pp. 277–78. [38] J. Johns, "Malik Ifrīqiya," pp. 92 and 93. [39] *Ibid.*, p. 91.

sovereign to each constituency among his subjects and dependents: Latinate, Byzanto-Christian, and Muslim (the latter including Sunnī, Shīʿī, and Khārijī Ibāḍis).[40] From the Fāṭimids he appropriated an entire chancery apparatus in Arabic and became – in the finest tradition of Islamic kingship – an active patron of Arabo-Islamic high culture. But this had roots in the policies of his father and his uncle. Robert Guiscard had minted coins as *malik* after the conquest of Palermo, while Roger Bosso referred to himself as *malik*, *sulṭān*, and, even, *imām* – a title that implied supreme religious authority over the Muslim *umma*.[41] The two Rogers also actively patronized Orthodox monasteries and churches in Sicily, both as an administrative strategy and in order to position themselves as patrons of the substantial Byzantine Christian populace, to whom they were presented as *anax* ("ruler") by the grace of God, or even *basileus* – "emperor."[42] For domestic administration Byzantine offices were adapted and Greek was used extensively. Finally, the d'Hautevilles and their proponents presented themselves as "defender[s] of the Pope of Rome and protector[s] of the Christian faith" and as "filled with zeal for God."[43] Hence, after the conquest of Palermo, the much-suffering Greek bishop was replaced by a Latin appointee. As Latinate settlement in Sicily intensified – particularly after the 1140s – the apparatus and regalia of Latin Christendom became more prominent in royal administration. An illustration from the *Liber ad honorem Augusti*, Petrus de Ebolo's 1196 history of the twilight of Norman power in verse, depicts a chancery still divided into Greek, Muslim (*saraceni*), and Latin departments.[44] For this monk from Campania, Palermo was a "fortunate city, endowed with a trilingual population" (*urbs felix, populo dotata trilingui*).[45]

The enthusiastic and very public Arabophilia of the Norman kings is one of their most enduring legacies: it amazed and impressed contemporary Muslim and Jewish observers and discomfited their Christian apologists. For Roger II and his successors, Palermo became a capital infused with what historians would have described until recently as "Oriental luxury." Their royal palace was a hybrid of Latin, Arabo-Islamic, and

40 See, for example, K.C. Britt's revisionist approach in, "Roger II of Sicily."
41 This is analogous to the approach taken by Alfonso VI of Castile; see, above, p. 44.
42 E. Kitzinger, "On the Portrait," p. 30.
43 See J. Johns, "Malik Ifrīqiya," p. 91, and H. Houben, *Roger II*, p. 111, respectively.
44 The lavishly illuminated manuscript of Petrus de Ebolo's verse-chronicle "Liber ad honorem Augusti sive de rebus Siculis" ("Book to the honor of the Emperor, or On the affairs of Sicily") was completed for Henry VI in the 1190s, and is available in facsimile, as T. Kölzer, *et al.*, *Liber ad honorem*. The plate in question can be found on p. 59 (f. 101r).
45 See B. Zeitler, "'Urbs Felix'."

Byzantine architectonic and decorative elements, run largely by a clique of crypto-Muslim former slaves, staffed in part by Arabic scribes and Muslim cooks, servants and entertainers, and frequented by Infidel literati, savants, and sycophants.[46] Among the physicians, astrologers, scientists, and poets who populated and visited the Norman court, the best known is Muḥammad al-Idrīsī, famous for the world atlas and planisphere he designed for his Christian patrons. Like many of his erudite co-religionists who enjoyed royal favor, al-Idrīsī was not a native, but had willingly immigrated from the *dār al-Islām* to the court of an Infidel. Here, he and his colleagues found enthusiastic patronage: virtually all of the literary and most of the cultural production of the Norman court was in Arabic or followed Arabo-Islamic models. Beyond the confines of the palace lay parks and gardens, with lodges and pavilions, either appropriated from the former rulers or built in emulation of their tastes, arranged – in the words of the contemporary Andalusī traveller, Ibn Jubayr – "like pearls encircling a woman's full throat."[47] One of the pearls on this necklace survives: the "Ziza" (from *dār al-ʿazīz*, or "noble house"), a keep-like lodge not far from the royal palace. Commissioned by William I and completed under William II in 1189 by Muslim workers and artisans, it interweaves Latin, Byzantine, and Fāṭimid stylistic elements, in a structure designed to cool through an elaborate system of evaporation and air-flow. This high-register Islamophilia was paralleled by a broader, more quotidian, acculturation, in which Arabo-Islamic fashions and cosmetics, musical styles, and cuisine were enjoyed and adapted by Latins both within Palermo and across the island.[48]

Clearly, there was a pragmatic dimension to this emulation and imitation of Arabo-Islamic culture, in that it would have served both to reinforce the dynasty's image as legitimate players in the Islamicized political culture of the Mediterranean and to engage with and reassure their own Muslim subjects. Beyond this, it can hardly be denied that Arabo-Islamic culture – in terms of cuisine, music, high culture, fashion, and virtually every realm of quotidian experience – offered a comfort, luxury, sophistication, and variety that Latinate culture simply could not match at that time. The overlap of the pragmatic and aesthetic dimensions of the Norman kings' tastes is evident in Roger II's regalia, which included

[46] For the Islamic elements of Roger II's cultural program, see M. Gelfer-Jørgensen and C. Henriksen, *Medieval Islamic Symbolism*, Part II, "The Sicilian Scene," pp. 149–78.

[47] Ibn Jubayr, *Travels*, p. 348. For the Islamicate architecture of Norman Sicily, see, for example, K. Mallette, *Kingdom of Sicily*, pp. 17–46; W. Tronzo, *The Cultures of His Kingdom*.

[48] See, below, pp. 437ff. and 495ff.

his royal parasol and the famous silk "coronation" cloak, manufactured at his own *ṭirāz*, or royal atelier. This stunning mantle of gilt-embroidered and gem-studded red silk, nearly 1.5 by 3.5 metres in size, depicts a lion pounced on the back of a camel, and is bordered by an Arabic inscription in Kufic script lauding the majesty of Roger's treasury.[49] Hence, the material vocabulary of Arabo-Islamic culture was converted into an expression of the king's own sovereignty over Muslims – the Norman lion gripping the Muslim camel. Roger's great parasol was a gift of the caliph, al-Ḥāfiẓ (1131–46), and evidently formed only one element of the formal court ceremonial the Norman borrowed from his Fāṭimid allies. It has been suggested that the construction of the 400-metre-long *via copperta* – a covered passage linking the palace to the cathedral – represented a deliberate emulation of caliphal isolation.

Indeed, so entrenched was this Islamophilia that it long outlasted its political and practical usefulness. By 1160 Ifrīqiya had been lost to the Almohads and along with it any real possibility that the Normans might constitute a pan-Mediterranean ruling dynasty. By this point the marginalization of the native Muslim population of Sicily was well underway, thanks to a growing wave of Lombard immigration – a process that was confirmed dramatically by the attacks and massacres waged on the Muslims in the course of the colonists' revolts against William I. And yet, the Kings continued to cultivate the "Palace Saracens," a cadre of freedman Muslim functionaries thinly masquerading as Christians. Nor did their rulers' patronage of and fascination with Islamicate high culture subside – William II (1166–89) was said to have been an Arabic speaker.[50] Land and tax registers (*jarīda*, plural: *jarāʾid*), which had been compiled by the Arabic chancery (*dīwān*) as consequence of the implementation of a "feudal" fiscal and land-tenure regime, continued to be maintained in that language long after it had become "unnecessary" in practical terms.[51] While it may be true that Arabic, for the Normans, had become a "prestige language," if only the palace cadres were in a

[49] The mantle is usually referred to as the "coronation mantle," but this is in reference to the Hohenstaufen Holy Roman Emperors who inherited it. It was produced by Roger's silk workshop in 1133/34, several years after his coronation. He almost certainly did use it as a ceremonial robe. See, for example, M. Gelfer-Jørgensen and C. Henriksen, *Medieval Islamic Symbolism*, pp. 166–67, and H. Houben, *Roger II*, pp. 124–25.

[50] Ibn Jubayr, who met the king, waxes glowingly regarding his Arabophilia. Ibn Jubayr, *Travels*, pp. 340–43.

[51] For the "feudalization" of Norman Sicily and its impact on subject Muslims, see H. Bresc, "Féodalité coloniale." Molinari suggests, however, that at times what appears to be a Norman process of *encastellamento* may actually reflect the spontaneous and independent movement of Muslim settlers to more secure hilltop sites. See A. Molinari, "The Effects," pp. 263–5 and 267.

position to read it, its continued use would have also had the effect of limiting the access to the chancery to a narrow, royally controlled, minority bureaucracy, thereby reinforcing the court's monopoly on the control of administrative intelligence – and this could be extremely useful.[52]

### *Roger II's legacy*

In February 1154 Roger II died, leaving his dominions to his fourth and eldest surviving son, William. The new King inherited the complex edifice of power that his father had constructed, but was ill equipped to manage the stresses and tensions that underlay it. Encouraged by the emergence of the Almohads, the subjects of Ifrīqiya rose up in revolt and welcomed the armies of ʿAbd al-Muʾmin (1130–63). Mahdia, the Norman "capital," fell in January 1160 after a six-month siege. Meanwhile, relations with the Fāṭimids turned increasingly hostile, and Byzantium's formidable Manouēl (Manuel) I Komnēnos (1143–80) launched an offensive, briefly recovering the Apulian coast. Religious rhetoric notwithstanding, Sicily and Ifrīqiya were simply too interdependent economically to remain at odds; by the 1070s the Normans and Almohads had settled into a working *détente* in loose conjunction with the Genoese; Sicilian agents returned to the African port cities, and North African Muslims traded once again in Sicily. In 1180, William's gallant return of an Almohad princess who had been captured at sea would be rewarded with a ten-year truce and a restoration of merchants' privileges in Mahdia and Zawīla, such as they had stood prior to the 1140s.[53] In this light, the Norman naval attack on Mallorca – the last remaining Almoravid emirate – in 1181, can be seen less as a manifestation of a Crusading impulse than the by-product of an Almohad-Norman alliance.

At home, Roger's centralizing programme – continued by Maio of Bari, his capable *amiratus* and chancellor – had engendered resentment among the Sicilian nobility and the lesser members of his own clan, who saw the

[52] Johns notes that the emergence of the Arabic-language bureaucracy was a late development, not a continuation of pre- or early Norman practice. Chancery records were generated in Arabic in the first twenty years after the conquest, but the practice was then abandoned. (J. Johns and A. Metcalfe, "The Mystery at Chùrchuro," p. 226.) For Mallette, it was a "prestige language." However, Takayama observes (H. Takayama, *The Administration*, pp. 81ff) that the foundation of the Arabic-language *dīwān al-taḥqīq al-maʾmūr* or *duana de secretis*, one of the kingdom's two financial supervision offices, dates from 1144 or 1145, and was part of Roger II's centralizing efforts in reaction to the previous decade's rebellions. Seen in this light, the trilingual administration policy may have served as a linguistic approach to "divide and rule." See B. Catlos, "'Accursed, Superior Men'."

[53] See D. Abulafia, *The Two Italies*, pp. 131 and 156ff; also M. Brett, "Ifriqiya as a Market."

royal functionaries, notably the *quwwād* or master chamberlains (who tended to be former Muslims), as their rivals. In November 1160, with the encouragement of Frederick I Barbarossa, the Latin aristocracy rose up, assassinating Maio and a number of the "Palace Saracens." The revolt that followed provided an opportunity for generalized anti-Muslim violence across the island. William himself was held captive as the rebels first proclaimed his young son Roger as the new King, and then his half-brother, Simon of Taranto. In 1162, however, the rebellion faltered and the King returned to rule for another four years until his death by an attack of dysentery. William would be known to posterity as "the Bad," yet even "Hugo Falcandus," the anonymous chronicler who vilified him, recounted how the king was mourned for three days in Palermo, and that

> Throughout these three days women and noble matrons – especially the Muslim ones, whose grief was not feigned – symbolically went around in sackcloth with their hair loose day and night, in groups, with a crowd of waving slave-girls preceding them, and filled the entire city with their wailing and rhythmic chanting in time to the beating of drums.[54]

The King was succeeded by his second son, William, who took the throne at the age of eleven, although control of the kingdom was left in the hands of a triumvirate of royal familiars, headed by the crypto-Muslim eunuch, Peter (see below, p. 118), together with the dowager, Margarita of Navarre. Stability returned to Sicily, and the reassertion of royal power brought respite to the suffering of the kingdom's Muslims. In 1189, however, with the death without legitimate issue of William – known as "the Good," perhaps only in contrast to his father – the kingdom was plunged into a succession crisis. The soon-to-be Holy Roman Emperor, Henry VI (1191–97), claimed the kingdom by virtue of his marriage to William's aunt, Constance; but this was contested by Tancred of Lecce (1190–94), an illegitimate grandson of Roger II, who seized the throne and gained the recognition of England and France.[55] Sensing the regime's vulnerability, some of the island's Muslims rose up as well. The Emperor's forces marched south, but were unable to take the kingdom until 1194, when Tancred died and his four-year-old son was crowned as William III (1194). Amidst the resulting disarray, Henry's armies swept

[54] H. Falcandus, *The History of the Tyrants*, p. 138.

[55] After taking power Tancred had imprisoned William II's widow, Joan Plantagenet. In 1190 her brother, Richard the Lion-Heart, *en route* with the Third Crusade, seized and sacked Messina in retaliation. In return for the release of her person and her dowry, Richard and his ally, Philippe Auguste, recognized Tancred. Once in the Levant, Richard proposed Joan as a wife for al-ʿĀdil, the brother and heir-effective of Ṣalāḥ al-Dīn, on the condition that they serve as joint rulers.

down through southern Italy and took Palermo on November 20, 1194. On Christmas Day, Henry was crowned king (1194–97) on the strength of his wife's claim to the throne; the next day Constance gave birth to a son, Frederick, who would be both vilified and romanticized for his own engagement with Arabo-Islamic culture and his cultivation of the Muslims under his rule. The Norman dynasty, which poets like ʿUmar b. Ḥuṣn had praised, was no more. But life for Muslims under the d'Hautevilles should not be viewed with nostalgia by modern scholars – those who fled the conquest recalled it with bitterness and held little admiration for the Infidel victors. As the poet-refugee Ibn Ḥamdīs (*c.* 1078/79) lamented, "I console my soul, since I see my land fighting a losing battle against a venomous enemy. What else, when she has been shamed, when the hands of the Christians have turned her mosques into churches."[56] That said, the polemical reaction of the self-exiles was also an exaggeration; it would be a full century and a half after Ibn Ḥamdīs's departure that Sicily's mosques would disappear. Until then, a remarkably diverse and dynamic Islamic society persisted under Infidel rule.

## Muslims under the d'Hauteville dynasty

The Muslims of the city [of Palermo] preserve the remaining evidence of their faith. They keep in repair the greater number of their mosques and come to prayers at the call of the *muʾadhdhin*. In their own suburbs they live apart from the Christians. The markets are full of them, and they are the merchants of the place. They have a *qāḍī* to whom they refer their lawsuits, and a cathedral mosque where, in this holy month [of *Ramaḍān*], they assemble under its lamps. The ordinary mosques are countless, and most of them as used as schools for *Qurʾān* teachers. But in general these Muslims do not mix with their brethren under infidel patronage, and enjoy no security for their goods, their women, or their children. May God, by His favor, amend their lot with His beneficence. (Muḥammad b. Jubayr, *Riḥla* (*c.* 1185 CE)[57])

When the Genoese ship conveying a homeward-bound Muḥammad b. Jubayr from Crusader Acre in late 1184 was wrecked off Messina, the pilgrim and courtier from Almohad al-Andalus was cast ashore on an island of apparent contradictions. The Sicily he found in his five months there, he claimed, was a Christian kingdom ruled by a king who spoke Arabic, consulted only Muslim astrologers and physicians, had Muslim cooks prepare his food, was surrounded by slave-girls, and whose palace was run by ex-slave functionaries whose continuing adherence to Islam

[56] K. Mallette, *Kingdom of Sicily*, p. 135. [57] Ibn Jubayr, *Travels*, pp. 348–49.

was an open secret.[58] Here, travelers from the *dār al-Islām* were welcomed with honor, and local Christians had begun to emulate Muslim customs and mores to such an extent that some were secretly converting. It was a land where Muslim subjects worshiped freely, followed their own laws, and lived in reasonable prosperity under royal protection.[59] Ibn Jubayr must have struggled to reconcile his impulse to optimistically present a triumphant Islam with Sicilian Muslims' undeniable position as vulnerable subjects in an infidel kingdom.

At the foundation of *mudéjar* experience in Sicily were the treaties of submission the Normans seduced, cajoled, and bullied the various communities of the island and their leaders to accept. As in the Christian conquest of al-Andalus, these were expressed in a conceptual language – *amān*, *jizya*, *dhimma* – that Muslims could understand, distasteful as it may have been for them to apply it to themselves. And as with al-Andalus, the application of these policies arose unpremeditated, as a consequence of the demands of pragmatism; Sicily's prosperity and stability depended on the maintenance both of external trade with the Islamic world and of domestic Muslim society. The Norman strategy was to maintain the outward appearance of continuity to the extent that this did not threaten their own position. Thus, it might have seemed for many Muslims that life under Norman rule would entail only the most minor of disruptions, and this seems to have been the case in the first generations. For his Muslim subjects, Roger II's legal reform of the 1140s, in which he promulgated his "Assizes," confirmed their juridical independence – except to the extent that it contradicted royal law – but said little more. Muslims would be forbidden from owning Christian slaves, and strict penalties were established for repentant Muslim converts who might commit apostasy, but otherwise were left to their own devices.

In thoroughly Islamic Ifrīqiya, the Norman approach was even more cautious. Only Mahdia and Jerba came under direct rule, while the other cities were in effect tributary clients. Islamic law and institutions remained intact here and were not to be subject to Christian administrative veto or legal superiority, although the mere notion that they functioned even abstractly under the authority of an infidel king provoked resistance among local jurists who questioned the legitimacy (*ʿadala*) of the practice of law under even these circumstances. Explicit interference, such as Roger II's order that the Almohads not only be omitted from, but cursed

[58] In the manuscript of Petrus de Ebolo's "Liber ad honorem Augusti," an illumination depicts the dying William II attended by a physician and astrologer who are evidently Muslim in appearance. See T. Kötzer, *et al.*, *Liber ad honorem*, p. 43 (f. 97r).

[59] For his account of Sicily, see Ibn Jubayr, *Travels*, pp. 335–63.

in the preamble to the sermon (*khuṭba*) at Friday prayer provoked outrage and revolt.[60] When the Normans were expelled from Ifrīqiya in the uprisings that followed Roger's death, local Muslims vented their wrath at these usurpations by massacring Christian communities at Sfax, Tripoli, and Tunis.

Naturally, in the aftermath of the conquest of Sicily the overwhelming bulk of the Kalbid political and cultural elite fled to Islamic lands – most to Ifrīqiya or al-Andalus and some to Egypt and Syria – although, in contrast to Spain, this flight was mitigated by the d'Hautevilles' emphatic propaganda of continuity and their efforts to style themselves as "Islamic" rulers. Hence, here some members of the military elite, as well as the literati and even Islamic jurists, remained. Perhaps more important was the Normans' continuing patronage of high Islamic culture – unique in the Latin West – which ensured that these individuals could continue to earn a living and enjoy some prestige and power. Indeed, the mounting crisis in early twelfth-century Ifrīqiya inspired some Muslims, including members of the courtly classes, to immigrate to Norman Sicily, particularly to Palermo and the royal court.

### *Emigration and reorganization*

The most famous of these opportunists was Muḥammad al-Idrīsī, a native of Ceuta who distinguished himself as a geographer of Roger II and William I, most notably producing a world atlas both in book form and as a silver planisphere. Practical and technical knowledge was clearly in demand, and so it is little surprise to find Muslim astrologers, physicians, artisans, artists, and musicians at the Norman capital. It is rather more remarkable that Roger and his successors became patrons of Arabic letters, supporting a bevy of Muslim poets who adorned their court, producing poetry in praise of the sovereigns and their realm, including a substantial collection of panegyrics in praise of members of the royal family. This patronage was undoubtedly rooted in a number of factors: the undeniable sophistication and cosmopolitanism of Arabo-Islamic culture, the rulers' determination to present themselves as universally recognized sovereigns before the audience of the Islamic Mediterranean, and simple consumerism. Roger's foundation (or continuation) of the *dār al-ṭirāz*, the royal silk-works – an installation staffed by Muslim artisans creating high-quality ornamental textiles for the royal household and sale – is emblematic of the complexity of the Norman ruler's relationship

[60] See M. Brett, "Muslim Justice."

with Islamic high and material culture and technology. The *ṭirāz* was an institution close to the palace and served as a stepping stone for Muslims into the administration, although by 1147 Muslim craftsmen were being replaced by Thebans.[61]

The entrenchment of Islamic arts and letters here undoubtedly provided a vector for the spread of their influence to the Christian heartlands of the north, both through the medium of the transmission of texts and the movement of people. Visitors from the Latin hinterlands would return from Sicily bearing the objects and impressions of Arabo-Islamic culture, not to mention slaves who, transplanted to the north, provided an important if historically obscure medium for the dissemination of artistic, musical, literary, and culinary styles, as well as technical knowledge, such as medicine and pharmacology. Nor were cultural links with the Islamic world severed by the Norman conquest: Sicily remained under the influence of Ifrīqiya and Fāṭimic Egypt, and Muslim courtiers, diplomats, hostages, merchants, and travelers continued to travel back and forth to the island.[62]

The appearance of continuity would have provided further encouragement to the productive classes to remain. Thanks in part to the fact that the conquest itself was not immediately accompanied by a large-scale colonizing movement, the general population distribution in the countryside stayed largely the same in the decades after the fall of Palermo. The north and eastern side of the island remained predominantly Greek Christian, and the south and western half, Muslim – although internal immigration may have had a polarizing effect. There were local relocations, some spontaneous, and some deliberate, notably the forcible resettlement of Muslims to Calabria by the new rulers. Aside from the households of the castellans that dotted the countryside, what Latin immigration there was initially focused on the main cities and towns. In the urban environment Muslim populations may have been displaced locally within and around the cities and towns they inhabited, but they persisted throughout the island in the 1180s. Again, this can be attributed largely to the persistence of pre-Norman economic structures and commercial relationships with Ifrīqiya; the livelihood of Muslim artisans and merchants was not immediately threatened. In sum, the transformation of

61 A. Metcalfe, *The Muslims of Medieval Italy*, p. 149; D. Jacoby, "Silk Economies," p. 227.

62 In addition to Ibn Jubayr, other Muslim visitors whose accounts have survived are the Zirid Prince ʿAbd al-Azīz ibn Shaddād, who visited in the 1150s, the poet Naṣr (Allāh) al-Qalāqis, who came in 1169/70, and the Syrian ascetic al-Harawī in 1175.

the Sicilian economy – and the social relationships it supported – would be gradual.

By the 1140s, however, changes were clearly underway. This can be seen in the countryside, in a process of administrative rearticulation associated with the transformation of the Muslim peasantry from free, land-owning and tax-paying subjects of an Islamic regime, into *dhimmiyyūn*, and then into "feudal" tenants of royal demesne lands and the island's major monasteries. Two types of Muslim tenants emerged: the "rough" and the "smooth" (*ḥursh* and *muls*, in Arabic, *rusticus* and *glaber*, in Latin). The former carried their seigniorial obligations by birth, and the latter, by contract. In other words, Latin concepts of servitude and serfdom were being imposed on a formerly free population.[63] There can be little doubt that this resulted in a loss of liberty for Muslim peasants, who were increasingly tied to the lands they worked, and burdened with service obligations to their landlords. For some, such as the villages granted in the 1090s to the Monastery Cathedral of Santa Agata in Catania, this process began soon after the conquest, whereas for most, this would not occur until several generations had passed.[64] These tendencies characterized the massive transfer of Muslim tenancies to Monreale in the 1160s, and contributed to Muslim rebelliousness here.[65] In this process, pre- and early post-conquest tax rolls were updated and regularized and gaps in the formal records were closed with the creation of the *dīwān al-taḥqīq al-maʿmūr*, the fiscal chancery. While records were kept also in Greek and Latin, the use of Arabic did not constitute a pre-conquest holdover, but an innovation. When Arabic documents began to be created in 1132, this was after a two-decade hiatus, and represents an attempt to emulate administration in contemporary Muslim kingdoms, particularly the Fāṭimid Caliphate. The institutionalization of Arabic in the royal administration coincided with the rise of an administrative clique of converted former slaves, known as the "palace Saracens."[66]

Those high-status Muslims who stayed behind after the conquest may well have seen a duty (to their co-religionists) as well as an opportunity (for themselves) to serve the new rulers. Juridical independence notwithstanding, to hold the position of *qāḍī* of Palermo or other major towns would have invited and demanded collaboration. One such

[63] See J. Johns, *Arabic Administration*, pp. 149–50.
[64] The Abbot of Santa Agata was specifically given the right to pursue and reclaim Muslim peasants who had left his lands. *Ibid.*, pp. 116–19.
[65] See, for example the *jarīda* described in *ibid.*, pp. 165–66. For the chronology of the rebellions, see H. Bercher, *et al.*, "Une abbaye latine," p. 539.
[66] See J. Johns, *Arabic Administration*, pp. 212–56.

individual who rose out of historical obscurity was Abū 'l-Ḍaw' Sirāj – scion of a family of Palermitan magistrates, poet and panegyrist of the d'Hautevilles, and Roger's chief secretary (*kātib al-inshā'*) – holder of the title *qā'id* ("commander"). Abū 'l-Ḍaw's connections to the Zīrid and Fāṭimid courts provided vectors for the Islamicization of the Norman administration. In 1151 – with the death of George of Antioch – the age of the "palace Saracens" was ushered in by the rise of Philip of Mahdia (Fīlib al-Mahdawī). This converted eunuch and former slave of African origin, raised since boyhood in Roger's intimate circle, was appointed to the positions of chamberlain and admiral. In 1153, having just completed the conquest of Ifrīqiya, Philip was put to a very gruesome and public death, ostensibly in punishment for his thinly veiled adherence to Islam, which included both the patronage of local mosques and the tomb of the Prophet at Medina.[67]

### *The "Palace Saracens"*

With the exception of the brief tenure of Maio of Bari, for the next three decades the Norman administration would be largely run by former or crypto-Muslim eunuchs, who held the title *qā'id* (*caid*) and served as military commanders, chamberlains, and prime ministers, as well as in a gamut of lesser positions, including administrators, scribes, bodyguards, interpreters, and footmen. If Ibn Jubayr is to be believed, their continuing adherence to Islam was an open secret. And, indeed, at least one of Philip's successors, Peter (Barrūn) – who had become the single most powerful man in the kingdom – avoided his unfortunate predecessor's fate by defecting to the Almohads.[68] Arabophilia aside, Roger and his successors saw advantages to stacking their administration with such individuals. Not only did they provide a counter within the administration to Latin elements who were in a position to outwardly challenge royal power, the Palace Saracens were utterly dependent on the kings. They were all the more vulnerable because as crypto-Muslims, they could be disposed of on charges of apostasy at their sovereign's will. Thus, although they had come to form a powerful and influential clique, their fate – like that of the Muslim community – depended almost entirely on royal good will. This was not lost on the barons, who resented royal power, or on the northern Italian "Lombard" settlers, who from the 1140s began to arrive

[67] See J. Birk, "From Borderlands," and B. Catlos, "Who was Philip of Mahdia."

[68] After his defection he became an admiral for the Almohads, and was known as "Aḥmad al-Ṣiqillī." For Peter's career, see J. Johns, *Arabic Administration*, pp. 222–28.

in increasing numbers. The colonists, who settled primarily in the center of the island, grated against the Muslim population, who themselves had become emboldened by their (secret) co-religionists' power at court.

Taking advantage of the disarray that followed Maio of Bari's assassination in November 1160, five months later Simon of Taranto and Tancred of Lecce captured William I and sacked the royal palace. The royal chancery records and the secretaries who kept them were singled out for destruction, as were the eunuch functionaries who ran the royal administration. Soon, factions within the Christian populace joined in what became a general assault against the city's Muslims, who defended themselves to the loss of much life and property. Tancred and Roger Sclavus, an illegitimate member of the del Vasto family, then headed for the east of the island, where they rallied "Lombard" settlers to rise up against the Muslim inhabitants and dispossess them of their land. Faced with indiscriminate massacre, those who were able escaped to the royal demesne lands in the south and west of the island, more densely populated by their co-religionists. Although by 1162 William had regained control over eastern Sicily and launched punitive attacks against the rebels, the refugees did not return. Indeed, the campaign served to heighten tensions within the royal army, and Christian soldiers turned on their fellow Muslim troops. However, despite these outcomes, it would be wrong to view these events solely through the lens of religious rivalry. Norman Sicily and southern Italy were inherently unstable and volatile, and at bottom this uprising represented an attempted coup by marginalized members of the leading Norman families along with a landed aristocracy resistant to royal centralization, rather than a confessional struggle. Nevertheless, thanks to the resentment towards the Palace Saracens and competitive tensions in the countryside, combined with anxieties raised by the Almohad advances and the loss of Ifrīqiya, for the rebels, attacking Muslims provided an opportunity to simultaneously harness popular discontent and strike at the roots of royal power.

With the re-establishment of royal authority, the Palace Saracens, reinstated by William I, struck back, together with the Muslim elite. According to the less than sympathetic account of "Hugo Falcandus," the *caids* and their Christian allies carried out a campaign of revenge against the supporters of the rebellion, and against Christians in general. In actual fact, the populace of Palermo seems to have been reconciled to their Muslim neighbors, whereas the "foreign" Latins' enmity towards the eunuchs and their co-religionists intensified. From the 1160s through the 1180s, the civilian Muslim elite became increasingly politicized; some, like Robert of Calatabiano and the *faqīh* Ibn Zurʿa, converted to Christianity – at least ostensibly – and became influential functionaries.

Remarkably, the converted Ibn Zurʿa apparently not only served as a Christian magistrate, but continued to function officially as a judge of *sharīʿa* law. Others, like the *qāḍī* and merchant, Abū ʻl-Qāsim b. Ḥammūd ("Bulcassim"), the *qāʾid* of Trapani (Aṭrābanish), another important figure in the island's fiscal administration, felt increasingly pushed to cast off the humiliation and vulnerability of *dhimma*. Abū ʻl-Qāsim allegedly went so far as to entrust the Syrian pilgrim, al-Harawī, with letters addressed to Ṣalāḥ al-Dīn, urging the Ayyubid *ṣulṭān* to conquer the island.[69]

Through the 1180s the Muslim upper and middle class remained remarkably robust, and wealthy enough to support an impressive array of native poets and *fuqahā*ʾ. And while these leading individuals tended to be associated with the royal court, Islamic high culture here was not an appendage of it. Members of the elite maintained independent commercial and cultural ties with the *dār al-Islām*, and – as in Kalbid times – patronized private mosques. Al-Idrīsī claims that in Roger II's time the congregational mosque in Palermo was still in use, and that Catania, in the Greek-dominated east, had "many mosques." A generation later, Ibn Jubayr noted the lively and open religious life of Muslims in Palermo and described a noisy, public procession in Trapani held to mark the *ʿĪd al-Fiṭr*. In addition to visitors and pilgrims from North Africa and al-Andalus, Islamic life here would have been stimulated by events such as the transportation of the population of Jerba to Sicily (as happened twice during Roger II's reign alone).[70]

There is little evidence of Christian missionizing or formal pressure to convert, although Roger is claimed by sympathetic chroniclers to have made this a personal cause in his final days. Nor does it seem that Muslims were subject to a discriminatory fiscal regime either in Sicily or in Malta, which maintained a majority Islamic population through the twelfth century. The liberties afforded to Muslims, along with the ease with which the island's natives blurred and crossed religio-cultural boundaries, however, generated anxieties among Christians, particularly peninsular newcomers. These were manifested in reports and rumors that apostate functionaries and Muslim aristocrats were conspiring to secretly violate Christian women.[71] With the riots of 1161 these tensions were pushed to the fore; as a consequence, the Muslim population seems to have split between those who began to convert and those who retrenched. Muslim insecurity and reaction, for its part, was likely intensified by the evolving commercial environment, in which the Islamic elite suffered financially,

[69] *Ibid.*, pp. 241. [70] A. Metcalfe, "Muslims of Sicily," p. 291.
[71] See, for example, H. Falcando, *The History of the Tyrants*, p. 166.

as their role in external trade was reduced. With the death of William II in 1189, armed insurrection must have seemed like one of the few viable options for survival. Hence, as Ibn Jubayr prepared to depart the island on board a Genoese ship in 1185, a desperate Trapanese Muslim begged for anyone among the pilgrim's companions to marry his young daughter and take her away in order to save her from the apostasy that seemed to be the inevitable fate of the Sicilian Muslim community.[72]

## The Hohenstaufens, the Angevins, and the end of Islamicate Italy

> We have heard, to our wonder and dismay, that the sons of perdition – namely the Saracens established at Puglia – with your consent (which does not seem believable) have transformed the dwelling of angels into a place of beasts of burden: that they have utterly demolished the Church of Saint Peter in Bagno Foietano, carrying away its stones and beams in order to build their houses in Lucera . . . (Pope Gregory IX, letter to Frederick II (December 3, 1232)[73])

In fact, the Muslim community would survive in Sicily for less than a half century after Ibn Jubayr's departure. Beginning in the 1220s the remaining population was transported to Lucera, an ancient settlement in the northern reaches of Apulia. The mass exile took place at the orders of Emperor Frederick II, the Middle Ages' most famous Islamophile – demonstrating the fact that admiration for and engagement with Arabo-Islamic culture should not be assumed equivalent with "toleration" of diversity or affection for Muslims *per se*.[74] But more than any individual sovereign's animus, it was the emergence of the Muslims of Sicily as a political force during the collapse of the Norman dynasty that all but sealed their fate.

The death of the childless William II in 1189 left the kingdom without a direct successor, which immediately sparked a struggle for power. The legitimate heir was Constance, a posthumous daughter of Roger II, and wife of Henry VI Hohenstaufen. Alarmed at the prospect of a powerful foreign king, the Sicilian grandees rallied behind Tancred of Lecce, and he was crowned in Palermo in 1190. After suffering the sack of Messina at the hands of Richard the Lion-Heart's Crusaders in 1191 and submitting to his terms, Tancred was recognized by England and France. Henry VI, however, now King of Germany and Holy Roman Emperor, was intent on pressing his wife's claim, and marched his armies south, for what turned out to be an inconclusive campaign. After

[72] Ibn Jubayr, *Travels*, p. 360. [73] K. Mallette, *Kingdom of Sicily*, pp. 164–65.
[74] See, for example, H. Bresc, "Frédéric II et l'Islam."

Henry's withdrawal, Tancred set out to reassert his authority over Apulia and Campania in 1192 and 1193, crowning his young son, Roger, as co-king. However, both father and son died in late February 1194, leaving the throne to a four-year-old William III, under the guardianship of his mother, Sybilla d'Acerra. By September Henry was in Sicily with his army, and having purged the palace functionaries and disposed of the young Norman King they supported, on Christmas Day 1194, he was crowned King of Sicily in Palermo cathedral. Far off in Jesi (Ancona), his forty-year-old wife, Constance, was in labor, and on December 26, she gave birth to the red-haired infant who would become known as "the wonder of the world" (*stupor mundi*) – Frederick II.

## Rebellion and resistance

Through of all of this, the island's Muslims were both pressed and drawn into political action. Sectarian unrest had flared up in Palermo during the interregnum as Christians struck at Muslims in the capital, many of whom fled. Relations between the Abbey of Monreale and the many Muslims under its seigniorial jurisdiction had also been pushed to the breaking point by the monks' increasing exactions; many tenants had sold or abandoned their lands, and those remaining were prepared to cede no more. In the more stable and prosperous west, local leaders rose up, taking advantage of Tancred's vulnerability. The new king was forced to buy their loyalty; a reversal of fortune which only emboldened them. When Henry's armies arrived, these would be resisted by Muslims and Christians fighting together under William III's banner. Although the Emperor triumphed, his own death in 1197 put the future of Sicily again in doubt, and held the promise of opportunity for local Muslims. An isolated Constance sought protection for her son and his realm by placing them under the protection of Innocent III (1198–1216), a move that sparked an uprising by the official regent, Markward of Annweiler.

Now it was Markward's vulnerability that provided an opportunity for the increasingly confident Muslims of western Sicily, whereas their collaboration presented Innocent III with justification for qualifying the campaign against the rebel as a Crusade, and Markward as "another Saladin" and "an infidel worse than the infidels."[75] Few signed up for the Crusade, but nevertheless, in July 1200 Markward's forces, which included Muslim troops, were defeated in battle at Monreale. But the

[75] J. Riley-Smith, *The Crusades: A History*, p. 163.

rebellious regent was subdued rather than expelled, and although he died only two years later, the Muslims managed to establish considerable political autonomy. The earlier Crusade notwithstanding, Innocent III wrote to their leaders in 1206, admonishing their rebelliousness, but inviting them to remain loyal vassals to Church and king. However, mounting tensions, and the division between papacy and empire further emboldened the Muslims, who began to raid Christian territory, notably attacking Palermo and kidnapping the Bishop of Agrigento. As Frederick II slowly consolidated his power as king and emperor, Muslim resistance reached its peak under Muḥammad b. ʿAbbād. This immigrant from Ifrīqiya, who styled himself as "the Commander of the Faithful in Sicily," established what was effectively an independent emirate based around Entella and Iato, going so far as to mint his own coins. Corralled by Frederick in his redoubt at Roca d'Entella, Ibn ʿAbbād sued for terms, and was granted safe passage to Ifrīqiya, only to be treacherously drowned by the King's men en route.[76]

In 1222, Frederick II, now King of Sicily and Germany as well as Emperor, undertook a brutal campaign to subdue the rebels, and re-engineered the relationship between the crown and its Muslim subjects.[77] Rather than enslave or deport them, Frederick reclassified them as *servi camere* ("servants of the royal chamber") – a status conceptually similar to that of the Muslims in the Crown of Aragon, which conferred protections under both canon and secular law.[78] Next he set out to establish a "Bantustan" at Lucera, on the northern frontier of Apulia, where ultimately all of his Muslim subjects would live.[79] This was a process that took several decades and involved the gradual transfer of these populations from the island. A community survived at Palermo until the mid thirteenth century, but its members were increasingly marginalized, and displaced from their role in commerce and urban industry by Jewish refugees welcomed from Almohad Ifrīqiya. Many converted to Christianity, perhaps under false pretenses at first, but ultimately

[76] A folk tradition recounts that Ibn ʿAbbād's daughter remained in Roca d'Entella, holding the fort as a guarantee of her father's safety. Following his betrayal, she baited Frederick into sending three hundred soldiers to the city, who she then had massacred before she herself committed suicide. See K. Mallette, *Kingdom of Sicily*, p. 108.

[77] See J. Powell, "Frederick II and the Rebellion."

[78] J. Taylor, "Lucera Sarracenorum," p. 117. "Servus" is a rather ambiguous term and can refer to anything from a client, to a servant, to a slave.

[79] It may be that, as Maier suggests, Frederick viewed his Muslim subjects as "polluting" the purity of his Sicilian kingdom, and this may have been a mitigating factor in his policies towards them, but ultimately it was the political threat they comprised that sealed their fate. See C. Maier, "Crusade and Rhetoric," p. 345.

with the effect of further debilitating the community.[80] The Muslims of Malta were transported to the Lucera in 1249, while those of Pantelleria escaped this fate, having come under a tributary co-dominion established by Frederick and the Almohad governor of Tunis in 1221.[81]

### *"Lucera of the Muslims"*

At Lucera, Frederick compensated Christian foundations and individuals for properties he assigned to the Muslims (a community now numbering less than 40,000), who came to be engaged primarily in cereal farming and urban crafts. For the emperor, the establishment of the Muslim colony held a number of advantages. It provided him with direct income (via the *terragium* tax), stimulated the economy of Foggia, and maintained a community of subjects over whom he had direct control, were vulnerable by virtue of their faith, and – in their isolation from the larger Islamic world – were in no position to rebel. Frederick continued to use Muslim soldiers in his personal bodyguard. And while, Crusading notwithstanding, Frederick certainly engaged positively with Islamic high culture and foreign Muslim elites, his court and his persona were resolutely Christian and Italo-Latin in orientation. Frederick spoke Arabic (as well as Greek), occasionally donned "Saracen" dress, and enjoyed Arabo-Islamic entertainments, such as music and dance. Despite this, unlike the Normans, he was a consumer and translator of, rather than a participant in Arabo-Islamic culture, and like the contemporary Castilian kings, preferred to access it through the medium of Arabized Jews.[82]

The papacy was bothered by the establishment of a new Muslim colony so deep in Latin lands and so close to Rome. Gregory IX (1227–41) dispatched a Dominican missionary to the colony in the 1230s, and ordered Frederick to "terrorize them into conversion," but the Pope's

80 Royal functionaries who converted could maintain their position and influence. Oberto Fallamonaca, the son of a *shaykh*, was one of Frederick's chief secretaries; his son became a cathedral canon at Palermo. See H. Bresc, "Pantelleria," p. 103.

81 L. de Mas-Latrie, *Traités de paix et de commerce*, pp. 153–55. The subject Muslims of Pantelleria would survive the collapse of Hohenstaufen rule and survive under the Aragonese into the fifteenth century. See H. Bresc, "Pantelleria."

82 For Frederick II, Islamic culture, and translation, see, for example, G. Gabrielli, "Frederick II and Moslem Culture"; D. Lomax, "Frederick II, His Saracens, and the Papacy"; K. Mallette, *Kingdom of Sicily*, pp. 47–64; M. Schramm, "Frederick II of Hohenstaufen"; S. Kinoshita, "Translation/N, Empire," p. 376; J. Taylor, *Muslims in Medieval Italy*, pp. 74ff. Frederick II purportedly sent a series of philosophical queries to the Almohad ruler, ʿAbd al-Wāḥid al-Rashīd (1232–42), to which the Andalusī refugee, Ibn Sabʿīn, was commissioned to respond; this, however, was most likely merely a literary conceit of the tract in question. See A. Akasoy, "Ibn Sabʿīn's Sicilian Questions"; M. Amari, "Questions philosophiques"; and Ibn Sabʿīn, *et al.*, *Las cuestiones sicilianas*.

interest in the colony seemed to be only as it served to underline the Emperor's greater disloyalties. The Muslims were "hapless pawns" in the political struggle between the papacy and the Hohenstaufen "anti-Christ."[83] Once tensions between Rome and Frederick warmed Gregory lost interest; broadly speaking, both he and Innocent IV (1243–54) took the view that as long as the existence of the colony did not violate canon law and remained docile, it was best left alone.[84]

However, with Frederick's death in 1250 the remaining Sicilian Muslims, now all corralled at Lucera, were once again swept up in political events which were beyond their control but which would have a profound impact on their future. Although Frederick's son, Conrad IV (1250–54), inherited the kingdom by right, in fact it came under the control of the latter's half-brother Manfred (eventually king: 1258–66), who attempted to establish independent rule. The split in the Hohenstaufen family was exploited by the papacy and its Angevin allies, resulting in a struggle that saw Charles d'Anjou (1266–85) take the kingdom of Sicily with papal blessing, after defeating Manfred in 1266. In 1268, Conradin (1254–58), Frederick's grandson and the last of his line, was defeated by Charles at Tagliacozzo, taken to Naples, and tried and executed as a traitor. Through all of this, the descendants of the Sicilian Muslims showed their characteristic if futile loyalty to the ruling dynasty, providing crossbowmen to both Manfred and Conradin. This prompted Clement IV (1265–68) to declare a Crusade against the Muslims of Lucera in 1255 on the grounds of their disloyalty and "wickedness." Eudes de Châteauroux, charged with preaching the Crusade, marshaled the most sensational rhetoric of Old Testament genocide, and alleged brutal violence on the part of Luceran Muslims against Christians, their clergy, and their women. According to Urban IV (1261–64), the Lucerans "had plunged their hands in the guts of the Church."[85] Even the Muslims' submission and payment of tribute was portrayed as an act of violence, as it "blinded" the Christians who received it. After Charles defeated in Manfred in 1266, the Muslim colony received clemency in exchange for handing over the pretender's treasure and dismantling their town walls. But in 1268, they rose up once more against the Angevin King, this time in support of Conradin. Final defeat came the following year.

However, once the rebellion was suppressed and Angevin power established, the colony at Lucera retreated into an unobtrusive, functional

83 See D. Lomax, "Frederick II," esp. pp. 184 and 188.

84 See C. Maier, "Crusade and Rhetoric," pp. 346 and 348, and generally, for the Crusade against Lucera.

85 *Ibid.*, p. 353.

autonomy. Charles evidently appreciated the practical advantages of maintaining his infidel subjects, and – in spite of the feverish rhetoric of the Crusades of the 1250s and 1260s – in the 1290s the Church showed little concern for the persistence of the colony.[86] Incredibly, in 1296 the Curia reiterated its position that the rights of Muslim subjects should be protected. Meanwhile, as a consequence of its isolation and ghettoization, the community began to diversify and stratify, and prosperous Muslim traders journeyed as far afield as Campania. At the same time, integration in the larger Angevin economy stimulated specialization, and the colony became increasingly important for the manufacture of arms. Given that it originated by the transportation of whole communities, Lucera would have had an active culturo-religious life, and there is evidence that a *madrasa* had been established in the 1230s, although nothing of this legacy survives.[87] Charles II, who succeeded to the throne of Naples in 1285 (Sicily having been lost to Aragon), cultivated the colony as a military reserve: Muslim infantry, crossbowmen, and even cavalry fought in his forces. Because of the privileges such service garnered, a new *mudéjar* elite with a clearly military vocation emerged here towards the turn of the century. For example, the Muslim officer, Leon de Lucera, served as captain ("governor") of the island of Pantelleria in the 1260s.[88] Ultimately, a certain wealthy *miles* ("knight") named Adelassius (ʿAbd al-ʿAzīz) was charged with assisting in the dismantling of the colony and the confiscation of his co-religionists' property and persons when the order came from Charles II in 1300.[89]

Within a space of months after that decree, *Lucera Sarracenorum* ("Lucera of the Muslims") was a memory. Swiftly resettled in temporary locations around Apulia, the majority of the populace was enslaved and sold, with only the wealthiest citizens and valuable craftsmen (notably arms-makers) permitted to ransom themselves. A few were allowed to escape bondage by converting to Christianity. With the city evacuated, Church and royal officials inventoried and redistributed land, property, and money to their own benefit and that of the crown. For the next half-century vestigial, unconstituted communities of free Muslims appear to have persisted scattered about the Kingdom of Naples, or so one may infer from an order issued in 1336 by Charles's successor Robert the Wise (1309–43) for his officials to respect their rights "so

86 Indeed, Charles I was accused of Islamophilia; the Provençal troubadour Austorc de Segret accused him of favoring Muslims over Christians at the very time his saintly kinsman, Louis IX, was on crusade in Tunis. See A. Barbero, *Il mito angioino*, p. 80.

87 J. Taylor, *Muslims in Medieval Italy*, p. 54.

88 H. Bresc, "Pantelleria," p. 106.

89 See J. Taylor, "Lucera Sarracenorum," p. 121; also pp. 122–25 for the fate of the Muslims after the colony was dismantled.

that they might live peacefully under the shadow of Our wings."[90] But by the late fourteenth century Islamicate Italy was no more.

## Isolation and decline

We have known for a good long time what a disgrace it is – indeed, what an offence to that aforementioned [Catholic] faith – that Saracens flourish in Our kingdom, inhabitants to this day of Lucera. And We have always planned in Our heart to depopulate that city and move the Saracens out of it, so that it might be populated with Christians. (Charles II, letter to his courtier, Giovanni Pipino de Barolo (August 24, 1300)[91])

The decision of Charles II to destroy the colony was undoubtedly informed by a sense of religious mission and the weight of his Capetian descent – the heavy presence of his paladin great-uncle, Louis IX of France (1226–70; canonized in 1297) – and it is certainly true that it followed close on the heels of his expulsion of the Jews from Apulia.[92] Like Jaume II of Aragon's foreclosure on Islamic Menorca in 1285, the appropriation of the colony provided a fiscal opportunity that could be presented as an act of virtue. In 1300 Charles II needed cash, and the dismantling of Lucera was too good an opportunity to pass up, whatever the mid- to long-term effects might be. Moreover, it was an act not inconsistent with the approach taken to Muslim subjects by the sovereigns of southern Italy since the time of the Normans. In any event, Charles's ideological posturing as regards the expulsion is all the more suspect, given that he himself allowed two hundred households of "free Muslims" (*Sarraceni libri*) to settle at San Pablo di Civitate, only 30km north of Lucera in 1302.[93]

The remarkable integration of Muslims into the society and political structure of Norman Sicily was a direct consequence of the size and productive capacity of the Muslim population at the time of the conquest, the d'Hautevilles' political vulnerabilities vis-à-vis the Latin elite of their kingdom and the peninsula, and their ambition to expand in a world characterized overwhelmingly by Islamic and Byzantine political culture and authority and commercial relations. The Normans were as enamored and sympathetic of Arabo-Islamic culture and society as the post-colonial dictators of our developing world are of what we call "the West." Under

90 *Ibid.*, p. 124.
91 P. Egidi, *Codice diplomatico*, pp. 127–28; K. Mallette, *Kingdom of Sicily*, p. 167.
92 Charles turned the Inquisition on the Jews of Apulia in 1293; many initially took refuge in Lucera, evidently hoping to hide among the Muslims. See J. Dunbabin, *The French*, pp. 184–85.
93 J. Taylor, "Lucera Sarracenorum," p. 124. The settlers were apparently forbidden from building mosques or calling the *'adhān*.

the Angevins, no more. Thus, the decline of Muslim society was a function of Muslims' declining usefulness, a process driven by Latin colonization, the reconfiguration of trade relationships, decreasing competition among Christian factions, and the cultivation of a less-threatening Jewish minority in Sicily. Muslims' active resistance to their own progressive marginalization merely undermined their value to the very kings who were their only effective protectors. A ruler like Frederick II could brook no resistance, nor risk any betrayal. For all the Arabic, Latin, and Greek he is said to have spoken, power was the language he understood. The quiescence of the colony at Lucera showed – as the Church recognized – that the Muslims here did not constitute a threat; but by the time of the Angevins, they were so isolated and numerically insignificant that they could be disposed of at the convenience and whim of a king, whatever rights and protections they were supposedly held to enjoy.

# 4 Infidels in the Holy Land

## The Latin East (1099–1291)

When they arrived in Syria, they saw divided sovereignties, conflicting opinions, and contending views, combined with hidden enmity, so that their ambitions expanded accordingly and extended to whatever their power could command. They [the Franks] continued zealously in the Holy War against the Muslims (*jihād al-Muslimīn*), while the Muslims were not inclined to wage war against them and did not join forces to fight them – with each [Muslim power] expecting the other one to take up their fight [for them] – until they [the Franks] made themselves rulers of lands beyond their wildest dreams and subjected the inhabitants to destruction and degradation far beyond what they had intended ... (ʿAlī b. Tāhir al-Sulamī, *Kitāb al-jihād* (1107)[1])

Preached over several days at the Umayyad mosque of Damascus in 1105, this perceptive, if vain, plea for Muslim solidarity and leadership against the Franks in Syria and Palestine came just eight years after the fall of Jerusalem. On the one hand, al-Sulamī's portrayal of the First Crusade as only one part of a larger campaign against Islam gives lie to the notion that the concept of military *jihād* developed *de novo* as a response by Islam to Crusader aggression in the Holy Land, while, on the other, it suggests an appreciation that the movement Urban II launched in 1095 was not entirely novel. Urban's Crusade drew together established theological strands of penance, pilgrimage and the struggle against Evil and the Infidel, giving them a concrete outlet in the shape of a deliberate military campaign against a specific enemy with a clear objective, at a time that Latin society was electrified by millenary anxiety, fraught with social tension, struggling with endemic violence and political crisis, and opening up to the opportunities and challenges presented by contact with Islamic world. Whatever the Pope's intentions were on that day at Clermont when he inveighed the princes and knights of Christendom to come to the aid of their "Eastern

[1] "The Book of Holy War," excerpted and translated in P. Chevedden, "The View of the Crusades," p. 290.

brethren," the time was ripe for what would eventually come to be called "Crusade."[2]

For a historical episode that lasted at most two centuries and had remarkably little direct and lasting impact on the region, the Latin adventure in the Holy Land has loomed disproportionately large in the European imagination, undoubtedly in part because it represented a "loss" (medieval Europe's "Viet Nam," perhaps), in part because it is challenging to reconcile its less savory aspects with the assumed moral position of Christianity and its self-declared representatives, and finally, because it has been seen as echoing in more successful, modern European colonial exercises in the same region. Historians critical of the movement and suspicious of the Church have enthusiastically written off the Crusades as brutal, hypocritical, and calculated campaigns of conquest, sustained by bigotry and driven by greed. On the other hand, whereas it well may be that contemporary Latin ideologues could present Crusading as an "act of love," scholarly apologists have taken positions no less disingenuous than to characterize Crusade as an act of self-defense against an Islam which was, it is absurdly alleged, "gunning for Christians."[3] This chapter is concerned with those Muslims who found themselves living under Latin rule as a consequence of the Crusades; therefore, the motivations behind the movement – which were undoubtedly too complex and varied to be rendered in such simple

[2] Urban's precise words are unknown. Several versions of his speech were recorded, some by witnesses, but none before the conquest of Jerusalem, and all with the benefit of hindsight and a view to justifying the venture. It is likely, therefore, Urban's "call" was rather vague, and focused on aiding the "Eastern brethren," and secondarily on the conquest of Jerusalem. Translations of various versions can be found in E. Peters, *The First Crusade*, pp. 25–36. Urban's contemporary letters (which can be dependably dated) are far more restrained in rhetoric and detail regarding the mission. See *ibid*., pp. 37–47. The revolutionary character of Urban's call has been exaggerated, as the movement clearly had religious, social, institutional, and economic precedents stretching back decades, and should be regarded as a dimension of the Gregorian reforms of the eleventh century. Contrast Chevedden's "gradualist" perspective, with that of Rubenstein, who portrays the Crusades as an explosive millenarian episode, in P. Chevedden, "The View of the Crusades," and J. Rubenstein, *Armies of Heaven*. If vocabulary is any guide, contemporaries did not see the Crusades as generically unique. For them Crusaders were "pilgrims," and the word "Crusade" did not appear until the thirteenth century (as the Old French *croisée*,) and is not attested to in English until the fifteenth century (see OED, s.v. "Crusade"). The Latin *crucisignatus* ("marked by the Cross") seems to have come into use in the 1190s at the time of the Third Crusade. See P. Chevedden, "A Crusade from the First"; C. Erdmann, *The Origin*; G. Constable, "The Historiography of the Crusades"; M. Markowski, "*Crucesignatus*"; J. Møller Jensen, "Peregrinatio sive expeditio"; and C. Tyerman, *The Invention of the Crusades*.

[3] See J. Riley-Smith, "Crusading as an Act of Love," and T. Madden, "The Real History."

terms – are considered only insofar as they shaped the experience of this community.[4]

As historians we can be sure that there were significant numbers of Muslims who remained under Christian rule in the aftermath of the Frankish conquest; however, investigating this population is an exercise fraught with frustration. Under the best of circumstances, sources for lower- and middle-class Christians in twelfth-century Latin Europe are thin, and there is little beyond chronicles and hagiography, legal codes and records of custom, and land-tenure and exchange documents to work with. The clerics and aristocrats who produced and maintained records were simply not interested in the details of peasant life – a lack of interest further magnified in this case, where the tenants and subjects in question were infidels. Moreover, the fact that Latins saw themselves as establishing a new, ethno-religiously defined political order here, and that this order was itself violently swept away in a little less than the span of a century, means that the institutions and organizations that might have safeguarded such records were themselves destroyed. Attempting to apprehend the history of the Muslims of the Latin East, therefore, is akin to reading a parchment twice scraped clean. In any event, the twelfth century was a time when Latin institutional development was still primitive. As a consequence, there are few surviving legal codes from the pre-1187 kingdom, and no significant administrative documentation that refers to the subject Islamic community. Nor were contemporary Muslim chroniclers interested in the lives of commoners, least of all

[4] Representative general works on the Crusades and the Latin East, include T. Asbridge, *The Creation of the Principality*; A. Atiya, *Crusade, Commerce and Culture*; A. Ben-Ami, *Social Change*; M. Balard, *et al.*, *Dei gesta per Francos*; C. Cahen, "Notes sur l'histoire," and *La Syrie du nord*; K. Ciggaar, M. Metcalfe, and H. Teule, *East and West*; P. Cole, *The Preaching of the Crusades*; P. Edbury, *The Kingdom of Cyprus*; A.-M. Eddé and F. Micheau, *L'Orient*; M. Gervers and J. Powell, *Tolerance and Intolerance*; C. Hillenbrand, *The Crusades: Islamic Perspectives*; P. Holt, *The Age of the Crusades*; C. Kostick, *The Social Structure*; C. MacEvitt, *The Crusades*; H. Mayer, *The Crusades*; A. Murray, *From Clermont to Jerusalem*; M. Shatzmiller, *Crusaders and Muslims*; J. Prawer, *The Crusaders' Kingdom*, and *The Latin Kingdom of Jerusalem*; J. Richard, *The Crusades*; J. Riley-Smith, *The Crusades: A Short History*, and *Crusades, Idea and Reality*; S. Runciman, *A History of the Crusades*; K. Setton, *A History of the Crusades*; R. C. Smail, *The Crusaders*; and C. Tyerman, *God's War*, to name a very few. Likewise a tremendous amount of primary source material is available in English and European languages, including many chronicles (Latin and Islamic), travelogues (Christian, Muslim, and Jewish), letters and documents. The collection *Recueil des historiens des croisades* is fundamental, some others relevant to the present chapter include Ibn Jubayr, *Travels*; Usāma b. Munqidh, *The Book of Contemplation*; H. A. R. Gibb, *The Damascus Chronicle*; F. Gabrielli, *Arab Historians*; J. Brundage, *The Crusades, a Documentary Survey* and E. Peters, *The First Crusade*; William of Tyre, *A History of Deeds*; B. Bacharach, *The Gesta Tancredi*; P. Edbury, *The Conquest of Jerusalem*; D. S. Richards, *The Chronicle of Ibn Al-Athīr*, and *The Rare and Excellent History*; and R. and C. Sweetenham, *Robert the Monk*.

those who chose to live under the yoke of the Infidel. Therefore, our history of this people must be built on whatever occasional and indirect evidence surviving Latin and Arabic chronicles and letters yield, occasional and exceptional travelogues and memoirs, and whatever can be gleaned from the meager and (until recently) neglected archeological evidence.[5]

### The *Bilād al-Shām* at the turn of the twelfth century

In this year [1101–2] reports were brought to the effect that the peoples of Khurāsān, ʿIrāq, and Syria were in a state of constant bickering and hatred, wars and disorder, and fear of one another, because their rulers neglected them and were distracted from the task of governing them by their dissensions and mutual warfare. (Abū Yaʿlā Ḥamza b. Asad b. al-Qalānisī, *Dhayl taʾrīkh Dimashq* (1160)[6])

Whereas, for the peoples of Latin Christendom Jerusalem and the Holy Land represented the center of the world, both in a religious and a geographic sense, for the world of Islam, the *Bilād al-Shām* (Syria and Palestine: the "land on the left side," for the early *émigrés* from the Arabian Peninsula) remained very much a frontier. The fortuitous victories of the Saljūqs, notably the Battle of Manzikert (1071), had pushed the *dār al-Islām* to the gates of Constantinople, but by the 1080s the threat to Byzantium had passed, and by the 1090s, Qilij Arslan (1092–1107), the *sulṭān* of Rūm ("Rome") in western Anatolia, had reached a not un-cordial accommodation with the Emperor Alexios I (1081–1118). Northern Syria, having fallen to Turkic warlords in the late 1080s, soon disintegrated, like Anatolia, into an array of autonomous city-states lorded over by Saljūq princes, their Central Asian clients and allies, and local Arab and Armenian petty lords, each paying lip-service, but little more, to the authority of the Great Saljūqs of Baghdad. In reality, the situation was essentially a free-for-all, with local strongmen jockeying for survival in a landscape of constantly shifting alliances and opportunities.

[5] The use of archeology by historians such as Pringle and Ellenblum has revised the previously dominant view of a highly divided and balkanized countryside, as held by Prawer and Smail. See, for example, A. Boas, *Crusader Archaeology*; D. Pringle, *Fortification and Settlement*, and *Secular Buildings*; R. Ellenblum, *Frankish Rural Settlement*; and T. Levy, *The Archaeology of Society*. Surprisingly, with all that has been written about the Crusades and the Latin East under Frankish rule, little work has been done on the Muslim minority. This is due chiefly to the paucity of sources available both in translation and in Arabic. Undoubtedly, there is much unedited material in Arabic manuscript collections that has yet to be studied. See the works of H. Dajani-Shakeel, J. Drory, A.-M. Eddé, B. Kedar, and D. Talmon-Heller referred to in this chapter and in the Bibliography.

[6] "Supplement of the History of Damascus," in H. A. R. Gibb, *The Damascus Chronicle*, p. 54.

Saljūq legitimacy had been founded on the notion of re-establishing a unified, orthodox Sunnī caliphate – a goal that focused primarily on the purging of Shīʿī elements at the ʿAbbāsid court and *jihād* against the schismatic Ismāʿīlī Fāṭimids, rather than on the conquest of Christian territory. In fact, the expansionary impulses of the sultanate remained oriented all but entirely towards Central Asia. In any event, the tenuousness of Saljūq unity was obvious even before the death of the second and last Great Saljūq, Malik Shāh (1072–92), and the assassination of his brilliant Prime Minister Niẓām al-Mulk, in 1092. As their struggles against the ʿAbbāsid caliphs they had allegedly come to support show, the Saljūqs and their Turcoman allies, like the Almoravids in the Maghrib and Iberia, had not come in reality to restore and rejuvenate a weakened Islamic order. Rather, these barely sedentary (and sometimes barely Muslim) horsemen had come to establish their own families and clans as the new overlords over urbane and sedentary subjects with whom, whether Muslim or not, they felt little solidarity or affinity.

### *The land and its people*

The zone south of the latitude of Tripoli (Ṭarābulus al-Shām) and Tiberias (Ṭabariyya), including Jerusalem, had traditionally been under Fāṭimid dominion, although as the political crisis of the Caliphate deepened in the eleventh century, Saljūq, Turcoman, and Kurdish *condottieri*, and Bedouin (*ʿArab*) tribesmen had seized control of much of this territory, while in the coastal towns local potentates and urban "republics" endeavored with varying success to shake off Egyptian rule and set up autonomous statelets. It was only in 1091 that Jerusalem (al-Qūds or Bayt al-Maqdis; "the Noble Sanctuary" or "the House of Holiness") was retaken by the *wazīr* al-Afḍal b. Badr al-Jamālī, in his campaign to re-establish Fāṭimid hegemony in Palestine and the Levantine coast. For their part, the Fāṭimids did not see Christianity and its world as an existential threat; Egypt would cast its lot with Norman Sicily against the Almohads and with Byzantium against the Franks and Saljūqs, and it was just beginning to appreciate the benefits of cultivating relations with the Italian trading cities. The world of Islam was certainly expanding, but not towards Europe; rather, it was spreading into the resource-rich lands of Sub-Saharan Africa, South and Central Asia, and across the Indian Ocean.

The Islamic society of Syria and Palestine was dizzyingly diverse, particularly in comparison to Sicily and al-Andalus. Although among Muslims there was a clear orthodox majority here, and the four *madhāhib* (singular: *madhhab*), or "schools of interpretation" of Islamic law, were all represented among the Sunnī population, there was also a considerable Shī'a element, both as a consequence of Persian immigration and influence, and of Fāṭimid domination and missionizing.[7] Further, the coastal mountains were haven for a number of secretive, heterodox sects including the Nuṣayriyyūn ('Alawiyyūn, "Alawites"), Nizāriyyūn (Bāṭiniyyūn, "Assassins"), and Durūz ("Druze"), none of which recognized the legitimacy of either the Fāṭimid or 'Abbāsid Caliphates, and one of which – the Assassins – was explicitly revolutionary.[8]

However, Muslims comprised only part of the population, and in many regions conquered by the Crusaders, they were in a minority.[9] Antioch (Anṭākiya) had been under Byzantine rule until 1084, and Armenian Edessa (al-Ruhā') had passed only fleetingly under Saljūq rule, and the populations of both cities and their hinterlands would have been primarily Christian. Indeed, the territory from the Orontes (al-'Āṣī) valley to the Mediterranean coast was home to significant Christian populations of the monophysite Syriac confession, along with Byzantine (or Melkite) Orthodox, Armenians (primarily in the North), and Maronites (around Mt. Lebanon). There were Muslim communities in the major towns and cities, but the countryside seems to have been largely unintegrated, characterized by villages and larger zones of settlement that were religiously homogenous. The coastal plain stretching north from Acre ('Akkā) and the Orontes and Biqā' valleys had substantial areas of Muslim rural inhabitation, as did the Jordan (al-Urdunn) valley north of Jerusalem, and the Galilee. But south of Acre and Jerusalem and west of the Dead Sea, the countryside was populated overwhelmingly by Arabized Syriac Christians.[10] Fiercely independent Bedouin nomads ranged not only

7 There were four orthodox schools (*madhāhib*) of legal interpretation (*fiqh*) in Sunnī Islam: Ḥanafī, Mālikī, Shāfi'ī, and Ḥanbalī – all of which were considered valid. Mālikī law exercised a near-monopoly in the Western Mediterranean, although there was some Shāfi'ī presence. In the East, all four schools had adherents. Shī'a legal interpretation differed essentially on questions of leadership of the community, but was generally compatibly with Sunnī law.

8 Ismā'īlism (the Shī'ism of the Fāṭimids) was important in Egypt and the Levant; see F. Daftary, "The Isma'ilis and the Crusaders" for an overview. The Assassins (Nizāriyyūn) arrived in Syria in the early 1100s, and from the early twelfth century were known pejoratively as "Ḥashīshiyya" (whence "Assassins"). They created a confederation of principalities in Syria and Persia that regarded both Sunnī princes and the Fāṭimid Caliphate as illegitimate. For this reason they were willing to engage productively and form alliances with the Franks, notably, the Hospitalers. See, generally, B. Lewis, *The Assassins*, and Y. Gautron, "Assassins, Druze et Nosayris."

9 See B. Kedar, "The Subjected Muslims," p. 149, for the distribution of the Muslim population in the Frankish Kingdom of Jerusalem.

10 See H. Dajani-Shakeel, "Natives and Franks," pp. 161–63 for al-Muqaddasī's and Nāṣir e-Khusrau's descriptions of the demography and inter-communal relations in the Sham just prior to the Frankish conquest.

around the desert periphery, but throughout the flat-lands of the Shām. There were Jews here also, as throughout the Islamic world (and including Rabbinical Jews, Samaritans, and Karaites), with notable communities at Jerusalem and Ascalon (ʿĀsqalān). On the other hand, much of the Jewish population of the Galilee seems to have converted to Islam and integrated with the Muslims in the preceding centuries. In sum, the Bilād al-Shām presented a complex and multi-layered array of ethnic, cultural, linguistic, and religious identity, characterized by ambiguity and acculturation. Seen in this light, the lack of "Muslim solidarity" in the face of the First Crusade which has so surprised European historians should actually come as no surprise at all – socio-cultural and political relations here were simply not imagined in terms of a strict Christian–Muslim binary.

Any potential Muslim solidarity was also undermined by the particular economic and political conditions of the late eleventh-century Levant. This was a period of economic and demographic contraction, prompted in part by the decline of the two caliphates and the disorder that followed. The emergence of a new, foreign military elite – the Saljūq and Turcoman warlords – encouraged the establishment of oppressive, extra-canonical taxes which, combined with the prohibition of indebted tenants from leaving their lands, rendered the rural population (*fallāḥīn*) in many areas here little more than serfs, thus driving a wedge of disinterest between ruler and ruled, and sharpening the division between urban and rural communities. The urban classes – the craftsmen and merchants, and the *quḍāt* who represented them – also viewed the new military elite with suspicion and alarm, but there was little they could do apart from vainly invoking Islamic solidarity and the rule of law.[11] The historian Ibn al-Qalānisī recounts how four years after al-Sulamī preached his "Treatise on Holy War" in Damascus a delegation from Aleppo led by a scion of the clan of the Prophet and accompanied by merchants, Sufis, and *ʿulamāʾ* arrived in Baghdad, disrupting prayer services and demanding relief from the depredations of the infidel Franks from the Great Saljūq, Muḥammad b. Malik Shāh (1105–18). However, when their monstrations disturbed the pageantry of the arrival of Khātūn al-ʿIṣma, wife of the Caliph al-Mustaẓhir bi'llāh (1094–1118), the ʿAbbāsid "Successor of the Prophet" – far from being shamed by the display – indignantly called for the culprits to be apprehended and punished.[12] But the attitude even of the lords of the Shām who faced Latin aggression first-hand was no less

[11] It was only in Tripoli, with the rise of the Banū ʾAmmār, that a dynasty of jurists, of the type that was so common in post-Almoravid al-Andalus, managed to gain power.

[12] H. A. R. Gibb, *The Damascus Chronicle*, pp. 111–12.

ambivalent than that of the Successor of the Prophet in Baghdad. The reaction of native Muslims to Frankish conquest and rule can only be understood in light of the diversity, divisiveness, and disarray, and the multiplicity of political agendas that characterized Syria and Palestine at the turn of the twelfth century.

## The Kingdom of the *Ifranj*

If only you had seen Syria and Iraq in the decade of 490 you would have seen an unconcealed religion, abundant knowledge, a secure, settled and united society, too splendid and perfect to be described because of the lustre of its condition and the brilliance of its perfection. But an evil fate brought a cold wind from the north and south which left Syria like a yesterday that has passed and gone. It erased the voice of Islam from the al-ʿAqṣā Mosque and executed there on Friday morning, the 18th of Shaʾabān 492 [11 July 1099], three thousand men and women, including God-fearing and learned worshippers, renowned for their spiritual state and noted for their religiosity. (Abū Bakr Muḥammad b. al-ʿArabī, *Tartīb al-riḥla* (*c.* 1100)[13])

The conquest of the Holy Land by Latin Christians contrasted sharply with their expansion into Islamic Iberia, southern Italy, and Ifrīqiya. Here, the conquest was driven by a conscious spirit of aggressive piety and unremitting brutality, and characterized by deliberate massacre and a calculated disregard for natives, whether these were Muslims, Jews, or Eastern Christians. In short, it had a sudden, catastrophic character that Latin expansion elsewhere lacked. The culmination of the Crusade was the capture of Jerusalem. When the walls were breached on June 15, 1099, the Crusaders poured into the city, and set out to purge it by killing its Muslim and Jewish inhabitants wholesale. Whatever complex bundle of motivations lies at the bottom of such deliberate cruelty, it is clear that there was a ritual component to this event. The Holy City, "Mother Jerusalem," was to be cleansed. Indeed, the plunder and rape were halted for a period of several days while the Muslim inhabitants were rounded up and systematically put to the sword: men, women, and children. Among the "wonderful sights" recorded by the witness Raymond d'Aguilers were the killing and torture of men, women, and children and the "piles of heads, hands and feet" that littered the streets.[14] The few who managed to

[13] "The Account of the Journey," in J. Drory, "Some Observations," p. 120. The famous Sevillan *ʿālim* (and, later, *qāḍī*) visited the Holy Land in 1096, just prior to the Frankish conquest.

[14] Raymond d'Aguilers, *Historia Francorum qui ceperunt Iherusalem* ("History of the Franks who conquered Jerusalem") in E. Peters, *The First Crusade*, p. 260. Contemporary Christian chroniclers are unanimous regarding the massacre, which must be regarded

save themselves from the initial carnage by taking refuge in the citadel were put to the grisly task of collecting the dismembered remains of the dead.

That said, the killing was not indiscriminate – the Fāṭimid governor negotiated his release and that of his entourage in return for handing over the citadel. High-status prisoners who could be expected to fetch large ransoms were saved, many sent back to Antioch in chains. After one of these, a famous jurist named Makkī al-Rumaylī, failed to generate the generous ransom hoped for, he was stoned to death by his captors, a fate suffered also by a respected *ʿālim*, ʿAbd al-Salām al-Anṣārī. Other *ʿulamāʾ* who had the misfortune to find themselves in the city at the time met no better a fate, and the number of clerics killed may have easily been several hundred.[15] In what was clearly a sign of the carnage to come, the Franks took a captured Muslim warrior, "a most noble man, clean-shaven, tall of stature, seasoned and robust," and after interrogating him on his beliefs and unsuccessfully inveighing on him to convert, they dragged him in front of Baldwin's forces assembled outside the Tower of David, and beheaded him.[16] As the death of that anonymous martyr showed, Frankish Jerusalem was to be a Christian city. The city had been cleansed by the massacres. As William of Tyre would put it, "It was indeed the righteous judgment of God which ordained that those who had profaned the sanctuary of the Lord by their superstitious rites and had caused it to be an alien place to His faithful should expiate their sins by death and, by pouring out their own blood, purify the sacred precincts."[17] Muslims and Jews were forbidden by decree from living in the Holy City. In sum Ibn al-ʾArabī's recollection of the concord of pre-conquest Palestine may have been exaggerated, but his account of the massacre was not.

The events at Jerusalem were consistent with the early phase of the First Crusade, which was characterized by a high degree of violence against both military and civilian populations and a deliberate, exemplary use of

as fact, even taking into account Old Testament-style rhetoric the chroniclers drew on. Several versions can be compared in E. Peters, *The First Crusade*, pp. 91–93, 248–49, and 256. See B. Kedar, "The Massacre of 15 July 1099," for a reassessment of the question of Muslim refugees. Jews, who apparently also defended the city, and some Eastern Christians were also killed, although many were enslaved, and some, who managed to ransom themselves by pledging their holy books to the Jews of Ascalon, withdrew with the Fatimids. See J. Prawer, *The History of the Jews*, pp. 19–45.

15 H. Dajani-Shakeel, "Natives and Franks," p. 164. Jerusalem had been something of a center of learning and religious debate, hence there would have been scholars from across the *dār al-Islām* living there at the time of the conquest.

16 The episode is recounted by Albert of Aachen, *Historia Hierosolymitanae expeditionis* (*c.* 1125), or "History of the Expedition to Jerusalem," translated in *Recueil des historiens des croisades*, vol. IV, p. 469 {5}.

17 William of Tyre, *A History of Deeds*, vol. I, p. 372.

brutality.[18] Muslims were the clear focus of this aggression, but Jews and even native Christians were targeted as well. This period, from 1097 to 1110, saw the establishment of the County of Edessa, the Principality of Antioch, the County of Tripoli, and the Kingdom of Jerusalem.[19] In this time, the Crusader principalities reached nearly their maximum extent; only the coastal enclaves of Ascalon and Tyre (Ṣūr), and the Transjordan remained in Muslim hands. With few exceptions, as the Crusader forces swept down the Orontes valley, and down along the Lebanese coast towards Jerusalem, the Muslim populations of the towns they conquered were put to the sword, without regard to age or sex. Local rulers and communities from Aleppo to Ascalon reacted to the conquest variably: by offering tribute, counter-attacking, allying with Latin leaders, or suing for peace (or combining all four approaches as circumstances changed). After 1099, Latin raiding and captive-taking continued in the north, while in the south, Baldwin de Bouillon, who emerged as the strongest leader of the Crusade forces and was crowned King of Jerusalem on Christmas Day 1100 (reigning to 1118), aimed for territorial consolidation.[20] As the coastal cities fell, the Muslim populations of some, like Arsūf, managed to negotiate safe evacuation, whereas others, like Caesarea (Qayūariyya), suffered deliberate annihilation. Even where clemency had been extended, the Crusade leadership could not always control the troops, as at Tripoli in 1109, when Genoese forces killed surrendering townsfolk indiscriminately, notwithstanding Baldwin's guarantee of safety.

The brutality of the Crusaders' *entrée* into the world of the Near East has sometimes been defended by the notion of a pious and "innocent" ignorance, but this applies at best only to those who came from northern Europe. Even among these, however, the leadership was not unfamiliar with the Islamic world. Noblemen and high clergy had been making the pilgrimage to the Holy Land in the previous decades, as had Peter the Hermit, the charismatic charlatan responsible for the disastrous "People's

[18] Cannibalism, not unknown in the Latin military tradition, was apparently practiced both out of necessity and as a weapon of terror in the first Crusade, as contemporary witnesses recount at Antioch and, famously, at Maʿarat al-Nuʿmān in 1098. The former episode was later celebrated in the French vernacular *Chanson d'Antioche*, which has the feasting pilgrims remark, "This is most tasty, better than any pork or even cured ham" as they tuck into the roasted Muslims. See J. Rubenstein, "Cannibals and Crusaders," p. 549, and generally.

[19] Even before the arrival of the Crusaders, an advance mission under the initiative of Raymond of Toulouse had taken the Rūj Valley, southeast of Antioch, and massacred the Muslim inhabitants. See T. Asbridge, *The Creation of the Principality*, p. 30.

[20] Baldwin succeeded his brother, Godfrey, who was the first ruler chosen by the Crusader nobility, but who refused to take the title "king." Baldwin had previously established the first Crusader principality when he seized power in Edessa from the Armenian ruler, Thoros, in 1098.

Crusade." Nor were the *Ifranj* ("Franks"), as the Muslims referred to the Crusaders, a coherent or unified group. The Provençals, Lorrainers, and northern French, who made up the bulk of the forces, were split into factions according to bonds of regional origin, family, and vassalage.[21] Some had cut their teeth fighting the Infidel in Iberia. The "Norman" bloc was, in fact, southern Italian. Its leader, Bohemond of Taranto (Prince of Antioch, 1098–1111), was the son of the same Robert Guiscard who conquered Islamic Palermo; his formative years had been spent invading the Byzantine West, and he would have fought alongside Roger Bosso's Muslim troops at Capua in 1098.[22] In this light, it comes as little surprise that Bohemond and his nephew, Tancred, would prove most adept at navigating the ethno-religiously complex waters of regional politics in the Levant.[23] For their part, Pisa, Genoa and Venice – whose support proved indispensible in the campaigns – had been raiding and trading with Muslim lands for generations. For each of these groups the disarray of the Islamic Shām, coupled with Urban II's call, provided that irresistible combination of raw self-interest and exculpatory virtue. The "cleansing" of its satanic denizens seemed not only a religious obligation but a practical necessity, were the Holy Land to be incorporated permanently into Christendom.[24]

### *Regional relations and* realpolitik

As early as 1105, however, the situation was changing. Most of the *peregrini* ("pilgrims") as the Crusaders called themselves, had returned home, and those few who remained faced the task of establishing functioning principalities in the complex environment of the Shām. There are indications that when Tancred briefly held Tarsus in 1097, he was prepared to allow even the Saljūq garrison to remain in place, as long as they acknowledged his sovereignty.[25] In any event, the Normans lost no time in integrating, and by

[21] Even at the time of the Frankish conquest, the various factions among the Crusaders: the northern French under the Bouillon brothers, the Provençals under Raymond IV of Toulouse, and the Normans under Bohemond of Taranto, had been competing and undermining each other. One thing they were unanimous on was their disdain and disregard for Eastern Christians, both Byzantines and Syriac Christians, whom they were ostensibly sent to rescue. Latin efforts to undermine the local Church and displace its clergy are well-documented. See MacEvitt, *The Crusades*.

[22] R. Rogers, *Latin Siege Warfare*, pp. 101 and 102.

[23] Tancred and some of the other Normans had evidently picked up Arabic and familiarity with Arabo-Islamic culture and habits in southern Italy and Sicily. See G. Beech, "A Norman-Italian Adventurer," pp. 28 and 39.

[24] For the widespread view among Frankish Crusaders of Muslims as "pollution," see P. Cole, "'O God'."

[25] T. Asbridge, "Knowing the Enemy," p. 23.

1105 they had learned that mistreating the local populace could result in either flight or rebellion, either of which was counterproductive.[26] Antioch, under Bohemond and Tancred (his nephew and, later, regent) attacked Christian Byzantines and Armenians, as well as the Muslim Danishmends, settling into a "hot peace" with Riḍwān b. Tutush of Aleppo (1095–1113) and the warlords and princes of the Orontes.[27] Apamea (Afāmiya) was taken with the collusion of native Christians and the sons of its assassinated ruler, Khalaf b. Mulā'ib, who appealed to Tancred and became his tributaries or vassals. In order to obtain Jabala in 1109, Tancred made an offer of vassalage to Fakhr al-Mulk b. 'Ammār (1091–1108), the *qāḍī*-prince who had just lost Tripoli. Once he had the town, Tancred reneged, but did allow Fakhr al-Mulk and the Muslim population to depart in peace.[28] Although cross-border raiding continued through the next decades, a measure of Antioch's integration can be seen in the triple alliance between the Turcoman warlord, Najm al-Dīn Il-Ghāzī b. Artuq (1107–22) of Mardin (Mārdīn), the Saljūq *atabeg*, Ẓāhir al-Dīn Tughtigīn of Damascus (1095–1118), and Roger of Salerno (Regent of Antioch; 1112–19), against Riḍwān of Aleppo in 1115. The Antiochene chronicler Walter the Chancellor recalled how Roger and Tughtigīn's troops seemed to meet with "a welcome, even a bond of complete love, like sons and parents in companionship."[29] Opportunity, not ideology, ruled; and in 1119 the same Il-Ghāzī killed Roger and wiped out the county's forces at the battle known as *Ager Sanguinis* ("the Field of Blood"), allowing Baldwin II of Jerusalem (1118–31) to take control of the Principality. Roger, an Arabic speaker, and Il-Ghāzī, had reportedly been friends, but sentimentality did not prevent the Turcoman prince from having the erstwhile count's head converted into a jewel-encrusted goblet for use at his table.

Indeed, Antioch was something of a model of political integration in the Crusader Levant.[30] Diplomacy with the Muslim powers began here even before the city had been taken, when on or about February 9, 1098, in the

[26] This can be seen in the case of Artah, a town inhabited mostly by Armenian Christians. Initially, the town had expelled the Muslim garrison and gone over to the Franks, but after suffering mistreatment by the Crusaders, they expelled the Latin garrison and shifted back to Riḍwān b. Tutush of Aleppo. After the Crusaders defeated Riḍwān in battle in April 1105, most of the area's Muslims fled to Aleppo, although they were pursued by the Latins and many were killed. T. Asbridge, *The Creation of the Principality*, p. 57.

[27] The thirteenth-century chronicler, Ibn Abī Ṭayyi' reports a treaty between Tancred and Riḍwān against the Banū Munqidh of Shayzar, in A-M Eddé, "Francs et Musulmanes," p. 164.

[28] H. A. R. Gibb, *The Damascus Chronicle*, pp. 74 and 89.

[29] T. Asbridge and S. Edgington, *Walter the Chancellor*, p. 89 {I.3}.

[30] For Antioch, see C. Cahen, *La Syrie du nord*; K. Ciggaar, "Adaptation to Oriental Life"; T. Asbridge, *The Creation of the Principality*, "The 'Crusader' Community," "The Jabal as-Summaq," and "Knowing the Enemy."

midst of the long siege, Fāṭimid envoys arrived to negotiate peace and spent over a month in the Crusader camp. As early as September 1098, ʿUmar, the leader of the Muslims of nearby ʿAzaz, became clients of Godfrey of Bouillon (later ruler of Jerusalem, 1099–1100), who swore to protect them against Aleppo.[31] And although Raymond of Toulouse's campaigns in the nearby Rūj valley and Jabal Summāq were extremely brutal, this was as much a consequence of his determination to undermine Bohemond as anything else. Once Norman rule was established and secure, the city became a center for industry – notable textile manufacture – and of cultural/literary initiatives in which Muslims also played a notable role.[32] Among the early Muslim sojourners in the city was al-Qayṣarānī, a poet from Caesarea, who had fled that city's conquest by the Franks, and evidently stayed long enough in Antioch in 1145/6 to become ensnared by the beauty of the blue-eyed Frankish women of the city.[33] Throughout the period Antioch managed to maintain both urban and rural populations of Muslim subjects, even in the face of Saljūq and Ayyūbid competition and encroachment. As late as 1186 Bohemond III (1163–1201) drafted a letter to the Hospitalers at Marqab that referred to "my villeins, or those of my men, who are Saracens . . ."[34]

Even prior to 1110, however, a similar spirit of pragmatism had taken hold in the kingdom of Jerusalem. Hence, when Sidon (Ṣaydā) surrendered in that year, the garrison was allowed to withdraw unharmed and the commoners, in particular the agricultural producers, were invited to stay under a pact of peace (*sub pactione . . . pacifica*).[35] Like the Normans in the north, the Crusaders in the south established diplomatic relations with Muslim powers, and as early as 1108 treaties were established between Jerusalem and Damascus.[36] At times, agreements included provisions for sharing tribute over areas that neither party could conquer and defend. One of these truces, negotiated by Baldwin and Tughtigīn for the period of 1108 to 1110, set up a tax-sharing arrangement in the lands east of the Sea of Galilee, whereby one third of the area's produce would go to Jerusalem and one third to Damascus, the rest remaining with the

[31] T. Asbridge "Knowing the Enemy," pp. 21–22. [32] See, below, pp. 143, and 152
[33] Hillenbrand, *The Crusades: Islamic Perspectives*, p. 347.
[34] J. Prawer, "Social Classes," p. 109.
[35] *Recueil des historiens des croisades*, vol. III, p. 342.
[36] For the early treaties, see H. Dajani-Shakeel, "Diplomatic Relations," pp. 202–12; Ibn al-Athīr, who may not be reliable on this point claimed that even prior to the taking of Jerusalem, the Crusaders had contacted local Muslim rulers to assure them that they had no intention to attack any towns except those that had once belonged to the Byzantine Empire. T. Asbridge, "Knowing the Enemy," p. 21.

producers.[37] This was the first of a series of bilateral truces upon which the survival of both the kingdom of Jerusalem and an independent Damascus would depend.[38] In 1124 Baldwin besieged Tyre for a third time, and when the defenders were pushed to the point of desperation, he offered them the choice of paying a ransom and remaining in their homes or leaving. Most, it seems, opted to leave, and headed for Damascus, but within a short time, a significant number had returned to their lands and homes. A similar arrangement held in the contested region of the Golan, in the area around the ancient shrine of Banyas (Bāniyās). Here, Ibn Jubayr reports, that under the shadow the Château Neuf (at Hūnīn), "The cultivation of the vale is divided between the Franks and the Muslims, and in it there is a boundary known as 'The Boundary of Dividing.' They apportion the crops equally, and their animals are mingled together, yet no wrong takes place between them because of it."[39]

### *Integration and fragmentation*

As a measure of the transformation of Latin society, even decades earlier, Baldwin's chaplain, Fulcher of Chartres, who had been on the Crusade since its launch, penned these oft-quoted lines:

> Consider, I pray, and reflect how in our time God has transferred the West into the East. For we who were Occidentals now have been made Orientals. He who was a Roman or a Frank is now a Galilaean, or an inhabitant of Palestine. One who was a citizen of Rheims or of Chartres now has been made a citizen of Tyre or of Antioch. We have already forgotten the places of our birth . . .

But Fulcher's glib evocation of ethno-cultural fusion and harmony – "Different languages, now made common, become known to both races, and faith unites those whose forefathers were strangers"[40] – cannot be taken at face value, even as regards Eastern Christians. He speaks from a position of privilege, as a member of the Frankish Christian élite living in a *volkstat* where only "Latins" (*Latini*) – as opposed to "Christians" – enjoyed full legal rights, political power, and social prestige. This was, after all, the same chronicler who assessed the Crusaders' treatment of Muslim women at Antioch as: "the Franks did them no evil but drove

[37] H. Dajani-Shakeel, "Diplomatic Relations," p. 202.

[38] The ill-conceived and disastrous attack on Damascus in 1148 that was the culmination of the Second Crusade spelled the end of Damascene independence and set the scene for the destruction of the Kingdom of Jerusalem four decades later.

[39] Ibn Jubayr, *Travels*, p. 315.

[40] A. C. Krey, *The First Crusade*, pp. 280–81. Book III of Fulcher's *Historia hierosolymitano* was composed between 1118 and 1127. See also C. Hillenbrand, *The Crusades: Islamic Perspectives*, p. 354.

lances into their bellies."[41] On the other hand, in contrast with Sicily and the Iberian Peninsula, there was virtually no Latin appropriation of Islamicate artistic and architectural styles here; perhaps a consequence of a heightened sense of ethno-cultural opposition and a sense of vulnerability and lack of confidence on the part of the *Ifranj*.[42] Moreover, his rosy view of *convivencia* did not necessarily reflect that consensus, particularly once Frankish fortunes had failed. Jacques de Vitry, Bishop of Acre from 1216 to 1228, took a rather different view, and in his incendiary sermons excoriated those who had grown Eastern-style beards and emulated and adapted other accouterments of Levantine culture.[43] As for literary/scientific engagement: with the possible exception of William of Tyre's now-lost history of the Muslim kingdoms, the enterprise of high-cultural exchange was apparently limited to the more cosmopolitan and regionally integrated court of Antioch – a point of encounter for Latins, Byzantines, Armenians, Syriac Christians, and Muslims that served as an eastern node for translation and adaptation.[44]

To a far greater degree than was the case of the Iberian and Norman expansions into the western Islamic lands, the establishment of the Crusader principalities was characterized by competing factions of foreign warrior families, united only in their determination to preserve their own status above that of all of the subject peoples. The highly fragmented and internally competitive character of the Latin élite, the absence of a pre-established political order and institutions, and the transitive nature of the Crusade experience (whereby pilgrims visited, fought, and returned home), meant that the kingdom of Jerusalem offered both challenges and opportunities for its Muslim subjects. Over the first half-century of Frankish occupation this political fragmentation intensified: landed lords resisted vulnerable monarchs, Italian trading states controlled enclaves in the most important ports, the newly founded Military Orders – the Hospitalers and Templars – came to pursue independent (and mutually antagonistic) policies, and a steady parade of independent Crusaders trickled in from the West seeking glory and booty, blissfully unconcerned with the effect their adventures might have on the stability of the kingdom. By the 1140s Latin power had spread to the north of the Transjordan, as

41 See Y. Friedman, *Encounter Between Enemies*, p. 89. This "lances in bellies" may be a metaphor for sexual assault.

42 See A. Boas, "Archaeological Sources." This is analogous to the situation in thirteenth-century Valencia, another region marked by an absence of cultural borrowing, at least in terms of architectural styles.

43 K. Ciggaar, "Adaptation to Oriental Life," p. 279.

44 See A. Krey, "William of Tyre," p. 154; C. Burnett, "Antioch as a Link," and "The Transmission of Arabic Astronomy."

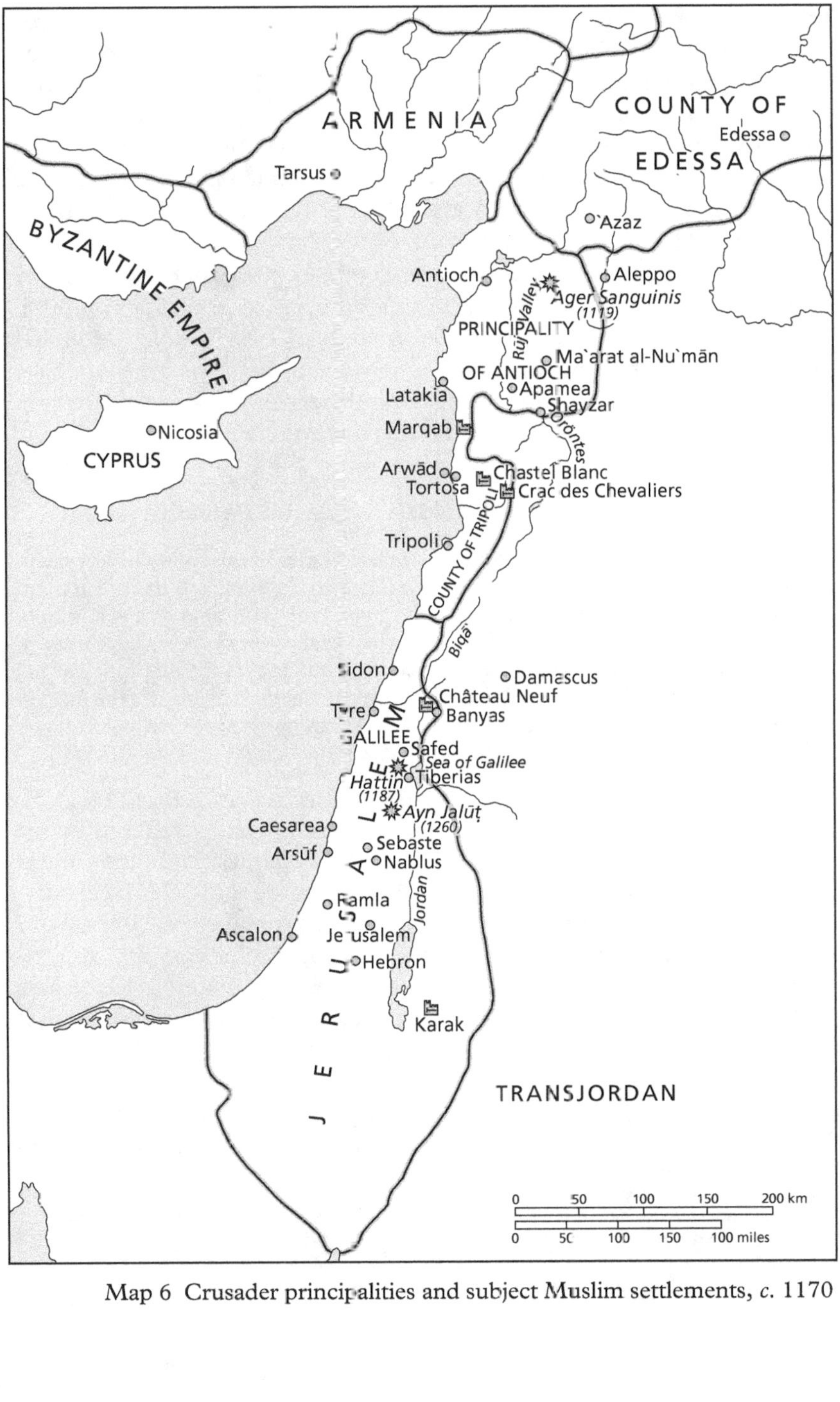


Map 6 Crusader principalities and subject Muslim settlements, *c.* 1170

much by osmosis as conquest, and when Ascalon, the Fāṭimids' sprawling military center and strategic port, was finally taken in 1153 after a hard-fought siege, the inhabitants were simply allowed to evacuate. However, the future of the kingdom already seemed doubtful. The Turcoman warrior ʾImād al-Dīn Zangī (1127–46) had captured Edessa in 1144, and the Second Crusade, called in response to this setback, not only failed in its ill-conceived attempt to take Damascus, but prompted the city's populace to submit to Zangī's son and successor, Nūr al-Dīn, in 1154. By this point Nūr al-Dīn (1146–74) had not only united Muslim Syria, but had taken the key towns of the upper Orontes, threatening the existence of the kingdom of Jerusalem and pushing the Assassins into an ever-closer alliance with the Crusaders.[45] It was only the triple détente of Nūr al-Dīn, Manouēl Komnēnos, and the Angevin Kings of Jerusalem that kept the Latin East secure. Through all this time Muslim subjects in the occupied Shām continued to live and labor under the rule of Latin lords.

## Muslim subjects of Frankish Syria and Palestine

> …. the Muslims fell under the domination of the Franks in the region of Jerusalem and its provinces, working the land for them. They used to punish them, jail them and levy a fee which resembles the *jizya*. The greatest of the Franks was Ahūmān b. Bārizān – may God curse him … It so happened that whereas the infidels used to collect one *dīnār* from everyone under their control, he – may God curse him – levied four *danānīr* from each of them. He used to mutilate their legs. Amongst the infidels there existed no more evil nor greater in violence than him – may God put a shame on him. (Ḍiyāʾ al-Dīn, *Sabab hijrat al-Maqādisa ilā Dimashq* (prior to 1245)[46])

The picture of Muslim life in the kingdom of Jerusalem painted by Ḍiyāʾ al-Dīn is not a happy one, as he recounts the indignities suffered by his forebears, the Banū Qudāma, in the region of Nablus (Nābulus) under the rule of Baldwin of Ibelin, Lord of Mirabel, in the mid twelfth century. In this passage and others Latin rule is depicted as oppressive, violent, and arbitrary. Leaving aside for the moment the particular agenda, circumstances, and dependability of this memoir, one immediately is led to ask: did this reflect the normal experience of Muslims in the kingdom? And, if so: why did they choose to remain and live under Christian rule?[47]

[45] See B. Smarandache, "The Franks and the Nizārī Ismāʿīlīs."

[46] "The Reason for the Migration from the Holy Land to Damascus," from J. Drory, "Ḥanbalīs of the Nablus Region," p. 95. This refers to Baldwin of Ibelin, the son of Barisan I, Lord of Mirabel.

[47] Indeed, one may ask if this represented the normal experience of Muslims in Nablus. Usāma b. Munqidh (see below, p. 148, n. 55) apparently visited frequently, where he lodged with a local Muslim innkeeper. He does not mention that the town had a particularly problematic or religiously charged atmosphere.

Certainly, many did not; not the least, the multitudes who were butchered during the conquest. Accounts of these massacres, however, refer to the walled towns, whereas the rural population seems not to have been targeted. While some refugees from the countryside fled the advance of the Franks to Damascus and Aleppo, it was evidently not a general trend.[48] By the second decade of the twelfth century, Latin seigniors were shifting to a more conciliatory policy, designed to maintain the native population, including Muslims; and areas such as the Galilee and Samaria were conquered with little fighting or purging of the populace. After the conquest of Tyre, some of the Muslims who had initially left for Damascus returned to their homes, as also seems to have occurred around Acre. The reasons for Frankish-Muslim accommodation are clear. The Christians needed a rural population to maintain the economic viability of their territory, and – according to contemporary sources – some Muslims found the rule of Frankish lords no less oppressive than that of the Saljūq and Turcoman lords who dominated Syria. In the century previous to the Crusade, the life of Muslim peasants seems to have become increasingly difficult, and for the poor *fallāḥīn* emigration to Muslim lands would have been at least as risky as remaining under Infidel rule. However, it was not just poor farmers who stayed, many Muslim craftsmen, townsfolk, and even men of religion either stayed or returned after the conquest.

Nevertheless, the Crusade was certainly catastrophic and provoked a demographic reconfiguration of the region. Although the view, championed by Prawer and Smail, that Latins remained a small minority confined to the cities and a few rural enclaves, has been discredited by subsequent historical and archeological research, so too was the earlier thesis of a confessionally integrated Latin Palestine and Syria.[49] The purging of the cities meant that the Muslim population disappeared from sections of the littoral, although within decades Muslim communities reappeared in some coastal towns and contemporary travellers report an almost exclusively Muslim countryside from Latakia (al-Lādhiqīya) down towards Tyre.[50] South of Jerusalem and Ramla (al-Ramla), the population remained overwhelmingly Syriac Christian, while the greatest concentrations of Muslims persisted in Samaria, Galilee, the Biqā' and Orontes valleys, and the Transjordan. Native Christians lived in these areas as well, although early in the twelfth century Christians from the Transjordan had been brought over to settle in Judea. Latins, particularly agriculturalists, tended to settle in the areas where native Christians were

[48] See D. Talmon-Heller and B. Kedar, "Did Muslim Survivors," for a revisionary view on the matter of refugees from Jerusalem.

[49] See above, p. 132, n. 5. [50] See B. Kedar, "The Subjected Muslims," p. 149 for sources.

most numerous; in Muslim-populated zones they lived in the new towns they established alongside existing settlements (some of which were simply abandoned). Native Christians probably tended to live in their own settlements, although there were also mixed Syriac–Muslim villages and towns. In sum, outside of the towns, there would have been relatively little interaction between Muslims and Franks – a state of affairs that would have suited both communities well.

### *Muslim subjects in the Latin East*

As elsewhere in Latin Christendom, Muslims here comprised a subject community, legally and socially subordinate, and liable for tribute – notably a head-tax modeled on the *jizya*.[51] Taxes do not seem to have been assessed communally, and given that it was Frankish identity that defined full participation in Crusader society, Muslims were lumped jurisdictionally and legally in with other non-Franks, including Syriac and Armenian Christians and Jews. Nor did kings succeed in acquiring direct fiscal and legal jurisdiction over minority subjects here, meaning that Muslims lacked the royal protection that was instrumental to their individual security and communal stability in Iberia and Sicily. Together with other non-Franks, Muslims were initially subject to the *Cour de Syriens*, which handled disputes among religious communities and was presided over by four Syriac and two Frankish jurors; by the late twelfth century this had been absorbed by the commercial court, or *Cour de Fonde*.[52] Given that there are few specific references to Muslims in the Frankish law codes or to the exercise of Islamic law, this clearly remained in the hands of local Muslim communities and was evidently subject to minimal interference and influence. Inter-Muslim disputes would have been resolved by a local *qāḍī* or *shaykh*, whose authority rested on his recognition by local Muslims rather than appointment by Frankish authorities.

At any rate, a sophisticated legal apparatus of the Latin kingdom did not develop until the early thirteenth century, a time when legists were preoccupied with the rights of the nobility versus that of the king, rather than the then all but non-existent Muslim minority. An early set of laws, promulgated at the Council of Nablus in 1120, contained only twenty-five statutes and most refer to sexual transgressions.[53] As far as the Islamic

[51] For Frankish seigniorial institutions and strategies and their relation to Byzantine and Islamic antecedants, see J. Richard, "La Seigneurie."

[52] For Franks, jurisdiction and legal rights were determined by social class. The nobility came under the jurisdiction of the *Haute Cour* and free subjects, the *Cour de Bourgeois*.

[53] For the Council of Nablus, see B. Kedar, "On the Origins."

minority is concerned, these included injunctions against the rape of Muslim slave women, Christian women having sex with Muslim men, and Muslims wearing Frankish clothes, alongside laws against sodomy and inter-Christian adultery.[54] In practice, however, through the twelfth century, law seems to have been exercised by local seigniors under the vague authority of the king, with a strong disposition towards trial by ordeal (and particularly, battle). Little wonder that Frankish legal custom provided no shortage of smug disdain for Usāma b. Munqidh, the Syrian soldier, diplomat, and memoirist who traveled extensively in mid twelfth-century Palestine.[55]

The administrative regime the Franks did establish for their minority subjects centered almost exclusively on the collection of rents and taxes. Villages, whether native Christian, Muslim, or mixed, were governed by a *rays* (from *ra'īs*, meaning "headman," or "mayor") appointed by the lord, and who acted as an intermediary between the former and the villagers. Typically, it seems each *rays* had responsibility for one village, but some governed several. Some villages also had an official *dragoman* (from *tarjumān*, or "translator"), as well as a scribe. Evidence for the distribution and competency of these officials is sparse, but one can say confidently that although this administrative structure may have been widespread, it was not systematized or standardized, at least in the twelfth century. There were certainly Muslim *rayses*, and some Muslim *dragomans* and scribes, but the existence of a large Arabic-speaking Christian minority meant that unlike in other conquered lands, the new rulers of the Latin East were not obliged to appoint Muslims to administrative positions for reasons of linguistic or cultural facility.[56] The degree to which the Crusaders adapted local Muslim administrative institutions – particularly those connected with revenue collection – meant that for many villagers the transition to Christian rule may have hardly represented a disruption. Taxes and *corvées* were levied, but it seems that Latin lords were no less capricious than Muslim lords, and the tribute they demanded no more onerous compared to their Saljūq counterparts. In any event, many Muslim

[54] The issue of clothing and appearance was tied to fears of miscegenation and apostasy; see below, p. 201.

[55] See Ibn Munqidh, *The Book of Contemplation*, pp. 144–54, for anecdotes under the rubric, "The "Wonders" of the Frankish Race." Usāma b. Munqidh (1095–1188) was raised in Shayzar in the Orontes Valley, and had a long career as a soldier, diplomat, and courtier. His autobiography, a unique document, recounts in very personal terms his memories, including relations both cordial and bellic with the Franks. For his life, see P. Cobb, *Usama ibn Munqidh*; Cobb also produced a new translation of the autobiography, Ibn Munqidh, *The Book of Contemplation*.

[56] In fact, as early as 1181 a Christian named "Sade" is referred to as "rays of the Muslims of Tyre." See M. Nader. "Urban Muslims," p. 250.

subjects would have little or no direct contact with their new lords or even their Latin agents. It is not clear that Muslim *rustici* ("peasants") were generally tied to their lands or prevented from purchasing or alienating property. In the thirteenth century, the kingdom's legists categorized free Muslims as *serfs du roi* ("serfs of the king"), a status roughly analogous to the *servi camere* and *moros de paz* of contemporary Italy and Iberia. The status of these *serfs*, who could be found in the thirteenth century in Nicosia, and likely in the mainland ports, represented a trade-off. In exchange for royal protection, they were prohibited from alienating their land (like *mudéjar* royal tenants in Aragon), and from marrying Christians – a curious qualification to specify, given that this would have been completely forbidden by contemporary canon law.[57] The status of the many Muslim subjects of the Military Orders and other ecclesiastical foundations in the Levant is much more obscure. They must have been very numerous, but virtually no documentary evidence remains of them.[58] A rare example is the confirmation by Baldwin IV (1174–85) of a sale of lands by Hugh of Ibelin to the Church of the Holy Sepulchre for lands at "Vuetmoamel" (Wādī al-Naml?) including the "peasants and all their properties, except the two *casales* belonging to an Arabic knight, namely Odabeb and Damersor."[59] Even so, the designation "Arabic knight" may well have referred to a native Christian.

### *Law and identity*

Frankish indifference to Islamic law was matched by an indifference to Islamic religious practice. Barring a few sensational episodes, no effort was made to convert Muslims or curb their worship. Certainly – above all, in the frenzy of conquest – many urban mosques were pillaged and converted into churches; however, mosques clearly survived not only in Muslim villages, but in cities with substantial Islamic communities, and the local and Biblical shrines and tombs scattered about the region continued to attract Muslim pilgrims both from within Latin lands and beyond.[60] Indeed, Ḍiyā' al-Dīn's memoir of the Ḥanbalī *shuyūkh* of the Nablus region portrays a vibrant and diverse Islamic community: one in

[57] See *ibid.*, pp. 248 and 266–68. It was unlikely that there were any cases of subject Muslims marrying Latin Christians; this likely referred to marriage of Muslim men to indigenous Christian women which undoubtedly did happen when the region was under Islamic rule.
[58] See P. Sidelko, "The Acquisition."
[59] "cum villanis et omnibus pertinentiis suis, exceptis duobus casalibus Arabici militis, scilicet Odabeb et Damersos …" M. E. de Rozière, *Cartulaire*, p. 110 {56}.
[60] See for example, the pilgrims' guide to Syria (*Kitāb al-Ziyārāt*), written by 'Alī b. Abī Bakr al-Harawī (d. 1215), J. Sourdel-Thomine, *Guide des lieux de pèlegrinage.*

which popularly recognized holy men could not only fill Friday mosques to overflowing and challenge the authority of Latin-appointed *rayses*, but also work miracles, and where scholars and pilgrims moved back and forth between Nablus and Damascus, and even Mecca. Tensions within the Muslim community are also revealed, ranging from condemnation and disdain for those who collaborated with Frankish rule, to the betrayal by Muslims of those who sought to resist it.[61] Indeed, it was the Ḥanbalī school, of which Ḍiyā' al-Dīn was an adherent, that was at the forefront of the ideological reconfiguration of *jihād* to mean military resistance to the Franks.[62] In an environment where there was a great deal of diversity of Islamic belief, where rural *shuyūkh* wielded considerable informal power, and in which socio-economic networks – even among the Sunnī majority – developed according to adherence to particular *madhāhib*, or interpretations of *fiqh*, a larger "Muslim solidarity" would hardly have manifested in the context of quotidian affairs.

This may account in part for the lack of local Muslim resistance to Crusader rule, but it must be remembered that the twelfth century was not an age known for popular peasant uprisings. There was certainly a lurking suspicion that Muslim subjects might collaborate with outside forces or rise up and rebel, but this happened rarely. In the first decade or so after the conquest, European pilgrims reported native Muslims in Galilee attacking travellers.[63] Nablus was apparently pillaged in 1113 by local Muslims, and the same area saw uprisings in the 1180s, but these were isolated events and both coincided with attacks from Damascus.[64] Otherwise, Muslims who were discontented with Latin rule whether for ideological or mundane reasons could either escape or become "bandits." And there were bandits aplenty in twelfth-century Palestine, both Christian and Muslim – many of whom exhibited little or no preference regarding the religious affiliation of their victims. Added to this were the frequent cross-border incursions by warlords and privateers. Even if their co-religionists spared their flocks and crops – and it was not always the case – such raiding would have still affected local Muslims by disrupting local economies.[65] But the greatest source of danger and anxiety for

61 See J. Drory, "Ḥanbalīs of the Nablus Region," and Talmon-Heller, "The Shaykh and the Community."
62 N. Elisséeff, "The Reaction of Syrian Muslims," p. 164.
63 H. Dajani-Shakeel, "Natives and Franks," p. 169.
64 H. E. Mayer, "Latins, Muslims and Greeks," p. 183.
65 H. A. R. Gibb, *The Damascus Chronicle*, p. 139. After the forces of Damascus defeated the Franks and pursued them deep into the Kingdom of Jerusalem, the Muslims of the area around Nablus sent envoys to the *atabeg* requesting that he and his men not plunder their property, and offering him tribute in exchange.

Muslim villagers were the bands of *bilghriyyīn* (Crusader "pilgrims") who continued to trickle in from the Latin West, and who raided, pillaged, and attacked even those who lived under the protection of Frankish lords.

Thus, the mutual antagonism and antipathy of Muslim peasants and their Latin seigniors was mitigated by the fact that the former provided revenue and the latter security. On the one hand, Latin lords had the power to aggressively exploit Muslim subjects and to engage in exemplary or punitive violence, as at Wādī Mūṣā in the Transjordan, when a peasant rebellion was pacified in 1144 by the deliberate destruction of local olive groves. For their part, the fact that Muslim subjects who felt ill treated could fairly easily escape eastwards induced those Latin lords who depended on them for revenue to adopt a moderate approach.[66] Moreover, because this was a relationship founded essentially on coercion, when the Franks appeared to be militarily weak or vulnerable, Muslim tributaries and peasants did not hesitate to simply withhold their dues.[67] For example, William of Tyre reported that in the years after the conquest many Muslim peasants resisted by refusing to raise crops, preferring to "endure famine themselves" rather than abet the enemy. After Baldwin of Bouillon's defeat in battle in 1113, William reported many subject Muslims went over to the Saljūqs; however, this indicated a shift of tributary contribution, rather than physical movement.[68] In areas of Frankish-Saljūq condominium the position of Latin lords would have been even more delicate and vulnerable in this regard.

### *Subject Muslims in the Frankish economy*

With an ongoing shortage of settlers and of agricultural output, the Latin economy needed Muslim manpower. But Muslims were not merely peasant farmers; in the balkanized Frankish realms native villages comprised complete local economies and included craftsmen, herders, and traders. The villages were socio-economically diverse; while there may have been no cohesive or self-conscious local elite class here, some villagers, even aside from those who held an official position like that of *rays*, were comfortably prosperous. There were no legal restrictions on acquiring and alienating land, and the most successful Muslim villeins and townsfolk engaged in a diversity of economic activities and were able to

[66] See E. Sivan, "Réfugiés syro-palestiniens."
[67] See B. Kedar, "The Subjected Muslims," p. 171.
[68] William of Tyre, *A History of Deeds*, vol. I, pp. 409 and 494–95.

accumulate houses and properties.[69] The German traveler, Wilbrand of Oldenberg, a canon of Hildesheim (in Lower Saxony), who passed through Antioch in 1211, observed many wealthy Muslims in the city.[70] Muslims undoubtedly continued to work in cloth and ceramic, although in these sectors it was difficult for the kingdom to compete with better and cheaper Syrian products. Nevertheless, Tripoli and Antioch remained important production centers (the former with some 4,000 silk weavers alone), and Muslims doubtless comprised part of this workforce.[71] Husbandry on a larger scale was a major activity of the "Arabs" – Bedouin tribes who ranged across the Holy Land. These were looked on with suspicion by their fellow Muslims, and were governed by Latins only to the extent that tribute could be exacted from them in exchange for access to pasturelands. The important sugar industry, taken over and expanded along the coast by the Franks, may also have relied to some extent on Muslim manpower and know-how. Finally, it is clear that urban communities were re-established, most importantly in Acre and Tyre, but possibly in other coastal towns as well. Here, Muslims were evidently engaged both in craft production and trade, both on the local and regional scale. As early as 1120 Baldwin II decreed *in perpetuam* that no merchant, Muslim or Christian, bringing foodstuffs ("wheat or barley, beans, lentils or chickpeas") for sale to Jerusalem should be hindered or taxed in any way.[72] Al-Idrīsī's characterization of Antioch as a center for production of fine Iṣfahānī cloth would suggest that there was a community of craftsmen there.[73] Not surprisingly, urban communities seem to have been most closely integrated with Frankish society, by virtue of close quarters, the absence of seigniorial apparatus, and the socio-economic integration that characterizes urban life. Ibn Jubayr remarked on the congeniality of the Franks of Tyre and observed Muslims there enjoying a Christian wedding procession, and outside Acre he visited a shrine that alternated between holding Christian and Muslim services.[74]

[69] See Ibn Jubayr, *Travels*, pp. 313–25, particularly p. 317, when Ibn Jubayr recalls being shown hospitality by a Muslim *rays* on the way to Acre. See also M. Nader, "Urban Muslims," pp. 248–49 and 267.

[70] S. Edgington, "Antioch," p. 251. For Wilbrand, see J. Folda, *Crusader Art in the Holy Land*, pp. 119–20.

[71] J. Prawer, *The Latin Kingdom of Jerusalem*, p. 393.

[72] H. Mayer and J. Richard, *Die Urkunden*, vol. I, p. 232 {86}. The decree was made at the request of the Latin Patriarch, Warmund of Picquigny (1118–28); the King specified that it should not be altered or violated by any of his successors.

[73] al-Idrisi, *Géographie*, vol. II, p. 330. Of course, non-Muslims can certainly produce items using "Islamic" styles and techniques, but technical knowledge in crafts tended to be practiced within and passed down through family networks.

[74] B. Kedar, "Convergences," p. 91

Indeed, this twelfth-century traveler's observations regarding the status and condition of Muslim subjects of the kingdom of Jerusalem is rather more optimistic than that of Ḍiyā' al-Dīn. As he transited Frankish lands from the lower Biqā' and Levantine coast, Ibn Jubayr was scandalized by a countryside of Muslims, content and secure under Frankish lordship, living in a better state than their Syrian brethren. Just east of Acre, he sojourned in the company of a Muslim *rays* who was wealthy enough to provide an evening of hospitality and entertainment for the entire caravan.[75] Several factors may lie at the root of the difference between these two accounts; however, simple piety is not among them. Ibn Jubayr, after all, was returning from the *ḥajj* and spared no sympathy for those Muslims who chose to live in the land of the Infidel. Ḍiyā' al-Dīn's account, on the other hand, was in essence a work of hagiography, praising the decision of Aḥmād b. Muḥammad b. Qudāma, a *shaykh* of the village of Jammā'īl, who led his family and followers on their own, personal *hijra* to Damascus in the 1160s.[76] Here, they settled in the suburb of Ṣaliḥiyya, which became a hotbed for the brand of anti-Frankish *jihādī* sentiment cultivated by Nūr al-Dīn, and of which they became vocal and visible proponents. However, it was not their stringent Ḥanbalī piety that prompted their self-exile from the Frankish Holy Land, rather they fled only as tensions rose with their fellow Muslims, and after their lord, Baldwin of Ibelin, had apparently resolved to kill Aḥmād.

Nablus was certainly not a center of determined resistance; in 1099, even before Jerusalem had fallen, representatives from the region came bearing gifts and offering their subjugation to the Crusade leader Godfrey of Bouillon. When Usāma b. Munqidh passed through Nablus several decades later, his only recollection of the town was an amusing (and hardly plausible) anecdote involving the wife of a Christian wine merchant who lived down the street from the Muslim-owned inn where he stayed.[77] Thus, if any coherent picture emerges from our fragmentary sources referring to free Muslim subjects of the Crusader principalities, it is that of a society that – in spite of its marginalization – had reached a situation of functional stability. Muslims here lived under varying degrees of security and prosperity, and – despite the violent and ideologically charged environment in which they lived – even the most

[75] Ibn Jubayr, *Travels*, pp. 316–17. He noted that they paid half of their produce in tribute, plus a poll tax.

[76] The Banū Qudāma became a tremendously influential family of mystically inclined Ḥanbalī jurists in Damascus; notably Aḥmād's son, Muwaffaq al-Dīn and the ascetic Shaykh Abū 'Umar.

[77] Ibn Munqidh, *The Book of Contemplation*, p. 148. The incident reads rather like a medieval "traveling salesman" joke.

stringently pious could apparently reconcile their religious convictions to the compromises (and in some cases, the benefits) inherent in life under Latin rule.

## Accommodation and détente in the age of *jihād*

I used to travel frequently to visit the king of the Franks during the truce that existed between him and Jamāl al-Dīn Muḥammad (may God have mercy on him) on account of an act of generosity that my father (may God have mercy on him) had done for Baghdawīn al-Bruns ["Prince" Baldwin II], the father of the queen, the wife of Fulk ibn Fulk. The Franks used to bring their captives before me so that I might buy their freedom, and so I bought those whose deliverance God facilitated. (Usāma b. Munqidh, *Kitāb I'tibār* (*c.* 1183)[78])

As much as Iberia and southern Italy, the Holy Land was a place where contemporaries saw little problem in reconciling the formal sectarian struggle of Christianity versus Islam with political, economic, and social realities that ignored or defied this division. On the one hand, it was the scene of constant and brutal raiding and pillage, where Muslim and Christian warriors took every opportunity for glory and plunder. Yet, when it came to kings, collectives, and corporations, *realpolitik* rather than ideology drove policy. Indeed, for much of its history, Jerusalem's survival as a kingdom depended on the truces that bound it to Damascus, and the overland trade that linked that city to the Christian-ruled ports of the coast. Aside from this agreement, temporary truces and alliances between local Christian and Muslim powers were common. For example, when shifting political fortunes left the Assassins – arguably the most "extreme" Muslim group here – isolated, they were drawn into an alliance with the Hospitalers, one of the most "extreme" Christian groups here. Most dramatically, as the Fāṭimid caliphate teetered on the bring of civil war in the 1170s, one of the contenders for power, the *wazīr*, Ḍirghām, showed no compunction in converting the caliphate itself into a Frankish protectorate in order to save his own position.[79]

As a result of the Crusader states' enmeshment in the larger world of the Islamo-Arabic Levant, the Muslim presence in Latin lands was not limited to those townsfolk and farmers who persevered in the wake of the Frankish conquest; it included members of military and professional

78 *Ibid.*, pp. 93–94. Jamāl al-Dīn Muḥammad ruled Damascus from June 1139 to March 1130. The favor he had done to Baldwin II was to have kept him in secret and under his protection when the latter was his prisoner at Shayzar.

79 See M. Baldwin, "The Latin States," pp. 555–56.

elites, and large numbers of slaves.[80] That said, however great the need on the part of the Franks for linguistic and cultural intermediaries, it was a demand that could be met easily by Arabic-speaking native Christians, whom the Crusaders obviously preferred over Muslims when it came to establishing a colonial administrative apparatus. Hence, it was only rarely that members of the Muslim military elite made the transition to Latin service. Tancred – perhaps influenced by his south Italian origins and experiences – evidently considered having Muslim vassals as feasible. He made such an offer, albeit in bad faith, to Fakhr al-Mulk b. ʿAmmār, and may have exercised it with the sons of Khalaf b. Mulāʿib of Apamea (ʾAfāmiya).[81] Otherwise, references to Muslim vassals are vague and inconclusive.[82] The only conclusive proof of a Muslim serving in the upper levels of Frankish administration comes in the case of Ḥamdan al-Athāribī (d. 1147/48), a poet and chronicler. He was a fixture at the court of Antioch for a time and received as a fief and resettled the abandoned village of Maʿar Bunīya near Aleppo from the Frank, Alan al-Athārib – an act which provoked the censure of his learned co-religionists, but for which Ḥamdan remained stubbornly unrepentant.

Ḥamdan, however, was not atypical of the adventurers and opportunists of this instable world, who readily laid aside religious prerogatives to forward personal agendas.[83] He was also a physician – a member of a profession whose members frequently served unbelievers and whose potential influence in infidel courts was nearly limitless. Coptic, Syriac, and Muslim experts trained in traditions of Eastern medicine – far more sophisticated than that of the Latins – were in high demand, and could transit or establish residence in Frankish lands relatively easily, and could have access to the highest echelons of the elite.[84] Undoubtedly, other learned professionals and skilled craftsmen enjoyed similar privileges.

### *Pilgrims and travelers*

Even in times of open hostility, foreign Muslims could travel in Latin territory, enjoying either the benefits of a truce or a document of

80 There are several references to the wholesale enslavement of local Muslim populations in the early phases of the Frankish conquest. See, for example, A.-M. Eddé, "Francs et Musulmanes," p. 165.

81 See above, p. 140. 82 See above, p. 149.

83 Ḥamdan, like his more famous contemporary Usāma b. Munqidh, was something of a renaissance man. This poet, physician, and Frankish vassal also wrote a now-lost "History of the Franks who invaded the *Dār al-Islām*." When he was sent as an envoy to the Fatimid caliph al-Amir (1101–30), the latter initially refused to admit Ḥamdan to his presence for fear he was an Assassin. See D. Morray, *An Ayyubid Notable*, pp. 88 and 149.

84 J. Prawer, *The History of the Jews*, pp. 107–9; and below, pp. 431ff.

safe-passage issued in the name of the king.[85] Ibn Jubayr bore testimony to the steady east–west trade from Syria to the Latin Mediterranean, and saw how in Acre the Franks had established a Muslim-style *dīwān*, staffed by scribes who kept accounts in Arabic.[86] He also observed, for example, how Maghribī merchants and pilgrims were charged a higher transit tax than other Muslims after fellow "Westerners" had been enlisting to fight the Franks alongside Syrians. The most eloquent testimony of the permeability of the frontier, however, is Usāma b. Munqidh's famous and unique memoir, which records his many sojourns in Frankish territory, where he hobnobbed with the elite, met local Muslims, observed with perplexity Frankish customs, and worshiped under Templar protection at the al-ʿAqṣā mosque in Jerusalem.[87] Indeed, the exclusion of non-Christians from the Holy City was neither complete nor permanent, and in the decades following the conquest Muslims established themselves in the environs, if not in the city itself, and pilgrims came to pray at the Qubbat al-Ṣakhrah ("Dome of the Rock"). The Anatolian *shaykh*, Rabīʿ al-Mārdīnī, not only worked for a time at as a laborer in Jerusalem and lodged in a Christian monastery, but his piety so impressed the Dome's Frankish gatekeeper that the latter dispensed with his customary demand of *baqshīsh*. Only a century after the liberation of Jerusalem by Salāḥ al-Dīn an anonymous pupil of the great Catalan rabbi Naḥmanides wrote a pilgrim's guide to the Holy Land in which he observed at the Dome of the Rock, Muslims "on the day of their festivity, around three thousand, and going around in a procession, as if dance, as the Jews – be sure to make a distinction between unclean and pure – used to go around the altar."[88]

The Bilād al-Shām was peppered with sites held sacred by Christians, Muslims, and Jews, either because of Biblical or mythical associations, or due to their connection to more recent figures. The church at Sebaste (Sabasṭiyya), outside Nablus – one of the reputed resting places of the head of John the Baptist (a prophet in Islam associated with the mysterious *al-Khiḍr*) – was one of the better-known sites, as was Hebron (al-Khalīl), where several Old Testament Patriarchs are said to be entombed. Al-Harawī's pilgrimage guide, written at the time of Salāḥ al-Dīn's victory, records dozens of lesser sites of pilgrimage for Muslims around

85 Mayer, "Latins, Muslims and Greeks,"p. 184.
86 The scribes themselves were likely indigenous Christians.
87 See Ibn Munqidh, *The Book of Contemplation*, throughout.
88 See the anonymous *Tōṣōth Eretz Israel* ("Comings and Goings in the Land of Israel"), quoted in J. Prawer, *The History of the Jews*, p. 240.

Palestine, some of which were also holy to either Jews or Christians. In the Galilee, a grove sacred to Jews was venerated by Muslims, together with a number of rabbis' tombs.[89] Both Usāma and al-Harawī mention the shrine at ʿAyn al-Baqr, outside Acre, where Muslims and Christians worshiped side-by-side. Some Muslims also attended the "miracle of the oil" that occurred at Easter in the Church of the Holy Sepulchre, and were even admitted, along with Jews, to the hospital in Jerusalem. Likewise, local Muslims do not seem to have been prohibited from making the *ḥajj* to Mecca any more than foreign pilgrims, like Ibn Jubayr, were from transiting Frankish territory for the same purpose. Conversely, Franks journeyed to the shrine of the Melkite monastery at Saydnaya outside Damascus, where they adored a miracle-working icon of the Virgin, alongside native Christians and Muslims. Genuine expressions of piety could elicit empathy in spite of difference, and the Latins could not but respect (if at times, grudgingly) the pious asceticism of Sūfīs and the powers of local *shuyūkh*.

Indeed, religious difference seems to have been largely ignored in quotidian affairs, except notably in the case of Latin *bilghriyyūn* freshly arrived to the Holy Land. These were reputed among Muslim observers to be particularly uncouth, uncomprehending, and bigoted, and were more likely to carry out acts of violence against any Muslims, even those living under the king's peace. In 1290 newly arrived Europeans apparently attacked and massacred Muslim peasants at Acre.[90] Indeed, the reality of constant conflict and violence – both in the form of warfare along the frontier and incursions deep into the interior – must have taken a psychological toll and contributed to tensions among communities. On the one hand, Usāma recalled the rescue of a servant of his by a mysterious Arabophile burgher from a near-lynching in Acre, after a raving woman accused him of having killed her brother in a recent battle. But on the other, he recounts with relish how a lost band of Latin pilgrims wandered into his hometown of Shayzar one night – the few who were not taken as slaves were either killed in the streets or hunted down on horseback the following morning.[91] Muslim campaigns of conquest were also characterized by the massacre of non-combatants, a fact obscured by – *inter alia* – the development of a historiographcial tradition in which Salāḥ al-Dīn is presented as rational, pacific, and humane, in contrast to the brutal and

[89] This may have been a consequence of the conversion of local Jews to Islam.
[90] M. Nader, "Urban Muslims," p. 269, n. 121.
[91] Ibn Munqidh, *The Book of Contemplation*, pp. 142 and 153–54.

superstitious Franks.[92] This was a world of visceral violence, and both Muslims and Franks not only killed women and children, but allowed their women to take part in killing enemy prisoners.

### *Captives and slaves*

Large numbers of captives were taken by both Christians and Muslims, either to be held as political capital, to be ransomed, used as domestics, sold on to the market, or put to work at hard labor. Here, unlike the rest of the Latin Mediterranean, raids were launched with the specific aim of taking Muslim prisoners. Wealthy or prestigious individuals could often fetch considerable ransoms. To this end, members of the aristocracy were naturally prized, as were men of religion – in 1177 two jurists fetched the hefty price of 60,000 *danānīr* plus a number of Frankish captives. But even large numbers of common prisoners could be used as bargaining chips: either to be exchanged, incorporated into treaty negotiations, or – as with Richard the Lion-Heart's 3,000 Muslim prisoners at Acre – slaughtered for effect. Women were captured for use as domestics, prostitutes, and in the cloth industry, and children who were taken were brought up as Christians. Italian merchants shipped Muslim captives westwards, although as supplies dwindled in the thirteenth century, more and more of the "Muslims" they sold were in reality unfortunate eastern or Balkan Christians. But here, slaves were also needed for labor, whether it was the skilled craftsmen who were used to rebuild the castle at Safed (Ṣafad) when the town was regained by the Latins by a treaty of 1240, or simply for building and repairing the walls and moats that the security of so many towns and cities depended on.[93] The twelfth century was a time of intense and regular seismic activity in the Levant, and an earthquake could easily breach or bring down walls that had kept a settlement secure for centuries. For example, the Persian poet Musharrif b. Muṣliḥ al-Saʾdī recalled how he had been forced to work digging a moat at Tripoli until he was recognized by a wealthy Aleppan traveler, who ransomed him, took him home, and had him marry his daughter (although al-Saʿdī observed wryly to his father-in-law that, with the

[92] For examples, see Y. Lev, "Prisoners of War."

[93] In the event, the Templars saw fit to massacre the thousand or so workers they had at Safed, when the latter, trusting in their greater numbers, plotted revolt. Ibn al-Furāt, "History of the Dynasties and Kingdoms" in U. Lyons, *Ayyubids, Mamlukes and Crusaders*, pp. 88–89.

marriage, he had merely been delivered from one form of unpleasant bondage to another).[94]

Ransoming captives is considered a form of alms in Islam, and high-status foreign Muslims like Usāma acted as both rescuers and intermediaries for foreign benefactors. Local Muslim communities undoubtedly provided shelter for and abetted escaping slaves, as Usāma reported those around Acre did, and some captives managed to negotiate their own release, even obtaining permission to return to Muslim lands to raise their ransoms. Otherwise, conversion and marriage were often the only possibilities for manumission, and not surprisingly both were sometimes undertaken with false pretenses. Tales of murderously vengeful false converts abound in both the Latin and Arabic sources. Perhaps because of this few converts here rose to high station. It was a remarkable rarity when a convert and favorite of Baldwin I attained a rank and influence almost equal to that of royal chamberlain; but he had to be hanged when it was discovered he was plotting to murder the king.[95]

Conversion – genuine, permanent, or both – certainly did take place, as reflected in the references to *batiés* ("baptized" converts) in the legal literature of the post-1187 period, but it was not widespread. The mixed marriages between Muslims and Christians to which Fulcher of Chartres cheerily refers in his evocation of the new Latin "Orientals" undoubtedly involved Muslim women for whom speedy conversion was an only opportunity to mitigate what would otherwise have been a life of sexual slavery. The mysterious *turcopole* auxiliaries – the Latins' own squadrons of Saljūq-style light, mounted archers – may have also included converts. Part of the problem here, of course, was that it was Latinity, rather than Christianity, that conferred full social and legal status on individuals. Therefore, for conversion to be worthwhile from a pragmatic sense, it would require not only a rejection of one's religion and community, but the successful adaptation of a new set of linguistic and cultural mores, and acceptance by the narrow and closed community of the colonial class.[96] This was a transition few would be in a

[94] A. J. Arberry, *Kings and Beggars*, p. 32. It should be noted that Christians were also pressed into labor repairing and building fortifications. The chronicler Michael the Syrian claimed that Renaud de Marash effectively enslaved the Christians whom he put to work on the castle of Cesson. See J. Richard, "Frankish Power," p. 181.

[95] William of Tyre, *A History of Deeds*, vol. I, pp. 487–89.

[96] The Crusader and chronicler, Raymond d'Arguillers, clearly sees Franks as a race apart (*gens*). Hence, he alludes to the plan of the "King of Babylon [to] ... mate the young Frankish males with women of his race and the Frankish women with young males of his land and there by breed a warrior race from Frankish stock." Y. Friedman, *Encounter between Enemies*, p. 228.

position to make – the challenges and tensions involved would have been tremendous. Usāma, for example, told of a relapsed Muslim he met in Nablus, whose mother had converted and married a Christian. At some point she killed her husband, and thereafter she and her son set traps for Latin pilgrims and lured them to their deaths. Once apprehended, the young man was evidently judged as a Latin and submitted to the ordeal of water. Having failed this, he had his eyes put out. Thereafter, he returned to Islam and, through Usāma's mediation, was sent to Damascus and assigned a pension.[97]

Clearly, there was a certain amount of acculturation among Christians and Muslims in the Latin principalities, both at a quotidian and a learned level.[98] Evidently, some Latins affected Arabo-Islamic styles of dress and cooking, some of the accouterments of Levantine urban life (such as bathing and depiling), and enjoyed some of its diversions, such as the singing, music, and dancing.[99] Some Arabic was undoubtedly spoken or understood by significant numbers of people of virtually all social strata, whether used to bark commands at slaves and *villani*, negotiate in the market or on the battlefield, or debate the finer points of theology or philosophy. Periods of captivity would have provided ample if uncomfortable opportunities to learn. However, here the current seems to have been almost entirely one way. It can be assumed that most urban-dwelling Muslims had a facility with Latin or some sort of Romance vernacular, but there is no evidence that Frankish culture, whether in substance or appearance, held any allure for them. Legends, such as that of Salāḥ al-Dīn's dubbing or of Bohemond's rescue from Danishmend captivity by Melaz, a Saracen Ariadne, reflect Frankish anxiety at how frustratingly little Muslims were drawn to Latin culture in reality. For despite their subjugated and marginalized status, the Muslims of Jerusalem and Antioch were hardly an isolated minority; they continued to live on the fringe of a vibrant and dynamic Islamic world and in a local environment in which the majority of Christians – the *Suriani* – were also Arabized and "Oriental." In any event, for most of them, the Frankish historical episode would last less than a century.

## The long dusk of the Latin Rule

You took possession of Paradises, palace by palace, when you conquered Syria fortress by fortress.

97 Ibn Munqidh, *The Book of Contemplation*, p. 152. 98 See above, p. 142.
99 See, for example, Ibn Munqidh, *The Book of Contemplation*, pp. 149–50.

Indeed, the religion of Islam has spread its blessings over created beings. (Ibn Sana' al-Mulk, ode to Salāḥ al-Dīn (*c.* 1187)[100])

On July 4, 1187 Salāḥ al-Dīn's troops wiped out almost the entire military force of the Latin kingdom at the Battle of the Horns of Hattin (Ḥaṭṭīn). The True Cross was lost, the king, Guy de Lusignan (1186–1192/94), was taken prisoner, and the captured Templars and Hospitalers were systematically exterminated. The towns and fortresses of the kingdom were left almost without garrisons. Within three months, the Holy City would be re-conquered, and the entire kingdom of Jerusalem, except for the enclave of Tyre and Guy's siege-camp outside Acre, would be back under Muslim control. In the north, only Antioch and the great fortresses of the Hospitalers and Templars – Marqab, Crac des Chevaliers (Ḥiṣn al-Akrād), Chastel Blanc (at Ṣāfītā), and Tortosa (Ṭarṭūs) resisted. In 1191, thanks to the efforts of Richard the Lion-Heart and Philip Augustus of France, Acre would be re-established as a Christian city. In 1229 Frederick II's "conquest" and short-lived "rule" over Jerusalem and a narrow corridor to the sea was established by virtue of his treaty with Malik al-Ṣāliḥ 'Imād al-Dīn of Damascus (1225–1231?), but the new King was so beloved by his Latin subjects that local butchers apparently showered him with entrails and offal as he boarded ship in Acre. Jerusalem would remain nominally Christian until 1244, Antioch would fall in 1269, Chastel Blanc in 1271, Crac and Marqab in 1281 and 1285 respectively, Tyre in 1291, and Arwād, the island 3km off of Tortosa, in 1302/3. In other words, with the exception of a few scattered enclaves under the Military Orders and the Lusignan kings, Frankish rule over the Holy Land and its people had come to an end in 1187. On the one hand, Salāḥ al-Dīn had built on Nūr al-Dīn's propaganda of *jihād* to reconfigure Jerusalem as the focal point of the struggle against Unbelief, and on the other, the Crusaders' own priorities had realigned to match their commercial interests, and they now looked to Byzantium, Egypt and the Maghrib. In the Shām itself, the political and ideological environment became increasingly charged. The idea of civilizational conflict which al-Sulamī had preached to deaf ears in Damascus in 1107 resonated ever more in the mid thirteenth century, when the Franks and indigenous Christians conspired with the Mongols – the fearsome "un-eyelashed Tatars" – to eradicate Islam. The Mamlukes of Egypt became not only the heroes of 'Ayn Jalūṭ, where they stopped the Mongols, but of Fāriskūr, in Egypt, where they destroyed the army of the Seventh Crusade and captured St. Louis.

100 C. Hillenbrand, *The Crusades: Islamic Perspectives*, p. 179.

Post-Hattin, few Muslims remained under Latin rule in the Levant, aside from captives and slaves, and those who chose to would have done so for the same reasons as their predecessors in the twelfth century: economic opportunity and reluctance to leave their homes. Undoubtedly, for these, like the ancestors of the Muslims of Tyre whom Ibn Jubayr interviewed, "love of native land ... impelled them to live amongst the infidels ..."[101] And some lived quite well, indeed. Muslim farmers in the environs of Acre must have throve supplying the isolated Crusader enclave, and the presence of well-to-do Muslims is attested to in thirteenth-century Antioch.[102] There were even, it seems, some living on Cyprus – the island that had been conquered from the Greeks by Richard the Lion-Heart, and had become the Kingdom of Jerusalem's "mainland" – although they were so few in number that they could hardly be qualified as a community.[103]

In sum, the experience of Muslims under Latin rule in the Crusader principalities and the approach taken by Western Christians to Islam in the Bilād al-Shām, is consistent with contemporary developments in Iberia and southern Italy, although there were important differences. Chief among these was the near-catastrophic character of the conquest: far more sudden, brutal, and disruptive than those to the West. The explicitly religious motivations and rhetoric of the conquerors and their unfamiliarity with the urbane and diverse environment of the Islamic Near East intensified this, as did their sense of being a people apart. For the Franks it was not merely religious affiliation that marked them as distinct from the indigenous, it was their identity as *Latini*. Once the Crusaders had established themselves in this environment, they took the same essentially *laissez-faire* approach to their Muslim subjects as Christians did in Iberia and Italy. In contrast, the insecurity and vulnerability of the Latin states here encouraged a much more polarizing view of religious identity, particularly as a consequence of warfare and raiding, but on the other hand, the mutual dependency, both economic and political, of Christian and Muslim powers, and the relative equality of power, led to the development of accommodations and compromises – not least the periods of Latin–Muslim condominium – that had little parallel elsewhere. Likewise, the heightening of religious sensibility that arose because of the Scriptural associations of the contested territories was counterbalanced to some degree by the compromises and empathies that derived from recognizing and sharing the same sacred geography. The most notable difference, however, is that here the history of the Muslim

[101] Ibn Jubayr, *Travels*, p. 321. [102] See above, p. 152.
[103] M. Nader, "Urban Muslims," pp. 265–66.

subjugation to Latin Christendom was truncated in the last quarter of the twelfth century, and it ended not with the expulsion of the Muslim minority but with the expulsion of the Christian "majority." Indeed, it was only in the Iberian Peninsula that Muslim communities proved capable of achieving a stable transition to Latin Christian domination into the fourteenth century.

# 5 Diversity in an age of crises

## The Christian Spains III (*c.* 1350–1526)

I ought then to visit Spain
for there some secrets to explain;
And through Aragon will I fare
and I will find great Muslims there.
There I will be well-maintained,
the festive welcome unrestrained.
Then I will visit the noble King
of powerful Granada, this I think . . .
(the "Sarrazin" in Honoré Bonet, *Apparicion de Mestre Jehan de Meun* (1389)[1])

By the mid fourteenth century the Iberian Peninsula represented an anomaly – it was the only region of Latin Christendom in which there remained substantial communities of Muslim subjects. The areas ruled by Castile, the mainland principalities of the Crown of Aragon, and the kingdoms of Navarre and Portugal all had considerable free Islamic populations. As will be seen in this chapter, on the one hand, the size and circumstances of these communities varied considerably from place to place, while on the other, certain general trends can be observed. By no coincidence, the peninsula was also the region with the greatest and most integrated Jewish minority of the Latin West, a situation recognized by contemporaries both at home and abroad as being related. Some of the anxieties provoked by the Muslim presence within the larger Latin world can be seen in the French cleric Honoret Bovet's *Apparicion*, a series of imaginary dialogues between the literary sensation, Jean de Meun (author of the *Roman de la Rose*), and three "outsiders": a physician, a Jew, and a Muslim. Here, the "Sarrazin" – dark-skinned, potent, and cultured – is an envoy sent by the Ottoman court across Europe, and whose ultimate mission is to plot against Christendom with the Muslim King of Granada. In the course of his journey he looks forward to passing through the lands of Aragon, home to a wealthy and confident Muslim community, living openly in their religion.[2]

[1] "The Specter of Master Jean de Meun," in Honoré Bonet, *Medieval Muslims*, p. 82 (author's translation).

[2] The notion in France of an Islamic conspiracy against Christendom involving Granada and Eastern Mediterranean powers goes back to 1321, when the well-poisoning that first

Viewed in general terms, by the early fourteenth century the *mudéjares* of the peninsula had apparently arrived at a situation of stable equilibrium vis-à-vis the Christian-dominated societies in which they lived. They had developed functioning administrative institutions, enjoyed a clearly defined and legitimate legal status with broad rights and privileges, had maintained their religious and personal liberties and cultural identity, and were engaged in a wide array of bilateral relationships with Christian corporations and institutions. They were not subject to systematic repression or violence, either official or popular, and seemed to exhibit a general confidence and satisfaction in their position. The mid fourteenth century, however, would precipitate a series of crises that transformed the Islamic and Christian worlds and undermined the environment that had sustained the diversity of the Iberian Peninsula. Most dramatic was the Black Death, which struck the Mediterranean lands with particular virulence. Upheaval both preceded the plague and would follow, in the form of warfare and rebellion, economic contraction and uncertainty, commercial realignments, millenary popular movements, and the emergence of charismatic Christianity.

In 1391 a wave of religious violence swept the peninsula. This was aimed at Jews, but in the decades that followed, in some areas anti-Islamic sentiments germinated and took root, even alongside a persistent Islamophilia. Although not targeted in 1391, *mudéjares* would have been concerned by the pogrom, and the days that followed were marked by occasional attacks on *morerías*.[3] With the rise of the Ottomans, the threat of attack from Granada and the Maghrib, and the economic marginalization of the *mudéjares*, Muslim and Christian communities disengaged – and relations became increasingly politicized. The surrender of the kingdom of Granada in 1492 brought a whole new population of Muslims under Christian rule, but the revolts that followed made of this a short-lived experiment. In 1499 the kingdom's population was ordered to convert to Christianity, to be followed by that of Castile in 1502. By this time Portugal, under Manuel I (1495–1521), had apparently already expelled its Muslim subjects. Spain – the accidental creation of dynastic caprice – would rid itself of the last of its *mudéjares* in 1526, in an act of mandatory conversion under the guise of an order of expulsion.

From the late fourteenth century, sources for the study of *mudéjares* throughout the peninsula increase dramatically in both quantity and variety, thanks largely to the development of bureaucratic regimes and commercial practices together with the increasing availability of paper, as well as the

lepers, and subsequently, Jews, were accused of, was said to have been carried out at the behest of "the King of Granada and the Sultan of Babylon" (i.e. the Mamluke Sultan of Egypt). See M. Barber, "Lepers, Jews and Muslims," p. 8.

[3] J. E. López Coca de Castaner, "Los mudéjares valencianos," p. 650.

increasing integration in and subjugation of Muslims to Christian institutions and jurisdictions, and the formalization of both Christian and *mudéjar* administration. That said, most of the surviving archival documentation prior to the fifteenth century relates to the Crown of Aragon. There is abundant information for the late fifteenth-century kingdom of Granada, thanks to the detailed *libros de repartimiento* and other royal and ecclesiastical records relating to its conquest. Concurrently, intensifying socio-cultural interaction led Muslims to play a somewhat more visible role in Christian chronicles, literature, and art. Economic integration spurred *mudéjar* craft and artistic production aimed at Christian markets, and thus a greater quantity of material evidence survives.

Nevertheless, from the historical perspective, the Islamic minority remains almost entirely mute. *Mudéjar* voices emerge only occasionally in Christian records, such as contracts, petitions, and trial transcripts, as well as in the smattering of Arabic-language texts – mostly religious in nature – that have been preserved and recovered only by chance. Beginning in the fifteenth century, a new indigenous Islamic literature appeared, *aljamiado*, in which Muslim and convert authors translated and composed in Romance using Arabic script or Latin characters, and which included legal, religious, and scholarly works, as well as literature and poetry. Even with this, however, *mudéjar* experience can only be apprehended almost exclusively through "Christian" sources.[4]

[4] There is an immense bibliography of studies on *mudéjares* in the fourteenth and fifteenth centuries. Overviews can be found in R. I. Burns, "Mudéjar Parallel Societies," and D. Nirenberg, "The Current State," as well as the various "state of the question" articles in the *Actas* of the *Simposios Internacionales de Mudejarismo*. Published bibliographies include M. de Epalza Ferre and L. Bernabé Pons, "Bibliografía de mudéjares y moriscos, I," "Bibliografía de mudéjares y moriscos, II," and "Bibliografía de mudéjares y moriscos, III"; A. Reyes Pacios Lozano, "Bibliografía de arte mudéjar. Addenda (1992–1995)," and "Bibliografía de arte mudéjar. Addenda (1995–1996)." There are scores of studies on local *mudéjar* communities; some important monographs and major articles include: M. B. Basáñez Villaluenga, *La aljama sarracena*; J. Boswell, *The Royal Treasure*; Á. Conte Cazcarro, *La aljama de moros de Huesca*; A. Collantes de Terán Sánchez, "La aljama mudéjar de Sevilla"; A. Echevarría Arsuaga, *Biografías mudéjares*, and "Las aljamas mudéjares"; M. Febrer Romaguera, *Les aljames mudèjars*; M. T. Ferrer i Mallol, "L'aljama islàmica de Tortosa," *Els sarraïns de la corona catalano-aragonesa*, *La frontera amb l'Islam*, "La moreria de Xàtiva," *Organització i defensa*, and *Les aljames sarraïnes*; Á. Galan Sánchez, *Los mudéjares del reino de Granada*; M. García-Arenal, *La aljama de los moros*; B. Leroy, *Moros y judíos*; F. García Marco, *Comunidades mudéjares*; M. Gómez Renau, "La aljama de Valladolid"; J. Hinojosa y Montalvo, *La morería de Elche*, and *Los mudéjares*; M. A. Ladero Quesada, *Los mudéjares de Castilla*; M. L. Ledesma Rubio, *Los mudéjares de Aragon*, and *Estudios sobre los mudéjares*; M. F. Lopes de Barros, "Las elites mudéjares," *Tempos e espaços*, and *A comuna*; C. López Martínez, *Mudéjares y moriscos sevillanos*; F. Macho y Ortega, "Condición social"; E. Marín Padilla, "Los moros de Calatorao (I)," and "Los moros de Calatorao (II)"; M. Meyerson, *The Muslims of Valencia*; J. C. de Miguel Rodríguez, *La comunidad mudéjar*; Á. L. Molina Molina and M. del C. Veas Arteseros, "Situación de los mudéjares en el Reino

## The bad fourteenth century

We have mentioned that the Christian King Alfonso had taken possession of Algeciras, in the year 743 [1344] and, that having achieved great power, died of the Plague, in the year 751 [1350], outside the walls of Gibraltar, the fortress to which he had laid siege. God thus rid the Muslims of a relentless enemy. (Walī al-Dīn ʿAbd al-Raḥmān b. Khaldūn, *Kitāb al-ʿibar* (after 1375)[5])

For contemporaries, one of the most disconcerting aspects of the Black Death, the series of plague outbreaks that swept across the Islamic world and Christendom beginning in 1348, was not only its terrifyingly high mortality rate, but the fact that it showed no regard to its victims' social status or vocation. Peasants, prelates, merchants, and royalty were equally vulnerable. Transported primarily by ship, the plague struck the Mediterranean islands and coasts hardest. In Mallorca the mortality in some settlements may have reached 90 percent; estimates put the peninsula's death rate at about 30 percent. At Gibraltar, the microscopic bacillus *yersina pestis* achieved what the Muslim defenders had been incapable of – killing Alfonso XI of Castile and lifting the year-long siege that had encircled the strategic stronghold.[6] Joan of England, fiancée of Alfonso's son, Pedro, had earlier been struck down en route to Castile. In Valencia, the burghers, afraid of becoming circumstantial regicides, freed their King, Pere II (Pere III in Barcelona, Pedro IV of Aragon; 1336–87), who had been suffering public humiliation as their captive during the uprising of the *Unions*. He would lose his wife, Elionor of Portugal, to the epidemic, but would live on to take exemplary revenge on the rebels. Throughout the peninsula, the plague wiped out families, neighborhoods, and villages, shattering communities, spreading terror, and forcing a series of economic reconfigurations and commercial reorientations.[7]

Already, by the third decade of the fourteenth century, the tremendous growth and dynamism of the previous hundred years was clearly faltering across the Latin West, and Iberia was no exception. Failed harvests in the first decades provoked famine, and royal authority was challenged by popular and noble uprisings. In the 1320s the *Pastoureaux* (the "Shepherds'

de Murcia"; D. Menjot, "Les mudéjares du Royaume de Murcie"; M. Monjo i Gallego, *Sarraïns sota el domini feudal*; J. Mutgé i Vives, *L'aljama sarraïna*; I. O'Connor, *A Forgotten Community*; M. Romero Sáiz, *Mudéjares y Moriscos*; and F. Soyer, *The Persecution*.

5 "The Book of *Exempla*," known as the "Universal History," adapted from Ibn Khaldūn, *Histoire des Berbères*, vol. IV, pp. 378–79.

6 The precise nature of the plague and the identity of the pathogen has been the subject of considerable debate. The latest research supports the case for *y. pestis*; see S. Haensch, *et al.*, "Distinct Clones."

7 For the general history of the Iberian Peninsula in the fourteenth and fifteenth centuries, see J. O'Callaghan, *History of Medieval Spain*, and J. N. Hillgarth, *The Spanish Kingdoms*.

Crusade") attacked the Jewish communities of the Pyrenees, and beginning in 1347 the *Unions*, in which municipalities and magnates rose up in the Crown of Aragon under the leadership of Pere III's half-brothers, nearly brought down the House of Barcelona.[8] Although the Banū Marīn had been effectively neutralized at 1340's Battle of Salado, and the Naṣrid Kingdom of Granada had become a tributary of Castile, tensions among the Christian dynasties of the peninsula were running high, aggravated by economic and territorial competition, a series of failed political marriages, the propagation of illegitimate children who fomented rebellion as pretenders, and the choleric personalities of rulers. Southern Valencia and Murcia were the focus of Aragonese–Castilian tensions, sparking the "War of the Two Peters" – between Pere the Ceremonious of Aragon and Pedro the Cruel of Castile, supported by Genoa and Granada – in 1356. The war, which was bitterly fought for the most part on Aragonese and Valencian territory, would last until 1369, when Pedro was killed and the Castilian–Leonese throne seized by his half-brother, Enrique de Trastámara, who was supported by Aragon, France, and the mercenary "White Companies." In the following years, Enrique entrenched his new dynasty through marriage alliances with Portugal, Aragon, and Navarre (under the rule of French dynasties since 1322). Meanwhile Portugal, aided by England, fought a series of wars against Castile until the victory of João I (1385–1433) at the Battle of Aljubarrota (1385). This, along with this King's impressive longevity, established the continuing independence of Portugal under the Aviz dynasty.[9]

### *Crisis and aftermath*

These political upheavals reflected larger social and institutional tensions. The move to end the Avignonese papacy sparked the Great Western Schism, when a vacillating conclave attempted to dethrone Urban VI (1378–99) by electing Robert of Geneva as "Clement VII" in 1378. The split, which divided the loyalties of the dynasties of Latin Europe, would not be resolved until the deposition of the anti-Pope "Benedict XIII" (the Aragonese cardinal Pedro Martínez de Luna, known commonly as "Papa Luna") and the election of Martin V (1417–31) by the Council of

8 For the Crown of Aragon, see also T. Bisson, *The Medieval Crown*, and for the *pastoureaux*, M. Barber, "The Pastoureaux," and J. Riera i Sans, *Fam i fe*. Despite the supposed role of Muslims in the poisoning plot that served as a rationale for the Shepherds' Crusade (see above, p. 163, n. 2), Muslim communities in the Crown of Aragon were not targeted, even those of towns the Jewish communities of which were attacked (cf. M. Barber, "Lepers, Jews and Muslims," p. 12).

9 For the "War of the Two Peters," see M. T. Ferrer i Mallol, "La frontera meridional."

Constance. This crisis only served to intensify widespread dissatisfaction with the Church, which was seen in many quarters as corrupt and having lost God's favor (not the least because of the manifest success of Islam). The rational optimism of the thirteenth century gave way increasingly to new modes of piety: introspective, ascetic, mystical, which found voice among charismatic popular preachers – notably Vicent Ferrer – and in the Franciscan Observant movement, as well as in more revolutionary-minded heretical groups. Within the Church, the ideal of a universal Catholic dominion continued to develop, as Canon Lawyers and theologians elaborated ever more restricting notions of what qualified as orthodox and the degree to which existence of non-Christians should be suffered. In the meanwhile, the scholastic tradition slowly mutated into Humanism, a literary-intellectual movement that prompted, *inter alia*, a reconsideration of the nature of sovereignty and citizenship and the relation of Man and Law; this, and the reaction against Humanism by pietists were matters of no small relevance to the religious minorities of late medieval Iberia.[10] Symptomatic of these various trends was the increasing persecution of Jews both through policies of isolation and expulsion in northern Europe, and in popular acts of violence, typically rationalized on the basis of alleged crimes, including host desecration, ritual murder, well-poisoning, and plague-spreading.[11]

The economic distress caused by these decades of plague and warfare can hardly be understated. Demand for foodstuffs dropped, but so did production, as a consequence of labor shortages. And while the market for certain manufactured goods declined, whole craft industries were wiped out or crippled. The demographic decline sparked inflation, traditionally seen as to the advantage of the peasants who had converted their terms of tribute to fixed cash payments, and to the detriment of the landed aristocracy whose rent-values plummeted and who were now at the mercy of a mobile peasantry and a hostile labor market. On the contrary, however, in the end it was the seigniorial regime that emerged more strongly entrenched as a consequence of the crisis. Across the Latin West, attempts by authorities to limit earnings and movement provoked peasant uprisings, such as the Jacquerie (1358) and the Peasants' Revolt (1381), but these were put down with unflinching brutality. Such uprisings did not occur in the peninsula, although the measures taken by Pedro the Cruel

[10] For the pietist view, see the statements by Francesc Eiximenis regarding the "Muslim danger" in his *Regiment de la cosa pública* ("The Administration of the Republic"), excerpted in J. Hinojosa y Montalvo, "Cristianos contra musulmanes," p. 352.

[11] For the increasing rigidity and exclusionary attitude among Latin Christian clergy and legists, see, for example, R. I. Moore, *The Formation of a Persecuting Society*, and D. Iogna-Pratt, *Order and Exclusion*.

and Pere III were, in fact, more stringent than those enacted in France and England and came within a year of the plague's arrival. Indolence was forbidden, mobility restricted, and prices, wages, and terms of employment were fixed, not only for agricultural and low-status urban works, but also for artisans, professionals, and men-at-arms.

In Iberia, it was the restive and eternally feuding nobility that most destabilized society and challenged the rule of law. The common people could only resist indirectly; the wave of anti-Jewish violence that swept across the Iberian Peninsula in 1391 was as much an attack on royal authority as an expression of religious hysteria or socio-economic malaise. Perhaps the most far-reaching consequence of these crises, however, was the aggravation of the divergence between the Crown of Aragon and Castile. The institutionally compartmentalized Crown of Aragon was increasingly locked into a contracting and competitive Mediterranean, vying against Italian trading states, such as Genoa, and establishing partnerships with the Banū Marīn, Granada, and the Mamlukes. Meanwhile, a nimbler, authoritarian Castile had become engaged in the new cloth industry, providing lucrative low-labor raw material in the form of wool to the now-booming textile sector of northern Europe, and had oriented its own maritime expansion towards Africa and the Atlantic.

By the mid 1390s the political situation in the Iberian Peninsula had begun to stabilize, or so it seemed. Under Pere III's successors, Joan I (1387–96) and his brother Martí (1396–1410), the Crown of Aragon continued to expand into the central Mediterranean, asserting its power over Sardinia and taking control over Sicily, although noble and urban factions in the kingdom of Valencia continued to spar. In Castile, the Trastámaras consolidated their position. Juan I (1379–90) died prematurely, but his young successor, Enrique III (1390–1406), proved a tenacious ruler, who not only tamed the nobility but determined to bring to heel an increasingly bold and independent Granada. His heir Juan II (1406–54) came to the throne an infant, a circumstance that sparked a struggle between the two regents, the dowager Catalina (Catherine) of Lancaster, and Juan's uncle, the *infante* Fernando. They soon reached an accommodation, splitting the kingdom, thereby allowing Fernando to continue the war against Granada. In 1410 he scored a major victory when the garrison of Muslim Antequera (Madīnat Antiqīra) surrendered. His greatest achievement, however, came with his election in 1412 as King of the Crown of Aragon as a consequence of "the Compromise of Caspe." Here, a jury of nine representatives of various estates of the main realms of the Catalan–Aragonese confederacy, including the charismatic Dominican preacher and missionary, Vicent Ferrer, had been charged with selecting a successor to King Martí, who had died without a legitimate heir. With their decision, Fernando de Antequera became "Ferran I" (1412–16), and the Crown of Aragon, like Castile, came under Trastámara rule. Navarre would follow in 1425. The rise of the Trastámaras paved the way for the eventual establishment of the Kingdom of Spain under the Hapsburgs, and the formal demise of the Muslim minority, each only a century away.

## *Mudéjares* and the "War of the Two Peters"

We, Pere, etc., desiring to provide a means by which our locale of Asp, situated within the Kingdom of Valencia, in which many Muslims used to live, and which was greatly depopulated as a result of the war with Castile, may be repopulated quickly, at the request of you, the *alaminus*, the elders, and the *aljama* of the said locale ... grant full license in perpetuity that you may, legally, without fear of incurring any penalty, call the *çala* [ʾ*adhān*], and pray openly within the mosque of the said locale, at the sound of the trumpet or the *nafil*, just like the Muslims of the city of Valencia and Xátiva ... (Pere the Ceremonious, King of Aragon, letter to the Muslims of Asp (November 25, 1366)[12])

The situation of the *mudéjares* of the Crown of Aragon during the "War of the Two Peters" provides an illustration of the dangers and opportunities presented to Muslims as a consequence of the turmoil of the fourteenth century. Pedro the Cruel launched a series of campaigns into Pere's domains, each of which saw significant territories in Valencia and Aragon fall temporarily under Castilian control. In 1357 Pedro took control of the area around Tarazona, the following year raids took place on the Murcian frontier, and in 1359 a Castilian and Portuguese fleet raided the Valencian coast and reached Ibiza, dropping troops at Alacant as it withdrew. In 1360 Castilian and Granadan cavalry invaded southern Valencia; where territory could not be held, crops were destroyed and prisoners taken. Meanwhile Pere struggled desperately to raise the money necessary to defend his lands. In the Aragonese interior, things were hardly more stable, as the mercenary White Companies, brought in in support of Enrique Trastámara's play for the throne of Castile, proved scarcely less dangerous and destabilizing than the enemy, both for their general unruliness and their attacks on local Jewish communities.[13]

After a brief peace, fighting resumed in 1362 as Castile, Portugal, Granada, and Navarre attacked the Crown of Aragon, seizing much of the upper Jalón valley, home to many *mudéjares*. In southern Valencia, the

[12] J. Boswell, *The Royal Treasure*, p. 474; translation by author.

[13] See *ibid.*, pp. 372–400; M. T. Ferrer i Mallol, *La frontera amb l'Islam*, and "La frontera meridional."

embattled Muslim inhabitants of Elx and Crevillent begged Pere's Queen, Elionor de Sicilia, for protection and support, which she promised – in exchange for hostages. But little help was actually forthcoming, and the townsmen of the frontier either resisted as they could or surrendered to Castile. As more of the *mudéjar* heartland of Aragon fell, Pere used his local Muslim officials in the kingdom of Valencia to make contact with anti-Castilian elements in Granada; at one point the self-aggrandizing *alaminus* of Xelva promised to deliver the Aragonese King a force of one thousand cavalry, but this came to nothing. Finally, by early 1363 almost all of the kingdom of Valencia, as well as Teruel in southern Aragon, had fallen to the enemy. Caught between Pere's incapacity and Pedro's proverbial cruelty, and fired by long-standing discontents, many locales in Valencia went over to Castile. Over the next three years, the *chevauchées* and raiding continued, as Castilian knights, Murcian irregulars, and Granadan mercenaries, aiming at crippling the kingdom, destroyed crops and carried off both property and prisoners. But by 1368 those tempted to side with the Castilian King had found his violent and unpredictable rule to be even less palatable than that of their own monarch, and they began to resist the occupation, and rebel. Finally, on March 23, 1369 Pedro was stabbed to death under a flag of truce by his half-brother, Enrique, thus bringing "the War of the Two Peters" to an end. Over the next two years, the frontier between Castile and the Crown of Aragon returned to the *status ante quem*, although the Trastamaran King was loathe to give up the territories in northern Murcia and southern Valencia taken by Pedro the Cruel, and sparring and raiding continued here through 1371.

### Mudéjares *at war*

In the wars of the late thirteenth century *aljamas* across Aragon had sent detachments to aid the defense of the realm, and Valencian-Muslim crossbowmen were feared and respected by the French Crusaders who invaded the Crown. In the fourteenth century *mudéjares* also played a military role, all the more so because the fighting was taking place in their own lands. *Mudéjares* joined royalist forces during the *Uniones*, although it may well be they also joined the rebels in some locales, whether out of obligation or preference. Muslims were required to contribute to civil defense, such as the upkeep of walls, and were used (occasionally alongside Jews) to garrison loyalist fortresses both in Aragon and Valencia. Further, an important component of royal taxation consisted of the *exercitum* – the right for the king to demand military service from local Christian, Muslim, and Jewish communities. Generally a cash payment in proxy was preferred, but Muslim communities certainly raised militias consisting both of foot soldiers and cavalry in the service of the king. By 1366 the *aljama* of Xàtiva had its own regiment, distinct from that of the local Christians. Occasionally, individual *mudéjares* were singled out for meritorious conduct, or rewarded with tax privileges or other benefits, and there were a number who were either professional soldiers or known primarily for their military vocation. As in the previous century, there is no indication that the monarchy considered its Muslim subjects any less loyal than Christians, and *mudéjares*, for their part, would have certainly appreciated the benefits, both as individuals and as a community, of participating in the kingdom's defense.

On the other hand, in Valencia, *mudéjares* (like Christians) at times went over to the enemy, as when *mudéjares* – in support of a local rebel, Rodrigo de Ganga – killed the castellan of Elda and brought his head and those of his murdered garrison as a token of submission to Pedro the Cruel.[14] A betrayal such as this must be seen in the context of an increasingly polarized Valencia – an environment in which both Christians and Muslims had for centuries exploited the political rivalries of princes by shifting allegiances for their own benefit. In occupied lands, Castilians also pressed local *mudéjares* into military service. As it was, over the last century Muslims had been increasingly displaced and mistreated by Christian townspeople, who maintained vivid folk memories of the Muslim rebellions of the 1270s. While economic opportunity was sufficient cause for the progressive marginalization of *mudéjares* here, particularly in rural environments, the fact that Pedro the Cruel made use of Granadan cavalry in large numbers, and gave these a free hand to carry off Christian captives, only fueled sectarian fear and animosity. In fact, Granadan raiding on the frontier had been constant through the 1300s, but after the war clerical and burgher factions who shared an increasingly anti-Muslim agenda cultivated a popular fear of *mudéjares* as an Islamic "fifth column." Whereas this was clearly not the case generally, such accusations were lent credence by the occasional complicity of Valencian Muslims in Granadan raiding and Moroccan spying, particularly in the early part of the century.[15] It would not be until the late 1400s that *mudéjares* here began to send pleas for military support to foreign Muslim powers.

[14] M. T. Ferrer i Mallol, "La tinença," p. 23.

[15] J. E. López Coca de Castaner, "Los mudéjares valencianos," p. 665. In 1332 "Abadal" confessed under torture that he was a Christian of Museros (Valencia) who had traveled to Sijilmasa and Granada, having converted to Islam, and returned to Valencia as a spy (ACA, C., Processos en Quart, 1332). Such fears would increase in the following centuries with the Ottoman expansion and the coastal raiding carried out by the "Barbary corsairs" they sponsored. See, generally, A. Díaz Borrás, *El miedo al mediterráneo*.

### *The situation in Valencia*

In fact, the *aljamas* of Valencia had been losing population in the decades prior to the war, thanks to Aragonese treaties with Granada – commercial agreements the Naṣrids used incidentally to position themselves as the legitimate sovereigns of all Iberian Muslims, countering the claims of their North African rivals. In the 1380s, the *aljama* of Zaragoza would establish independent diplomatic relations with Granada. As a consequence of diplomatic pressure, the kings of Aragon were not only obliged to allow *mudéjares* to travel and trade with Granada, but to emigrate.[16] The many who did leave would have come from the most prosperous of the farmers and from the artisans and traders who made up the "urban middle-classes" – those who had the means and initiative to undertake emigration. Others left "illegally," escaping under cover of Granadan raiders. In 1331 and 1333 the apostate Christian freedman and *ḥājib* of the kingdom of Granada, Riḍwān, led two major invasions of Valencia, the first against Guardamar, and the second besieging Elx.[17] Not only were many Christians captured and much booty taken, but many Valencian Muslims – embittered by the heavy subventions they had been forced to pay to support the Crown's invasion of Sardinia of 1323 – left the kingdom. Once hostilities cooled, however, a significant number of these were evidently disappointed by life in Granada and asked for, and received permission from Alfons III of Aragon to return to their former homes.[18]

As a result of all this, *mudéjar* society here became progressively more hollow – made up increasingly of a small privileged elite and a large rural underclass. Pushed out of the best lands by Christian encroachment, and with the irrigation systems that provided a framework for rural Muslim society abandoned or transformed, the coherence of *mudéjar* peasant society in the kingdom was eroded, contributing further to alienation, vulnerability, and impoverishment. On the other hand, some larger towns like Xàtiva maintained diverse and substantial populations and remained centers of trade, craft, and industry – notably paper-making and ceramics.

Following the War of the Two Peters, the Aragonese monarchy's goal was to re-establish the economic viability of the region. As a result, generous tax reductions were given to Muslim communities, as well as assurances of protection from Christian abuse and encroachment, and

[16] For Naṣrid advocacy of *mudéjar* rights, see J. E. López Coca de Castaner, "Granada y el Magreb," pp. 661–65.
[17] For Riḍwān's origin, see Ibn Khaldūn, *Histoire des Berbères*, vol. IV, pp. 327 and 429.
[18] For the context and effect, see J. Hinojosa y Montalvo, "Las relaciones entre Elche y Granada."

from usury.[19] Pardons were issued for communities that had collaborated with the occupation or had surrendered to Pedro. Returning refugees were to be allowed to reclaim their lands, and royal authorities funded and facilitated missions to Castile to ransom and repatriate captured *mudéjares*. Parallel to this, Muslim rights and privileges – at least those relating to religious law – were not only confirmed but broadened, as local communities capitalized on Pere III's vulnerability to lever greater freedom. Mosques were to be repaired, religious rights extended, the "*sunna* and *xara*" to be respected, and *mudéjar* jurisdictions protected. These provisions were aimed at the remaining *mudéjar* elite, the patronage of whom was seen as key to the re-establishment and maintenance of Muslim society here; for while such liberties did indeed hold a general appeal, they were direct sources of religio-social prestige and financial benefit for the families who dominated local *mudéjar* administrations.

On the other hand, emigration from the kingdom came to be prohibited, and freedom of movement and residence – once established on royal lands – severely curtailed. In 1363 Pere the Ceremonious declared that any unlicensed *mudéjar* travellers would be judicially enslaved, although only eight years earlier he had confirmed in law their right to move freely.[20] In 1404 Martí I would further restrict internal migration by forbidding any Muslim woman from marrying outside of her own *aljama*.[21] Still, repressive measures were risky to undertake, given the propensity of Muslims here simply to flee when pressed too hard – a further indication of the increasing disengagement of Valencian *mudéjares* from the larger society of the Crown. And in any event, emigration, clandestine, or merely discrete, continued.[22] Although credible population figures are non-existent, it is clear that it was over the course of the fourteenth century that Muslims in Valencia finally became a numerical minority in the kingdom.

### *Aragon and Catalonia*

The Muslim communities of Aragon and Catalonia also suffered the effects of plague and war, although they weathered them far better than those of Valencia. The loss of population and the damage to the economy and infrastructure here was also considerable, as borne out by the increasing and successful petitions made by Aragonese and Catalan *aljamas* for

[19] In fifteenth-century Navarre, Carlos III would make similar concessions for Muslim communities that had suffered from the plague. See M. García-Arenal and B. Leroy, *Moros y judíos en Navarra*, pp. 111–12 {XXXIV}.
[20] J. E. López Coca de Castaner, "Los mudéjares valencianos," pp. 656ff.
[21] M. B. Basáñez Villaluenga, *La aljama sarracena*, p. 69.
[22] See M. T. Ferrer i Mallol, "L'emigració dels sarraïns."

tax relief in the second half of the century. And although it seems Muslims suffered a proportional decline in population relative to Christians, massive dislocation or emigration do not seem to be the cause. Their population enjoyed greater freedom of movement than in Valencia, but exercised it less. *Mudéjares* here were more confident and constant, undoubtedly as a consequence of their long-standing and profound integration with local Christians. To be sure, they were a people apart, and a subject people at that, but their level of linguistic and social acculturation as well as their integration in local political and economic structures was deep. Reports of sectarian violence and religious pressure are all but non-existent. Occasionally local Jewish and *mudéjar* communities chafed, typically as a consequence of credit relationships, or as their leaders jockeyed for prestige – hence, the occasional scrums between Jews and Muslims regarding precedence in royal funeral processions.[23] Indeed, tensions and violence tended to manifest themselves within Muslim communities, as family-led factions competed, corrupt officials held onto power, or wealthy *mudéjares* conspired to evade their communal tax duties.[24] Christians were not infrequently involved in these struggles, but as allies, patrons, and partisans of various factions; Military Orders, bishops, seigneurs, local officials, and royal functionaries all found themselves caught up in inter-Muslim disputes – a dynamic the monarchy decried, but also actively participated in.[25]

The impoverishment of Aragonese and Catalan *aljamas* in the fourteenth century is indisputable, but it should not be equated necessarily with the impoverishment of Muslims. A numerous and prosperous *mudéjar* middle class of artisans, craftsmen, and merchants survived the vicissitudes of the 1300s. It was the *aljama* as the incorporation of the community that was formally liable for taxes, but its capacity to raise taxes was eroded by the increasing number of Muslims who could claim exemptions, or *franquitas*, which were granted by the kings in recognition of individual service. The problem was that these exemptions were perpetual and heritable and therefore the number of individuals who could claim tax exemptions grew exponentially over time. Moreover, these were

[23] See below, p. 411.

[24] This was one of the factors that exacerbated the factionalism that increasingly characterized *aljamas* around the peninsula from the late fourteenth century on. See, for example, M. F. Lopes de Barros, *Tempos e espaços*, p. 383, and "Las elites mudéjares"; E. Cantera Montenegro, "Las comunidades mudéjares," p. 173, and, generally, R. Salicrú i Lluch, "Sarraïns desaveïnats," and M. T. Ferrer i Mallol, "Francos pero excluidos." Ferrer i Mallol presents a case study from Elx (Valencia) in detail in "L'alfaquí Mahomat Alhaig."

[25] These bitterly fought intra-communal disputes were not a particular characteristic of *mudéjar* society; local Jewish and Christian communities were wracked by the same or similar tensions and factionalism.

typically the wealthiest members of the community. *Mudéjar* families carefully guarded these royal privileges – whether genuine or spurious – and lawsuits and counter-suits over tax liability stretched out over centuries, occasionally descending into violence. The de Rey family of Huesca, which battled its own *aljama* for over two hundred years, was not exceptional.[26] Royal and local officials and Christian communities added to the problem by attempting to take a share of the revenues *aljamas* generated, infringing on the *mudéjar* jurisdictions, or by attempting to shift some of their own community's tax liability onto local Muslims. The monarchy, for its part, worked to extend the seigniorial monopolies that Muslims were subject to (e.g. mills, ovens, baths, butchers shops), and levied all sorts of extraordinary and occasional taxes, which further undermined community finances. The cash-strapped kings also used *aljama* tax liabilities as collateral for loans, or sold, rented, or granted out communities' tax-rights. This, together with communal insolvency, left *aljamas* vulnerable to speculators and usurers, both Jewish and Christian. Hence, when the nobleman Blasco de Alagón sold the hamlets of Sàstago and Cinquelinas to the Barcelona merchant, Arnau Betran, in the 1360s, the local *alaminus* cautioned that the Muslim community was at risk of abandonment due to the unbearable cost of maintaining its fiscal obligations.[27]

But Muslim communities in Aragon and Catalonia also were able to exploit the political and financial vulnerabilities of the monarchy to maintain or recover privileges and rights they had enjoyed earlier. In 1356 – as the tide of the war turned against Aragon – representatives of the Muslim community of Ricla presented Pere III with an original parchment, signed a century and a half earlier by his great-great-great-grandfather, Pere "the Catholic," and still bearing the Crusader-King's leaden seal. It enumerated a diverse array of rights that had been conceded to the Muslims of the Jalón valley in 1210: drastically limiting the *corvée* that Muslims owed the king (a maximum of six days per year and only for those who owned oxen), giving the community rights to the estates of intestate Muslims (contrary to seigniorial practice and royal statute), assenting to the authority of the "çunia" (*sunna*) in various criminal matters relating to "personal law," and confirming Muslims' hunting and fishing rights in the region. Pere "the Ceremonious" confirmed it in its entirety and in perpetuity.[28]

26 See B. Catlos, "The de Reys (1220–1501)."
27 See M. D. López Pérez, "Las repercusiones económicas," p. 212.
28 See E. Lourie, "An Unknown Charter." In 1365 the same King had to tempt the rebellious Muslims of Castro and Alfandeguilla to return to their homes, by acceding to their demands vis-à-vis their rights and privileges. See J. Boswell, *The Royal Treasure*, pp. 494–97.

There has been a tendency by historians to focus closely on the amount of taxes in cash that Muslim communities paid the crown and, after comparing this to the dramatically higher amounts extracted from much smaller Jewish populations, to conclude that the Muslim minority was of less consequence and was less prosperous than the Jewish minority. Any such argument must consider, however, that royal tax yield is only one metric of economic utility, and it has one specific beneficiary. Although Muslim communities' direct tax yield may have been lower, they would have offered other compensatory benefits to the Crown, both in terms of providing an economic base and a subject constituency that could be managed directly. Moreover, utility to the crown was only one factor contributing to a minority's stability and security – more important was the breadth of integration and variety of connections a subject community had with the majority society, and in this sense the *mudéjares* were quite robust. Moreover, because they were "less important" to the kings, the Crown would have felt less need to control or intervene in the internal affairs of Muslim *aljamas* than in Jewish ones.[29] And finally, the wealth of a formally constituted community does not necessarily reflect the wealth of its members. In the late fourteenth century many *aljamas* may have stood on the brink of insolvency, but many of their members – taken as families and individuals – were quite clearly comfortable, or even prosperous.

## Royal treasures: *Mudéjar* integration in the Christian kingdoms

Since it is expected of the power of princes to protect subjects from future danger, and defend the weak and unarmed from the artifice of men, so that by such a provision offence may be withheld from those striving with good purpose, and free them from the oppressions of the wicked, it is proper for Us to constitute the Muslims settled in Our cities, towns and other places, amongst others of those peoples of Our realms, under Our general and special protection ... for they all pertain to the greater treasure of the king ... (Pere the Ceremonious of Aragon, a letter to the Muslims of Xàtiva (September 16, 1366)[30])

Pere III, known also as *el Punyalet* ("the Little Dagger"), after the knife with which he publicly shredded the "magna carta" of the Aragonese *Union* after the rebels' defeat at Épila in 1348, was an individual who did not mince words or let principle stand in the way of the practical. Hence, the charter of protection he granted to the *aljama* of Xàtiva in Valencia in 1366 not only emphatically ensured his Muslim subjects' security and

[29] See J. Riera i Sans, *Els poders públics*, and A. Blasco Martínez, "Los malsines."
[30] ACA, C., reg. 913, ff.33r–v; author's translation.

autonomy, but laid out in equally strict terms their obligations to pay him tribute and taxes. *Mudéjares* were to be protected, officially on principle because they were weak and vulnerable subjects – as Jaume I's 1248 *fuero* maintained – but in fact because they constituted an important part of the "royal treasure." This turn of phrase reflected Muslims' position across the peninsula; in Portugal, Castile, the Crown of Aragon and Navarre, the kings consistently presented themselves as the particular and direct sovereigns of their Muslim subjects. Both the *Fuero General* of Navarre and the Portuguese *Ordanações Afonsinas* were explicit in this regard.[31] This is not to say that *mudéjares* all lived under direct royal fiscal and judicial jurisdiction; in fact, Muslims can be found subject to the authority of and paying taxes to lay lords, municipalities, dioceses, monasteries, and Military Orders as well as to the monarchy. At times, fiscal and judicial jurisdiction coincided, at times it did not; at times it fell upon all members of a locale equally, at times it adhered to individuals. Moreover, in many circumstances the same communities or individuals were subject to multiple fiscal and judicial jurisdictions.[32] Taken together, the principle of direct royal sovereignty and the reality of *mudéjar* implication in a broad array of Christian power structures, were essential factors in sustaining these communities. It meant that a wide range of Christian institutions and collectives benefited from the existence of *mudéjar* communities, and ensured that the principle of their continued existence would be supported by law. Meanwhile, the situation engendered competition among Christian powers for authority over Muslims and gave rise to ambiguities. Whereas such rivalries may have encouraged the increasing regulation of Muslims and their communities, as seen above, it also provided opportunities for *mudéjares* to mitigate their situation by exploiting their own usefulness and value, and skillfully playing competing Christian authorities against one another.

### *The Crown of Aragon*

This dynamic is most clearly seen in the Crown of Aragon, which not only had the largest Muslim minority in the peninsula, but also the best documented by far. Here, in general terms *mudéjares* were broadly integrated in Christian society, administrative structures, and economies.

[31] See M. R. García Arancón, "Marco jurídico," p. 497 and M. F. Lopes de Barros, *Tempos e espaços*, pp. 121–22.

[32] See M. Febrer Romaguera, "Los tribunales," esp. pp. 47–57, for jurisdictional ambiguities and conflicts, and the tenuous nature of the *mudéjar* judicial hierarchy in the Crown of Aragon.

Certainly Muslims were objects of "exploitation," but so was the rest of the huge common class of medieval society. In some ways they were more vulnerable to violence, abuse, and enslavement than their Christian neighbors, but they also enjoyed protections – such as from torture and execution, and the right to appeal at royal court – that Christian peasants did not. Overall, the diverse networks of interdependence, subjugation, and mutual benefit that marked their interaction with Christian collectives, individuals, and institutions in the Crown endowed *mudéjar* society with a remarkable stability and security.

This was particularly true in the Kingdom of Aragon and "New Catalonia," where Muslims remained a numerically robust minority in most of the major towns as well as through the fertile valleys of the Ebro, Jalón and Jiloca, and the foothills of the Pyrenees. As the War of the Two Peters showed, in the kingdom of Valencia, where Muslims were more numerous and occupied economic positions that were both narrower in range and less complementary to Christian interests, the situation was more volatile. It would be here that Christian–Muslim "convivencia" in the Crown of Aragon would begin to break down in the fifteenth century. In Old Catalonia, including Barcelona and Girona, and in Mallorca, there were scatterings of free Muslims, as well as passers-by and slaves, but no formally constituted communities. Sometimes these groups were co-opted into Jewish *aljamas* for tax purposes, but for the most part, these small communities or isolated families of *mudéjares* were evidently regarded by both the authorities and their Christian neighbors as *vecinos* – ordinary inhabitants. They appear in the historical record only by the sheerest of chance, if at all.[33]

The Crown of Aragon's particular political structure favored the survival and prosperity of Muslim communities. A dynastic aggregate of independent kingdoms governed by autonomous *cortes* (or parliaments) with separate laws and fiercely independent estates, the Crown was governed by a system the influential theologian and political theorist, Francesc Eiximenis (*c.* 1330–1409), described as "pactist." The kings could not tax without the assent of the *cortes*, where they had to contend with a powerful landed nobility, strong municipalities, and rich Military Orders, monasteries, and dioceses. As a consequence they were cash-poor – so much so that in the late fourteenth century, the crown jewels were broken up and pawned out to merchants, to be hastily recovered when required for ceremonies of state (if not merely substituted with "paste" replicas). Hence, Muslim *aljamas* formed an important and

[33] See, for example, the lone Muslim family in early fourteenth-century Girona (below, p. 392, n. 154.

flexible component of the royal fisc. These provided direct sources of taxes, fees for licenses (such as for *ḥallāl* butchers), judicial fines, and income from the royal monopolies to which they were subject. Moreover, these various assignations could be rented out or alienated either temporarily or permanently to meet the kings' financial obligations or as acts of favor. Muslim *aljamas* were often allocated wholly or in part to support the households of queens, who became powerful patronesses and protectors of these communities and their leaders. On the other hand, with no formal representation in the *cortes*, Muslims were in little position to contest new taxes or irregular levies demanded of them, and wealthy Muslims, like wealthy Jews, could be occasionally inveighed upon to make "donations" or loans of cash to the crown.

### *Diversity and prosperity*

But it was not only the Crown who benefited directly from Muslim subjects. Landed lords needed their labor and sought out Muslims both as vassals and tenants. The Islamic sharecropping arrangement, *shārik*, was so widely adapted that its Latin and romance cognate *exaricus*/*exarico* became a functioning synonym for "Muslim farmer."[34] These various arrangements bound together Muslim peasants and Christian lords. At times the latter certainly used coercion – lobbying successfully, for example, to impose prohibitions and penalties on the common *mudéjar* strategy of changing residence or vassalship in order to obtain better conditions. Generally, however, Christian lords saw their interests best served by protecting their Muslims against abuse by the Crown or royal officials, rival lords, municipalities, and other *mudéjar* factions. The fact that lords had only limited success in obtaining criminal and civil jurisdiction (*merum et mixtum imperium*) over Muslims meant that *mudéjares* had ample opportunities to play seigniorial and royal authorities against each other, particularly as emigration brought the kings and magnates into competition for Muslim manpower.[35] These seigniorial authorities included aristocratic families, military and monastic orders, bishops, and even the anti-Pope, Pedro Martínez de Luna ("Papa Luna"), who lived out his post-Avignon days as lord of Penyiscola. To a reader today it may seem remarkable that a Crusading order used its *mudéjar* subjects to beat up on local Christians, as the Order of Calatrava at Alcañiz did, or licensed and taxed Muslim prostitutes, as did the Templars at Tortosa;

[34] See B. Catlos, *The Victors and the Vanquished*, pp. 181–88. For the traditional view, see E. Hinojosa, "Mezquinos y exáricos."

[35] See S. Ponsoda López de Atalaya, "Migracions mudèjars."

however, such positions were completely consistent with these Christian parties' role as lords and agents of local ecclesiastical corporations. Adding to the ambiguities, the monarchs themselves were seigniors, and therefore bound to inconsistent and conflicting agendas as regards the Muslims of their realms.[36] When Pere III's son, Martí I, came unexpectedly to the throne in 1396, the combined properties of the Duke and his wife, Maria de Luna, comprised the largest seigniorial patrimony in the Crown – and included both urban *aljamas* and extensive agricultural lands farmed by Muslims. As a consequence, when acting as seigniors they frequently contradicted the very orders and policy decisions towards *mudéjares* they had issued as monarchs.

Through the fourteenth and fifteenth centuries *mudéjar* prosperity was linked to diversity. Muslims not only dominated certain craft sectors, including building and decorative trades, but occupied strong niches in trades such as paper-making, soap-manufacture, leather and shoemaking, ironworking, carpentry, luxury-cloth tailoring, ceramics, and transport, and practised a broad range of non-exclusive trades. Muslim master builders and artisans worked on the renovations of the Aljafería (the former Hūdid palace in Zaragoza), on Papa Luna's building projects in Zaragoza, Penyiscola, and Calatayud, and on churches and secular buildings throughout the Crown. The family-oriented organization of ateliers and the low index of conversion helped keep technical knowledge and special skills specific to the community. Further, specialization would have helped to counteract the increasing competitive disadvantage Muslims faced from Christians, as the latter increasingly organized trades into explicitly religiously flavored confraternities or family-dominated guilds, which not only regulated the practice of crafts but took a growing role in municipal and local government. Likewise, there is no reason to suspect that Muslim artisans suffered as tastes in building shifted away from the "mudéjar" styles that had dominated the thirteenth century; Muslim artists and stone- and woodworkers were capable of a wide repertoire of styles and techniques, including "Christian" styles that involved representative portraiture.[37]

## *The economy and the* mudéjar *elite*

Although with the commercial realignment of the peninsula and the growth of a Christian trading culture, fewer Muslims were engaged in large-scale and "international" commerce, they did remain very active in

[36] See, for example, below, p. 481. [37] See below, chapter 10.

retail and local trade, and participated in strong regional economic networks. Some Muslim traders journeyed from Aragon to Castile and Navarre, or from Valencia to Granada; but crossing borders, and long-distance travel was risky for Muslims, who might be arrested as fugitive vassals by over-enthusiastic or corrupt Christian officials even if they were carrying royally secured letters of transit (*guidatica/guiatges*) or were protected by treaty. Throughout the century, however, Muslims, particularly in Valencia, but also in Aragon, came to be involved in partnerships with both local Christians and foreign merchants, serving as middlemen between their own communities and distant markets. The most successful of these medieval "bazaaris" were frequently the *alcaydi* and *alamini* of their communities, the local *mudéjar* juridical and administrative elite.[38] They would not be inclined to perceive of their own economic collaboration with Christians as ideologically or culturally problematic, and as long as they remained in charge, commercial concerns would drive formal community consensus. By the late fourteenth century, *mudéjares* were becoming increasingly active in this trade, leading to the emergence of a clutch of extremely successful trading dynasties, such as the Ripolls of Valencia, in the 1400s.[39]

Two factors that were key to the *mudéjar* economy were adaptability and access to credit. Across the socio-economic spectrum many individual *mudéjares* and their families engaged simultaneously and succesively in a number of professions and activities, such as craft, agriculture, animal husbandry, commerce, administrative work (whether royal, seigniorial, or local), money-lending, and property speculation. Notarial records, bills of sale, and even the continual series of lawsuits between borrowers (frequently Muslim) and creditors (usually Jewish), show that through the fifteenth century Muslims could raise capital with relative ease – capital that was at times needed in order to meet their communal fiscal obligations, but at others was invested by individuals either in raw material for craft or land for speculation. *Mudéjares*' economic activities bound them also to Christian townsfolk and farmers, as landlords and tenants, creditors and debtors, partners in ventures, employers and employees, and customers and suppliers. The places they occupied in chains of production and distribution helped to establish a fundamental interdependency between Christians and Muslims that discouraged the former from attacking or marginalizing the latter.

38 J. Soler Milla, "Commercio musulmán," esp. pp. 239–45. For an example in Castile, see A. Echevarría Arsuaga, "Los Caro de Ávila."
39 See M. Ruzafa García, "Els orígens," and "Las relaciones"; and see, below, p. 222, n.158.

The fourteenth century represented a turning point for the *mudéjar* elite in the lands of the Crown of Aragon. Not surprisingly, local *aljamas* tended to remain in the control of their most prosperous families, whose wealth was generally anchored in a trade and boosted by the hereditary tax exemptions they were often awarded as a consequence of serving as community officials. But few families were successful in establishing long-standing dynasties as had been common in the thirteenth century – a notable exception being the corrupt and abusive Abenferre family, who ruled the *aljama* of Lleida through most of the 1400s. Others, such as the Avinholes in Tortosa, the de Abdellas in Daroca, the Ballestarius of Zaragoza, the Xupiós, Ripolls, and the Fusters in Valencia, and the de Reys, de Albahos, and de Marguáns in Huesca, drifted in and out of influence, clashing, allying, and intermarrying with rival local families, none of whom obtained a clear domination over the *aljama*.[40] Occasionally, *mudéjares* emerge in high-status or royally connected positions, as physicians, tailors, or builders to the kings. Arabophone Jews were apparently preferred as diplomats to the Islamic world and translators of Arabic, at least until the mid fourteenth century, by which time they had been effectively pushed out of the upper administration of the Crown. By this time, *mudéjares* – who had previously performed these services locally or on an *ad hoc* basis – were filling these roles with increasing frequency, whether they were local officials, members of higher professions, or merchants and craftsmen.[41] Hence, Mahoma Albaho of Huesca served as translator to the Catalan consulate in Damascus in the 1390s, Abraham Abenxoa as envoy to Granada, and Ali Abencomixa as ambassador to Granada and Morocco, both in the 1360s, and the Bellvis family as envoys to Granada in the 1400s.[42] The wealthiest families (although not necessarily the most pious) had the resources to

[40] See J. Mutgé i Vives, "Els Bimferre"; M. T. Ferrer i Mallol, "The Muslim *Aljama* of Tortosa"; B. Catlos, *The Victors and the Vanquished*; M. Ruzafa García, "La familia Xupió," and "Alí Xupió"; and M. Ruzafa García, "Élites valencianas," esp. pp. 197–85; B. Catlos, "The de Reys (1220–1501)"; and Á. Conte Cazcarro, *La aljama de moros*, respectively.

[41] See R. Salicrú i Lluch, "Intérpretes y diplomáticos," for an overview, and many examples. For *mudéjar* officials acting in this capacity locally and at the royal court, see M. V. Febrer Romaguera, "Los tribunales," p. 67.

[42] M. B. Basáñez Villaluenga, *La aljama sarracena*, p. 67; and J. Boswell, *The Royal Treasure*, p. 43. For the Bellvis family, see below, pp. 185 and 194. Further examples can be found in M. T. Ferrer i Mallol, *El sarraïns*, pp. 141–42 and 177. It has been suggested that Jews were preferred as diplomats because Muslims were viewed as too unreliable or potentially disloyal to serve in this capacity, but this was clearly not the case. Few subject Muslims had a level of linguistic and cultural sophistication suitable for the job; those that did tended to find employment in the Islamic world. Moreover, Jews had better access to and were better connected to the royal court, and were, therefore, simply more adept at landing these lucrative and influential posts.

make the pilgrimage to Mecca, as did the Abenferre family in 1375, the Cordovís in 1361, and Aḥmād b. Fatḥ b. Abī al-Rabīʿ of Tortosa in 1396 – the latter leaving an account of his journey in Arabic.[43] Others had to be content with local pilgrimage sites, such as the tomb of the Sufi mystic Abū Aḥmad Jaʿfar b. Sid-Bono al-Khuzaʿi (d.1227) at Atzeneta in the Vall de Guadalest (Valencia), one of the many such *qubbāt* that were undoubtedly scattered throughout the peninsula.[44]

Whereas the Jewish minorities in Iberia were anchored by sets of extremely wealthy and powerful families, well connected to the monarchies, and who moved in a larger Mediterranean and European worlds, *mudéjar* society in the Crown of Aragon remained highly localized, with no effective centralized institutions or hierarchy of authority. This was due, in part, to the fact that seigniors had the right to appoint their own *alcaydi* in the communities under their power, but even among royal *aljamas* there was no real hierarchy.[45] For example, the *alcaydus Sarracenorum* of Zaragoza, the capital of Aragon, may have been above the kingdom's local Islamic magistrates in a vague sense, but in fact he had no authority over them and it was not his jurisdiction under which they fell or with whom appeals against their decisions were to be lodged. It was the king or his representative, the royal bailiff, who appointed them (or ratified their election), deposed them (at his pleasure), and with whom judicial appeals or official complaints were lodged. In the thirteenth century, one family, the Bellidos of Zaragoza – builders to the kings and protégés of the Dominicans – moved in the highest circles of the realm, lending money to courtiers and establishing interests in Tunisia, but by 1300 they had retreated into a wealthy but anonymous prosperity in their home city.[46] The Abenxoas of Valencia gained royal confidence and influence serving

43 See M. de Epalza Ferre, "Dos textos." There are many instances of *mudéjares* obtaining permission to make the pilgrimage. See, for example, M. T. Ferrer i Mallol, *Els sarraïns de la corona catalano-aragonesa*, pp. 107 and 144–46. In 1357 Pere the Ceremonious granted a *guidaticum* to the Navarrese Muslims Mahoma Alcordoueri (Cordobí?) and Abdela Tinic, to pass through his lands on their way to the Holy Cities, along with their wives sons and families. See J. Boswell, *The Royal Treasure*, pp. 446–47. López Coca de Castaner cautions that historians have overestimated the frequency of these voyages, forgetting the expensive exit tax that the pilgrimage was subject to. See his "Los mudéjares valencianos," p. 655.

44 M. Meyerson, *The Muslims of Valencia*, p. 257. In 1337 Pere the Ceremonious had ordered Bartholomew Carrasqueri, the owner of the land where the shrine stood, to stop charging an entry fee to Muslim visitors. See ACA, C. reg. 862, f.121r (January 15, 1337). Later, Pere started charging a fee himself; see p. 482.

45 Seigniorial *alcaydi* even overtly defied or poached the jurisdiction of their royally appointed counterparts, as Mahomet de Bellvís learned in 1453, when the *alcaydus*, Ali Alaça of Quart de Valls, tried a case which was actually under the *alcadí-general*'s jurisdiction. V. Febrer Romaguera, "Tribunales," 51–53.

46 Catlos, *The Victors and the Vanquished*, pp. 217–19, and 331–37.

as grooms to the household of Queen Leonor de Sicilia; Abraham, the *paterfamilias*, obtained the post of *alcaydus* of no fewer than seven *aljamas* simultaneously, including Xàtiva, Elx, and Crevillent.

Out of all of these, one particular family stands out. From the mid fourteenth century the Aragonese Bellvís family used its position as royal grooms to the kings and princes, and its contacts with powerful Christian families, to build a veritable empire. Faraig (Faraj) de Bellvís, who had been in the service of Pere III since the latter's youth, assembled a portfolio of lifetime administrative benefices that allowed him to rule major *aljamas* across Aragon, Catalunya, and Valencia. In the style of the Jewish elite, he parlayed his ability to raise money for the Crown and his service as an envoy into further privileges, dispensations, and appointments. He placed his son, Ovechar (Abū Baqr), in the household of the *dauphin* and future King, Joan I, while his brother, Jahia (Yaḥyā), established himself in Castile, where he undoubtedly made the match that married Ovecar into another prominent *mudéjar* family from that kingdom. When Faraig's attempt to take over *mudéjar* Valencia by marrying into the Fuster family stumbled, he embarked on an aggressive campaign against his ex in-laws in the courts.[47] As early as 1355 he had been named "*alcaydus* of all of the Muslims of the Kingdom of Aragon," and soon after in Valencia he was styled "*alcaydus* of the King," a designation the family would bear in the 1400s. Here, the family would forge an alliance with the Christian Mercader family, who dominated the position of royal-bailiff of the kingdom until 1490.[48] These appointments did not reflect a policy on the part of the Crown to centralize and organize *mudéjar* administration; rather, they invested Faraig and his descendants with imprecise but potent titles that would allow them a free hand to interfere in the affairs of local Muslim communities, and attempt to appropriate fines and dues from the *aljamas* in those kingdoms. In the fifteenth century the family continued to thrive, serving as envoys to Granada, and establishing a commercial concern that traded throughout the Western Mediterranean.[49]

The emergence of this narrow elite was one of the ways in which the *mudéjar* situation was transformed in the fifteenth century. On the one hand, town-based Muslim society remained reasonably prosperous and dynamic, given the times, although communal life would have been put under strain by constant crises of leadership rooted in Christian

47 J. Boswell, *The Royal Treasure*, pp. 44ff.
48 M. V. Febrer Romaguera, "Los tribunales," pp. 53–55.
49 For the Bellvís family in the fifteenth century see A. Echevarría Arsuaga, "De cadí a alcalde mayor (I)," 152–68; M. V. Febrer Romaguera, "Los Bellvís"; and M. Meyerson, *The Muslims of Valencia*, pp. 102–08, 142, 195, 243, 256, and 258.

administrative encroachment and economic competition, local factionalism, and the abuses of their small but powerful regional elite. Poorer Muslims, particularly peasants, may have become poorer, squeezed ever harder by Christian lords who increasingly saw their best interests in limiting the freedom of movement and alodial rights that these had traditionally enjoyed. But on the other hand, seigniorial lands offered refuge from the dangers to the faith and to the faithful that Christian-dominated town society posed. As a consequence, many *mudéjares* arrived at the conclusion that country rather than city air "makes you free," and there was a drift of population into more homogenously Muslim rural enclaves, particularly in the kingdom of Valencia. By the mid fifteenth century *mudéjares* in the Crown of Aragon were retrenching, resisting these destructive trends by increasingly focusing on their distinctive culture and religious identity. This approach would help to stabilize community life, but would aggravate tensions that were developing with Christian society.

### *The Kingdom of Navarre*

In Navarre, the Muslim population remained concentrated in the river valleys of the southern sector of the kingdom, with a large community at Tudela (comprising perhaps half of the total population). *Mudéjares* may have amounted to up to 20 percent of the population in mid-century, living in communities that were completely Muslim, mixed with Christians and Jews, or as small minorities. Most lived under royal or seigniorial jurisdiction, although some were subjects of the Hospital. Some communities experienced a significant decline as a consequence of the plague and wars, but their situation was remarkably stable, although there were dramatic local fluctuations and adjustments. *Mudéjar* prosperity here is reflected in Muslims' easy access to regular credit, which supported both rural and urban economies. The former was based both on profitable horticulture and cereal crops, while the latter included commerce and a range of trades, notably ironworking, livery, tack, transport, and the building-related trades. In the late fourteenth century Carlos III (1387–1425) employed many Muslim craftsmen in the construction of his palace-castle at Olite. Several families emerged as particularly wealthy and propertied, including the Alpelmí, Alfayat, Alcordobí (evidently of Andalusī origin), and Xetení. Some, like the Alpelmí, whose most visible member was the crossbowman, Muza (also an "alfaque" or *faqīh*) had strong connections in royal circles.[50]

[50] The *alfaquí* Caet Alpelmí was also very close to the royal household in the fourteenth century. See H. Ozaki, "El régimen tributario," pp. 453 and 457; J. Carrasco Pérez, "Los Mudéjares de Navarra," p. 93.

Indeed, the Alpelmís remained the most powerful Muslim family in the kingdom through the fourteenth and into the fifteenth century, dominating the administration of the *aljama* of Tudela.

The leading Muslim families of the kingdom came both out of professional backgrounds (such as engineers and physicians), and out of the craft sector, which was extremely important both for *mudéjar* society here and for the kingdom as a whole. In the early fourteenth century Tudela was a hive of Muslim industry, with dozens of carpenters, smiths, and shoemakers working the *aljama*, and evidently serving a large Christian market.[51] The kings were keen to exploit the potential of Muslim crafts and technical know-how. Hence, when Carlos II (1349–87) wanted to modernize the cloth industry in 1372, he paid 14,000 *dineros* to send Çalema Çaragoçano, the royal carpenter, down to Zaragoza, to recruit a wool dyer, a washer, and a carder, and to inspect the structure and function of Aragonese watermills, so that he could construct similar mills back home in Navarre.[52] It was not only the kings, but also seigniors and other notables, including bishops, who used *mudéjares* as messengers and envoys to Aragon, and perhaps beyond.[53]

There is no evidence of friction among the communities or of pressure on the part of elements in the Christian majority in Navarre for Muslims to convert or leave. Muslims collaborated alongside Christians (and Jews) in local defense and fought in the royal army.[54] In 1363 Muslim crossbowmen and armorers were even dispatched to support Jean II of France (1350–64), and fought alongside Castile in the War of the Two Peters. By mid-century, Navarrese *mudéjares* distinguished themselves as masters of the new-fangled *ballesta de trueno* ("thunder cross-bow": a musket or small cannon).[55] In fact, the office of royal artillery master was held by Halí Aludalí, who was succeeded by his son, Hamet, and then by Aliot (likely a grandson). Muslim engineers like Zalema Alpuliente, "master of works of the castles of La Ribera," constructed and maintained the kingdom's fortresses, and Muslims served as physicians, veterinarians, grooms, falconers, and envoys for the royal family and for bishops, and as armorers and goldsmiths to the royal court.[56]

51 A. Ozaki, "El régimen tributario," p. 445.

52 F. Serrano Larráyoz, "Viajeros navarros," pp. 370, 374, and 391.

53 A. Ozaki, "El régimen tributario," p. 458.

54 See A. Malalana Ureña and I. Muñoz Cascante, "Mudéjares."

55 This complicates and contradicts the accepted chronology of the introduction of the handgun to Europe, which is usually attributed to Granadan forces fighting against Castile at the Battle of Egea in 1391. See J. Vernet Ginés, *La cultura hispanoárabe*, p. 232.

56 A. Malalana Ureña and I. Muñoz Cascante, "Mudéjares," p. 528; Ozaki, "El régimen tributario," pp. 457–58; C. Conde Solares, "Social Continuity," pp. 315 and 318–19.

Conditions varied by locale, but mosques and formal *aljama* structures are attested to in significant settlements, such as Corella, Ablitas, and Cascante. Tudela was home to a diverse population of artisans and traders. In 1309 the *aljama* had no fewer than nineteen *procuradores* (representatives), a sign, perhaps, of a community prosperous enough to mitigate the influence of the elite families. As the century descended into disorder, Muslims were given permission to fortify the *morería*, and were granted tax relief to compensate for the fiscal crisis. Concessions to the independence of Islamic jurisdiction ("çuyna") continued to be made by the monarchy, and when in 1392 the King's visit to Tudela was greeted by rioting on the part of some *mudéjares*, the matter was set right with a fine of 500 *florines* (reduced from the original sentence of 3,000). Although, as in Aragon, statutes were in place to limit *mudéjares*' rights to alienate land to non-Muslims (which would represent a loss of revenue to the King), the population remained mobile. The frontiers were porous, criss-crossed by smugglers shuttling contraband, and by runaway slaves and fugitives from the law. Conditions here evidently attracted Muslim settlers from Castile, as well; in 1371 the master engineer, Mahoma de Burgos, settled in Tudela in the salary of the Queen, Jeanne de Valois.[57]

### *The Kingdom of Portugal*

The proportion and distribution of Portugal's Muslims was similar to that of Navarre; they comprised a clear numerical minority concentrated in a few zones – here, the area stretching from Coimbra to Beja, and along the Tagus (Tejo), and a cluster of settlements on the Atlantic coast. The kings endeavored to maintain direct jurisdiction over their *mouros* so as to benefit from the revenue they generated. Hence, Pedro I's requirement of 1361 that Muslims and Jews live in segregated neighborhoods (*mourarias* and *judiarias*). Nevertheless, some Muslim communities slipped under the control of the Order of Avis or of cathedral chapters. *Mudéjares* here seemed to prefer the rule of kings, who apparently did not interfere inordinately in communal affairs, but could be counted on in times of dispute, such as when in 1362 the Muslims of Évora petitioned for their *alcaide* to be deposed, alleging he was illiterate and unfit for office. Thirty years earlier they had brought a suit at royal court, complaining that the Master of Avis had usurped their right to elect their own magistrate, Mafamede Francelho – an appeal that, in the end, the community did not win.[58]

[57] See M. García-Arenal and B. Leroy, *Moros y judíos*, pp. 69–71, 87, and 102 and, generally, J. Carrasco Pérez, "Los Mudéjares de Navarra."

[58] F. Soyer, *The Persecution*, pp. 28, 38 and 39.

*Mudéjar* administration also remained local in nature here. In the mid 1400s, a royal physician named ʿAlī served as ambassador to the Marīnids and was apparently named chief magistrate of the *mouros* of the kingdom. In 1451 a certain Saʿīd Caciz from Lisbon was appointed as representative of the kingdom's *comunas*. But these evidently represented acts of patronage to well-connected Muslims rather than a turn in policy towards centralization of *mudéjar* administration.

As in Navarre, Muslims' economic role and fiscal contributions were what ultimately determined their value to Christian society and their experience as a minority. They were active in agriculture and viticulture, as producers of grain, grapes, olives, and figs. Fishing was an important activity on the Algarve coast. Muslims were also highly active in a number of trades and crafts, including ironworking, shoemaking, carpentry, and cloth-making, as well as commerce, both local and foreign. Evidence of a privileged set emerges occasionally, as in the case of the Láparo family – Lisbon cork-makers who found fortune and favor in the fifteenth century, using their industrial activities as an expansion into other spheres and zones.[59] Muslim traders from the Maghrib circulated in the kingdom with royal permission, while Portuguese Muslims, *naturalls destes nossos Reignos* ("natives of these Our kingdoms"), journeyed to Castile.[60] Unlike in the Crown of Aragon, there does not seem to have been a policy of restricting Muslims' movement; a study of the *comuna* of Lisbon shows that Muslims from the city had properties and relationships with locales all over the southern half of the kingdom.[61] As in Navarre and the Crown of Aragon, Muslims here performed military service, both on foot and horse – indeed, some were explicitly designated as *fidalgos* ("knights") in the 1400s.[62] As in Castile, they also served in municipal militias, but here, much later – well into the fifteenth century.[63] Late in the same century, when initiatives and laws were proposed or promulgated (unsuccessfully) in Aragon and Castile to disarm subject Muslims, in Portugal *mouros* were successfully petitioning against local prohibitions for the right to bear arms.[64]

Here, as elsewhere, when royal favor was returned in the form of communal tax exemptions, wealthy *mudéjares* could find themselves in

59 M. F. Lopes de Barros, *Tempos e espaços*, pp. 548–51. 60 *Ibid.*, p. 157.

61 M. F. Lopes de Barros, *A comuna*, pp. 122–30.

62 See M. J. da Silva Leal, *Livro do almoxarifado*, pp. 35 and 45, and F. Soyer, *The Persecution*, pp. 57–58.

63 F. Soyer, *The Persecution*, p. 58. Jews also served in militias in Portugal, whereas they did not in Castile or Aragon.

64 M. F. Lopes de Barros, *Tempos e espaços*, p. 580; F. Soyer, *The Persecution*, pp. 57–58. In fact, as early as 1369–70 the Valencian *corts* of San Mateu had prohibited Muslims from bearing arms except in the presence of the kingdom's bailiff, but this was simply not observed. See M. T. Ferrer i Mallol, "Frontera, convivencia y proselitisme," p. 1584.

conflict with their own communities – particularly when hard economic times increased the fiscal burdens on *comunas*. Ordinary Muslim craftsmen seem to have benefitted from the labor shortage in the wake of the plague. In 1359 the *comuna* of Moura succeeded in having legal requirements regarding the long-sleeved robes they were required to wear as Muslims altered on the basis that they interfered with their work, and consequently, their ability to generate tribute. A century later, the townsmen of Mourão succeeded in obtaining privileges of legal equality conceded to Jewish and Muslim craftsmen who were willing to settle there, and in 1459, the authorities in Elvas obtained tax exemptions for Muslims – both local ones and the Castilian *mudéjares* they hoped to lure as immigrants.[65] The same town recognized the service and sacrifice rendered by Muslims and Jews in the wars with Castile. Although conditions varied locally, from the 1360s through the 1400s *mouros* served as royal and local forces as foot soldiers, musketeers, and cavalry, both on campaign and on garrison duty. Here, there is virtually no evidence of sectarian or ideological tension or violence directed at Muslims at this time.

Islamic society in Portugal was anything but static through the fourteenth and fifteenth centuries. Economic and administrative integration drew Muslims into Christian society and culture, diluting what remained of distinctively Islamic commercial and occupational practices and administrative institutions. Labor-hungry monasteries, such as Alcobaça and Chelas, together with noble landlords, benefited from their mobility and initiative, and Muslim families spread out from urban enclaves into the countryside, not as owners, but as tenants and sharecroppers. And yet, the Muslim population seems to have been voting with its feet, and illegal emigration took its toll. Some, like the convicted murderers Azmede of Avis (1383), Focem Picom of Santarém (1443), and Focem of Évora (1472), fled to Castile to evade justice; others in response to hostile or repressive legislation.[66] Most clandestine emigrés headed for Granada or North Africa, but a significant number made for Christian lands. Their flight represented a short-term gain for the crown, which by law took ownership of the property of those who fled, but *comunas* were impoverished and pushed towards social and economic crisis as a result. Other communities, such as that of Avis, simply disappeared. As a response to this decline, in the second half of the fifteenth-century several of the more important *comunas* requested and gained the right to purchase and manumit slaves in order to marry them into their communities – an influx of

[65] F. Soyer, *The Persecution*, pp. 65–66, and 73–74.
[66] M. F. Lopes de Barros, *Tempos e espaços*, pp. 165–66.

foreign-born co-religionists that would not only help to sustain the population in numerical terms, but reinforce (and transform) Muslim culture here religiously and culturally.[67] In the late 1460s and 1470s a number of documents refer to Moroccan Muslims who received permission to settle or trade in Portugal, or who, like the *mouro forro* and native of the "kingdom of Fez," Omar, received royal dispensation to return to his homeland in spite of legal prohibitions against emigration.[68]

### *The realms of Castile-León*

Although there is an abundance of documentary material for the late fifteenth century, evidence relating to the *mudéjares* of the realms of Castile-León remains sparse for the 1300s; however, they certainly constituted a larger segment of the population than either Portugal or Navarre both in terms of number and proportion.[69] And despite a lack of direct evidence, most historians credit the rebellions of the Guadalquivir of the late thirteenth century to an influx of Muslims in the lands to the north, where sizable *aljamas* had long been established at sites including Ávila, Segovia, Madrid, Arévalo, and Toledo, as well as Burgos, Palencia, Toro, Tordesillas, Madrigal, Valladolid, and Medina del Campo, among others. Many of these were quite substantial; Ávila, for example, had no fewer than three mosques. How the "native" Muslims interacted with these newcomers cannot be said, although the latter seem to have established new extramural settlements, and it can be expected that the former endeavored to maintain a competitive advantage over their co-religionists.

Apart from the larger communities, there was also a considerable Muslim presence in the countryside, hamlets, and smaller towns, stretching down from Burgos to Madrid, as well as in the Castilian Extremadura, to the southwest.[70] Some were organized into *aljamas* under the control of lay and ecclesiastical seigneurs, whereas others do not seem to have been formally constituted at all. Major communities in the Extremadura included Alcántara (governed by the Military Order of the same name), Mérida, Llerena, and Hornachos, each of which had dependent villages and hamlets. In the Guadalquivir and to the south there were small communities at Córdoba, Seville, Écija, and La Algaba, and in the late

[67] F. Soyer, *The Persecution*, p. 44. [68] M. F. Lopes de Barros, *Tempos e espaços*, p. 155.

[69] See, for example, A. Echevarría Arsuaga, "De cadí a alcalde mayor (I)," "De cadí a alcalde mayor (II)," and "Las aljamas mudéjares"; I. Montes Romero-Camacho and M. González Jiménez, "Los mudéjares andaluces," and I. Montes Romero-Camacho, "Las comunidades mudéjares."

[70] See for example E. Cantera Montenegros, "Las comunidades mudéjares."

fourteenth century thriving new *aljamas* were established under the Trastámaras at Palma del Río, Archidona, and Priego, to accommodate refugees from the Castilian civil wars and the fighting along the Granadan border. The Order of Santiago at Uclés was also patron and lord of a number of substantial communities. In Murcia, immigration helped to reconstitute *mudéjar* society, although Muslims here preferred seigniorial lands and the rural environment to the city. Through the fifteenth century the Muslim population in the capital declined by 95 per cent.

As in the rest of the peninsula, the crown's interest in cultivating and maintaining the Muslim population related to their contribution to the royal fisc and the larger economy. Here, Muslims were subject to three royal taxes: the *servicio* or *medio servicio*, a poll-tax paid by men aged over twenty, the *cabeza de pecho*, a fee levied in exchange for their religious liberties, and – in the fifteenth century – the *castellano de oro*, a hearth tax that subsidized the war with Granada. Over time there was a tendency for these taxes to become more onerous, a factor that contributed both to the movement of Muslims off of royal lands, and to emigration, legal or not. The minority of Juan II, which lasted from 1406 to 1418, also provoked reconfigurations. The Queen Mother, Catalina of Lancaster, clashed with her co-regent, Fernando de Antequera, and the two eventually divided the realm into two independent zones. Although both passed restrictive legislation regarding the religious minorities, Catalina's initiatives were much more stringent and applied with more rigor, a fact that encouraged the movement of *mudéjares* from the north towards Ferdinand's lands in the south.

Overall, the *mudéjar* population here seems to have grown strongly through the mid fifteenth century, before dropping off rapidly in the last decades of the 1400s. Internal migration led some *aljamas*, such as Talavera, to disappear, whereas others, like Toledo, experienced growth – the latter largely as the consequence of the manumission and settlement of prisoners of war. In sum, far from representing the fossilized remains of a defunct caliphate, the *mudéjares* of Castile-León comprised a mobile and evolving population, responding to changing conditions and opportunities both on their own initiative, in reaction to seigniorial powers, and under the coercion of royal authority.

Naturally, agriculture figured as the leading occupation of Castilian Muslims, although here – perhaps due to the relative importance of the larger *aljamas* – their domination of certain key trades, and notably in building and decorative crafts, appears to have been even clearer, particularly in the north. Muslims were also engaged in commerce, both locally, in Aragon and Portugal, and with Islamic Granada and North Africa. Most remarkably, there was significant presence of Muslims in high-status, educated professions, particularly medicine; and these physicians were popular among the Christian elite.[71] This is curious, not so much because it flew in the face of legal prohibitions on Muslims exercising this vocation, but both because, typically, *mudéjares* did not have access to advanced education, and as educated Muslims, they had the option of, and tended to prefer pursuing their vocations in the *dār al-Islām*. In any event, these activities, together with the more effectively autocratic tendencies of the Castilian monarchy, helped to sustain a middle and upper class that was proportionately larger than that of the other kingdoms and which was more actively engaged in with the upper classes of Christian society – although the success of this group was not necessarily to the benefit of *mudéjares* as a group.

Alfonso X's mid thirteenth-century legal compilation, *Las Siete Partidas* ("The Seven Divisions"), had aimed for the establishment of a hierarchy of authority among his *mudéjar* communities. Each would be under the supervision and control of an *Alcalde Mayor*, who paid a license fee for the privilege, while these would answer to "the chief *alcalde* of all of My realms," whose dues were correspondingly heavier.[72] This institution may have indeed been inspired by the Islamic *qāḍī al-quḍāt*, which Alfonso would have been familiar with from his relations with Naṣrid Granada, but it was also consistent with Castilian policy vis-à-vis the kingdom's Jewish communities, which were overseen by a Chief Rabbi (*Rabí Mayor* or *Rab de la Corte*).[73] However, *mudéjar* administration did not necessarily function according to the legal ideal. A town like Ávila had several *alcaldes* – apparently, one for each of its three major mosques. Although it is not clear that they each enjoyed the same juridical power, their mere existence undermined the authority of the office of *qāḍī*, which was predicated on the notion of unipersonality, which is to say, one magistrate per locale.[74] Nor is it clear that the *Alcalde Mayor* took any active role in the activities of the *alcaldes* of the smaller communities scattered across Castile.[75]

71 See, below, chapter 10.

72 J. Torres Fontes, "El alcalde mayor," p. 143. In 1369 the annual dues for a local *alcalde* was set at sixty *maravedís*, whereas that of the *alcalde del regno* was to be 600. See also Partido III, Title XX, Law VIII, in Alfonso X, *Las Siete Partidas*, vol. III, p. 772–73.

73 Echevarría argues for institutional continuity in A. Echevarría Arsuaga, "De cadí a alcalde mayor (II), pp. 275–79, but this argument holds at best for form rather than function. The office of *alcalde* was fundamentally and essentially different from that of *qāḍī*, a point on which contemporary Islamic jurists were adamant. See, below, p. 316.

74 For the Ávila, see p. 191, above. Not surprisingly, this led to competition and tension. See, for, example, S. Abboud Haggar, "Diffusión del tratado jurídico," p. 7.

75 See E. Cantera Montenegro, "El apartamiento de judíos y mudéjares," and J.-P. Molénat, "*Alcaldes* et *alcaldes mayors*."

*Elite and hierarchy in Castile*

Be that as it may, this administrative hierarchy provided a framework for a relatively broad and wealthy *mudéjar* upper class, although to characterize either these Muslims or the judicial apparatus in which they served as "autonomous" would be a mistake. The interpretation and execution of Islamic justice remained subject to Christian authority and control, albeit less directly than in the Crown of Aragon, and the individuals and families who ascended the administrative and economic ladder did so largely as a consequence of the influence of powerful Christian allies and patrons. This can be seen in the contest for control of the office of *Alcalde Mayor* in the fifteenth century, which pitted the Xarafís against the Bellvís family. The Xarafís were a family of jurists whose pedigree may have stretched back to tenth-century Sevilla. They gained control of the *aljama* of Toledo in the fourteenth century, and reinforced their position by cultivating connections with the Christian clerical and noble elite. For example, Abrahem Xarafí was not only *Alcalde Mayor* of the realms of Castile, but also the physician to Alfonso Carrillo, Archbishop of Toledo.[76] His appointment as titular head of the kingdom's Muslims in 1475 marked the family's victory over their Aragonese rivals. As for the Bellvíses, Jahia de Bellvís, the brother of Faraig, Pere III's groom and *alcadi regis*, had been settled at Medinaceli, on the frontier with Aragon, by the early 1360s. This provided a Castilian base for the family, whose commercial and diplomatic operations played out across both Castile and the Crown of Aragon, as well as in Granada and North Africa.[77] By gaining the favor of the Trastámaras (who ruled both Castile and Aragon from 1414), and of magnates, including the powerful Mendoza family, and Alváro de Luna, Master of Santiago and Constable, favorite and *eminence grise* of Juan II, the Bellvíses obtained control first of the *alcaldia de moros* of Guadalajara, and, later, with the appointment of Farax de Belvís as chief Islamic magistrate, for all of Castile. Thus, the rivalry of leading *mudéjar* families was not such much a contest within the Muslim community, but rather among a narrow *mudéjar* elite. In any event, it was enabled, if not driven, by the partisan rivalries of the Christian factions who were their patrons and for whom they served as proxies.

Below these *mudéjar* "magnates" there existed a fairly broad class of educated and relatively affluent Muslims, who surface frequently in the abundant documentation of the late fifteenth century. They served in more prestigious professions (such as medicine), or prospered as master

[76] J.-P. Molénat, "Une famille d'élite," p. 768.
[77] A. Echevarría Arsuaga, "De cadí a alcalde mayor (I)," pp. 152–53.

craftsmen or merchants – influence-currying and capital-generating activities that allowed them access to official positions, such as that of local *alcaldes de moros*.[78] Like their more prosperous co-religionists, members of these families competed for local influence and advantage, sparking a series of conflicts within the *aljamas* in the fifteenth century that frequently required royal intervention to defuse. On other hand, they helped to sustain a literary and religious culture that seems to have been more productive than those of the other Christian kingdoms.

Surviving *mudéjar* literature from this period consists of religious and secular texts, including sermonaries, didactic manuals, *ḥadīth* (both canonical and apocryphal), poetry, exegesis, editions of the Qur'ān, and treatises on Islamic law – both idealized, and as practiced under Christian rule.[79] These continued to be written in Arabic, although by the fourteenth century they were being produced increasingly in Romance (here in Castilian, but elsewhere in Valencian and Aragonese) as well as in *aljamiado*, or Romance written with Arabic characters. Indeed, a letter written by a medical student at the *madrasa* of Zaragoza to the *alfqui* of Belchite in the late fourteenth century reveals not only that there was a rural literary elite in the Kingdom of Aragon, but that its members were in contact with their counterparts in Navarre and Castile.[80] Evidence of this can be seen in the found *Poema de Yuçuf*, composed by an Aragonese *mudéjar* in the fourteenth century in a heavily Castilian-influenced *aljamiado*.[81] The culmination of the *mudéjar* literary movement in Castile can be seen in ʿĪsā ("Jesus") b. Jābir, *faqīh* from late fifteenth century Segovia, who produced a translation of the Qur'ān commissioned by the cardinal and theologian, Juan de Segovia, as well as an extensive manual of *mudéjar* law, the *Suma de los principales mandamientos y debadamientos de la Ley y Sunna*.[82]

[78] The same dynamic, in which commercial/professional activities, religious authority and administrative office correlated, can be observed on both a local and regional scale throughout the Iberian kingdoms.

[79] Evidence of a broad *mudéjar* literary culture, and one which was in dialog with contemporary Christian culture in fourteenth-century Castile is hinted by the appearance of the Guadalajaran poet Mahomat al-Xartosi in the fifteenth-century anthology of courtly poetry known as the *Cancionero de Baena*. The "Maestro Mahomat el Xartosse de Guardarfaxara" is described as physician of the admiral Diego Hurtado de Mendoza, and is said to have written in a "subtle and very literary" style. See J. A. de Baena, *El cancionero de Juan Alfonso de Baena*, p. 565 {522}; G. Wiegers, *Islamic Literature*, p. 61.

[80] L. García Ballester, *Historia social de la medicina*, pp. 68–70; also, P. S. van Koningsveld, "Andalusian-Arabic Manuscripts," p. 14.

[81] This poem represents the Islamic narrative of the Old Testament figure Joseph. See R. Menéndez Pidal, *Poema de Yuçuf*, pp. 62–63.

[82] The standard work on *mudéjar* and Morisco literature is G. Wiegers, *Islamic Literature*. See also his "Mudejar Biographies," and "The Persistence of Mudejar Islam?," as well as P. S. van Koningsveld, "The Polemical Works"; V. Barletta, *Covert Gestures*; C. López-Morillas, *Textos aljamiados*; and D. Zuwiyya, "A Typological Approach."

### *Intermediaries*

The circulation of merchants, pilgrims, refugees, migrants, and captives kept *mudéjares* throughout the peninsula connected with the larger Muslim world and living Islamic traditions. Hence, the work of the late fourteenth-century Damascene *faqīh* and *ḥadīth*-scholar, Muḥammad b. al-Jazarī, not only circulated among *mudéjares*, but was translated (into Aragonese Romance) within the lifetime of the author or soon after.[83] But in Castile the rapprochement between Islamic and Christian culture was particularly broad and deep. The translation of works of high Arabic culture, philosophy, and science had a long history here; the "school of translation" at Toledo had been active since the twelfth century and patronized by figures no less than the crusader and historian, Archbishop Rodrigo Jiménez de Rada (d. 1247), and Alfonso X.[84] *Mudéjares* and converts took an active role in the endeavor, which was not restricted to Toledo; in Murcia, the King founded a *madrasa* which served as a translation – an act of formal Islamic patronage that had no parallel in the other Christian kingdoms. The establishment of Naṣrid Granada as a vassal kingdom and Castile's political ambitions in North Africa further encouraged engagement with the Muslim elite both at home and abroad, and a recognition of Arabo-Islamic culture as valuable on its own terms.

Hence, the Castilian elite, and in particular, the monarchs, embraced "Moorish" styles of decoration, architecture, dress, and diversion to the point of notoriety and scandal at a time when "*mudéjar*" styles had largely passed out of fashion in the rest of the peninsula. Pedro the Cruel, for example, built a series of buildings in the most exuberant Islamicate styles, including the Alcázar in Sevilla, with its stunning pseudo-Naṣrid "Patio de las Doncellas," and the elaborately renovated *mudéjar*-style palace at Tordesillas.[85] This self-described *ṣulṭān* even attempted (unsuccessfully) to recruit no less a figure than the noted Maghribī *litterateur* and *faqīh* Ibn Khaldūn to his court. A century later, the embattled Trastámaran ruler Enrique IV (1454–74) was lampooned by domestic enemies both for his

[83] See S. Abboud Haggar, "Una muestra de transmisión."

[84] For an overview, see L. P. Harvey, "The Alfonsine School of Translators," and C. Burnett, "The Coherence"; for a case study, see O. R. Constable, "Chess and Courtly Culture." For the relation of the Alfonsine school to contemporary developments in the Islamic world, see M. I. Fierro Bello, "Alfonso X." The singularity of the "Toledo school" has been exaggerated, a misconception the work of Burnett has done much to correct; see C. Burnett, "The Translating Activity," and other works cited in the Bibliography. Murcia and Sevilla were also important centres of transmission, at least during the reign of Alfonso. See F. de la Granja, "Una polémica religiosa."

[85] See A. Almagro Gorbea, "El Alcázar de Sevilla," and C. Robinson, "Mudéjar Revisited." The palace at Tordesillas became a Clarissan convent after Pedro's death.

alleged homosexuality and his Maurophilic predilections.[86] When in 1458 his half-brother rose up against him in Burgos, the rebellious Don Alfonso asserted his claim to the throne on the basis that Enrique was showing favor to the "Muslim enemies of the faith, traveling with them, hosting them, and paying them double the salary of Christians."[87] In Castile, this attraction to Islamic culture was for the most part confined to the aristocratic elite; ordinary Christians saw Muslims, whether *mudéjares* or foreign, as too much of a threat to engage in such confident cultural appropriation.[88]

In the fourteenth and fifteenth centuries Castile was intermittently at war with Granada and with the Marīnids, and all three faced ongoing rebellions and insurrections. Thus, it was common for Christian and Muslim renegades, political refugees, rebels, and soldiers of fortune to seek refuge and find employment on the far side of the frontier. Hence, the Castilian nobility experienced Islamic society and culture first-hand, through the medium of a shared military vocation and common aristocratic mind-set, while Castilian *mudéjares* were exposed to the example of an independent Muslim military elite. The most striking manifestation of this was the establishment under Juan II and Enrique IV of a regiment of Muslim cavalry, the *cavalleros moriscos* – a praetorian guard made up primarily of volunteers from Granada who settled around Castile.[89] They were active throughout Castile and against Granada, and as the kingdom spun into chaos during Alváro de Luna's struggle for power in the 1440s, members of the guard took sides among the noble factions or passed over to the service of Juan II (1405–54) of Navarre. By 1466 the company had been disbanded. In the surviving pay registers, most *cavalleros* are indicated by Romance names, and it is likely they converted on or soon after recruitment, although some may have been converting superficially or temporarily, or may have simply adopted "Christian" *noms de guerre*. High status *mudéjares* also joined the guard, with varying outcomes. For example, Hamede al Cabrí, a Muslim from near Lucena, converted as "Juan Fernández de Aguilar," and came to enjoy the personal favor of King Enrique, while Farax de Bellvís, the son of Jahia, kept his faith. Farax not only survived the disgrace and execution of his patron, Alváro de Luna, but remained active as the *alcalde de moros* of Guadalajara and in his clan's commercial ventures for the rest of his days.[90]

86 See B. Fuchs, *Exotic Nation*, pp. 17 and 43.
87 See L. Torres Balbás, *Algunos aspectos*, p. 26.
88 S. de Tapia Sánchez, "Los mudéjares de la Extremadura," pp. 101–02.
89 See A. Echevarría Arsuaga, *Knights on the Frontier*.
90 See A. Echevarría Arsuaga, "Conversión y ascenso," pp. 557–61, and, "De cadí a alcalde mayor (I)," 159–60.

Castile seems to have seen a greater rate of conversion among *mudéjares* than the other kingdoms of the peninsula, a fact which is likely rooted in the relative wealth and influence of the Muslim upper classes here, and their capacity to transition into comparable positions in Christian society, rather than being a consequence of repression, segregation, or proselytizing. This is not to say that these were not features of the *mudéjar* experience in the fourteenth and fifteenth centuries. Although there was a general tendency towards the physical segregation, isolation, and differentiation of Muslims across the peninsula, in Castile religious and legal pressure seems to have been particularly acute. Nevertheless, as *mudéjares* increasingly came to be regarded as alien, their reaction here, as in other Christian realms, tended to be either to retrench or depart, rather than abjure.

## Familiars and aliens: cultivating difference in late medieval Iberia

Thus declares the wise and honored *mufti* and *faqīh* of the *aljama* of the Muslims of the noble and loyal city of Segovia, *Don* Iça Jedih ... And because the Muslims of Castile, under great subjection and great obligation, and under heavy tribute, suffering and obligations, have declined in their wealth and lost their schools of Arabic ... they begged me to undertake to recopy and translate in Romance the famous text of our Holy Law and *Sunna*, of that which every good Muslim ought to know and follow ... (ʿĪsā b. Jābir, *Brevario sunni* (1462)[91])

Although their experiences in the various kingdoms of the peninsula varied, the fourteenth and fifteenth centuries were a time when *mudéjares* across the peninsula became simultaneously both more engaged in the Christian-dominated societies in which they lived and more detached from them. This can be seen most clearly in legal developments. The translations and redactions in Romance of Islamic legal texts, such as ʿĪsā b. Jābir's *Brevario*, or the anonymous fourteenth-century Valencian digest edited as *El llibre de la çuna e xara* ("Book of the *Sunna* and *Sharīʿa*") were clearly meant for Christian as well as Muslim readers – a consequence of the former becoming more involved and interested in the function and supervision of Islamic jurisdictions.[92] In this spirit, in the 1460s Afonso V of Portugal commissioned Yūsuf Ibrāhīm b. Yūsuf al-Laḥmī of Lisbon, "a jurist certified in the laws of the Muslims," to undertake a similar project, which he

[91] "Abridgement of the *Sunna*," in P. de Gayangos, *Las leyes de los moros*, pp. 247–48.

[92] The *Brevario* and the "*Leyes de moros*" ("Laws of the Muslims"), a second, purportedly early collection of contemporary Castilian Islamic law, are edited in *ibid.* The so-called *Llibre de la Suna e Xara* is edited and studied in C. Barceló Torres, *Un tratado catalán*, and V. Garcia Edo, *Suna e xara*.

called the *Declaração dos direitos dos mouros forros.*[93] These legal manuals consciously followed the traditions of the Mālikī *madhhab* that had exercised a practical monopoly over Andalusī jurisprudence; but, as their authors surely knew, these works represented truncations and distortions of Islamic law, the scope and competency of which was drastically limited in practical terms by the rights and powers of Christian rulers and institutions over free Muslim subjects. In other words, these treatises represented, in a sense, damage control – an attempt to salvage what could be preserved of the legal jurisdiction that is central to Islam, and present to Christian authorities those aspects of the law *mudéjares* considered most at risk.

In Navarre there were no significant innovations in royal law codes concerning Muslims after the great compilations of the mid to late thirteenth century. On the other hand, in Castile – perhaps as a consequence of the high visibility of *mudéjar* society, together with the pretensions of the monarchs to universal authority over the peninsula based on the twin claims of pre-Islamic, Visigothic pedigree and the exercise of Crusade (and "Reconquest") – jurists focused ever more closely on their Muslim subjects. Here, Alfonso X's voluminous *Las Siete Partidas* had established the subject and secondary status of non-Christians.[94] But in the Middle Ages, laws were often little more than declarations of the ideals of jurists, and frequently collided with the demands of politics; hence, the restrictions in the Alfonsine code were undoubtedly enforced unevenly, if at all. Nevertheless, these were repeated and extended by subsequent edicts, such as those of the Cortes of Alcalá in 1348, which limited, *inter alia*, Muslims' ability to own land and serve in administrative posts. However, these restrictions, along with those of the *Partidas*, were rolled back by Enrique II in the wake of the Black Death.[95] Likewise, in 1408 and 1412 rigorously segregationist laws were laid down by the Dowager-Regent, Catherine of Lancaster, limiting *mudéjar* economic and social interaction with Christians, excluding them from a range of professions, and establishing a range of laws aimed at segregating Muslims.[96] But these were likely never enforced; at any rate, Juan II's majority and Alváro de Luna's ascendency marked a return to a pragmatic and conciliatory approach towards *mudéjares*. The Constable's fall provoked 1465's *Sentencia de Medina del Campo*, a revision of the kingdom's government, which necessarily included a reappraisal of Muslims' (and Jews') place in Castilian society, and reiterated Catherine of Lancaster's prohibitions. But the

[93] M. F. Lopes de Barros, *Tempos e espaços*, p. 61, and "A comuna," pp. 63–64.
[94] See M. Ratcliffe, "Judios y musulmanes."
[95] See S. de Tapia Sánchez, "Los mudéjares de la Extremadura," 105.
[96] See A. Echevarría Arsuaga, "Catalina of Lancaster," pp. 97–102.

repressive measures advocated here were neither ratified by Enrique IV, nor enforced with any consistency.

Similar legislation was promulgated in Portugal at the royal, ecclesiastical, and municipal level, from the mid fourteenth century onwards. Here, it seems that efforts at enforcement were somewhat more consistent, a circumstance that sparked protests not only from Muslims, but from Christian parties (including municipalities) who saw the maintenance of a prosperous, content Muslim population as being in their interests. In the Crown of Aragón, on the other hand, legal innovations of this type were few, although rulers of religious temperament, notably Martí I, ordered drastic restrictions on the public practice of Islam. However, these prohibitions – reiterated in mid-century by King Joan II (1458–79; of Navarre, 1425–79) – apparently went ignored. Even in the late fifteenth century, a series of foreign travelers to the peninsula echoed the sentiments of Honoré de Bovet's "Sarrazin," singling out Aragon as a place where there was an abundance of Muslims who freely and openly practiced their faith.[97] Islamic culture was particularly vibrant in the countryside, as attested to by the survival of religious and secular texts written in Arabic, *aljamiado*, and Romance that were composed and read in hamlets throughout the kingdom.[98] This is not surprising, when one recalls that King Martí himself, and his wife, Maria de Luna, were also seigniors with significant Muslim communities, and in that role, they adopted flexible and liberal approaches to the regulation of non-Christian religious practice that went against the spirit of their own royal decrees.

As a seignior in 1381, for example, Martí ordered anyone daring to call the *ʾadhān* on his estates to be punished with a lashing and by having their tongue pierced with a spike, and yet in 1385 he gave permission for the *aljama* of Benaguasil to summon local *mudéjares* to prayer using a trumpet (*anfīl*) from atop the minaret, or chanting the *ʾadhān* at the door of the mosque. The *infant* was merely emulating his father, Pere the Ceremonious, who had himself rejected the *Cortes* of Valencia's ban of the *anfil*, on the grounds that playing the trumpet "is not a sign of disloyalty," and out of concern that such a ban would simply drive *mudéjares* off royal lands.[99] Similar bans were promulgated in Castile and Portugal, and

97 For an overview, see J. Hinojosa y Montalvo, "Cristianos contra musulmanes," pp. 351–56; many accounts are edited in J. García Mercadal, *Viajes de extranjeros*.

98 For the Muslims of Christian Iberia, literary culture, which we usually associate with cities and centers of formal patronage, was evidently largely a rural and village phenomenon, as demonstrated by the discovery of caches of manuscripts in villages such as Sábiñan, Ocana, and Almonacid de la Sierra.

99 M. T. Ferrer i Mallol, "Frontera, convivencia," pp. 1589–90.

with similar results.[100] Hence, throughout the peninsula, mosques continued to be repaired, Muslims prayed in public, and in many locales the *mu'adhdhin*'s call echoed five times per day calling the faithful to worship.

### *The weight of the law*

Enforced or not, the cumulative effect of such legislation, whether sponsored at the royal or local level, coupled with a grating awareness that Islam-in-the-world continued to be a force to be contended with, together with the determination of lords and rulers to keep a grip on their revenue-producing subjects, and the increasing sense of economic competition between Christian and Muslim subjects in some sectors and locales, took its toll. By the fourteenth century Muslims in the various kingdoms were generally required, and increasingly chose, to live in separate *morerías* for their own security, to more clearly maintain separate fiscal regimes, and to ensure that the rights and revenues of the holders of communally defined monopolies (such as butcher shops, inns, and baths) were guaranteed. This was a gradual process, beginning with some locales as early as the 1270s but stretching out late into the 1400s in others.[101] In the name of preserving the tax base, Muslims were typically forbidden under penalty of dispossession (except with dispensation) from selling property to non-Muslims, and Christians from buying Muslim property. On the other hand, while the principle that non-Christians should not be subject to the tithe continued to be upheld in principle, land was held to be subject to Church taxes if it had passed under Christian ownership at any time. Savvy ecclesiastical lords could engineer a temporary "expulsion" of their Muslim tenants in order to bring the lands they occupied under the tithe. In sum, *mudéjares* found themselves increasingly disadvantaged in and edged out of the land market.

Independent of the innovations of Church law – notably the canons of Lateran IV (1215) – from the late thirteenth century *mudéjares* across the peninsula became increasingly subject to vestimentary rules, the aim of which was to distinguish them visually from Christians and prevent unwitting inter-communal sexual intercourse. These laws varied greatly in terms of content and application over time and from locale to locale. In some regions, the *garceta* (a soup-bowl haircut) was mandated, while in others particular items or cuts of clothing (e.g. capes, robes, or hoods of certain styles or materials), and/or badges of various colors (e.g.: blue,

[100] In 1390 the *cortes* held at Coimbra prohibited the call to prayer. See M. F. Lopes de Barros, *Tempos e espaços*, p. 198.

[101] See, for example, M. L. Ledesma Rubio, "Marginación y violència," p. 205.

red) and shapes (e.g. crescents, disks, half-moons) were mandated.[102] These rules should be understood not only in terms of minority status, but as a manifestation of the sumptuary laws that applied to subjects of all faiths and banned the use of luxury materials by all but the upper (Christian) classes.[103] The application of these laws, however, was capricious, and the fines and enslavement prescribed for their violation seem to have been seldom imposed. Moreover, both entire communities and specific individuals received relaxations or dispensations from these laws, as acts of grace, signs of favor, as a result of lobbying by powerful Christian patrons and allies, or merely due to official indifference.[104] As it was, to the extent that such laws were enforced, they may have met with the satisfaction of religiously inclined *mudéjares* who would see them, like the segregative laws, as a means of marking off and preserving Islamic identity. Others, however, either defied the orders passively, or resisted openly.[105]

The chauvinistic tone of the legislation reflected and resonated with the anti-rational and millenarian trend that swept through the Church in the century after the plague, and which inspired preachers ranging from St. Vicent Ferrer (1350–1419), miracle-working ascetic, adviser, and confessor to royals, and converter of Jews and Muslims, to Ferrán Martínez, the incendiary Archdeacon of Éjica, who sparked the anti-Jewish pogroms of 1391. Local Church councils, such as 1312's Synod of Zamora, had been advocating social restrictions on non-Christians for some time. As a result, constraints against the public practice of Islam, which had been mandated by Canon Law since the late 1100s, gradually and fitfully came to be imposed across the peninsula. The construction and repair of mosques became increasingly problematic, prohibitions against the call to prayer were extended, public alms-collecting (practiced by slaves for the purpose of ransoming oneself) was restricted and regulated, and Muslims (and Jews) were increasingly obliged not to visibly break the Christian Sabbath and to yield or conceal themselves when Christian religious processions passed in the street. Over time, such restrictions were increasingly incorporated into municipal law codes; the sound of the industrious hammering of Muslim smiths during Sunday Mass seems to have been a

[102] See the discussion in M. F. Lopes de Barros, "Body, Baths and Cloth," pp. 9–11.

[103] For example, if wealthy *mudéjares* in Old Castile were forbidden from dressing in gold, silk, scarlet, or camelote (a silk, camel-hair mix), these were also restrictions lower-class Christians would have been subject to. See L. Torres Balbás, *Algunos aspectos*, p. 31.

[104] See M. T. Ferrer i Mallol, *Els sarraïns*, chapter 3: "La imposició de distintius," pp. 41–60.

[105] From the 1350s Portuguese Muslims were protesting the requirement to wear special badges and clothing.

particular point of irritation for Christian burghers. Nevertheless, later fourteenth-century "reiterations" or promulgations of these types of decree show that in many locales they were little observed.

The impact of the laws aimed at the social segregation of and discrimination against Muslims is difficult to gauge. There is considerable evidence, however, that it was limited.[106] With remarkable frequency, Muslims, Christians, and Jews continued to socialize, live amongst each other, commit crimes together, have sex with each other, drink and gamble and disport with prostitutes together (and in the case of Muslim prostitutes, serve Christian and Jewish clients). Even when malefactors were caught *in flagrante*, the gruesome corporal punishments prescribed by law could usually be avoided by payment of a fine or commuted by enslavement – a fact that would have disconcerted pious *mudéjares* as much as their Christian oppressors.[107] Muslims continued to construct mosques, worship publicly, openly practice forbidden professions, including medicine, dress and pose as Christians, and travel with or without permission. Together, all of this reflects the fundamental disconnect between legislation and social and economic realities in the Middle Ages.[108]

The tension between *mudéjar* integration and segregation reached the critical point in Valencia in the 1450s. The kingdom was a powder-keg – combining a large population of Muslims, geographic proximity to the *dār al-Islām*, and a violently divided Christian society, with a history of *mudéjar* insurrection and Islamic resistance. The *guerra Sarracenorum* of the 1200s and the repression that followed was a formative episode that loomed large in both the Christian and Muslim imaginations here. The traumatic forced relocations and the steady discplacement and marginalization of Muslims that characterized the conquest of the kingdom and its aftermath may have left *mudéjar* society here less stable and more reactionary. In early 1360 simmering resentments led Çilim [Sālim], a

106 The broad nature of Muslim–Christian social interaction, particularly in Navarre, Castile, and Aragon, but also in Portugal and Valencia, is manifest across a whole range of sources that survive in abundance from the late fourteenth century, including notarial registers, municipal records, land transfer and loan documents, chancery documents (in particular, royal responses to complaints and petitions, royal account books, and trial records).

107 See, below, p. 457.

108 Some laws, such as the oft-repeated injunctions against Christians serving as wet-nurses and servants in Jewish (and Muslim) households, seem to have been little more than formulaic recapitulations of late Roman law codes. See H. Gilles, "Législation et doctrine canoniques," p. 195. Others, such as the novel injunction that Muslims and Jews should be executed by being hung upside down, either represented the fantasies of jurists or occasional and localized customs. See, below, p. 367.

Muslim from the hills north of Xàtiva, to lead a significant *mudéjar* revolt. For his followers – who appear to have been many – he was a prophet-like figure, while for Pere III he was a mere criminal and a "perfidious Muslim."[109] The violent insurrection took two years to quash, ending in 1362, when Çilim and his leading accomplices were captured and burned at the stake. The King granted the rebellious communities amnesties, but fresh revolts broke out only two years later.

### *An anti-Muslim turn*

Episodes such as these, together with coastal and cross-border raiding by Muslims, and lingering memories of the thirteenth-century *guerra Saracenorum*, contributed to suspicions here that *mudéjares* were acting as a "fifth column," as did the growing proportion of Granada and Maghribī Muslims who joined Valencian society as slaves. These anxieties were, in turn, encouraged by reactionary members of the clergy and elements of the urban population who saw anti-Muslim sentiment as serving either their heavenly or earthly agendas. López de Coca Castaner discerns two Christian attitudes towards Muslims in Valencia after the mid fourteenth century: a "philo-Muslim" approach exhibited by rural seigniors, and an increasingly antagonist attitude that characterized the clergy and urban classes.[110] In 1386 the *morería* of Xàtiva was both devastated by a severe earthquake and attacked by the local townsfolk. King Pere promised exemplary retribution and compensation for the afflicted, but as in the case of Çilim's rebels, the infractors went all but unpunished. The hills south of Valencia continued to be a flashpoint, and attacks on Muslim communities continued through the 1390s. In Valencia itself there were attacks on the *morería* in 1391 and 1399, although they did not prove catastrophic.[111] Ideologues, like the Franciscan political theorist and reformer Francesc Eixmenis, began to pressure the city council of Valencia to ban public manifestations of Islam and disarm the *mudéjares,* not only for Christians' safety, but so that "God may not be angered at you or this land."[112]

As the fifteenth century progressed, economic competition and depression, religious reactionism, papal Crusade rhetoric, continuing civil disorder, and the growing threat of war with Granada undermined

109 See J. Boswell, *The Royal Treasure*, pp. 376–78 and 489–90; M. T. Ferrer i Mallol, *Els sarraïns*, pp. 164–65, 288 {77} and 291 {81}.
110 J. E. López Coca de Castaner, "Los mudéjares valencianos," p. 644.
111 See M. Ruzafa, "Élites valencianas," pp. 172–73.
112 J. E. López Coca de Castaner, "Los mudéjares valencianos," pp. 652–53.

the stability of Christian–Muslim relations in the kingdom, stoking the perception of Muslims as disloyal, generically distinct foreigners. Contemporary Valencian literature, ranging from Jaume Roig's moralizing bourgeois novel, *Espill* ("The Mirror", 1460) to Joanot Martorell's chivalric tale, *Tirant lo Blanch* ("Tirant the White", 1490), reflected and reinforced such stereotypes and advocated for the establishment of a homogenously Christian society. In 1451 the city council demanded Alfons the Magnanimous disarm the Muslims, who they declared "are our enemies openly and by their prophecies" and were waiting for the opportune moment to strike.[113] On the policy level, these suggestions that the kingdom's *mudéjares* should be disarmed by law came to little. Finally, tensions boiled over into religious violence in June 1455, when the city's Muslim *aljama* was attacked by mobs to cries of "May the Muslims convert to Christianity or die!"[114]

In a progression that will seem all too familiar to students of the Jewish history of Christian Iberia, the pogrom unfolded in stages. That May, rumors were circulated that Calixtus III (1455–58; the Aragonese prelate Alfonso de Borja) had promised indulgences to anyone who killed Muslims, while gangs of youths celebrated his election by harassing and threatening *mudéjares*. The city authorities stood idly by as crowds of angry, disaffected townsfolk grew. On June 2 violence erupted, and the *morería* was sacked. Most of the inhabitants had fled so there were few deaths, but much material damage – including to the house of Mahoma de Bellvís, which was looted and burned. The Corpus Christi celebrations of June 5 brought larger crowds into the city, and as new rumors spread of an impending Muslim counter-attack, the revolt resumed, threatening to spread through the kingdom. The monarchy and municipal oligarchy saw the uprising for what it was: a challenge to their authority and the established order. Hence, the repression was swift and decisive, including massive arrests, general confiscations, selective executions, and the establishment of a royally sponsored inquisition into the events. Finally, by 1460, when it was clear that order had been re-established, Alfons V (1416–58) authorized a general pardon for the city-folk, including all but ten of the leaders of the pogrom, in exchange for a substantial payment to the treasury and reaffirmation of royal authority.

Unlike the anti-Jewish violence of 1391, the Valencian uprising of 1455 did not represent a transformative moment. Rather, it was one localized episode in the process of alienation and separation of Christians and Muslims, particular to that kingdom, that did not find echo among

[113] *Ibid.*, p. 653. [114] See M. Ruzafa García, "Façen-se cristians."

Christian townsmen elsewhere. It did, however, reverberate in far-off Granada, from where the Sultan, Sa'd (1453–64), demanded explanations. The city council responded in flattering tones, making light of the attack, congratulating the Sultan on his recent usurpation of the throne, and expressing the hope "in good confidence that all of our merchants [in Granada] ... will be treated well." A similar backlash had occurred after the pogroms of 1391, when Yūsuf II of Granada (1391–92), took advantage of the situation to demand concessions from Joan I. At the request of the Naṣrid ambassador, the King rescinded the sumptuary laws that applied to the *mudéjares* in his realms, relieving them of the obligation to wear "the *garceta* or any other distinguishing sign."[115] Singular as it may have been, the episode of 1455 was characteristic of a growing alienation of the Muslim subjects of Valencia from the Christian majority.

Partly as a consequence of their marginalization, partly in response to their continuing contact with a powerful and dynamic Islamic world, and in the face of an undeniable decadence and decline, many *mudéjar* communities began to retrench in terms of religious and social identity in the fifteenth century, both in the Crown of Aragon and across the peninsula. In some locales, attempts were made by Muslims to reorganize *aljamas* and to re-establish the religio-juridical integrity of their communities by spurning the Christian-imposed elite who ruled over them in favor of unofficial, popular religious authorities. Naturally, not all *mudéjares* stood to benefit personally from these developments – which at times provoked resistance and generated internal conflict. Community cohesiveness also emerged out of the increasing solidarity of *mudéjares* with Muslim slaves and fugitives, whom they helped to ransom or escape, and it reflected the low-level but widespread patronage of literary and religious culture. Meanwhile, commercial activities provided a conduit for communication and the strengthening of relations with foreign Muslim regimes, notably the ever-more powerful Ottomans, whom *mudéjares* courted as advocates and protectors. In 1487 the *aljamas* of Xàtiva and Paterna would send envoys to the Ottoman Bāyazīd II (1481–1512) seeking protection and military aid against the Christians of the kingdom of Valencia.[116]

## The conquest of Granada and the end of Islam in Latin Christendom

And once the fortresses have been handed over, Their Highnesses and the Prince, *Don* Juan, their son, will receive as native-born vassals, for themselves and the

[115] J. E. López Coca de Castaner, "Los mudéjares valencianos," p. 664.
[116] M. D. Meyerson, *The Muslims of Valencia*, pp. 67 and 68.

kings who succeed them, on their word, and royal security and protection, King Abí Abdilehi, and the *alcaides*, *cadís*, *alfaquís*, *meftís*, *sabios*, *alguaciles*, *caudillos* and *escuderos*, and all of the commoners, young and old, men and women, inhabitants of Granada and the Albaicin and suburbs, and the strongholds, towns and locales of its territory and of the Alpujarras, and the other places that are covered by this agreement and surrender, in any way; and they will leave them in their homes, estates and properties, for now and for all time and forever, and they will not allow them to suffer any ill or harm without cause or justice, nor will they let them be deprived of their goods or estates nor any part of them – rather, they will be obeyed, honored and respected by these their subjects and vassals, like the others who live under their government and rule . . . (Ferdinand (Ferran II) of Aragon and Isabel I of Castile, *Protocols for the Surrender of Granada* (November 25, 1491)[117])

For all the Crusade rhetoric that was associated with it, and the air of historical finality and inevitability with which it has been imbued, the surrender of the city of Granada by Muḥammad XII (1482 and 1486–1492; "Abū ʿAbd Allāh" or "Boabdil") to the "Catholic Monarchs" on January 2, 1492, marked neither the end of Islam in the peninsula, nor the end of Muslim rule here. As the text of the agreement shows, the intention was that the kingdom's inhabitants would remain as loyal, Muslim subjects of their new Christian lords. Nor is the conquest best understood as the culmination of a centuries-long "reconquest"; it was, on the contrary, a response to very contemporary challenges and opportunities faced both within the peninsula and in the context of a changing Europe and Mediterranean by the now jointly ruled Crowns of Aragon and Castile. Nevertheless, by 1526 the last significant Muslim community in the peninsula (and in Latin Christendom) would formally cease to exist, when the *mudéjares* of the Crown of Aragon were ordered to convert to Catholicism.

## *The road to Granada*

On October 19, 1469 the second cousins, Isabel of Castile (d. 1504) and Ferran II of Aragon (d. 1516), married in secret, in violation of the pact the *infanta* had made with her half-brother, Enrique IV, who had fought unsuccessfully against a coalition of Castilian noblemen to have his own daughter, Joanna "La Beltraneja," rather than Isabel, confirmed as heir to his kingdom. In 1474 Isabel would become Queen of Castile and León, while Ferran, King of Sicily since 1468, would go on to become King of the Crown of Aragon (1479) and Naples (1504), and Regent of Castile

117 M.A. Ladero Quesada, *Los Mudéjares de Castilla*, p. 173 {50}. For the full text, see J. Cowans, *Early Modern Spain*, pp. 15–19.

(1504), eventually forcing Navarre to submit to that kingdom (1512). The immediate consequence of the marriage, however, was war with Portugal, as the *infanta* Joanna's husband, Afonso V (1438–81), proclaimed himself King of Castile, and attacked. The invasion failed, and Isabel and her King-Consort were confirmed as separate rulers over their various kingdoms. Ferran and Isabel's momentous reign would see, *inter alia*, the expulsion of the Jews from their lands and the launching of Columbus's mission to "the Indies" in 1492, and the partition of the non-European world between Portugal and Castile with 1494's Treaty of Tordesillas, not to mention the conquest of Naṣrid Granada. It was as a consequence of their union that their realms would pass in 1516 into the hands of a foreign dynasty, the Hapsburgs, who would lay the ground work for a new political entity that would eventually be called the "kingdom of Spain."

In fact, the second half of the fifteenth century was marked by a general reconfiguration of the Mediterranean. In the west, both Portugal and Castile launched campaigns against Morocco, as the decadent Banū Marīn were overthrown by the insurgent Banū al-Waṭās. The Crown of Aragon expanded its influence in Italy and Ifrīqiya, while Venice struggled to hold its empire against both European powers and the Ottoman Turks. The latter had survived the Mongol and Timurid upheavals to emerge under the Sultan Mehmed I (1451–81) as the major power in the eastern Mediterranean. Constantinople would fall to him in 1453, although his subsequent campaigns against Italy were unsuccessful.[118] The Ottomans would drive into Persia in the 1510s, and the Balkans and Hungary in the 1520s. In 1517 the Mamluke Sultanate of Egypt, the Crown of Aragon's long-time trading partner, would succumb to the Turks, while the Ottomans, with the occasional collaboration of the so-called "Barbary corsairs," began a struggle with Castile over disintegrating Ifrīqiya and Barr al-Jazā'ir (Algeria). Ottoman iridescence had stirred anxieties in Spain since the late 1400s, and the anti-Turkish propaganda that began to emerge across Europe resonated strongly in the peninsula. In Europe, the Bourbons of France wrestled with the Hapsburg Holy Roman Emperors for control of the Catholic world, while the papacy's rhetoric of universal authority became progressively more strident the more that authority diminished in real terms, and even as a then-obscure German monk, Martin Luther, was formulating his "Ninety-Five Theses" for the reform of the Church. In the meanwhile, Portugal had also established bases in North Africa and beyond; in 1510 Afonso de Albuquerque took Goa (where he massacred the Muslim population), Muscat (Masqaṭ), and

[118] The town and fortress of Otranto were taken in 1480, but the occupation came to a negotiated end the following year.

Hormuz (Hurmuz), as well as Java and Sumatra, in the heavily Islamic Malay Archipelago. Missions of diplomacy, trade, and exploration had sent Europeans into the New World, around Africa, into the Indian Ocean, and to the Far East, revealing to them a world larger, richer, and more complex than had been previously imagined. With all of this, the centrality of Jerusalem and the simple binaries that characterized the medieval world seemed less and less appropriate; the concept of Latin Christendom, like the Tau-maps that once described its world, was a notion that had become obsolete.

Although the Naṣrid kingdom had effectively been a vassal state since its inception, its relations with Castile had been fraught since the outset, as the Christian kings sought to impose their political will and extract tribute, and the Granadan rulers, for their part, endeavored to shake off Christian influence and power. The stakes were high, as Granada's thriving silk industry, agriculture, and trade generated tremendous income. Moreover, the continuing existence of the kingdom presented a danger to Castilian stability and security. In times of confidence, Granadan forces attacked Castile, and rebellious Christian noblemen took refuge across her frontier, and raiding and captive-taking continued. The image of the Christian slave languishing in a Muslim *mazmorra*, enduring hard labor, or (in the case of women) being forced into concubinage, loomed ever larger in the Castilian imagination. Through the 1400s continuing unrest in Castile had prevented any following-up of Fernando de Antequera's early victories, but the situation in Granada was no better. Conflicts among the kingdom's leading clans and within the royal family kept Granada in a constant state of civil war and increased the political, economic, and military embroilment of factions within the Christian kingdom and within the Naṣrid elite. Conflicts among rival claimants for the throne were common, as uncles conspired to depose nephews, and the rival wives of reigning kings intrigued for the succession of their own offspring. All the while, powerful, independent families, like the Banū al-Sarrāj (romanticized as the "Abencerraje" in sixteenth-century literature), endeavored to take control of the kingdom or carve out their own principality with Castilian support.

In the interim, the border between the two kingdoms was stabilized by a series of truces, aimed at maintaining the territorial status quo, preventing raiding and slave-taking in times of peace, redeeming captives, and mediating disputes between Christian and Muslim parties. Formal protocols were established, overseen by officials known as *Acaldes entre moros y cristianos* ("magistrates [for disputes] among Muslims and Christians"); these supervised the activities of professional slave-ransomers (*alfaqueques*), and organized parties to pursue cross-border bandits. Land-based trade continued between the kingdoms, but this too was regulated and limited to specific ports of entry. Overall, relations between Granada and Castile were both adversarial and interdependent, with the fifteenth century representing a period of *entente*, although the end-game for Castile – the conquest of Granada – was never in doubt.

### *The final crusade?*

Conditions for the conquest would begin to converge with the defeat of Portugal in 1476, the conclusion of the Castilian civil war, Ferran's accession to the throne of the Crown of Aragon, Sixtus IV's (1471–84) concession of Crusade bull in 1479, and a coup d'état in Granada in 1482. In that year, Abū 'l-Ḥasan ʿAlī (1464–85) was briefly overthrown by the Banū al-Sarrāj, who placed his son, Boabdil, on the throne as Muḥammad XIII. The rightful King, together with his brother, Muḥammad al-Zaghal, took refuge in Málaga, effectively splitting the kingdom. However, the following year, an overconfident Boabdil was captured on a raid against Castile, to be released only after the Catholic Kings had extracted a pledge of vassalage from him – an act which earned him a formal *fatwa* of condemnation by the kingdom's religious elite.[119] In the interim al-Zaghal was recognized as King, but in 1492 he sailed for Oran (Wahrān), having sold to Ferran his remaining estates in the Alpujarras (al-Bushārrāt), the little princedom he had been granted by Castile in exchange for the surrender of Guadix (Wādī 'Ash) and Almería. His erstwhile enemies, the Banū al-Sarrāj, who had also found themselves confined to the tiny puppet state on the southern slopes of the Sierra Nevada, would emigrate the following year. Meanwhile, Boabdil remained as the sole, unpopular ruler over what little remained of the Naṣrid kingdom.

The previous decade had seen relentless campaigns led personally by Ferran II and Isabel to subdue the sultanate. The approach combined large-scale conventional warfare, the use of the latest, wall-busting heavy artillery, and *chevauchées* designed to undermine the capacity of the Andalusīs to mount a mobile, guerilla-type defense, and to demoralize the populace. Nevertheless, resistance was determined, and ordinary subjects fought tenaciously against the Castilian invaders. The fall of Ronda (al-Runda) represented a turning point. Although the defenders were determined, the reputedly impregnable town was no match for the Christian artillery, and on May 22, 1485 the inhabitants surrendered.

[119] See F. de Granja, "Condena de Boabdil."

Ferran granted generous terms, allowing the townsfolk to take their moveable goods and settle to where they wished, within or outside his realms. The commander, Ibrāhīm al-Ḥakīm, was provided with a financial settlement, and retired to Seville.[120] Those who chose to stay were designated as *sierbos mudéjares* – "Muslim serfs" – who were direct subjects of the monarchs. For their part, the local religious authorities swore an oath both to uphold Islamic law, which Ferran pledged to protect, and to serve faithfully their new rulers. Likely as a consequence of the conquerors' largesse, other towns – like Marbella (Marbil-la) on June 11, 1485 – yielded without a fight. The campaign continued the following year, bringing more successes, including the capture of Loja (Lawsha), at which Boabdil once again fell prisoner to Ferran.

At al-Zaghal's stronghold of Málaga, however, Ferran would trade carrot for stick. In spring 1487 he assembled a massive force to besiege the town, in what became undoubtedly the most viscerally fought battle in the war. Under the commander Aḥmad al-Thaghrī, the garrison and inhabitants resisted valiantly, fighting hand-to-hand and house-to-house and holding out in the face of starvation. Atrocities were threatened and committed against prisoners on both sides, and at one point an infiltrator claiming to be a turncoat almost succeeded in assassinating Ferran and Isabel in their own tent. Indeed, had it not been for Boabdil's complicity and assistance, a relief force sent by al-Zaghal might have broken the siege. As it was, worn down after more than three months, a faction within the leadership of the city lobbied for peace, and having secured their own amnesty, surrendered the city on August 18.[121] Alí Dordux, who led the negotiations, was rewarded with the lucrative post of *alcalde* of the *mudéjares* of Ronda, Marbella, Málaga, and Vélez Málaga. Opportunist he may have been, but no traitor to Islam; not only did he not convert, but he determined to disinherit his own son, who did accept baptism.[122] Ferran and Isabel showed little mercy to the rest of the inhabitants, who were enslaved *en masse*. Most were sold, while others – particularly women – were sent by the score as gifts to foreign luminaries, including Innocent VIII (1484–92), Queen Leonor of Portugal, and Queen Joana of Naples. In the meanwhile, Boabdil desperately sent Abū ʿAbd Allāh Muḥammad b. al-Azrāq, the chief *qāḍī* of Granada, to petition

[120] See L. P. Harvey, *Islamic Spain*, pp. 285–87, and, in general, chapter 10, "The Final Decade of Granadan Independence (1482–1491)," pp. 275–306.

[121] See M. T. Martín Palma, *Los repartimientos de Vélez-Málaga*, and F. Bejarano Robles, "El Repartimiento de Málaga."

[122] See I. Montes Romero-Camacho, "Las comunidades mudéjares," p. 426, and M. del C. Pescador del Hoyo, "Alí Dordux."

the Mameluke sultan, Qayt Bay (1468–96), and another envoy to the Ottoman, Bāyazīd II, for help.[123]

After Málaga there were few towns that would resist Ferran's combination of intimidation and largesse. The Andalusī leadership despaired, and either headed for North Africa (via the Alpujarras), or accepted honorable retirement in Castile. Some went one step further. At Baza (Basta) in 1489 the commander Sīdī Yaḥyā al-Najjār became "Pedro de Granada Venegas," converting to Christianity in exchange for estates, special privileges, and cash payments after a series of secret negotiations.[124] The rest of the population was granted broad liberties and protections, and it seemed that daily life for the local Muslims would hardly change. Yet, as what little of his kingdom remained collapsed around him, Boabdil abandoned his Castilian patrons and attempted to rally a counter-offensive. Inspired by decades of Naṣrid propaganda of Islamic resistance, in 1490 ordinary subjects, new *mudéjares*, and a scattering of North African volunteers rose up against the thinly spread Christian forces. But all this was to little effect, and the revolt was swiftly repressed, leaving Boabdil to retreat into a capital city contested between his supporters and the established elite. Little else of the kingdom remained, and in 1491 Ferran and Isabel established a massive military camp in the broad valley below Granada.

There was no doubt regarding the ultimate outcome of the campaign; as forces gathered and the sparring and raiding wore on, the siege took on an air of theatrical inevitability.[125] Meanwhile, two parallel but separate processes of negotiation got under way. The first, with the support of the urban elite and the less reactionary among the general populace, was aimed at negotiating the precise terms and conditions under which the city would be delivered, the war concluded, and the townsfolk governed. Among those in the "pacifist camp" were Abū 'l-Qāsim Venegas, Alī Sarmiento, and Yūse Banegas – the first, the former *wazīr* of Abū 'l-Ḥasan, the latter two, both well-respected members of the *'ulamā'*.[126] The

[123] J. E. López Coca de Castaner, "Mamelucos, otomanos," p. 223.

[124] The generous terms Yaḥyā/Pedro negotiated included exemptions from certain taxes and from the obligation to billet royal troops, the right to maintain his own armed guards, and a gratuity of 10,000 *reales* for facilitating the surrender of Guadix. See L. P. Harvey, *Islamic Spain*, pp. 301–04.

[125] The exaggerated praise of the contemporary Almerian *faqīh*, ᶜAbd Allāh b. Ṣabbāh, for Granada's stout defenses turned out to be little more than whistling by the graveyard. See F. Franco Sánchez, "El reino nazarí," p. 206.

[126] See L. P. Harvey, *Islamic Spain*, p. 275, and "Yuse Banegas." The Banaghash family consisted of a powerful faction in pre-conquest Granada, and had played politics in their own kingdom and Castile since the early fourteenth century. See L. P. Harvey, *Islamic Spain*, pp. 251–53.

second were the secret negotiations undertaken by Boabdil to secure his own future and fortune – a personal arrangement that effectively guaranteed the other, public negotiation. In November 1491 the first agreement was finalized, the "Protocols" for the surrender of the city were signed, and hostages were duly handed over by the Muslims. Faced by the prospect of radical elements slipping out of his control, Boabdil moved forward the date of the handing over of the city and its fortress-palace, the Alhambra. This was carried out in a choreographed public ceremony on January 1, 1492, followed by the new monarchs' triumphal entry into the now-Christian city the next day.

The *Capitulaciones* themselves were essentially a far more detailed and more generous version of the surrender agreements that had been current in the peninsula since the late eleventh century, and resembled closely the privileges that had been granted at Huéscar three years earlier. An amnesty was announced for combatants and prisoners, security and freedom of movement for all Muslims were granted, Islamic law in its broadest possible sense – judicial, fiscal, administrative – was to be preserved, property titles including grants made by the Naṣrids were to be considered legitimate, and the visible signs of Christian dominion were to be minimized. Clauses regarding freedom of emigration and facilitating the sale of property and estates were clearly aimed at encouraging the military elite and their families to depart. Contrast these with Ferran's position on the Muslims of Valencia, who in 1488 justified penalties legislated against those who abetted illegal emigration as "for the greater public good (*per benefici de la cosa pública*), which depends much on the case that the Muslims not depart from the said kingdom."[127] On the other hand, those relating to religious practice and law and the regulation of Christian–Muslim–Jewish *convivencia* represented a deliberate effort to tempt the pious, the mid-level administrators, and the productive classes to stay. This remarkable treaty would effectively create a functioning Islamic principality – a *mudéjar* kingdom – under Christian rule. It would remain in force for only eight years.

The success of the Crusade brought considerable security, wealth, and prestige to Ferran and Isabel, who by the end of the century, on account of this and other triumphs for the faith, would be designated by the Valencian Pope, Alexander VI (1492–1503), as "the Catholic Monarchs." With this victory, "profligate Hispania" – that had been, in the view of an eighth-century Christian chronicler, cast to the mercy of the Muslims – had been restored.[128] But for all that the propaganda of *Reconquista* served the

[127] G. Colón and A. Garcia i Sanz, *Furs De València*, vol. VI, p. 126 {VI:1:XXXIV}.
[128] See, for example, "The Chronicle of 754," in K. Wolf, *Conquerors and Chroniclers*, p. 133 {55}.

Castilian rulers at home, it did not necessarily play well in the complex world in which they lived. So while they basked in and took advantage of the good will and appreciation of the Church for having concluded this Holy War, they presented the campaign to their Muslim allies as an internal affair – their legitimate treatment of their client, Boabdil, who had breached his duties of vassalship by attacking them in 1491. This, at least, was how their envoy, Pedro Mártir de Anglería, argued the case to the Mamluke Sultan of Egypt, al-Ashraf Qānṣuh al-Ghawrī (1501–16) in 1502, when the latter had threatened reprisals against Christians in the Holy Land as a consequence of the conquest.[129] Nor, for that matter, did the "Reconquest" end with Granada – in 1494 and 1495 Ferran and Isabel received Crusading bulls for conquests in "Africa." Melilla (Mlīlya), on the African coast, was taken in 1497, and in 1505 Cardinal Francisco Jiménez Cisneros, the reactionary Archbishop of Toledo, Inquisitor and former confessor to Isabel, launched a crusade against Oran, in which the city was taken and thousands of inhabitants massacred. Following up on this in 1510, Pedro Navarro, Count of Oliveto, captured a string of coastal strongholds for Ferran, including Bougie, Algiers, Tunis, Tlemcen (Tilimsān), and Tripoli.

### *Mudéjar Granada*

Initially, the situation in Granada appeared to hold. Boabdil retired to an estate at Andarax (Andarash) in the Alpujarras, and Hernando de Talavera, Isabel's confessor, was installed as the new Archbishop – the head of an archdiocese the incomes of which, thanks to its rights and appropriations, dwarfed those of even Toledo – and the effective representative of royal and Christian authority in the city. The *santo alfaquí*, as he was popularly known to Muslims, scrupulously and enthusiastically adhered to the spirit and letter of the capitulations, taking an optimistic and inductive attitude to missionizing, and an open approach to the maintenance of local folk customs.[130] His personality became all the more important after Boabdil abandoned the Alpujarras, sailing for

[129] See L. García y García, *Una embajada*, and P. Liss, *Isabel the Queen*, "Prologue: An Embassy to Egypt," pp. 3–7. For the larger context of these negotiations, see J. E. López Coca de Castaner, "Mamelucos, otomanos." Since the late thirteenth century, relations between the Crown of Aragon and the Mamelukes had been based on a reciprocity of rights of Muslims living under the dominion of the Crown and Christians living under Mameluke rule. See P.S. van Koningsveld and G. Wiegers, "An Appeal," 179–180. Hence, a century previous, the Mamelukes had threatened to demolish the Church of the Holy Sepulchre in Jerusalem in retaliation for Joan II's destruction of two mosques in Valencia.

[130] See D. Coleman, *Creating Christian Granada*, pp. 84ff.

Tlemcen and into obscurity in 1493. The majority of the remaining Muslim aristocrats followed the example of their former King; those who did not were incorporated into the elite of Christian Castile, either as Muslims, like Alí Dordux, or as converts. For example, "Zuraya" (Zuhraya?), a former Christian and convert to Islam who had been captured as a young girl and went on to become the second wife of Boabdil's father, Abū 'l-Ḥasan ʿAlī, successfully sued in Castilian courts to retain her queenly title and her landed estates in Granada. She settled in Seville, where her sons, the former Princes Naṣr and Saʿad, converted as Juan and Fernando of Granada, and the apostate dowager recovered her Christian faith and the name she had borne as a girl: Isabel de Solís.[131] In sum, Ferran and Isabel followed a similar strategy with the Muslims of Granada as they had with the Jews of Castile vis-à-vis conversion. The idea was to remove or co-opt the elite and leave the bulk of the population docile and leaderless in order to facilitate their willing conversion. However, the very limited success of this policy vis-à-vis the Jews was demonstrated by 1492's Edict of Expulsion. In Muslim Granada it would do no better.

With its privileges and prosperity, in the years immediately after the conquest Granada attracted Muslim immigrants from around the kingdom, creating what was in effect a hugely populated and dynamic *morería* in a city where the Christians were represented only by a tiny colonial elite – a state of affairs that Ferran and Isabel's secretary and their representative there, Hernando de Zafra, regarded with no small measure of unease.[132] The Islamic administration of the city seems to have hardly changed at all. Like the political-military elite of Naṣrid Granada, the reaction of the religious elite to the Christian conquest was varied – a state of affairs reflected in the choices made by some of the sixteen members of the *ʿulamāʾ*, who had crafted the *fatwā* condemning Boabdil for his collaboration with Ferran and Isabel and their circle.[133] The *muftī* Abū ʿAbd Allāh al-Mawwāq, whose name appears first on the list of signatories, appears to have remained in the city after 1492, although he died soon after the conquest. Ibn al-Azraq, the chief *qāḍī*, left for Tlemcen, and from there to Cairo; after failing a second time to inspire the Mamluke sultan to recover al-Andalus for Islam, he moved to Jerusalem, where he was appointed chief *qāḍī*. Finally, there was Abū Jaʿfar Aḥmad al-Baqannī, a close relative of the "*cadí*" or "*alfaquí*," Mahomad el Pequenní. This el Pequenní served as an intermediary,

[131] See J. E. López Coca de Castaner, "The Making of Isabel of Solis."

[132] See de Zafra's letter of August 28, 1493, in F. de Zabálburu, *et al.*, *Collección de documentos inéditos para la historia de España*, vol. XI, pp. 533–37.

[133] See F. de la Granja, "Condena de Boabdil."

agent, and later, spy for the Catholic Kings, until he converted in 1500 as "Fernando Enríquez."[134]

Ultimately, because most (or at any rate, very many) of the religious elite and functionaries stayed, and many served in official posts, there was an institutional continuity here uncharacteristic of *mudéjar* societies. This was true of social and economic associations as well, including craft guilds, pious foundations (*ḥubus*), and unofficial networks of lineage and patronage. Indeed, in the capital city and across the kingdom the determination of the religious class to remain and to deepen its influence and power under Christian rule resulted in its coalescence as a clearly defined and self-conscious *mudéjar* elite – the *alfaquíes*. This was very much in line with Ferran and Isabel's goal, which was to maintain the tremendous productive capacity of the kingdom. What they endeavored to establish was a "dual society," wherein the Muslim and Christian societies and economies functioned side-by-side but clearly separated.[135] Of the commoners, many stayed, and some who left found conditions so difficult in Morocco that they willingly re-immigrated to Christian Granada.[136]

However, the equilibrium established under Talavera and Zafra began to break down by 1498. By this time the cumulative effect of Christian colonization provoked a reorganization of the city. As a consequence, Muslims were banned from the city itself and corralled into the hillside suburbs of Albaicín and Antequerela. This policy not only ran counter to the spirit of the *Capitulaciones*, but would have undermined both the initial socio-economic continuity of the community and the integrity and prestige of the *mudéjar* elite. This order was followed by a series of ecclesiastical decrees designed at limiting Christian–Muslim social and economic interaction, by separating the two communities. In more militant quarters of the Church, Talavera (himself of Judeo-converso origin) was seen as suspiciously soft on Muslims and utterly remiss in his duty to convert them. Chief among his critics was Cisneros, who determined to take control of the situation himself. Among the protocols of the treaty were clauses protecting the rights of *elches* – Christians, like Isabel de Solís, who had converted to Islam in Granada – to remain Muslim should they choose.[137] This was an unquestionable violation of Canon Law and

[134] See A. Galán Sánchez, "*Fuqahā'* y musulmanes."

[135] See A. L. Cortés Peña, "Mudéjares y moriscos," and A. Galán Sánchez, "El dinero del rey."

[136] So, at least, claimed the nineteenth-century historian, Ibn al-Ḥājj al-Sulamī. See P. S. van Koningsveld and G. Wiegers, "An Appeal," p. 162.

[137] A significant number of these *elches* were women who had been captured as girls and subsequently converted to Islam. See, for example, M. Ladero Quesada, "Las relaciones," pp. 52–53.

contemporary sensibilities, and this proved to be the wedge issue justifying Cisneros's intervention in the city.[138] But the Cardinal interpreted his pious duty to convert Muslims to the True Faith in the most zealous and uncompromising spirit, and set out not only to abrogate the *Capitulaciones* as he saw fit, but to obtain "successful" conversions through torture, imprisonment, and coercion. Moreover, he understood that to undermine the Granadans' religious affiliation could not be separated from their ethnic identity, and he set out to suppress public manifestations of Arabo-Islamic culture, most notably by confiscating and publicly burning Islamic religious texts.

### *The end of Islam in Latin Christendom?*

Cisneros's policies are often blamed for the upheaval that followed. On December 18, 1499 the Muslims of the city rose up in revolt. The uprising was successfully quashed in only three days by Talavera and the Captain-General, Iñigo López de Mendoza, Count of Tendilla – thanks largely to Talavera's promises of absolute clemency for those who would convert to Christianity. But the rebellion soon spread to the Alpujarras and beyond. In fact, tensions in the kingdom were not limited to the capital, and had been building for some time. Indeed, the surrender of the kingdom had never been absolute, and since 1492 guerilla-style resistance had continued in the hills around Ronda. Policies relating to taxation and colonization were at the root. The *mudéjares* had hoped that Castilian overlordship would free them from the onerous Naṣrid tax system; however, not only was this maintained, but new taxes were added, notably the *farda* – a levy Muslims paid to maintain the coastal defenses. As early as 1488 there had been organized resistance to taxation, and in 1497 a tax revolt in the Albaicín. Not surprisingly, Christian colonial administrators not only acted arbitrarily, but sought to enrich themselves at the cost of the *mudéjares*. Finally, lands were confiscated to accommodate the influx of tens of thousands of Christian settlers, pushing Muslims out of the towns and into the countryside and into a few protected enclaves like Granada. Many had evidently begun to despair at the situation, and in the decade between 1490 and 1500 more than 40 percent of the population fled.[139]

[138] On the contrary, a twelfth-century Catalan treaty with conquered Muslims (renewed in 1276) explicitly stated that Muslims who converted to Christianity could convert back with no penalty, and Christians who had previously fallen captive to Muslims could choose whichever faith they would like, also without penalty. See J. M. Font i Rius, "La carta de seguridad," p. 283.

[139] For population estimates, see I. Montes Romero-Camacho, "Judíos y mudéjares," p. 263.

Moreover, even prior to the Granadan revolt of 1499, a growing stream of Muslims of all social classes had sought baptism; this became a wave in the days that followed the failure of the revolt. Some 50,000 were baptized, and all of the city's mosques were reconsecrated as churches.[140] In sum, the uprising had provided a pretext for the annulment of the *Capitulaciones* as well as the other treaties and privileges extended to Muslims in the Kingdom of Granada. Islam was proscribed.

No sooner was the situation under control than a fresh revolt broke out in the Alpujarras under the *alguacil* (from the Arabic, *al-wazīr*) Abrahem aben Humeya (Ibrāhīm b. Umayya) in January 1500.[141] Some converts and collaborators were killed, and it was rumored that help was on the way from North Africa. In desperation the rebels appealed for help to the Ottomans.[142] No sooner was this crushed – with brutal and exemplary violence – that Almería and eastern Granada rose up (in October), and Ronda (in January 1501).[143] Although the rebels scored a notable victory at Málaga in March 1501, the divided and disorganized *mudéjar* forces were no match for Ferran's military machine. But crushing the revolt was only part of the solution. Talavera, mindful of the history of the Jewish *conversos* and the dangers of proselytization by coercion, became increasingly concerned by the possibility of false conversion and contamination by contact with outside Muslims. Hence, from July 1501, Muslims – including those of Castile – were no longer allowed to enter the kingdom. For their part, many former Muslims soon learned that conversion did little to change their status as marginalized second-class subjects. Meanwhile, Isabel's *mudéjares* in Castile were given assurances they would not be subject to similar measures. In 1493, the monarchs had attempted to calm nervous Muslim communities, who had been alarmed by false rumors that they were to be subject to an order of expulsion similar to that promulgated the previous year against the Jews of Castile and Aragon. "Our will and

[140] See A. Pérez Ordóñez, "Viejas Mezquitas."

[141] For a detailed study of revolt, resistance and repression on both a popular and official level, see R. G. Peinado Santaella, *Los inicios de la resistencia*.

[142] See J. Monroe, "A Curious Morisco Appeal," and Á. Galan Sánchez, "Turcos y Moriscos." The rebels were certainly in contact with the Ottomans, but the appeal referred to, composed in the form of a poem, may have been composed after 1517 – later than Monroe believed. See P. S. van Koningsveld and G. Wiegers, "An Appeal," p. 175. Nevertheless, the Muslims of Granada had been seeking aid from the Ottomans as early as 1477. See A. Temimi, "Une lettre," p. 101.

[143] Contemporary sources report the massacre of Muslim inhabitants, including at Andarax, where the mosque in which the women and children had taken refuge was set alight. See P. S. van Koningsveld and G. Wiegers, "An Appeal," p. 178.

desire has not been, and is not, to order the said Muslims to leave these Our said kingdoms . . ." they vowed.[144]

By 1500, however, many Muslims gave such promises little credence. On April 25, 1500, for example, the entire community of Palencia accepted baptism – obviously a calculated attempt at self-preservation. By September, encouraged in part by promises of fiscal equality with the Old Christian subjects, the entire Muslim population of Murcia had converted; similar incentives were offered to other communities. Finally, on February 12, 1502, Ferran and Isabel promulgated a decree ordering the conversion or departure of all of the Muslims remaining in the Crown of Castile, a population that numbered then perhaps 25,000.[145] By March 1502 the order had been carried out. Most stayed and converted – officially, the Islamic minority of Castile was no more.

### *Portugal and Navarre*

The Muslims of Portugal had already suffered a similar fate in 1496–97 under Manuel I, although the details and motives remain obscure. The consensus is that they were expelled by fiat, without provocation, sometime between May and September 1496, at about the same time that the Jews of the kingdom were ordered to convert to Christianity. Evidence is sketchy, and no record of an edict of expulsion has survived, but it appears clear from the secondary evidence and from Inquisition records that by the end of 1497 virtually no Muslims remained in Portugal, and that few had converted.[146] Evidently, most sold their property in the kingdom and emigrated to Granada or North Africa, while others went to Castile.[147] The *aljamas* of the Extremadura had long had ties with and been a destination for Portuguese *mouros*, and in a decree of April 12, 1497 Ferran and Isabel welcomed the refugees to their realms, granting them permission either to settle or transit, as they desired. Manuel's motivations remain somewhat of a mystery, but the most likely hypothesis is that this was a gesture intended to bolster his reputation as a defender of the faith before the papacy as he struggled against the Catholic Kings to obtain rights of sovereignty over the kingdom of Fez, which Ferran and

[144] M. A. Ladero Quesada, *Los mudéjares de Castilia*, pp. 115–16.

[145] For the order of expulsion, see *ibid.*, pp. 148 and 320–24. For the population estimate, see I. Montes Romero-Camacho, "Judíos y mudéjares," p. 257.

[146] In the mid sixteenth century *mouriscos* and *mouriscas* appear in Inquisition trials, accused of crimes such as magic, but these appear to have been almost all immigrants or the children of immigrants from North Africa or Spain. See I. M. Mendes Drumond Braga, "Os mouriscos," and "Relaçoes familiares."

[147] See J. E. López Coca de Castañer, "La migración mudejar," p. 206.

Isabel also claimed.[148] It was a gesture that would cost him little, given that the community had been atrophying for some time; indeed, the fact that the expulsion of 1497 left so little historical record is testament to Portuguese Muslims' growing irrelevance to both the royal fisc and the economy as a whole.[149] The capriciousness of the policy is also reflected in its lack of thoroughness. In spite of the edict, a handful continued to live as *mouros forros* in his lands, including Muḥammad Láparo, the former head (*capalão* or "chaplain") of the Lisbon *comuna*, who was still there as late as 1507.[150]

Through all of this, life continued uninterrupted for the *mudéjares* of Navarre. Neither the titular rulers, Catherine de Foix (1483–1517) and her consort, Jean d'Albret, nor Ferran II of Aragon, who exercised effective control over the kingdom, had any interest in pursuing a policy of expulsion or conversion. In the end, the Muslims here, like those of Castile, were victims of "collateral damage" occasioned by the colonization of Granada. In the late fifteenth century, as the kingdom was pulled into the orbit of Castile, the Inquisition arrived and began to harass local Muslims, and by 1498 warning had been issued by the royal court to Christian authorities to cease badgering the *alcadi* of Tudela.[151] In 1512 Ferran conquered Pamplona and the southern half of the kingdom, and was acclaimed King in 1513. As a consequence of this union, in 1515 Navarre was irrevocably absorbed into the Crown of Castile and became subject to its laws, including 1502's edict of conversion. Few Muslims here, it seems, opted for baptism; the high volume of land sales by Muslims listed in property records of 1516, together with the absence of baptismal records for *mudéjares*, strongly suggests that most simply abandoned the kingdom and moved south to the more hospitable Kingdom of Aragon, or to Valencia, and then onwards to the Maghrib. Others, apparently, simply stayed on in defiance of the order: in 1520 there were still at least two hundred Muslims in Tudela who were wealthy enough to figure in the notarial registers. These included Yayel Cortobí, a successful cloth merchant, who still held the titles of *alcadi* and *alfaquí*.[152] Such was the resentment that the edict of conversion and the Inquisition that was charged with enforcing it generated, that in 1521 former Muslims and Jews greeted the invasion of the kingdom by Henri d'Albret, who ruled

[148] See F. Soyer, *The Persecution*, chapter 5, pp. 241–80 and esp. pp. 258–60, for the date; also F. Soyer, "The Expulsion."

[149] Hieronymus Münzer, who traveled in the peninsula in 1494–95, speaks of the Jews of Lisbon at length, but mentions no Muslims there. See J. Münzer, *Viaje por España*, pp. 69–75.

[150] See M. F. Lopes de Barros, *Tempos e espaços*, pp. 548–60.

[151] M. García-Arenal, "Los moros de Tudela," pp. 88–89.

[152] *Ibid.*, p. 78.

French Navarre as Henri II (1517–55), with celebrations and declarations of loyalty. After this the Moriscos of Navarre drifted into obscurity; it can be assumed that they either eventually left or gradually converted under pressure from the Inquisition, only ultimately to be expelled in 1610.[153]

### *The Crown of Aragon*

With substantial *mudéjar* populations in Aragon and Valencia, the Crown of Aragon was to prove to be the last redoubt of medieval European Islam, and a refuge also for Muslims fleeing Castile in 1502.[154] Among these was no less a figure than Mancebo de Arévalo ("The Youth of Arévalo), who would go on to become the most prolific Morisco theologian.[155] In Aragon, foreign visitors remarked on the size and piety of the *mudéjar* population, as well as its docility. In 1495, after lodging in a Muslim home and attending a *mudéjar* wedding in Arcos de Jalón just over the Castilian frontier, the German traveller Hieronymous Münzer proceeded to Zaragoza. Here he found a populous and dynamic community, still worshiping publicly, calling the *'adhān* from their minarets, and even continuing to pray at what was likely the *miḥrāb* of the former mosque, then converted into a chapel to the Virgin and located in the cathedral cloister. He had interviewed one of the Muslim "priests" at length, and had been left impressed by this people's sobriety, industry, and physique. For Münzer there was no doubt that the continuity of *mudéjar* society was grounded in the community's economic value as tenant farmers, and he noted the popular refrain "He with no Muslims, has no money" ("Quien no tiene moro, no tiene oro").[156] Other visitors were left with the same impression, including the Florentine ambassador Francesco Guicciardini, who in 1513 observed that the royal policy of tolerance was a consequence of the taxes Muslim subjects paid, and in 1502 the Netherlandish knight, Antonio de Lalaing, was told by the future king, Philip the Fair (r. 1506), that the Muslims were tolerated "because of the great sums of money they pay as tribute."[157]

In Valencia, the situation was somewhat less stable. *Mudéjares* were now firmly in the minority, amounting to some 30 percent of the kingdom's

153 *Ibid.*, pp. 79–82.

154 See J. L. Corral Lafuente, "El proceso de repression," p. 349, n. 27. The census of 1495 counted 5,674 Muslim households, or about 25,000 individuals, in Aragon, but this is clearly far too low.

155 See L. F. Bernabé Pons, "Una fama sin biografía."

156 See J. Münzer, *Viaje por España*, pp. 120–23.

157 See J. H. Robinson, *Readings in European History*, pp. 242–45; J. L. Corral Lafuente, "El proceso de repression," p. 347.

population. In the towns they continued to practice trade and commerce, particularly with the Maghrib, but were coming increasingly into competition with Christians, precisely at a time when the artisanal sector there was suffering contraction. *Mudéjar* merchants were very active in the grain trade, working independently and forming partnerships with local and Italian Christians. Moreover, they enjoyed clear advantages in North Africa thanks to their ability to communicate, network, and move freely, their familiarity with the culture, their status as religious "insiders," and their favorable tax and tariff status.[158] Their successes, however, provoked accusations of unfair competition and embargo-flouting on the part of Valencian merchants, and fueled economic tensions that would be expressed in terms of religious difference, or even violence.[159] In the countryside the nobility had come to depend ever more heavily on Muslim labor, drawing them into a close symbiotic relationship of collaboration and protection. Thanks to the support of seigniors, the *mudéjares* of Valencia remained armed, in spite of increasingly credible reports that some had been contacting the Ottomans, and that Granadan *fuqahāʾ* had been raising money by popular subscription for the Naṣrid kingdom's defense.[160] Nevertheless, they had been put on edge both by the Castilian edict of 1502 and by Ferran's attempts to limit their mobility and liberties. Meanwhile, the craftsmen of Valencia had obtained permission to form popular militias – *germanías*, or "brotherhoods" – associated with their guilds, for defense against the North African coastal raiders who had been receiving increasing support from local Muslims.

Through Ferran's reign, the Muslims of the Crown of Aragon had been spared the threat of forced conversion by the King's commitment to upholding the *mudéjar* policy in his realms. It was after his death that a power struggle would flare up amongst the Aragonese nobility, the Castilian elite, and the reactionary wing of the peninsular Church, represented by the Inquisition, in which the Muslims of the Crown would be the pawns. The death of Ferran in 1516 provoked yet another political

158 The cultural affinities and social bonds between *mudéjar* and Maghribī trading elites may have acted to overcome the challenges of agreement enforcement, in a way that foreign Christian merchants were unable to. For underlying principles, see A. Greif, "Contract Enforceability." Constable, although highlighting the economic transformations brought on by the Christian conquest of al-Andalus, seems to underestimate the continuing importance of trade with the Maghrib and the role played by *mudéjares* in that trade. See, for example, O. R. Constable, *Trade and Traders*, p. 140.

159 See, for example, M. Ruzafa García, "Els orígens," and R. Salicrú i Lluch, "Mudéjares y cristianos en el comercio." When Christians attacked the *morería* of Valencia in 1399, their avowed target was the house of the *mudéjar* merchant and patrician, Jucef Xupió. See M. Ruzafa García, "Élites valencianas," pp. 172–73.

160 See M. D. Meyerson, "The War Against Islam."

transformation in the peninsula, with the succession of his grandson, the son of the Catholic King's sole heir, Juana "the Mad" (1504–55), and the Hapsburg Prince, Philip the Fair. With this, Carlos I (1516–58) became sole sovereign of Castile, Aragon, and Navarre, as well as Naples and Sicily, and from 1520, lord of the Low Countries and Austria, King of Germany, and Holy Roman Emperor (as Charles V). Spain was transformed into the center of a Hapsburg power bloc that would be fueled by the tremendous wealth of the Americas and set against an equally powerful Ottoman Sultanate, and its ally France. Between Carlos's northern origins, his messianic and universal pretensions, new and potentially mortal challenges to the monopoly of the Catholic Church, political resistance in the Spanish kingdoms, and war against Islam in the Mediterranean, "His Caesarian Majesty" would be little disposed to tolerating subjects who were "enemies of the faith."

However, for the *mudéjares* of Valencia, trouble came first from the city craftsmen, who in 1520 turned the armed militias of their guilds against the kingdom's nobility and the local *aljama* in a revolutionary movement that was also a challenge to the new Emperor's authority. As royal forces fell back, the movement spread through the countryside, where the palaces and hamlets of the aristocracy and the communities of Muslims who were seen as their confederates, were attacked. Thousands were killed, and many were forcibly baptized.[161] The nobles and their Muslim vassals resisted, as royal forces struggled to regain control of the kingdom and eliminate the movement's leadership. The imperial army, however, did not come as saviors of the Muslims; in 1521 Carlos's troops mercilessly plundered *mudéjar* properties around the capital. By 1522, the rebellion had been defeated, although the pacification of the countryside and the official reprisals would continue into 1528. During the uprising many Muslims had been baptized at the point of the sword and the harquebus, raising the sticky legal and moral problem of how to deal with less than legitimate converts who wished to return to their original faith.[162]

In the midst of this, Carlos, himself no sympathizer of the chronically ungovernable Valencia nobility and their proudly independent Aragonese counterparts, acted against the Muslims of the Crown of Aragon. On January 5, 1526 an edict was issued at Zaragoza that ordered the closing

161 M. D. Meyerson, "Slaves and Solidarity," p. 307.

162 In 1524 Charles V convened a commission to study the validity of these baptisms, which were *prima facie* contrary to Canon Law. The Inquisitor General, Bishop Alonso Manrique de Lara of Seville, judged them legitimate on the precedent of the forced conversions of Jews carried out by the Visigoths in the seventh century. See G. Magnier, "The Controversy," pp. 206ff.

of the mosques and the suppression of Islamic worship and folk traditions. *Mudéjares* were to be disarmed and to wear the distinguishing blue half-moon patch. Finally, all were to be catechized – the Emperor "had resolutely and irrevocably determined that in all of his kingdoms and lordships, only one evangelical law should be held and observed, and that all of the Muslims of the said kingdoms and lordships should convert to Our Holy Catholic faith."[163] It was a fate foretold, when six months earlier the Emperor had announced his plans, and embarked on a series of repressive measures, having obtained from Clement VII (1523–34) a dispensation absolving him of the obligation to honor the treaties and guarantees made to the Muslim subjects of his kingdoms. Faced with the passive resistance of the *mudéjares*, their lords, the royal functionaries, and many municipalities, who delayed in implementing the new decrees or complied to the literal minimum in the hopes that Carlos would relent, imperial forces fanned out through the territory to ensure the law would be carried out to the letter.

### *A last gasp*

While increasing numbers of Muslims despaired in the years leading up to 1526 and went willingly to the font, in Valencia many were determined to resist what amounted to an unprovoked and undeserved betrayal of the custom and the *modus vivendi* that had been long established in law. Even "modern" political theorists and theologians like Eiximenis had not disputed the existential right of the Muslim community. As the Valencian city council was pushed to implement Carlos's decree, outlying Muslim communities either refused to comply or played for time, and the fortified town of Benaguasil, twenty-five kilometers northwest of the capital, became a refuge and a focus of organized resistance. Envoys traveled back and forth to the imperial court, then at Toledo, but Carlos was inflexible – those Muslims who refused to convert would be given until January 22 to travel to A Coruña, in the far northwest, where they could embark by ship for exile. Obviously, they were meant to stay. Still refusing to comply, on January 17 the Muslims of Benaguasil were declared "traitors and rebels"; Carlos mobilized the army, even as he sent a mission offering a full pardon should the *mudéjares* relent.[164] However, when the royal notary, Miquel Dorta, rode up to the town walls with the King's letter, and respectfully called out for the *alamín* and the representatives

[163] J. L. Corral Lafuente, "El proceso de represión," p. 350.
[164] J. F. Pardo Molero, "*'Per salvar la sua ley'*," p. 128.

(*jurats*) of the *aljama*, the *alfaquí*, "One-Eyed" Mahomet Moferrig answered,

> Here there is neither *alamín*, nor *jurats*, nor *aljama*. There is no leader, because these are matters of the Law, and in matters of the Law, each person is a *jurat* and an *aljama* unto himself.

The populace crowding along the walls then called out, "As the *alfaquí* says, so say we all!" There would have to be battle, and the Emperor would oblige. But not all of the inhabitants agreed; the *cadi* Abdalá Abemamir, for example, believed that they should surrender, as did the *alfaquí* Amet Alacoch, who refused to take up arms.[165] This is not to say they were ready to abandon Islam – *taqiyya*, or occultation of the faith, was as valid a response to repression as was military *jihād* and martyrdom, and ultimately more responsible as regards the integrity of the community as a whole.

As the siege got underway, accompanied by fierce and deadly skirmishing and shootouts, the royal forces cut off the town's water supply and brought forward heavy artillery. This was used to bombard the walls until the cannons themselves split from fatigue. Sensing defeat, and feeling community opinion turn against them, Mahomet Moferrig and his resolute followers took to the hilly maquis of the Serra d'Espadà to the northwest of Valencia. Here they would rally with other resisters and carry out a short-lived and futile guerrilla war. On January 17 a delegation of the town's Muslims offered to surrender and to pay the Emperor for the cost of the siege; the next day royal troops entered the town and the entire population was baptized. With the affair under control, neither the Emperor nor the Valencian officials were vindictive – terrorizing, provoking, or crippling the new Christian community was in no one's interests. For his part, Carlos passed the cost of the siege on to the City of Valencia, which, as seignior of Benaguasil, could be held legally and financially responsible for the rebellion. An investigation and a series of trials were held under the kingdom's and city's jurisdiction, with the result that the former Muslims were levied a 12,000-*ducat* fine as a community. Moferrig, then a fugitive, was condemned to death, but the other resisters were eventually pardoned. Only the foreign fighters (likely escaped slaves) who were captured were put to death, and a handful of Aragonese *mudéjares* were imprisoned until they could be auctioned off as slaves. Thus, by early 1526 the Crown of Aragon, like the rest of the new "kingdom of Spain," was formally a nation of Christians, and Christians alone.

165 *Ibid.*, pp. 129–130.

## Conclusion: the failure of *mudéjarism*

And he continued, "Son, I don't cry for the past, to which there is no return, but I cry for what you will see in your lifetime, and what awaits you here in this Island of Spain . . ." (Yūse Banegas, Morisco *grandée*, bidding farewell to the "Mancebo de Arévalo" (*c.* 1500)[166])

*Mudéjarism* – the arrangement between Christian rulers and Muslim subjects that had preserved these communities, normalized relations between Christians and Muslims, and legitimized the latter's place in Christian society – had failed. This was not because of some inherent debility in the situation, nor was it an inevitability. It happened here in Spain in the sixteenth century because of a conjunction of political circumstances and shifting social, economic, and cultural contexts.[167] The net result of these changes was the erosion of the networks of relationships of mutual interest that had bound members of the minority to institutions and interest groups in the majority, and had thereby sustained ethno-religious diversity. It was a crisis of *conveniencia*; a divergence of interests and agendas, that left Islamic society in the peninsula increasingly irrelevant, if not threatening – anomalous, if not provocative. If anything, it was Muslims' increasing integration in Christian society that had led them to this juncture. *Mudéjar* institutions did not fail because they were the crystalized relics of a medieval past; *mudéjar* society was not static or disengaged. And while it may have been that the idea of religious diversity did not square with the new Europe of the sixteenth century, this was not sufficient cause for the elimination of the minority communities.[168] From Portugal to Valencia, Christian rulers and ideologues acted because they saw they had nothing to lose by forcing the Muslims' conversion or expulsion, whereas those few Christian parties who did stand to suffer as a result did not have the power, support, or the will to resist.

For the Muslims of the Crown of Aragon, the edicts of 1525 and 1526 were catastrophic. In a six-month period their entire society was transformed – ancient places of worship were shut down or destroyed, the administrative–social elite was disempowered and the religious elite driven underground, religious books were hurriedly ferreted away, complex socio-religious structures were delegitimized, first and family names were changed, and entire communities were placed under the obedience of a clergy which with rare exceptions did not sympathize with them, and pressed into a society which would not accept them. Thanks to Carlos's

166 L. P. Harvey, "Yuse Banegas," p. 301. For Banegas, see above, p. 212.
167 See below, chapter 7: Christians in name: The *Morisco* problem (1499–1614).
168 I. Montes Romero-Camacho, "Las comunidades mudéjares," p. 441, and, generally, A. Galán Sánchez, *Una sociedad en transición*.

conditions, exile was not a viable option, and Muslims had to choose between the fate of Mahomet Moferrig and that of Abdalá Abemamir. Catalano-Aragonese Islam, however, could weather a cataclysm even of this magnitude. The tensions of the fourteenth and fifteenth centuries had rejuvenated the indigenous religious culture here – the *fuqahā*ʾ were rooted in villages and hamlets, discreetly supported by popular initiative, and if *mudéjar* institutions had failed, the Muslim family had not.[169] Islam was merely driven underground. The lull after the edict before the Inquisition turned to the Moriscos gave Muslims time to regroup, and when the new repression began, it would only drive them closer together as a group.

In the "dual society" of Granada, on the other hand, Islamic social institutions and hierarchies had remained largely intact, if under a veneer of Christianization. The *alfaquíes* who converted generally maintained their power and prestige and their incomes. Contrary to the situation after the thirteenth-century conquests, where the artisanal class moved into royal administration and filled the vacuum left by the departed religious elite, the ʿ*ulamā*ʾ here stayed put and became the new mercantile and administrative elite. The tremendous importance of the Muslim economy in Granada mitigated Christian interference in Morisco affairs. Opportunists and survivors could not only go from being Muslim *quḍāt* and *muftūn* to Christian *corregidores* and *alguaciles*, but enrich themselves in the process. Hence, in 1502, Mahomad el Pequenní was granted as his own personal property the mosques and *ḥabūs* and *waqf* foundations he would have once served as custodian over for the Islamic community.[170] Across the peninsula, Talavera's misgivings regarding forced conversion would be vindicated. Many, if not most Muslims became Christian in name – but the history of the Islamic communities of Latin Christendom had not yet come to an end.

169 See, for example, M. Meyerson, "The Survival of a Muslim Minority," p. 377.
170 F. de Granja, "Condena de Boabdil," p. 175.

# 6 Strangers in strange lands

## Foreign Muslims and slaves in Latin Christendom (*c.* 1050–*c.*1550)

The Sixth Climate [*Iqlīm*] is even colder and rougher, farther from the sun and excessively humid. Here live the Turks, the Khazars, the Franks, the French, the Kashgards and all those living at the same latitude. They are called "red." The relationship of these people to the Slavs is the same as that of people of Sind to the Blacks. Their color is, at bottom, white. They live like animals, without cares or concerns, except for war, raiding, and the hunt. They have received no Revelation and have no religion.

(Shams al-Dīn Abū ʿAbd Allāh Muḥammad al-Dimashqī, *Nukhbat al-dahr fī ʿaj āʾib al-barr wa ʾl-baḥr* (1325)[1])

It seems remarkable that an educated Muslim living near Damascus at the turn of the fourteenth century would have so little to say and be so poorly informed about Latin Europe and its inhabitants, given the history of conflict and interaction that had played out in his own homeland over the previous two hundred years. Part of this may be due to the stylized and derivative nature of the genre of geographical digests, but it also reflects the general rule that Latin Christendom figured only slightly in the Arabo-Islamic imagination.[2] This is not the consequence of an Islamic culture that lacked curiosity, enterprise, or the spirit of exploration, as embarrassingly ignorant Anglo-European scholars have occasionally suggested – Muslims were ranging far and wide across Asia and the Indian Ocean, and across the Sahara long before Latin Christian "Europeans" had set foot beyond the former limits of the long-extinct Roman Empire which still largely defined their world. Marco Polo trod along trails well worn

[1] "A Selection of Treasures of the Marvels of the Land and the Sea," in A. F. Mehren, *Manuel de la cosmographie*, pp. 399–400.

[2] See J. A. Boyle, "Rashīd al-Dīn and the Franks," pp. 62 and 63. According to Bernard Lewis (cited here), Rashīd al-Dīn's "History of the Franks," compiled *c.* 1306 for the Il-Khan Öljeitü is the only work on the history of Christendom written by a Muslim during the period covered by the present study. In any event, some other geographers were better informed than al-Dimashqī. Zakariyyāʾ b. Muḥammad al-Qazwīnī (d. 1283), for example, described "Frank-land" (which he locates in the fifth *Iqlīm*) in detail, noting its Christian faith, cold climate, fertility, and the strength of the swords manufactured there. He characterizes the Franks as extremely brave and fierce, but filthy, and of mean character. See C. Hillenbrand, *The Crusades: Islamic Perspectives*, p. 272.

by Muslim travelers (if he did indeed tread along them at all!).[3] Latin Christendom – with the exception of those formerly Islamic lands around the Mediterranean and the Italian port cities – was *terra incognita* for Muslims because it was a poor, inhospitable, and underdeveloped region with virtually nothing to offer the Muslim traveller or merchant except danger.[4] The Syrian poet and warrior Usāma b. Munqidh could hardly contain his self-assured contempt when a Frankish friend had offered to take back his son to be raised among the *Ifranj*, a people who – despite his friendships with some of them – he considered "to be mere beasts possessing no other virtues but courage and fighting."[5] Those commodities, such as slaves and furs, and eventually cloth and grain, which the Islamic world did import from the Christian north were brought to the *dār al-Islām* for the most part by Christian, Jewish, or *mudéjar* merchants, thus relieving foreign Muslims of the need to risk themselves in this barbarous *thule*.[6]

Most Muslims who found themselves in the Latin Christian lands beyond Iberia and Southern Italy had come there unwillingly, as hostages or slaves. In the Middle Ages there were no significant or durable communities of free Muslims in the lands that would become France, Germany, Britain, or northern Italy. Those few who did come of their own volition did not come to settle, but rather to do business, whether commercial or official, and return to their homelands. The only significant exception to this are the *Bashghird* and other Muslim peoples apparently originating in the area of the lower Volga, who emigrated to the recently Christianized Hungarian kingdom and surrounding lands in the eleventh century. Unlike the other Muslim minority communities, the Bashkurts did not in any way self-identify as Arabs, nor did they feel the same solidarity or share in the same cultural affinities as their co-religionists of the lower latitudes. Their ties with the Arabo-Islamic heartland were tenuous. When they disappeared – at about the time al-Dimashqī was writing his digest – they left virtually no trace and no record of their fate.

The present chapter examines the little we know of the Muslims of medieval Hungary and the Latin Christian lands to the north and east, as well as the individuals who, as slaves, travelers, or merchants, found

3 Lewis clearly exhibits the Eurocentric and Orientalist perspective regarding the Islamic world's engagement with Europe in B. Lewis, *The Muslim Discovery of Europe*.

4 Contrary to the contentions of some twentieth-century historians, the absence of Muslim merchants and travelers in Latin lands, however, was neither absolute nor due to any supposed Islamic religious prohibition – contra, for example, F. Cardini's contention in *Europe and Islam*, p. 186.

5 See Ibn Munqidh, *The Book of Contemplation*, p. 144.

6 That said, prior to the eleventh century, evidently some Muslim merchants were reaching Central Europe.

themselves living temporarily or permanently in the *bilād al-Rūm* – the "land of the Christians."[7] Although the slaves and travelers did not constitute communities in a coherent, self-conscious sense, a survey of the experience of Muslims in the Latin West until the turn of the sixteenth century would be incomplete without taking their role into account. This section will conclude with that most famous late medieval Muslim immigrant to Europe, al-Ḥasan b. Muḥammad al-Wazzān al-Zayyātī – better known after his conversion to Christianity as "Giovanni Leo Africanus" – who died in obscurity *c.* 1554. By this time the presence of Ottoman, Maghribi, and the Safavid exiles, merchants, and diplomats in Latin lands, had come to mark a new and modern phase of Christian–Muslim engagement.

We have few sources at our disposal for the study of the Muslims of medieval Hungary – a late incorporation into the world of Latin Christendom. These include Christian chronicles and law codes, occasional notices in Arabic geographies, and little else. The panorama for the northeast is even more barren. The sources for Muslim slaves and travelers in the Latin West are somewhat more abundant and varied, although – with the exception of Christian Iberia, where we can sometimes reconstruct in rich detail the experiences of slaves – our evidence is largely restricted to financial accounts, deeds of sale, notarial documents, and ocasional anecdotes which surface in chronicles and other works of literature. These sources permit us to trace general trends, but seldom allow the slaves themselves to rise out of the anonymity that was their fate both in life and in history.

### Hungary and the east (*c.* 1000–*c.* 1550)

In the city of Aleppo, I met a large number of persons called Bashkirs, with reddish hair and reddish faces. They were studying law according to the school of Abū Ḥanīfa (may God be well pleased with him!) I asked one of them who seemed to be an intelligent fellow for information concerning their country and their condition. He told me, "Our country is situated on the other side of Constantinople, in a kingdom of a people of the Franks called the Hungarians. We are Muslims, subjects of their king, and live on the border of his territory, occupying about thirty villages, which are almost like small towns ... Our language is the language of the Franks, we dress after their fashion, we serve with them in the army, and we join them in attacking their enemies, because they only go to war attacking the enemies of Islam ..." (Yāqūt al-Rūmī, *Al-muʿjam al-buldān* (1224 CE)[8])

[7] See al-Idrisi, *Géographie*, vol. II, p. 34. "Al-Rūm" means "the Romans," and usually referred to the Byzantines, but was also used as a synonym for "the Christians," particularly when referred to as a broad ethno-religious group. In religious contexts *Naṣrānī* ("Nazarenes") or *Masīḥī* ("Messianists") were the preferred terms.

[8] "The Dictionary of the Lands," excerpted in T. Arnold, *The Preaching of Islam*, pp. 193–94. For the *Bashghird* see al-Gharnāṭī, *Abu Hamid el Granadino*, p. 65 (Arabic, p. 27).

From the eleventh to the thirteenth centuries, Hungary (*Unqūriyya, Madjaristān, Bashghirdiyya*) was undoubtedly the most ethno-religiously diverse kingdom in Latin Christendom. It was a latecomer to the faith, having become Christian only when the Magyar potentate, Vajk, Grand Prince of the Hungarians, was baptized as "István" (Stephen) in 1000 CE, and thus became king (1000–38, and later, saint). Located at the western terminus of the great Eurasian plain, Hungary was the natural landing point for the periodic waves of Central Asian "pony peoples" who had been heading westwards across the steppes from the time of the Hittites to the time of the Mongols, and which included the Magyar Hungarians themselves.[9] Indeed, some Muslim geographers did not distinguish the Hungarians as a separate people.[10] In the century after István's conversion Latin Christianity came to define Hungarian religious identity, but the kingdom maintained significant populations of Jews, pagan Cumans and Pechenegs, and Muslims, not to mention immigrant individuals and communities from all around Latin Christendom and Byzantium. By 1300, of the non-Christians, only the Jews remained as an unconverted minority, and they would be subject to orders of expulsion beginning in 1349.[11] At about the same time, and independent of this, Muslim Qipchak Turks ("Tatars") were settling in the Catholic lands to the north, where they were welcomed as soldiers by the rulers of Poland and Lithuania.[12]

### *Infidel guests in a Christian kingdom*

Unlike the other Muslim communities studied in this book, the Muslims of Hungary were not indigenous. According to the unreliable and often contradictory sources, the *Bashghird* (*Bashjird*, or "Bashkurts") consisted of Muslims and pagans of various tribes (Káliz, Pechenegs, Volga Bulgars, and so on) originating around the southern Urals and north of Khurāsān. They were classified in the Hungarian kingdom as *hospes* – medieval *Gastarbeiter* – little different from the other groups, Christian or not, that

9 Medieval Muslim geographers were unanimous in considering the Magyars a Turkic people.

10 See *Encyclopedia of Islam*, s.v. "Madjar, Madjaristān."

11 J. Reinaud, *Géographie d'Aboulféda*, vol. II, pp. 294–95.

12 As a consequence of the lack of sources, scholarly bias and linguistic challenges, little scholarly work has been done on the Muslim minority of medieval Hungary and Eastern Europe. Notable exceptions include N. Berend, *At the Gate of Christendom*, and H. Norris, *Islam in the Balkans*, and *Islam in the Baltic*. Also of note are I.-A. Pop, "The Religious Situation," M. Lower, "Negotiating Interfaith Relations," and S. Sroka, "Methods of Constructing."

settled in the kingdom in the service of the kings.[13] The Magyars referred to them as *Böszörmények*, a corrupted Persian loanword (appearing in Latin as *Bissermini*, and other variants), or as *Ismaelitiae* (*Hysmaelitae*; "Ishmaelites"), or *Saraceni*, in Latin (Hungarian: *Szereczen*).[14] Muslims had, however, settled here as early as the ninth and tenth centuries, arriving soon after the pagan Magyars.[15] By the eleventh century the Muslim population seems to have concentrated in a few huddles of villages and towns in the far south of the kingdom (Syrmia and Bodrog, in modern Croatia and Serbia); the northeast, near Debrecen; Pest, in the center; and likely in the region of Turiec (modern Slovakia); as well as smaller communities scattered throughout the kingdom. The pagan Pechenegs who were welcomed into Hungary through the twelfth century, and settled in the western parts of the kingdom or along the frontier with Byzantium, also included Muslim or Islamicized families and individuals, and there are references to *fuqahā*ʾ living among them. There is no basis for making a concrete estimate of the Muslim population, but they could only have represented a small portion of the total, somewhere in the tens of thousands. In the twelfth century some sources suggest latecomers arrived, described as Turkic Muslims and "Maghribians." The former groups probably included the Khwarezmian (in Hungarian: *Káliz*, with many Latin variants) traders, who had first reached the area in the tenth century.[16] While historians debate the significance of the latter term, in this context, it likely refers to Muslim Pechenegs (Arabic: *Bajana*; Hungarian: *Besenyö*) who had come to Hungary from the area around Kiev, rather than Muslims from the Maghrib.[17] Abū Ḥāmid

13 *Gastarbeiter* is the modern German expression for foreign, termporary "guest-workers" that were recruited in large numbers from the Islamic West, particularly Turkey, from the early 1960s. For *hospes*, see I. Petrovics, "Foreign Ethnic Groups," and for Muslims, N. Berend, *At the Gate of Christendom*, pp. 105–6. For a detailed discussion of origins, see H. Norris, *Islam in the Balkans*, pp. 27–31.

14 See A. Csaba, "The Way Leading," p. 9. For a comprehensive overview of these peoples and how they figure in Arabic and Hungarian sources, see *Encyclopedia of Islam*, s.v. "Maḏjar, Maḏjaristān."

15 According to the thirteenth-century (*c.* 1220?) *Gesta Hungarorum*, during the reign of István's grandfather Taksony in the tenth century, two lords from the land of Bular, "Billa" and "Baks," came with a "a great host of Muslims" and "were granted lands in various parts of Hungary, and he gave them in perpetuity, the castle that is called Pest." They were followed by another "most noble warrior" from Bular, name Hetény. The descendants of Billa and Baks apparently later converted, but at what date, it is not specified. See Anonymous and Master Roger, *Gesta Hungarorum*, p. 127.

16 Substantial hoards of Islamic coins have been found in Hungary, Lithuania, and Poland; see, for example, G. Székely, "Les contacts," p. 71.

17 See H. Norris, *Islam in the Balkans*, pp. 28–29. It is possible that small groups of Muslims from the Mediterranean had settled in Hungary in the thirteenth century as a consequence of the kingdom's conquest of the Dalmatian coast and its diplomatic and marital ties with Norman Sicily, but the fact that the traveler Abū Ḥāmid reports many thousands of those he identifies as "Mahribians" in Kiev makes this hypothesis all the more unlikely. That

al-Gharnāṭī, an Andalusī traveller who passed through and settled briefly in Hungary during his wanderings north of the Black Sea, stayed with this community, which he described as quite substantial.[18] Al-Idrīsī, whose twelfth-century geography covered the Frankish lands in considerable detail, lists and describes the major settlements of the kingdom, but makes no mention of any Muslim community here or any place else in the Sixth *Iqlīm*.[19]

### *Guest-workers*

Although there is little direct evidence, Hungarian Muslims must have lived, like other *hospes* (and like ethno-religious minorities across the pre-modern West), as juridically and fiscally autonomous communities.[20] They figure in Hungarian royal law only in the context of conversion and apostasy, legal cases between Muslims and Christians, and in statutes that limited their participation in Christian society and the outward manifestation of Islam as a faith. Likewise, we may deduce from the fact that most lived in fairly homogenous rural enclaves, that they were engaged in agriculture as well as a range of craft industries. Muslims had served on the frontier since the time of István, and Hungarian *Saraceni* communities were called up in times of war and for raiding by the kings and nobility. Like their Aragonese and Valencian homologues, they were renowned for their archery.[21] This role would have endowed these communities with a considerable cachet among the powers-that-be – a reliable and dependent military contingent was an extremely valuable resource in the context of the intermittent noble revolts and wars with Byzantium, Bohemia, and eastern princes of the twelfth and thirteenth centuries. Indeed, Béla IV (1235–70) invited the pagan Cumans back into his kingdom for this

said, on a separate occasion he refers to "Arabs of the Maghrib" (*awlād al-ʿarab bi-ʾl-Mughrib*) in this region, which may, indeed, be a reference to North Africans. See al-Gharnāṭī, *Abu Hamid el Granadino*, pp. 50 and 64 (Arabic: pp. 5 and 25).

18 See al-Gharnāṭī, *Abu Hamid el Granadino*, pp. 64–73 (Arabic: pp. 27–39). His account is entitled *al-Muʿrib an baʿḍ ʿajāʾib al-Maghrib* ("Report on the Marvels Far from the West"). For Muslim travelers' and geographers' impressions of Hungary, see B. Nagy, "The Towns of Medieval Hungary," pp. 169–71.

19 Al-Idrisi, *Géographie*, vol. II, pp. 352–41, for the sixth clime. Following the Ptolemaic tradition, Arabic geographers divided the world into seven latitudinal "climates."

20 N. Berend (*At the Gate of Christendom*, pp. 102–04) points out that it was not only Muslims, Jews, and pagans that had separate law codes in Hungary, but also the communities of foreign Christian *hospes*. This, however, was not a unique situation; in eleventh- and twelfth-century Aragon and Castile, foreign Christians (here, *Francos*) enjoyed similar privileges, which derived at bottom from the conception of law as being custom.

21 See H. Norris, *Islam in the Balkans*, p. 27, and T. Arnold, *The Preaching of Islam*, pp. 193–94.

reason, even after they had been expelled in the course of a bloody oppression in reaction to their alleged support of the Mongols.[22]

We know that Muslim soldiers were used with great success in Hungarian conflicts with the Byzantines in the twelfth century, as well as against pagans to the east.[23] Géza II (1141–62), who was accused of "loving Muslims," reputedly sent 500 in support of Barbarossa's siege of Milan in 1161.[24] They fought alongside German and Hungarian knights against the Tatars at Šibenek in 1241, and against Bohemia in 1260. Military service, particularly among the higher status cavalrymen, would have fostered a sense of community with Christian countrymen of similar vocation and station. Hence, Muslim soldiers are found intervening to help secure the ransom of Hungarian Crusaders who had been captured by the Muslim enemy in the Holy Land.[25] Either out of sentiment or pragmatism, *Böszörmények* frequently placed loyalty to homeland (*waṭān*) above that to the foreign co-religionists of their *umma*, defending the kingdom also against Muslim raids.[26] Loyalty and trust were not necessarily reciprocated, however, and – at least by the thirteenth century – Muslim settlements were specifically forbidden from constructing defensive walls, in case they should be tempted to revolt.[27]

The *Böszörmények* must have also had homegrown religious, administrative, and economic elites – the great eleventh-century Andalusī geographer Abū ʿUbayd al-Bakrī claimed that Muslims here had their own *fuqahāʾ* (jurists) and *qurrāʾ* (Qurʾān reciters).[28] There are indications that Hungarian Muslims occasionally made the *ḥājj*, and Yāqūt's red-haired "Bashkir" had evidently been sent to Syria to train as a jurisprudent – one may assume, at no small expense. While this individual's lack of a beard and Frankish attire may suggest he was a warrior by vocation, it would not be surprising if his family's wealth was the result of trade; Muslim traders ranged back and forth within the kingdom in the eleventh and twelfth centuries, if not beyond its boundaries.[29] That said, the depth and orthodoxy of Islam as practiced here is subject to some

[22] The Cumans had been blamed for the Mongol attacks; see N. Berend, "Medieval Patterns," p. 158.

[23] See A. Madgearu and G. Martin, *The Wars of the Balkan Peninsula*, pp. 68ff; N. Berend, *At the Gate of Christendom*, p. 141.

[24] G. Székely, "Les contacts," p. 72; see also p. 247, below.

[25] N. Berend, *At the Gate of Christendom*, pp. 96 and 240. [26] *Ibid.*, p. 240.

[27] *Ibid.*, p. 141.

[28] See H. Norris, *Islam in the Balkans*, p. 27, and T. Arnold, *The Preaching of Islam*, pp. 193–4.

[29] The custom of wearing a beard may have been current in the Eastern Mediterranean, but there is no evidence that beards were commonly worn by subject Muslims in the Iberian Peninsula or Italy in the twelfth and thirteenth centuries.

question – steppe-dwellers are notoriously open in matters of religion: reluctant to give up their traditional shamanistic practices or to commit clearly to a single, coherent orthodoxy. Thus, among the nominally Muslim clans that settled here in the late tenth and early eleventh centuries, there were some who immediately converted to Christianity – some along with István – although it is clear that many of these continued to practice Islam in secret.

## *Muslim society and culture*

There is also evidence for the existence of a kingdom-wide Muslim elite, of the sort found in Iberia and Sicily, although its scale and influence here was far narrower. Aside from those soldiers who may have moved in privileged Christian circles by virtue of their class and profession, Muslims were also employed in fiscal and royal administration. There are indications that the merchants who arrived in the early twelfth century became involved both in royal finance and the lucrative domestic salt trade.[30] Indeed, by mid-century the Hungarian rulers were being reprimanded by the papacy for employing Muslims and Jews in the administration. One hundred years later, Pope Gregory IX went so far as to excommunicate briefly Béla IV for his refusal to dispense with his Muslim and Jewish officials.[31] The extent of this alleged patronage is difficult to gauge, as individual officials are not attested in the surviving sources and papal decrees of this type were frequently based on policy positions rather than political reality. But in the thirteenth century several converts from Islam, unnamed, are reported in high office.[32] Under Béla III (1172–96) Arabo-Islamic-style coins were minted, a fact that has led some historians to conclude that Muslims were employed as royal minters, but there is no direct evidence.[33] What is certain is that Islamic society here was evidently incapable of sustaining a substantial literary class or high culture; neither artifacts nor reports of scientific, literary, religious, or artistic achievements survive.[34] This is likely a consequence of the community's isolation from the larger Islamic world and its small size – the socio-economic elite was not substantial enough to generate the "critical mass" required for cultural

[30] N. Berend, *At the Gate of Christendom*, p. 113. See also I. Vásáry, "Western Sources," p. 264.
[31] N. Berend, *At the Gate of Christendom*, pp. 153, 155, and 157.
[32] *Ibid.*, pp. 86 and 120. The one individual named is "Misze," see below, p. 240.
[33] The hypothesis is certainly not unlikely, and there is some circumstantial evidence; see, for example, Anonymous and Master Roger, *Gesta Hungarorum*, p. 127, n. 3, and G. Székely, "Les contacts," 72.
[34] N. Berend, *At the Gate of Christendom*, p. 210.

production, and these descendants of steppe nomads were not bearers of the sophisticated and cosmopolitan Arabo-Islamic culture that characterized the indigenous Muslim minorities in the Latin Mediterranean.[35]

Our clearest and, indeed, the only substantial portrayal of Muslim society here by a contemporary eyewitness is provided by Abū Ḥāmid al-Gharnāṭī, who came from al-Andalus to Hungary in 1150/1 and stayed until 1153. His account, which appears remarkably reliable, reports two discernable groups among the *Bāsghird*: crypto-Muslim "Khwarismians" (*Awlād al-Khūwārizmiyyin*) and the openly-Muslim "Maghribians" (*Awlād al-Mughāriba*). He tells of many substantial Muslim towns, walled and surrounded by gardens and hamlets. By this account they were a prosperous community, esteemed by the King. Many were wealthy enough to own slaves, and some proudly traced their ancestry to the "nobles" who had come generations before to fight for the Hungarian kings. During his stay, Abū Ḥāmid claims to have re-acquainted the *Böszörmények* with Islamic practices and customs, including the Friday prayer and polygamy, and weaned them off their love of wine.[36] This was allegedly done with the consent of King András I (Andrew; 1047–61), whom Abū Ḥāmid interviewed, convincing the King that permitting his Muslim subjects to practice polygamy would breed him a larger army.[37] He copied out books in Arabic for local Muslims at their request, and assured them that serving the Hungarian king against his Christian enemies constituted a legitimate form of *jihād*. Al-Gharnāṭī settled in here, purchasing his own slaves, including a Byzantine (*Rūmī*) boy of eight, and a beautiful fifteen-year-old pagan girl, who bore him a son. The infant died, and when Abū Ḥāmid left the *Bilād 'Unqūriyya* he manumitted her, now a Muslim, bearing the name of Maryām. Al-Gharnāṭī was also obliged to leave his own son, Ḥāmid, as a hostage in the kingdom, having married him off to the daughters of two local Muslim notables. He then returned to his base at Sajsīn, on the lower Volga, in the company of a royal

35 That said, Hungary may well have been an occasional conduit for Islamic culture. In 1094, for example, the monks of Korvey (in Westphalia) claimed to have acquired a book in Arabic via Hungary. See G. Székely, "Les contacts," p. 62.

36 Abū Ḥāmid undoubtedly over-generously credits himself with having established what might be called "normative" Islam among his Hungarian co-religionists. Intriguingly, the analysis of discarded animal remains discovered at a recent archeological dig of an Arpadian-age village at Hajdúböszörmény (Hungary) – a site suggested as a probable Muslim settlement – has revealed that almost no pork was consumed here, in contrast to the usual contemporary consumption patterns. The results have been disseminated as L. Szolnoki, *et al.*, "A Hajdúböszörmény Téglagyár." [Thanks to József Laszlovszky for bringing this to my attention, and summarizing the findings.]

37 This claim is certainly a stretch, and there can be little doubt that Abū Ḥāmid exaggerated his influence on Hungarian Muslim society.

envoy, Ismāʿīl b. Ḥasan, and his entourage, with the aim of recruiting more Muslims for the King's army.[38]

### *The decline of Hungarian Islam and the Muslim Tatars of the Catholic northeast*

Unlike the other Muslims of Latin Christendom, those in Hungary were immigrants, who had no claim to any historical "right" to exist as a community. Perhaps for this reason, they seem to have come under pressure very early on to convert to Christianity, as the recently pagan Magyar ruling class had itself done. Backsliders among the early converts were targeted by István, and in 1092, by László (Ladislas) I (1077–95). In that year the Diet of Szabolcs decreed that those returning to Islam should be subject to internal exile. In the twelfth century Hungary also became the focus of concerted efforts on the part of the papacy to reduce the influence of or eliminate minority religious communities – significantly earlier than in the Latin Mediterranean. Hungary was of particular concern to the papacy, not so much because of the Muslim or Jewish communities, which were less active and important than in many contemporary Latin kingdoms, but because of the strong and resistant pagan Cuman (Qipchak) presence in the kingdom. As late as 1253 the young heir, István (István V, 1270–72), married a Cuman princess who had been raised a pagan; their son, László IV (1272–1290), was known as "the Cuman," and preferred the nomadic lifestyle. This, together with the danger posed by Byzantium and the presence of heretical Bogomil communities, put Hungary on the frontline of the battle for Christendom in the mind of the Roman Curia.[39]

Nevertheless, at times royal policy in the twelfth century also targeted Muslims. Kálmán (1095–1116), for example, passed a series of discriminatory decrees. Each Muslim community was to build a church, after which half of the population was to resettle in a new location and build another church. He forbade the observance of *ḥallāl* dietary customs and bathing and other "misdeeds" – going as far as prohibiting "Ishmaelites" from eating any meat *except* pork – and mandated Muslim women to marry *only* Christian men.[40] Not only is it unlikely that such laws were observed or enforced (despite the provision that informants would gain half the confiscated property of those caught violating them), one suspects

[38] Abū Ḥāmid never returned to the West, but eventually settled down into retirement in Damascus, where he died in 1169/70 at the age of ninety. See Abū Ḥāmid and I. Bejarano, *Al-muʿrib*, p. 30.

[39] See I.-A. Pop, "The Religious Situation," pp. 78–90.

[40] C. d'Eszlary, "Les musulmans hongrois," p. 383; J. Bak, *et al.*, *The Laws of the Medieval Kingdom of Hungary*, pp. 29 and 30.

that their promulgation may have been little more than an act of show, or a response to papal pressure.[41] Kálmán was married, after all, to Felicia, a daughter of Roger I of Sicily, and therefore was well aware that there were other Latin rulers who adopted conciliatory and flexible policies towards their Muslim subjects.

This, however, was a curious moment. In 1095 Urban II had sparked what would be known as the First Crusade, and in summer 1096, fresh from massacring the Jews of the Rhineland, the unruly rabbles of the "Peoples' Crusade" entered Hungarian territory under the monk Gottschalk and began to plunder as they made their way southeast. Kálmán's forces contained and disarmed them at Székesfehérvár, and then massacred them; a few weeks later a larger group under Count Emich of Leisingen was also routed.[42] When the main body of Crusaders arrived under Godfrey of Bouillon, it was allowed to cross the kingdom only under strict conditions, after leaving hostages and under escort of Hungarian forces. Thus, in one of those apparent paradoxes so typical of the history of Muslim–Christian relations, the Crusaders' first contact with Muslim warriors was, it seems, in a Latin kingdom, where the latter either had been given the opportunity to slaughter unarmed Latin "pilgrims," or had facilitated the passage to Byzantium of those very warriors who three years later would conquer and massacre the Muslim population of Jerusalem. Such an irony may not have been lost on either Kálmán or his Latin contemporaries, and it may be that his legislation was a gesture designed to confirm his commitment to the Christian cause in view of his use of Muslim soldiers against Christians.

### *Papal pressure*

Such repression of Muslims as took place in Hungary was likely periodic in nature. Nevertheless, it is remarkable for a law code as early as that of Kálmán to take an interventionist approach to a Muslim minority, and to link so clearly social custom and cultural practice with religious identity as a strategy for forced conversion. For his part, half a century later, Abū Ḥāmid reported that the Hungarian kings favored their Muslim subjects and granted them broad liberties, at least those that the author identified as "Maghribian" – a group welcomed for their military vocation.[43] Likewise, the individual Yāqūt interviewed half a century later in Aleppo innocently characterized life for Muslims under Hungarian rule as

[41] See, for example, J. Bak, *et al.*, *The Laws of the Medieval Kingdom of Hungary*, pp. 29, 30 and 57; N. Berend, "Medieval Patterns," p. 173.

[42] S. Runciman, *A History of the Crusades*, vol. I, pp. 140–41 and 147–48.

[43] For an overview of royal policies, see C. d'Eszlary, "Les musulmans hongrois."

unproblematic, although he notes, in contrast to al-Gharnāṭī's report, that they were not permitted to construct defensive walls around their settlements – an indicator, perhaps, of a shifting of attitude on the part of the Christians.

Indeed, pressure mounted in the thirteenth century, and the papacy, alarmed at the great numbers of Jews and Muslims said to be living in the kingdom, pushed for the restrictions on minority groups established at Lateran IV to be applied in practice.[44] In 1232, with the "Oath of Bereg," András II (1205–35) was obliged by Gregory IX to promise to dismiss the Jews and Muslims serving in his royal household, whom the pope accused of corrupting the regime and usurping power.[45] The Oath relieved András from the interdict the kingdom had been placed under eighteen months before as a consequence of his refusal to conform to previous calls to dismiss non-Christian officials. A decade earlier he had been forced by his own nobility to sign the "Golden Bull" – a Hungarian "Magna Carta," which extended aristocratic privileges and rights at the expense of the monarchy. Among these was the exclusive prerogative for noblemen to serve in royal administrative positions; as a corollary, the Bull explicitly forbade Muslims and Jews from these offices, as well as ordering the offspring of Christian women who had married Muslims to be baptized.[46] Gregory's determination to marginalize the Muslims and Jews in Hungary was implacable. Concerted efforts were made to force Muslims to wear a distinguishing badge (here, a yellow circle), as part of a general policy of social separation.[47] Evidently, these pressures began to yield results; by mid-century accusations of secret apostasy were being aimed at Muslim converts, backsliding that was attributed at least in part to the persistence of the Turko-Islamic social customs that the papacy lobbied to repress.[48]

[44] For Lateran IV, see p. 372.

[45] N. Berend, *At the Gate of Christendom*, pp. 153 and 155.

[46] C. D'Eszlary, "Les musulmans hongrois," p. 383. The author here refers to women who had married "blacks," but this is a mistranslation of the word *szerecsen*, which refers to "Arabs" or Muslims (see G. Székely, "Les contacts," p. 70). See also M. Lower, "Negotiating Interfaith Relations." The near-contemporary *Privilegium general* forced on Alfons the Liberal of Aragon in 1287 by the rebels of the first "Union" (see above, p. 78) contained similar provisions but aimed only at Jews. Muslims were not competing with Christians for administrative positions here.

[47] N. Berend, *At the Gate of Christendom*, pp. 127, 128, and 159. Interestingly, Gregory was somewhat less concerned about the Muslims of Lucera, much closer to home (see above, p. 124).

[48] N. Berend, *At the Gate of Christendom*, pp. 201 and 212, as well as p. 237, for the persistence of folk customs.

### *The end of Islam in Christian Hungary*

In the mid thirteenth century Muslim society in Hungary would suffer catastrophe, not at the hands of the papacy and its agents, but at those of the Mongol armies, who overran the kingdom after the disastrous Battle of Muhi on April 11, 1241. Losses were heavy, and would have included contingents of *Böszörmények*. In the aftermath, the Mongols devastated the Hungarian plains, killing perhaps one quarter of the population and displacing many more.[49] It would have been difficult for the small Muslim minority to survive such a trauma and, indeed, late medieval Islamic historians attribute the demise of the community here to the Mongol invasion.[50] In fact, the Muslims persevered for another half-century or so. Muslim contingents apparently formed a substantial part of Béla IV's forces when they were routed by Přemysl Otakar II of Bohemia (1253–78). In 1279, Pope Nicholas III's (1277–80) legate, Philip of Ferma, complained that Muslims were still not being required to wear the badges of distinction that had been mandated by Gregory IX, and in 1286, the paganophile Lászlo IV explicitly restored Muslims' access to royal administrative offices. Four years later the same King named to the post of Palatine – the highest position at court – a Muslim named "Misze" (Mūṣā?), who converted to Christianity immediately on his appointment, and served as regent when the King abandoned the sedentary life of court to live with his nomadic pagan Cuman kinsmen.[51]

In 1308, with the accession of Károly (Charles I, or Charles-Robert; 1308–42), Hungary came under the rule of the Angevins, the same dynastic family that was responsible for the final destruction of the Muslim community of mainland Italy – a process that was underway at this very time. By this time, however, the Muslim community of Hungary was no more. This does not seem, however, to have been the consequence of deliberate policy, whether of conversion or expulsion. Rather, it was a case of attrition; this community was simply too small and too isolated to survive the violence of the Mongol invasion and the cumulative effect of the Church's pressure – however half-heartedly the latter may have been applied.[52] Moreover, the *Böszörmények* did not fill any unique niche in the socio-economic or

[49] For an evocative, contemporary account of the Mongol campaign, see the contemporary "Master Roger's Epistle to the Lament upon the Destruction of Hungary by the Tatars written to the Reverend Lord James, Bishop of the Church of Preneste," in Anonymous and Master Roger, *Gesta Hungarorum*, pp. 133–227, esp. pp. 213–27.

[50] N. Berend, *At the Gate of Christendom*, p. 242.

[51] N. Berend, "Medieval Patterns," p. 161. For the pro-Muslim policies of Lászlo IV, see C. d'Eszlary, "Les musulmans hongrois," p. 384.

[52] N. Berend, "Medieval Patterns," p. 174.

political environment of the kingdom; they came to be seen as extraneous, superfluous, and anomalous – conditions under which few minority communities can survive. As it was, under the Angevins, Hungary would become a homogeneously Catholic kingdom; the Jews – the last significant minority – were expelled first in 1349 in the aftermath of the Black Death, then re-admitted, only to be expelled again in 1360. By then, a process had been set in motion by which Islam would re-establish itself in Hungary, not as a "guest" community but as the herald of a new order. By 1355 the Ottomans had pushed into the Balkans, and by 1389 they had crossed the River Tisza. In 1526 the Hungarian army would be routed at the Battle of Mohács by the forces of Sulaymān the Magnificent (1520–66). Lajos II (1516–26), the last uncontested King of an independent Hungary, died in ignominious retreat. In 1541, Buda, the kingdom's former capital, fell.

### *The* Lipqa *(1383–)*

Even as the Ottomans were embarking on their conquest of the Balkans, and a full century after the *Böszörmények* had been absorbed into the society of Christian Hungary, new Muslim populations were coalescing just within the northeastern frontier of Latin Christendom. These too were immigrants: Muslim Tatars (*al-Tatār*) of Qipchak ethnicity, fleeing the first of the depredations of the Golden Horde and, after 1391, of Tīmūr Lang. These were welcomed into the Grand Duchy of Lithuania, most notably under the rule of Vytautas (1392–1430), who valued them as warriors in the face of the threat both of the Mongols and the Teutonic Knights, whose Crusading zeal was undampened by the conversion of the pagan ruler.[53] Indeed, the history of the Muslim minority here began with Vytautas's conversion to Catholicism as "Witold" in 1383, followed soon after by that of his cousin, Jogaila, King of Poland, in 1387 (Władysław II Jagiełło; 1386–1434). The early history of these communities, known as *Lipqa*, or *Lubqa*, is even more obscure than that of the Hungarian Muslims, and they represent an even clearer anomaly.[54]

Tatar clans, who maintained their own tribal social organization, settled first in the eastern frontier regions as well as the major towns, including

[53] Tellingly, Vytautas/Witold, who was known in contemporary Muslim sources as "amīr Watad," became a folk hero among the Tatars. In 1519 a local Muslim writer described him as "a defender of Islam, whose name we respect like our caliphs"; see A. B. Kopanski, "Muslim Communities," p. 92, and G. Mickūnaitė, "Ruler, Protector and Fairy Prince." For the Muslims of Lithuania and Poland, see H. Norris, *Islam in the Baltic*, and, particularly, A. B. Kopanski, "Muslim Communities," who synthesizes Polish and Lithuanian historical research.

[54] H. Norris, *Islam in the Baltic*, pp. 37, 50, and 58.

Vilnius, where they lived alongside the natives but in separate communes, receiving tax exemptions in exchange for military service. These comprised the local elite; others, of various non-Qipchak extractions, were known for their skill as craftsmen, whereas the lowest order were the descendants of freed captives. As in Hungary, Muslims here practiced agriculture, trades, and transport – "good farmers and fearless Muslim fighters who recognize the Polish king as their own ruler."[55] Each settlement, or *djemat* (from *al-jāmiʿ*), was endowed with its own mosque, and the community was substantial enough to have a chief-*qāḍī* (*kaji*). These were humble settlements; a local pilgrim to Mecca described in 1558 his people's "poor, simple and small mosques, made of wood, without minarets and niches."[56] Older urban communities, such as that of Lvov, founded in the 1300s, were wealthier and had better-appointed brick mosques. Eventually, settlements were established as far west as the Belorussia and Volhynia regions of Poland (*Lehistān*) – a consequence of the union of the Polish and Lithuanian crowns, and by the early seventeenth century there were some sixty communities scattered across the kingdom.

Connected to the greater *dār al-Islām* primarily through the mediation of peripatetic Sufis, native pilgrims, and missionaries from the Crimea, their Islam was clearly that of a steppe people – they drank alcohol with gusto, and their women enjoyed the liberties and independence characteristic of nomadic societies.[57] They persisted in their Islam, and survived by acculturating – quickly adopting the Slavic vernacular of the region and the outward appearance of the Christian peoples among whom they lived.[58] They were not isolated, however; as individuals and groups they moved back and forth across the ill-defined frontiers of the expanses west of the Urals; this was particularly true of the warrior clans, and especially from the 1500s as Ottoman influence north of the Black Sea increased. It was reported in the sixteenth century that the wealthiest were sending their children to study "in Arabia."

The importance and efficacy of the *Lipqa* cavalry bestowed the elite of this community with a prestige and social standing that approached that of their Christian counterparts, and insulated them to some degree from the vicissitudes of late medieval and early modern identity politics. Their loyalty was tested and survived on occasions, as in the early 1500s, when they helped repulse a Tatar invasion. Others served as envoys and liaisons

[55] This, according to the late-sixteenth century Polish chronicler, Aleksander Gwagnin, referring to the period two centuries earlier. See A. B. Kopanski, "Muslim Communities," p. 92.
[56] *Ibid.*, p. 89.
[57] This tendency was encouraged by their close proximity to (and intermarriage with) pagan Nogai and Altaic nomads.
[58] See A. Danylenko, "On the Language of Early Lithuanian Tatars."

with the Ottomans and the people of the steppes. More refugees arrived in the mid 1500s, fleeing Ivan the Terrible (1547–84); Sigismund II (1548–69) increased their privileges and went so far as to openly proclaim his "love for the religion of Islam." In the late sixteenth century, however, it was precisely *Lipqa* success in these roles that put them in the sights of the Christian elite, who came to perceive them as a competitive threat, and of a Catholic clergy fired up by the Catholic Reformation. Pressure on the community reached its apogee late in the century under Stefan Batory (1576–86) and Sigismund III (1587–1632). Although the Ottoman Sultan Murād III (1574–95) lobbied the King to moderate his stance, the *Lipqas* became increasingly estranged from their host society, and began to aspire to liberation, occasionally abetting Turkish attacks, or rising up in revolt.[59]

Over the following centuries the fate of the Polish-Lithuanian Muslims fluctuated according to the politics of the day. They were scapegoated for the victories of Mehmed IV (1648–87), and many fled, but 1677 saw their rights restored and they were given representation in parliament. Another bout of persecution followed in the 1710s during the Polish Civil War, with popular violence fanned by demagogic clergy. Through all of this, however, the community persevered, and in the end the Tatars comprised the only Muslim community of medieval Latin Christendom that did not either outlast Christian rule (as in Ifrīqiya and the Levant), or was not absorbed or expelled (as in Hungary, Italy and the Iberian Peninsula). Indeed, they survive to this day.

## Travelers, traders and seekers of fortune (*c.* 1050–*c.* 1500)

Lord Jaume, etc. to His noble and esteemed and faithful vassal, Alabez Abenrraho, etc., Know that We saw the letter sent by Our dear P. de Montagut, Our agent in the Kingdom of Murcia, in which he gave Us to know how you and your knights and your companies, together with the Master of the Temple ... raided the Kingdom of Granada, and how you made easy work of the guards and troops of the King of Granada, and how by the grace of God you vanquished and destroyed them, for which We give thanks, praising God for your goodness and faithfulness, which you have clearly shown to us by your deeds, with the help of God ... (Jaume II, King of Aragon, Letter to al-ʿAbbās b. al-Raḥūa (May 31, 1304)[60])

The historical research on the Mediterranean region of the Middle Ages in the last three or so decades has put the lie to the idea that the "frontier" between Christendom and Islam was some sort of impenetrable wall of

[59] A. B. Kopanski, "Muslim Communities," p. 96; see *Encyclopedia of Islam*, s.v. "Lipqa."
[60] A. Giménez Soler, *La Corona de Aragón y Granada*, p. 369.

opposition and difference. On the contrary, it provided an environment in which persons, goods, ideas, and techniques circulated back and forth across confessional frontiers that were often blurred, if perceptible at all.[61] Indeed, it was often difficult to determine where this frontier was, particularly in Iberia, where for centuries amorphous protectorates, defined by the tenuous authority of opportunistic Muslim warlords, drifted in and out of Christian lordship. Nowhere is the porous and ambiguous nature of the religio-political frontier more evident than in the case of Muslim warriors and diplomats who served in Latin courts; their presence signals the degree to which Muslim and Christian regimes were prepared to recognize each other as legitimate, religious ideology notwithstanding, and "do business" with each other.

### *Soldiers of fortune*

As has been noted in the previous chapters, Christian rulers in Iberia, Hungary, and Southern Italy showed no qualms in using Muslim troops, whether their own subjects, or allies, in battle against both Muslim and Christian enemies. Indeed, these warriors offered advantages, including the sort of loyalty – based on their own isolation and vulnerability – that foreign, infidel troops have been valued for throughout history. Moreover, unencumbered by any moral reservations with regard to Christian enemies, they could be unleashed with devastating effect. During the war between Alfonso I and Urraca of Castile in the early 1100s, for example, the Aragonese King's Muslim troops attacked the monasteries of the Rioja and Old Castile, without any of the compunction that might have conceivably restrained Christian warriors. It was only in the Crusader principalities that local Muslims were not regularly recruited. An almost singular allusion appears in the fourteenth-century *Gestes des Chiprois* ("Deeds of the Cypriots"), which describes how in response to an attack by the Venetians in 1264, the lord of the city mustered defenders including "Saracen archers and peasants from the countryside around Tyre."[62] Another possible case is that of the "Turcopoles," the enigmatic light cavalry auxiliaries of the Frankish forces in the Holy Land, who it has been suggested were either Muslims, Eastern Christians, converts from Islam, or the offspring of converts.[63]

[61] Indeed, Muslim religious and judicial authorities could not agree amongst themselves as to how to define the boundary between the Islamic and Christian worlds. See below, p. 316.

[62] P. Crawford, *The "Templar of Tyre,"* p. 43 {322}.

[63] See J. Richard, "Les Turcopoles," and Y. Harari, "The Military Role of the Frankish Turcopoles."

Even in the Latin East, however, alliances between Muslim and Christian powers not infrequently saw their knights fighting side-by-side against common enemies, and Bedouin did serve with Frankish forces.[64] When Adelaide del Vasto journeyed to Jerusalem in 1112 for her short and unhappy marriage to Baldwin I of Jerusalem, she brought with her a considerably dowry and a large body of Sicilian troops, including Muslim archers. In 1127 her son Roger II sent a force including Muslim infantry to aid his kinsman Bohemond II in an unsuccessful attempt to retake Antioch.[65] If there was irony inherent in the use of Infidel warriors against fellow Christians, or for the Military Orders, the sworn paladins of the Crusades, to fight alongside the Infidel, it was clearly lost on many contemporaries. Indeed, the German pilgrim Ludolph of Sudheim described the late thirteenth-century Master of the Temple at Acre as "[the Sultan's] own very special friend."[66] Religious agendas and ideologies certainly informed policy, but did not necessarily shape it. Hence, in 1291, as Acre, the last refuge of the mainland Latin East, fell to the Mamelukes, Alfons the Liberal of Aragon wrote to his ally, Muḥammad II of Granada, excusing himself for having been obliged to commit to the Crusade in the East.[67]

The trend for foreign Muslim soldiers-of-fortune to serve Christian princes after 1050 CE was a continuation of the same dynamic that had for centuries seen Christian knights – the most famous of whom was Rodrigo Díaz de Vivar, "el Cid" – enlisting in the forces of Islamic kingdoms.[68] Only now the balance of power was changing, and Muslims were drawn increasingly into Christian service. This was a phenomenon that extended across the Latin Mediterranean, Hungary, and the East, and even into the European hinterland, as clients, mercenaries, and subject Muslims served their Christian rulers or fought for hire. The phenomenon is mostly clearly observable in the Iberian Peninsula. Here, in addition to deposed kings and governors – people like ʿImād al-Dīn b. Hūd, al-Qādir of Toledo, or "El Rey Lobo" – individual privateers from foreign Muslim lands were regularly recruited by Christian sovereigns. This was a phenomenon related to but distinct from the enlistment of native Muslim subjects as soldiers, a common occurrence in all of the Latin lands where Muslims lived, with the exception of the Crusader principalities in the East. The chief exception was the in the Holy Land, where Latin and

[64] Curiously, this is not unlike the situation in Israel today, where Druze are allowed to serve in the IDF, and Bedouin are used as scouts and irregulars.
[65] See G. A. Loud, *Roger II*, p. 251.
[66] S. Menache, "When Jesus Met Mohammad," p. 81.
[67] See B. Catlos, "Mahomet Abenadalill," p. 269.
[68] See, above, pp. 26ff.

Muslim allies at times fought side by side, but there is no clear evidence that native Muslim subjects regularly served under Latin command.

From the 1270s through the 1320s a series of Muslim noblemen came with their households and dependants to the Crown of Aragon. In the 1290s Abraham Abenamies, a Jewish diplomat, recruited Muḥammad b. al-ʿĀdil, a refugee nobleman from the kingdom of Granada. He not only brought over a substantial company of fighters, but he and his son were made formal, lifetime vassals of Alfons II, who appointed Muḥammad head of all of the mercenary companies, Christian and Muslim, of his realm.[69] The skill of these *jeneti* ("Berber-style light cavalry") was particularly suited to the lightning cross-border raids intended to weaken the enemy – a favored and effective tactic.[70] Muḥammad acquitted himself well in the war against Castile, capturing booty and slaves, which he sold or ransomed back in Aragon with the aid of royal officials. When he left the King's service, he was sent home with valuable gifts, including falcons – a testament to the personal favor he enjoyed. Nor was he exceptional; several other Muslim commanders brought their troops to the Crown at this time. Royal chancery registers record numerous gifts of expensive cloth and tack bestowed on them by the kings as tokens of their service. In the same period, exiled princes of the deposed Almohad dynasty settled with their families in Valencia, and they too served in the royal forces.[71]

A temporary peace with Castile sent the Granadan mercenaries home, but in the first decade of the fourteenth century, some Moroccans crossed over to serve the House of Barcelona. One such was Ibn al-Raḥūa, a scion of the Marīnid ruling family, who acquitted himself with distinction against Muslim Granada until he was suddenly summoned back by the Sultan, Abū Yaʿqūb Yūsuf (1286–1307), in 1304.[72] During those decades Muslim mercenaries served alongside Christian warriors against France, Navarre, and in the Crown's Mediterranean campaigns. The Crown's adversaries took righteous umbrage when they were at the receiving end of these operations; after the Angevin loss of Sicily to Pere II, for example, the Cardinal of Sainte-Cécile complained, "he has taken up with Muslims

69 See, for example, B. Catlos, "Mahomet Abenadalill," and F. Gazulla, "Las compañías de zenetes." Jewish mercenaries also served in Aragon, but these were rare. See E. Lourie, "A Jewish Mercenary," and B. Catlos, "Mahomet Abenadalill," pp. 278–79.

70 The term is derived from the name of the Zanāta Berber tribe (J. M. Alcover, *Diccionari*, s.v. "genet"), but came to be synonymous for "mercenary" as well as "(light) cavalryman" (Castilian: *jinete*). A parallel borrowing occurred in the lands where the *Lipqa* lived: the Polish term *ułan* (*ulan*, in German) referring to a "light cavalryman" derives from the atar word meaning "brave warrior" or "young man."

71 See F. Gazulla, "Las campañías de zenetes," 179–80.

72 For Ibn al-Raḥūa, see M. T. Ferrer i Mallol, "La incursió de l'exèrcit de Granada."

in order to destroy Christendom ..."[73] Indeed, in the Crusade called against the Crown of Aragon in response to the Sicilian Vespers, a detachment of Zanāta cavalry on loan from the Marīnids helped defend Pere's realms.[74] However, when given the opportunity, Latin European princes including the kings of England and France and the Holy Roman Emperors were happy to make use of Muslim soldiers that were occasionally sent on loan, whether from Iberia, Sicily, or Hungary.[75] In 1161, for example, Muslim troops from Hungary helped Frederick Barbarossa (1155–90) – the Emperor who would die twenty-nine years later as a Crusader *en route* to relieve the siege of Acre – win a crucial victory over forces supporting the papacy at Milan. These troops may have included the Turcoman Muslim mercenaries from Konya (in Anatolia), who were coming north at that time to serve the Hungarian King.[76] As for the Crown of Aragon, after the departure of Ibn al-Raḥūa, foreign Muslim fighters continued to come, although in much smaller numbers. Documentary evidence of these mercenaries is rare, but foreign Muslims and *mudéjares* are recorded as serving in the royal bodyguard, known as *La Genata*, in the mid fourteenth century; and in the 1350s and 1360s Pere the Ceremonious used Muslim mercenaries from Granada and North Africa against Castile.[77]

In Castile, foreign Muslim knights (along with some *mudéjares*) comprised the fifteenth-century praetorian guard, the "Guardia morisca" – a number of whom evidently settled permanently in the kingdom and converted to Christianity.[78] The relationship of reluctant clientage which bound Granada to Castile from the time of its inception meant that soldiers from the Naṣrid sultanate regularly crossed over to the north, whether they were sent as allies or came as political refugees and rebels. Alfonso X evidently had sizeable contingents of Granadan soldiers in his army, and Pedro the Cruel apparently had some 2,000 Muslim troops in his service during the War of the Two Peters, although whether these were *mudéjares*, foreigners, or both, is not noted.[79] Although sources are often scant, there can be little doubt that the presence of foreign Muslims in the forces of Christian Iberian kings was a constant feature through the Middle Ages – just as Christians served in Muslim armies in al-Andalus and the Maghrib. Earlier in the century the Angevins of "the Regno" (the

73 B. Desclot, "Llibre del rei en Pere," p. 328 {146}.
74 M. Shatzmiller, "Marīnids (Banū Marīn)."
75 See, above, pp. 187ff. Even Charles II, who, with a great show of piety, dismantled the colony at Lucera, used subject Muslims as troops.
76 al-Gharnāṭī, *Abu Hamid el Granadino*, p. 68.
77 See M. T. Ferrer i Mallol, "Évolution du statut," 451, "La organización militar en Cataluña," 186; and J. Boswell, *The Royal Treasure*, p. 186.
78 See, above, p. 197.
79 M. T. Ferrer i Mallol, *Entre la paz y la guerra*, pp. 406–07.

mainland rump of the kingdom of Sicily) continued Frederick II's custom of employing the Muslims of Lucera as soldiers. The use of minority groups to constitute a "praetorian guard" is a traditional Mediterranean practice, from the use of Germanic barbarians in Rome, the Scandinavian Varangarian Guard in Byzantium, and the Christian *al-khurs* ("the mute ones") of the Caliphate of Cordoba. Employing foreign, out-group soldiers offers clear advantages as a strategy.[80] The regiments in question are vulnerable, by dint of their minority status, and are, therefore, dependent on and loyal to their ruler; moreover, in the absence of any sense of religio-cultural solidarity with the larger population, their capacity for independent political action (revolt) is minimized, and they will act without restraint or compunction against the subjects of the kingdom.[81]

There is evidence, also, that Muslim soldiers served in Christian armies both on Crusade and deep in the European hinterland. As has been noted above, Muslim troops were used on the Italian mainland, not only by the rulers of Sicily and the "Regno" from the eleventh through at least the fourteenth century, but also by their allies; while both indigenous and foreign Muslims fought with the forces of Hungary and Lithuania.[82] Sicilian Muslim archers took part in William II of Sicily's unsuccessful attack on Alexandria in 1174.[83] Christian rulers resisting Crusaders also employed Muslim troops: Markward in Sicily, Alfons III in Aragon, and the Grand-Duke Władysław II, who made a series of alliances with foreign Tatar mercenaries – a force that was instrumental in his watershed defeat of the Teutonic Knights at Tannenburg in 1410.[84]

In the later Middle Ages, France received regular support from *mudéjar* soldiers and technicians originating in the Iberian peninsula. In the 1360s, for example, Pere the Ceremonious of Aragon sent a detachment of Granadan cavalry to Jean II of France (1350–64).[85] Jean and his successor, Charles V (1364–80) also received Muslim troops from Navarre. In 1353 a group of Muslim crossbowmen were sent to serve in France, and in 1365 and 1368 more were sent on loan, including a local notable, Muça Alpelmi. *Mudéjar* soldiers served as far afield as Normandy, and as close to home as Aragon. Navarrese Muslims also provided infrastructure support

[80] The Frankish and "Slavic" praetorian guard of Córdoba was referred to as "the mute ones" in reference to their lack of Arabic.

[81] For the politics of minority administration in the medieval Mediterranean, see Catlos, "'Accursed, Superior Men'".

[82] See F. Soyer, *The Persecution*, pp. 54–58 for Muslim military service in Portugal, and A. Metcalfe, *The Muslims of Sicily*, p. 143. See D. Abulafia, "The Italian Other," p. 227, for Roger's use of Muslim troops to quell mainland rebellions.

[83] C. D. Stanton, *Norman Naval Operations*, p. 146.

[84] See A. B. Kopanski, "Muslim Communities," p. 89; cf. above, p. 241.

[85] J. Boswell, *The Royal Treasure*, p. 187.

for French forces. In 1353 a certain Muça Toriel was sent along with other lance-makers, and *mudéjares* also worked as sappers and military engineers: making and maintaining pontoons, siege engines, and campaign tents.[86] A document of 1363 refers to "those who accompanied the *alfaquí* of Tudela" as he went to France in the service of the King with a detachment of *mudéjar* horsemen, crossbowmen, and armorers.[87] Carlos II of Navarre even went so far as to grant a special subsidy to the wives that the *mudéjares* who were serving in France had left behind on the farm.[88]

### *Envoys and diplomats*

Other high-status foreign Muslims also found themselves sojourning in Latin lands, either willingly, as diplomats and dignitaries, or unwillingly, as exiles or hostages. Castile, the Crown of Aragon, Portugal, Sicily and the Crusader principalities – even the papacy – all received regular visits from Muslim ambassadors and envoys. Trade and political alliances linked Norman Sicily to Ifrīqiya and Fāṭimid Egypt, the Crusader principalities to their Muslim neighbors, and the Iberian kingdoms to virtually the whole of the Islamic Mediterranean, all of which resulted in a steady traffic of envoys, aristocrats, and literati back and forth across Christian–Muslim frontiers. Figures such as Ibn Khaldūn, the diplomat and scholar, and Usāma b. Munqidh, the warrior and poet, moved within both Muslim and Christian circles in the lands they visited. Only a few years after the great *mudéjar* uprisings of 1264 Naṣrid dignitaries participated in the service that consecrated the great congregational mosque of Seville as a Christian cathedral, and the King, Muḥammad II al-Faqīh, was a dubbed a knight by Alfonso X.[89] From the late thirteenth century, the Mongols (particularly the Il-Khans) sent envoys to Latin courts in order to negotiate alliances against the Mamlukes; diplomats who were – to judge by their names – themselves Muslim.[90] Through the fifteenth century, foreign Muslim knights and nobles attended and participated in courtly ceremonies and entertainments in the courts of the Iberian kings.[91] Countless other foreign Muslim dignitaries, whose names figure briefly, if at all, in the sources traveled in Latin lands. Some remained as diplomatic hostages, including the Naṣrid prince, Abū 'l-Ḥasan ʿAlī (or *Muley*

86 A. Malalana Ureña and I. Muñoz Cascante, "Mudéjares," p. 526.
87 M. García-Arenal and B. Leroy, *Moros y judíos*, pp. 77–78 {VI}.
88 A. Malalana Ureña and I. Muñoz Cascante, "Mudéjares," 529.
89 P. Linehan, *Spain, 1157–1300*, p. 96.
90 See J. A. Boyle, "Rashīd al-Dīn and the Franks," pp. 64–65.
91 R. Salicrú i Lluch, "Crossing Boundaries," p. 43.

*Hacén*), who settled in Arévalo (Castile) in 1454.[92] Tangential references to such individuals appearing in local *aljamas* and intervening in their affairs pepper the chancery registers of the fourteenth- and fifteenth-century Crown of Aragon.[93] Given the political embroilment of Muslim and Christian kingdoms around the Mediterranean, we can be all but certain this was typical; what makes the Crown unique is only that such voluminous and detailed records have survived.

Most of the Latin powers around the Mediterranean had relations with the Mameluke dynasty, but it seems, for the most part, that it was Latins who sent envoys (including Christians, Jews, and *mudéjares*) to the Sultanate, and not vice versa. Until the post-Timurid period, Muslim ambassadors were a rare sight in the lands of Western Christendom. Whereas Venice had been receiving regular embassies from the Ottomans since the 1380s, diplomatic missions from Islamic lands were making regular appearances in northern Europe, in particular, in Hungary and the Holy Roman Empire by the late fifteenth century.[94] Formal Turkish embassies appeared in German lands as early as the 1480s, and in 1524 an envoy from the Ottomans' rival, Safavid Persia, also attended the gathering of the Imperial estates at Nürnberg. This was at the very moment that France was courting Sulaymān the Magnificent as an ally against the Emperor Charles V (1519–56) – who, as Carlos I of Spain, had ordered the conversion of the *mudéjares* – and only two years before Hapsburg-allied Hungary would be mortally wounded by the Ottomans at Mohács.[95] Regular Safavid embassies had begun arriving in Venice from 1509, and in the second quarter of that century, there was a steady flow of envoys, notables, and translators being sent from the Maghrib and Ottoman lands to Spain, Italy, and France.[96] By the 1580s ambassadors of the Saʿdī Moroccan dynasty and of the Ottomans, together with their retinues, were present at the English and French courts, and Turkish envoys could be found meeting with the Dutch.[97] By the 1600s independent Muslim

92 L. P. Harvey, "El Mancebo de Arévalo," p. 254. For hostages and diplomacy in the twelfth-century Levant, see A. Kosto, "Hostages during the First Century of the Crusades."

93 See, for example, M. T. Ferrer i Mallol, *El sarraïns*, p. 164, and B. Catlos, *The Victors and the Vanquished*, p. 286.

94 See, for example, J. Wansbrough, "A Mamluk Ambassador."

95 C. Finkel, *Osman's Dream*, pp. 121–23. Lajos II (Louis; 1516–26) was married to the Hapsburg Princess Mary; he died retreating from his defeat at Mohács.

96 Claire Gilbert's working paper, "Language Liquidity in Empire: A Mediterranean Question," presented at the Fall 2011 workshop of the Mediterranean Seminar/ UCMRP, details these (pp. 2–4). This will feature in her forthcoming doctoral dissertation (History, UCLA).

97 See, generally, S. Faroqhi, *The Ottoman Empire*. In the early 1600s the Ottoman envoy Ḥāj ʾIbrāhīm ʾAghā was sent to England to request help regarding the Moriscos. See A. Temimi, "Une lettre," p. 260.

travelers, exiles, notables, and spies were journeying throughout northern Europe.[98] In 1611, for example, the former Morisco of Hornachos, Diego Bejarano, returned as Aḥmād al-Hajarī, an envoy from Morocco, and traveled across Europe.[99] The diplomatic and economic integration which prompted the appearance of Muslims in these lands, and the perception of Islam it provoked on the part of Europeans from the late fifteenth century onwards, was a phenomenon quite distinct from the attitudes of the Middle Ages; it coincided with the obsolescence of the notion of "Latin Christendom," and the abeyance of the idea of a fundamentally opposed binary of Islam and Christianity.

### *A question of class*

With rare exception, Muslim knights, princes, diplomats, and dignitaries, and even high-status captives who visited Latin lands, were treated first and foremost as warriors and aristocrats.[100] Usāma b. Munqidh referred to the Templars as his "friends"; they allowed him to pray on the Temple Mount in a little mosque that been converted to a church and that stood beside the al-ʿAqṣā Mosque.[101] The class affiliation of the elite and the common inclinations of the nobility trumped confessional identity, just as it did in many cases when Christian and Muslim peasants, merchants and scholars found themselves interacting in contexts relating to vocation.[102] As such, they were not only respected, but often esteemed, both as individuals and as adornments to princes that aspired to project cosmopolitanism and power through courtly display. Ṣalāḥ al-Dīn's power over the Latin imagination as a model of pious chivalry was so great that he was eventually assimilated as a romanticized literary figure – albeit typically reconfigured as somehow Christian of spirit or origin.[103] Tughtigīn of

98 Nabil Matar's work runs directly against that of Bernard Lewis in this respect. See B. Lewis, *The Muslim Discovery*.

99 Aḥmād was sent to investigate goods that had been stolen from Morisco refugees. He journeyed through France and the Netherlands, disputing on religion with Christians and Jews. See G. Wiegers, "Managing Disaster," pp. 142 and 161, n. 4; L. P. Harvey, "The Morisco," pp. 69–73; and C. Sarnelli Cerqua, "Il morisco ispano-marrochino." The memoir he wrote records his impressions; see al-Hajarī, *Kitāb nāṣiral-dīn*, and L. P. Harvey, "The Morisco," pp. 86–97.

100 See above, p. 111.

101 Ibn Munqidh, *The Book of Contemplation*, p. 147. Usāma uses the anecdote to contrast the behavior of acculturated Franks with those who had recently arrived in the Holy Land, and who were hostile to Muslims and uncomprehending of their culture and religion.

102 See, for example, J. Hysell's observations regarding Sicily in "Pacem Portantes Advenerint," pp. 153–54.

103 See, generally, M. A. Jubb, *The Legend of Saladin*.

Damascus was similarly romanticized as the hero of the *chanson*, *Ordene de chevalerie*, which had him (here styled as "Huon of Tabarié") convert to Christianity and fight in the ranks of the Kingdom of Jerusalem.[104] Nor were they alone; by the thirteenth century the figure of the chivalrous Saracen was popping up in the most unexpected of fictional milieux, from Provence to King Arthur's Round Table.[105] But these were not mere literary conceits – Crusade chroniclers, like Joinville, St. Louis's biographer and witness to the Seventh Crusade, and William, Archbishop of Tyre and Chancelor of the kingdom of Jerusalem, recognized the chivalric character of infidel warriors and their rulers.[106] In the fifteenth century, the kings of Granada were even called on by Christian knights to serve as judges at tournaments, duels, and staged battles.[107] Moreover, members of vanquished Muslim rulers who on rare occasions converted to Christianity were welcomed by royal courts and rapidly absorbed though marriage by the local aristocracy. Hence, in the early thirteenth-century Crown of Aragon, both the children of the apostate Prince of Valencia formerly known as Abū Zayd, and the orphaned son of the last Muslim ruler of Mallorca, were married into the Christian elite and went to become seigniors whose tenants included both Christians and *mudéjares*.[108]

In the same spirit of class and vocational solidarity, foreign Muslim dignitaries were typically held to be exempt from the various limitations and restrictions regarding clothing or comportment that lower-status Muslims may have been subject to. Such exemptions are not infrequently made explicit in royal charters. Powerful Jewish and *mudéjar* courtiers

[104] See J. Richard, "Huon de Tabarié."

[105] See A. Hatem, *Les poémes épiques*, esp. "La vie franque en Syrie," pp. 279–324. The knight Palamede or Palomides, a convert from Islam, appears in Arthurian romances from the thirteenth century, while the good, former Muslims Rainouart and Orable-Guibourc figure in the Guillaume d'Orange cycle of *chansons*. See D. Schenk, *The Myth of Guillaume*, pp. 22 and 28–29, and N. Dulin-Mallory, "Seven trewe bataylis." The best general study of the figure of the Muslim in the *chansons de geste* is N. Daniel, *Heroes and Saracens*.

[106] For Joinville, see M. A. Jubb, "Enemies in the Holy War," p. 257, and throughout. William eulogized Nūr al-Dīn as "the greatest persecutor of the Christian name and faith, yet a just, shrewd and provident man, and religious according to his people's tradition." See R. C. Schwinges, "William of Tyre," p. 128.

[107] R. Salicrú i Lluch, "Crossing Boundaries," pp. 42–43.

[108] See B. Catlos, *The Victors and the Vanquished*, p. 103, and Burns, "Almohad Prince," and "The Daughter of Abū Zayd." Not all such converts were so lucky. Martin Sanchez was a former Muslim nobleman from Portugal who, after surrendering his castle to Afonso III and receiving baptism in the presence of the King, moved to Navarre. There, he was accused in 1263 of being a crypto-Muslim, was tortured, and had his property confiscated. Eventually, he made his way to Rome, where he appealed his conviction and was absolved. See M. R. García Arancón, "Origen y azares," 693.

and functionaries received similar privileges from Christian rulers, as did pagan war-leaders and dignitaries in the eastern fringes of the Latin world.[109] These individuals moved within the rarified air of the aristocratic, cultural, and economic elite – an atmosphere in which the legitimacy of infidel sovereigns and the value of high culture were recognized irrespective of the chauvinistic and exclusionary ideologies that were formally espoused, and in which Christian and Muslim rulers were prepared to concede that their infidel homologues were, like them, legitimate rulers. Through the exchange of gifts, the appreciation of learning and luxury, and shared aristocratic sentiment and military vocations, diplomats helped to disseminate tastes and technical knowledge from across the Islamic world and beyond throughout Latin Christendom.[110]

When Sirāj al-Dīn Urmavī, an Azerbaijani scholar who had formerly served as ambassador to the Mongol khan, Hülegü (1256–65), was sent to Frederick II's court, he came into contact with notables and functionaries from across Latin Christendom.[111] After Fernando III of Castile allowed his son Alfonso to seize the kingdom of Murcia from his vassal Aḥmad b. Hūd, the Muslim ruler dispatched an envoy to Rome to complain to Innocent IV that the Christian king had broken his word.[112] *Mudéjares* in the service of Iberian royal houses, the Church, and nobility would have also circulated in the larger Latin West, but few records remain. For example, ʿĪsā b. Jābir, the *faqīh* of Segovia, was ordered to settle in Aynton, in Savoy, in the 1450s, while he worked on the Qurʿān translation commissioned by Juan de Segovia.

Lower-level functionaries and agents, such as the official captive redeemers (the *exea*, *alfaqueque*) and the borderland sheriffs (the *alcalde entre moros y cristianos*, *adalid* and *almocadén*), who included merchants from the Islamic world, and who had been circulating on both sides of the Iberian frontier since the eleventh century, may not have enjoyed the same prestige and privileges as royal envoys, but they were protected by law and enjoyed a certain diplomatic immunity. The most remarkable example of this class solidarity can be observed in the diplomatic correspondence between Christian and Muslim

109 For a *mudéjar* who purchased such an exemption, see M. T. Ferrer i Mallol, *Els sarraïns*, p. 48.

110 See R. Salicrú i Lluch, "La diplomacia y las embajadas." For a general study of diplomatic, political, and economic relations between the Crown of Aragon and Granada, see Salicrú i Lluch, *El sultanat de Granada*, and M. D. López Pérez, *La Corona de Aragón y el Magreb*; for documents, see À. Masià i de Ros, *Jaume II: Aragó, Granada i Marroc.*

111 L. Marlow, "A Thirteenth-Century Scholar," pp. 290–97.

112 The envoy Abū Ṭālib b. Sabʿin, the brother of the renowned Sufi and philosopher, ʿAbd al-Ḥaqq b. Sabʿin, apparently succeeded in meeting with the Pope, who praised his learning. See M. Amari, "Questions philosophiques," pp. 251–52.

sovereigns, wherein the former express their "love" and "friendship" to the latter, and call them "brothers" and rulers "by the grace of God."[113]

### *Exiles and renegades*

Even as policies and attitudes towards Muslims and Moriscos at home tightened up, both Portugal and Hapsburg Spain became refuges for Muslim political exiles from the Maghrib, just as the earlier Crowns of Castile and Aragon had been in preceding centuries.[114] Although class and vocational affinity were a *sine qua non* for such relationships, welcoming the exiled royalty of the Maghrib presented a way of destabilizing the Islamic West, tenuously extending Hapsburg power and the Catholic faith into North Africa, and interfering with the Ottoman advance. As the power of the Marīnids collapsed beginning in the late fourteenth century, and those of their successors and rivals, the Banū Waṭṭās and the Saʿdids, rose and fell in the fifteenth and sixteenth, a series of dispossessed princes paraded north to seek aid and shelter from the Avis and Hapsburg dynasties.[115] Likewise, the Ḥafṣid princes of Ifrīqiya came to see the Ottomans ultimately as a greater enemy than their infidel neighbors. In 1548 Abū Ḥasan, "King of Velez," crossed over to petition Charles V for aid, and found himself and his family living in Brussels and Augsburg, kept effectively as hostages. He was followed in 1550 by Mulay Amar, "King of Debdū," who was kept "safe" in Melilla with his retinue of 300 kinsmen, together with the Waṭṭāsid prince, Abū Ḥassūn, "King of Bādis." Most of these refugees and their families, particularly those who settled in Europe, ended up converting and living off of the mercy of the monarchs, or carving out military careers in the service of the emperors. In the late sixteenth century, the former Waṭṭāsid princess, Juana Brandonia, "she who is called 'Queen of Fez,'" could be found with her children making the rounds in the kingdom of Castile.[116] Gaspar de Benimerín

[113] See, for example, C. Conde Solares, "Social Continuity," p. 313; and B. Catlos, "Mahomet Abenadalill," p. 257, and *The Victors and the Vanquished*, p. 75. In 1309, in a typical exchange regarding the return of subjects captured in times of truce, Jaume II of Mallorca wrote to Abū 'l-Juyūsh Naṣr (1309–14) addressing him as "The very high and powerful *Don Naçer*, by the grace of God, King of Granada, of Malaga, Almería, Algeciras, of Ronda, Guadix, and Lord of Ceuta and Commander of the Muslims [*Amir Almoçlemi*] . . ." [ACA, CRD, Jaume II, caja 29, no. 3643 (June 18, 1309).]

[114] See, for example, above, p. 246. In 1421 the dispossessed heir of the kingdom of Tlemcen fled prison in Granada, first for Castile, and then the Crown of Aragon, from where he planned to launch a mission to claim his throne from his illegitimate brother. See R. Salicrú i Lluch, "Fugues, camuflatge i treball," p. 436.

[115] After 1581 and Felipe II's takeover of Portugal, the North African princes could no longer play the Avis and Hapsburg kings against each other.

[116] B. Alonso Acero, *Sultanes de Berbería*, p. 82.

(Bani Marīn) – one of the many of his dynasty who fought under the Hapsburgs – lived for many years in Flanders. Carlos of Africa, the last of the Zayyānī dynasty of Tlemcen, joined the Order of Santiago. Felipe of Africa, the last King of the Saʿdids, lived in luxury in Madrid, served in the imperial Infantry of Milan, and retired in Vigévano, Italy in 1610. His daughter and heiress, Josefa of Africa, ended her days as a nun at the Convent of St. Paul in Zamora. In 1612 an imposter, "Mahamete ben Mulay Naçar," was condemned to the galleys after a long run claiming to be the former "King of Fez." Given their own evident lack of religious integrity, it is no surprise that few of these refugees demonstrated solidarity or concern for their Morisco cousins. A rare exception was Felipe of Aragon, who, having settled in Elche, evidently fell in with fellow crypto-Muslims and was condemned in an *auto da fé* by the Inquistion of Málaga for sheltering heretics, and for being a schismatic, a witch, a minion of the Devil, and a Muslim. He was sentenced to three years in prison and, thereafter, permanent exile.[117]

The emergence of the Ottomans as the pre-eminent power in the eastern Mediterranean brought Turkish and Safavid Persian merchants, envoys, refugees, and pretenders to Latin shores.[118] The most famous of these was "Cem Sultan" the deposed son of Mehmed II (1444–46/1451–81), who fled the Ottoman Empire in 1482 under the supposed protection of the Knights of St. John.[119] The latter, however, had made a secret deal with the usurper, Cem's half-brother, Bāyezīd II. As a consequence, Cem was taken captive, and sent to a specially built prison in the Savoyard Alps to avoid his falling into Venetian or Hungarian hands. In 1489 he was transferred to Rome and the custody of Innocent VIII, who hoped to convert him to Christianity and use him as a propaganda tool in the service of a new Crusade. After this came to naught, Innocent's successor, Alexander VI, planned to use him to help leverage an alliance with Bāyezīd against Charles VIII of France (1483–98).[120] In 1495, however, the French King recovered Cem from the Pope and took him along on his campaign against Naples, where the unfortunate pretender succumbed to illness on February 25, 1495. Four years later, his body was returned to Sultan Bāyezīd, who had him interred with full pomp and honors – in recognition, perhaps, of Cem's constancy. This was considerably greater than that displayed by his exiled uncle, Bāyezīd Osman. Also a refugee

[117] For the preceding, see *ibid.*, esp. chapter 2: "Exiliados regios del Magreb en tierras de la monarquía durante los siglos XVI y XVII," pp. 61–174.

[118] See, for example, N. Matar, *In the Lands of the Christians*, and G. Rota, *Under Two Lions*.

[119] See J. Freely, *Jem Sultan*.

[120] See F. Inalcik, "A Case Study."

from the intrigues of the Ottoman court, Bāyezīd had submitted to baptism by Calixtus III in 1456 and joined the court of Frederick III (1452–93), who touted him as the legitimate successor to the Ottoman Sultanate. Known as "Calixtus Ottomanus," he was assigned a fief at Bruck an der Leitha (in modern Austria), where he lived out his years, occasionally to be trotted out by the Hapsburg emperors when it suited them, often in full Turkish regalia for maximum effect.[121]

### *Merchants and travelers*

Prior to the late fifteenth century, few Muslims reached northern Europe, and those that did tended to come unwillingly, as slaves. Muslim merchants and travelers transited the Latin Mediterranean on board Christian-owned vessels and passed by land through Latin principalities, but the only areas they visited with any frequency or duration were those which had a subject Muslim population.[122] The reasons were manifold. With the exception of the Mediterranean shores, Latin Europe had little to offer the Muslim merchant or traveler, and those commodities that the continent provided were conveyed to the Islamic world by Christian and Jewish traders. The land of the *Ifranj* was a hostile and dangerous environment, where Muslim travelers would be at constant risk of violence, and where there would have been no Islamic infrastructure to sustain them or to provide a frame for their commercial activities. Travelers like Ibn Baṭṭūṭa and Abū Ḥāmid al-Gharnāṭī supported themselves on their journeys by working in Islamic administrations, by serving local Muslim communities as jurisprudents and judges, and through their dependence on Islamic charitable institutions and networks – none of which was possible in the Latin hinterlands.[123]

Such foreign Muslim travel and trade as there was in Latin lands prior to the Ottoman era, then, was confined effectively to the Mediterranean, and overwhelmingly to those areas with subject Muslim communities.

121 See C. Johnson, *Cultural Hierarchy in Sixteenth-Century Europe*, pp. 201–03; F. Babinger, *Mehmed the Conqueror and His Time*, p. 238, and "Bajezid Osman."

122 See O. R. Constable, *Housing the Stranger*, pp. 328–29; and H. E. Mayer; "Latins, Muslims and Greeks," p. 187.

123 Shams al-Dīn Abū ʻAbd Allāh Muḥammad b. Baṭṭūṭa (1304–1368/77) is the most famous of medieval Muslim travelers. His *rihla* (memoir) records his purported travels to China, India, the Indian Ocean, and Sub-Saharan Africa, as well as Central Asia. See R. Dunn, *The Adventures of Ibn Battuta*, and Ibn Baṭṭūṭa, *The Travels of Ibn Battuta*. During his travels Ibn Baṭṭūṭa sailed sometimes on Christian ships, but only set foot on Latin soil once – a brief stop in Cagliari (Sardinia), which he was happy to leave, as he heard the natives planned to pursue his ship and capture him. See Ibn Baṭṭūṭa, *The Travels of Ibn Battuta*, p. 307.

Thanks to its position between the Mediterranean and the markets and trade termini of the East, the Crusader Levant was a regular stopping point for Muslim merchants originating from Morocco to Iraq. Ibn Jubayr marveled that "although the fires of discord burn between the two parties, Muslim and Christian ... travelers will come and go between them without interference," and that "Muslims continuously journeyed from Damascus to Acre" even as Ṣalāḥ al-Dīn was waging war on the kingdom of Jerusalem.[124] Only rarely do exceptions appear in the documentation. For example, in 1401, the Navarrese Muslim smith Ybrayn Madexa is mentioned as living in Cherbourg, where he had evidently been for some time, and Carlos III took his master carpenter, Lope Barbicano, with him to Paris in 1405.[125] The safety and security of Muslim travelers was guaranteed either by truces and treaties between Muslim and Christian rulers, or by royally issued letters of passage, known as *guidatica* (singular: *guidaticum*) in Christian Iberia; to travel without such protection meant to risk arrest or abuse at the hands of local seigniors and officials, and even such documents were no guarantee.[126] Finding acceptable and appropriate lodging and dining also presented challenges for travelers, except in areas where there were indigenous Muslim populations, and in Iberia, where many towns had *fanādiq* (merchants' inns or caravanserais), run by and specifically catering to Muslims.[127]

Generally, these "civilian" travelers consisted almost exclusively of merchants, although pilgrims, like the *ḥājjī* and diarist Ibn Jubayr, and scholars and literati, like Ḥamdan al-Athāribī, were often obliged or chose to travel through Christian lands or on the Latin Christian ships that dominated the Mediterranean from the twelfth century onwards.[128] It is clear that Muslims also worked as crew members and pilots on these vessels,

[124] Ibn Jubayr, *Travels*, pp. 300–1.
[125] H. Ozaki, "El regimen tributario," pp. 442 and 452.
[126] See R. I. Burns, "The *Guidaticum* Safe-Conduct."
[127] See O. R. Constable, *Housing the Stranger*, chapter 5, "Conquest and Commercial Space: the Case of Iberia," pp. 158–200, especially pp. 164–69. In the Crown of Aragon there was a network of royal caravanserais (*alhóndigas reales*) that represented the continuation of a network that had existed in Almohad times, if not earlier. For example, in 1284, Pedro Fernández el Hijar received a privilege to administer these inns that were on his seigniorial lands, according to "Muslim law, and just as had been done in the time of the [Almohad] Amīr al-Mu'minīn" ("'Çuna', secundum usum temporis de Miramamolin"). See M. V. Febrer Romaguera, "Derecho común," pp. 310 and 313–14.
[128] For Ḥamdan al-Athāribī, see p. 155. See, also, p. 116, n.62. There are abundant references to late medieval Muslim pilgrims; see for example, P. S. van Koningsveld and G. Wiegers, "The Islamic Statute," p. 39. For Muslim merchants traveling and sojourning in Italy through the fourteenth century, see, for example, H. E. Mayer, "Latins, Muslims and Greeks," p. 184; D. Abulafia, "The End of Muslim Sicily," p. 133; and J. A. Taylor, "Lucera Sarracenorum," p. 117. For notices of Muslim traders going from Spain on Christian ships, see, for example, O. R. Constable, *Trade and*

most likely with greater frequency than the surviving sources suggest.[129] In twelfth-century Sicily trade remained largely under the control of Muslim and Jewish merchants, who received associated agents from the *dār al-Islām*, while the employ of Arabophone customs scribes in Crusader Acre confirms the activities of Muslim traders there.[130] There are notices of a Muslim resident in Tyre who carried on shipping trade with Egypt, and it is reasonable to presume that such individuals were scattered up and down the Levantine littoral.[131]

Nevertheless, some Muslims settled temporarily in Latin lands that lacked *mudéjar* communities, particularly in the port cities that had strong links with the Islamic world, like Barcelona, Mallorca, Montpellier, Narbonne, Venice, Marseilles, Pisa, Salerno, and Genoa.[132] The conversion of the apostate Muslim and monk of Monte Cassino, Constantinus Africanus, was prompted by a visit he made to Salerno as a merchant in the 1060s.[133] In the 1190s, Donizone, a monk from Canossa and the biographer of Mathilda of Tuscany (1076–1115), was scandalized by the Muslims he saw in Pisa: "Whoever reaches Pisa will see there monsters from the sea. That squalid city has Turks, Libians, and even Parthians. Foul Chaldeans traverse her shores."[134] The first Muslim envoy to Genoa is attested in 1238, but it is clear that merchants and notables had been coming to the city for at least a century previously. The port cities of the Italian littoral, whose fortunes depended on trade with Byzantium and the Islamic world, were home to Muslim slaves, artisans, artists, and merchants since the late eleventh century. Generic allusions to these communities crop up only occasionally in the historical record, and references to individuals are even more rare. Even higher-status individuals, such as the Sicilian *mudéjar* grandee Abū 'l-Qāsim, who maintained a presence in Genoa and carried out business there in the 1160s, are exceptional.[135] In the thirteenth century, the commune employed both Arabic

*Traders*, p. 253; C.-E. Dufourcq, "Chrétiens et Musulmanes," pp. 217–18; R. Burns, "Los mudéjares de la Valencia," pp. 15–16 and 19–20 {1}; and J. P. Madurell Marimón, "Un convenio," p. 40. Christian-domination of the sea notwithstanding, Muslims, including *mudéjares* continued to own ships. See, for example, M. T. Ferrer i Mallol, *El sarraïns*, p. 156.

129 Arab crewmen and navigators contributed to the success of the European "voyages of discovery," including, perhaps, that of Columbus. See A. Hamdani, "An Islamic Background," especially pp. 281–83.

130 D. Abulafia, *The Two Italies*, p. 249.

131 H. E. Mayer, "Latins, Muslims and Greeks," p. 184.

132 For Narbonne and Montpellier, see J. Lacam, *Les Sarrazins*, p. 207.

133 See below, p. 337.

134 Donizone di Canossa, *Vita Mathildis*, p. 52. For Pisan trade with the Islamic West, see, for example, T. Bruce, "The Politics of Violence."

135 D. Abulafia, *The Two Italies*, pp. 248–49; and p. 120.

notaries and language teachers.[136] Genoa, of course, had exercised direct sovereignty over Muslim populations since the 1140s, when it briefly ruled over captured Tortosa and Almería.

### Mudéjar *merchants*

The Mediterranean expansion of the Catalan dynasty that began in the thirteenth century would prompt *mudéjar* merchants to establish themselves in territories where there had hardly been a free Muslim community, such as at Sardinia, or where it had long ceased to exist, such as at Palermo.[137] From the late thirteenth century merchants from Ifrīqiya were trading in Latin ports.[138] Mallorca, in particular, became an important center of activity for merchants from Tunis and Bougie in the fourteenth century, and an entrepôt that linked various ports along the northern and southern shore of the Mediterranean. Commodities including leather, oil, silk, wool, and wax traveled between North Africa and Latin Europe. With the decline of the Islamic merchant marine, much of this trade would have been carried out on Christian ships, and *comendas* and trade agreements between foreign Muslims, and local and North African Jews, Christians, and *mudéjares* were evidently common. Hence, in 1318 we find Zohra, the wife of a Mallorcan cobbler, borrowing money from a certain Ṭāhar b. ʿAbd Allāh of Tunis to invest in oil for export to North Africa. Nearly half a century later, in 1354, Hamet Atzuahi, from Bougie, accepted a *commenda* of five *reales* on behalf of Bernat Bru of Mallorca, and promised to deliver it to his countryman, Antoni Garcia, when he returned home. Like so much of the quotidian history of the *mudéjares* and Muslim–Christian relations, the frequency of such arrangements is obscured by the paucity and the nature of the surviving sources, both in the Christian and Islamic worlds.[139]

From the fourteenth century Venice was embroiled politically and commercially with Naṣrid Granada and the Maghrib, but for the most part, Venetian policy was oriented more towards Byzantium and the Levant, and from the 1430s numbers of Anatolian Muslim traders began to arrive at the Serenissima.[140] The situation in the other cities of the Italian coasts would have been no different. The fact that such individuals appear so

[136] G. Jehel, "Jews and Muslims," pp. 122–23.

[137] See G. Oman, "Vestiges arabes en Sardaigne"; T. Bruce, "The Politics of Violence," pp. 132–39; and C. Verlinden, *L'esclavage*, vol. II, p. 142.

[138] Conversely, Jews and Christians from the Iberian peninsula were active in the Maghrib. See J. L. Soler Milla, "Relaciones comerciales," and, above, p. 222.

[139] For an overview, see D. Valérian, "Ifrîqiyan Muslim Merchants"; for Zohra, p. 54.

[140] See C. Kafadar, "A Death in Venice," 193; and G. Rota, *Under Two Lions*.

infrequently in the historical record is likely a consequence of the nature of the surviving sources rather than indication of a complete absence of long- and mid-term Muslim visitors, who would have included members of other professions such as translators and interpreters, physicians, and musicians – experts who enjoyed a technical advantage due to the education available in the Islamic world.[141] That said, much of the demand for such specially trained vocations would have been filled by slaves, the captive Muslims who most certainly formed part of the quotidian social fabric not only around, but beyond the shores of the Latin Mediterranean, and who – as they converted, were manumitted, and absorbed into Christian society – acted as a potent vector of acculturation and the transmission of knowledge, technique, and cultural practice and preference.[142]

### *Immigrants and travelers*

Most surprisingly, at times there were significant voluntary movements of Muslim populations to Christian lands. While most of these took place between Christian lands, as when Portuguese *mudéjares* emigrated to Castile, and Castilian *mudéjares* settled in Navarre or the Crown of Aragon, they reflect a decision on the part of Muslims to remain in familiar lands under Christian rule rather than take on the risks inherent in emigration.[143] Likewise, a number of the Muslims who had fled the upheavals of the Castilian campaign in Almería in the 1140s, or Valencia's "Muslim War" of the late thirteenth century, opted to repatriate themselves when favorable conditions were extended to them by Christian rulers.[144] Some fifteenth-century Andalusī refugees in Fez were adamantly vocal regarding the preferability of life under Christian rule.[145] Nevertheless, there were also times when Muslims left unconquered Islamic lands to settle in Latin principalities. For example, the political

[141] See, generally, R. Salicrú i Lluch, "Intérpretes y diplomáticos." Christian rulers were keen to cultivate these skills among their own Muslim subjects. In 1434, Maria de Castilla, Queen and Lieutenant-General of the Crown of Aragon, petitioned for the liberation of one of her *mudéjar* subjects from Valencia who had been captured by Portuguese pirates when he was en route from Almería to Tlemcen, where he was going to "study and learn." See F. Lopes de Barros, *Tempos e espaços*, p. 169.

[142] See, for example, P. S. van Koningsveld, "Andalusian-Arabic Manuscripts," p. 91.

[143] Similar movements took place towards Norman Sicily as Ifrīqiya went into crisis. It was not only members of the intellectual elite, like al-Idrīsī, but ordinary Muslims who chose to immigrate. See L. C. Chiarelli, "The Ibadiyah in Muslim Sicily," p. 11.

[144] See, for example, p. 192.

[145] This may have represented rhetorical posturing on the part of the refugees, but the alleged preference among some Muslims for life under Christian rule did provoke a vehement *fatwa* against *mudéjares* from the great Maghribī jurist al-Wansharīsī. See K. Abou el Fadl, "Islamic Law and Muslim Minorities," p. 154; see, also p. 315.

crisis of late thirteenth- and early fourteenth-century al-Andalus prompted numbers of ordinary Granadans, which is to say members of the productive classes, to move north to Valencia.[146] The most remarkable and sustained episode of Muslim immigration to Latin lands, however, took place in the first half-century or so after the d'Hautevilles' conquest of Sicily, when members of the literary, scientific, and religious elite settled in Palermo. Muḥammad al-Idrīsī, the Andalusī geographer and cartographer, is only the best known of the scores of learned, foreign Muslims who found patronage and prosperity at the Norman court. This singular chapter in the history of Muslim–Christian relations was due to the convergence of three factors: the instability and uncertainty in al-Andalus and North Africa that followed the rise of the Almoravids and the Almohads, the fact that Norman rulers were prepared to patronize this Islamic elite on their own terms, and the presence of a broad, secure, and prosperous indigenous Muslim community in Sicily.

The presence of high- and middle-status foreign Muslims in Christian lands helped reinforce the identity of native Islamic communities and provided subject Muslims a connection with the larger Islamic world. It also offered a model of prestige for communities that were confronted continually with their secondary and subject position. For isolated populations, like the *Böszörmények*, the occasional visits of travelers like al-Gharnāṭī might seem to be all that was staving off conversion by attrition; in Iberia and Italy, where the presence of foreign Muslims, whether royalty and warriors, merchants or settlers, was part of the normal backdrop of daily life, their influence would have been profound. Influential foreign Muslims married into local Muslim families, positioned themselves as patrons over individuals and communities, and strengthened social, economic, and cultural bonds between *mudéjar* communities and the larger *dār al-Islām*. This is not to say that all of them were conscious agents of ethno-religious solidarity; many noble Muslims, like Usāma b. Munqidh, who scarcely mentions his subject co-religionists in his lengthy memoirs, probably held humbler *mudéjares* in no less contempt than they regarded the Muslim lower classes at home. Nor could the pilgrim Ibn Jubayr, who was no aristocrat, suppress his disapproval of those who submitted to infidel rule from occasionally bubbling up – "There is no excuse in the eyes of God for a Muslim to stay in an infidel country" – amidst his descriptions of the prosperous *mudéjares* of Palestine and Sicily.[147]

[146] See, for example, M. T. Ferrer i Mallol, "Les phenomènes migratoires."

[147] Ibn Jubayr, *Travels*, p. 321. This was a sentiment apparently shared by some of those same *mudéjares*, including ʿAbd al-Massih, a Muslim Ibn Jubayr met in Messina who,

But in the final analysis, as will be described below, the foreign Muslims who exercised the greatest impact on the evolution of subject Muslim communities were not the handfuls of travelers and diplomats who transited and sojourned in Latin lands, but rather the masses of foreign captives who fed the booming slave markets of western Christendom.

## Muslim slaves in Latin Christendom (*c.* 1050–*c.* 1550)

And the said *justicia mayor* had the said Muslims questioned by Per de Gudar, squire of Daorca, who knows Arabic very well, as to who these Muslims were and if they had been captured or stolen, to which, according to the said Per de Gudar, the said Muslims said that one was from Morocco and the other two from Granada, and that they were captured by mercenaries [*almogavers*]of the noble *infant Don* Pero, the day the said prince [*infant*]vanquished the Muslims and killed Hamo, and four other Muslim princes, and many other Muslims, and those mercenaries had sold them in Castile, and they know no more, neither where they had been, nor for how long they had been captives of the said Domingo Gomez, nor who had sold them to him ... (Tomas Lopez del Gras, notary, trial transcript (May 2, 1318).[148])

Although we are conditioned to think of slavery in the Christian West as an early modern phenomenon, in fact, the widespread trade and ownership of slaves by Christians was a prominent feature of the medieval Latin economy and society, particularly in the Mediterranean. During the great age of Latin aggression against the *dār al-Islām*, from the mid eleventh through the mid thirteenth century, the overwhelming majority of slaves sold and held were culturally Arab prisoners originating in conquered territories or their environs.[149] In twelfth-century Portugal and Castile Muslim slaves were freed in order to increase the base of settlers, but by the following century, the development of a functioning market in the Latin West had acted to commoditize captives.[150] In any event, from 1300

despite his own evident prosperity, disclosed that he felt "bound in the possession of an infidel who has placed on our necks the noose of bondage." *Ibid.*, p. 324; discussed in C. Dalli, "Contriving Coexistence," pp. 36–37. This contrasts markedly with Ibn Jubayr's own description of Muslim life in Messina; it is possible that rather than feeling this way, ʿAbd al-Massih thought he *ought* to feel this way, or was embarrassed by his own complacency in this regard, and felt obliged to put on a front before his distinguished visitor.

148 ACA, C., Pr. 1318E, f. 13v. See B. Catlos, "Tyranny and the Mundane," and M. Sánchez Martínez, "Aspectos del cautiverio," p. 275.

149 Muslim slaves are attested to in Latin lands at least as early as the 900s. See S. Bensch, "From Prizes of War," p. 67. By the 1080s Muslim captives figure as a commodity in an Aragonese customs schedule; see M. Gómez de Valenzuela, "Esclavos moros," p. 117.

150 C. Verlinden, *L'Esclavage*, vol. I, p. 143. Muslim slaves were offered freedom in exchange for settling in Freixo, Portugal in 1159; *ibid.*, pp. 153ff. For captives in the early period, see also R Fletcher, *The Quest for El Cid*, p. 179.

or so onwards, slaves of eastern origin, including Balkan Slavs, Bulgars, Greeks, Turkic peoples, and Tatars (or eastern Christians passed off as such) began to overtake Muslims in terms of volume.[151] Nevertheless, piracy and raiding ensured a steady, if reduced, supply of North African Muslims for the Latin market through the sixteenth century, as both Muslim shipping and settlements were targeted for abduction by Iberian, French, and Italian corsairs, and conquest continued to generate captives.[152] Shipwrecks also provided an occasional and fortuitous source of slaves for coastal villagers, who were entitled to treat the survivors as salvage subject to the payment of a fee to the Crown. The Catalan commercial/political expansion in the late thirteenth and fourteenth centuries stimulated the trade and distribution of Muslim slaves in the south of France, Italy, Sicily, and Sardinia.[153] It was thanks largely to the Catalans that Genoa emerged as a slave *entrepôt* as early as the twelfth century, but by the late 1300s few Muslim slaves were traded there. As the Ottomans emerged as a regional power in the late fourteenth century, raiding and military engagements brought Muslims from Anatolia and Central Asia into the slave markets of the central and eastern Mediterranean.[154] By the early fifteenth century, however, sub-Saharan "blacks" were the most visible if not the most voluminous contingent on the market. While many of these would be categorized as Muslims, as often as not their exposure to Islam was superficial – a consequence of their capture by Muslim traders who "converted" them to Islam as a matter of course.[155] Finally, alongside these foreign slaves, were indigenous Muslims who had been enslaved juridically, either as a consequence of debt or some violation of Christian or Islamic law.

### *Slavery in the Latin Mediterranean*

Bondage, like freedom, was a relative condition in the Middle Ages, and Muslim slaves in Latin Christendom lived in a diverse range of

[151] For the shift towards non-Muslim slaves, including Greeks and Sards in the Eastern Mediterranean, see A. Luttrell, "Slavery at Rhodes." For Italy, see C. R. Backman, *The Decline and Fall*, pp. 247–68, esp. 266, for the shift to Greek slaves, and D. Abulafia, "The End of Muslim Sicily," p. 131. Among the 5,000 transactions involving slaves recorded by Barcelona notaries, only 1079 refer to Muslims. See F. Guillén Diop, "Esclavage et métissages," p. 2.

[152] See, generally, C. Torres Delgado, "El Mediterraneo nazarí."

[153] C. Verlinden, *L'Esclavage*, vol. I, pp. 750ff, vol. II, pp. 142 and 344.

[154] From the thirteenth century Venetians were purchasing slaves of various provenances, including Christians. For the Venetian slave trade at Alexandria, see G. Christ, *Trading Conflicts*, chapter 7, "Slavery and Solidarities," pp. 121–42.

[155] See K. Lowe, "Black Africans," p. 68, for example.

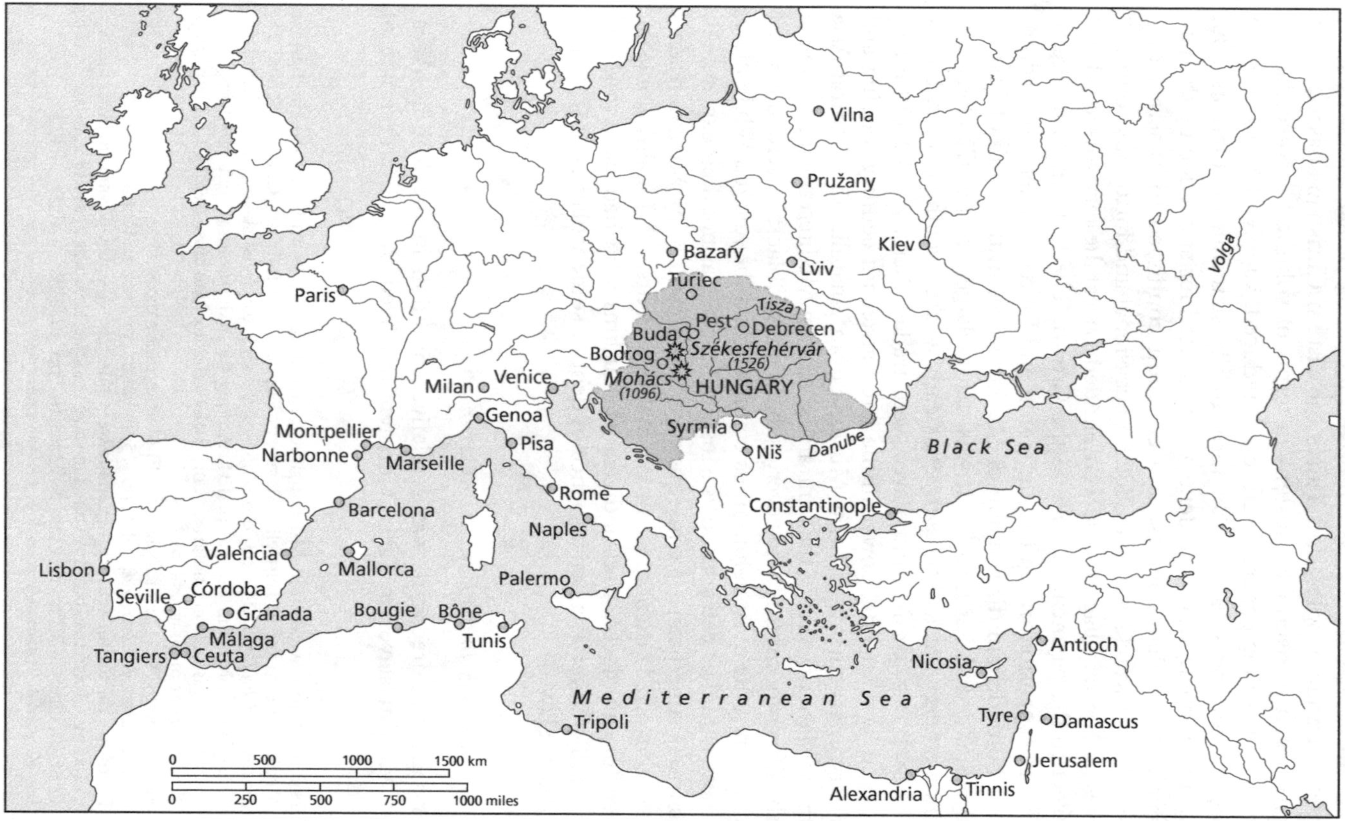


Map 7 Muslim settlement in Hungary and the north-east; centres of Muslim slavery and Islamic commerce (*c.* 1300)

circumstances and experiences. With the exception of sugar and cotton production in some areas (notably Crete and Cyprus), large-scale agricultural, "plantation-type" slavery was not a feature of the economy of the Latin West.[156] That said, rural slavery was not unknown; in fifteenth-century Mallorca, much of the agricultural labor force – perhaps 7 percent of the population as a whole – were slaves belonging to urban-based smallholders.[157] In any event, Muslim captives were used for large-scale manual labor throughout the Middle Ages.[158] In the twelfth century Muslim prisoners, including the elderly, women, and, children, were pressed into service building and repairing churches and fortifications – particularly in the Holy Land, where Latins were constantly on the defensive, and where a series of earthquakes gave the repair of defenses a special urgency.[159] In the assault on Jerusalem, Muslim captives were conscripted to help build the Crusaders' siege towers.[160] In Iberia, from the thirteenth century onwards the burden and cost of the repair of municipal fortifications fell on the reluctant shoulders of free subjects, including local Christians, Muslims, and Jews; but for seigniors (whether secular or clerical), slaves – often kept in the most miserable conditions – continued to provide hard labor through the fifteenth century.[161]

Apparently, at the conquest of Tyre in 1124 the Muslim women of the city were spared death in order to be condemned to a life in the textile works. While it is not clear whether these women were enslaved, it was certainly not uncommon for female slaves to be put to work in manufacturing or artisanal activities.[162] The use of slaves to power galleys did not become widespread until the later sixteenth century; by this time the free Muslim communities of the Latin West had disappeared, and the supply of galley-slaves was met largely by convicted Christian criminals. However, throughout this entire period slave markets were a common feature of Latin towns and cities on the Mediterranean shore, and throughout

156 See C. Verlinden, "L'esclavage agricole" for Muslim and Greek slaves on Crete; also C. Verlinden, *L'Esclavage*, vol. II, pp. 436ff. Most slaves on Cyprus were not Muslim; see N. Coureas, "Christian and Muslim Captives." There were few slaves engaged in the sugar industry, even in Valencia; see D. Abulafia, "Sugar in Spain," pp. 192 and 198, and, generally, J. H. Galloway, "The Mediterranean Sugar Industry."

157 See C. Verlinden, "Aspects quantatifs," p. 771.

158 See, for example above, p. 25, n 16.

159 See, for example, H. E. Mayer, "Latins, Muslims and Greeks," p. 187, for the Frankish Levant, C. Verlinden, *L'Esclavage*, vol. I, p. 131, for Muslim slaves building churches and fortifications in eleventh-century Portugal. See also p. 158.

160 R. Rogers, *Latin Siege Warfare*, p. 54.

161 For municipal fortifications, see B. Catlos, *The Victors and the Vanquished*, pp. 269–70; for slave labor, M. Gómez de Valenzuela, "Esclavos moros," pp. 122–24.

162 See H. E. Mayer, "Latins, Muslims and Greeks," p. 187.

Christian Iberia, at which a substantial proportion if not the overwhelming balance of the merchandise on offer consisted of foreign Muslims. It was not only private individuals who kept slaves, but also ecclesiastical institutions, including Military Orders and monasteries and convents (both male and female), for whom it was common for unfree Muslims to serve as laborers.[163] There is no indication that the clergy involved in such relationships felt any moral duty to convert and manumit their slaves.

Although its prevalence may be exaggerated by historians, domestic slavery on the "Mediterranean model," in which slaves served in and were incorporated into their owners' households, was common, particularly but not only in the case of women, who served in the most intimate of domestic contexts as nursemaids, and chamber-servants, and who were privy to their owners' most delicate and dangerous secrets. The fourteenth-century Valencian noblewoman Isabel Cornel discovered this to her regret, when two of her slave girls (a Muslim and a Tatar), testified in graphic detail in court regarding an illicit *ménage-à-trois* in which she was involved.[164] Muslim slaves' knowledge of family secrets and indiscretions could act as a counter-balance to the otherwise arbitrary and little-restrained authority of their owners. The genuine esteem in which Muslim domestics slaves were often held by their owners can be seen in Christian last wills and testaments, which not infrequently make provision for slaves, including both gifts of cash and kind, and manumission – although the latter was almost invariably contingent on the slave's willing conversion to Christianity. Once emancipated, slaves that did not return to the *dār al-Islām* often came to form part of their former owners' network of patronage and dependence. Whether as a strategy for survival or symptomatic of a sort of "Stockholm Syndrome," slaves in Valencia came to see themselves as sharing in and benefitting from the honor and prestige of their owners' families and, as a consequence, became active protagonists rather than merely accessories, in inter-Christian feuds.[165] Indeed, the Muslim household slaves of powerful Christian owners may have enjoyed more prestige and real power in many contexts than a poor but free Christian – not to mention a generally better lifestyle.

163 See, for example, M. Gómez de Valenzuela, "Esclavos moros," pp. 122–25. High-ranking clerics in Aragon, including abbots, bishops, and even the schismatic Pope, Benedict XIII, made use of Muslim slave labor on building projects.

164 See N. Silleras-Fernández, "Failed Expectations."

165 For the relationship of slaves to their owners' households in fifteenth-century Valencia, see D. Blumenthal, *Enemies and Familiars*, chapter 4, "Enemies or Extended Family," pp. 122–53. Earlier examples of the integration of both free and slave Muslims into their owners' households can be found in R. I. Burns, "Los mudéjares de Valencia," p. 25.

*Sex and the Muslim slave*

The most intimate role that Muslim slaves played, of course, was that of sexual object, whether used as concubines or obliged to engage in prostitution.[166] Indeed, this became an enduring image of the Muslim woman in Christian society.[167] Although later medieval legislation in some regions, notably Valencia, where slave-owning was ubiquitous, formally prohibited sexual relations between owners and slaves, the nature of the master–slave relationship and the incredible vulnerability and disorientation of the young foreign girls and women who so often found themselves abducted and sold, meant that coerced sex was a terrible reality for many, and that consensual or semi-consensual relations could be an important strategy for survival and advancement.[168] Giving birth to a master's child could sometimes be a route to manumission for female slaves. However, from the fourteenth century, legislation eliminated the obligation for such manumissions, or placed increasing restrictions on such liaisons – not only in the kingdom of Valencia, but also in other principalities of the Latin West.[169] For example, in the thirteenth century, pregnant slaves could not be sold, and children fathered by any Christian would be free *de jure*; however, a century later, such a rule applied only in cases where it was the owner who was the father, and where this could be proven (i.e. admitted).The effect (if not the intention) of such legislation would have been to undermine any legal claims made by slave women who bore their masters' children. Not surprisingly, here and elsewhere, many men repudiated such children, denying them the right to the free, Christian status they deserved by law, or claimed (honestly or not) that a third-party Latin male had been to blame. Slave men and boys were undoubtedly also the subject of sexual abuse and violence at the hands of their owners and third parties, but this is a matter on which the sources are, not unpredictably, silent.

Muslims owned by Jews were subject to the same abuses and mistreatments, aggravated by the additional danger (in the view of Muslim and Christian authorities) that these slaves might convert to Judaism either through coercion or domestic acculturation.[170] Such a conversion qualified as apostasy (on the part of the slave) and of proselytism (on the part of

[166] See, for example, M. Meyerson, "Prostitution of Muslim Women."
[167] Shakespeare, for example, refers to Muslim concubinage and sexual slavery in his work. See M. Kahf, *Western Representations*, p. 90.
[168] From the late thirteenth to the early fifteenth century, virtually all of the new legislation incorporated into the *Furs* of Valencia referred to the sexual relations between Christian men and Muslim slaves. See B. Catlos, "A Genealogy of Marginalization?"
[169] See p. 365. [170] See D. Nirenberg, "Love Between Muslim and Jew," p. 29.

the owner), and was considered a capital crime by both Christian and Muslim jurists. Cases of Jewish–Muslim miscegenation in which offspring resulted were conceived of along the same lines. Such cases, which were prosecuted in the royal courts with some frequency, provided an opportunity for royal authorities to confiscate judicially the property of wealthy Jews accused of these crimes, or obtain payments in exchange for absolution.[171] By the thirteenth century Jews in Iberia were major holders of Muslim slaves, bought to serve as domestics (driven in part, undoubtedly, by Sabbath work restrictions), laborers, or investments. In 1360, Samuel ha-Levi, Pedro the Cruel's treasurer, owned some eighty.[172] Cultural, linguistic, and culinary affinities led Jews to prefer Muslim women as domestic slaves, a state of affairs that would have caused considerable distress among free Muslim communities, not only because some surrender agreements had specifically established that Jews would not hold Muslim slaves, but – as royal inquests of the Crown of Aragon attest – Jewish men had sex with their Muslim slaves, and occasionally these were tempted or coerced to convert.

The sexual abuse of female slaves was institutionalized in the Crown of Aragon, where both captives and judicially enslaved Muslim women often suffered the fate of being consigned to royally operated brothels. This was normally a fate reserved for Muslim women who had been convicted of some sort of sexual crime either under Christian or Islamic law, whether it was infidelity, promiscuity, prostitution, apostasy (to Judaism), or ethno-religious miscegenation.[173] Such crimes were considered *ḥadd* (grave moral/religious breaches), and were often subject to the death penalty under Islamic law – a punishment *mudéjar* authorities were prohibited from applying, on the grounds that Muslim bodies were the special "property" of the kings. The fourteenth-century Valencian manual of Islamic law, the "Llibre de la çuna," specified enslavement as the punishment for female adultery.[174] Hence, the "social death" of enslavement served to satisfy both the Islamic sensibilities and the royal fisc in such situations.[175] Indeed, the profit motive was such that royal officials aggressively sought out and prosecuted female offenders. In fourteenth-century

171 In December 1321, two wealthy Jews of Girona obtained a pardon for having circumcised and converted to Judaism a boy that one of them had fathered with his Muslim slave. See ACA, C, Reg. 385, fol. 19r (Girona, December 7, 1321).

172 C. Verlinden, "Esclavage dans la péninsule," p. 580.

173 Men were also subject to judicial enslavement. A number of Muslims from the County of Denia died as slaves in Mallorca in the early fourteenth century, after which their landed properties (*casas*) were sold off to other *mudéjares*. See J. Argente Vidal, "Un libro de cuentas," pp. 299–301.

174 C. Barceló Torres, *Un tratado catalán*, p. 95 {335}.

175 M. Meyerson, "Slaves and Solidarity," p. 168.

Aragon, royal bailiffs sometimes met with the active resistance of local Christian communities, who did not want local Muslim prostitutes to be arrested. On the other hand, at times Muslim women went willingly into bondage, rather than face the opprobrium of their own community. Thus, in 1337 Fatima of Benisalim chose enslavement over the one hundred lashes she had been sentenced to for adultery; Alfons III of Aragon made a gift of her to his Jewish courtier, Jacob de Oblitas.[176] Outside of Iberia there were no such restraints, and slaves could be punished by death or dismemberment by their owners or judicial authorities.

### *Slaves in society*

In Iberia, Christian authorities were also prohibited from executing or dismembering *mudéjares* without royal authorization and, hence, Muslim men were also judicially enslaved when convicted of a capital crime. They could lose their freedom for a variety of offenses, but sometimes only temporarily, and with the specification that they serve the Christian party who had been injured by their comportment. In 1300, thirteen Muslims in Aragon were enslaved for ten years for illegally transferring their vassalage from the Abbot of Rueda to an unnamed nobleman. They were ordered to be kept in chains and to serve as laborers or in any other capacity the Abbot chose.[177] Sometimes, it was the children of convicted Muslims who were seized and sold into slavery – a form of collective punishment that protected the interests of the offenders' present lord by relieving him of a liability (an unproductive child) rather than a revenue-generating Muslim tenant or vassal.[178] At other times Muslims gave up their own children as slaves, as collateral, or in payment of debts.[179]

Men and boys served as apprentices and laborers for craftsmen, as general laborers and factotums, and could provide occasional muscle as proxies in feuds against rival households. In Valencia and Mallorca slave-owning was common even among the lower or middle classes; artisans and smallholders not only bought slaves, but actively moonlighted as corsairs themselves.[180] Not infrequently unscrupulous or

[176] C. Verlinden, *L'Esclavage*, vol. I, pp. 865–66 {XIV}.

[177] B. Catlos, *The Victors and the Vanquished*, p. 223.

[178] See M. T. Ferrer i Mallol, *La frontera amb l'Islam*, pp. 329–31 {104} for Muslim children being sold into slavery as a means of punishing their parents.

[179] M. Meyerson, "Slaves and Solidarity," p. 160. For an overview of slavery in the Crown of Aragon and the ambiguities of this status, see J. Torró i Abad, "De bona guerra."

[180] M. Meyerson, "Slaves and Solidarity," p. 291. Some of the slaves here were *mudéjares* enslaved judicially or voluntarily; see above, n. 73, and E. Lourie, "Free Moslems," pp. 634–35.

over-enthusiastic privateers captured shiploads of traveling or legally emigrating *mudéjares*, or foreign Muslims protected by truce, and a considerable amount of diplomatic effort was expended tracking down and liberating such illegal captives.

Muslim slaves who had special knowledge or skills were particularly prized and valuable, whether they came with those skills or their owners invested in their education. For, example, in 1296 Abdella, a "white" Muslim described as a physician, sold in Barcelona for 2,000 *solidi*, approximately five to fifteen times the going rate for a garden-variety slave.[181] When the Mallorcan Franciscan tertiary, theologian, and missionary Ramon Llull determined to learn Arabic, he obtained a slave for that purpose, retaining him even after the latter attempted to murder him.[182] Foreign Muslim captives were also apparently employed as copyists, if not translators, of Arabic manuscripts at Toledo and elsewhere.[183] In 1294 Jaume II of Aragon (1291–1327) sent out an order to look for chess masters among the captives that had been taken that year.[184] A Valencian silk merchant, Guillermus Straery, promised to manumit his slave, Mahomet Abendenu, after twelve years of service if the latter would teach him his secret techniques for silk dyeing and promise to refrain from practicing them once he was free. However, Alfons III (1327–36) ruled in 1335 that the then-free Mahomet, who had remained in Christian lands as a settler and sued Guillermus, remained free to practice the art himself.[185] Raymond Bertrandi, a merchant from Barcelona, gave his slave Julian, "a black of the Muslim race," absolute liberty to manage his affairs "on land and sea," with the promise that he would be freed in five years, and allowed to keep whatever he had earned, if in the interim he would pay Raymond twenty *solidi* per month.[186]

Both male and female slaves (Muslim or not) were used for manual labor, although – aside from cloth manufacture – men were preferred. Hence, in the fifteenth-century Crown of Aragon, male slaves far outnumbered women, in contrast to Genoa, where slave labor was less common and the female slaves predominated.[187] In the Crown of Aragon slaves became a

[181] "Sarracenus albus Abdella metge." See S. Bensch, "From Prizes of War," 93, cf. Table 2, pp. 92–93.
[182] Muslim slaves were often used as copyists and translators. See P. S. van Koningsveld, "Andalusian-Arabic Manuscripts," p. 91.
[183] *Ibid.* [184] B. Catlos, *The Victors and the Vanquished*, p. 236.
[185] C. Verlinden, *L'Esclavage*, vol. I, pp. 877–78 {XXIII}.
[186] *Ibid.*, vol. I, pp. 875–76 {XXI}.
[187] See R. Salicrú i Lluch, "Slaves in the Professional and Family Life," esp. pp. 326–39. In Genoa the proportion of female slaves varied from 62.9 percent in the thirteenth century to 85.5 percent in the fifteenth. See M. Balard, "La femme-esclave," as discussed in M. Green, "Conversing with the Minority," pp. 112–13.

leading commodity for investment and were so ubiquitous and were so widely employed as laborers that guilds were prompted to enact legislation to limit their use, both in craft and industry and in ancillary and service sectors. For example, in 1455 slave trumpet-players were prohibited from playing on the Feast of Corpus Christi and from accompanying heralds making royal and municipal public announcements. The ultimate reflection of the commoditization of slaves here came with the establishment of the *Guarda d'esclaus* – an insurance fund against loss of slaves through escape, which was paid for by subscription.[188]

Clearly, some Muslim "slaves" in Iberia were not slaves at all in the conventional sense. In Christian Iberia it was possible for free Muslim men and women willingly to formally endenture themselves to a Christian third party, a fact that tended to blur the line between slaves and free Muslims.[189] In effect, these slaves put themselves up as collateral or their labor as repayment against loans. A typical enslavement agreement would specify that the individual would be manumitted either after serving for a set number of years, or after a certain amount had been rendered to the "owner." During the interval these "fiscal slaves" did not lose their property, were generally not subject to sale, and often continued to practice the same economic activity they had done previously.[190] Nor did they necessarily lose their legal rights and royal protections. Slaves or not, Muslims in the Crown of Aragon, for example, had the right to appeal to the king – their direct sovereign – and many petitions survive in the royal chancery in which male and female slaves appeared before the king, contesting their status and demanding their manumission on the grounds that they had fulfilled their debt to their owner or had been enslaved illegally.[191]

However, the situation of foreign captives, prisoners-of-war, and judicial slaves, who were effectively non-persons, was much more grim; physical and sexual abuse and restraint, deprivation and isolation, humiliation and suffering marked the lives of many of these unfortunates.[192] In Mallorca, where the existence of a large population of unfree Muslim men had nearly led to an uprising in 1374, slaves were subject to increasingly harsh conditions, including a prohibition of carrying arms, a curfew, and the obligation to wear iron chains (later specified as weighing at least three kilograms) in public.[193] In most areas, however, risk of revolt was low; mitigated either by the presence of free Muslim communities who

[188] See R. Salicrú i Lluch, "L'esclau com a inversió?," "La implantació de la Guarda d'Esclaus," and *Esclaus i proprietaris d'esclaus.*
[189] See, generally, B. Catlos, "Esclavo o ciudadano."
[190] See, for example, E. Lourie, "Free Moslems," pp. 629–30 and 634–35.
[191] B. Catlos, *The Victors and the Vanquished*, p. 233.
[192] See, generally, C. Verlinden, "Esclaves fugitifs." [193] *Ibid.*, p. 309.

provided some sort of a socio-cultural network for slaves, or by the fact that slave populations were themselves diverse and therefore lacked the solidarity and cohesiveness required to plot and carry out an uprising.

### *Paths to freedom*

For most slaves, therefore, the three routes to freedom were ransom, escape, and conversion. Muslim complicity in the escape and liberation of their enslaved co-religionists was acknowledged in the earliest law codes of the Christian conquest, which – remarkably – set strict limits on the ability of Christian officials to search for escapees. Typically, these laws limited the number of free Muslims' homes that could be searched by local authorities, and specified that Muslim officials were to be present. By the thirteenth century, however, such rights had been lost.[194] Without the assistance of local Muslims, escape would have been extremely difficult, especially for those slaves of foreign origin. When slaves escaped, posses were set out to comb the countryside; some fugitives turned themselves in out of hunger and desperation, and those that were recaptured were subject to torture in order to locate their still-at-large companions.[195]

In the fifteenth century, as Muslim and Christian society in Iberia became progressively estranged and ordinary Muslims came to see religious solidarity as increasingly important, the ransoming of Muslim slaves became a favored act of communal almsgiving and piety, and an act of ethno-cultural solidarity and resistance. It has been suggested that *mudéjares* came to see such acts of manumission as a form of *jihād*, waged against an increasingly antagonistic and chauvinistic Christian society.[196] Many freed slaves who had converted to Christianity continued to maintain contacts with Muslims, and demonstrated a certain sense of solidarity and responsibility towards their former co-religionists, especially those who were unfree.[197] With permission from their owners, slaves could also obtain

[194] This can be seen clearly in the municipal *fueros* of the Kingdom of Aragon. The twelfth-century *fuero* of Jaca, for example, sets a limit of three Muslim homes that can be searched for fugitives. See M. Molho, *El Fuero de Jaca*, pp. 161–62 {A: 313}. Others specified that search parties had to be composed of members of both religions. The royal law code of 1247, however, mandated an absolute and unlimited right of search, including in the homes of noblemen. See G. Tilander, *Vidal Mayor*, vol. I, p. 476 {VIII: 8}; and *Fori Aragonum*, p. 104. That said, the privileges of the Muslims of the lower Ebro in Catalonia, granted in 1153–59 and renewed in 1276, stated that any fleeing Muslim slave who reached the area would be considered free (*solutus et libere*), and exempt from recapture. See J. M. Font i Rius, "La carta de seguridad," p. 283.

[195] See, for example, M. Gómez de Valenzuela, "Esclavos moros," pp. 125–27.

[196] See the discussion in Miller, *Guardians of Islam*, chapter 5, "Captive Redemption," pp. 151–76; also R. Guemara, "La liberation et le rachat."

[197] See, for example, F. Plazolles Guillén, "Trayectorias sociales," pp. 632–34.

permits to beg for alms for their own manumission; those who begged without royal licenses were liable to prosecution.[198] In Valencia, laws were eventually passed prohibiting such begging, and requiring that any capital used for redemption be raised in the *dār al-Islām*.[199] Foreign captives were also freed through the agency of diplomats, Christian religious orders such as the Mercedarians, private agents, or merchants, who facilitated exchanges for Latins held in the Islamic world, or conveyed ransoms raised by captives' families at home.[200] In Valencia, local Christians and Muslims formed a co-operative "brotherhood" (*hermandad*) to facilitate the liberation of co-religionists.[201] Indeed, the *Llibre de la çuna e la xara* placed a legal obligation on Muslims to redeem their enslaved family members.[202] Interestingly, fleeing Muslims did not always head for the coast and for the *dār al-Islām*; in Iberia, escapees sometimes settled down in neighboring kingdoms, or even went over the Pyrenees to the Midi.[203]

Conversion to Christianity was an option that tended to be exercised by the most isolated of slaves and those who had the slimmest hope of returning home. Although conscience may have suggested that Christians should not remain as slaves under any circumstances, the authorities of the Crown of Aragon established obstacles and conditions to deter would-be converts in the thirteenth century. This was partly in response to Jewish lobbying; the slave economy was undermined by the tendency for captives – particularly those held by Jews – to seek conversion to Christianity as a quick path to manumission. Measures included the obligation of converted slaves to pay a remission to their owners before they would be freed, and the institution of waiting periods of varying length, in order to ensure, in the words of the legists, that these neophytes were genuinely moved to conversion by religious conviction (i.e. whether they "walk in shadow or in light"), and the stipulation that even converted slaves of Jews would remain as such until they paid a redemption fee to their master.[204] However, Christian

198 M. Meyerson, "Slaves and Solidarity," pp. 315–26, and P. López Elum, "Apresamiento y venta."

199 G. Colón and A. Garcia, *Furs de València*, vol. I: pp. 219–21 {I:3:lxxxvii, I:3:lxxxviii, and I:3:lxxxxix}.

200 For the Mercedarians, see J. Brodman, *Ransoming Captives in Crusader Spain*.

201 M. Meyerson, "Slaves and Solidarity," p. 295; J. Torres Fontes, "La hermanidad."

202 C. Barceló Torres, *Un tratado catalán*, pp. 92–92 {326–27}.

203 See B. Catlos, *The Victors and the Vanquished*, pp. 230–31, and C. Verlinden, "Les esclaves musulmans," p. 226.

204 J. Pons i Marquès, *Cartulari de Poblet*, p. 63 {147}. Some converted slaves evidently did feel a calling. Bernat Sans, a converted slave who had been captured during a raid on Cherchell (Sharshāl, in Algeria) in 1412, not only converted, but was ordained as a priest. He eventually held three benefices. See M. N. Munsuri Rosado and F. J. Marzal Palacios, "Los esclavos sarracenos," for this case, and on the conversion of slaves in general.

authorities and slave-owners were no less eager to prevent such losses. In Crusader Palestine both the Church and Frankish law supported the principle of manumission for converted slaves, but this was opposed by noblemen, who conspired to keep their slaves clear of churches.[205] In the Crown of Aragon, lords placed disincentives on conversion for both free and bonded Muslims, by claiming – contrary to law – that they should lose the property they held as Muslims.[206] Similar obstacles to conversion were instituted in Cyprus, whereas in the south of France and Italy, it was never assumed conversion should entail manumission – a position confirmed by a succession of popes.[207] Echoing the early Church Fathers, the famous fifteenth-century missionary and mystic Vicent Ferrer held that baptism "frees the soul, not the body."[208] In 1310 when Fadrique (Frederick) III of Sicily (1295–1337) introduced reforms to curb the abuse and mistreatment of slaves, these were primarily aimed at unfree Christians (they did not, for example, prohibit the pimping out of non-Christian women as prostitutes), and in fact, served at bottom to reaffirm and reinforce owners' rights and prerogatives.[209]

In any case, conversion did not result in full membership in the Christian community; even before the mass conversions and the "Morisco problem" of the sixteenth century, former Muslims were referred to as *baptizati* ("the baptized," *batiés* in the East) – a socio-judicial category which set them apart from born Christians, and which typically endured for a generation or so.[210] Nor did manumission necessarily imply full acceptance in Christian society or the breaking of previous bonds of dependency and subordination.[211] In any case, indigenous Muslim slaves were less likely than foreign captives to choose conversion because of the opprobrium this provoked among both community and family. Apostasy was often seen as an act of betrayal and could sunder all family and social relations; hence, when Abduzalem Escausseri learned that his daughter, Fatima, who was owned by a Christian of Penyiscola, had abjured her faith, he not only refused

205 See B. Kedar, "Ecclesiastical Legislation," p. 226, and "Multidirectional Conversion," pp. 191–92.

206 M. T. Ferrer i Mallol, "Frontera, convivencia y proselitismo," p. 1594.

207 N. Coureas, "Christian and Muslim Captives," p. 530; C. Verlinden, *L'Esclavage*, vol. I, pp. 750ff; S. Epstein, *Speaking of Slavery*, p. 175; and also C. Verlinden, "Esclaves musulmans."

208 M. T. Ferrer i Mallol, "Frontera, convivencia y proselitismo," p. 1593.

209 S. Epstein, *Speaking of Slavery*, p. 95.

210 See B. Catlos, *The Victors and the Vanquished*, pp. 258–59. In the Crown of Aragon, *baptizati* were sometimes subject to the same restrictions on change of residence that had been instituted vis-à-vis *mudéjares*. See, for example, M. T. Ferrer i Mallol, *El sarraïns*, p. 133.

211 See, for example, F. Soyer, "Muslim Freedmen."

to ransom her, but sued to have the down payment he had paid for her redemption refunded.[212] Christians generally thought little better of converts; stiff fines were prescribed for calling them "turncoats" (*tornadizos*), or otherwise insulting them, and incidents of anti-convert violence are confirmed in court records.[213] Of course, not all converts from Islam became Catholics; in Sicily, in particular, many went over to the Greek Church.[214]

The presence of a substantial population of Muslim slaves impacted *mudéjar* society in different ways. The sight of the public sale and purchase of foreign and local Muslims must have constituted a serious humiliation to *mudéjares* on the communal level and an undeniable reminder of all Muslims' status as vulnerable, second-class subjects under the Christian regime. On the other hand, the support of slaves, whether through raising ransoms or abetting escape, reinforced religious and social solidarity in *mudéjar* communities.[215] Moreover, the continual in-flow of foreign Muslim captives, many of whom were educated practitioners of skilled crafts, or members of the religious or socio-economic elites, would have served continually to reinvigorate free Muslim society in Christian lands in terms of language, religious practice, and cultural development. Indeed, a *faqīh* from Fez, captured in the eastern Mediterranean in the early 1400s

[212] See B. Catlos, *The Victors and the Vanquished*, p. 253. In 1383 in the Crown of Aragon, a certain *mudéjar*, Maria Fernandez, had converted to Christianity, after which her father, Abrahim de la Puerta, seized her property and sold it to her husband's brother. In order to recover it, Maria returned to Islam, at least outwardly. When her seigneur, the *infant* Martí (later, King of Aragon) was made aware of this, he ordered the property returned and Maria reinstated as a Christian. [ACA, C., reg. 2063, f. 166r–v (December 14, 1383).] In the Middle Ages the four Sunnī schools of jurisprudence agreed that the unrepentant, deliberate male apostate (*murtadd*) of sound mind should be punished by death. This appears to have derived from Jewish law. See W. Heffening, "Murtadd," in *Encyclopaedia of Islam, Second Edition*. Nevertheless, in situations where large numbers of Muslims within a *mudéjar* community were led to convert through fear or pressure, this could be viewed with some sympathy (see p. 341, below). It was individual, uncoerced conversion that was regarded as beyond the pale.

[213] See, for example, J. Boswell, *The Royal Treasure*, p. 379. In 1281 Pere the Great warned Muslims who had been "presuming to disparage the Catholic faith" and insulting converts were to lose the protections of Islamic law and face Christian justice. See B. Catlos, *The Victors and the Vanquished*, p. 253.

[214] There has been a long history of acculturation, accommodation, and intermarriage among Muslims and Greek Christians in Sicily under Islamic rule, which made conversion to Orthodoxy an attractive and natural option. See J. Johns, "The Greek Church."

[215] See, for example, F.J. Marzal Palacios, "Solidaridad islàmica." See I. O'Connor, "Mudejars Helping," p. 104, for the case of Nuça, a slave who was rescued by *mudéjares* of Xàtiva, who helped her escape to Castile in 1315. Foreign Muslims were also involved. In 1424 two fugitives hid for seven months in the castle of Tortosa within the entourage of a prince from Tlemcen who was visiting the Crown; as the circle closed around them, they escaped by descending ropes they hung from the castle toilets (which overhung the walls). See R. Salicrú i Lluch, "Fugues, camuflatge i treball," pp. 440–42 {1}.

and sent to market in Mallorca, recalls in his memoir how he was eventually redeemed by *mudéjares (mudajjanīn)* of Lleida so that he could instruct them in the faith.[216] A century earlier, the captive *ᶜālim* Muḥammad al-Qaysī had been put to work to similar ends, but by Christians, who forced him, in the course of a trajectory of captivity that led him around the south of France and Aragon, to discuss theology and dispute the merits of Islam over Christianity.[217]

### *The impact of slavery*

In sum, the dynamic of redemption reinforced a whole range of connections with the free Islamic world beyond the frontier, both through the slaves themselves and networks of redemption. This impact would have been most dramatic in the cases of large influxes of captives produced by episodes of mass enslavement, such as occurred during the conquest of the Guadalquivir in the mid thirteenth century, Alfons II of Aragon's confiscation of the entire population of Islamic Menorca in 1287, or the punitive enslavement of Granadans after the Second Revolt of the Alpujarras in 1499.[218] In late fourteenth-century Portugal *mouros* petitioned for the right to purchase and redeem foreign slaves not so that the latter could return home, but in order to integrate them and replenish their own communities.[219] In the kingdom of Valencia, slaves redeemed by *mudéjares* sometimes stayed on as free Muslims themselves and married local Muslim women, so that ransoming became a means by which *mudéjares* could establish or extend their own networks of patronage and dependence.[220]

Slavery was also an important feature of Islamic societies, and Muslims in Latin lands also purchased or were granted slaves, sometimes to manumit them and sometimes to keep them.[221] Although prior to the fifteenth century, for the most part it is visiting foreign Muslims who crop up as slave-owners in the documentation, there are clear indications that *mudéjares* both in Iberia and Sicily kept their co-religionists in bondage.[222]

216 M. de Epalza Ferre, "Dos textos," 103 (Arabic: p. 62).
217 See P. S. van Koningsveld, "The Polemical Works."
218 See p. 77 and p. 217, above.
219 F. Soyer, *The Persecution*, p. 44, and F. Lopes de Barros, *Tempo e espaços*, p. 570.
220 M. Meyerson, "Slaves and Solidarity," pp. 317 and 322ff; M. T. Ferrer i Mallol, "L'emigració dels Sarraïns," p. 25.
221 In 1364, for example, the Aragonese *mudéjar* magnate Faraig de Bellvís was granted a female Muslim slave worth 300 *solidi*. See J. Boswell, *The Royal Treasure*, p. 493.
222 See, for example, B. Catlos, *The Victors and the Vanquished*, pp. 231–32; A. Echevarría Arsuaga, "Esclavos musulmanes," pp. 465–66. In 1355 Faraig de Bellvís filed suit to reclaim a Muslim slave belonging to his brother Jahia, who had been stolen and resold in Valencia. See J. Boswell, *The Royal Treasure*, p. 415.

How they approached this situation is impossible to say; perhaps they rationalized it as an act of protection and patronage for fellow Muslims who would otherwise be owned by Christians or Jews, or perhaps, in some instances, they simply perceived of slave-owning as a sign of economic status and social station which they should aspire to in spite of being Muslims themselves. Like their Christian and Jewish counterparts, high-status *mudéjares* received female Muslim slaves as boons from indulgent monarchs, and pursued their escaped servants with all of the resources the law afforded.[223] Hence, we should not be too ready to assume that Muslim slaves owned by *mudéjares* or foreign Muslims were necessarily better treated as a consequence of religious solidarity – after all, according to Islamic law, Muslims should not acquire other Muslims as slaves, and the inherent power imbalance in the slave–master relationship would have made coercion and abuse all but inevitable. In the fifteenth century, *mudéjares* – including *fuqahā'* and officials who might be expected to exercise a higher moral standard – were holding significant numbers of sub-Saharan Muslim Africans as slaves, and it was widely recognized that they treated their black slaves more poorly than non-blacks.[224]

As Meyerson provocatively and convincingly suggests, enslavement became a potent tool for *mudéjar* religious and administrative authorities, both to the extent that the threat of enslavement could be used to enforce communal discipline, and that the act of enslavement of free Muslims was coercive strategy they could employ with the ready consent of royal authorities. Christian and *mudéjar* elites, agendas coincided in their aim to manage and control the Crown of Aragon's free Muslim population, leading them collaborate in the use of enslavement as a domestic political tool.[225] The situation of Morisco slave-owners was rather more complex. At times Moriscos and their Muslim slaves secretly worshiped together, at other times slaves betrayed their crypto-Muslim owners; in recognition of the potential danger to the faith, Morisco ownership of Muslim slaves was forbidden in the omnibus act (the *Congregación*) of 1526.[226]

The ownership and circulation of Muslim slaves also had an impact on Latin Christendom. First and foremost, this was economic. The sale, resale and ransoming of slaves, together with the taxes and duties charged on their importation (in the Crown of Aragon, the *quinta*: 20 percent of their value), represented an important source of income for warriors,

223 See J. Boswell, *The Royal Treasure*, pp. 415–416, and 493.
224 M. Meyerson, "Slaves and Solidarity," pp. 330–32.
225 M. Meyerson, "Slavery and the Social Order," p. 173.
226 J. L. Cortés López, *Los moriscos*, pp. 13–15 and 20. For the *Congregación*, see below, p. 289. This law was not put in effect, however, until 1566.

merchants, speculators, and officials, as well as royal and municipal regimes. In the Crown of Aragon, slave-owners were expected to keep *alabarana* (singular: *albaranum*), or duty-receipts, both to ensure that slaves were indeed slaves and not free Muslims, and that the *quinta* had been paid. Periodically, kingdom-wide inspections were ordered, and undocumented slaves confiscated or freed. A vigorous resale market fed a trade in undocumented or illegal slaves; criminal bands and opportunists, including Christians and Muslims working in collaboration, sometimes kidnapped *mudéjares* or free Christian children, and sold them on as slaves.[227]

The port cities of Iberia and northern Italy, where much of the slave trade was centered, had substantial populations of slaves, but captive Muslims were also distributed throughout Latin Christendom. Crusaders and *condottieri* had been taking home slaves since the mid tenth century. Many of the Muslims of Barbastro, conquered in 1064, ended up in Latin Europe, even if the "thousand slave girls" Guillaume de Montreuil was said to have taken back to Provence on that occasion was an exaggeration.[228] Often these came in the form of gifts between monarchs or high clergy. Abū Ḥāmid, for example, remarks that the Byzantine Emperor Manouēl I Komnēnos sent Muslim slaves as gifts to the King of Hungary, and after the conquest of Granada the victorious Ferran and Isabel dispatched scores of Muslim men and women as gifts to other Christian rulers and to the papal court. In smaller numbers, individual Muslim slaves were sold on northwards, or taken home by returning Crusaders, clergy, pilgrims, and functionaries who had spent time in the Latin Mediterranean. But records of such individuals are almost non-existent; they appear only by chance, as when an "Ethiopian" named Bartholomew, "formerly a Saracen," went on the lam from his master in 1259, or a "Mahumet" was found to be living in late thirteenth-century Wiltshire.[229] Indeed, those few slaves and captives who found themselves in northern Europe would have either come as converts, having been baptized as a formality by traffickers, or succumbed to apostasy as a consequence of their isolation.

Through the Christian Mediterranean, but particularly in regions like Iberia, where slave-owning was widespread, trade and ownership of Muslims would have served to objectify them and helped to sustain a perception that they were generically inferior. This can be observed both in areas where there was no *mudéjar* community to provide a model for the legitimate Muslim subject, as in the south of France, or in areas where a

227 See, for example, Lourie, "Anatomy of Ambivalence," pp. 69–72, and B. Catlos, "Four Kidnappings."
228 M. R. Menocal, *The Arabic role*, p. 27.
229 M. Lower, "A Black Slave on the Run," and Ricard Cassidy, personal communication.

superabundance of slaves engendered anxieties among the free Christian population and provoked the development of an aggressively anti-Muslim sentiment in compensation, as in Mallorca.[230] As for the slaves themselves, their testimony survives in a variety of forms, including memoirs, poetry, and their depositions as witnesses (and objects) in Christian inquisitions and trials. Each of these genres is biased and distorting, but it is clear that slaves' reactions to their predicament were as varied as their circumstances, ranging from the defiant confidence of the domestic slaves of Valencia, to the numb resignation of the three prisoners interrogated at Daroca, and to the indignant defiance of the *faqīh* of Fez and the other members of the *ᶜulamāʿ* who left records of their captivity in Christian lands.[231]

Those slaves who lived in areas that did not have free Muslim populations can hardly be said to have constituted communities, even in those port cities where they could be found in considerable numbers. Isolated and disempowered, unable to marry or to reproduce, they were in no position to sustain what might be described as an Islamic society. This is not to say that they were historically insignificant. Difficult as it may be to quantify, it cannot be doubted that Muslims who served Christian masters and households as cooks, musicians, dancers, tailors, craftsmen, nursemaids, physicians, and tutors, and those who converted and married into Christian families, together constituted a potent vector of cultural transmission and contributed to the transformation and enrichment of Latin culture in medieval and early modern eras.

One of the few of these individuals to rise out of historical anonymity was "Leo Africanus." Born in Granada in 1492, al-Ḥasan b. Muḥammad arrived in Fez an infant refugee, and went on to become a diplomat, functionary, and envoy in the service of a series of North African princes.[232] This career came to sudden end when he was captured by Spanish corsairs – likely in June 1518. Sensing his abilities and value, his captor, Pedro de Bobadilla, gifted him to the Pope. After a brief confinement, al-Ḥasan consented to convert to Christianity, and on January 6, 1520 took the birth and regnal names of his patron Giovanni de Medici, Pope Leo X (1513–21), becoming "Giovanni Leo, the African." Over the course of the following decade he lived in Rome and Bologna, where he worked as an Arabic teacher and produced or undertook a number of literary projects, including a comprehensive "Description of Africa" based on his

230 C. Verlinden, "Esclavage dans la péninsule," p. 582.
231 See, for example, above, p. 262; M. de Epalza Ferre, "Dos textos"; and P. S. van Koningsveld, "The Polemical Works."
232 See N. Zemon Davis, *Trickster Travels*, and P. Masonen, "Leo Africanus."

own travels, an Arabic–Hebrew–Latin medical dictionary, an Arabic grammar, a book of exemplary lives of Muslim and Jewish sages, and a history of North Africa.

Nothing is known of his fate after the late 1520s, and competing traditions describe him as either dying in Rome or abjuring Christianity and returning to his native North Africa. The significance of "Leo Africanus" – beyond the fame of his exceptional *Descrittione* – is that he was neither singular nor unique. The life of the Tunisian prisoner Ḥajjī Aḥmad presents an analogous case. Captured in 1559, he too passed on geographic knowledge to his captors.[233] Joannes Latinus/Juan Latino is a similar figure. In the 1570s this freed sub-Saharan slave composed the *Austrias carmen*, a poem which is ostensibly a panegyric on the occasion of the victory of Juan of Austria and the Holy League over the Ottomans at Lepanto, but it is, in fact, rather ambiguous.[234] In sum, the enigmatic al-Ḥasan/Leo represents only the best known of the multitudes of captured Muslims who lived out their lives in the obscurity of foreign bondage – "tricksters" and survivors who anonymously but relentlessly, if subtly, reoriented European culture over the course of six centuries.

233 See P. Masonen, "Leo Africanus," p. 126.
234 See E. Wright, "Narrating the Ineffable Lepanto."

# 7 Christians in name

## The *Morisco* problem (1499–1614)

A scholar of this kingdom [Aragon] when speaking of the sufferings we are undergoing said: "I know very well that we are going through a period of terror, but God will still not fail to punish us if we neglect the service of his kingdom insofar as our legal obligations are concerned. As for hiding our true intentions, we can still make use of this as is our privilege. [We can worship through] the singing of the foreigners whereby the Christians seek salvation, for it all may be classed as allowable dissimulation . . ." ("El Mancebo de Arévalo", *Breve compendio de nuestra santa ley y sunna* (*c.* 1533 C.E.)[1])

Between 1499 and 1526, one by one the various principalities of the Iberian Peninsula – the last refuge of indigenous Muslim communities in Catholic Europe – ordered the conversion or expulsion of their Muslim subjects. The overwhelming majority stayed in the peninsula, whether remaining in their ancestral lands, or fleeing ahead of persecution for what they hoped would be safe haven in other Christian kingdoms. Thus, within a generation, hundreds of thousands of Muslims converted to Christianity by *fiat* and under duress, becoming "New Christians," or "Moriscos" ("Moorish").[2] Although some may have converted in good faith or with good intention, and some of the subsequent-generation Moriscos must have been genuine Christians, it is clear that many, if not most, were merely driven underground religiously, becoming crypto-Muslims. Indeed, as van Koningsveld points out, "Morisco" is a Christian term – Spanish Muslims did not recognize the edicts of conversion as

[1] "Short Digest of the Holy Law and Custom"; this excerpt adapted from L. P. Harvey, *Muslims in Spain*, p. 184. The "Young man of Arévalo" was a crypto-Muslim (possibly a former Jew) from Castile, who became an important religious authority among Moriscos in Castile and Aragon, and authored several works, including the "Short Digest," the *Tafsira* ("Commentary"), and the *Sumario de la relación y ejercicio espirtual* ("Summary of the Account, and Spiritual Exercise"). See L. P. Harvey, "El Mancebo de Arévalo and his Treatises."

[2] The term "New Christians" (*Cristianos nuevos*) included converts from both Islam and Judaism and their descendants. Jews were also known as *conversos* and *Marranos* (a pejorative term, from the Arabic *muḥarram*). "Old Christian" referred to those without Jewish or Muslim ancestry.

having changed their religious identity.[3] Indeed, García-Arenal suggests that by the sixteenth century, the syncretic influence of Christianity on Morisco belief was so pervasive that the very categories of "Christian" and "Muslim" may no longer be appropriate for understanding Morisco religiosity.[4] As it was, Islam had developed a doctrine for the survival of communities facing such mortal oppression. *Taqiyya*, or "prudence" – the outward denial of the faith and dissimulation of unbelief – originates in the Qur'ān.[5] Persecuted Muslims could be excused from all sorts of violations of Islamic law and tradition in the name of preserving their community and their faith – even drinking wine and eating pork. And from across the Straits, this is precisely what some local and Maghribi *muftūn* recommended to the former *mudéjares*.[6] A third possibility is that for many Moriscos, the oppositional binary of Christianity and Islam simply did not define their religious experience, and they had moved into a vaguely defined hybrid position, perhaps anchored in Marian-centered mysticism.[7]

The success of the conversion policy was further undermined by the fact that, for a number of reasons, Moriscos continued to live as a distinct people, and were regarded with suspicion by "Old Christians" – circumstances that undermined any process of assimilation that may have taken place in subsequent generations. Moreover, ordinary folk are not necessarily systematic in their approach to religion, and some Moriscos undoubtedly shifted back

[3] P.S. van Koningsveld, "Andalusian-Arabic Manuscripts," p. 88. Indeed, New Christians themselves considered the term "Morisco" to be an insult. See A. García López, "Moriscos andalusíes," p. 164. When faced with expulsion, some Moriscos went to great lengths to establish their credential as good Catholics; such protestations, however, fell on deaf ears. See, for example, the case of the Gausqui family of Benissanet (Tortosa) in J.-H. Muñoz Sebastià, "Actitud dels Moriscs."

[4] See the intriguing case study in M. García-Arenal, "A Catholic Muslim Prophet." In the 1530s the Morisco boy Agustín de Ribera from Aljofrín (near Toledo) began to experience visions of the type common among Old and New Christian mystics and clairvoyants (*illuminados* and *alumbrados*) of the time, and which combined elements of Christian and Muslim imagery. He was charged by the Inquisition with being a "Prophet of Islam" and a "dogmatizer." For Moriscos' combination of baptism with Islamic prayer rituals see S. Abboud-Haggar, "Ibn al-Ǧazarī," pp. 21–23.

[5] *Taqiyya*, the dissimulation or occultation of Islamic religious identity in the name of the preservation of self and community, included the adoption of non-Muslim religious, dietary, and social practices. Together with *kitmān* ("the action of covering, dissimulation"), it is sanctioned in the Qur'ān itself. Even more latitude – *muwāfaqa* ("connivance") – is permitted to women, children, the infirm, and those who have responsibility for their care. See *Encyclopedia of Islam*, s.v. "*Taḳiyya*."

[6] See the *fatwa* promulgated by the *muftī* of Oran (May 3, 1563) in M. García-Arenal, *Los Moriscos*, pp. 43–45; and, below, p. 319. See also, L. P. Harvey, "Una referència explícita." Through the sixteenth century many clerical writers were adamant that Moriscos were merely hiding their faith; and, indeed, many revealed their true beliefs once the edicts of expulsion had been publicized. See L. Cardaillac, "Un aspecto de las relaciones."

[7] See M. García-Arenal's reflections in "Religious Dissent." See, for example, pp. 307 and 322, below.

and forth between the two religions, or inhabited some sort of ambiguous middle ground. This was not lost on the Church and royal authorities, who continued to see the "Muslim problem" as unresolved, while Moriscos' dissatisfaction with their own ongoing status as second-class subjects bred dissention and revolt. Finally, in 1609 Felipe III of Spain (1598–1621) ordered all of the descendants of the peninsula's *mudéjares* to leave the kingdom. Hence, the story of Islam in Latin Christendom would not be complete without the present brief chapter, for it cannot be said to have concluded until at least 1614, when the last of these communities – neither fully Christian, nor fully Muslim – departed their ancestral lands for foreign exile.[8]

Modern institutions that practice systematic oppression tend to have remarkably well-developed bureaucracies, and the Iberian Catholic Church and royal administrations of the sixteenth and seventeenth centuries were no exceptions. As a consequence, historians have abundant and rich sources for the study of the Moriscos, including archival records, official correspondence, policy papers, baptismal records, and inquisition trial transcripts, many of the latter containing first-person testimony from the converts and the descendants of converts who were investigated for heresy or apostasy. Aside from this, a substantial body of Morisco literature survives, including works in *aljamiado*, Latin, Castilian Spanish, Aragonese, Catalan, and even Arabic. Ironically, it is precisely when this community was no longer formally Islamic that we can hear its members speaking most eloquently in their own voices. Nevertheless, the historiography of the Moriscos remains highly charged; issues relating to the interpretation of these various sources have divided historians among those who see the Moriscos as committed crypto-Muslims, as genuine Christians, as both, or as something in between.[9]

[8] Thanks in part to the abundance of source material, there is an immense body of scholarly literature focusing on the Moriscos. Works consulted for this chapter include, for example, V. Barletta, *Covert Gestures*; M. Barrios Aguilera, *Granada morisca*; L. F. Bernabé Pons, *Los moriscos*; A. Bū Sharab, *Os pseudo-mouriscos*; L. Cardaillac, *Moriscos y cristianos*; M. S. Carrasco Urgioti, *El problema morisco en Aragón*; D. Coleman, *Creating Christian Granada*; A. Domínguez Ortíz and B. Vincent, *Historia de los Moriscos*; M. F. Fernández and Rafael M. García Pérez, *En los márgenes de la ciudad de Dios*; M. García-Arenal, *Los Moriscos*, and "Religious Dissent"; M. H. Halavais, *Like Wheat to the Miller*; A. K. Harris, *From Muslim to Christian Granada*; L. P. Harvey, *Muslims in Spain*; F. Janer, *Condición social*; H. C. Lea, *The Moriscos of Spain*; M. Lomas Cortes, *La expulsión de los Moriscos*; L. López-Baralt, *La literatura secreta*; F. Márquez Villanueva, *El problema morisco*; I. M. Mendes Drumond Braga, *Mouriscos e Cristãos no Portugal*; J. del Olivo, *Los moriscos de Calatayud*; J.-M. Perceval, *Todos son uno*; M. E. Perry, *The Handless Maiden*; S. de Tapia Sánchez, *La comunidad morisca*; J. M. Usunáriz, "Entre dos expulsions"; and B. Vincent and A. L. Cortés Peña, *El río morisco*. For general context, see H. Kamen, *Spain, 1469–1714*, or J. Elliot, *Imperial Spain 1469–1716*.

[9] Inquisition trial records lend tremendous insight into Morisco religiosity, but these must be used critically and with caution. See, for example, M. de Epalza Ferre, "Los Moriscos frente a la Inquisición"; K. Garrad, "La Inquisición," and M. García-Arenal, *Inquisición y*

## Morisco nations

It has been explained to me on the part of the New Christians of the Kingdom of Granada that recently they were ordered by Us not to gather to play their instruments and sing and dance, nor to hold any gathering where they do this, not even at their weddings, because they sing some songs that call to Muḥammad, and likewise because the *gazís* and *harbis*, who are slaves and captives, put on spectacles in which there is much vice and evil acts, and that if good and honest people are exposed to this it will cause them great harm … (Empress Isabella of Portugal, Letter to the Royal Administration and Chancery of the City of Granada (March 10, 1532)[10])

With historical hindsight, it may seem obvious that the forced conversion of the Muslims of Spain would create more problems than it would resolve. Such problems would result not only from the coercive nature of that policy, or the capacity of clandestine Islam to persevere in a hostile environment, but because theological affiliation was only one aspect of *mudéjar* religious and social identity, and – as is the case in virtually any religious culture – it is not necessarily foremost in the minds and lives of common believers. Social customs, informal economic networks, charitable mechanisms, and relationships of clientage and patronage were all aspects of religious identity that had a very real, quotidian impact. Thus, the success of a policy of conversion would necessarily depend not only on effective and consistent religious instruction, but on a program of social, cultural, and economic integration. None of these, however, was pursued with any consistency, and there was little will to do so, among either Old or New Christians. As a result, Moriscos continued to exist as a nation apart in Christian Spain – or, rather, as nations, given that there were significant differences between the Morisco experience in Granada and the rest of the kingdom, and among Moriscos of different social classes and ethnic origins.

In Granada, the determination of the Catholic Kings to preserve the Naṣrid economy and fiscal system had provided a means for higher-status Muslims to maintain (and expand) their power, wealth, and prestige after their conversion to Christianity, and discouraged intervention in Morisco religious, cultural, and social affairs. In the first decades of the sixteenth century the kingdom generated one-fifth of the total tax income of the Crown of Castile, and members of the formerly Islamic elite were instrumental in maintaining the flow of revenue. As a reward for their collaboration, Naṣrid nobles went on to become *alguaciles* and *hidalgos*, and members of the *fuqahāʾ* became influential courtiers and advisors in

*Moriscos*. In her seminal article "Religious Dissent," M. García-Arenal reviews recent works on Morisco and Converso religiosity, outlines the various "schools" of Morisco historiography, and discusses problems relating to the interpretation of sources.

10 A. Gallego y Burín, *Los Moriscos del Reino de Granada*, p. 234 {44}.

royal circles, particularly as translators of Arabic.[11] Having converted to Christianity, at least outwardly, the members of this elite became the regime's greatest defenders; optimistically confident that integration was a real possibility, they sought actively and innocently to claim a place for Moriscos as full and legitimate subjects in the new Spain. While some of these courtiers and officials actively embraced their new faith, others determined to carry on as secret Muslims, and refused to relinquish their culture. Regardless of their true convictions, these high-status *cristianos arábigos* ("Arabic Christians") served as advocates and protectors of the Morisco population as a whole.[12] In the meanwhile, royal and Church authorities would turn a blind eye to the crypto-Islam of the population. Among the lower classes, both Islam and Arabo-Islamic folk traditions were more persistent, not only among the farmers and herders of the countryside, but – as reflected by the Empress Isabella's dismay – even in the capital itself.

Here, where colonists and Moriscos cohabited in the compartmentalized city, the persistence of Arabo-Islamic custom was all the more obvious and grating, just as was Old Christians' determination to maintain the converts as a people apart and of lower status. As New and Old Christians came to find themselves competing in commercial and artisanal sectors, the ethno-religious divide provided a framework for articulating and channeling economic competition.[13] Ironically, as Moriscos were brought into the Church through the formation of parishes and the foundation of confraternities and the ordination of clergy, the reaction of Old Christians intensified – a consequence not of their suspicions regarding Morisco religiosity, but rather of alarm at the growing influence of New Christians in ecclesiastical circles. The rest of the kingdom was balkanized, alternating between zones that were homogenously Morisco and others that were homogenously Christian – the colonists often preferring to found new towns rather than move into existing settlements. In mixed areas, Moriscos were more likely to find themselves the vassals or tenants of predatory and chauvinistic Old Christian officials and lords. The additional tax burden that second- and third-generation New Christians continued to bear both reminded them of and reinforced their distinct identity.[14] It also had a dampening effect on integration through

[11] See E. Soria Mesa, "De la conquista a la asimilación." For a typical case, see M. Espinar Moreno, "Abulcaçen aben Cohbe"; also M. García-Arenal, "*Shurafā* in the Last Years of al-Andalus," p. 176.

[12] Contrast the equally impassioned declarations of Francisco Núñez Muley (below, p. 291) with those of Yūse Banegas (see p. 212).

[13] See, for example, L. García Ballester, "The Minority of Morisco Physicians," pp. 214ff.

[14] See J. Torró i Abad, "Vivir como cristianos."

marriage, which was exceptional, despite the express efforts of Charles V to promote such unions as a motor of religio-cultural integration.[15] Old and New Christians tended overwhelmingly to marry within their own communities, and in the post-conversion period endogamous marriage practices, which seem to have declined across the peninsula in the *mudéjar* era, apparently intensified, despite the efforts of the Church to suppress them.[16] Over the course of the sixteenth century tensions between the two communities would build, fueled by Old Christian suspicions and New Christian frustrations, until they exploded in 1568's Revolt of the Alpujarras.

### *Beyond Granada*

In the rest of Spain continuity between *mudéjar* and Morisco communities was also clear, at least until 1570. Populations remained concentrated in certain areas of Castile, along the Ebro and Jalón in Aragon and Catalonia, around Tudela in Navarre, and were spread throughout the Kingdom of Valencia. Here, Moriscos continued to be important both in craft and agricultural sectors. The descendants of these old *mudéjar* communities were thoroughly acculturated to Christian society, although not at the cost of their own cultural or religious identity. Most crucially, they were integrated in the larger economy and Christian networks of patronage, which provided them with advocates and protectors. Such was the determination of Christian lords to defend their crypto-Muslim vassals that some Old Christian nobles were targeted by the Inquisition. In 1570, no less a figure than Sancho de Cardona, Admiral of Aragon, was brought up by the Holy Office on charges of having allowed his Morisco vassals to openly practice their old faith.[17] Whether or not the accusations made against the Admiral can be taken to the letter, it is clear that many seigniors were willing to protect their crypto-Muslim tenants and allow

[15] For Charles's decree to this effect, see F. Á. Pareja Pareja, "Los matrimonios mixtos," pp. 171–73. The pro-miscegenation policy would meet with resistance in reactionary Christian quarters (see, below, p. 290, n. 29).

[16] G. López de la Plaza, "Las mujeres moriscas," p. 316. These customs had evidently persevered in Granada. See B. Vincent, "La famille morisque." The expulsion of the Granadan Moriscos may have served to bolster or revive these practices in other parts of the peninsula (cf. below, p. 297).

[17] M. García-Arenal, *Los Moriscos*, pp. 135–56. The accusations are stunning. Cardona was accused by the witnesses for the prosecution (themselves, Moriscos) of having allowed his Morisco vassals not only to continue the pilgrimage to Atzeneta but to build a new mosque there. They allegedly worshiped openly and chanted the call to prayer. The Admiral, who was sentenced to life imprisonment and the *sanbenito*, or robe of the penitent, was even said to have counseled them to pretend to be Christians on those occasions when they were required to attend church.

them to practice their faith in order to maintain a stable and productive peasantry. Indeed, even local clergy were apparently complicit in such acts on occasion.[18]

In these lands there was no equivalent of the converted Naṣrid elite of Granada, who could act as a hinge group between the Christian administration and the Morisco masses. Previously, the *mudéjar* elite had consisted primarily of middling to wealthy local families of craftsmen who served as royally appointed functionaries. Although often their Islamic credentials and piety seem to have been dubious, and they tended to serve themselves as much as their constituents, they helped to preserve and protect their communities. With the edicts of conversion, however, this class lost its usefulness to the Christian rulers, and disappeared. This had two effects. First, it robbed this elite of their protection from the chauvinistic Christian parties; in Aragon and Navarre, the Inquisition became a means to eliminate the former-Muslim economic elite – whose continuing prosperity rankled anti-Morisco pietists and those Christians who were in economic competition with them.[19] Second, it allowed the informal but popular pious elite that they themselves had endeavored to suppress – the ilk of Mancebo de Arévalo, and the Aragonese "alfakís"whom he observed – to become the new, clandestine leaders of crypto-Islamic society.[20] The continuing production and circulation of *aljamiado* and Arabic religious texts, evidence of underground madrasas (*madāris*) in rural Castile, Aragon, and Valencia, the circulation of popular *muftūn*, mystics, and *curanderos*, and the active involvement of women in these activities, is proof of the authority, appeal, breadth, and vigor of this cryto-*ʿulamāʾ*. The formidable Cuencan *shaykha* and midwife, Nuzaya

[18] In 1587 Llorenç Casals, the local vicar of Benissanet (Tarragona) was accused of failing to force local Moriscos to attend mass on the accusation of Antoni Domenech, the official entrusted with ensuring their attendance. See J.-H. Muñoz Sebastià, "Actitud dels Moriscos."

[19] This can be seen in post-conversion Huesca, where prosperous Morisco families were systematically eliminated. See Á. Conte Cazcarro, "La inquisición y los moros," and "La decadència." In the 1580s the prosperous Morisco master builders of Zaragoza, including members of the Gali and Compañero families, were brought before the Inquisition; many were burned as *relapsos*. See C. Gómez Urdáñez, "El Morisco, la doncella y el fraile," esp. pp. 324–28. For the Compañeros, see J. Fournel-Guérin, "Un famille morisque." In Navarre, even before the edict of conversion, the heavy-handed action of the Inquisition had driven *mudéjares* to rebellion, and discouraged conversion. As early as the thirteenth century charges of apostasy were frequently leveled against former-Muslim converts, who were subject to torture and confiscation as a matter of procedure. See F. Segura Urra, *Fazer justícia*, p. 380.

[20] See L. Bernabé Pons, "Una fama sin biografía," and L. P. Harvey, "El Mancebo de Arévalo." El Mancebo's *tafsīr* (exegesis) is edited as M. T. Narváez Córdova, *Tratado*.

Calderán, was only the most famous of the female religious authorities in Morisco Spain.[21]

In sum, the conversion, it seems, did little to dampen popular piety – quite the contrary, it may have fed it, particularly in the context of the millenarian fever that swept through the Mediterranean world in the late sixteenth century. Andalusī religiosity had exhibited a strong mystical streak since the 1100s, one that was resisted by the more legalistically minded Muslims who tended to dominate official positions through the *mudéjar* period. Seen in this light, the Morisco period may be seen as the final victory of indigenous Sufism and mystical Islam over *fiqh*-oriented Mālikī orthodoxy.[22] Those *aljamiado* texts that have survived – many of them anthologies which constitute, as it were, comprehensive cultural primers – present, through their reworking of Qur'ānic texts, *ḥadīth*, and tales drawn from Arabic, Jewish, and Christian traditions, an active response to the Moriscos' situation, with their apocalyptic themes providing a solution to the predicament of New Christian suffering.[23] Coming and going under the flimsy cover of their new faith, Moriscos continued to travel and do business in the Islamic world, to study religion, and even to participate in the *ḥajj*, thereafter returning to Spain and to their concealment as Muslims with the blessing of North African *muftūn*.[24] Although here it was tensions between seigniors and townsmen that had been at the root of anti-Muslim violence, as in Granada, the social and economic friction that had prompted the edicts of conversion remained unaddressed. Thus, both religious authorities and the Old Christian populace as a whole came to see Morisco social customs as an offensive and dangerous mark of apostasy and disloyalty. Then, as in the Europe of today, Morisco women's custom of covering their faces was regarded as particularly subversive and offensive, and was repeatedly legislated against.[25]

[21] See L. P. Harvey, "El Mancebo de Arévalo," pp. 270–73.

[22] For the anti-Sufi prejudices of the *fuqahā'*, see R. El Hour, "The Andalusian Qāḍī," pp. 73–74, and M. García-Arenal, "*Shurafā* in the Last Years of al-Andalus," pp. 162–64. The robust Sufi tradition of al-Andalus produced figures such as Ibn al-ʿArabī (d. 1240) and Ibn Sabʿīn (1269–71).

[23] The corpus of literature in *aljamiado* is quite broad, including, among other things, a treatise on sex; see L. López Baralt, *Un káma sútra espanyol.*

[24] See L. P. Harvey, "The Moriscos and the Hajj," and P. S. van Koningsveld and G. Wiegers, "The Islamic Statute," p. 39. In the late sixteenth/early seventeenth century the Aragonese poet Muhammad Rabadán not only made a secret pilgrimage to Mecca, but recorded his experiences in a poem composed in *aljamiado*. See R. Zuñiga López, "Un morisco."

[25] In the face of this prohibition Morisco women in Granada took to wearing a broad mantle which extended past the shoulders and at times almost to the ground, and which could be easily held over the face. See K. Mills, *et al.*, *Colonial Latin America*, pp. 88–89; C. Weiditz, *Authentic Everyday Dress of the Renaissance*, plates LXXIX–LXXXVIII.

From the 1520s onward, the question of socio-cultural integration and Morisco piety would become ever more important.

## Integration and exclusion

Can we say there is a lower race than the black slaves of Guinea? Why are they allowed to sing and dance to their instruments and songs, and in the languages in which they normally sing them? . . . So why must one defend all of the aforesaid with respect to the natives of this kingdom? As I have said, they commit no offense against the Holy Catholic faith; rather, through playing the *zambra* and its instruments they merely practice the usages of the kingdom and the customs of the province with respect to merrymaking at weddings . . . (Francisco Núñez Muley, New Christian and royal courtier, "Memorandum" presented to the Royal Audience (1567)[26])

In June 1526 the churchmen assembled in a conclave (*congregación*) of the royal chapel of Carlos I proposed measures that would effectively outlaw Morisco culture – mandating, *inter alia*, the suppression of folk customs, the interdiction of "Moorish" costume (notably the veil, for women), the prohibition of the use of Arabic, restrictions on the practice of medicine and midwifery, and the requirement of Moriscos to take "Christian" (i.e. Spanish) names. This was passed into law on December 7, but in the event, the Morisco communities convinced the Emperor (by way of a bribe of 8,000 *ducats*) to suspend enforcement for forty years. Nevertheless, by November 1526 the Inquisition had been dispatched to Granada. As it was, Inquisitors had been targeting converted Muslims and proselytizers in Aragon since the late 1400s, and since 1523 in Castile. Although they acted with some circumspection and restraint in Granada, the methods the Holy Office employed, including secret arrests, anonymous denunciations, torture (even of women and minors), and the awarding of confiscated goods to informants, established a dynamic that encouraged Old Christians to launch accusations of apostasy against Morisco neighbors, and prompted members of New Christian communities and families to betray each other, whether warranted or not.[27] In the end, repression had the opposite effect of what its best intentions might have been, and crypto-Muslims were pushed ever closer together, while genuine converts were alienated.

Most seriously, this assault on Arabo-Iberian culture was not accompanied by an opening up of Old Christian society. Moriscos remained

[26] F. Núñez Muley, *A Memorandum*, p. 81. For the *zambra*, see p. 491, n. 270.

[27] See, for example, M. E. Perry, "Between Muslim and Christian Worlds." For the toxic effects of Inquisitional violence and torture on a Morisco community, see R. Yassine Bahri, "L'organisation interne."

subject to a distinct and onerous tax regime, and were vulnerable to all manner of discrimination, including prohibitions, whether formal or informal, on bathing with Christians, being buried in churches, and so on. In Valencia, for example, seigniors continued to be given legal jurisdiction over Moriscos on the basis that it "would not be just nor conform to reason or equity that, the said Muslims having converted to the Christian faith and religion . . . that [these lords] ought to lose the said criminal jurisdiction which they have."[28] Although over the previous century a positive distinction had developed in Christian lands between *naturals* – or indigenous, native-born Muslims – versus aliens and captives, this was giving way in many Old Christian circles to the notion that all Muslims and their descendants were "foreigners." Controversial legislation relating to "blood cleanliness" had been proposed since the fifteenth century as an attempt to exclude the descendants of Jewish *conversos* from high-status administrative positions. These were incorporated into law in 1556 and, thereafter, increasingly deployed against Moriscos.[29]

Thus, from the mid 1500s the Morisco elite – even those who had fully acculturated – came under threat. A century earlier, a combination of suspect conversions, together with the survival of Jewish culture and community, had acted to increase Christian anxieties and had, in fact, intensified the social stresses and economic competition that also drove anti-Jewish discrimination. As a result, by 1492 the maintenance of a Jewish minority came to be seen as untenable, and Jews were ordered to convert or depart. Moriscos were now in a similar situation – they were all Christians, and therefore could not be marginalized on the basis of religion, but they remained distinct, and their conversion had changed neither their cultural identity nor their fiscal status. Nor did it change their place in the political and economic environment of the kingdom. In their case too, conversion did little to dampen the tensions at the root of anti-Muslim sentiment. Rather, by eliminating the religious barrier, it introduced new ambiguities and, therefore, fed Christian anxieties. Conversion in absence of integration was simply not a situation that could hold.

[28] Similar arguments were used to restrict Moriscos' right to move their domicile or to approach coastal areas without permission. G. Colón and A. Garcia i Sanz, *Furs de València*, vol. III, pp. 146–47 {III:5:xci}, vol. V, pp. 107–09 {IV:1: xxvii}, and pp. 109–10 {IV:1: xxviii and xix*bis*}.

[29] In the early 1600s Pedro de Aznar Cardona, the author of "The Justified Expulsion of the Spanish Moriscos" (*La expulsión justificada de los moriscos españoles*, 1612) would argue for the expulsion of the children of Moriscos on the grounds that if they were to stay they would contaminate the "clean" or "heathly" blood (*sangre sana*) of the Old Christians they would eventually marry. See G. Magnier, "The Controversy," p. 199.

Through all of this, Moriscos, whether Christian or crypto-Muslim (or both), endeavored to establish a position for themselves in this increasingly repressive environment. For Muslims, this involved active resistance, through the covert maintenance of Islamic judicial and theological networks, the support of popular religious figures (both men and women), and recourse to prophetic, mystical, and messianic strands of piety. Moreover, this was a process that was fed by contemporary currents in the Christian and Jewish worlds; Muslim thinkers drew on sources as diverse as Isadorean prophecy, popular Marianism, and Thomas à Kempis's *Imitation of Christ*, in their efforts to construct a viable, new theology.[30] Morisco messianism was the product of a hybrid of Islamic, Jewish, and Christian cosmological, astrological, political, and theological influences, but addressed the very particular circumstances of their community.[31] It was also a reaction on the part of proponents of the messianic Hapsburg ideology and the increasingly exceptional and narrow notion of Spain and Spaniards that was emerging in royal circles and among pietist elements at court.[32]

### *The Morisco elite and the "lead books"*

Highly placed Morisco courtiers, such as Francisco Núñez Muley, saw the danger of the culturally repressive edicts, and advocated the acceptance of Moriscos – even those who maintained their folk traditions and language – as full subjects of the Catholic Emperor.[33] After all, he and his ilk reasoned, their customs were not incompatible with Christianity, and Arabic was the language of long-standing Christian congregations in the East.[34] Loyalty to their king should be the measure of their legitimacy. However, such a "modern" view of the relationship between conscience and citizenship was simply not tenable in sixteenth-century Europe, where millenarian anxieties were being fed by the explosion of politicized heresy in the form of the Reformation, and the very future of Christendom was seen as threatened by the Muslim Ottomans.

[30] Messianism was a powerful strand of devotion among common Christians also. See, for example, the case of the would-be prophet Miguel de Piedrola, tried by the Inquisition in 1587, in R. L. Kagan and A. Dyer, *Inquisitorial Inquiries*, pp. 60–87.

[31] See G. Magnier, "Millenarian Prophecy," and L. M. Alvarez, "Prophecies of Apocalypse." For Messianism as a form of Morisco resistance, and reciprocal links between Jewish and Muslim thought, as well as portentous astrological omens observed in the 1580s, see M. García-Arenal, *Messianism and Puritanical Reform*, esp. pp. 300 and 313.

[32] See G. Magnier, *Pedro de Valencia*.

[33] For the figure and family origin of Francisco Núñez Muley, see L. P. Harvey, *Muslims in Spain*, pp. 211–14 and M. J. Rubiera Mata, "La família morsica de la Muley-Fez."

[34] F. Núñez Muley, *A Memorandum*, p. 92.

The last, desperate gambit on the part of the Morisco courtly elite to carve out by hook or crook an equal place for New Christians in the new order took the form of an unlikely forgery – the "lead books of Sacromonte." Over the course of eleven years, a series of twenty-two collections of apparently ancient lead tablets was discovered in the caves of this hillside Granadan suburb. Written in Arabic and Latin and peppered with mysterious symbols, the "books," ostensibly dating from the first century, claimed to relay various Apostolic prophecies, including instructions originating with the Virgin Mary for the evangelization of Spain. These were presented as having been recorded by Spanish, Arabic-speaking Christians. Clearly, their authors' aim was to establish a pedigree for the legitimacy of Arabic language and culture as part of the Christian Iberian tradition, and to present a primitive Christian doctrine that was not in conflict with the tenets of Islam. The latter is a manifestation of the Islamic principle of *tahrif* – the conviction that Jesus's teachings could not be in conflict with Islam, and that therefore the Christian Gospels represent a corruption of the original message. Seen by scholars today, the tablets are obvious forgeries, and the consensus is that the two individuals charged with translating them, Miguel de Luna and Alonso del Castillo, were likely themselves the forgers.[35] Both were physicians, writers, and courtiers, who served as translators of Arabic for Felipe II (1556–98), and both were second-generation crypto-Muslims. Miguel de Luna was best known for his work, *The True History of King Rodrigo*, a history of medieval Spain, which portrayed the Muslim rulers of the peninsula and the cultural synthesis the conquest provoked in a most favorable light.[36] His father-in-law, Alonso del Castillo, was a poet who was commissioned by the King to collect and translate Arabic inscriptions and texts and to catalog the Arabic language holdings of the library of the Escorial.[37]

Although the "discovery" of the lead tablets, along with various other items purported to be relics of the Virgin (not the least a veil!), provoked a sensation across western Christendom, neither they nor other contemporary texts that were produced with the aim of Islamicizing Christianity met

[35] See, generally, M. García-Arenal and F. Rodríguez Mediano, *Un oriente español*. For Miguel de Luna and Alonso del Castillo, see G. A. Wiegers, "The Persistence of Mudejar Islam?," pp. 515–18, and M. García-Arenal and F. Rodríguez Mediano, "Médico, traductor, inventor."

[36] The full title of the work is *La verdadera historia del rey Rodrigo, en la cual se trata de la causa principal de la pérdida de España, y la conquista que della hizo Miramamolín Almançor Rey que fue del Africa, y de las Arabias, y vida del Rey Iacob Almançor. Compuesta por el sabio Alcayde Abulcacim Tarif Abentarique, de nación Arabe, y natural de la Arabia Petrea. Nuevamente traduzida de la lengua Arabiga por Miguel de Luna vezino de Granada, interprete del Rey don Phelippe nuestro Señor*. It was published in Granada in two parts, in 1592 and 1600.

[37] See G. A. Wiegers, "The Persistence of Mudejar Islam?"

with success. Nor did those Moriscos who were attempting to Christianize Muslims fare much better. For Ignacio de las Casas, a contemporary Jesuit of Morisco origin, the failure of the evangelization movement rested on the chauvinistic attitude of Old Christian clergy, the repression and marginalization of Moriscos (and in particular, the policies of the Inquisition), the failure to use Arabic effectively as a missionizing tool and to educate young Moriscos, and the continuing appeal of the crypto-*ʿulamāʾ*. His proposals for remedying this situation were set out in a series of essays he wrote between 1605 and 1607, including a letter to Clement VIII (1592–1605). But they fell on deaf ears; indeed, the fact that his own Company of Jesus adopted blood purity policies in 1593 indicates how determined the leading men of the Church were to exclude converts and their descendants in Spain – the voices of the Talaveras were being drowned out by those of the Cisneroses.

## Repression and resistance

Having seen the great number of converted Muslims and their descendants there are in this kingdom and region, who are known to all to be so vile as to live as Muslims; and having seen how many times in recent years fleets of Turks, the enemies of our Holy Catholic Faith, have come to the shores of these kingdoms, and you, the said new converts have celebrated ... and desired ... to join with them ... We order that from here on, no convert nor descendant of a convert ... may hold in his power or of another, nor fire nor provide: harquebuses, rifles, pistols, or crossbows, nor any other type of firearm, nor have gunpowder, musket balls, shot, darts or any arms of this type, which may be set up to fire ... (The Inquisitors of the Kingdom of Aragon, edict prohibiting Moriscos from bearing arms (November 5, 1559)[38])

Of course, Moriscos were not merely the passive victims of Old Christian discrimination; and whereas some, like Francisco Núñez Muley and Miguel de Luna, fought the system from within, others – whether openly or under cover of *taqiyya* – actively resisted, at times, with violence. Indeed, the "banditry" for which Granadan Moriscos came to be known was essentially a continuation of the defeated uprising of 1500, carried out by small groups of *monfíes* (a Castilianization of the Arabic *munfī*, or "outlaw") who refused baptism and carried out a small-scale guerilla war.[39] Others took advantage of the growing power of the Ottomans to escape; in 1526 Khayr al-Dīn, the *Beylerbey* of Algiers, sent six missions to

[38] M. García-Arenal, *Los Moriscos*, pp. 223–25.

[39] In a later parallel, Republican, Anarchist, and Communist partisans who continued to resist the Fascist government after the conclusion of the Spanish Civil War were labeled as garden-variety "bandits" by the official media, rather than resisters.

the Granadan coast, from where some 70,000 New Christians were said to have been evacuated.[40] The deportation of all of the remaining Moriscos from the kingdom of Granada to other parts of Spain in the early 1570s only served at once to disperse and intensify this type of resistance.

However, the most widespread mode of fighting back against religious and social oppression was secrecy. The fact that Moriscos continued to live in discrete neighborhoods both provided cover for underground Islamic networks and served to intimidate genuine converts from betraying apostates. In the 1540s, in the extremely prosperous Morisco town of Arévalo in Castile, Inquisitors unearthed what was apparently a regional network of secret Muslims united around the figure of a young boy they described as a "prophet."[41] Inquisitions in Valencia and Aragon also uncovered networks of secret *fuqahā*ʾ. Women played a surprisingly active role in religious resistance: not only do we find them acting as popular *muftūn* and mystics, such as "the *Mora* de Úbeda," or the widely respected midwife and *ʿālima* Nuzay Calderán, but ordinary women showed great heroism in resisting Inquisitors and the soldiers who searched their homes for prohibited works.[42] Several are recorded as stuffing copies of the Qurʾān up their skirts in an effort to protect them from confiscation. Women's resistance was particularly entrenched in Valencia, where, as Labarta notes, there is no record of any nuns of Morisca origin.[43] And, of course, it was women who most visibly and willingly wore the mark of their community by covering their heads and wearing traditional clothes, whereas Morisco men had largely assimilated in terms of personal appearance. Between 1566 and 1620 more than one quarter of the suspects brought before the Inquisition were Moriscas.[44]

The Morisco commercial class also became an important source of community solidarity and resistance, far more than the *mudéjar* "patriciate" had been in preceding centuries. Wealthy families of merchants of silk and other high-margin commodities established networks of marriage and clientage that spanned the peninsula, from Granada to Zaragoza, and beyond. Whereas some of these families attempted to obtain royal privileges exempting them from their onerous "New Christian" status, most rose to the challenge of protecting their communities, providing a conduit

[40] See A. Temimi, "Une lettre," p. 102.

[41] For this episode and the possible connection to El Mancebo de Arévalo, see L. P. Harvey, *Muslims in Spain*, pp. 110–17.

[42] See *ibid.*, pp. 185–91, for *La Mora* and Nuzay.

[43] A. Labarta, "La mujer morisca," p. 24.

[44] See R. Surtz, "Morisca Women"; also A. Labarta, "La mujer morisca," p. 221, who notes that men far outnumbered women; 525 Moriscas in total were put on trial by the Inquisition.

for the movement of information and people (particularly covert religious figures), and launching diplomatic initiatives with the French and with foreign Muslim powers. It is for this reason – as well as their wealth – that families such as these were so frequently targeted for prosecution by Inquisitors and local Old Christian clans. Moreover, theirs was a solidarity that outlasted even the expulsion; wealthy Morisco families that settled in France, such as the Chapiz and the Cardenas, provided support for their co-religionists who were sent into exile beginning in 1609.[45]

In Aragon and Valencia, as well as much of Castile, Moriscos' most active protectors remained the seigniorial powers, whether lay lords or Military Orders, who continued to issue their Morisco subjects arms and turned a blind eye to the public practice of Islam and traditional customs. Sancho de Cardona, for example, allegedly allowed his Morisco vassals to have a mosque, and encouraged them to resist efforts to convert them.[46] In the Vall d'Uxó the Duke of Segorb allowed a *madrasa* to operate, and in Cortes, the Moriscos' seignior not only allowed them to follow their customs in exchange for payment, but personally attended their festivities. Thus, as a consequence of their mutual interests, New Christians came to be identified in the eyes of the Crown with the insolently independent Aragonese and Valencian aristocracy, and the ever-present threat of noble rebellion. As a consequence, from the early sixteenth century, there were repeated calls to disarm the Moriscos but, with the exception of local successes (as at the Aragonese hamlet of Burbáguena in 1526), to little result.[47]

In the meanwhile, royal officials became ever more abusive and dishonest towards their Morisco subjects, particularly in Granada, where New Christians lodged a formal complaint with the royal court in 1561, stating that "they were receiving severe harassment and vexations from the *alguaciles* and the ministers of justice," right up to the Corrigedor ("chief justice") of Granada, Hernando Carrillo de Mendoza.[48] Then, in 1566, the forty-year exemption granted by Carlos I expired and, over the objections of some of his leading statesmen, Felipe II passed into law the recommendations made by the conclave of the royal chapel. According to the Pragmatic, which was to come into force at the beginning of 1567, written and spoken Arabic and Berber would be banned, together with traditional Muslim dress and customs, and all documents and books

[45] See, for example, F. L. Bernabé Pons, "Notas sobre la cohesion," and "On Morisco Networks"; W. Childers, "An Extensive Network"; and J. Abella Samitier, "Una família."
[46] For Sancho de Cardona, see above, p. 286. These examples are taken from S. Haliczer, *Inquisition and Society*, p. 256.
[47] M. Halavais, *Like Wheat to the Miller*, p. 91.
[48] A. García López, "Moriscos andalusíes en Pastrana," p. 167.

written in Arabic. New Christian children were to be handed over to the Church for their education. But the decree also had an economic impact: a ban on the use of silk by Moriscos undermined an already depressed industry, and the blanket annulation of all deeds and contracts written in Arabic instantly deprived many New Christians of their property and wealth.[49]

### *Rebellion and repression*

The reaction was swift. In 1568 rebellion once again flared up in Valencia's Serra d'Espadà, while Granada became the scene of a kingdom-wide uprising. The revolt opened on Christmas 1568 when a rebel leader, Farax ben Farax, made a brief incursion into the capital before embarking on a campaign of violence against Old Christians and clergy in the countryside of the Alpujarras. He and his followers cast off any pretensions of conversion, declaring themselves openly to be Muslims. Soon after, a certain Fernando de Valór or Aben Humeya ("Ibn 'Umayya") was declared "King" and crowned according to the "rite of the Granadan kings" by the rebel forces.[50] Soon Ottoman irregulars and Maghribī volunteers were crossing over from North Africa to join the fight. They were met by the weight of the veteran imperial army under the leadership of proven commanders, overseen by Felipe's brother, Don Juan of Austria. By late 1569, a rift among the Muslim forces resulted in the murder of Aben Humeya and the installation of his cousin, Aben Abóo, as leader. Although set-piece battles, like the siege of Golera in 1570, would be decided by the unstoppable power of the Spanish heavy artillery, Morisco forces proved adept at guerilla warfare, and scored a series of successes against the imperial troops. However, even as Don Juan's columns poured over the hills of Andalucía in pursuit of the evasive rebels, Felipe II undertook to exile the entire New Christian population of the kingdom and disperse them throughout his lands. Meanwhile, negotiations were undertaken with the rebel leaders to end the war and establish a new protocol for Christian–Muslim relations. At first these showed promise, but Aben Abóo was determined to fight on, and the war ended only when he was murdered on March 15, 1571 at the hands of the moderate faction in his camp.

The war may have meant the end of Morisco society in Granada – about 84,000 were sent into exile – but if Felipe II had hoped that scattering the kingdom's natives would dilute their influence, the opposite occurred. Despite tensions and differences between the *Moriscos antiguos* ("old

49 The Pragmatic is published in J. Bleda, *Corónica de los moros*, pp. 657–59.
50 See J. Acosta Montoro, *Aben Humeya*, pp. 121–29.

Moriscos") and the *Moriscos granadinos* ("Granadan Moriscos") in Castile, the net effect of the diaspora was, as Harvey characterizes it, a "consciousness raising" among the New Christians of Spain, not to mention a tremendous injection of cultural and religious capital into the Spanish Morisco communities.[51] Morisco "banditry," which had been previously confined to Granada, now became a problem elsewhere. The dispersion of the Granadans must have also been a strong breath of air on the fading embers of Arabic culture and Islamic learning, particularly in Castile. The exiled crypto-Muslims would have brought with them books and ideas that reflected the latest developments in Islamic political and religious thought, as well as first-hand news of the possibility of liberation that the Ottoman rise seemed to herald.

Meanwhile, the pitch of the reactionary secular and clerical ideologues in Hapsburg Spain reached feverish heights. Moriscos now came to be portrayed as almost a species apart: smelly, dirty, noisy, abstemious, carnal, ugly, and "black" – a foreign substance in the body Christian that needed to be "vomited up."[52] This fed anxieties among the Old Christian common classes; and as these intensified, the specter of Morisco revolts and conspiracies gripped the popular imagination, encouraged by unscrupulous individuals who stood to benefit.[53] Moreover, 1580 marked a period of increased tension in Spain, a time of famine, plague, and war with Portugal. In that year, rumors of a plot to revolt in Sevilla and neighboring areas led to vigilante attacks that provoked Morisco retaliation.[54] In Valencia, in 1581, rumors of a rebellion led to mass arrests and a three-year Inquisition – that eventually found that the "plot" was a fabrication.[55] In 1600 posters appeared in parishes of Sevilla ostensibly advertising a coming uprising, but even some Old Christians decried these as a hoax. In Aragon, a violent opportunist, Lupercio Latrás, harnessed the discontent of Old Christian upland shepherds and led them on a campaign of violence against Morisco cultivators in the mid-Ebro region. In a medieval "Srebrenica moment," the civil authorities and the Monastery of Rueda – the Moriscos' seignior – stood by as New Christian townsfolk were massacred.[56] In the meanwhile, efforts to disarm the Moriscos, particularly in Valencia, which was seen as vulnerable to foreign Muslim attack, were stepped up. Such efforts

[51] L. P. Harvey, *Muslims in Spain*, p. 215; G. Wiegers, "Moriscos and Arabic Studies," pp. 594ff.

[52] See J.-M. Perceval Verde, "Asco y asquesidad," p. 23, and throughout.

[53] Suspicion of Morisco plotting was fed by the fact that the regular meetings that many communities held were convened at night, and often had a religious element. See L. F. Bernabé Pons, "On Morisco Networks and Collectives," pp. 124–26.

[54] See M. Bogelin, "Between Rumor and Resistance."

[55] S. Haliczer, *Inquisition and Society*, pp. 263–64.

[56] See V. Ara Otín, *Lupercio Latrás*.

continued to be resisted by the New Christians' patrons among the landed nobility, but increased in frequency and determination. In 1593 tens of thousands of weapons were seized in Aragon alone.

By this point, the Crown and its Old Christian subjects had become convinced that the Morisco population constituted a grave threat. Of course, not all New Christians were "fifth columnists," but many had been attracted by this possibility or driven to this point. In 1575, it was emerging that the Moriscos of Aragon and Valencia had been plotting an uprising with the aid of the French Protestants and the Ottomans.[57] In Aragon, Moriscos publicly celebrated Ottoman victories, and there were suggestions that an uprising was in the works. In 1585, Henry Cook, an archer and notary in the service of Felipe II, visited the Jalón Valley and reported that New Christians were keeping *ḥallāl*, and that the churches of the zone remained locked, even on Sundays.[58] Not only did Moriscos actively maintain contacts with North African *fuqahā'* and lobby the rulers of North Africa and the Ottoman Empire, some were clearly implicated in the increasingly damaging raiding of the "Barbary corsairs," which included not only attacks on shipping, but the terrifying raids in which towns were attacked and inhabitants carried off into captivity.[59]

But Moriscos also made common cause with other religious nonconformists in Christian Europe, notably the Protestant Huguenots. Despite the violence of the Wars of Religion, France's conciliatory policies, such as 1562's Edict of Saint-Germain, and 1598's Edict of Nantes, would have seemed like admirable models. By 1595, however, France and Spain were at war, and the French connection – not to mention overtures made to other enemy powers, such as England – further cemented the Moriscos' reputation as traitors. As early as the 1570s, Aragonese Moriscos were in contact with French agents, and had promised to rise up in the event of an invasion, and to declare Henri IV (1589–1610) king.[60] By the early 1600s both the English and the newly independent Dutch were also negotiating with Morisco emissaries with an eye to supporting a Moroccan invasion of Spain. The fact that Valencia, widely regarded as the underbelly of the Spanish kingdom, was where the Morisco population was now most

[57] See, for example, L. P. Harvey, *Muslims in Spain*, p. 343; L. F. Bernabé Pons, "On Morisco Networks and Collectives," p. 130 (but n.b. n. 53, above). The Compañero family of Zaragoza, merchants, and *alfaquíes*, were found to be at the heart of this conspiracy; they were hunted down, tortured, and put to the stake. See J. Fournel-Guérin, "Un famille morisque."

[58] J. L. Corral Lafuente, "El proceso de represión," p. 353.

[59] See, for example, above, p. 218, for requests for aid during the first War of the Alpujarras, and A. Temimi, "Un lettre," for a subsequent call in 1541.

[60] The Moriscos undoubtedly imagined that Henri would take a similar approach to Islam as he did to Protestantism and the issue of a multi-confessional kingdom.

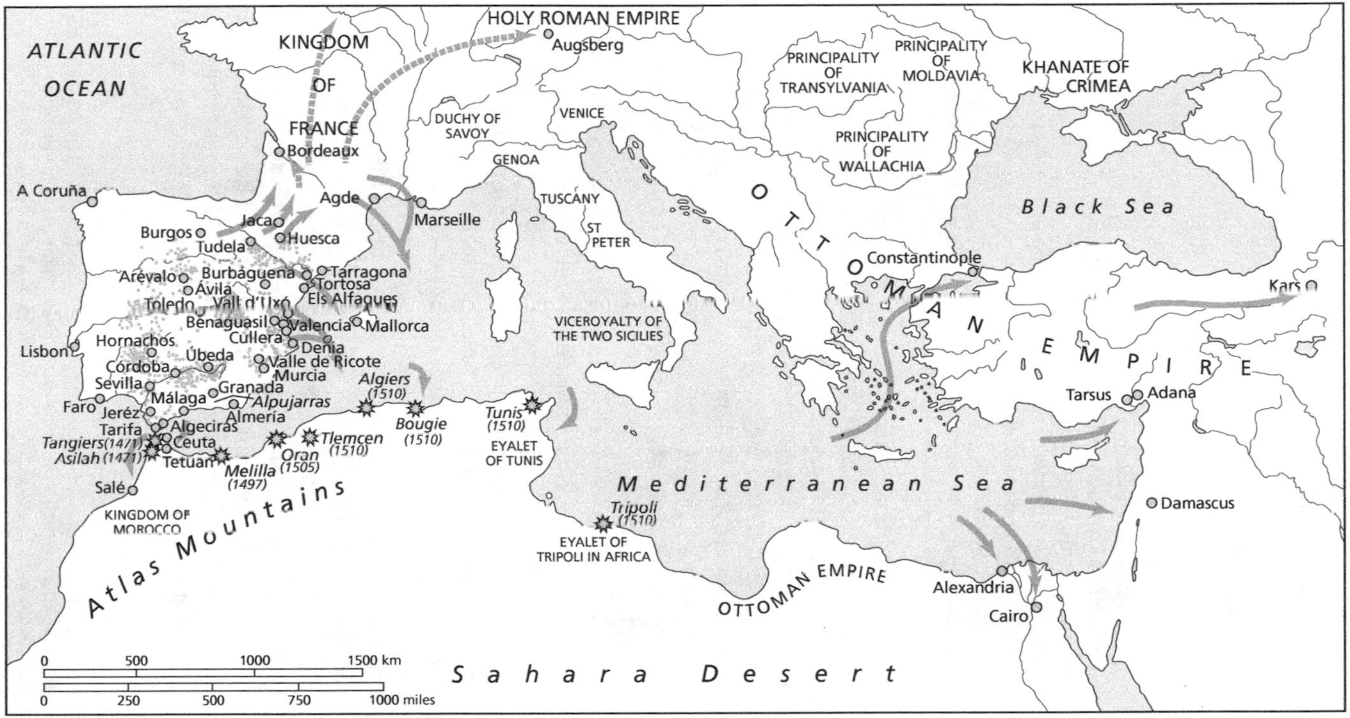


Map 8 The Morisco diaspora

concentrated, only underscored a sense on the part of the Crown that action needed to be taken.[61]

## Expulsion

Descendants of Ishmael
now that beautiful Spain
by the inspiration of God
and His Holy Providence
has banished you from Her service
because She does not want in Her Homeland
those who in their rites and apostasies
show such perseverance . . .

Francisco de Aguirre, *Romance del consejo que dio un soldado a los Moriscos para que empleasen sus dineros en mercaderías, que se gastasen en África* . . . (1612)[62]

The idea of seeking a final solution to the Morisco problem had been settled by Felipe II as early as 1581, but it was under his son and successor, the anemic Felipe III, that the idea gained real traction. On the initiative of a clutch of influential courtiers, including the royal favorite, Francisco Gómez, Duke of Lerma, and the powerful Juan de Ribera (later sainted), Archbishop and Viceroy of Valencia, a number of propositions were tabled with the aim of permanently disposing of the New Christians. The most gruesome of these ideas – to drown the entire Morisco population by loading them onto ships that would be sunk offshore – was floated several times. A more moderate proposal was to castrate the men and sterilize the women, and then exile them all to the northeast of the Americas ("the Coast of Cod and Newfoundland"), where they would simply die out.[63] These and other drastic plans ran up against declared Christian principles of mercy and justice, not to mention the possibility that the Islamic powers of the Mediterranean would retaliate. Thus, the prelate de Ribera offered the more charitable proposition of mass enslavement and forced labor. However, by the end of the first decade of the seventeenth century, Felipe III had been convinced that forced exile of the entire Morisco population was the most viable solution. The consensus among the most influential courtiers and clerics was that the New Christians were incorrigible rebels and apostates. The moderate clergy and advisors who opposed the plan were ignored.[64] All that remained was to work out the details, and decide how to handle the delicate matter of the

[61] See B. J. García García, "La cuestión morisca."
[62] "Romance of the Advice that a Soldier Gave to the Moriscos to Spend their Money on Supplies to be Used in Africa . . ." edited in M. Ruíz Lagos, *Moriscos*, p. 264.
[63] L. P. Harvey, *Muslims in Spain*, p. 296. [64] See H. Kamen, *Spain, 1469–1714*, p. 232.

Morisco children, whom some felt were not beyond correction, and who were owed mercy as Christians.[65]

In the first decade of Felipe III's reign, the matter was subjected to a lengthy cost-benefit analysis, and in the end it was determined that the only people who would be seriously inconvenienced would be the Aragonese and Valencian nobility. The *cortes* of these kingdoms had stubbornly insisted on their autonomy and refused to grant the new King tax subsidies, so striking a blow at the seigniorial economy here was seen as a benefit. Further, Felipe's advisors insisted that the confiscation of the property and estates of the exiled New Christians would bring considerable profit to the royal treasury. In order to assuage the papacy and those among the clergy who were discomfited by the notion of exiling Christians *en masse* to Islamic territories, where they would undoubtedly apostatize, the royal court presented the policy on political, rather than religious terms. It was not the solution to a religious problem, but rather to an intractable rebellion.

### *Finalizing the solution*

And so by 1609 a policy had been drafted in careful secrecy. It was promulgated first in the kingdom of Valencia on September 22, with the intention of taking the New Christians there by surprise – although it seems some Castilian Moriscos had foreseen what was to come and were quietly leaving Spain.[66] According to the decree, on pain of death all Moriscos were to assemble at their place of residence in three days' time with the property they could carry, in order to receive orders from local commissioners. As they assembled they were not to be molested or harmed by Old Christians, nor were they to be abetted in avoiding the order. Six of every hundred were to be obliged to remain behind long enough to instruct the Christians who would be moving onto their property as to how to run their irrigation systems and mills. Other exceptions

[65] Opinions among Catholic ideologues ranged from that of Aznar Cardonas, who believed that the sins of Moriscos were visited on their children, and that for the latter to die would constitute a blessing, and Pedro de Valencia, who opposed what he characterized as collective punishment, and urged mercy, especially on Morisco children. See G. Magnier, "The Controversy," pp. 200–03.

[66] For the decree, see M. García-Arenal, *Los Moriscos*, pp. 251–55, trans. in J. Cowans, *Early Modern Spain*, pp. 145–48. See G. Wiegers, "Managing Disaster," p. 143, for Moriscos surfacing in Rome in 1608, and, generally for Moriscos' responses first to the tightening of conditions on their communities, and finally to the expulsion. For the latest research on the Morisco expulsion and diaspora, see the studies in M. García-Arenal and G. A. Wiegers, *Los Moriscos* (work which was published too late to be incorporated into this study).

included children under six who had been born to New Christian mothers, Moriscos who had not taken part in communal assemblies for at least two years, and those bearing an exemption from their bishop. In practical terms, however, there were no exceptions. Remarkably, almost all went willingly, and only a few took refuge in the hills to resist. Having been marched to their designated ports of departure, by October 11 the first of tens of thousands of Moriscos were arriving in Oran, where they were escorted to the limits of this Spanish enclave and simply turned loose. By late November, the Valencian expulsion was complete, with 116,000 individuals having been sent into exile.

Over the objections of the local nobility and clergy, the Aragonese and Catalan expulsions began in April 1610. The element of surprise had been lost, but there was little resistance from the 60,000 or so New Christians here; in fact, the only one who refused to comply was the Bishop of Tortosa, who maintained that the 2,000 or so Moriscos on his lands were all good Christians and would not be deported. The rest, having had time to wrap up their affairs as they could, were directed either towards Jaca, where they would cross the Pyrenees into France, or to the port of Els Alfaques near the mouth of the Ebro. A request by the Ottoman Aḥmād I to James I of England (1603–25) to allow the Moriscos to shelter in England and then transit to the Empire went unanswered.[67] Those who crossed to France had been offered the possibility of settling in the north of the kingdom by Henri IV on condition that they would be good Catholics, but all but a few took the route to the port of Agde, and on to Tunis.[68]

The Moriscos of the Crown of Castile were the subject of several different edicts promulgated between September 1609 and July 1610, each of which affected different groups and regions. Generally, Moriscos here were given thirty days to comply with the order and were encouraged to depart willingly, although in Murcia they were allowed as little as ten.[69] They wound up their affairs and sold what they could for cash – a 50 percent duty would be charged on any money that they took out of the kingdom. Contemporaries reported a trickle of wealthy Moriscos from Old Castile and Toledo trundling towards France in their carriages, amongst the plodding lines of poorer refugees. Most, however, were ordered to the coast, leaving on foot with what little they could carry, to be borne by ship to Africa. Many, of course, were victims of piracy, banditry, and theft, whether

[67] See, above, p. 250, n. 97.
[68] See L. Cardaillac, "A propósito"; for the text of Henri's promolugation, see A. Berthier, "Nouveaux documents," p. 25, n. 1.
[69] L. Lisón Hernández, "Mito y realidad," pp. 149–50.

they made their way to Islamic lands by sea or land.[70] Aside from the New Christians of Tortosa, the only exceptions made were for North African renegades who had recently converted to Christianity, for slaves of Christian masters, and for the Moriscos of the Canaries.[71] From 1611 onwards, royal authorities scoured the countryside for evaders and for those who, having been expelled, had sneaked back into the kingdom. The communities of the Valle de Ricote (some fifteen kilometers north of Murcia) simply ignored the order, insisting on the authenticity of their Christian piety. But to no avail: in December 1613, the Moriscos who lived here – some 2,000 in number – were turned out by force.[72] These were the last of the Moriscos, and on February 20, 1614, the Count of Salazar, who had overseen the expulsion, reported to Felipe III that his mission had been completed.

### *After the expulsion*

In the decades that followed, occasional reports surface of Moriscos who had avoided the expulsion, or who, like real-life versions of Cervantes's fictional Morisco, Ricote, covertly returned to the kingdom, or were sent back as envoys.[73] Indeed, the characters' name was no coincidence – many Moriscos returned to Ricote, where they sacked the local archives to prevent their detection. Considerable numbers from other locales petitioned for permission to return, citing their separation from their wives and children, but to no avail.[74] Recent research suggests that a substantial and affluent crypto-Muslim community survived in Granada until a final Inquisitional purge of 1727.[75] But for all intents and purposes, by 1615 Islam had disappeared from Western Europe, and substantial Muslim communities would not reappear in these lands until the twentieth century. Clearly, by the late sixteenth century, Spain – the last kingdom of what was once Latin Christendom in which the medieval Islamic community had not been extinguished – was no longer able to sustain this minority. This was the result of a conjuncture of circumstances and

70 After receiving complaints from exiles of their suffering at the hands of pirates, the Ottoman Aḥmād I sent envoys to France and Venice, requesting that the Moriscos be allowed to transit eastwards by land, and that their safety and property be guaranteed. See A. Temimi, "Une lettre."

71 The Moriscos of the Canaries had a distinct provenance and identity; they successfully petitioned the crown for regularization, and were not expelled. See L. A. Anaya Hernández, "The Canary Moriscos," esp. pp. 46–47.

72 F. J. Flores Arroyuelo, *Los últimos Moriscos*, p. 171.

73 See the case of Diego Bejarano/Aḥmād al-Hajarī, above, p. 250.

74 See L. Lisón Hernández, "Mito y realidad," pp. 147–48.

75 See E. Soria Mesa, "Los moriscos que se quedaron."

causes, just as it had been a conjunction of circumstances that had allowed this anomalous situation to continue so long after the formal ideology of the Church had precluded the possibility of *convivencia*. Iberian Islam outlived its homologues by three centuries. But religion itself had rarely been an issue – proof of this is not only how little religious ideology affected the lives of Muslims under Christian rule, but how conversion, whether genuine or feigned, made so little difference.

Moreover, new notions of race were emerging and displacing the medieval concept of law (and religion) as the essence of ethnicity. One can convert to another religion, but not to another race. Finally, the shift in political structure and ideology from the Middle Ages, with its overlapping patrimonial structures based on bonds of personal loyalty, to the early modern empires and republics of the European West, together with the universal aspirations of the Church and emperors, introduced principles of moral consensus and ideological homogeneity that were apparently incompatible with religious diversity. The upheavals of the Reformation, the French Wars of Religion, and the Thirty Years' War would bear this transformation out. In this sense, one might see the Moriscos as victims of "collateral damage." Yet this would be innaccurate; it is clear that the Muslims of Latin Christendom and the Moriscos of Spain were anything but passive as historical actors. Over the course of six hundred years they reinvented themselves and renegotiated their position within their host societies with dogged determination and remarkable ingenuity, surviving as a community under Infidel rule, while keeping faithful on the best terms they could manage to the religious identity that defined them as individuals and as a society.

Thus, what failed was the integration of two communities that were unable or unwilling either to come to equal terms or to merge. Hence, the forced conversions of the early sixteenth century exacerbated rather than alleviated tensions between them, by effacing or softening the formal boundaries and introducing an uncomfortable ambiguity – new aspirations for the underclass, new fears of competition for the majority. Much as the Restoration in the post-Civil War American South led to the development of an ideology of segregation and the emergence of reactionary groups like the Ku Klux Klan, here the elimination of formal religious difference between the two communities demanded the articulation of a new ideology to rationalize their separation. Simultaneously, the disengagement of minority and majority societies and the weakening of bonds of economic and social interdependence, asymmetrical as these may have been, transformed the Muslims of Iberia into competitors and enemies for the greater part of Christian society and encouraged the perception of these indigenous peoples as foreigners. Yet, this broad estrangement was neither sufficient nor necessary cause for the elimination of these Muslim communities. It was the disengagement of Muslims from the institutions of power – royal, municipal, ecclesiastical, commercial, and seigniorial – that was the crucial factor in sealing their destiny. By the late sixteenth century, only the aristocracy and certain ecclesiastical/seigniorial corporations had any interest in maintaining and nurturing Morisco communities. The rest were indifferent or hostile. The Moriscos had become dispensable, and therefore ethno-religious diversity could no longer be sustained – this was a crisis of *conveniencia*.

## Coda: al-Andalus abroad

> And don't think, my lord, that it was the hand of the King of Spain, he who has exiled us from his land; rather it was Divine Inspiration. For I have seen predictions made more than a thousand years ago, which tell of all that has happened to us, and that will happen: that God will take us from this land, and that to this purpose God would set himself in the heart of the king, and that many of our people would die on land and sea. And in the end this is what happened. But at any moment, God will intervene, and send a king to subdue the entire world with nothing more than the Word of God, against whom neither siege nor artillery might prevail. (Molina (a Morisco), Letter to Jerónimo de Loaysa, knight of Trujillo, from exile in Algiers (July 25, 1611)[76])

Altogether, some 320,000 Moriscos were marched into exile – perhaps eight times as many as the Jews who had chosen to leave under duress just over two hundred years earlier.[77] The sudden departure of 3 percent of the Spanish kingdoms' total population would have a devastating effect on the regions where the Morisco population had been most dense: Valencia, Murcia, and parts of Aragon. The local nobility who ran both their own estates and those of the Military Orders would suffer, but that was of little concern to a monarchy focused on Protestant Europe, the Ottoman East, and the New World. Those few Moriscos who moved to other parts of Christian Europe – like Cervantes' Ricote, who had been drawn to the freedom of Augsburg – were soon absorbed into the local population and disappeared from the historical landscape.[78] Those who were sent to the Islamic world, and in particular, Ifrīqiya and the Maghrib – the

[76] M. García-Arenal, *Los moriscos*, pp. 264–65.

[77] For the number of Jews sent into exile, see H. Kamen, "The Mediterranean." For an overview of the Morisco diaspora, see L. Bernabé Pons, "Las emigraciones moriscas."

[78] The Moriscos of France present something of an exception. In 1668 "a Muslim merchant" from Bordeaux "disguised as a Christian" was intercepted in Marseille as he tried to board ship to Tunis with eighteen members of his family. An investigation, launched at the behest of the Prime Minister, Colbert, and with the active interest of Louis XIV

vast majority of Moriscos – maintained a distinct identity for a considerable time.[79]

The Moriscos had long maintained contact with the Ottoman Empire, and although the Ottomans failed to rescue Spain's Muslims or launch an invasion of the mainland, they did recruit and welcome Spanish refugees, who served them as guides, interpreters, and soldiers. In 1613 an edict was published which set aside certain areas of Anatolia for Morisco settlement, including Adana, Tarsus, and Kars – zones that had only recently come under Ottoman control.[80] Refugees also headed for Egypt and Syria, lands with which *mudéjar* and Morisco merchants and craftsmen had maintained ties for centuries. The proliferation of the *nāsib* "al-Andalusī" and "al-Maghribī al-Andalusī" attests to this immigration, although it seems that Spanish Muslims quickly intermarried with local families, and disappeared as a distinct community.[81] The overwhelming majority, however, went to the western Ottoman provinces.

Ifrīqiya was not only the point of disembarkation for the exiled Moriscos; it was also a long-standing destination for Andalusī refugees. Since the twelfth century, Iberian Muslims fleeing the Christian advance had settled here, including leading families amongst the religio-cultural elite. These had been welcomed by the Ḥafṣid princes, for whom they had helped to develop a political ideology and literary culture that legitimized Ḥafṣid rule and Ifrīqiyan distinctiveness.[82] In the seventeenth century, Morisco refugees were protected both by the local Ottoman governor, ʿUthmān Dey, and Muḥammad Abū'l-Ghayz "Siti Bulgaiz" – a wealthy and well-connected ʾ*ālim*, who assisted the refugees both materially, in the form of provisions, and communally, by helping them establish mosques and charitable networks and to maintain a separate community hierarchy.[83]

(1643–1715), apparently revealed a network of hundreds of crypto-Muslims and Jews scattered across the kingdom, who were indistinguishable in manner and appearance from the French. See A. Berthier, "Nouveaux documents," pp. 26–27.

[79] For post-expulsion Morisco solidarity, see L. Bernabé Pons, "Notas sobre la cohesión." Apparently, few Moriscos reached the Americas. From 1501 Muslims and Jews were forbidden from going to the Americas, a ban that was broadened to include slaves in the decades that followed. Prior to 1700 there were only twenty-seven cases of Moriscos being brought up before the Inquisition in all of the Indies. See R. Qamber, "Inquisition Proceedings," pp. 29 and 41. Nevertheless, a copy of the *Brevario sunni* can be found among the Inquisition documents in Mexico City. (Archivo General de la Nación, Mexico, Ramo Inquisición vol. 1528, expediente 1, ff. 1–109; thanks to Robin Vose for this reference.) However, it seems the recent fashion among Latinos to "discover" a purportedly crypto-Muslim heritage has much to do with modern politics of identity and little or nothing to do with history.

[80] A. Temimi, "La politique ottoman," p. 167.

[81] See A. Abdel-Rahim, "Al-Moriscos Settlement."

[82] See R. Rouighi, *The Making of a Mediterranean Emirate*, chapter 6, "Emirism and the Writing of History," pp. 148–72.

[83] See M. de Epalza Ferre, "Sidi Bulgaiz."

Such support was completely in keeping with the Ottoman policy of ethno-religious fragmentation, and when tensions between local Muslims and "Andalusīs" came to a head in 1613, the Sultan Aḥmād I (1603–17) issued an order to both the *Beylerbey* ʿUthmān and the chief *qāḍī* of Tunis, reiterating his support for the Morisco community.[84] Here, as elsewhere, the refugee community was heavily involved both in craft industries and in maritime commerce; they were particularly useful and influential as intermediaries in Muslim–Christian trade. As war broke out with Algeria in mid-century, Morisco irregulars under Mustafá de Cárdenas, the "alcaide de los Andalusíes," formed an important part of Tunis's forces.[85]

Moriscos also arrived in numbers in the Maghrib, at a time that coincided with the decadence and decline of the Saʿdī dynasty, which was facing attacks both from the Ottomans and Spain. Here, there were two major zones of settlement. Most Moriscos joined an established expatriate community at Tetuan (Tiṭwān), where they ultimately proved incapable of resisting local forces and were eventually assimilated. Relations with indigenous Muslims – who referred to the newcomers as "Christians of Castile" – were strained and often violent. Andalusīs, however, were no pushovers; they gained renown as warriors, and many carved out their own place in the Islamic Maghrib.[86] The proverbially tough Moriscos of Hornachos set up at Salé, from where they initially served the Saʿdī *sharīf*, Zaydān (1608–27), as soldiers, fighting against the rebellious tribes on the Eastern slopes of the Atlas and in the sub-Sahara.[87] From 1627, however, they endeavored to establish themselves as a politically autonomous republic, and carried out a *jihād* of piratical attacks of legendary fierceness on Christian shipping from their base on the coast.[88] By the late seventeenth century the Moriscos had disappeared as a distinct community in Morocco, although they exercised a lasting cultural influence.[89]

Although some Moriscos clearly dreamed of returning home in the context of an Islamic *reconquista*, and a few braved death to return illegally to their homeland, others, as Molina showed in his letter to Jerónimo de

[84] For the decree, see A. Temimi, "Politique ottoman," p. 169.
[85] J. D. Latham, "Mustafa de Cardenas."
[86] See for example, M. García-Arenal, "Vidas ejemplares."
[87] For their service to the Saʿdīs, see L. Bernabé Pons, "Las emigraciones moriscas," pp. 75–77. On Hornachos, see L. P. Harvey, *Muslims in Spain*, pp. 369–77, and J.-P. Molénat, "Hornachos fin XV$^{e}$-début XVI$^{e}$ siècles."
[88] For the brutality of the exiles towards the Spanish, see L. Bernabé Pons, "Las emigraciones moriscas," p. 84.
[89] See M. Razūq, "Observaciones," and M. García-Arenal, "Los Andalusíes en el ejército saʿdī."

Loaysa, took solace in a new messianism inspired by Islamic notions of the Hidden Imamate conflated with prophecies attributed to St. Isadore of Seville.[90] But the vast majority undoubtedly felt powerless and regretful in the face of historical forces that were absolutely beyond their control. Hence, on March 30, 1611, the exile, Antonio de Abila, wrote to his "dear and loyal friend," Sebastián Redondo of Arévalo, recounting the Expulsion and his travels through France where, along with "twenty and five thousand men from the Kingdom of Aragon and two thousand Castilians," he was loaded on a ship for Tunis at Agde. Antonio lamented the fate of the innocent women and children suffering on account of the exile, and assured his friend that unlike the dissimulating Granadans, he and the "Moors" were great and genuine devotees of Mary – *La Birxen Ssantisima del Rrosario* – although he is not clearly explicit regarding his own religious orientation, or whether Mary was seen as the prophetess of the Qur'ān, the Mother of an incarnate God, or something in-between.[91] Be that as it may, facing the prospect of permanent exile from his homeland, he bade his friend, and a long list of others, farewell: "I kiss your hands one thousand times ... May God preserve [you all] from the enemies of the Holy Catholic faith and guide me in His holy service ..." – the words of an infidel, perhaps, but hardly an enemy.[92]

[90] M. García-Arenal, *Messianism and Puritanical Reform*, p. 296.

[91] Mary, the mother of Jesus, is also esteemed by Muslims; indeed, she is the only female figure mentioned by name in the Qur'ān, and has a *sūra* ("chapter") devoted to her. Indeed, Antonio does not mention belief in the Trinity, or Jesus's identity as God incarnate – two doctrines that distinguished Christianity from Islam.

[92] S. de Tapia, "Los moriscos de Castilla," pp. 194–95.

*Part 2*

# Living in sin

## Islamicate society under Latin dominion

As the foregoing chapters have shown, Islam and Muslim communities were features of Latin Christendom from the mid eleventh century through to and beyond the end of the Middle Ages. And whereas the experience of each Muslim community varied from region to region, and was related to the particular circumstances of the kingdom or principality within which each existed, many commonalities and constants can be observed. These derive, in part, from the internal characteristics of both Christian and Islamicate society and culture, each of which manifests an ambiguous but undeniable coherence, and from the fact that the repertoire of relationships that both bound and divided Muslims and Christians was remarkably consistent across the breadth of Latin Christendom. That said, the arc of experience of these various communities was not identical, nor was their durability: for some, Latin occupation ended rapidly, others were expelled or absorbed soon after the turn of the fourteenth century, and still others survived into the age of the Reformation and the establishment of a contested, vernacular Christian Europe. While to a degree, the fortunes of these Muslim communities were related to the internal evolution of Christendom and Islam, their experiences do not map consistently onto the supposed development of an increasingly more reactionary Christianity or a progressively more rigid Islam.

If over these centuries Latin Christendom was indeed transformed into a "persecuting society," this was evidently neither a necessary nor a sufficient cause for the oppression or marginalization of Muslims. The various communities throve and atrophied, were cultivated or suppressed, and opened up or retrenched, in manners that were neither constant nor consistent with a narrative of inevitable exclusion. Nevertheless, the rationale or chronologies of their oppression does not correspond to that of the other non-Christian and dissenting communities of the Latin West: whether Jews, pagans, heretics, homosexuals, or lepers. And, in any event, factors contributing to the repression or accommodation of out-groups were strongly determined by local circumstances.[1] Thus, scholarly discussion that focuses on "toleration" as an underlying source of social relations between ethno-religious groups in the Middle Ages is not only built on anachronistic concepts, but mistakes a symptom for a cause.[2]

Both in medieval Christendom and the contemporary *dār al-Islām*, religious affiliation was the primary means of social, legal, and cultural differentiation. Language and nation, which came to define ethnicity in the modern world, did not function either practically or formally as primary poles of communal identity.[3] Both the vernaculars and the confessional languages (Arabic, Hebrew, Latin, and Greek) were used and esteemed by members of all of the various religious communities. And, whereas *natio* (birth, or origin) was recognized as a source of custom, its

[1] See, generally, C. Ames, *Righteous Persecution*; R. Chazan, *The Jews of Medieval Western Christendom*; J. Elukin, *Living Together, Living Apart*; D. Iogna-Prat, *Order and Exclusion*; J. Muldoon, *Popes, Lawyers and Infidels*; R. I. Moore, *The Formation of a Persecuting Society*, and "Heresy, Repression, and Social Change"; D. Nirenberg, *Communities of Violence*; and J. Tolan, *Saracens*. Edward Said's *Orientalism* is provocative, but its view of the Middle Ages is anachronistic and rather misconceived. Recent scholarship by medievalists has offered a more nuanced and accurate view of the cultural and intellectual perception of Islam in the Middle Ages, without rejecting Said's vocabulary. See, for example, S. Akbari, *Idols in the East*; D. Blanks, "Western Views of Islam"; and J. Moran Cruz, "Popular Attitudes."

[2] In Spain, the debate was framed in the mid twentieth century by Américo Castro, who established the term *convivencia* ("convivial living together") to describe Muslim–Christian–Jewish social relations and cultural development in medieval Iberia, and by Claudio Sánchez-Albornoz, who countered with the idea of the "eternal Spaniard," whose character developed in reaction to "foreign" elements. Each school of interpretation attracted its disciples, and the debate soon stagnated between two entrenched positions, each of which bears the strong imprint of (rival) modern political sensibilities. See A. Castro, *España en su historia*, and C. Sánchez-Albornoz, *España: un enigma histórico*. T. F. Glick perceptively outlines the contours and problems of the controversy in *Islamic and Christian Spain*, "Cultural Contact and the Polemic of Spanish Historiography," pp. 6–14. Some recent works that argue in terms of "toleration" or *convivencia*, or respond to these paradigms, include S. Boissellier, "Une tolérance chrétienne"; G. Cipollone, "From Intolerance to Tolerance"; M. Launay, "Tolérance et dialogue"; M. Menocal, *The Ornament of the World*; C. Nederman, "Introduction," and *World of Difference*; A. Novikoff, "Between Tolerance and Intolerance"; J. Ray, "Beyond Tolerance"; S. M. Soifer, "Beyond Convivencia"; R. Szpiech, "Convivencia Wars"; A. Testas, "Models of Cultural Exclusion"; K. Wolf, "*Convivencia* in Medieval Spain"; and P. Zagorin, *How the Idea*. Both the introduction and the various chapters in C. Robinson and L. Rouhi, *Under the Influence*, are useful. I. Bejczy ("*Tolerantia*," p. 371) argues against the grain, that *tolerantia*, even applied to Jews and Muslims, did indeed come to be seen as virtuous in itself by the mid thirteenth century, but his evidence in this regard is rather circumstantial and not compelling on the whole. More convincing is S. B. Schwartz in *All Can be Saved*, here using evidence from popular culture to argue for a current of ground-up tolerance developing in early modern Iberia.

[3] Bartlett characterizes "customs, language and law" as the "primary badges of ethnicity" in the Middle Ages. See R. Bartlett, *The Making of Europe*, p. 197. For a discussion of the concepts of *natio, gens*, and *populus* in the early Middle Ages, see P. Geary, "Ethnic Identity."

use to define "national" communities was limited for the most part to the fantastical Biblical and Virgilian genealogies that the cleric-historians of the Latinate kingdoms felt obliged to preface the "national" chronicles they were crafting from the twelfth century onwards with. These represented a literary conceit, rather more than a symptom of an incipient, genetically-defined proto-nationalism.[4] And while there was certainly a sense of "race" in both Christendom and Islam – which is to say, that a conjunction of physical appearance and geographical provenance influenced personal characteristics and attributes, the idea of race (*genus*, or *gens*) was vague and inchoate at this time.[5] Although, in artistic representations in the Middle Ages dark skin color was sometimes used to signal moral deficiency or inferiority, the physical reality of skin color was usually held to be an arbitrary external characteristic that had little or no relation to character or, even, provenance. Thus, whether he or she was black, white or dark (*llaurus*, *olivetastrus*), a Christian was first and foremost a Christian, and a Muslim, even if he or she was a native (e.g. *naturell*) of a Christian realm, was first and foremost a *Saracenus*.[6] It was this categorization that most dramatically shaped his or her experience and determined his or her possibilities and limitations.

Nevertheless, it would be misleading to characterize these social groups merely as "religious communities." While religious affiliation was the foundation of the legal status, social position, and economic potential of their constituents, religion itself was only one factor in shaping their identity; it was not necessarily always first and foremost in these Muslims' own conception of who they were as individuals and communities. The term "Islamicate," coined by Hodgson to "refer not directly to the religion, Islam, itself, but to the social and cultural complex historically associated with Islam and the Muslims, both among Muslims themselves and even

[4] For a critique of the manufactured genealogies of European nations, see P. Geary, *The Myth of Nations*.

[5] This is not to say that race was not conceptualized in either Christian or Islamic society – both drew on Hellenistic thought and their own particular innovations. The standard work on race in Islam is B. Lewis, *Race and Color in Islam*, but see also the discussion in R. Zorgati, *Pluralism in the Middle Ages*, p. 130. For an example of contemporary Christian attitudes, see Fulcher of Chartres' comments regarding the purported eugenics project of the Fāṭimids, p. 159, n. 96. This reflects a particular and problematic Frankish conception of *gens*. See A. V. Murray, "Ethnic Identity." As P. Geary notes for the early Middle Ages, concepts of ethnicity cannot be ascribed causes of conflict at this time ("Ethnic Identity," p. 12).

[6] In the Crown of Aragon a distinction was made between foreign Muslims and those "Muslims who were born in this kingdom" ("moros qui en aquest regne son nats"). See R. Salicrú i Lluch, "Mudéjares y cristianos en el comercio," p. 298. For Portugal, see M. F. Lopes de Barros, *Tempos e espaços*, pp. 155–6. Christians were not sensitive to the internal divisions of Islam, such as the difference between Shīʿī and Sunnī Muslims.

when found among non-Muslims," is a more appropriate descriptor.[7] Theirs were cultures and communities that were strongly informed by religion, but not necessarily "religious" *per se.* Moreover, Muslims interacted with each other and with the Christians and Jews who were their neighbors, enemies, and collaborators in a broad range of contexts, in many of which religion and religious identity were quite simply not at issue. Members of each of these faiths interacted as tenants and landlords, customers and vendors, debtors and creditors, locals and foreigners, and superiors and subordinates, and often shared interests and agendas with individuals and collectives of other religions that put them in direct and violent conflict with their own co-religionists. Nor were these groups monolithic – for example, Christian society might have been more wealthy and powerful than *mudéjar* society, but there were many *mudéjares* who were more wealthy and powerful than most Christians; many of these identified with Christians on the basis of status or profession, as much as they did with fellow Muslims. Identity was situational rather than absolute.

This is all the more remarkable because on a formal, ideological level the mere existence of Muslim communities under Christian rule should have been awkward, if not untenable, for members of both faiths. Unlike the case of the Jews, there was no direct Biblical rationale or classical precedent that Christians might draw on that advocated for the existence of an Islamic minority in Christian lands.[8] For Muslims, on the other hand, for them to live under the authority of the Infidel was directly contrary to the spirit, if not the letter, of divine revelation and law. This is to say, both *mudéjares* and their Christians hosts were all, by virtue of their *convivencia,* living in sin. Hence, the second part of this book looks at Muslim and Christian perceptions of the situation of the Islamicate minority in the Latin West, the formal structures which framed Muslim minority society, and Muslim–Christian–Jewish interaction, in terms of the Augustinian ternary of transgression: thought, word, and deed – which is to say ideology, administration, and practice.

[7] M. Hodgson, *The Venture of Islam,* vol. I, p. 59.

[8] Because of their role in the Revelation of St. John (e.g. Revelation 3:9), for example, Jews had a place in Christian eschatology that precluded their total elimination. On the other hand, Jews' purported role in the crucifixion of Jesus and their refusal to acknowledge him as Messiah (seen increasingly by Christian polemicists after 1300 as "stubborn" or deliberate) made them a particular target for Christian aggression and anxieties. Hence, laws relating to segregation tended to explicitly target Jews, while sometimes ignoring Muslims. See the discussion in Zorgati, *Pluralism in the Middle Ages,* p. 163.

# 8 Thought

## Images and ideals of Muslims and Islamicate society in Latin Christendom

On a theological and ideological level the situation of the Muslim minorities was incompatible with both Islam and Christianity. On a formal level, Islam is more accommodating of confessional diversity, at least within Islam, and in terms of non-Muslim communities. The latter, or at least "the People of the Book" (*ahl al-kitāb*) – those who shared in the same Prophetic tradition out of which Islam emerged, or belonged to revealed religions which Muslims were prepared to regard as well-intentioned – were eligible for inclusion within the pact of *dhimma*, or "protection," under which communities that remained loyal to the Muslim regime and recognized the superior jurisdiction of Islamic law could live as semi-autonomous and subordinate confessional communities. Islamic ideology, however, was founded and elaborated in an age of exuberant success and expansion, and therefore did not contemplate the possibility that Muslims might one day live under the authority of Latin Christian princes.

### Islam and Muslim minorities

He who lives in Christian lands does not care for what is sacred. He turns from guarding the faith because he mingles in the feasts of the infidels and openly worships images. With respect to their women, his wife is a slave to the Christian and she subjects herself to him every day. If it should happen that misfortune befall her husband, she must seek refuge in the house of her lord and request favors from him, and his power prevails. O what evil fortune! (Abū Zayd ʿAbd al-Raḥman al-Ṣinhājī "Ibn Miqlāsh," *fatwa* (Oran, late fourteenth century)[1])

[1] Adapted from K. Miller, *Guardians of Islam*, pp. 34–35; cf. G. Wiegers, *Islamic Literature*, p. 83, n. 58. The prospect of the dishonor and abuse of women struck a deep chord (see below, p. 474). Poets tried to use it to shame authorities into action against the Franks in the twelfth century, and it figures in the sixteenth-century *qaṣīda* (ode) sent by the Moriscos to the Ottomans. See H. Dajani-Shakeel, "Jihād in Twelfth-Century Arabic Poetry," pp. 100–01; and P. S. van Koningsveld and G. Wiegers, "An Appeal," p. 171.

Muslim jurists were first explicitly confronted with this situation in ninth-century Spain, when the rebel and alleged apostate, ʿUmar b. Ḥafṣūn, set up a briefly independent principality in the Andalusī province of Reiyo (Málaga).[2] At issue was whether it was licit for Muslims to live under his rule. The response of the *fuqahāʾ* was a resounding negative: the *ahl al-dajn* ("people who remained") were living in sin. The reason for this was that the notion of a just, Islamic society hinged on the authority of properly invested Islamic magistrates, and it was held to be impossible for a non-Muslim prince to legitimately appoint a *qāḍī*. Moreover, the obligation of emigration was also supported by the example of the Prophet and His Companions, whose striking out (*hijra*) from pagan Mecca in September 622 CE to establish a new Islamic community at Yathrib (Medina) marked the end of the age of Ignorance (*jahiliyya*) and the beginning of the era of Islam.[3] But the episode of Ibn Ḥafṣūn was a local affair, and by 916 CE, thirty-six years after his rebellion was launched, and seventeen years after he had allegedly abjured his faith, the aged rebel was reconciled with the Umayyad *amīr*, ʿAbd al-Rahmān III (912–961), and the issue became moot.[4]

## *Questions of legitimacy*

Only a century or so later, however, in the face of apparently durable Latin conquests in al-Andalus, Sicily, Southern Italy, Ifrīqiya, the Mediterranean islands, and the Holy Land, Islamic jurisprudents were forced to confront the fact that significant numbers of Muslims had not only been conquered by Latin princes, but had made the deliberate choice to remain in their homes under Christian rule. The overwhelming consensus was that all Muslims should abandon Christian lands and emigrate to Muslim-ruled territories, but there was a broad range of interpretation and some dissent. Part of this was due to differences among the orthodox schools of legal interpretation. The Mālikī *madhhab*, which exercised a near-monopoly in the western Mediterranean, was adamant on the issue of obligatory emigration, whereas Ḥanafī *muftūn* regarded it as permissible to remain in formerly Muslim territory, and the Ḥanbalī and Shāfiʿī schools permitted Muslims to live wherever they could practice their religion. In other words, the world was not perceived as a clear binary consisting of the *dār al-Islām*

[2] Jurists in al-Andalus had been forced to face this problem even earlier; for example a *fatwa* of 801 was promulgated regarding a Muslim who was residing in Barcelona. See P. S. van Koningsveld and G. Wiegers, "The Islamic Statute," p. 49.

[3] According to tradition, previous to this, early Muslims had left the persecutory environment of Mecca for exile in Ethiopia.

[4] For Ibn Ḥafṣūn, see M. Acien Almansa, *Entre el feudalismo*.

and the *dār al-ḥarb* ("the abode of struggle") or the *dār al-kufr* ("abode of polytheism"). The lines between these and the intermediary *dār al-ahd* ("abode of truce") were subject to interpretation. For some, *mudéjar* communities continued to form part of the *dār al-Islām*, while for others even Christian protectorates and vassal states, like Naṣrid Granada, were to be excluded. Some held that Muslims should not even travel beyond the boundaries of the Islamic world; others, that obeying the laws of Infidel kings presented no moral dilemma, so long as they did not intrude on intra-Muslim affairs. Moreover, many *fuqahāʾ* were sensitive to the difficulties and dilemmas that migration posed for ordinary Muslims whose livelihoods and families were rooted in conquered territory. A few went so far as to enjoin Muslims to remain in occupied territories as a moral imperative to reinforce Islam there, and perhaps convert Christians.[5] The Andalusī *muftī* Muḥammad b. Rabī (d. 1319), who served as *faqīh* and *wazīr* of Málaga, wrote a lengthy *fatwa* on the topic of *mudéjares* in which he proposed a typology that corresponded to a gradation of sinfulness. The most sinful were those Muslims who lived dispersed among the Infidel, the next, those who lived as a minority but in closed enclaves, and finally, those who remained a numerical minority under Christian rule and still controlled the countryside and towns in which they lived.[6]

The notion of the legitimacy of *mudéjar* magistrates was a major concern, for if they were indeed illegitimate and their legal decisions and opinions void, Muslims in these lands would not be living under Islamic law. Al-Wanshirīsī, the great fifteenth-century jurist of Fez, who was adamant on the absolute duty of emigration, represented the consensus in the Muslim West. In fact, he went so far as to characterize any Muslim's willingness to live under Christian rule as "manifest proof of his vile and base spirit," and *mudéjares* as "almost Infidels."[7] Al-Mahzūnī of Ifrīqiya declared that Sunnī Muslims should not even correspond with *quḍāt* from Aragonese Jerba, the inhabitants of which he considered "heretics" (*ahl al-ahwāʾ*).[8] His countryman Ibn ʿArafa (d. 1401) agreed, calling into question the declarations of "magistrates of the *ahl al-dajn*, like the magistrates of the Muslims of Valencia, Tortosa and Pantelleria" on the

[5] See, generally, P. S. van Koningsveld and G. Wiegers, "The Islamic Statute"; K. Miller, "Muslim Minorities"; K. Abou el Fadl, "Islamic law and Muslim Minorities"; J.-P. Molénat, "Le problème"; M. Fierro, "La emigración." For jurists who did not emphasize emigration, see for example, K. Miller, "Muslim Minorities," p. 273.

[6] See P. S. van Koningsveld and G. Wiegers, "The Islamic Statute," esp. p. 34.

[7] K. Miller, "Muslim Minorities," p. 258, and L. G. Jones, "Retratos de la emigración," 28. For a thorough study and reappraisal of al-Wanshirīsī's *fatwa*, and its legacy, see J. N. Hendrickson, "The Islamic Obligation."

[8] V. Lagardère, *Histoire et société*, pp. 31 {I: 73} and 33 {I: 88}.

grounds that they were likely not "appointed by someone who is entitled to do so."[9] The uncompromising insistence of the Maghribī *'ulamā'* may have been rooted in Mālikī doctrine, but it was also undoubtedly inspired by the reactionary attitudes of the many members of the religious elite who had fled the Christian advance and had chosen piety over place, risking the dangers of exile over the complacency of occupation. Some North African *muftūn* were exiles themselves.

But their position also reflected the realities of *mudéjar* administration. In the first one hundred and fifty years or so of Christian domination, most Muslim communities enjoyed near-total autonomy as regards the internal workings of their *aljamas*. At this time, those who functioned as magistrates and legists did so with the broad recognition of their own communities. Hence, in the early twelfth century, al-Imām al-Māzarī of Mahdia could qualify the Norman-appointed chief *qāḍī* of Sicily as legitimate on the basis of a dubious Muslim authority being better than none, yet prohibited Muslims in the *dār al-Islām* from traveling to or trading with the island, which was a matter of choice.[10] However, by the mid thirteenth century the increasing integration of *mudéjares* in Latin administrations and economies pushed Christian rulers to take an increasingly active role in managing *aljamas* and appointing Muslim officials. It was becoming less and less common for local Muslims to have a say in the appointment of local *alcadis*. Hence, those *mudéjares* who received commissions as local magistrates were successful not as a consequence of their education, erudition, or popular recognition, but rather on the basis of how wealthy they were, how much influence they carried in Christian circles, and how the kings perceived they would serve royal interests. Seen in that light, except when they were appointed with the assent of the community, a *mudéjar alcaydus*, *alcait*, or *çaualquem* was not a *qāḍī* in any real sense.[11] This was the opinion of the early fifteenth-century *muftī* of Fez, Abū Muḥammad 'Abd Allāh al-'Abdūsī, for whom the legitimacy of a *mudéjar qāḍī* rested precisely on his free and uncoerced election by the local *aljama*.[12] Even in these cases, however, it was Christian authorities who ultimately determined how justice would be administered.[13] In

[9] Adapted from P. S. van Koningsveld and G. Wiegers, "The Islamic Statute," esp. p. 51.

[10] See S. Davis-Secord, "Muslims in Norman Sicily." Al-Māzarī, however, was hardly conciliatory towards the Christian conquerors, whom he considered "Infidels, nothing less than impurity." See H. Idris, *La Berbérie orientale*, vol. II, p. 666.

[11] For *mudéjar* administration, see pp. 390ff, below.

[12] A. Echevarría Arsuaga, "De cadí a alcalde mayor (II)," p. 276.

[13] For example, in 1361, the *infant* Ferran, acting in his capacity as Governor-General of the Kingdom of Aragon, absolved the Muslims of Daroca (with the exception of a certain Iacem de Moncayo) of almost all criminal liability as individuals and as an *aljama* in exchange for a donation of 1,400 *solidi*. See R. Esteban Abad, *Estudio histórico-político*, pp. 396–8 {20}.

effect, it was virtually impossible for a subject Muslim magistrate to meet the criteria set by more rigorous jurists for a legitimate *qāḍī*.[14]

Needless to say, *mudéjares* and their officials did not necessarily share the opinions of these foreign jurists. It is clear that *mudéjares* were willing to concede a working legitimacy to the religious figures in their communities, whether these were local officials appointed or ratified by Christian kings, or the independent *muftūn* and mystics who circulated throughout the Muslim communities of Latin Christendom and occasionally competed with and challenged the authority of Christian-appointed magistrates. In any event, even in the Islamic world, there was a long-standing distrust of magistrates appointed by Muslim rulers, who were viewed as potentially corrupted by the conflict of interest that receiving a stipend from the *sulṭān* inevitably entailed. Thus, some highly esteemed *ʿulamāʾ* living in the Islamic world were known to have refused official commissions on principle.[15] Moreover, the Christian occupation did not provoke a mass emigration of pious Muslims. Some – like al-Mawwāq, a noted *muftī* of Granada – chose to stay behind in 1492, even though he himself had advocated emigration.[16] In fact, as early as the twelfth century some Mālikī jurists, including Ibn al-Ḥājj al-Tujībī, the Almoravids' chief *qāḍī* of Córdoba, took a more realistic and conciliatory position, ceding *mudéjares* the right to live under Christian rule on the grounds that they did so under what amounted to duress.[17] Indeed, it came to be recognized that duress, necessity, and the public welfare of Muslims could justify not only living under Christian rule, but even false conversion.[18] When questioned by a Morisco on pilgrimage in the early sixteenth century, the Shāfiʿī *muftī* of Cairo (Miṣr) opined that Islam in Aragon was robust enough that *mudéjares* there should be under no obligation to leave.[19]

[14] See R. El Hour, "The Andalusian Qāḍī," pp. 67–69 and 72. According to authorities including Ibn Khaldūn, in order to function properly, a *qāḍī* had to fulfill a specific range of roles, including acting as the judge should the prince (*sulṭān*) commit a crime – something that was clearly impossible under Christian rule. Similarly, under Christian rule the *qāḍī*'s potential for independent political action (as demonstrated by their establishment of popular "republics" in the twelfth century) was lost. See, for example, above, pp. 30, 57, 95, and 140.

[15] See, for example, M. Marín, "Biographical Dictionaries," p. 255. There was good reason for this, as even in Islamic lands the judiciary was in constant danger of losing whatever independence it had, as a consequence of patronage. See M. I. Calero Secall, "Rulers and Qāḍīs."

[16] Miller notes him as chief-*qāḍī* of Granada, but the *fatwa* edited by de la Granja refers to him as a *muftī*. See K. Miller, "Muslim Minorities," p. 277; F. de la Granja, "Condena de Boabdil," p. 159; and, above, p. 210.

[17] P. S. van Koningsveld and G. Wiegers, "The Islamic Statute," p. 49.

[18] K. Abou el Fadl, "Islamic Law and Muslim Minorities," p. 179.

[19] *Ibid.*, pp. 159–60; for a translation and study of the document, see G. Wiegers, "Islam in Spain."

Representatives of the other three schools were also asked their opinions; they were more circumspect, however, and spoke of the option of "postponing" emigration.[20]

Van Koningsveld and Wiegers attribute the varying opinions of jurists vis-à-vis the legitimacy of *mudéjar* society as reflecting the particular historical contexts within which they made their pronouncements. In times of war and threat they tended to adopt more rigid positions regarding the unacceptability of the *mudéjar* situation, whereas in times of peace or truce, they tended to be more pragmatic.[21] Distance was probably also a factor; the moderate chief *quḍāt* of Cairo were under no risk of invasion themselves, whereas the reactionary al-Wanshirīsī lived in a land under direct threat of military attack by Christians. The *fatāwa* of North African *ʿulamāʾ* were undoubtedly aimed as much at a domestic audience as at subject Muslims abroad – intended to fortify the formers' resolve to resist the Christians and to dissuade them from yielding or collaborating. Correspondingly, some expatriate *ʿulamāʾ*, and even at least one *mudéjar*, attributed the Christian conquest to divine punishment for the Andalusīs' lack of piety and rigor.[22]

Other writers, on the other hand – both foreigners and subject Muslims – praised the steadfastness of *mudéjares* and Moriscos. Such declarations, whether positive or negative, cannot be taken as mere observations or detached from the rhetorical objectives and particular socio-religious agendas of their authors. Contrary to the opinion of expatriate *mudéjar* jurists, foreign *ʿulamāʾ* who spent time as captives in Christian lands tended to express a more sympathetic and charitable view of the Islam of subject Muslims, both in terms of their intentions and its practice. Such was the impression garnered by an anonymous jurist from Fez who was captured at sea off Anatolia in 1407 and redeemed by the *faqīh* of Muslim Lleida in Catalonia, that he dedicated twelve couplets of his verse account to praising the faith of "the many [*mudéjares*] who are very good, confessing the unity of God and are governed and guided by the laws of the Apostle . . ."[23]

[20] P. S. van Koningsveld and G. Wiegers, "The Islamic Statute," p. 41.

[21] *Ibid.*, pp. 54–55.

[22] This was the opinion, for example, of the late fifteenth-century Almerian *faqīh*, ʿAbd Allāh b. Ṣabbāh al-Aṣbaḥī. F. Franco Sánchez, "Los mudéjares," p. 380. He traveled the breadth of the Islamic Mediterranean and his *riḥla* (*c.* 1460), the *Minsāb al-akhbār*, was meant to inspire subject Muslims by the greatness of the Islamic world – a popular genre among late-period *mudéjares* and Moriscos (see M. García-Arenal, "*Shurafā* in the Last Years of al-Andalus," pp. 171–65).

[23] M. de Epalza Ferre, "Dos textos," pp. 106–07 (Arabic: p. 63).

The culmination of the conciliatory trend can be seen in sixteenth- and seventeeth-century *fatāwa*, including the 1504 dictum of al-Maghrāwī of Oran, himself a former *mudéjar*.[24] This *muftī* advocated Moriscos' full outward compliance with Christian social and religious practices – an exhortation to *taqiyya* that Morisco religious leaders would wholeheartedly embrace.[25]

However, in the final analysis, the opinions of foreign jurists would have little effect on decisions that *mudéjares* made, or the way they lived their lives, and *mudéjar* and Morisco religious authorities adopted, out of necessity, a realist position. For example, in the thirteenth-century Ebro valley in Aragon – the locus of numerous and well-established *mudéjar* communities known for their stability and integration – sermons emphasized forbearance and resoluteness in the face of Christian domination and the pressures of acculturation.[26] Such a moderate stance served not only to protect the community from the worst excesses of integration, but also to preserve the preachers' own relevance and influence. Calling down fire and brimstone on ordinary Muslims striving to cope with Infidel domination would have likely served to alienate the native *ʿulamāʾ* from their own constituents – particularly the wealthiest of these, who owed their position and enjoyed influence and authority specifically to their close relationship with royal, ecclesiastical, and local Christian authorities. Indeed, these same individuals were often *also* local religious authorities. From the outside, however, an *ʿālim* like Ibn Miqlash would have viewed such quietism as shameful and humiliating acquiescence. Nevertheless, it was an effective strategy for survival, as evidenced by the fact that learned Islam could continue to flourish for centuries in Castile, Aragon, and Navarre in the absence of the aristocratic patronage that sustained high culture within the *dār al-Islām*. This is reflected not only in the observations of travelers and the writings of figures such as the Mancebo de Arévalo, but in occasional details that emerge in fragments of surviving documentation, such as when in the town of Aranda, in Castile, no fewer than seven local *fuqahā* competed for the privilege of leading the prayers during the holy month of Ramaḍān at the local mosque.

### *Assimilation and resistance*

But calls for dissimulation and advocacy of collaboration would have played into the fears of foreign *ʿulamāʾ*, who saw the contaminating

[24] See D. Stewart, "The Identity of 'the Mufti of Oran.'" [25] See p. 282, above.
[26] This is studied in L. G. Jones, "The Boundaries of Sin." Miller provides a summary of this dimension of Jones's research in K. Miller, *Guardians of Islam*, pp. 144–45.

potential of associating with Christians. In the fourteenth century, the self-exiled Andalusī Ibn Rabīʿ warned Latinate Muslims of the consequences of living under Christian domination: Islam would lose its pride of place over the other religions, *mudéjares* would collaborate with Christians, Islamic norms would be difficult to maintain, Muslim women might marry Christians, and Muslims would imitate Christian dress and language, to end up ultimately as apostates – consequences that did, indeed, come to pass.[27] This was not a dilemma unique to subject Muslims; peninsular Jews, too, had long grappled with threat of acculturation, and rabbinical *responsa* from the twelfth century forward emphatically prohibited Jews from socializing with Christians, or affecting their mores and fashions.[28]

But the acculturating influence of Christian society posed a more explicitly religious threat, albeit indirectly. Although Arabic did not disappear altogether as a written or spoken language among subject Muslims, its decline as a vernacular from the thirteenth century onwards demanded that Islamic "liturgy" and Scripture make accommodations. As early as the late fourteenth century, Andalusī *muftūn* like the Granadan al-Ḥaffār (d. 1408) were voicing concern that the *khuṭba* – the mandatory Friday sermon – was being delivered in Romance rather than Arabic.[29] This would have seemed particularly threatening given that the Romance vernacular was seen specifically as a Christian language, and is referred to in some contemporary documents as "Cristianego."[30] Indeed, in the mid thirteenth century, Ibn ʾAmīra al-Makhzūmī of Valencia saw in the decline of Arabic grammar the decadence of Islamic practice.[31] However, by this time a process of linguistic adaptation which was getting under way would see a whole range of material, including the Qurʾān, *ḥadīth*, and exegetical and folkloric texts translated into Romance or *aljamiado*, either under the

[27] P. S. van Koningsveld and G. Wiegers, "The Islamic Statute," p. 28; cf. B. Catlos, *The Victors and the Vanquished*, pp. 407–8.

[28] These prohibitions, of course, were largely ignored. Even more than with the *mudéjares*, Jewish religious leaders were closely involved with Christian institutions and centers of power. By way of example, the brother of the great thirteenth-century Rabbi Moshe ben Nachman (Nachmanides) served Jaume I as bailiff-general, to whom he was known as "Beneviste ça Porta." For the profound implication of the Jewish elite in the administration of the Crown of Aragon, see for example, E. Klein, *Jews, Christian Society, and Royal Power*, pp. 192–96.

[29] See K. Miller, *Guardians of Islam*, pp. 141–42.

[30] See, for example, ACA, C., reg. 2063, f. 156r–v (November 15, 1382).

[31] For his lament, see F. N. Velázquez Basanta, "Ibn ʿAmira, Abu L-Mutarrif," p. 113. For language anxiety, see the discussion in G. Wiegers, "Language and Identity," pp. 309ff. Such complaints, however, must be taken with a grain of salt. By this time, there were many "normative" Muslim peoples living in the *dār al-Islām* who did not speak Arabic, including Berbers, Turks, and Circassian Mamlukes.

instigation of Christian missionaries, or as a response to the needs of the faithful. Despite the banning and destruction of Arabic texts that was ordered in the sixteenth century, over seventy *aljamiado* editions of the Qur'ān survive, many surviving fortuitously, having been plastered into the walls of Morisco homes.[32]

Still more threatening and insidious was the effect on *mudéjar*-Morisco religiosity provoked by the shared socio-cultural environment of late medieval and early modern Iberia and, in particular, the obligation to attend Christian sermons and mass. Not only were subject Muslims swept up by the same millenary and Messianic trends as their Abrahamic cousins, but they came to be directly influenced by new trends in Christian religious thought, such as the *Devotio Moderna*, as expressed by writers like Thomas à Kempis, Marianism, the Protestantism of Luther, and the moral sentiments expressed in secular literature, such as *La Celestina*.[33] The atmosphere of confrontation with Christianity also influenced *mudéjar* devotional practices; the emphasis, for example, on performing *tasliyya*, the ritual blessing on Muḥammad, mirrored the increasing emphasis in Christian devotion on the figures of Jesus and Mary, while the emergence of the hagiographical genre in twelfth- and thirteenth-century al-Andalus was a response to Latin veneration of saints.[34] What is the reader to make, for example, of the tale in *Cántiga* 167, when a *mudéjar* woman of Borja prays to the Virgin to raise her dead son?[35] Is this a parable of Christian superiority, or a reflection of genuine quotidian worship and syncretism? Indeed, *mudéjares* in Iberia increasingly turned

[32] See, for example, I. Hofman Vannus, "Historias religiosas," and "El manuscrito mudéjar-morisco"; C. López Morillas, "El Córan romanceado," and "Textos aljamiados"; and J. Vernet Ginés, "La exégesis musulamana." Some copies of the Qur'ān were redacted in Arabic with an intralinear translation; see, for example, M. J. Hermosilla Llisteri, "Una traducción aljamiada."

[33] See G. Wiegers, "The Persistence of Mudejar Islam?" and L. P. Harvey, "El Mancebo de Arévalo and his Treatises," esp. pp. 259ff, for the relation to Christian practice. The work of à Kempis was a major source of el Mancebo's Morisco theology, but this is only one example of the influence of Christian mysticism on late medieval Islamic thought among subject Muslims. See G. Wiegers, "Jean de Roquetaillade's Prophecies," p. 229, and throughout; and above, p. 282, n. 4, for Morisco *alumbradismo*. A modern parallel can be seen in modern Britain, where some Muslims are being drawn to anti-evolutionary or creationist ideologies as a consequence of contact with Evangelical Christian culture. See, for example, S. Jones, "Islam, Charles Darwin and the Denial of Science," The *Daily Telegraph*, December 3, 2011 [online].

[34] L. G. Jones, "The Boundaries of Sin," pp. 442 and 420–22 for Christian influence; also her discussion of the "personification of religion," pp. 361–63. See, also, the prayers edited in X. Casassas Canals, *Los siete alhaicales*. For hagiography, see M. I. Fierro Bello, "Christian Success," pp. 174–78.

[35] See R. Zaid, "The Muslim/Mudejar," p. 149, and J. Guerrero Lovillo, *Las Cántigas*, p. 143 {183}.

towards Marianism – a fact that was not lost on Christian polemicists, like Oldradus de Ponte, who consequently judged Muslims to be superior in God's eyes to Jews.[36] On the other hand, in some areas, either out of a sense of mutual sympathy or common resistance, some Moriscos allegedly began to take part in Jewish rituals with their *converso* neighbors.[37]

Active armed resistance to Christian rule and proselytization of Christians (and Jews) on the part of *mudéjares* are not matters that concerned the *fuqahā'* of the *dār al-Islām*, although the personal and political rebellions such as that of al-Azrāq in thirteenth-century Valencia or Abū 'l-Qāsim in twelfth-century Sicily were enthusiastically portrayed in religious terms by their participants. On the other hand, on at least one occasion, a *muftī* acknowledged the possible benefits of reaching out religiously to Christians, not so much with the aim of converting them, but of establishing a relationship of mutual respect.[38] This, however, was risky, as it could be interpreted as proselytizing, a crime that, as Yuçe de la Vaçía, the *alfaquí* of Molina (in Sigüenza), found out in 1495, would be punished by Christian authorities in an exemplary manner.[39] Perhaps advocating quietism merely reflected a realist approach to these matters – except in times of exceptional confidence or exceptional duress, *mudéjares* were little disposed to armed revolt, and Muslims abroad would have understood that missionizing among Christians was a capital crime. In any event, *jihād* was considered a "collective duty" (*farḍ kifāya*) incumbent only on communities of believers when there was some reasonable chance of success. Even in the Holy Land at the height of the Frankish

36 See D. Nirenberg, *Communities*, pp. 191–95, for the curious "Disputation of Talavera" which was provoked by the conversion of a female Muslim slave to Judaism in the early 1500s. The issue on trial was whether Jews or Muslims were closer to Christ and, therefore, if such conversion was licit. The Muslim side was represented by two Christian clergymen, who argued their case based on the Islamic recognition of Mary and Jesus as Prophets. Such a conversion of a Muslim concubine by a Jewish master, which here sparked such an extraordinary reaction, was in fact a fairly common occurrence in the peninsula. For *mudéjar* and Morisco Marianism, see R. Barkaï, "Une invocation musulmane," pp. 264–65, and, generally, A. G. Remensnyder, "Beyond Muslim and Christian," and M. de Epalza Ferre, *Jésus otage*, chapter 5, "Jésus et sa mere Marie," pp. 170–99. For Morisco popular veneration of Jesus, see, for example, I. Hofman Vannus, "La figura de Jesús."

37 E. Cantera Montenegros, "Las comunidades mudéjares," pp. 164–65.

38 For resistance, see pp. 71ff, and 125ff. For reaching out, see K. Miller, "Muslim Minorities," p. 276.

39 This curious case is recorded in a unique *aljamiado* transcription of an Inquisition trial. Yuçe was convicted of tempting converted Muslims back to Islam by welcoming them into the mosque. He was convicted, and sentenced to be paraded through the town of Molina in humiliation, sitting on an ass, to pay a fine of fifty golden *florines*, and to suffer perpetual exile from the kingdom of Castile. See M. García-Arenal and Ana Labarta, "Algunos fragmentos."

threat, religious thinkers were divided on the nature of *jihād* and the virtues of its handmaiden, martyrdom. While the latter was certainly praiseworthy, it was not generally seen as a fate to be deliberately sought.[40]

Thus, *jihād*, to the extent it was practiced by subject Muslims, would be the "greater struggle" (*al-jihād al-akbar*) – internalized and aimed at improving oneself, rather than the "lesser struggle" (*al-jihād al-asghar*) of conquest and the imposition of the divine moral order in the world.[41] Such was the consensus among both *mudéjar* and Andalusī *ʿulamāʾ* – the cultivation of Islamic virtue was seen as a mode of resistance.[42] Nevertheless, *Al-Tafrī ʿ*, a tenth-century Mālikī treatise on *jihād* that was not only popular in al-Andalus but was translated into *aljamiado* and circulated widely among Spanish *mudéjares* and Moriscos, focused on the violent, external alternative.[43] However, it emphasized *jihād* as a means of maintaining the moral propriety of the Muslim community, and thus resonated with both the aspirations and the practical capabilities of *mudéjar* and Morisco religious leaders. The struggle was also tied to emigration; and to the extent *mudéjares* were exhorted to fight the Christians, it was specified that this should be waged from the Islamic world, rather than in the form of rebellion from within.[44] Nevertheless, it is not unlikely that subject Muslims would have conceived of any undertakings which either reinforced their own community or undermined that of the Christians, whether this was redeeming slaves, collaborating with raiders and foreign Muslim powers, or engaging in armed rebellion, as part of a larger moral/religious struggle. In this light, it is not surprising that *sabr*, or "forbearance," became a pillar of *mudéjar* religious ideology.[45]

Polemic was another matter. Leaving aside the lively tradition of anti-Christian polemic which throve in the *dār al-Islām*, subject Muslims were obliged to engage in the defense of their faith and the refutation of rivals, on the one hand, because they were occasionally forced to take part in religious disputations with Christians, and on the other, because polemical literature serves to fortify vulnerable minority populations against the

[40] See D. Talmon-Heller, "Muslim Martyrdom."

[41] Miller suggests communal captive redemption was seen by *mudéjares* as a way of performing *jihād*. See K. Miller, *Guardians of Islam*, chapter 5, "Captive Redemption," pp. 151–76. For *jihād*, see R. Firestone, *Jihād*.

[42] K. Miller, *Guardians of Islam*, p. 129; L. G. Jones, "The Boundaries of Sin," pp. 453ff. As seen in chapter 10, however, many *mudéjares* fell far short of the ideal.

[43] See S. Abboud Haggar, "Al-Ǧihād " "Al-Tafrīʾ," "Diffusión," and "*Las leyes moros.*"

[44] See K. Miller, *Guardians of Islam*, p. 129 for the fifteenth-century *mudéjar* preacher ʿAlī al-Barmūnī from Barcelona, who advocated emigration as a precondition for waging war against the Infidel. In contemporary Granada, by contrast, military *jihād* was seen as laudatory. See, for example, O. Herrero Soto, "La arenga," p. 51.

[45] For *sabr*, see L. G. Jones, "The Boundaries of Sin," p. 485.

threat of conversion by attrition.[46] Here, again, the Jews of Christian Iberia provide an obvious parallel case. Subject Muslims had a deep tradition of polemic on which to draw, not the least being the works of the Andalusī polymath Abū Muḥammad ʿAlī b. Ḥazm (d. 1064), whose pioneering work on comparative religion necessarily comprised an indictment of Christianity and Judaism; and the writings of his countryman and contemporary, Abū 'l-Walīd Sulaymān al-Bājī (d. 1081), who famously refuted the proselytizing overtures of the enigmatic "monk of France" towards the *taifa* King of Zaragoza, al-Muqtadir.[47] Under Christian rule, there were few disputations between subject Muslims and Latin authorities of the grandly staged variety that Jews were obliged to take part in from the thirteenth century onwards.[48] Rare exceptions include a debate between a native *ʿālim*, al-Ḥusayn b. Rashīq, and a group of Dominicans, that was apparently sponsored by the then-*infante* Alfonso X of Castile in his newly conquered kingdom of Murcia, around the year 1243, and another between the Qurʾān translator, Juan de Segovia, and an envoy from Naṣrid Granada in 1431.[49]

On the other hand, informal disputations were clearly an uncomfortable and potentially dangerous feature of daily life for Muslims of any rank or station. The imbalance of power between Christians and *mudéjares* obviously precluded the latter from engaging in frank debate; but the pressure to defend their faith, particularly for captives, would have been impossible to resist. Thus, the Tunisian *ʿālim*, Muḥammad al-Qaysī, who spent part of the early fourteenth century as a captive in and around Catalonia, was obliged on occasion to defend Islam in the face of Christian criticism.[50] Not only did he manage to survive the experience among "the gang of Satan," but, once free, set down his Christological

[46] Such was the case of Muḥammad al-Anṣārī al-Andalusī, held captive in Castile, who later wrote a memoir of the debates and disputes he was forced to take part in with members of the court and clergy. See G. Wiegers, "Biographical Elements," p. 500.

[47] See, for example, I. Zilio-Grandi, "Le opere di controvèrsia," and M. de Epalza Ferre, "Notes pour une histoire." Ibn Hazm's work was well known among late medieval Iberian Christians, Muslims, and Jews, who drew on it in fashioning their polemics. See H. Hames, "A Jew amongst Christians and Muslims." For the "monk of France," see A. Cutler, "Who Was the Monk," and D. Dunlop, "A Christian Mission to Muslim Spain."

[48] The two great disputations held in Iberia, the Barcelona disputation of 1263, and the disputation at Tortosa (1413–14), were each convened by individuals (Jaume I and pseudo-Benedict XIII, respectively) who took a determinedly neutral approach to the matter of Islam and Muslims in their lands. For a survey of the disputations, see H. Maccoby, *Judaism on Trial*.

[49] The text is edited and translated in F. de la Granja, "Una polémica religiosa," and D. Cabanelas Rodríguz, *Juan de Segovia*, pp. 100–07.

[50] The text is edited and translated in M. Asín Palacios, "La polémica anti-cristiana"; see also, P. S. van Koningsveld and G. Wiegers, "The Polemical Works."

and Trinitarian arguments in the form of memoir, which was duly copied and circulated among subject Muslims in the succeeding centuries.[51] Such works represent the literary tip of what must have been a thriving, if discreet, oral tradition – one that existed alongside the polemical subterfuge of high-status Moriscos, who couched their refutations and polemics in pseudo-Christian apocrypha such as the "lead books" of Sacramonte, or the spurious *Gospel of Barnabas*.[52] Although dangerous and, by necessity, discrete, anti-Christian and anti-Jewish polemics were also composed by *mudéjares* from the 1200s onwards, these works, many of which were recopied in subsequent centuries and translated into *aljamiado*, were undoubtedly intended to buttress *mudéjares*' own faith with counter-arguments against Christianity, rather than to be used in debate against actual Christians.[53]

Over the course of six centuries of Latin domination, both Islamic perceptions of the subject Muslim communities and those communities' engagement with Islam as a religion varied. However, this was not the simple consequence of isolation from the Islamic world, or of cultural crystallization, as has been suggested; nor can the larger narrative be characterized in terms of decline.[54] Recent research has established that the world of Iberian Muslims (the only major indigenous Muslim minority communities remaining after the early fourteenth century) was not completely cut off from the *dār al-Islām*: not intellectually, not culturally, not socially, not economically, and not religiously.[55] For example, in 1392, three *mudéjares*, each from separate towns in Aragon (Daroca, Calatayud, and Borja) journeyed to Granada to consult the *muftī*, al-Ḥaffār, regarding various matters concerning both Islamic doctrine and Christian–Muslim relations.[56] They continued to read the latest Islamic religious treatises, some of which were translated into *aljamiado*.[57] In sum, *mudéjares* and Moriscos responded to their religious predicament by engaging with Islamic thought in creative ways and in response to trends

[51] P. S. van Koningsveld and G. Wiegers, "The Polemical Works," p. 177. In a late version in *aljamiado*, al-Qaysī deflects a monk's arguments regarding the nature of Jesus and the nature of the Trinity – a work clearly intended to provide Moriscos with arguments to resist pressure to convert. See D. Cardaillac, "'Alcayçi et le moine de Lérida.'"

[52] See G. Wiegers, "The Persistence of Mudejar Islam?" and "El contenido."

[53] See G. Wiegers, "Biographical Elements," for an overview.

[54] T. F. Glick and O. Pi Sunyer's seminal article "Acculturation as an Explanatory Concept," remains important, but presents what is, perhaps, an exaggerated rigidity in the final centuries of the Islamic presence in Iberia.

[55] The Tatars of the northeast also survived (see above, pp. 241ff, but as a community, they were far less numerous than the Muslims of the Iberian peninsula.

[56] See Wiegers, *Islamic Literature*, p. 83, n. 58.

[57] Works authored as late as the fifteenth century were translated by *mudéjares* and Moriscos in Spain. See, for example, S. Abboud-Haggar, "Ibn al-Ǧazarī."

in the wider Islamic world in order both to preserve their religious identity in the face of infidel domination and maintain their own sense of validity as communities. Nor was their response simply one of retrenchment. Muslims were profoundly enmeshed with Christian (and Jewish) society, both on the socio-economic plane and on the intellectual and cultural level. Therefore, their reactions drew not only on Islamic ideology and religious concepts, but appropriated or adapted elements of Christian and Jewish thought (notably early modern Messianism) and religious practice, both as a consequence of existing within a common socio-cultural environment, and in response to specific challenges posed by innovations developed by their theological adversaries. In sum, the position of these communities cannot be fully understood without reference to Christian approaches to Islam and Muslims.

## Christianity, Islam, and Muslims

> The second step shows the error of Muhammad's law. Whence all the old dregs that the Devil had disseminated were collected and renewed by him in Muhammad and his law. For he denied ... the Trinity ... he taught that Christ was a plain creature ... he said the Jews did not kill Christ .... he denied all sacraments of the Church ... he said [that] he traveled to God and God laid his hands on him ... that the Holy Ghost was a creature ... that the ultimate human beatitude is eating, having intercourse and precious clothes and watered gardens ... he taught having several wives was permitted ... [and] that sodomy was allowed with both men and women ... (Riccoldo da Monte di Croce, *Disputatio contra Saracenos et Alchoranum* (*c.* 1299)[58])

Christian approaches to Islam and Muslims in the Middle Ages were mostly oriented towards – and a response to – the existence of a dynamic and, therefore, threatening, foreign Islam. A consistent and well-informed approach to Islam as a religion did not coalesce until the early thirteenth century, and for the theologians of the great centers of Christian thought in the north of France, Islam remained a foreign and abstract phenomenon. Nevertheless, the development of anti-Muslim thought would have an effect on subject Muslim communities, if not as a cause for the decline of their status and condition, then at least by providing a conceptual vocabulary for legitimizing their exclusion that could be drawn on by those who had an interest in marginalizing Muslims. And yet, Islam presented to medieval Christianity a culture that was clearly intellectually and technologically more sophisticated, not to mention wealthier, more

[58] "Against the Muslims and the *Qur'ān*" was first published in Seville in 1500 as *Reprobatio Alchoranis* ("The Refutation of the *Qur'ān*"); it is quoted here from A. Echevarría Arsuaga, *The Fortress of Faith*, pp. 165–6, n. 78.

expansive, and one that embodied an impressive religious coherence and popular piety. The conflicted attitude to Islam is dramatically evident in the life of the Florentine Dominican, Riccoldo da Monte di Croce, an Arabist who travelled to Baghdad and studied the Qur'ān in that "garden of delights . . . watered by the rivers of Paradise" and was left "stupefied, to ponder God's judgment concerning the government of the world . . . What could be the cause of such massacre and such degradation of the Christian people? Of so much worldly prosperity for the perfidious Saracen people?"[59] For this polemicist, and for his antecedents and successors, Islam represented either a polytheistic aberration or the sum of all Christian heresies (with a few novelties thrown in for good measure).[60] But the way they chose to present it depended less on the information they had at their disposal than their rhetorical objectives and their own anxieties – in fact, it is clear that polemicists regularly and deliberately misrepresented Islam and Muslim beliefs in the defense of Christian doctrine, and represented Islam in contradictory, although inevitably pejorative, terms. The Florentine Dominican would have known better than to believe that Islam advocated sodomy, but still he could not resist alleging it.[61]

## Islam and Muslims in the Christian imagination

This trend can be seen from the earliest Christian ideological engagements with Islam, whether by the likes of the Syrian Christian functionary, John of Damascus (676–749) in the eastern Mediterranean, or the eighth-century Mozarab chroniclers of Spain in the west, or the author of the apocryphal ninth-century *Risālat al-Kinaī* at the ʿAbbāsid court. Latin thinkers from Baetica to Britain portrayed Islam as a Christian heresy, pagan idolatry, or a herald of the Apocalypse, and the Prophet Muhammad as a fraud, the Antichrist, a false prophet, magician, hypocrite, and letch.[62] That said, a figure like Gregory VII (1073–85) could

59 "Epistolae v de perditione Acconis" ("The fifth letter, on the loss of Acre"; 1291), quoted in J. V. Tolan, *Saracens*, p. xiii.

60 Incredibly, polytheism was among the charges leveled against Muslims. See, for example, *ibid.*, p. 125.

61 For Muslims as heretics, see for example, M. Frassetto, "The Image of the Saracen." To be fair, Riccoldo may have been using "sodomy" in its broadest sense, to refer to any immoral sexual act, or he may have presumed that the Eastern Mediterranean culture of ephebophilia was permitted under Islam (whereas, in fact, it was condemned). In the course of his mission to France in 1612, al-Hajarī debated this very point with his French interpreter. See al-Hajarī, *Kitāb nāṣir al-dīn*, pp. 108–13.

62 See, generally, K. Armstrong, *Muhammad*; R. Barkaï, *Cristianos y Musulmanes*; T. Burman, *Religious Polemic*; N. Daniel, *Islam and the West*; A. Echevarría Arsuaga, *The Fortress of Faith*; B. Kedar, *Crusade and Mission*; P. O'Brien, *European Perceptions*, esp.

concede in a candid moment that Christians and Muslims worshiped the same God.[63] Indeed, it was this realization that made religious dialogue and synthesis among Muslims and Christians possible.[64] Yet, even after the launch of the Crusade, when Latin polemicists had gained first-hand insights as to the practice and tenets of Islam, they continued to present baffling mistruths, such as that "Mahummet" was, in fact, a huge gem-encrusted cast-silver idol encountered by Tancred in the Temple of Solomon as Jerusalem fell, or the notion that Muslims imagined God as a sphere of solid "hammer-beaten metal."[65] Latin ideologues, aspiringly celibate if not misogynous or closeted, found Islam's approach to sexuality particularly offensive, and much of the personal vitriol against the Prophet of Islam was centered on the permissibility of polygamy, the practice of endogamy, the sensuous Qur'ānic invocations of the afterlife, and the awkward aspects of Muḥammad's relationship with Zaynab, wife of Zayn (Islam's "Bathsheba moment").[66] Muslim women, too, were at times imagined as wanton, hyper-sexual beings – a quite remarkable perception given the formal cloistering, both socially (for example, the forbidding of unchaperoned travel and inter-gender socializing) and personally (with the prevalence of the head-cover or veil) that Muslim women were commonly subject to as a consequence both of Islamic law and Western Asian and North African folk customs.[67]

By the thirteenth century the stereotypes of an effete Eastern culture that were beginning to coalesce intersected with those of the "Saracen" either as a barbarous savage or a chivalric noble. Nowhere are the various modes of imagining Muslims more clear than in Christian Iberia, which

chapter 2: "The Quest for Subjective Eurocentrism," pp. 19–44, and chapter 3: "The Discovery of Islamic Superiority (1095–1453)," pp. 71–89; P. Sénac, *L'Image de l'autre*; M. Tarayre, "L'image de Mahomet"; J. V. Tolan, *Saracens*; and J. V. Tolan, G. Veinstein, and H. Laurens, *Europe and the Islamic World*, as well as the works cited in n.1, above.

63 D. Freidenreich, "Muslims in Western Canon Law," p. 42; see Gregory's letter to the Ḥammādid prince of Ifrīqiya, al-Nāṣir b. 'Alennās (1062–88) in C. Courtois, "Gregoire VII," p. 100.

64 This was particularly the case among the mystically inclined, the Sufis, and the Kabbalists, who were less constrained by dogma, as well as in the realm of symbols and signifiers. See, for example, the discussion in M. R. Menocal, *Shards of Love*, "Love and Mercy," pp. 57–90; C. Robinson, "Trees of Love, Trees of Knowledge," and *Imag(in)ing Passions*, as well as the works of H. Hames, including "A Seal within a Seal," "From Calabria," and *Like Angels on Jacob's Ladder*.

65 Raoul de Caen, *Gesta Tancredi* ("The Deeds of Tancred"), quoted in J. V. Tolan, *Saracens*, p. 119. See also C. Hansen, "Manuel I Comnenus," p. 64; as well as J. V. Tolan, *Saracens*, pp. 109ff and 119, for the lies of Christian polemicists.

66 See, for example, the eloquent expression of these attitudes cited in J. M. Perceval Verde, "Asco y asquesidad," pp. 33–37.

67 M. Kahf, *Western Representations*, p. 36. This is somewhat ironic, given Muslims' popular perception of Frankish women as "loose." See C. Hillenbrand, *The Crusades*, pp. 347–49.

not only was defining itself in terms of its interaction with foreign Islam, but which had significant domestic Muslim populations, both free and enslaved. Here, both in the *romances* and chronicles, Muslim men are presented in each of these modes, but most strikingly as a feminized, passive "sheep" fit for conquest, while those who are praised in the ballads of the frontier are those who rise above the humiliation of defeat, by displacing the same volatile masculine characteristics idealized in the broadly militarized "frontier" society of Castile and the Crown of Aragon.[68] Muslim women, too, were portrayed variably as conniving resisters, whose duplicity vindicated a sexualized and violent domination, as precious, virginal objects to be appropriated, or as actively prepared for and desiring the violent seduction of conquest.[69] In short, independent of whatever evidence was a hand, Islam came to be imagined as everything Latin thinkers imagined Christianity was not, or what they fancied Muslims might be.[70]

Nevertheless, the vitriolic and willfully distorting portrayals of Islam and Muslims must be understood as manifestations of the polemic genre, the expectations it generated, and the audience it was aimed at, just as the wistful, romanticized portrayal of Muslims suited other genres and agendas. They do not necessarily reflect the candid opinions of their authors or audience. Hence, St. Francis of Assisi expressed respect for the broad-based popular piety of the Islamic world, and Francesc Eiximenis was forced to recognize *mudéjares*' hygiene and express his admiration for the authority of their religious magistrates.[71]

These literary approaches represent the various ways in which Latin Christians grappled with a multiplicity of anxieties, questions, and issues raised by the existence of Islam and Muslims in their midst, and the potent but often ambiguous communal hierarchy that characterized their societies.

68 See L. Mirrer, *Women, Jews, and Muslims*, chapter 3, "Muslim Men in the Ballad," pp. 47–65. The Turnerian concept of "frontier" is useful, but has enjoyed a rather too durable and enthusiastic popularity as applied to the historiography of ethnic and communal relations in medieval Iberia (and subsequently, Sicily, Hungary, and across medieval Europe). C. J. Bishko's seminal article, "The Castilian as Plainsman," is worth noting. Father Burns used the paradigm of the frontier as an analytical and organizational principal for his tremendous and exhaustive work on Muslim–Christian relations in post-conquest Valencia (e.g. in *The Crusader Kingdom*). Historians are now taking stock, and realizing that it is a rather nebulous concept. Frontiers can be found just about anywhere, depending on how one defines them, or where one regards the "center."

69 See L. Mirrer, *Women, Jews, and Muslims*, chapter 1, "Of Muslim Princesses and Deceived Young Muslim Women," pp. 17–30, and p. 51 (for sexual predation of Muslim women). See also S. Kinoshita, "The Politics of Courtly Love."

70 J. V. Tolan, *Saracens*, p. 109.

71 J. Puig Montada, "Francesc Eiximinis," pp. 1575–6. These were clearly not false archetypes set up to shame Christians into better behavior. For Eiximenis's views on Muslims, see D. J. Viera, "The Treatment of the Jew and the Moor," pp. 207–13.

Beginning in the mid eleventh century a new trend can be observed in Latin Christian approaches to Islam with the elaboration of Canon Law, the coalescence of the notion of universal papal sovereignty, Latin engagement with Arabo-Islamic high culture and learning, Latin colonization of formerly Islamic lands, and the articulation of an ideology of exclusion – none of which can be separated from the monastic reform movement centered at Cluny. In the 1140s Peter the Venerable, Abbot of Cluny, journeyed to Christian Toledo – a center for translation activities carried out by Muslims, Jews, and Christians, and commissioned the English monk, Robert of Ketton, to produce a translation of the Qur'ān into Latin. This translation, once derided by scholars as "inaccurate" has been revealed to be a remarkably sensitive and sophisticated exercise of *tafsīr*, or exegesis – an attempt to render the Qur'ān not literally, but as it was understood as a living text by contemporary Iberian Muslims.[72] As the title, *The Law of the False Prophet Muḥammad* (*Lex Mahumet pseudoprophete*), shows, however, this was a political and polemical text, the aim of which was to contribute to the intellectual arsenal being assembled against Islam – one that included translations of Islamic law, *ḥadīth*, and Arabic folklore also commissioned by Peter the Venerable.[73] By the thirteenth century, indexed, pocket translations of the Qur'ān were circulating, apparently intended for missionaries and preachers, who needed to have easy and rapid access to the various "errors" it contained.[74]

As early as the twelfth century, thanks in part to the efforts of converted Jews like the Aragonese Petrus Alfonsi, Christian polemical approaches towards Jews were also deployed against Muslims. Hence, the (likely) *converso* Alfonso de Spina's vitriolic *Fortress of the Faith* (*Fortalitium fidei*), which first appeared in 1458, took on not only Jews, but Muslims and "heretics." At this time, new and improved Latin and vernacular editions of the Qur'ān were appearing, including Juan de Segovia's version, which was translated to Castilian by the Segovian *faqīh* 'Īsā b. Jābir (Yça Gidelli). In this case the *mudéjar*'s and the missionary's commitment to producing the most accurate result possible would have coincided: the latter to produce an effective tool for disputation, and the former to provide the Scripture to those subject Muslims who no longer spoke or read Arabic.[75]

72 See T. Burman, *Reading the Qur'ān*.

73 For Cluny's role in shaping anti-Islamic polemic, see D. Iogna-Prat, "The Creation of a Christian Armory."

74 See T. Burman, *Reading the Qur'ān*, chapter 3, "Polemic, Philology and Scholastic Reading," pp. 60–87.

75 Late fifteenth-century missionaries not only endeavored to use the Qur'ān to convert Muslims, but also the same commentaries that were circulating among *mudéjares*. See J. Vernet Ginés, "*Le Tafsir*," p. 420.

Indeed, ʿĪsā's translation seems to have been the basis of an early seventeenth-century version of the Qurʾān produced in Aragonese – one that was certainly meant for Morsicos.[76] In any event, the entire polemical impulse and translation movement involved subject Muslims only peripherally. They may have collaborated on translations, but the polemical thrust of these works was aimed explicitly at foreign Muslims, and implicitly at Latin Christians' own anxieties. They may have colored Christian opinion in the broadest sense, but had little direct effect on policy vis-à-vis *mudéjares*. The same can be said for the increasingly precise and elaborate position on the matter of Islam, Muslims, and *mudéjares* that was developed by the papacy and Canon Lawyers over the course of the thirteenth century – their provisions represented an abstract ideal and had little direct effect on policy.[77]

## Crusade and *Reconquista*

A similar observation can be made regarding the ideologies of Crusade and holy war that developed among Christians from the early eleventh century onwards. Although Islam was the formal object of these movements – Urban II's relief of Byzantium and the oppressed Christian brethren of the East – Crusade developed in response to internal developments of Latin Christian society and cult, as much as to any foreign Muslim threat, real or imagined.[78] It was an amalgamation of pilgrimage, penitential practices, and warfare, that coalesced precisely at a time when Latin Christendom was becoming politically and economically engaged with Byzantium and the Islamic world, while endeavoring to limit violence within Christian society, and that very time the papacy was grasping towards universal, secular sovereignty. While it may be that the Emperor Alexius called for military assistance against the Turks from noblemen in the Latin West, he did not ask them to conquer Jerusalem or the Holy Land on his behalf or anyone else's. Neither Islam nor Muslims provoked the Crusade directly; Islam was neither a necessary nor a sufficient cause for the phenomenon. Clearly, the restoration of a (Latin) Christian Jerusalem was the declared objective of the Crusades, but after the successes and failures of the twelfth century, the movement shifted focus to Byzantium, the pagan northeast, and to domestic heretics and rebels. Islamic Egypt and the western

[76] See C. López-Morillas, "El Córan romanceado."
[77] See, below, p. 372. In contrast to Jews, who were viewed as a religious rivals, Islam tended to be seen as a political rival. See M. D. Bollo-Panadero's reflections on the *Cantigas* in "Heretics and Infidels," p. 169.
[78] See Baldric of Dols' version of Urban II's speech, in E. Peters, *The First Crusade*, p. 31.

Mediterranean remained targets because of their economic value rather than their religious significance.

It may be true that the Crusade ideal encouraged a particularly brutal approach to conquest and an intense, generic hostility towards Muslims, notably among northern European Crusaders, as evidenced by the massacres committed in the course of military campaigns, such as at the siege of Jerusalem (1099) or the sack of Lisbon (1147). But such excesses were exceptional, and they pale before atrocities committed against fellow Christians, as in the course of the Albigensian Crusade in Languedoc during the early 1200s. It was the political power of Islam and its intellectual elite, rather than run-of-the-mill Muslims, that were the targets of Crusaders and ideologues. As is evident from the preceding chapters, subdued Muslims were incorporated as legitimate subjects in Latin regimes with remarkable facility even at the height of the Crusades. This was as true in Iberia, where a deliberate ideology of "Christian Reconquest" developed, as in the rest of the Latin Mediterranean. From as early as the 1050s, holy war provided a conceptual framework for Christian expansion across the Iberian peninsula, and was a powerful tool for maintaining noble and popular commitment to these campaigns; and yet this ideology had incredibly little impact on the either the formal policies adopted towards subject Muslims, or the informal social and economic relations that developed between the victors and the vanquished.[79]

On the domestic front, it was Jews, rather than Muslims, who found themselves the victims of Crusader and popular violence in the Latin West, from the massacres of the Rhineland in 1096 to the attacks of the *Pastoureaux* in upland Aragon in the early 1300s – a zone in which the considerable *mudéjar* population was left unmolested. Non-Latin Christians, whether Greek or "Oriental," often fared little better. In the Latin imagination, they too were practically "infidels," to be deprived of ecclesiastical dignities and political authority, subject to enslavement, and deserving of correction.[80] Small wonder some chose to conspire with local Muslim powers against Frankish invaders. In fact, prior to the particular case of Iberia from the late fourteenth century forward, the ideology of Crusade and holy war had virtually little effect on the formal status or quotidian experience of the Muslims of Latin Christendom, even on those *mudéjares* who were vassals and tenants of the Military Orders. The language of Crusade certainly colored pronouncements on policy, and may have inspired reactionary attitudes and narrowed the consensus in the

[79] See C. Laliena Corbera, "Guerra santa." [80] See C. MacEvitt, *The Crusades.*

Latin West on the character of Muslims and how they should be treated, but, although it was deployed occasionally to justify exclusion or expulsion, such as Charles of Anjou's dissolution of the colony of Lucera, it is far from clear that these ideologies prompted policy decisions, rather than serving as *post hoc* rationalizations for programs undertaken at bottom for practical and material motives.

### *Dreams of conversion*

Likewise, prior to the thirteenth century there was virtually no interest on the part of Latin Christians in converting Muslims. Unlike the case with Jews, the conversion of Muslims would not imply a vindication of Jesus's status as Messiah, nor was the mere existence of Islam construed as an affront and threat to Christianity as was that of Judaism.[81] It was the effervescent and innocent optimism of thirteenth-century clerics and philosophers, electrified by Islamo-Aristotelian rationalism, that led to the misplaced conviction that Muslims and Jews could be convinced of the truth of Christianity (or at least the falsehood of their own faiths) based on evidence found within their own Scriptures. The optimistic and generous-spirited approach of rationalist ideologues can be seen in the polemical genre of the dialogue – from Petrus Alfonsi's *Dialogue against the Jews* (*Dialogus contra judaeos*, 1110) through Ramon Llull's *Book of the Gentile and the Three Wise Men* (*Llibre del gentil e dels tres savis*, 1274–1276), and his *Debate between Raymond the Christian and Hamar the Muslim* (*Disputatio Raymundi Christiani et Hamar Saraceni*). In such works Muslims, Jews, and pagans were led to Christianity by measured and cordial persuasion.[82] As early as 1259 the Dominicans established *studia Arabicum* in Barcelona and Tunis, and soon after in Murcia, Valencia, and other locations, in order to train missionaries to preach and dispute in the Muslims' own language. Although the scale and importance of these academies has been exaggerated by historians, some did function, evidently with the collaboration of *mudéjares*.[83] The object was to convince Muslims (and Jews) of the truth of the Trinity, the Incarnation, and the

81 For Bernard of Clairvaux, advocate of the Military Orders and preacher of the Second Crusade, Muslims were not to be converted, but rather killed, as a necessary step in defending the Holy Land. See J. Kroemer, "Vanquish the Haughty," especially pp. 72–84.

82 For Petrus Alfonsi, see J. V. Tolan, *Petrus Alfonsi*. The best recent study of Llull is H. J. Hames, *The Art of Conversion*. Llull's writing is translated in R. Llull, *Doctor Illuminatus*, and *Ramon Llull: A Contemporary Life*. For the *Disputatio*, see J. Vernet Ginés, "La exégesis musulmana," p. 128. See, generally, R. I. Burns, "Christian–Muslim Confrontation."

83 For a revisionist view of the *studia*, see R. Vose, *Dominicans, Muslims, and Jews*, pp. 104ff.

identity of Christ as Messiah – the three issues seen by Christians as dividing the Abrahamic religions.[84]

However, as these efforts failed to yield results, and the "dream of conversion" soured, missionaries became increasingly frustrated and disillusioned, and came to attribute Muslims' and Jews' failure to convert to willful stubbornness or outright malice. Blinded by their own presumptions and caught in the double bind engendered by their respect for Muslim philosophers' skills and these same philosophers' rejection of Christianity, some Latin thinkers began to imagine that rational Muslims were, in fact, crypto-Christians, who persisted in Islam only from fear of persecution.[85] As a result, coercion came to be seen as an increasingly valid approach to missionizing. Thus, the legendary Dominican Ramon Martí (d. *c.* 1285) produced not only an Arabic lexicon for missionaries but his chauvinistic masterwork, *The Dagger of the Faith ... Against Muslims and Jews* (*Pugio Fidei Raymundi Martini Ordinis Prædicatorum adversus Mauros et Judaeos*), as well as as a widely circulated anti-Muslim polemic. In contrast, Ramon Llull, committed at one time to peaceful conversion, became an advocate of armed Crusade late in life in the face of the failure of the application of reason to bring an end to Islam.[86] Indeed, the fall of Acre in 1291 precipitated a flurry of polemical tracts and essays aimed at recovering the Holy Land from the Muslims (and eradicating the Greeks, who were seen as their collaborators), most of which combined a spirit of *realpolitik* with proclamations regarding the moral virtue of killing Muslims.[87]

Conversion, however, was essentially seen as an effort to expand the sovereignty of Christendom rather than save individual souls; thus, like Crusade, it was aimed almost exclusively at foreign Muslims, and for the most part, at princes who it might be hoped would bring about the conversion of their subjects by fiat. Hence, St. Francis of Assisi's famous, if futile, interview with the Ayyūbid Sultan of Egypt, al-Malik al-Kāmil (1207–37), in 1219 during the course of the ill-fated Fifth Crusade, and the efforts of friars like William of Rubruck, who accompanied Louis IX's (1226–70) Seventh Crusade to Egypt in 1248, and was later sent, again in vain, to Karakorum to preach to the pagan Great Khan of the Mongols, Möngke (1251–59), in 1253. Of course, Latin missionaries were prevented from preaching to common Muslims in the *dār al-Islām* both by Islamic law – which forbade preaching against Islam on pain of death – and by the

[84] See H. J. Hames, *The Art of Conversion*, p. 192.
[85] See J. V. Tolan, "'Saracen Philosophers'".
[86] See R. Harvey, *Raymundus Martini*, and J. Hernando, "De nuevo."
[87] See G. Constable, *et al.*, *William of Adam*, pp. 5–6.

animadversion of their would-be converts. But this did not necessarily stop them. Many, like Bernard of Carbio, who had been sent to Morocco on St. Francis's orders in 1220 as part of a general program to evangelize the Muslims, were martyred; others, like Llull, the Mallorcan tertiary, suffered merely a good stoning and expulsion from Muslim lands. In the 1300s Dominicans and Franciscans dodged Islamic legal prohibitions by obtaining permission to preach to subject Christians and take up posts as bishops, but the chief result of this was that more Christian clergy – like Monte di Croce – became familiar with and impressed by Islam, rather than the reverse.[88]

Aside from some half-hearted missionizing in Lucera and Hungary, the little missionary work that was directed at subject Muslims was carried out in Iberia. In the Crown of Aragon for instance, the Mendicant Orders (and, specifically, Llull) repeatedly obtained royal privileges that obliged Muslims and Jews to give them access to their places of worship and to attend the friars' sermons.[89] Royal law, however, could hardly oblige *mudéjar* congregants to pay attention, and, apart from slaves, and from those free Muslims who converted out of despair at the Christian subjugation of Valencia in the late 1200s, results were negligible.[90] This can be attributed to two factors. First, despite their rhetoric, royal authorities and ecclesiastical corporations were rather ambivalent regarding the conversion of *mudéjares*, who offered clear fiscal and political advantages as subjects and vassals precisely because of their religious identity. Abbots, bishops, and the commanders of Military Orders almost never worked for the conversion of their Muslim charges; quite the contrary, they tended to be stalwart advocates of *mudéjar* rights. The kings were also sensitive to any threat to public order, and on more than one occasion, converted Muslims who had taken up the calling of unofficial evangelists to their erstwhile co-religionists were ordered silenced on pain of prosecution. Nor did such efforts generally have the support of the local lords, who preferred to leave their Muslims in peace, even at the cost of their eternal salvation. In 1398, when Martí "the Ecclesiastic" of Aragon got word that a converted Muslim had arrived in one of the towns he held as seignior and demanded the local *mudéjares* attend his sermons, such "grave commotions, upheavals, scandals, and irreparable damages" resulted at the

88 See A. Jotischky, "The Mendicants as Missionaries."
89 See B. Catlos, *The Victors and the Vanquished*, pp. 250–51; and M. Barceló i Perellós, "'...Per sarraïns a preïcar.'"
90 That said, common converts appear in the historical register rarely, and often only by chance. See for example, the convert Pere Andreu, a farmer in rural Valencia, in M. T. Ferreri Mallol, "Un procés per homicidi," pp. 139–40.

hands of the inhabitants that he ordered local officials henceforth "not to permit or suffer such preachers in the said *morería*."[91]

Second, the friars' dialectical, intellectual approach to missionizing was misplaced; it failed to address the social, economic, and cultural underpinnings of religious identity, factors that were far more prominent in the minds of ordinary believers than the finer points of theology or the supposed corollaries of Scripture. Nor did it address the spiritual or ecstatic aspects of religious devotion.[92] Hence, by the late 1200s conversions had slowed to a trickle.[93] There would be a brief flare of success in the late fourteenth century with the popular Valencian Dominican preacher, Vicent Ferrer (late saint, d. 1419), whose intense charisma, coupled with the broad millenarianism of the post-Plague years and the growing threat of popular Christian violence, is said to have resulted in the conversion of no fewer than 8,000 Muslims in one mission to Granada alone.[94] While this tale may be apocryphal, Ferrer certainly had successes, both among the slaves and lower classes and educated Muslims, such as Hazmet Hannaxa, *alfaquí* of Alfándec (Valencia), who converted in 1413.[95] In a metaphor all too appropriate for his post-Plague times, Ferrer's sermons presented Jews and Muslims as contagions in the body Christian.[96] Hugely influential in royal circles around Latin Europe, it was largely thanks to his personal influence that the dowager-regent of Castile, Catalina of Lancaster, legislated a dramatic reduction of *mudéjares*' rights in her kingdom, including their obligatory quarantine in *morerías*.[97]

91 ACA, C., reg. 2335, f. 76r (9 May 1398). On the other hand Martí's wife, Maria de Luna, supported converts. In 1398, for example, she ordered a mule and herd of sheep returned to her tenant, Assensio Danadón. The animals had reverted to Maria as a consequence of his conversion to Christianity. ACA, C., Reg. 2105, fol. 65r-v (May 20, 1383).

92 In Alfonso X's *Cantigas*, when Muslims (whether foreign or *mudéjar*) are depicted as converting, it is never as a consequence of rational debate, but rather thanks to divine inspiration through the medium of the Virgin. In *Cantiga* 167, for example, a *mudéjar* woman of Borja converts after the Virgin miraculously raises her son from the dead. In another case, a Muslim slave is enveighed on by Mary to convert, and does so. See J. Guerrero Lovilla, *Las Cantigas*, p. 413 and 418 (láms. 183 and 210). The *Cantigas de Santa Maria* is a collection of over 400 parable-like poems written in Galician relating to the Virgin Mary, credited to Alfonso X of Castile, and compiled in an illustrated volume *c.* 1284.

93 For example, from 1355 to 1365 Boswell found only one case of conversion in the Crown of Aragon, and this was under duress. See J. Boswell, *The Royal Treasure*, p. 379. That said, see the comments below, p. 340, regarding low-status converts.

94 For an analysis of Ferrer's proselytizing strategy, see L. G. Jones, "The Boundaries of Sin," pp. 435–41.

95 M. T. Ferrer i Mallol, "Frontera, convivencia y proselitisme," pp. 1595–96.

96 He was not the first to use this metaphor; in 1266, when Clement IV wrote to Jaume I demanding he expel his Muslim subjects from Valencia, the Pope characterized the latter as a "poison" in the body. See P. Santonja, "Arnau de Vilanova," p. 423.

97 See J. K. Stearns, *Infectious Ideas*, chapter 2: "Contagion as Metaphor in Iberian Christian Scholarship," pp. 37–66.

Leaving aside purely religious experiences and group conversions that took place in the immediate aftermath of conquest, such conversions as took place in this period, whether to Christianity, Judaism, or Islam, seem to fall into two broad and not mutually exclusive categories: intellectual and opportunistic. Given the intellectual thrust and scholarly orientation of contemporary missionizing and polemic, it was bound to appeal primarily to the educated. Hence, there was some conversion among the intellectual classes – individuals such as Constantinus Africanus, the Tunisian refugee and convert, who gained fame as a medical authority in eleventh-century Salerno, or "Master John, once a Hagarene, who recently came to the faith of the Christian religion," and who in 1114/15 was at the siege of Mallorca, helping Rusticus of Pisa translate a medical treatise.[98] But, whereas Jewish examples, such as Petrus Alfonsi or Pablo Christiani, are many, there are few reports of subject Muslim religious leaders and scholars converting to Christianity prior to the repression of the 1499 revolt in Granada, and even fewer who went on to become anti-Muslim polemicists.[99] A possible exception is the anonymous author of the eleventh-century *Liber denudationis*, who may have been a converted Andalusi *faqīh*.[100] Until 1500 forced conversion was not considered legal or legitimate either by the Church or princes, and when it was carried out on the independent initiative of Christian clergy or popular mobs, kings reacted with legislation and even allowed converted Muslims to return to their faith.[101]

On the other hand, those Christian thinkers who worked so diligently to undermine Islam were occasionally seduced by the faith they sought to destroy. For example, the Mallorcan Franciscan, Anselm Turmeda

[98] Constantinus's defection was premeditated. He arrived as a merchant in Salerno in the 1060s, where he noted a demand for medical texts. Having returned to Ifrīqiya, he gathered a library and returned three years later, converted and entered Monte Cassino as a monk. Here, he set out to translate and adapt (and claim credit for) a number of key Arabo-Islamic medical texts. See M. R. McVaugh, "Constantine the African." For Master John, see C. Burnett, "Antioch as a Link," p. 7.

[99] Pablo Christiani was a Provençal Jew and student of the Talmud, who after converting joined the Dominican Order and took part in the famous Disputation of 1263 convened by Jaume I in Barcelona alongside Ramon de Penyafort.

[100] The full title of the work is *Liber denudationis sive ostensionis aut pateficiens* (*The Book of Denuding, or Exposing, or "The Discloser"*). The identification of the author is hypothetical; he was more likely a Mozarab than the converted *qāḍī* of Toledo, as has been claimed. See the discussion in T. E. Burman, *Religious Polemic*, pp. 37–62.

[101] See G. Magnier, "The Controversy," pp. 195–96. For annulations of such conversions, see B. Catlos, *The Victors and the Vanquished*, pp. 255–57; L. Torres Balbás, *Algunos aspectos*, p. 29. As R. Zaid ("The Muslim/Mudejar," p. 148) points out, this eschewal of coercion is reflected in works like Alfonso X's *Cantigas*. By the sixteenth century, Spanish clerics were arguing (against Canon Law) that forced baptisms were indeed valid (see above, p. 223, n. 162).

(d. 1423), fled to Tunis, where he abjured and took the name, ʿAbd Allāh al-Tarjumān, going on to become a prolific and popular anti-Christian polemicist. But ʿAbd Allāh was rather exceptional, and aside from a few other missionizing friars for whom the prospect of polygamy proved irresistible, most Christians who converted to Islam did so in the context of captivity in Islamic lands, or were renegades or political refugees, who decided to seek their fortune as Muslims.[102]

The fact that few learned Muslims were drawn to Christianity is likely a consequence, *inter alia*, of their lack of engagement with Christian doctrine, and the deeply ingrained resistance on the part of religious Muslims to aspects of Christian theology and devotion that smacked of anthropomorphism (e.g. the incarnation of God), polytheism (e.g. the cult of saints, the Trinity), and idolatry (e.g. Christian sacred art) – all of which were anathema to the pure monotheism of Islam. There is considerably more evidence of Muslims who converted opportunistically, whether this was from free and deliberate choice, by coercion, or out of desperation. Captives, whether anonymous slaves, or dignitaries, like Leo Africanus, often converted out of resignation, or in the hopes of bettering their position or gaining their freedom, although in the case of low-status slaves this was certainly not guaranteed. Most notably, the slaves of the royal household of Norman Sicily rose to the heights of power and influence, thanks to their thinly veiled false conversion to Christianity.[103]

Some free Muslims converted in an effort to escape criminal justice, a bad marriage, an oppressive family, or other obligations that would be discharged or dismissed as a consequence of their apostasy. Still others, including professional warriors, middling local officials, and ambitious

102 For Anselm Turmeda, see R. Boase, "Autobiography of a Muslim Courtier." Conversions of Christians to Islam emerge occasionally in the records. Those that occurred in Latin lands, among the humbler classes, and as a consequence of contact with *mudéjares*, were more likely to be motivated purely by religious concerns (particularly in view of the risk). See, for example, J.V. Cabalzuelo Pliego, "Cristiano de Alá." This is a distinct phenomenon from that of the opportunistic, politically motivated conversions of renegades and refugees from the Latin West, who included ex-Templars, after the dissolution and persecution of that order, and the many former Christian privateers and statesmen of the Ottoman era, such as the fifteenth-century Bosnian convert Stjepan Hercegović/Hersekli Ahmed Pasha and the Romanian noble Radu cel Frumos/Radu Paha, not to mention the many Christian boys converted as a consequence of the *Devşirme* system. From the 1380s the Ottomans conscripted and forcibly converted young Christian men for service in the army and administration. Quite independently of actual cases of conversion to Islam, the specter of conversion to Islam was deliberately manipulated by Christian authorities. See J. Rodríguez, "Conversion Anxieties." There are occasional reports of Jews living under Latin rule converting to Islam also; in Aragon, this was a capital crime that tended to be punished by judicial enslavement. See, for example, B. Catlos, *The Victors and the Vanquished*, p. 254.

103 See, p. 110, above.

entrepreneurs and professionals, converted in order to enjoy the benefits of full participation and security in Christian society, and full access to political and economic institutions that were restricted formally or in practice to members of the True Faith. Nevertheless, with the exception of the Muslim population of Hungary, which was apparently absorbed *en masse c.* 1300, remarkably few Muslims elsewhere in Latin Christendom abandoned their faith willingly. That is not to say converts were non-existent: we have notices of conversion taking place in Iberia, Sicily, and the Latin East. The twelfth-century land registers of the Abbey of Monreale refers to families split up over the issue of conversion, and the contemporary traveler Ibn Jubayr recounts how he met a former trader from Bône who spent so much time in Christian company, he converted and eventually became a monk.[104] On the other hand, the fantastic accounts of Muslim women who converted, and like medieval Ariadnes, facilitated the liberation of a Christian hero from captivity, are just that – a literary trope and nothing more.[105]

Except as noted above, conversions were rare in Iberia prior to the mid fourteenth century, when opportunities and liberties for *mudéjares* began to decline, but even thereafter they were uncommon.[106] From that point there are occasional notices of members of local *mudéjar* elite families converting, particularly as their clans' fortunes failed. Hence, as the power of the Abenferre family waned in fourteenth-century *mudéjar* Lleida, one of the sons of the *alcaydus*, Ali Abenferre, converted to Christianity, to became "Bernat Cortit."[107] On the one hand, Bernat was rewarded with the promotion to the post of *porterius* of King Pere the Ceremonious – a position he could not have held as a Muslim – but on the other, he was boycotted by his former family and his wife, who abducted his children and refused to pay him money they allegedly owed him.[108] Similarly, two sons of the *Alcalde de los Moros* of Tudela converted, along with their wives,

104 See A. Metcalfe, *The Muslims of Medieval Italy*, p. 222; Ibn Jubayr, *Travels*, p. 323; H. Salvador Martínez, *Alfonso X*, p. 172; B. Kedar, "Multidirectional Conversion," pp. 192–93.

105 M. Kahf, *Western Representations*, p. 33. See, however, the analysis of the story of the captivity of Bohemond of Taranto in G. Beech, "A Norman-Italian Adventurer," pp. 31–33.

106 There were evidently a number of conversions in Navarre in the thirteenth century, and in Zaragoza and the kingdom of Valencia in the fifteenth. However, the conversion of low-status Muslims left little mark in the records, and it is only by chance that we learn of them at all. See, for example, A. Altisent, "Conversión de un Sarraceno aragonès"; M. T. Ferrer i Mallol, "Un procés per homicidi," p. 139 (for the convert Père Andreu).

107 For the Abenferre family, see J. Mutgé i Vives, "Els Bimferre."

108 Also, below, p. 114, and see J. Mutgé i Vives, *L'aljama sarraïna*, pp. 363–6 {184–6} for Bernat's attempts to recover his children and money.

in 1400.[109] As it was, however, there were few incentives and considerable disincentives to conversion. On the one hand, the social, cultural, and economic integrity of subject Muslim societies proved remarkably durable, and they continued to offer considerable economic and social opportunities to their constituents. On the other, the social and cultural exile that conversion would entail represented a tremendous loss for apostates, both in abstract and real terms. Prior social networks were put under stress or sundered, and new ones difficult to establish in the face of popular disdain for "turncoats" and official marginalization as *baptizati.*[110] Furthermore, in the absence of royal orders and dispensations to the contrary, converts to Christianity lost the right to receive their part of family inheritances.[111] It was significant, however, that unlike Islam, which adapted *walāʾ*, the Arabo-Islamic institution of clientage as a vector for assimilating converts, Christian society lacked mechanisms for the social and economic integration of new Christians into established networks of familial patronage. Indeed – as the Morisco experience would confirm – in the Latin West, conversion to Christianity alone was no "passport to citizenship."[112]

## *Ethnic and religious identity*

The whole issue of conversion was complicated by that of ethnic identity, and – towards the sixteenth century – emerging notions of race. On the most informal level, ethno-religious identity shaped individuals' social and cultural habits, from style of dress, to dietary and culinary predilections, and sensibilities regarding sexuality, marriage, family relations, and the place of the individual in the community. It structured one's social and economic relationships both by circumscribing marital opportunities and through informal, but powerful, networks centered on communities of worship. Thus, changing religion implied much more than merely changing habits of worship; it meant leaving all that was familiar both in terms of personal and family relationships, social prestige, community standing, and cultural values. This created very direct problems, in the case, for example, of married couples, where one partner wanted to convert, or which were considered consanguineous by Rome, or in the case of

109 L. Torres Balbás, *Algunos aspectos*, pp. 81–82. 110 See p. 274, above.

111 One of the first peninsular monarchs to respond to this was Portugal's Afonso II, who ruled that Jews and Muslim who converted must be entitled to inherit property from their unconverted parents. See M. F. Lopes de Barros, *Tempos e espaços*, p. 133.

112 Mark Meyerson sketched this out in his talk "Conquest, Kinship, and Conversion."

polygamous families – problems Canon Lawyers and judicial authorities were forced to grapple with from the late eleventh century onwards.[113]

Hence, in 1383, that same Bernat Cortit petitioned the Crown to recognize as legitimate the children he had sired by his four wives before "he departed from Infidel error to the true faith." Once this had been granted, further royal charters were required to allow him to search his former neighborhood, where his erstwhile co-religionists and family members were hiding the children in question.[114] Changing religion, therefore, demanded both social marginalization and cultural conversion – a daunting prospect few were prepared to undertake and which was viewed with a jaundiced eye even by the Christian majority.[115]

As a consequence, the ethno-cultural element of religious identity tended to discourage individual conversion, and reinforced the religious sentiments of Muslim communities as these became increasing marginalized. That said, although the rejection of converted family members is widely attested, it was not universal. As pressure on *mudéjares* increased in the late 1400s and conversions took on an increasingly coercive aspect, their attitudes may have become more flexible. Documentation from Zaragoza, for example, shows that family and personal networks, including intimate relationships, could survive the conversion of one party to Christianity.[116]

The socio-cultural dimension of confessional identity, coupled with the Christians' and Muslims' (and Jews') communal endogamy, reinforced the correlation of religion, social and cultural customs, and birth, led to the development of a malleable and elusive concept of "nation" (*natio*, *nação*, etc., from the Latin for "birth") which conflated ethnicity and religion, and further complicated the subject of conversion.[117] As the case of the Moriscos demonstrates, difficult as cultural conversion may have been, ethnic conversion – particularly as ideas of "race" emerged from the sixteenth century – would prove all but impossible. That said, it is true that in the Middle Ages, ethnicity and race were subordinated to religion in terms of the formal hierarchy of identification. Skin color, thus,

113 See B. Kedar, "Muslim Conversion in Canon Law."

114 J. Mutgé i Vives, *L'aljama sarraïna*, pp. 363–66 {184–86}. For another example of family animosity towards a convert, see above, p. 274.

115 See above, p. 275. It was only when Muslim communities felt they faced imminent extinction, such as in Sicily in the 1200s, Valencia in the last 1300s, or Spain in the final decade of the 1400s, that there were substantial movements of voluntary conversion to Christianity.

116 E. Marín Padilla, "Notas sobre la relación de Moros." The situation was similar in late thirteenth-century Valencia, another scene of large-scale conversion. Here, converts and Muslims continued to socialize and even cohabit. See, for example, M. T. Ferrer i Mallol, "Un procés per homicidi."

117 See, for example, F. Soyer, "'It Is Not Possible,'" p. 88.

remained a simple descriptor through the fifteenth century, and was not generally understood as corresponding to an ethno-racial typology or a hierarchy of racial categories. Rather, color was understood as physiological, and attraction or aversion to a particular skin color reflected esthetic preferences and little more.[118] Muslim captives, for example, were described as black (*negrus*), white (*albus*), or darkish (*laurus*, *olivetastrus*), whether they were European, North African, or Eastern, and were qualified separately by their place of origin or ethnic orientation (*de genere*).[119] Thus, it was understood that Muslims did not constitute "a people" in a generic (or "genetic") sense. Many Latin observers, particularly those in Mediterranean lands, were sensitive to the ethnic varieties of Muslims (*Saraceni*, or less commonly, *Mahometani*), distinguishing, for example, between Berbers (*Mauri*) and Arabs (*Hysmaelitae*, *Hagareni*, *Arabes*, or simply, *Saraceni*).[120] Many artists, even in the context of religiously charged works such as Alfonso X of Castile's thirteenth-century *Cántigas de Santa María*, or his more mundane *Book of Chess, Dice and Games* (*Libro de axedrez, dados e tablas*), not only portrayed Muslims in a realistic, non-caricatured manner, but took pains to illustrate their diverse ethnic origins and cultural orientations.[121] For their part, Crusaders in the East understood the distinction between Bedouin and sedentary Arabs, as well as Arabs and Turks. And finally, from the fourteenth century it was clear to virtually all Europeans that the Turks (and, later, Persians) represented a completely distinct Muslim people.

Through the Middle Ages and beyond, the extent to which Muslim peoples were vilified, objectified, or discriminated against in generic or racialized terms was generally restricted to specific contexts and circumstances characterized by political conflict and socio-cultural anxiety,

118 See D. Goldenberg, *The Curse of Ham*.

119 The term "brown" (*laurus*, *lauro*, *llor*, *olivestratus*) did not mean "mulatto," but referred only to skin tone. It carried no racial connotation (nor did "black," or "white" necessarily). *Genus* and *natio* were used in ethnic rather than racial terms, and could refer to "Arabs," "Barbaries," "Turks," and so on. References to slaves of the "nation of the Blacks" (*nationis negrorum*; as in C. Verlinden, "Esclavage noir," p. 336) also had an ethnic sense, referring to Sub-Saharans.

120 See, for example, the chronicles of Norman Sicily, as analyzed in J. Hysell, "Pacem Portantes Advenerint," pp. 143–44. See above, p. 1, n. 2, for the origin of these terms.

121 See J. Guerrero Lovillo, *Las Cántigas*, and Alfonso X, *Libro del axedrez*. See, for example, Constable's remarks regarding the outcome of the matches illustrated in the *Libro*, in O. R. Constable, "Chess and Courtly Culture," p. 341. According to Zaid, Muslims appear in three scenarios in the *Cántigas*: converting to Christianity, being foiled by the power of Christian spirituality, or as temporarily politically ascendent (in which they are manifestations of God's righteous punishment of Christians). See R. Zaid, "The Muslim/Mudejar," p. 147.

whether this related to the Turks in the period after the conquest of Constantinople in 1453, or "the Moors," in the age of the Barbary Corsairs. Hence, the tendency to conflate all Muslims as dangerous foreigners in post thirteenth-century Valencia, where the political theorist Francesc Eiximenis justified the suppression of Muslim worship and the abrogation of the treaties of surrender on the grounds that the Valencians were "mixed up with all sorts of infidels, from whom derive innumerable dangers to the republic."[122] That said, "Muslim" was evidently used as a common term of derogation among Christians as early as the mid fourteenth century – because of their generic identification as enemies and slaves.[123]

Similarly, the construction by humanists in late fifteenth-century Italy of a generic, pejorative image of "Muslims" was based on their reaction to Ottoman irredentism, and Malory's presentation of the Muslims in the *Morte d'Arthur* (1485) was conditioned by his anxieties regarding the Turks of his own time.[124] But particular strands of ethno-racial theorizing that were related to specific circumstances should not be construed as necessarily reflecting general trends or shifts in the perception of religion and race.[125] As the situation with the Ottomans stabilized and settled down into a functional entente, the rhetoric of race gave way to equivalence and indifference as regards the supposed generic difference between Muslims and Christians.[126] For example, the late-fifteenth century "Pastrana Tapestries" – four massive silk works produced by Flemish artists in commemoration of Afonso V of Portugal's conquests of Asilah (Aṣīla) and Tangiers (Ṭanja) in 1471 – portray the citizens and soldiers of Morocco as visibly indistinct from European Christians.[127] It was not until the mid sixteenth century that Muslims were being consistently represented in terms of racial difference, but even then, these depictions

[122] Francesc Eiximenis, *Regiment de la cosa pública* (*The Ordering of the Republic*; 1383), quoted in J. Hinojosa Montalvo, "Cristianos contra musulmanes," p. 352.

[123] In Cervera, in the Catalan interior, far from any Muslim community, in 1356–57 alone, two Christian women were each fined (40 and 27 *sous*, respectively) for insulting their neighbors (also women), shouting "Whore! Muslim woman (*Sarraynaça*)! Muslim-like!" and "Wicked woman! Muslim woman born of Muslims!" See P. Bertran i Roigé, "Conflictes socials," pp. 59 and 60.

[124] See, for example, N. Bisaha, *Creating East and West*, and P. Goodrich, "Saracens and Islamic Alterity."

[125] The danger lies in presuming that the perspectives of particular authors (for example, Zurara, as presented in J. Blackmore, "Imagining the Moor") were universal.

[126] M. Kahf, *Western Representations*, pp. 60–70. Indeed, as notions of race coalesced, Mediterranean Muslims and Christians coincided in their antipathy towards sub-Saharan "blacks." See p. 277, above.

[127] See the reproductions in M. A. de Bunes Ibarra, *et al.*, *The Invention of Glory*.

were qualified and nuanced by social class – the upper classes were presented as less distinct, less dark, and less distorted, than lower-class Muslims.[128]

Nonetheless, Biblical notions of genealogy, coupled with neo-Aristotelian ideas of race and physiology and framed within the Ptolemaic geographical tradition, encouraged the development of an idea of Muslims as a generically distinct and inferior "race," although until the end of the Middle Ages, such ideas seemed to be largely restricted to members of the educated Latin elite, religious and secular polemicists, and in particular, to those members of these groups who lived in lands where contact with actual Muslims was unlikely.[129] While some learned Latins, such as William of Tyre (d. 1186), Chancellor of the kingdom of Jerusalem, or the Crusader and Archbishop of Toledo, Rodrigo Jiménez de Rada (d. 1247), undertook academic and relatively detached histories of Islam and the Arabs, many chroniclers and authors of Romances, notably the redactors (and many of the illuminators) of the *Song of Roland*, painted Muslims as near-monsters.[130] From the twelfth century on, Muslims were frequently depicted by Latin artists variably as dog-men, demons, monsters, and minions of the Devil.[131] Whereas such depictions – including presentation of skin color, gesture, and features – may have been intended as semiotic cues to indicate otherness and opposition, rather than as realistic representations, readers in the Latin north may not have been equipped or disposed to make such a distinction.[132] Northern Europeans are widely attested as being more

128 M. Kahf, *Western Representations*, p. 92. Nietzsche observed a general tendency in Western cultures for both "southerners" and the lower classes among conquered peoples to be idealized as small, dark, and monstrous. See F. Nietzsche, *On the Genealogy of Morals*. For the racialization of the Moriscos, see J. M. Perceval Verde, "Asco y asquesidad," pp. 39–42.

129 See D. Goldenberg, *The Curse of Ham*, esp. chapters 12 and 14, "The Curse of Ham," and "The New World Order: Humanity by Phsysiognomy," pp. 168–77 and 183–94; as well as S. Epstein, *Purity Lost*, esp. chapters 1 and 5, "The Perception of Difference," and "Human and Angelic Faces," pp. 9–51 and 173–203; and G. Heng, "The Romance of England." As Goldenberg points out, Islamic thought certainly contributed to the emerging European conceptualization of race.

130 See L. Pick, *Conflict and Coexistence*, esp. chapters 1 and 2: "Introduction: Themes and Arguments," and "Conquest and Settlement," pp. 1–70. For the *Song of Roland*, see D. Strickland, *Saracens, Demons, & Jews*, p. 180 {figs. 87 and 88}.

131 D. Strickland, *Saracens, Demons, & Jews*, esp. chapter 5: "Saracens, Tatars, and Other Crusade Fantasies," pp. 157–210, and pp. 221–29.

132 See S. Luchitskaya, "Muslims in Christian Imagery." Hence for example, as Zaid notes: in Alfonso X's *Cantiga* 167, a *mudéjar* woman takes on more "occidentalized" features after she converts to Christianity (R. Zaid, "The Muslim/Mudejar," p. 150; cf. J. Guerrero Lovillo, *Las Cántigas*, p. 413 [lám. 183]).

uncomprehending of, and aggressive and violent towards, Muslims than the Christians who lived among them.[133]

In any event, the supposed natural savagery of Muslims emerges in increasingly graphic terms in the early twelfth-century versions of Urban II's call to the Crusade, and in the racializing strands of thirteenth- and fourteenth-century English romances.[134] The subjection of Africans, and by extension all "dark" peoples, came to be justified on the basis of their supposed origin with Noah's voyeuristic son, Ham, while the contrast between Asians' Semitic (that is to say, "from Shem") pedigree and Europeans' imagined descent from Japheth, provided a rationale for understanding Muslims as physiologically distinct beings.[135] Early on a tradition had developed in Islam, which was echoed in Jewish and Christian thought, wherein Arabs and, by extension, Muslims, were imaged as the descendants of Ishmael (Ismāʿīl).[136]

This medieval "Orientalism," however, was distinct from and of dubious relation to that modern phenomenon described by Edward Said. Moreover, its relationship to formal policy and popular attitudes was tenuous – like the religious polemic described above, it was the fruit of certain genres, with specific aims and audiences. Nevertheless, at times it did indeed filter down to the broader public, as can be seen, for example, in Christians' eschewing Muslim nursemaids in thirteenth-century Perpignan, on the basis that the latters' milk would imbue infants with an "Islamic" character.[137] Undoubtedly, it also provided common Christians with a self-affirming justification on those rare but consequential occasions when they were drawn or driven to commit acts of violence and oppression against their subject Muslim neighbors and acquaintances. On the other hand, the characterization of Muslims as monstrous was

133 The violence of northern European Crusaders became proverbial thanks to episodes such as the Siege of Lisbon, or the massacres of the First Crusade. Usāma b. Munqidh reports being assaulted while praying by a new Frankish arrival, much to the embarrassment of his Templar hosts (see Ibn Munqidh, *The Book of Contemplation*, p. 147). The fifteenth-century Andalusī *mudéjar*, Ibn al-Ṣabbāh, was verbally accosted and interrogated by some knights and a priest speaking Frankish while visiting a church in Constantinople. See F. Franco Sánchez, "Los mudéjares," p. 385. The Netherlandish knight Antonio de Lalaing records how, in passing through Áriza in Aragón in 1501, some of his traveling companions made a point of trashing the town's mosque. See J. L. Corral Lafuente, "El proceso de represión," p. 348.

134 The evolution of the accounts of Urban's speech can be seen in the four versions in E. Peters, *The First Crusade*, pp. 25–36. For England, see G. Heng, "The Romance of England," and F. Quinn, *The Sum of All Heresies*, pp. 48–56. This should be contrasted with the rather more neutral tone of literature produced in Iberia by authors in actual contact with Muslims, including Iberian *cantares de gesta*, and the *romancero*.

135 See D. Goldenberg, *The Curse of Ham*, and S. Akbari, *Idols in the East*.

136 In the Islamic tradition, Ishmael, rather than Isaac, was the favored son of Abraham.

137 R. Winer, *Women, Wealth, and Community*, p. 150.

counter-balanced to some degree by the occasional recognition of their martial vocation and noble virtues in certain chivalric romances.[138] In any event, the flipside of the "othering" of Muslims was the allure that their objectification engendered, as reflected in the currents of Maurophilia, Arabophilia, and Turkophilia that occasionally welled up in Christian society throughout this period, and in the late medieval and early modern penchant for adorning courts with slaves and dignitaries as living exotica, bedecked in brilliant colors, or what was imagined to be Muslim garb.[139]

### *Emulating the Infidel*

Islamic learning, for its part, had exercised a long-standing and a deep fascination on Latin scholars in the West, and as early as the tenth century al-Andalus and its Christian periphery had become a destination for students of science, letters, and philosophy. No less a figure than Gerbert of Aurillac was said to have studied in Córdoba and Seville – experiences that gave rise to the legend that Gerbert, later Pope Sylvester II (999–1003), had studied sorcery in league with the Devil.[140] The transformative impact of Islamic learning on Latin society was as broad and deep, ranging from the introduction of a decimal number system ("Arabic numerals"), to technological innovations, such as the astrolabe, theories and techniques of medicine, magic, engineering, optics, botany, agriculture, the practice of industrial and artisanal crafts, and the adaption of genres and styles of music, literature, costume, and art. Later Christian polemicists were correct when they perceived that what separated Islam, Judaism, and Christianity on a theological level came down to a few specific doctrines relating to the Trinity and the nature of Jesus; and it was thanks to the similarities among the three faiths that philosophical and religious currents could connect philosophers and theologians, despite the formal gulfs between them.[141] Were it not for the fact that such matters largely

[138] See G. Allaire, "Noble Saracen or Muslim Enemy?"; see above, pp. 257, and 330.

[139] See N. Silleras-Fernández, "Nigra sum." This was a phenomenon related to the fashion among fourteenth- and fifteenth-century monarchs to keep menageries of exotic animals as manifestations of their power.

[140] See, for example, M. Zuccato, "Gerbert of Aurillac."

[141] See, for example, A. Samarrai, "Arabs and Latins." There has been a tremendous amount of scholarly work done on the scientific and philosophical influence of the Islamic world on that of Latin Christendom. See, for example, the works on science noted below in n. 143, as well as R. Boase, "Arabic Influences"; M. Cruz Hernández, "Islamic Thought"; and L. García Ballester, "A Marginal Learned Medical World." For art, music, and literature, see below, pp. 490ff. Implicit or explicit in much of this work is a critique of the idea of "Europe" as a coherent, substantive and distinct historical actor; see, for example, C. Giordano, "Interdependent Diversities." The last decade has seen a

transcended the confessional divide, the new Aristotelianism of the Latin Averroists, the Kabbalistic musings of Llull, and the Sufi-tinged mysticism of Joachim di Fiore would have all been impossible.[142]

The process of Latin appropriation and adaptation of Arabo-Islamic science and culture was tied directly to the process of conquest and colonization, and the persistence of Muslim communities under Latin rule.[143] The most striking example of this can be found at Toledo, where a formal enterprise was launched in 1130 under Archbishop Raymond, and continued to the late thirteenth century under such patrons as Rodrigo Jiménez de Rada and King Alfonso X. Careful research has laid to rest the myth that Toledo in Castile was the sole center of translation or node of acculturation in the Latin West, or that these activities reflect a situation of *convivencia* that was unique to Spain. In the Iberian Peninsula there were other centers of translation and transmission, whether formally constituted as "schools" or not – including Tudela, Tarazona, and Murcia, and much later, the Escorial – as well as in France (Montpellier), Sicily (Palermo), Italy (Salerno and Pisa), and the Latin Levant (notably, Antioch).[144]

This scientific enterprise was carried out to a great extent, of course, by the same clergy who were involved in developing anti-Muslim polemic. Robert of Ketton, the Qurʾān translator, had been drawn to Arabic and the Islamic world out of his interest in astrology, and after completing his commission for Peter the Venerable, served as Archdeacon of Pamplona. Arnau de Vilanova, who translated a series of medical treatises in Montpellier in the late 1200s was a fervent anti-Muslim.[145] But science comprised a sort of intellectual "neutral zone," all but devoid of polemic, in which intellectuals of different faiths could collaborate without evoking

reaction by a handful of scholars against what they perceive as a positively biased view of the role of Islam in the development of European science and culture, notably S. Gougenheim and S. Fanjul. Admittedly, certain authors (primarily non-scholars and non-specialists) may have presented a nostalgia-tinged, oversimplified, and anachronistic picture of Muslim–Christian cultural exchange, however, the works of those "occidentalizing" revisionists, following in the spirit of the later work of B. Lewis (e.g. *What Went Wrong?*), are clearly politically motivated (if not polemical) and run against an overwhelming and undeniable body of evidence that supports the positions they set out to deny.

142 See the works of Hames cited above in n. 64; also, T. F. Glick, "Sharing Science."

143 For the appropriation and impact of Arabo-Islamic science and learning in the Latin world, see, for example, H. Daiber, "Islamic Roots"; T. F. Glick, *Islamic and Christian Spain*, especially Part 2: "Movement of Ideas and Techniques," pp. 247–371; J. M. Millás Vallicrosa and T. Carreras y Artau, *Nuevas aportaciones*; G. Saliba, *Islamic Science*; J. Vernet Ginés, *Lo que Europa debe*, and "Un texto árabe"; and M. Watt, *The Influence of Islam.*

144 See, for example, C. Burnett, "Antioch as a Link," and "The Transmission of Arabic Astronomy."

145 See below, p. 433.

their ideological personae.[146] And whereas, previously, the translation effort was imagined as being carried out by Christians with the collaboration of Islamicate Jews, it is clear that subject Muslims were also engaged in this process, and to a far greater degree than is acknowledged in the texts themselves.[147] This was the case not only in Palermo, where the Norman court carried out an explicit program of patronage of Arabic arts and letters practiced by Muslims, but across the Latin Mediterranean, where both free scholars and slaves either collaborated willingly or were pressed into service. Here, translation was sponsored not only by Arabophiles such as Roger II and Frederick II, but even by less personally sympathetic figures, like Charles II.[148] In the Iberian kingdoms many Muslims served as official, royal translators of Arabic (as did Jews), and in the sixteenth century the program to catalog and translate the Arabic holdings of the imperial library was entrusted to Moriscos.

Nor did Latin interest in Islamic science and intellectual culture wane after "Greek" philosophy had been "recovered," and once the Renaissance was underway in the late fifteenth and early sixteenth centuries there was a second wave of translation and appropriation of scientific, medical, and religious texts from the Arabo-Islamic world.[149] As a result of all of this, individual subject Muslims benefited directly from the move to disseminate Islamic culture in the Christian West, while the Muslim community as a whole may have enjoyed a certain buoying of prestige, at least in certain Christian circles, thanks to their association with the intellectual and cultural desiderata of the *dār al-Islām*.

The development of scholarly Orientalism and of new humanistic approaches to Islam from the late sixteenth century onwards merely magnified the ambiguities of Christian views of Islam and Muslims that had been evident since the earliest era of contact.[150] From the late 1500s, Islam and Muslim cultures may have become objects to Europeans, but if

146 See B. Goldstein, "Astronomy as a 'Neutral Zone.'" Christian laymen were also involved in translation, for example, William II of Sicily's admiral, Eugenius of Palermo. See E. Jamison, *Admiral Eugenius*.

147 See, for example, P. S. van Koningsveld, "Andalusian-Arabic Manuscripts," pp. 90 and 91, and, generally, G. Wiegers, *Islamic Literature*, esp. chapter III.2: "The Involvement of Mudejars in the Transmission of Learning," pp. 47–56.

148 See K. Mallette, *Kingdom of Sicily*, chapter 2: "Frederick II and the Genesis of Sicilian Romance Culture," pp. 47–64; A. Metcalfe, *The Muslims of Medieval Italy*, pp. 256ff; J. A. Taylor, *Muslims in Medieval Italy*, pp. 74ff; and S. Kinoshita, "Translatio/N," pp. 376 and 387.

149 L. García Ballester, *Historia social de la medicina*, p. 72. See also T. E. Burman, "Cambridge University Library"; C. Burnett, "The Second Revelation"; and G. Wiegers, "Moriscos and Arabic Studies."

150 See M. Tolmacheva, "The Medieval Arabic Geographers," as well as D. Blanks, "Western Views of Islam," and J. Moran Cruz, "Popular Attitudes."

so, they were objects worthy of interest and study.[151] Even in the age of intense confessional competition and political conflict, Christian missionaries and ideologues, whether St. Francis or da Monte di Croce, could hardly help but admit a grudging admiration for the evident enthusiasm of Muslim popular piety (even if only to pose this as a shameful counter-example to Christian laxity). Ibn Rushd ("Averroës"), Ibn Sīnā ("Avicenna"), along with a whole host of Islamic philosophers were read with admiration and respect in medieval Christendom, while a Latin-imagined Ṣalāḥ al-Dīn could be presented as a paragon of chivalric virtue, and Muslim queens as powerful and independent.[152] Reflecting such mixed impressions of Islam and Muslims, the spurious fourteenth-century memoir, *The Travels of John Mandeville* – a medieval bestseller – portrayed Muslims in a surprisingly candid and positive light.[153]

The broad spectrum of formally articulated Christian opinion and the apparently contradictory attitudes which it expressed corresponds to a similar diversity of approaches to Muslims and Islam as is evidenced in Christians' legal and administrative policies, and in their social and economic relations with subject Muslims (these are the subjects of the final two chapters, respectively). However, it is not clear that there is a causal link between the ideological and intellectual approaches to Islam outlined above, and the policies and practices of Christian domination as they played out on the ground. Just as the pronouncements and fulminations of foreign *fuqahā'* had little if any bearing on subject Muslims' sense of themselves and their deployment of strategies for survival, the various vectors of Christian engagement with Muslims – ideal, institutional, and practical – do not seem to have followed parallel courses. Both hostility and sympathy arose out of cultural convergences between Christendom and the Islamic world, and seem in the end to have been symptoms, rather more than causes, of *convivencia* and conflict. On an ideal and ideological level the existence of subject Muslim societies was unsustainable from both a Christian and Muslim point of view, yet such societies persevered for up to six centuries. Not unlike Jews, Islam and subject Muslims became an "indispensable enemy" for Latin Christendom societies.[154]

151 For late medieval and early modern perspectives, see for example, N. Bisaha, "'New Barbarian' or Worthy Adversary?" and D. Viktus, "Early Modern Orientalism."
152 For Ṣalāḥ al-Dīn, see p. 251, above; for Muslim queens, see M. Kahf, *Western Representations*, p. 40.
153 See J. Mandeville, *The Travels*, pp. 24–27, and for examples, pp. 105 and 107.
154 I borrow the term from A. Saxton, "The Indispensable Enemy."

# 9 Word

## Law, administration and Islamicate society under Latin rule

Religious affiliation may have been the principal mode of individual and community identification in pre-modern Christendom, but it was understood in a manner quite distinct from that of today. It was not thought of merely as a reflection of one's individual approach to spirituality and the divine, but rather it indicated the community one belonged to in a moral, fiscal, administrative, and juridical sense. Hence, in the multi-confessional societies of Latin Christendom this affiliation is not normally referred to in terms of *religio*, but of *lex*. Thus, Muslims and Jews were those who governed by the "law of the Muslims" (*lex Saracenorum*) and "the law of the Hebrews" (*lex Ebraicum*), respectively.[1] As in the *dār al-Islām*, society was imagined in terms of a hierarchy of semi-autonomous religious communities, with religious minorities occupying a subordinate and secondary position. As a consequence, minority communities were subject both to the laws of the dominant society and those of their own confession – the latter understood as including not only "personal law," but taxation, civil, and criminal law as well. Each Muslim community (*aljama*, *comuna*, etc.) had its own administrative and fiscal institutions, and judicial apparatus, which were autonomous in principle. However, none of these systems functioned in isolation, and, in practice, the situation was much less clearly defined – with Muslim and Jews often coming under Christian jurisdictions, and occasionally, Christians being subject to Muslim courts, and Muslims to Jewish judges. The present chapter surveys the formal manifestations of Christian–Muslim interaction in Latin Christendom, and the institutional character of subject Muslim societies.

### Subject Muslims and Christian law

In principle, the plaintiff submits to the law of the defendant. Thus, if a Christian is the defendant and a Jew or Muslim the plaintiff, the judge in the case ought to be

[1] See, for example, L. Pick, "What Did Rodrigo Jiménez de Rada Know . . .," esp. pp. 232–35. Jewish law was also referred to, *inter alia*, as *lex Judaycorum*.

Christian . . . But if the plaintiff were a Christian or a Jew, and the defendant were a Muslim, the judge over them ought to be Muslim, which is to say, the *çaualchén*. Now, despite this being mandated by right and reason, because of the disloyalty of the Muslims and the Jews . . . and because there is nought among them but falsehood and vanity . . . it remains the Christians' option to take the cases brought against them by a Muslim or Jew before a Christian judge. (Vidal de Canellas, Bishop of Huesca, *In excelsis Dei thesauris* (1247–52)[2])

The thirteenth century represented a turning point in the legal history of Latin Christendom, characterized by the reformulation and articulation of kingdom-wide, royally sponsored law codes, based on the revived principles and precedents of the Roman *Codex juris civilis* – a process that had been sparked a century earlier by the Church's development of a coherent and cohesive corpus of Canon Law, and driven by the struggle for authority between the kings and the nobilities of Latin Christendom, and the development of an institutionally complex administration. It was a trend that affected all of the territories in which there were subject Muslim communities, and can be seen in the entrenchment and refinement of the earlier *Usatges* of Barcelona in the Catalan counties, the promulgation of the Golden Bull (1222) and Oath of Bereg (1232) in Hungary; the "Constitutions of Melfi" (1231) of Frederick II; the *Fuero General* of Navarre (1237); the *Fori Aragonum* and "*Vidal Mayor*" (1247) of Aragon; the *Livre de Forme de Plait* and the *Livre des Assises de la Cour des Bourgeois* in the rump kingdom of Jerusalem (1250s); the *Siete Partidas* ("The Seven Divisions," 1252–84) and the *Fuero real* (1255) in the Crown of Castile; and the *Furs* of Valencia (1261); as well as the legal reforms embarked on by King Diniz in Portugal (1280–90s).[3] It was a

2 G. Tilander, *Los fueros de Aragon*, Vol. II (2): 24 (2–7), and *Vidal Mayor*, Vol. II. p. 182 {II: 22, "De eodem"; "De foro competenti: De fuero que conuiene a cada uno"}. *In excelsis Dei thesauris* (*In the Treasuries of God on High*) is the compilation of the the *Fori Aragonum* (Fueros of Aragon) of Vidal de Canellas, also translated into Aragonese as the "*Vidal mayor*" ("*The Greater Vidal*").

3 Some modern editions and translations of these royal law codes include: D. Kagay, *The Usatges*; J. Powell, *The Liber Augustalis*; M. J. Brito de Almeida Costa and E. Borges Nunes, *Ordenações afonsinas*; F. Waltman, *Textos y concordancias*; A. Pérez Martín, *Fori Aragonum*; G. Colón and A. Garcia i Sanz, *Furs de València*; P. Edbury, *John of Ibelin*; Filippo di Novara, *Le Livre*; and Alfonso X, *Las siete partidas*. Many population charters (*cartas-pueblas*) municipal law codes (*fueros*) and acts of parliament (*cortes*) of the Iberian kingdoms have been published. Some major *fueros* include, for example, J. Powers, *The Code of Cuenca*; A. M. Barrero García, *El fuero de Teruel*; A. García Gallo, "Los fueros de Toledo"; J. Algora Hernando and F. Arranz Sacristan, *Fuero de Calatayud*; J. Massip i Fonollosa, *Costums de Tortosa*; M. Molho, *El fuero de Jaca*; and J. J. Morales Gómez and M. J. Pedraza García, *Fueros de Borja y Zaragoza*. For earlier *fueros* and *cartas pueblas*, see M. Febrer Romaguera, *Cartas pueblas*; J. M. Font y Rius, "Notas sobre algunas cartas pueblas" and *Cartas de población*; M. L. Ledesma Rubio, *Cartas de población*; and T. Muñoz y Romero, *Colección de fueros*.

trend that was also related to the emergence of a more commercialized and town-oriented society, with a blossoming vernacular culture, and a broader-based sense of "citizenship" and popular political community.[4]

Each of these law codes was obliged to consider and define the place of religious minorities, both because of the comprehensive and systematic nature of the exercise, and the fact that by this time – with the exception of Jerusalem (which had virtually no Muslim subjects left) – the Muslim minorities had become profoundly enmeshed in Christian-identifying societies that were engaging in their own processes of self-realization. Hence, as in the excerpt above, these codes express the tensions and challenges inherent in integrating Infidel religio-juridical communities in a framework of universal sovereignty, and within a culture predicated on absolute truths. This had not been a problem in the previous centuries, when the Latin legal apparatus was primitive and underdeveloped: a rough quilt of local custom, *ad hoc* royal and noble grants and privileges, local and regional conciliar decrees, and seigniorial custom, all hanging on the dilapidated frame of the *Codex juris civilis* and its early medieval (and pre-Islamic) descendants, such as Iberia's Visigothic *Forum judicorum*. And yet, even as each of the kingdoms developed legal apparatuses to accommodate the existence of Infidels in their midst, the legal codes that were promulgated remained remarkably restrained and free of chauvinistic rhetoric (the occasional grand declarations of Christian preeminence aside). Indeed, the legal culture of the Latin Mediterranean remained extraordinarily resistant to the intrusion of chauvinistic religious ideology in terms of both form and practice.

### *Legality and legitimacy*

Throughout this entire period – up until the end of the fifteenth century in the Iberian Peninsula – Muslims continued to be considered legitimate, albeit subordinate, subjects of the kingdoms that they inhabited. As Alfonso X of Castile put it: "Although [Muslims] do not acknowledge a good religion, so long as they live among Christians with their assurance of security, their property shall not be stolen from them or taken by force; and we order that whoever violate this law shall pay a sum equal to double the value of what he took."[5] True, Charles of Anjou would disenfranchise and enslave the Muslims of Lucera only two generations later, but even then the papacy was still maintaining their right in principle to live as free subjects

[4] D. Kagay, "The *Usatges* of Barcelona," p. 51. The *Usatges* date prior to the thirteenth century, but did not come to be applied consistently until after 1200.

[5] Alfonso X, *Las Siete Partidas*, vol. v, p. 1438 {vii:xxv:1}.

as long as they remained loyal and peaceful. Other episodes of communal enslavement or expulsion, such as that of Menorca in 1287 and Granada in the 1490s, were rationalized on the basis of political disloyalty and rebellion on the part of these particular Muslim communities, and did not entail or propose a reconsideration of the legal status of Muslims as a group. Of course, there were strong practical reasons for kings to support and sustain Muslim communities in their realms. *Mudéjares* fell outside the customary institutional and legal framework and, therefore, kings could claim special and direct fiscal and judicial jurisdiction over them in principle.[6] As a consequence, their status also served as a wedge to weaken the nobility, the municipalities, and the Church relative to the monarchy.[7]

Thus, they constituted a "royal treasure" or were described as *servi regis*, a term which could be interpreted variously from "wards of the king" to "slaves of the king," or just about anything in between. Not only did subject Muslim communities yield direct benefits to the monarchy in the form of taxes, rents, and other obligations but, because they had no unalienable "constitutional rights," they could not develop an independent institutional platform for defending themselves against the king. They never comprised an estate, nor were they represented formally in parliaments (*cortes*, *corts*). Indeed, their secondary, "minor" status formally justified their exceptional position – like women, orphans, and the poor, they were not full subjects and, therefore, required and deserved special royal protection.[8] Moreover, Christian officials were enjoined to protect and serve them.[9] While this granted them important protections as individuals – in principle, for example, in some kingdoms they were exempt from seigniorial jurisdiction and could not be tortured, dismembered, or killed without royal permission – it could leave them vulnerable as communities, dependent as they were on the good will of kings.[10] In times of royal weakness and need Muslim communities could negotiate privileges and extensions of autonomy, and in times of royal confidence these privileges could be eroded or

6 Even when Muslims did live under a seigniorial legal regime, their right to be judged by their own laws and magistrates tended to be observed, even in cases involving Christians. See, for example, J. M. Font Rius, *Cartas de población*, vol. I, p. 445 {303}.

7 For example, when in 1282 a *mudéjar* in Ascó (Catalonia) assaulted a Templar, the King ordered the local Commander not to interfere in the case. See C. Biarnes i Biarnes, "Tres motius," p. 235.

8 This is made explicit in the Aragonese law code. See G. Tilander, *Vidal Mayor*, vol. II, p. 463 {VIII: 4.5a}.

9 See, for example, the *Costums* of Tortosa, which emphasized that the local Chrisitian judicial officer (the *veguer*) was to swear to "hold and safeguard the rights and justice for Christians, Jews and Muslims . . . within his jurisdiction." See *Consuetudines Dertosae*, f. 9r.

10 Such was the case in late twelfth-century Sicily according to at least one contemporary observer. See G. Loud, *The Latin Church*, p. 519.

withdrawn.[11] On the other hand, at times when royal power was seen as weak, Muslims were more at risk of abuse by Christian parties.

The legal legitimacy of Muslim minority communities was predicated on the notion of a legal-religious hierarchy. Muslims (and Jews) would be permitted to follow their own laws to the extent that these did not directly undermine the secular law of the Christians or breach or offend the mandates of Canon Law. In these cases Muslims were not outside the law but subject to Christian law, and entitled to most of the same protections as Christian subjects.[12] The operating principle was one of "balance of convenience." As Roger II himself put it in his *Assizes*, the first significant legislative work of Norman Sicily: "Because of the variety of different people subject to Our rule, the usages, customs and laws which have existed among them up to now are not abrogated, unless what is observed in them is clearly in contradiction to Our edicts here."[13] This sentiment was echoed in later Iberian legal works, including the *Siete Partidas*, which stated: "We decree that [Muslims] shall live among Christians in the same way that we mentioned in the preceding Title that Jews shall do, by observing their own law and not insulting ours."[14] As the oft-repeated Iberian dictum maintained, Muslims were to be judged "according to their own legal custom" (*secundam suam zunam*).[15] As a consequence of this general approach, until the late twelfth century, Muslims rarely appear at all in Christian law codes – even those municipal codes developed in areas with abundant Muslim populations, including the Ebro and Jalón valleys in Aragon. For example, the earliest *fuero* of Tudela (1127) makes no mention of Muslims, although the community here had received its own laws from the king twelve years earlier.[16] Likewise, the twelfth-century *fueros* of Zamora, Mirando de Ebro, Zaragoza, Barbastro, and Belchite, as well the overwhelming bulk of *cartas pueblas* promulgated for Christian colonizers on the Iberian frontier, make no mention at all of *mudéjares*, despite the ubiquity of indigenous Muslims in these lands.[17]

[11] Virtually every one of the regional and studies of *mudéjares* and their communities includes a section on legal status. Refer to the studies noted, above, at the beginning of chapters 1–6.

[12] In Navarre, for example, Muslims were explicitly entitled to the same procedural guarantees and rights of appeal as Christians. See F. Segura Urra, *Fazer justícia*, p. 119. In Aragon, Jewish and Muslim criminal suspects were refused the right of sanctuary in churches by the kings on the grounds they were not Christian (see p. 369).

[13] A. Metcalfe, *Muslims*, p. 151.

[14] Alfonso X, *Las Siete Partidas*, vol. v, p. 1438 {VII:XXV:1}.

[15] See B. Catlos, "*Secundum suam zunam*," p. 14.

[16] T. Muñoz y Romero, *Colección de fueros*, p. 420.

[17] See A. Castro and F. de Onís, *Fueros leoneses*, T. Muñoz y Romero, *Colección de fueros*, and J. M. Font i Rius, *Documents jurídics*, pp. 54–57; also B. Catlos "*Secundum suam zunam*," pp. 12–15. Lleida's *carta-puebla*, promulgated in 1150, made no mention of the substantial Muslim community in the city. See J. M. Font i Rius, *Documents jurídics*, pp. 51–62.

In all of the Latin kingdoms, however, acts that broke the king's peace or affected the king's property would be subject to Christian law, as would – in the great majority of jurisdictions – crimes in which Christians were victims. Certain offences against public morality (such as ethno-religious miscegenation) or religious law (including apostasy and blasphemy against Christianity) came under the automatic jurisdiction of secular and/or Church law. Jurisdiction in legal conflicts between Muslims and Jews was somewhat less clear: whereas criminal cases would tend to fall under the purview of royal authorities, civil disputes between minority parties might be heard by either a Jewish, Muslim, or Christian magistrate, depending on the politics of the kingdom in question, local municipal law, and on specific privileges these communities or their members had obtained.[18]

In Iberia from the late thirteenth century on, Jewish communities lobbied kings strenuously and largely successfully to exempt their members from Islamic civil jurisdiction – an initiative that was driven by a general determination to maintain the integrity and authority of Jewish law, and because Jewish creditors frequently found themselves locked into drawn-out legal suits against Muslim debtors that would have otherwise been assigned to less-than-detached *mudéjar* magistrates. And while Vidal de Canellas might have felt that Christians should be exempt from *mudéjar* jurisdiction, this was not necessarily the case. In the twelfth century as Christian colonizers were integrated piecemeal into rural and urban Muslim property grids, they were forced to recognize the legal custom and authority of those larger networks.[19] Well into the fourteenth century, Christian plaintiffs in Iberia continued to find themselves, on occasion, having civil suits against Muslims judged by a *mudéjar* magistrate or subject jointly to *mudéjar* and Christian law.[20] Although there is no

[18] Circumstances in specific locales could vary widely. In 1359, for example, Pere the Ceremonious granted privileges to a whole number of rural *aljamas* in Valencia, exempting them from the obligation to be judged by the *Furs*, reaffirming the unique jurisdiction of the *sunna*, and even striking down the validity of Christian testimony. The same year, he confirmed a privilege of Lleida dated 1202 that said that Muslims could only be judged by the *zalmedina* or *alcaydus* of the *aljama*, even in cases involving Christians or Jews. See, for example, J. Boswell, *The Royal Treasure*, pp. 365–68.

[19] This can be observed clearly in Sicily, where by virtue of such a purpose the Archbishop of Palermo found himself subject to the jurisdiction of a *qāḍī*. See J. Johns, *Arabic Administration*, pp. 316–17, and generally, O. R. Constable, "Cross-Cultural Contacts."

[20] For example, this principle was reiterated in fourteenth-century Huesca by Queen Blanche d'Anjou (who had been apportioned the *aljama*); see B. Catlos, *The Victors and the Vanquished*, p. 164. In Lleida the Muslim community's right to have cases, even those involving Christians, tried by their *alcadius*, was explicitly reaffirmed in the 1350s by Pere the Ceremonious, and in subsequent decades by his successors. J. Mutgé i Vives, *L'aljama sarraïna*, pp. 103–07. In 1374, a Muslim of Beniguazir sued a Christian for unlawfully appropriating lands assigned to Muslims after the War of the Two Peters. The case was ordered to be resolved according to the *forum* and *sunna*. See ACA, C., reg. 2064, f. 1r.

evidence that Muslims necessarily received preferential treatment when mixed cases came before Islamicate magistrates, this situation did provoke some anxiety, at least in certain Christian circles. Hence, in his sermons, the thirteenth-century Dominican preacher Étienne de Bourbon would trot out a parable involving a *mudéjar* who, having converted to Christianity, left his property to the local diocese. On his death, however, his unconverted sons sued to assert their rights as heirs and landed the unfortunate bishop in the town's *sharīʿa* court.[21]

Needless to say, whatever anxieties this situation generated among the guardians of Christian society, the effect would have been far more dramatic on their subject Muslim counterparts. The overriding power of Christian law not only sapped the authority and executive force of subject Muslim judicial institutions and undermined Islamic principles of ownership and inheritance, it also provided an alternative that savvy *mudéjares* could manipulate through "jurisdiction shopping," launching appeals (spurious or legitimate) against the sentences of Islamic magistrates to Christian authorities, or simply by applying to have their cases heard in a Christian court if this was likely to bear a more favorable outcome.[22]

### *The development of municipal and royal law*

As law codes in the Iberian Peninsula became increasingly elaborate from the mid twelfth century onwards, commercial and economic interaction was one of the main contexts in which Muslim–Christian relations came to be explicitly addressed in both municipal and royal law codes. *Fueros* like that of Teruel, a town located on the frontier of al-Andalus in the twelfth and thirteenth centuries, had provisions relating to trade and transhumance taking place in Muslim lands – activities that were clearly well established and well organized.[23] These codes, too, tended to legislate regarding commerce's close sister, cross-border raiding – a major economic activity and vector for social advancement in these "societies organized for war" in which the fundamental municipal institutions were

[21] See de Vitry, *Exempla*, p. 175. The incendiary bishop of Acre, Jacques de Vitry, liked the tale so much, he made it his own.

[22] See M.F. Lopes de Barros, "A mulher," 111–12; B. Catlos, *The Victors and the Vanquished*, pp. 169–72 and 348; and J. Boswell, *The Royal Treasure*, p. 132, n. 80. C.f. below, p. 384. To be sure, Muslims living in the Islamic world also engaged in "*fatwa* shopping," whereas Jews would sometimes seek repeated Rabbinical opinions or go to Muslim courts in hopes of obtaining a favorable *responsum*. See M. Rustow, *Heresy and the Politics of Community*.

[23] See M. Gorosch, *El fuero de Teruel*, pp. 371 and 396 {718 and 784}.

the town council and the urban militia.[24] Laws addressed the sharing out of booty (including the obligation to give the "royal fifth" to the king), and the taking and redemption of Muslim prisoners and slaves.[25] Raiding was bilateral and, therefore, laws were put in place to ensure that captured Christians would be ransomed, with rules for the officials who mediated such exchanges.[26] Tellingly, it was the town's *axea*, or chief herder, who originally carried out such transactions.[27]

Concurrently, *fueros* across the peninsula began to develop laws relating to the Muslim–Christian–Jewish interaction in small-scale, local commerce, industry, and credit, outlining common rules that for the most part did not give Christians any particular advantage. Because of the nature of commerce – which does not function well in an atmosphere of coercion – the economic integration of Christians, Muslims, and Jews demanded that mechanisms develop to put members of the various faiths on a reasonably equitable footing before the law. Hence, law codes emphasized the rights and protections to which all merchants, creditors, and debtors were entitled regardless of their religious identity, and explicitly included Muslims in provisions regarding freedom of trade and the practice of crafts.[28]

Both giving testimony in court and signing legal contracts required the swearing of an oath before God. Since it would have been offensive to all concerned to have Muslims swear on the Gospels and to the Trinity, as was the Christian practice, and because such an oath would hold no coercive power over an unbeliever, Islamicate oaths and swearing rituals were not only permitted but came to be enshrined (and crystallized) in

24 See, generally, E. Lourie, "A Society Organized for War," and J. Powers, *A Society Organized for War*. The taking of prisoners and booty as well as rewards for the bounty killings of Muslims in raids, were means by which a low-status Christian *peon* ("foot soldier") could acquire the horse and armor that would qualify him as a *caualler*o ("horseman"). *Caualleros* were recognized as *infanzones*, in the Crown of Aragon, the broad class of lower nobility (or knightly class), who enjoyed significant tax exemptions and protections from seigniorial law.

25 The right of kings to claim a fifth of war booty was likely based on the same Islamic custom.

26 See M. T. Ferrer i Mallol, "Els redemptors de captius."

27 See J. Caruana Gómez de Barreda, *El fuero latino de Teruel*, p. 409 {507}, cf. M. Gorosch, *El fuero de Teruel*, p. 376 {732}. In Teruel, his recompense for "herding" a Muslim was the same as for herding one hundred sheep, and marginally more than for herding one cow or ox.

28 See, for example, J. I. Algora Hernando and F. Arranz Sacristan, *Fuero De Calatayud*, p. 41 {34}; J. Caruana Gomez de Barreda, *El fuero latino de Teruel*, pp. 11, 331, and 411 {79, 409 and 510}; M. Gorosch, *El fuero de Teruel*, pp. 137 and 250 {115 and 378}; M. Molho, *El Fuero de Jaca*, p. 85 {A 139}; *Suma de fueros*, ff.XIVv, XXIXr–v, XXXIV; *Fori Aragonum*, p. 102; G. Tilander, *Vidal Mayor*, vol. II, p. 181 {132}; E. Sarasa Sánchez, *El privilegio general*, pp. 69 and 86.

Christian law codes. In many legal codes it was merely indicated that Muslims should swear "according to their custom," while in others a precise oath was specified, either in the garbled Arabic of a Christian scribe – as one legist prescribed: "*berelle yale aylle illen*; these words are Arabic" – which was more common in the Crown of Aragon, or as a formula in Romance, as in Castilian laws.[29] In Aragonese lands the oath was essentially a variation on the *shahāda*, "There is no God, but God . . .," whereas in Castile it could involve a lengthy recitation of Islamic tenets, or some other Christian-invented incantation, sometimes accompanied by some sort of ritual choreography.[30] In some areas it was specified that the oath should be sworn at the mosque (reflecting Mālikī preferences), as in Aragon, Navarre, and Castile; holding a Qur'ān (a Christian innovation), as in Jerusalem and Navarre; or in the presence of local *shuyūkh*, or other Muslims of good repute, as in Valencia.[31]

In sum, as a consequence of the ethno-religious diversity of the societies over which they ruled, Christian authorities were obliged to acknowledge the good intentions and integrity of Muslims and Jews and their oath-swearing apparatus, as misguided or diabolical as Christians may have considered their religions to be – a "willing suspension of *belief*." The validity of the testimony of Muslims in Christian civil and criminal court, however, was subject to change. Naturally, in the earlier period, when trial by battle was common, Muslims were excluded from this remedy, even among themselves.[32] The possibility that a Muslim might vanquish a Christian in a judicial duel (even via a proxy) was highly problematic on a number of levels, and it was all but universally prohibited.[33] Well into the twelfth century Muslim testimony seems to have been regarded as equal to Christian evidence in many

29 J. M. Ramos y Loscertales, "Recopiliación," p. 510 {83}. For a detailed study of Islamic oaths in the Christian Iberia, see, B. Vicéns Sáiz, "Swearing by God," also the remarks by B. Catlos, *The Victors and the Vanquished*, p. 397.

30 See for example Alfonso X's *Espéculo (Mirror)*, R. MacDonald, *Espéculo*, p. 258 {V.II.17, Ley XVII "Como deuen jurar los moros"}.

31 For Jerusalem, see M. Nader, "Urban Muslims," 256.

32 See, for example, the *Fuero general de Navarra*, in B. Catlos, "Fuero General," f. 26v, which states, "Entre christian y iudeu et moro no a logar torna a bataylla ..."; cf. M. Molho, *El fuero de Jaca*, p. 56 {A 61}. This can hardly be regarded as discriminatory, given that Islamic law did not allow for trial by battle or ordeal, and Muslims – like Usāma b. Munqidh – considered this a barbaric and illegal custom. See Ibn Munqidh, *The Book of Contemplation*, pp. 151–53.

33 Jerusalem's *Livre des Assises* recognizes Muslims' right to trial by battle in cases of murder, treason, or heresy, but this likely represented legal theory never put into practice. See M. Nader, "Urban Muslims," 258. Indeed, the possibility that a Muslim would possibly by tried for "heresy" in a Christian court is very remote, unless it was undertaken on the initiative of Muslim authorities.

jurisdictions, and *mudéjares* could appear in court on their own and others' behalf. For example, the twelfth-century *fuero* of Salamanca's only clause that refers to the not insignificant number of Muslims and Jews who lived in the city and its environs was that they could represent themselves in court against accusers of any religion.[34] In fact, many early local codes in Iberia even specified that *mudéjares* could only be convicted on the testimony of other Muslims. Typical of the early spirit of the law, legists at the thirteenth-century kingdom of Jerusalem's *Cour de la Fronde* recognized the principle that testimony for the prosecution could be admitted only if the witness was of the same religion as the accused.[35] But there was a progressive erosion of Muslims' testamentary power, and by the fourteenth century it was widely held that it could not be used against Christians, or if it was admitted, did not have the same strength as Christian evidence – requiring, for example, two *mudéjar* witnesses in the place of one Christian. The testimony of Christians, on the other hand, gained weight over time, and came to be seen as sufficient proof for convicting *mudéjares* of crimes even in the absence of other evidence – Muslim witnesses were no longer required.[36]

This gradual loss of testamentary legitimacy mirrors the overall evolution of the status of Muslims in Christian legal regimes. Initially, *mudéjares* were governed by the *ad hoc* surrender agreements and settlement charters they negotiated with Christian powers; these provided them with near-total judicial autonomy.[37] Occasional thirteenth- and fourteenth-century confirmations of such privileges reveal that *aljama* officials had the authority to impose a range of sanctions and mete out corporal punishment in both civil and criminal (*ḥadd*) cases.[38] Such arrangements were negotiated on a local basis, and therefore, varied markedly even within a given kingdom. Although evidence is lacking, it is clear that in Hungary, Sicily, and the Latin East, local Muslim judicial institutions – whether formally constituted or not – functioned with considerable autonomy. In Iberia, Muslims appear in municipal law codes of the time only in specific contexts, such as, for example, the religious segregation of municipal baths (with Muslims and Jews typically limited to one day per week), the ransoming of captives, the protection of *mudéjares* (e.g. *moros de paz*, *mouros forros*, *moros de palio*) from Christian violence, searches for escaped

[34] A. Castro and F. de Onís, *Fueros leoneses*, p. 80 {CCLXXIX}.

[35] M. Nader, "Urban Muslims," 253. [36] See below, p. 367.

[37] See B. Catlos "*Secundum suam zunam*," and *The Victors and the Vanquished*, pp. 96–103, as well as M. T. Ferrer i Mallol, "La capitulación."

[38] See, for example, E. Lourie, "An Unknown Charter," and J. Mutgé i Vives, *L'aljama sarraïna*, pp. 108–110 and 120.

slaves, and jurisdiction and protocol in cases between members of different religions.[39]

In the late twelfth century, as municipal law codes became more elaborate and were standardized, and as Christians and *mudéjares* became increasingly integrated economically and engaged socially, more provisions appeared, including the regulation of Muslim (and Jewish) butcher shops, and the first secular statutes relating to miscegenation and sexual contact between Muslims and Christians. As specific local laws became model codes, such as the *fueros* (*foros, furs*, i.e. "laws") of Lisbon (in Portugal), Sepúlveda (in Old Castile and León), Cuenca (in New Castile), and those of Jaca and Calatayud (in Aragon), Teruel (in lower Aragon and northern Valencia), Muslims' place in Christian law was gradually idealized, and more standardized approaches developed that did not necessarily reflect the circumstances of local Muslim communities.[40] For example, the clauses that appear in northern Spanish *fueros* forbidding non-Christians from employing Christian servants and nursemaids do not necessarily indicate that this was a current practice – the prohibition is merely an echo of the fourth-century Theodosian Code.[41] Moreover, discriminatory legal innovations, particularly those related to the types of businesses *mudéjares* could patronize or pursue, were often driven by economic concerns or by the interests of specific Christian corporations (*inter alia* royal institutions, guilds, cathedral chapters, and monasteries) or individuals, specifically those who held the right to license baths, butcher shops, *fondaci*, and other revenue-generating utilities.

### *Muslims and royal law*

It was the legal revolution of the mid thirteenth century and the formulation of systematic and exhaustive royal law codes that forced Christian legists to theorize formally Muslims' place in the legal landscape of Christendom. This task involved both affirming and limiting Muslims' rights and place in Christian society while articulating and reinforcing boundaries between ethno-religious communities. In kingdoms where there was only a residual Islamic population, what little attention Muslims received from jurists

39 These terms: "Muslims of the (king's) peace," "protected Muslims," "Muslims of the (king's) robe," each referred to free Muslims who lived under royal protection, as to be distinguished from slaves (*cautivos*) and belligerent, foreign Muslims. For baths, see pp. 469ff.

40 For example, J. Lalinde Abadía traces the dissemination of three models of *fuero* in Aragon, originating in Jaca, Zaragoza, and Teruel, in *Los fueros de Aragón*, pp. 22–39.

41 Cf. T. Ruíz, "Trading with the 'Other'", p. 67. Complaints by churchmen of this practice must be taken with a grain of salt; see L. Torres Balbás, *Algunos aspectos*, p. 78.

tended to reflect local conditions and agendas. Hence, in Hungary, the little legislation that applied to them focused on limiting non-Christians' participation in the royal and municipal administration and marking them off as visibly distinct from Christians. On the other hand, Frederick II of Sicily, for whom the Muslims of Lucera comprised a "praetorian guard" and a political counter-balance to Christian factions, focused on affirming Muslims' rights to exist as a community.[42] For its part, the legalistic and commercial-oriented aristocracy of the (nominal, post-1187) kingdom of Jerusalem focused on strictly circumscribing Muslims' rights as witnesses and their potential to act in business and property cases.[43] It was in Christian Iberia, where substantial and robust *mudéjar* populations continued to thrive, that elaborate legal regimes for Muslims were established. The catalyst to this success was the integration of *mudéjar* communities into the broader regional economies and Christian institutions – a process that entailed a loss of autonomy (both formal and actual) and provoked the articulation of principles of marginalization and subjugation.

Even in the peninsula, however, such developments were uneven, and reflected the general state of the legal culture of each kingdom. For example, as late as 1296 only a few clauses of Portuguese royal law referred to Muslims: confirming their general privileges, rights and autonomies, and their obligation to render a poll tax to the king.[44] In the fourteenth and fifteenth centuries, the legal position of *mouros* varied across the kingdom – depending, for example, on whether they lived in a locale where there was a royal *alcaide*. In some cases they were subject to Christian common law, whereas in others the jurisdiction of Islamic law remained in force. The *fuero* of Navarre was more elaborate, establishing rules for contracts, trials, and criminal justice involving members of different faiths, and for the exchange of captives and the search for and recovery of slaves. Penalties were established for Christians who assaulted Muslims, and a series of clauses refer to conversion to Christianity: both the right of Muslims to convert and be protected from abuse and slander, and in relation to their right to inherit property from unconverted parents. Muslims' rights to alienate their own property was restricted to prevent the loss of royal tax revenue, which might result from the sale of *mudéjar* land to the Church or the broad class of lower nobility (*infançons*).[45] These fundamental issues

42 See C. Maier, "Crusade and Rhetoric," p. 344.
43 A. M. Bishop, "Criminal Law," p. 67.
44 See the table of comparison in M. F. Lopes de Barros, *Tempos e espaços*, p. 52.
45 This was the standard law across the Crown of Aragon, and is repeated frequently in royal declarations and legal codes. A corresponding decree was made in Navarre in 1275. See M. García-Arenal, "Documentos árabes," p. 35. Such restrictions also prevented

were also covered in the royal law codes of the Crowns of Castile and Aragon, but both the *Siete partidas* and the *Fori aragonum* were far more detailed and elaborate – a reflection of the energy and determination of their patrons, Alfonso X and Jaume I, to exert royal authority through the entrenchment of Roman-style law.

These two codes share much in common, although each reflects the particular political orientation of the realm – that of Castile emphasizing the privilege of the monarch, and of Aragon, the institutional structure of *mudéjar* society. In the *Siete partidas* the king's absolute authority is stressed. All mosques, for example, are said to be his property, to be disposed of at his pleasure. The exceptional and anomalous position of Muslims in Castile is reflected in the fact that their status is treated in a separate unit of the code – the seventh *Partida*. The relevant section, "*Oluidança et atreuimiento*" ("Heedlessness and insolence"), covers "offences which men commit" – criminal acts including fraud, adultery, incest, sodomy, procuring, and witchcraft, as well as laws governing Jews, Muslims, and heretics.[46] The *Fori Aragonum*, on the other hand, has no chapter that specifically covers *mudéjares* and the rules that bound them. Rather, they are considered pragmatically over the course of the various books that comprise the compilation. In other words, Muslims here are seen as much more integral to the legal structure of the realm, and a considerable amount of material outlines their institutional status and the administration of their communities, whereas their moral status tends not to be addressed directly. Nor is the king's absolute authority over them stressed, as it is in Castilian legal texts – Muslims in the Crown of Aragon were, indeed, the special subjects of the king, but they were not conceived of as his chattel.

Nevertheless, both Castilian and Aragonese royal law were rooted in the same principles and confronted similar legal dilemmas. Both agreed that Muslims were legitimate subjects of the realm and worthy of royal protection, but that they were not full members of society and their participation in the public, institutional, and social life was to be limited. Each had to establish protocols for the swearing of oaths and the admission of testimony of Muslims, and the consequences of inter-communal crimes. Each made provisions for the ransom of captives, the apprehension of escaped slaves, issues relating to conversion and manumission, the protection of *mudéjares* who converted to Christianity, and the punishment of

Muslim-owned land from falling under the tithe (see below, p. 376), and might have acted to ensure the stability of these communities (and their revenue-generating capacity) by acting as a brake on *mudéjar* emigration.

46 Alfonso X, *Las Siete Partidas*, vol. v, p. 1303.

apostates to Islam (and Judaism). The matter of maintaining social boundaries between the religious communities and reinforcing the hierarchy of religious identity also appears in both, although this receives much more attention in the Castilian code. Matters such as the requirement for Muslims to wear distinguishing clothes or hairstyles and the consequences of inter-communal miscegenation are emphasized in the *Partidas*, but do not appear in the *Fori*.

On the other hand, these subjects tended to be treated in detail in Aragonese municipal law For example, the issue of Muslim–Christian adultery is not referred to in the corresponding chapter of the *Fori*; however, the *Fuero* of Teruel examines the issue in detail – prescribing a public and exemplary death, if both parties were complicit.[47] Conversely, the Aragonese code emphasized the administrative structure of *mudéjar* society, systematically articulating the offices and jurisdictions of the various Muslim officials – a matter scarcely alluded to in the *Partidas*. Similarly, Aragonese law showed an ongoing preoccupation with the rules governing the manumission of converted Muslim slaves, and the rules governing interest rates, the repayments of loans, and the adjudication of credit disputes – all of which reflected preoccupations of an influential Jewish elite that was deeply embroiled with *mudéjar* society in these spheres.

Although the fundamentals of the thirteenth-century compilations were not disputed until the forced conversions of the late fifteenth and sixteenth centuries, through the 1400s and 1500s royal laws became increasingly restrictive and repressive vis-à-vis *mudéjares*. This is most evident in Castile, where in 1408 and 1412 the dowager-regent, Catalina, promulgated two sets of decrees which mandated the strict marginalization of Jews and Muslim through the rigorous application of principles embodied in the *Partidas*.[48] These would be echoed in Portugal's *Ordenações afonsinas* (1446), while in Castile they were reiterated and expanded in 1465's *Sentencia de Medina del Campo*.[49] These codes mandated the physical separation of Muslims (and Jews) from Christian society, including their ghettoization in *morerías* (*mourarias*) and the reclusion of Muslims during certain high Christian holidays (e.g. Easter and Corpus Christi), officially prohibited them from certain professions (notably, medicine) and all official posts, and prescribed penalties for dressing as

[47] See, for example, J. Caruana Gómez de Barreda, *El fuero latino*, p. 325 {385}. That said, run-of-the-mill inter-Christian adultery was also typically a capital crime.

[48] See A. Echevarría Arsuaga, "Catalina of Lancaster," pp. 97–102; and p. 192, above.

[49] See above, p. 199. See V. Silva Conceição, "Mouros, judeus." Muslims are referred to primarily in Books Three and Five of the Portuguese royal law code. See Afonso, King of Portugal, *Ordenações afonsinas*.

or impersonating Christians.[50] Nevertheless, they maintained the principle of juridical autonomy for Muslim officials and the validity of Islamic laws and customs in cases not under Christian jurisdiction, freedom of worship, the protection of Muslims' lives, property, and places of worship, and the illegality of forced conversion.[51]

In the Crown of Aragon, on the other hand, the status quo seems to have held, at least in terms of formal legislation, and there were few kingdom-wide legal innovations as regards *mudéjares*. For example, the *Furs* of Valencia, established by Jaume I beginning in the 1230s, incorporated almost no new legislation regarding Muslims in the fourteenth and fifteenth centuries. The few new laws that were instituted dealt almost exclusively with matters concerning jurisdiction over Muslim criminal and civil law. Through the 1300s the kings endeavored to prevent seigniors and municipalities from establishing their right of *merum et mixtum imperium* over local *mudéjares* – a development that would compromise both Muslim communal integrity and the royal fisc. A considerable amount of jockeying back and forth occurred as a consequence of the shifting political advantage between the Crown and the other estates. The seigniors gained ground over the course of the century and in the first decades of the fifteenth century; but when Martí I struggled to reassert the royal prerogative over *mudéjar* justice, the Muslims themselves were beginning to see that their own agendas were often better served by pragmatic seigniorial justice than that of a crown increasingly under the sway of Christian ideologues.[52] Further revisions were instituted concerning Christian men having sex with Muslim slave women, and the legal status of the resulting issue.[53] Over the course of these centuries, women's rights in this respect steadily declined, as a higher burden of proof was

[50] Muslims may have been forbidden from practicing medicine on Christians, but they remained important practitioners; see pp. 431ff, below. In Portugal the penalty for passing as a Christian was judicial slavery. See Afonso, *Ordenações afonsinas*, vol. II, pp. 536–9 {II: CIII "Dos trajos, que haõ de trazer os Mouros"}; vol. V, p\. 96 {V: XXVI "Do Judeu, ou Mouro, que anda em avito de Christaão, nomeando-se por Christaão"}; vol. II, p. 543 {II: CVII "Que os Mouros nom sejam Officiaaes d'El Rey, nem de nenhuum dos Iffantes, nem d'outros quaaesquer Senhores"}.

[51] *Ibid.*, vol. II, pp. 532–35 {II: CI "Que os Alquaides dos Mouros guardem em seus Julgados antre sy os eus direitos, usos, e costumes"}; vol. II, p. 561 {II: CVXIIII "Que nom façam tornar Mouro Chrisptaaõ contra sua vontade"}; vol. II, pp. 562–63 {II: CXX "Que nom mate alguum, ou feira o Mouro, nem lhe roube o seu, nem violle suas sepulturas, nem lhes embergue suas festas"}. See also Alfonso X, *Las Siete Partidas*, vol. V, pp. 1438–39 {VII:XXV:2}.

[52] See *Aureum opus*, pp. 163, 201, 213, 264, 266, 395–96, and 398 {LIIr/LII, LXIIr/CXXXI, LXXVIIr/CXVI, CIIv/VI, CIIIv-r/X, CLXVIIIr–v/XI, CLXVIIIv/XXII, CLXIXv/XXV}. This is the subject of B. Catlos, "A Genealogy of Marginalization?"

[53] G. Colón and A. Garcia, *Furs de València*, vol. V, pp. 109–11 {VI:I:XVIII–XXI}.

placed on them to establish paternity, and restrictions were placed on their rights and those of their children to emancipation.

Such formal promulgations and grand compilations of law, however, represent only one vector of royal legislation in the Crown of Aragon and the other peninsular kingdoms. Most legislation was promulgated in a piecemeal fashion, in the form of acts of parliament (the *cortes*, or *corts*), and *ad hoc* charters, privileges, sentences, and letters, dictated by the kings and their vassals, agents, and officials issued in response to the specific petitions lodged by their subjects. These acts, which do not necessarily appear in formal digests, reflect measures similar to those being promulgated in Castile. For example, a privilege granted in 1436 by Maria de Castilla, Queen of Aragon, to the city of Lleida (Catalonia) proscribed fines of up to 10 *lliures* (pounds) or thirty lashes, to Muslims who did not live within the confines of the *morería*, who failed to genuflect as the Corpus Christi procession passed, who sold meat to Christians, or worked on the Christian high holidays.[54] Concurrently, municipal codes and privileges – to the extent that they regarded the Muslim minority at all – focused on the cultural and economic boundaries between Christian and Muslim communities and reinforcing the Christians' position at the top of the ethno-religious hierarchy, two impulses that were certainly interrelated. When these are surveyed, a progressive decline of *mudéjares*' formal rights can also be discerned, although only as a general trend.

### *Marginalization and discrimination*

From the late thirteenth century onwards, royal dispatches restated with increasing frequency Muslims' obligation to wear distinctive clothes and hairstyles, restricted their right to move and change seigniors, imposed limits on the public display of Islam (such as the calling of the *ʿadhān*), discouraged social interaction with Christian subjects (including gambling and drinking, and Muslims' use of Christian prostitutes), limited their right to bear arms, and mandated their segregation into Muslim-only neighborhoods. In some areas, Muslims – particularly those who practiced metalworking and other noisy crafts – were forbidden from working on Sundays and holidays. Some legislation of this type was clearly aimed at reducing Muslims' economic capacity and preventing inappropriate social contact; other laws were intended to ensure they paid the taxes and

[54] J. Mutgé i Vives, *L'aljama sarraïna*, pp. 380–2 {199}. In the kingdom of Valencia beginning in 1314 Muslims and Jews were required to hide themselves from the Corpus procession, or if they could not, kneel before the host. See *Aureum opus*, p. 172 {LVIV/LXXII}.

fees they were liable for. In Braga, for example, the Archbishop forbade Muslims and Jews from working in any stores or workshops outside of their own neighborhoods.[55] In Castile, Muslims were only allowed to sell "live" meat to Christians – a rule that was perhaps justified by spurious suspicions of poisoning; in Valencia "security" was used as an excuse to ban *mudéjares* from a whole range of mundane professions.[56] In late fifteenth-century Burgos a penalty of seventy lashes was set for Muslim plasterers who were apparently employing Christian women as assistants to mix their paste.[57]

In addition, regulations were promulgated limiting access to baths, markets, and other utilities. Laws referring to Christian–Muslim adultery became increasingly elaborate in terms of the punishments they prescribed, and in some locales Muslims were expressly forbidden from serving as executioners. In others, non-Christians were specifically required to sit on the floor rather than on benches in town council meetings.[58] However, all of this should not be construed as comprising a coherent program of marginalization, as sentences and privileges were extended and retracted in a manner that can only be described as capricious. Restrictions or demands put on Muslims were typically aimed at specific locales – even if they were not so worded – and were frequently contradicted by subsequent privileges granted to Muslims in different, or even the same locales. In the Kingdom of Aragon alone, contradictory royal orders relating to each of these various matters were promulgated throughout the fourteenth century.[59] The legislative system, to the extent that it can be described as such, was characterized by a high degree of disorganization and inconsistency. Moreover, the kings and their agents were only too ready to grant or repeal privileges and restrictions in exchange for payment or the promise thereof on the part of their subjects.[60] As it was, given the inherently chauvinistic and hierarchical nature

[55] See M. F. Lopes de Barros, *Tempos e espaços*, p. 201. Here, the Muslim community would have been tiny and such restrictions would have little impact on the local economy. By contrast, in Elvas, where there was a large community of *mouros*, the municipality underlined its appreciation of Muslim mercantile and artisanal activities. See *ibid.*, p. 164.

[56] C. Conde Solares, "Social Continuity," p. 315; M. Meyerson, "Slaves and Solidarity," p. 301.

[57] L. Torres Balbás, "Algunos aspectos," pp. 28 and 30. This appears to be a measure to discourage inappropriate inter-communal relations, but this may have also acted to put Christian plasterers at a competitive advantage, or encourage conversion of Muslim plasterers.

[58] See F. Sabaté i Currell, "La pena de muerte," pp. 241–44 for adultery; for the council meetings, J. Massip i Fonollosa, *Costums de Tortosa*, p. 71 {1.9.5}, discussed in B. Catlos, *The Victors and the Vanquished*, p. 272.

[59] See, for example, above, pp. 201, below, pp. 375ff., and below, pp. 480ff.

[60] See pp. 170.

of these societies, for example the fact that Muslims were permitted to participate in town council meetings at all is perhaps more remarkable than the fact they were obliged to sit on the floor.

Nevertheless, discriminatory attitudes were certainly built into the Christian legal culture; the mere fact that Christians regarded themselves as inherently superior invited arbitrary acts of repression and violence. Muslims were not full and equal subjects, a fact reflected in the relatively lower price that municipal law codes tended to place on the crimes against them. Typically, assaulting, wounding, or killing a free Muslim, drew a far more lax sentence than killing a free Christian. Undoubtedly the conviction rate in such cases was also lower, in part due to the often-cited requirement for the prosecution to produce Christian witnesses, and because in the absence of witnesses some *fueros* allowed Christians accused of this crime to absolve themselves merely by swearing an oath of innocence.[61] Similarly, a Muslim who attacked a Christian would generally be subject to heavier penalties than would a Christian in municipal *fueros*. That said, because of the interest kings had in maintaining and protecting their Muslim subjects, some royal law codes, like the *Vidal Mayor*, mandated heavier penalties for those who killed *mudéjares*.[62]

Likewise, inter-communal adultery was not generally regarded as a crime for a culprit who was a Christian male, and a Christian woman could always hope to absolve herself by claiming she had been duped.[63] Muslim men, on the other hand, were technically subject to capital punishment if caught (although this was normally commuted by the payment of a hefty fine), and *mudéjar* women – with the exception of the wealthy and well connected – were all but inevitably sold into slavery in such cases.[64] Perhaps the most dramatic legal expression of disdain towards non-Christians was the custom (attested to in late fourteenth-century Valencia) of hanging condemned Muslims by their feet, rather than by their necks – a much more drawn-out, painful, and collectively

[61] See, for example, M. Gorosch, *Fuero de Teruel*, p. 108 {37}. This is fundamentally equal to the Mālikī position on unwitnessed homicide as observed in al-Andalus. See S. Abboud Haggar, "Diffusión del tratado jurídico," p. 2.

[62] The *Vidal Mayor*, remarkably, prescribes a higher fine for the Christian who kills a Muslim: one thousand *sueldos*, but this amount is later admitted to be discretionary and was likely rarely imposed. G. Tilander, *Vidal mayor*, p. 510 {IX: 22}.

[63] In Alfonso X's *Cantiga* 186 a jealous woman orders her Muslim slave to lie with her sleeping daughter-in-law, who is then accused of having sex with the "Mouro." Both are sent to the stake but the pious and innocent woman is saved by the intervention of the Virgin. See J. Guerrero Lovillo, *Las Cántigas*, p. 417 {lám. 202}. In Tortosa women who were raped, or who were seduced by a Muslim who lied regarding his identity or was dressed as a Christian, were pardoned. See J. Massip i Fonollosa, *Costums de Tortosa*, p. 415 {9.2.7}.

[64] For the actual application of these laws, see below, pp. 474ff.

humiliating death, and one that was more typically reserved for Jews and traitors.[65]

Yet, in practice, remarkably few Muslims went to the gallows or the stake – at least in the Crown of Aragon, which is the only principality for which we have rich and detailed sources prior to the fifteenth century. When they did, here or elsewhere in Latin Christendom, it tended to be for offenses considered beyond the pale, such as homosexual sex or treason – crimes for which subjects of any faith were put to a painful and exemplary death.[66] Hence, for example, the allegedly traitorous eunuch, Philip of Mahdia, was killed by public immolation on the orders of Roger II of Sicily in 1153. But, aside from the occasional exemplary execution, kings had little interest in liquidating potentially productive members of a community that comprised a "royal treasure," and it was, therefore, forbidden for any authorities to execute *mudéjares* without the express and individual permission of the king. Occasional extra-judicial killings did indeed occur, but these were rare events, and the monarchs regarded them as serious acts of defiance. For example, in 1308, the lynching of an insane, itinerant Muslim tinker in the town of Épila (Aragon) for assault and the theft of an ass provoked a lengthy judicial inquiry, carried out in person by the Bailiff-General of the kingdom.[67]

By the same rationale, *mudéjares* were generally protected from torture and punitive dismemberment – a privilege enjoyed also by knights and noblemen.[68] All Muslims had the right to appeal judicial convictions to the king personally, and many – even women and slaves – did.[69] Together with the kings' determination to exempt *mudéjares* from all seigniorial jurisdiction, both civil and criminal (*merum et mixtum imperium*), these rights could in some contexts give subject Muslims a decided advantage before the law over common Christians. In the fourteenth century

[65] See J. Riera i Sans, "Penjat pels peus," p. 612. The practice is confirmed in a judicial sentence for the murder of Cilim, a *mudéjar*, in 1315 in Alacant, where two guilty parties were ordered hung until dead: a Christian by the neck, and a Muslim by the feet; see M. T. Ferrer i Mallol, "Un procés per homicidi," p. 144.

[66] In Navarre, for example, few Muslims were executed, and those that were, were killed for specific crimes: rape of a Christian woman (rather than a Muslim), sodomy, bestiality, and secret apostasy. See F. Segura Urra, "Los mudéjares navarros," pp. 255ff.

[67] M. Ledesma Rubio, *Vidas mudéjares*, "El Ollero Loco," pp. 9–31. Thirty years earlier, the Templar commander Pere de Moncada had been strongly reprimanded by Jaume I for having hung "unjustly and without cause" a leading member of the Muslim community of Aiora (Valencia), "in contempt and prejudice of Us and Our jurisdiction." R. I. Burns, "Los mudéjares de Valencia," pp. 27–28 and 34 {10}.

[68] See, for example, J. Massip i Fonollosa, *Costums de Tortosa*, p. 12 {1.1.14}. Similarly, the Cistercians of Veruela successfully lobbied Jaume I to exempt their Muslim vassals from imprisonment by royal officials. See M. García-Arenal, "Documentos árabes," p. 34.

[69] See B. Catlos, "Esclavo o ciudadano," pp. 152–53.

*mudéjares* were so confident of the protection of the monarchy that they did not hesitate to brandish their royal privileges (along with their swords) against the injustices of Christian officials, and fleeing Muslim felons occasionally claimed the legal right of sanctuary . . . in churches.[70] Moreover, whereas requirements for Muslims to dress in a distinctive manner, and to disengage physically, culturally, and personally from Christian society may seem offensive to modern sensibilities, there can be little doubt that the moral authorities of *mudéjar* society would have been strongly in favor of any measures that might mitigate the acculturation and integration of their charges and reduce the risk of apostasy. Likewise, local *mudéjar* authorities sometimes petitioned for the creation of separate Muslim neighborhoods, whether for physical protection, religio-cultural preservation, or fiscal expediency – *aljama* officials were responsible for collecting tribute from their constituents, a task simplified considerably by the establishment of separate residential and business quarters.[71]

In any event, the relationship between legal statutes and social reality in the Middle Ages was often quite tenuous. The formal legal codes referred to above were not applied with any consistency, and often – as was the case with both the *Partidas* and Catalina of Lancaster's "Pragmatics" – they were not applied at all. Medieval law codes were aspirational in nature, and reflected the preoccupations and agendas of the jurists who formulated them, or post-*hoc* attempts to impose a rationale on diverse practices that developed organically with no consistent policy framework. Even when there was a determination on the part of kings to enforce royal laws (whether in order to protect, or to repress their Muslim subjects), it often proved impossible. This was an age of slow and imprecise communication, and of primitive institutional capacity. Carrying out a royal decree over any distance required the mediation and cooperation of a whole series of intermediaries – royal functionaries, municipal officers, noblemen and clerics, and local communities – each of whom had their agendas, which often ran contrary to the interests of the king, and all of whom were keenly aware of the practical limitations of royal power.[72] As a consequence, it is very risky to use legal and administrative texts as sources for understanding the experience of subject Muslims, or to do much more than generalize regarding the way that the law was applied. However, the very fact that even "secular" law was structured according to

70 B. Catlos, *The Victors and the Vanquished*, p. 249. Eventually, the *fueros* of Aragon were amended to prohibit this. See M. Gómez de Valenzuela, "Esclavos moros," p. 121.

71 B. Catlos, *The Victors and the Vanquished*, p. 302.

72 See D. Kagay, "The Treason of Center and Periphery."

religious affiliation, meant that ethno-religious identity would be a factor in social, economic, and legal contexts that were not *per se* "religious," and that both Christian and Muslim subjects would be constantly reminded of the of the boundaries that separated them and the imbalance of power that characterized to some degree virtually every transaction and exchange they participated in. These boundaries were further reinforced because, as subjects of Christian princes, *mudéjares* came also under the jurisdiction of Church law.

### *Muslims, morality, and Church law*

The evolution of the status of Muslims in Canon Law followed a course congruous to developments in royal legislation; this should hardly surprise, given that the legists who drafted the secular law codes tended to be clerics, and that that elaboration and reform of ecclesiastical law was based also on the revival of the principles and precedents of Roman law.[73] Hence, until well into the thirteenth century Church legislators showed remarkably little regard for subject Muslims. Even in territories with significant Muslim populations, local episcopal councils and the missions of papal legates tended to focus instead on questions of clerical discipline, Christian heresy, and (in Iberia) on discrediting the local "Mozarabic" liturgy. The notable exception to this was the kingdom of Hungary, where the papacy and its agents took an active and aggressive role in the legal marginalization of Muslims. Otherwise, subject Muslims drew the attention of early Church councils and legists only in matters involving social and sexual boundary-marking, particularly prohibitions on minority men having intercourse with Christian women and on the ownership of Christian slaves, as well as conversion and apostasy. These were matters of concern for secular legislation as well; hence, the handful of clauses in Roger II's mid-twelfth century *Assizes* relevant to Muslims focuses on these matters.[74] In the same spirit, many municipal law codes from Iberia legislated the religious segregation of public baths.[75]

Not surprisingly, the besieged and isolated churchmen of Crusade Jerusalem were the most reactionary in this regard. But while five of the twenty-five Canons of Nablus promulgated in 1120 refer to Muslims,

[73] For Muslims and Canon Law, see, for example, D. Freidenreich, "Muslims in Western Canon Law"; J. Gilchrist, "The Papacy and the War"; H. Gilles, "Législation et doctrine"; B. Kedar, *Crusade and Mission*; J. Muldoon, *Popes, Lawyers and Infidels*; and J. Tolan, *Saracens*.

[74] See A. Metcalfe, *Muslims*, pp. 151–52.

[75] See J. Powers, "Frontier Municipal Baths," and M. F. Lopes de Barros, "Body, Baths and Cloth."

these focus all but exclusively on miscegenation. Moreover, another ten of the canons refer to sexual crimes among Christians, including adultery, sodomy, and clerical concubinage. Punishments prescribed included castration, rhinotomy, death at the stake, and judicial enslavement. Clearly, the driving force behind the legislation was not concerns regarding the Muslim population, but a clerical obsession with sexual deviance. Such measures were neither innovative nor an expression of a Frankish "frontier mentality" – rather, they are rooted in Byzantine law, which had a profound influence across the central and eastern Mediterranean.[76] In Christian Iberia, on the other hand, where there was much more of a "Muslim problem," the rare conciliar acts that address *mudéjares* generally consist of nothing more than warmed-over Theodosian promulgations regarding Jews and pagans.

Indeed, Church lawyers had little to say about Islam prior to the mid thirteenth century, and as they worked to incorporate Muslims into the emerging system of Canon Law, the consensus was that – legally speaking – they were considered "pagans." Hence, when late antique Christian law codes referred to "Jews and pagans," medieval decretalists would understand these laws to apply to Muslims, however well they may have understood that Islam was not, in fact, idolatry.[77] Alexander II's (1061–73) decree, *Dispar* ("Jews and Muslims are certainly different"), rationalized the conquest and expulsion of Muslims (*Sarraceni*), while advocating Christian toleration of subject Jewish communities, on the basis that Jews "are prepared to serve."[78] Hence, while Muslims continued to be characterized as a violent people against whom it was both legitimate and recommendable to wage war, the general opinion among both legists and the papacy was that peaceful Muslim subjects should be not be persecuted, expelled, nor forcibly converted (although some advocated deliberate coercion as regards the latter). Around 1200, the influential decretalist Alanus Anglicus advocated compulsion "just short of death" to achieve conversion, yet argued also (on the basis of Theodosian precedents vis-à-vis pagans) that law-abiding Muslims should not be repressed.[79] A century later, while decrying Muslims' irrational and violent nature, the legist Oldradus de Ponte admitted Christian rulers' right to expel Muslims, but said that this should not be done without just

[76] See the table in B. Kedar, "On the Origins," p. 335.
[77] See B. Kedar, "De Iudeis et Sarracenis," and p. 330.
[78] Text in J. Hankins, *Humanism and Platonism*, p. 355. In Herde's view this was the crucial distinction that Canon Law turned in respect to the differing approaches to Muslims and Jews. See P. Herde, "Christians and Saracens," p. 364.
[79] J. P. Lomax, "Frederick II, His Saracens, and the Papacy," p. 192, and H. Gilles, "Législation et doctrines," p. 200.

cause.[80] Christian theorists were driven to enunciate these apparently paradoxical approaches because they were caught between an ideological/theological tradition that precluded compromise or relativism and a pragmatic/legislative program that demanded it.

Papal rhetoric and legislation followed the same pattern. As late as 1179, the Council of Lateran III scarcely mentioned Muslims and Islam, and apart from a decree forbidding Jews (and Muslims) from having Christians as domestic servants, the statutes in question referred to the war against Islam. They included an embargo on trading arms and strategic commodities with the *dār al-Islām*, and a prohibition on serving on Muslim "pirate" ships.[81] It was at Lateran IV (1215), the general council convened by that most imperial of popes, Innocent III, that the status of subject Muslims was first addressed substantially. The context was not Islam *per se*, but the status of non-Christians and the preservation of the primacy and integrity of the Christian community.

Thus, on the strength of Deuteronomical precedent, Muslims and Jews were ordered to wear distinctive (but unspecified) garments. The fear was that, unless they were clearly identifiable, Christians might accidentally have sex with them, which would open the door to apostasy. The same canon demanded they remain indoors from Good Friday to Easter Sunday, and commanded the "secular princes" to punish them should they "blaspheme Him who was crucified for us." Finally, the proscription on Jews from serving in positions of political authority, first established at Toledo in 589, was extended to "pagans."[82] A few decades after Lateran IV, Gregory IX's *Decretals* confirmed previous prohibitions and added new ones, including a ban on the construction of "synagogues" (a word sometimes extended to mean also mosques), and a belated response to a complaint by the Bishop of Palermo, dating a half-century earlier, that under "King William of Sicily," Muslims had been abducting and abusing Christian women and boys – presumably referring to events during the uprisings of the second half of the twelfth century.[83]

Yet, Gregory also reiterated the right of non-Christians (specifically, Jews) to be free from persecution and forced conversion, and secure in the practice of their religion.[84] His second successor, Innocent IV, went even further, admitting that infidel rulers could be considered legitimate, as

80 D. Freidenreich, "Muslims in Western Canon Law," p. 51; Oldradus de Ponte held that "those [Muslims] willing to live in peace and quiet ought not to be harassed . . ." See N. Zacour, *Jews and Saracens*, pp. 80–82 {LXII}, and pp. 19–28, generally.

81 As early as 1195 merchants of Montpellier were being prosecuted for embargo-busting. See J. Lacam, *Les Sarrazins*, p. 207.

82 See H. J. Schroeder, *Disciplinary Decrees*, pp. 236–96.

83 See C. Maier, "Crusade and Rhetoric," p. 372. 84 *Ibid.*

long as the lands they ruled had not been conquered from Christians, and that they allowed Christian missionaries into their kingdoms and did not impinge on the religious rights of their Christian subjects. For the thirteenth-century popes, enthusiastic advocates of Crusade as they may have been, heresy was perceived as a far greater threat than Islam.[85] The trend to see compliant Muslims as legitimate, if subordinate subjects who were not to be unduly interfered with was only departed from at the Council of Vienne (1311–12), where Clement V (1305–14) dictated two canons relating to the practice of Islam. The first ordered the establishment of schools of "Hebrew, Aramaic and Chaldean," in the name of "propagating the saving faith among the heathen peoples," while the second banned the call to prayer (*'adhān*) in the "parts of the world subject to Christian princes where Muslim live," and forbade popular pilgrimages to the tombs of Muslim "saints."[86]

By this time, however, the only subject Muslims left in Latin Christendom were those of the Iberian Peninsula, and it is curious that a council called by Philippe le Bel (1285–1314) with the express purpose of dissolving the Templar Order would bother to address two concrete aspects of Muslim worship directly. It may have been a reaction to the recent Muslim triumph at Acre (1291), or – more likely – a response to the specific complaint of some indignant Spanish cleric. The ululating and singing of pilgrims and celebrants at the tombs of local holy men, and the trumpet-blowing and chanting of the *mu'adhdhin* – like the Sunday hammering of Muslim smiths – would have rankled pious Christians, all the more so, when it was carried out with extra energy and exuberance on Christian feast days – as seems to have been the case in some locales in the Crown of Aragon.[87] Again, however, the moral guardians of *mudéjar* Islam might not have found themselves at odds with at least some of Clement's commands – the practice of *ziyāra* (pilgrimage to saints' tombs) and the more libidinous aspects of popular celebrations were also regarded with suspicion by orthodox Islamic authorities.[88]

In any event, as with secular law, by the mid thirteenth century the principles by which Canon Law would approach Islam and Muslim subjects had been established, and there would be little substantial change

[85] See J. Muldoon, "Tolerance and Intolerance," pp. 122ff. For an overview of thirteenth-century papal decrees regarding Muslims, see S. Domínguez Sánchez, "Cristianos y musulmanes."

[86] See O. R. Constable, "Regulating Religious Noise," pp. 74–75, for the Latin text and an English translation.

[87] H. Gilles, "Législation et doctrine," p. 203. For the issue of noise and religious identity, see O. R. Constable, "Regulating Religious Noise."

[88] See, for example, J. W. Meri, "The Cult of Saints," pp. 135ff; and below, p. 481ff.

thereafter. The preservation of the faithful (religiously, socially, and sexually), the prevention of intermarriage and miscegenation, providing an atmosphere conducive for Infidels to convert, and ensuring that they heard the Word of God remained the Church's preoccupations. Forced conversion and arbitrary expulsion were never presented as religiously legitimate, although they could be rationalized in non-religious terms. In the century following Vienne, local synods, municipal codes, and royal legislation would echo and elaborate on the restrictions that were supposed to apply to *mudéjares*, but with little practical effect. Kings were hardly consistent; however, among Pere the Ceremonious's many concessions to Valencian *mudéjares* during his war with Castile, was the right to call the faithful to prayer openly.[89]

Hence, Francesc Eiximenis's fervent attack on the *ʾadhān* in his devotional *summa*, *Lo Crestià* ("The Christian"; *c.* 1379–91). According to the friar, any Christian ruler who permitted "the public honoring of that villain Mafomet" or allowed Muslims to climb to high places "to laud and praise their strange gods ... especially that traitor, abomination, son of the Devil and deceiver of the World, named Mafumet of Mecha," would find his dynasty cast down Israelite-style by a vengeful Yahweh.[90] Such warnings notwithstanding, subject Muslims' relationship to Canon Law would change only in the 1400s and 1500s as some individuals who converted willingly backslid into Islam, or when whole communities were converted by *fiat*, and thereby came under full Church jurisdiction, as Christians.

Prior to that, Canon Law had very little direct power to influence subject Muslims. Like royal law, its enforcement in real terms was dependent on the willing collaboration of intermediaries for its execution, and in this case neither secular authorities nor local ecclesiastical corporations had a great interest in enforcing regulations that would make their Muslim subjects uncomfortable or restless. The financial and political agendas of local rulers and princes were too bound up with those of their *mudéjar* dependents. This was a world in which Military Orders earned money from licensing Muslim prostitutes, kings used Muslim officials and soldiers to their advantage, and lords, bishops, and abbots collected rents and dues in direct relation to the contentment and prosperity of their Muslim tenants and vassals.[91] This is not to say there was no effect. Any

89 See, for example, J. Boswell, *The Royal Treasure*, pp. 364–69 and 474.

90 Quoted in M. T. Ferrer i Mallol, "Frontera, convivencia y proselitismo," pp. 1587–88.

91 In the mid fifteenth century, the Monastery of Chelas in Portugal actively pursued policies that support and empowered Muslim tenants and artisans (including women) – priorities shaped entirely by the short-term economic benefit of the chapter, rather than by religious issues. M. F. Lopes de Barros, *Tempos e espaços*, pp. 248–49. For prostitutes, see below, p. 439.

interference with Islamic ritual, including the *ʾadhān*, would impact Muslims' ability to perform the *ṣalāt* properly, just as the absence of a legitimate ruler (and hence, of a legitimate religious authority) would make accurately calculating the *zakāt* ("alms tax") or the beginning of Ramaḍān impossible.[92] Each of these counted among the "Five Pillars of Islam." Still, as a general rule, in the lands where there actually were significant Muslim minority communities, the sumptuary mandates of Lateran IV, the restrictions on mosque building, and the edicts of Vienne simply went ignored, when it was not in local, seigniorial, or royal authorities' interest to enforce them.[93]

The issue of Muslims' obligation to wear distinctive clothing or badges was even more ambivalent. Officially, this had been established by Innocent III at Lateran IV as mandatory for Jews and Muslims in order to avoid accidental sexual encounters between Christians and non-Christians.[94] In some areas, including the Kingdom of Aragon, there are indications it was implemented sporadically as law as early as the late thirteenth century, although Muslims living on the frontier had apparently been exempt by virtue of the war with Castile.[95] In Lleida these laws had first been mandated in 1301, although the royal authorities continued to grant this *aljama* exemptions until the 1390s.[96] Muslims in Catalonia, Valencia, and Portugal resisted the implementation of such laws and protested against them in the mid and late fourteenth century, a fact that suggests they had not been previously enforced.[97] There is abundant evidence that Muslim men in the Crown of Aragon, Castile, and Portugal often defied these rules, and at times did, indeed, take advantage of appearing as Christians to have sexual liaisons with Christian women,

92 Discussed in L. G. Jones, "The Boundaries of Sin," p. 473.

93 Examples abound. In 1221, for example, the Count of Urgell, who owned the site of the Friday mosque of Lleida, ceded the property to a certain Lleonard de Safareig, on the condition that the latter find a suitable place for the local Muslims to construct a new mosque, complete with minaret. See J. Mutgé i Vives, "La aljama sarracena," p. 103. Much later, in 1360, Pere the Ceremonious granted the Muslims of Benavent the right to construct both a new mosque and a cemetery. See J. Boswell, *The Royal Treasure*, p. 467. Zorgati notes that when the provisions of Lateran IV relating to miscegenation were adapted in the *Siete Partidas*, it was only Jews and not Muslims who were included in the legislation, suggesting that in Castile, Muslims did not provoke the same level of anxiety as Jews. See *Pluralism in the Middle Ages*, p. 138.

94 A. García y García, *Constitutiones concilii quarti*, p. 107 {68}; confirmed by Gregory IX in *Decretales D. Gregorii Papae IX*, pp. 1665–6 {15}.

95 B. Catlos, *The Victors and the Vanquished*, pp. 300–05; cf. pp. 201–02, above.

96 See J. Mutgé i Vives, *L'aljama sarraïna*, pp. 375–78 and 380–82 {194, 197 and 199}.

97 M. T. Ferrer i Mallol, *Els sarraïns*, pp. 284–85 {73}, and "The Muslim *Aljama* of Tortosa," 160; M. F. Lopes de Barros, "Body, Baths and Cloth," p. 9, and *Tempos e espaços*, pp. 189–97.

both prostitutes and otherwise.[98] It is not clear, however, that *mudéjares* necessarily viewed these requirements as an imposition, particularly when they referred to "traditional costume" and were applied to Muslim women. Whereas, in Portugal, some *mouros* protested the requirement to wear Andalusī-style robes, those of Lisbon complained that they had been forbidden from doing so; and when the Granadan Moriscos petitioned the Ottomans for aid in the face of Spanish oppression, they cited the legal obligation that their women cease wearing the veil as one of their grievances.[99]

Such sumptuary regulations, based on communal identity, resonated with Islamic law and practice. In the *dār al-Islām* analogous requirements were placed on Christians and Jews, and the law prescribed punishment for those *dhimmī*s who ignored them, or who attempted to pass as Muslims.[100] In any event, the arbiters of *mudéjar* morality would have agreed that Muslim men should not wear luxurious materials, such as gold and silk, and would have favored measures which restricted Christian–Muslim fraternization. And if such laws do not figure in the law codes of Sicily and Jerusalem, it is likely because it was not Muslims who were dressing as Christians, but the contrary.[101]

As it was, one of the only contexts in which the institutional Church stood on something resembling principle as regarded Canon Law and *mudéjares* was in its insistence that Muslim landowners and tenants should be subject to the tithe, a matter that the Church was never able to resolve decisively in its favor. This was an initiative that was resisted fiercely by royal and seigniorial powers (both lay and ecclesiastical) – who sought to protect (and thereby better exploit) their Muslim vassals and tenants by relieving them of any tax obligations which they themselves would not profit by. Hence, the restrictions in most of Iberia placed on the sale of Muslims' property to Christians. The rule of thumb was that *mudéjares* were not liable for canonical taxes themselves, but once a property had passed into or through Christian hands, it would be forever subject to the tithe, regardless of who subsequently owned it. Therefore, the Church had a strong interest in dislodging Muslim landholders, even temporarily, or

[98] For Portugal, see the *Ordenaçoes afonsinas* as cited in M. F. Lopes de Barros, *Tempos e espaços*, p. 195. Some Muslim craftsmen complained the long sleeves mandated by law interfered with their dexterity and impinged on their ability to work.

[99] M. F. Lopes de Barros, *Tempos e espaços*, pp. 189–90; G. López de la Plaza, "Las mujeres moriscas," p. 308.

[100] See L. García Ballester, *Historia social de la medicina*, p. 52.

[101] By way of comparison, the situation for Jews vis-à-vis the promulgations of Lateran IV and Vienne was little different. In many realms they continued to build synagogues, serve in positions of power, lend at usurious rates, and keep Christian domestics, well into the fifteenth century.

as an administrative fiction, so as to bring land irrevocably under the ecclesiastical fiscal regime.[102] If in Ávila *mudéjares* owed the tithe as early as 1175, it was because these were likely newcomers rather than natives.[103] In Portugal, *Mouros* were only obliged to pay tithes in the 1370s, while on at least one occasion, exemptions from the tithe that had been granted to land worked by *mudéjares* in Aragon in the 1200s continued to be considered valid more than a century after the expulsion of the Moriscos.[104] In Navarre in 1478, no less a figure than the King's brother confirmed the exemption of the Muslims of Tudela from the tithe.[105] Across the peninsula, Christian landowners and Muslim farmers conspired together to evade ecclesiastical taxes by claiming the lands the latter worked were exempt; a prospect that led some Christians to prefer *mudéjar* tenants.[106]

## Subject Muslims and Islamic law

If any *qāḍī [alcadí]*, for money, hatred or ill will, love or fear, corruption or deception, deliberately pronounces sentence against anyone contrary to the *sunna [Çuna]*, or the opinions of those sages named "Almelich," *[Mālikī]* "Reffemi," *[Shāfiʿī?]* "Fambeli" *[Ḥanbalī]* and "Abofani," *[Ḥanafī]*, he must make restoration to the party against which he has given the sentence; and he shall also be punished with the appropriate penalty as assessed by the *qāḍī* or

102 The ideology of the "Reconquest" notwithstanding, land conquered by Christian kings but that had remained uninterrupted in Muslim possession was considered not to be subject to canonical taxes. However, once a parcel of land had been held by a Christian, it would be subject to the tithe forever onwards, regardless of the communal identity of the tenant or owner. As a consequence, local "expulsions" of Muslims were at times undertaken by churchmen merely to make the land liable to ecclesiastical taxation. The principle of Jewish and Muslim exemption was stated in both royal and municipal laws; for example, M. Molho, *El Fuero de Jaca*, p. 85 {A 133} and G. Tilander, *Los fueros de Aragón*, p. 11 {5}. The Church's position was formalized at the Council of Lleida (1229). See J. M. Pons Guri, "Constitucions conciliars," p. 83 {XIV}. For Navarre, see M. R. García Arancón, "Los mudéjares de Navarra," pp. 387–89.

103 See M. García Arancón, "Los mudéjares de Navarra," p. 399; the same is likely the case for the Muslims of Cantillana, who in 1345 made a pact with the Archbishop of Seville to pay.

104 M. F. Lopes de Barros, *Tempos e espaços*, pp. 404–05; for Aragon, see the case referred to in B. Catlos, *The Victors and the Vanquished*, p. 338, n. 54.

105 M. García Arancón, "Los mudéjares de Navarra," p. 403.

106 This dynamic led to numerous complaints and legal suits on behalf of the Church to collect these tithes and establish clear rules to avoid evasion. See, for example, M. García-Arenal and B. Leroy, *Moros y judíos en Navarra*, p. 118–19 {XXXVI}, and E. Lourie, "Anatomy of Ambivalence," p. 47. Evasion of canonical taxes was one of the reasons some Christian landowners preferred Muslim *exarici* (sharecroppers) as tenants. See B. Catlos, *The Victors and the Vanquished*, p. 181. Similar collusion between Christian officials and *mudéjares* aimed at avoiding secular taxes. See, for example, M. T. Ferrer i Mallol, *El sarraïns*, p. 265 {57}.

seignior, according to the *sunna*. (Anonymous Valencian *faqīh*, untitled treatise on the "*Çuna e Xara*" (fourteenth century)[107])

In theory, the jurisdiction and legal culture that most affected subject Muslims in Latin Christendom was Islamic law (Arabic: *sharīʿa*; Romance: *xara*) and custom (Arabic: *sunna*, *sunnat al-muslimīn*; Romance: *assuna*, *çuna*, etc.), but it is not clear what this meant in practice.[108] Aside from Iberian surrender treaties and population charters, and occasional anecdotes, we have virtually no sources for the practice of Islamic law by subject Muslims in Latin Christendom prior to the mid thirteenth century. Moreover, those treaties themselves say little other than to confirm the principle of judicial autonomy which Muslim communities were granted both as a *sine qua non* to their peaceful submission to Christian rule and as a consequence of the contemporary conception of religious identity as being correlative to legal community. This leaves us with little more than conjecture to work with as regards the communities of Sicily, the Holy Land, and Hungary, and the Iberian kingdoms prior to the late 1200s. In each of these cases, the survival and the integrity of Islamic jurisprudence would depend on a number of factors, including: the persistence of pre-conquest elites in Christian-occupied territories, proximity to the *dār al-Islām*, and ability to maintain cultural connections with it, and the degree of interference exerted by Latin rulers and seigniors on free Muslim subjects.

### *Isolation and entropy*

For the most part, it seems that Latin rulers did not take much of a role in intra-Muslim legal affairs in the early centuries of Christian domination. "El Cid," for example, may have appointed or confirmed the judiciary of Valencia during his short-lived domination of the city (1094–1100), but did not, as has sometimes been imagined, act as *qāḍī* himself. Rather, he took a supervisory role over the city's Islamic judges – undoubtedly with an eye to appropriating part of whatever fines they levied and maintaining control and oversight over what constituted a potent branch of government with a long tradition of independence and dissent. Similarly, at Burgos (Castile) – a locale which had an émigré rather than a "native" *mudéjar* community – a charter of Sancho IV of Castile (1284–95) dated 1293 explicitly stated that inter-Muslim disputes had always and would always come under the jurisdiction of the (Christian) *alcaldes* of the city. This undoubtedly refers, however, to their right to oversee and collect the

107 C. Barceló Torres, *Un tratado catalán*, pp. 8–9 {32}.
108 See R. García de Linares, "Escrituras arabes," p. 183 {8} (1181) for *sunnat al-muslimīn*.

revenues from these cases, which one must assume was decided in consultation with local Muslims.[109] Such was the case two centuries later in Segovia and Madrid, where the Christian *justícia ordinaria* was the official who technically decided Muslim disputes.[110] In Navarre, by the thirteenth century, *mudéjar* magistrates had lost criminal jurisdiction, but remained the arbiters of civil and "personal law," although cases where the fines exceeded sixty *soldi* came under the purview of the bailiff, and the kings occasionally made *ad hoc* interventions.[111] However, by the 1500s even these cases were being heard by a Christian official.[112] Further east and back in the late twelfth century, the diarist Ibn Jubayr observed that the Muslims of Palermo were under the jurisdiction of their own *qāḍī*.[113] In Ḍiyāʾ al-Dīn's memoir of Frankish Nablus, we read of a feudal seignior dealing rough justice to local Muslims, but it is also clear that this was an exceptional event and that both officially recognized and popularly supported *fuqahā* functioned.[114]

In each of these scenarios a pious Islamic elite had remained under Christian rule and provided both continuity and integrity to the administration of Islamic justice; moreover, each of these locales maintained close connections to the larger Islamic world. Thus there is little reason to doubt that Islamic law continued to function in form, if not – when the objections of foreign *ᶜulamāʾ* to the legitimacy of Christian-appointed *quḍāt* are accepted – in essence.[115] The kingdom of Hungary was the exception. Here – if the traveler Abū Ḥāmid al-Gharnāṭī is to be believed – the *Böszörmények* of the mid thirteenth century had only the most tenuous grasp of Islamic dogma. Nevertheless, Muslims here were apparently governed by *fiqh* as they understood it. In Christian Iberia, the corruption of Muslim law would have become increasingly marked from the mid thirteenth century onwards, as Christian and Islamic law ceased to function as two independent, parallel systems, and the latter was drawn under

[109] See G. Wiegers, *Islamic Literature*, p. 58.
[110] G. Wiegers, "'Isà b. Yabir," p. 168. In Castile, *mudéjar* legal autonomy was curtailed under Juan I. See F. Segura Urra, "Los mudéjares navarros," p. 242.
[111] F. Segura Urra, *Fazer justícia*, pp. 117–18.
[112] When Axa Granada sued her husband, the crossbowman Yayel Cortoví, for divorce and the return of her dower on the grounds of abuse in 1509, her case was heard by Garcí Perez de Barayz, "standing magistrate of the Muslims of the city of Tudela" (*juez hordinario de los moros de la ciudad de Tudela*). She hired a Christian attorney (*procurador*), and sentence was passed down (in her favor) in a court convened in the Church of Santa María. M. García-Arenal and B. Leroy, *Moros y judíos en Navarra*, pp. 124–26 {XLIII}.
[113] Ibn Jubayr, *Travels*, p. 348.
[114] See for example, B. Catlos, *The Victors and the Vanquished*, p. 156.
[115] See above, pp. 316ff.

the domination of the former, as a consequence of the administrative, economic, and institutional convergence of *mudéjar* and Latin societies.

It is in those areas of Iberia that were conquered and remained under Christian control that the impact of Infidel domination can be best apprehended. Here, the surrender agreements concluded by local Muslim authorities – local military commanders (*quwwād*), magistrates (*quḍāt*), judicial officials (e.g. Latin: "algalifos," "alforques," "alfaques," and "alguaziles") and elders (e.g. *shuyūkh*, "bonos moros," "senes Saracenorum") – seem to indicate a presumption of continuity, particularly as the authority of the these same individuals is sometimes confirmed in the treaties.[116] Nevertheless, it is clear that across the peninsula there was an exodus of members of the religio-cultural elite in the wake of the conquests. Unlike Sicily, where Norman rulers patronized Islamic high culture, here, learned Muslims would find their sources of support had vanished, and as the permanency of the conquest became clear, they moved south to seek their fortune in the *dār al-Islām*, taking their books and their expertise with them.

Yet, despite interference and distortion, Islamic law evidently continued to function in Christian lands between the time of the conquest and the era when *mudéjar* legal digests first begin to appear – a period of nearly three centuries.[117] Moreover, these later treatises make it clear that subject Muslims remained conscious of the fundamentals of *fiqh*, and that they recognized its governing principles, including the existence of four accepted schools of interpretation (*madhāhib*). This can be accounted for in part by the continuing contacts between Muslims in the Iberian kingdoms and the larger Islamic world – through pilgrimage and travel, trade and commercial links, diplomatic missions and slavery. Moreover, it is clear that the departure of the urban elites did not provoke a collapse of religious culture among *mudéjares*; even prior to the conquest, many areas (notably the Ebro and Jalón valleys in Aragon) had been characterized by a firmly entrenched network of rural mosques and schools – the type of organic institutional framework that could survive the disappearance of central authority. In Iberia the potential for Islamic magistrates to take on independent political leadership was made clear in the century prior to the

[116] See the surrender document of Tudela (1115), in T. Muñoz y Romero, *Colección de fueros*, p. 415; for the "Muslim elders" (*senium sarracenorum*), see R. I. Burns, *Diplomatarium of the Crusader Kingdom of Valencia*, vol. III, p. 321 {765}. Muslim elders (and later Christian elders) were commonly consulted to resolve boundary disputes, especially those relating "to the time of the Muslims." This was the case also in Sicily; see J. Johns, *Arabic Adminisration*, p. 309. "Bonos moros" or "good Muslims," echoes the Latinate concept of "boni homines," or "good men," who were given an analogous position in *fueros* promulgated for Chrisian communities.

[117] See A. Carmona González, "Textos jurídicos-religiosos islámicos," for an overview of the judicial literature.

Christian conquest, and was facilitated by the consensus of the uniformly Sunnī, and all but exclusively Mālikī orientation of the populace.[118]

The greatest threat to the integrity of Islamic law in these lands came as the consequence of the imposition of Christian legal systems as higher jurisdictions, and of the proprietary/protective relationship that the kings maintained with *mudéjares*. Obviously, any aspects of Islamic law that stressed the primacy of Islam and the jurisdiction of the *sharīʿa* over non-Muslim communities had to be discarded – this applied both to relations with Christians and with Jews (with whom Muslims were held now to be on an equally subordinate footing). The independent application of capital and permanently damaging corporal punishments was also now prohibited in the absence of royal dispensation, a change that would have a tremendous impact on the administration of law relating to *ḥadd* offences (approximately, criminal law), including crimes against the person (such as murder and assault), and property, including theft.[119] Laws governing inheritance were impinged upon by royal and seigniorial prerogatives, including lords' rights to appropriate the property of "intestate" Muslims.[120] Economic and commercial law would also be subordinated to Christian rules, except perhaps in concrete transactions limited strictly to Muslim parties and partners. The Islamic taxation system, enshrined in the *sharīʿa*, and consisting principally of the *khums* ("fifth"), *ʿushr* ("tenth"), *zakāt* ("alms-tax"), and other assorted canonically legitimate levies, would also be compromised, or entirely set aside.

Muslim communities went from being taxed under Muslim regimes to paying tribute under Christian rule – the latter in amounts negotiated with their new sovereigns, and which needed to be raised without regard to Qurʾānic mechanisms of assessment or limits on individual contributions. Many Muslim communities likely continued to administer an internal levy (perhaps, the *zakāt*) to finance communal institutions, but little trace of this remains in the documentation. Pious foundations (*waqf* and *ḥubus*) almost certainly continued to function and be founded. Typically these were classified as "mosques" by the conquerors and seized by royal or ecclesiastical authorities, but this appropriation would have been fiscal in nature in many cases, allowing foundations to maintain what would be in

118 See M. I. Fierro Bello, "The *Qāḍī* as Ruler," and "Alfonso X "The Wise"," pp. 179–82.

119 In 1337, for example, Pere the Ceremonious specifically granted certain *aljamas* the right to put to death Muslims who apostatized by converting to Judaism. See J. Boswell, *The Royal Treasure*, pp. 379–80 and 436–37.

120 This points to another structural divergence between Islamic and Latin legal culture. Given the rigid and precise rules of inheritance in Islamic law, a written will was not seen as necessary, whereas in Christian practice it was.

effect *dominium utile* (effective ownership) over their endowments, while paying rent or tribute to their new lords.[121]

The impact of Christian domination was no lighter in the sphere of "personal law," which remained, in theory, the particular jurisdiction of *mudéjar* communities. Family and gender law would have been impacted as the Christian concepts of commercial and property law, standards of evidence, and other procedural norms were imposed on Islamic communities. Islamic prohibitions against drinking alcohol and gambling, which were probably enforced with great difficulty even prior to the conquest, would have been all but impossible to apply afterwards – the popularity of taverns and gambling houses, particularly Christian-owned establishments, is well attested in the archival sources. From the late 1300s seigniors and kings increasingly felt the right or responsibility to intervene personally in specific cases relating to communal morality. Hence, in 1393 we find Carlos III of Navarre pardoning and absolving Yça de Garças, a young Muslim of Marchante, and his servant (*manceba*), who had been imprisoned for living together as man and wife contrary to the "çuyna."[122] Conversely, when the Muslims of Lucernich (or at least the most pious among them) petitioned their lord (and, later, Queen) Maria de Luna to shut down the local tavern, she refused.[123]

Likewise, the religious aspects of Islamic law, such as the obligation to observe established holidays and festivals would have been dramatically encroached on. Islamic festivals are public in nature, and from the thirteenth century onwards ecclesiastical and municipal authorities sought to limit such expressions, although royal privileges specifically recognized *mudéjares*' right to observe major public feasts such as the *ʿĪd al-aḍha* (or, as Christians understood it, "your [the Muslim] Easter").[124] Such considerations did not come free; Muslims paid taxes and fees specifically for the right to observe their religious rituals and festivities.

[121] Typically all religious properties (referred to generically as *mezquitas*, or "mosques") were granted to the Church at the time of conquest, but this did not necessarily indicate a change of purpose, merely that the Church became the new owner of the concerns. References to post-conquest pious foundations are rare, although sometimes fields belonging to mosques are mentioned. This is explicit in the population charter granted to the Muslims of the Vall d'Aiora (Valencia) in 1328, in which each mosque of the region is to be allotted three *tafulles* (a unit of area) of irrigated farmland free of any fiscal obligation, and evidently in order to generate income for upkeep. See M. T. Ferrer i Mallol, "La carta de població," p. 92 {20}. The *convenienҫa* granted to the Muslims of the lower Ebro by Ramon Berenguer IV in 1153–59 and confirmed in 1276 states explicitly that "the mosque will remain just as it is with all of its incomes and buildings." See J. M. Font i Rius, "La carta de seguridad," p. 282.

[122] M. García-Arenal and B. Leroy, *Moros y judíos en Navarra*, p. 104 {xxv}.

[123] ACA, C., reg. 2335, f. 76r (9 may 1398).

[124] See A. Canellas López, *Colección diplomática*, vol. I, p. 132 {41}.

The impact on the Islamic legal system, however, was far more profound than even these examples indicate. Christian lay jurisprudence, with its essentially secular orientation, its increasing emphasis on written evidence (as opposed to the Islamic insistence on the primacy of oral deposition), its dependence on royal authority, and the role of precedent (custom) and decree in what might be described as the "legislative process," all set it apart from the foundation and elaboration of Islamic law. Ideally, Islamic jurisprudence was elaborated independent of binding precedent (apart from the *sunna*) and without the interference of secular authority (*sulṭān*). Rather, it evolved as the consequence of accepted systems of scriptural interpretation and the legal *responsa* (*fatāwa*) that they inspired. Islamic jurists tended to see their own resistance to the interests of rulers as proof of their integrity, and in any event, multiple interpretations of the law (four alone, in medieval Sunnī law) were regarded as equally legitimate. And whereas, in the Islamic world, chief magistrates were indeed nominated by princes, to a great extent their actual authority depended on their recognition by the *umma* as a whole (or the more powerful elements within it), who could either accept or reject the validity of their pronouncements (and dispense or withhold patronage), based on what they perceived of as individual jurists' level of integrity and knowledge. For their part, beyond what they could accomplish by coercion and force, Muslim princes' legitimacy and popular authority depended on their recognition by the *ʿulamā*. In other words, there existed in the Islamic world a separation or balance of power and an element of popular consensus that served to reinforce the integrity and independence of Islamic law.

All of this would change under Christian rule. Christian princes saw their Muslim subjects essentially as a source of revenue with whom they shared no moral or religious consensus and to whom they felt no obligation other than that expressed by the letter of the treaties they signed or ratified. Their interest in Islamic justice went only as far as this would reinforce the stability of these subject communities and maintain the revenue stream they produced. Apart, perhaps, from the moment of conquest and the brief interval before Christian dominion was consolidated, these Infidel rulers' authority and legitimacy were not based in any way on their maintenance of Islamic law or patronage of a legitimate culture of *fiqh*. Therefore, the individuals they appointed as magistrates would be promoted on the basis of their capacity to serve the royal, Christian agenda, rather than any Islamic one. Moreover, having abrogated to a great extent their executive power, and with Christian officials enjoying an effective monopoly on legal coercion, *mudéjar fuqahāʾ* could hardly function with integrity, even when Christian and Jewish officials were not actively seeking to undermine their authority or to appropriate their jurisdictional rights.[125] In cases of such interference or when they felt their judicial liberties otherwise infringed, *mudéjar* communities and their officials did not hesitate to fight back, lodging counter-suits and complaints with the royal court.[126]

Were all of this not enough, the authority of the *sharīʿa* and the power of those who wielded it were further undermined by the fact that, unlike in the Islamic world, subject Muslims could simply opt out of the system. *Mudéjares* who were dissatisfied with the outcome of judicial decisions generally had the right to appeal these – ultimately to Christian judicial authorities, and in many jurisdictions to the king himself. Those who were convicted of serious crimes and who had exhausted their appeals could often simply purchase a pardon from the Crown, if they had the means. Finally, apostasy to Christianity was not only no longer prohibited, but encouraged by the highest powers of the land. Hence, *mudéjares* could also opt out absolutely by converting, thereby effectively wiping clean their slate as Muslims.[127] For petty criminals, disgruntled heirs, and dissatisfied *mudéjar* wives, conversion represented a drastic, but guaranteed tactic for obtaining a more favorable share of an estate or a divorce from an unwilling husband. The gravity of this situation was not lost even on a traveler like Ibn Jubayr, who shuddered: "Should a man show anger to his son or his wife, or a woman to her daughter, the one who is the object of displeasure may perversely throw himself into a church and there be baptized and turn Christian. Conceive now of the state of one so afflicted in his family, or even in his son."[128] Muslim men, for their part, could convert as a tactic for divorcing a wife without having to pay the *mahr* (*ṣadāq*), or dower, that would be due to her family in such a case.

Muslims became extremely adept at manipulating the weakened Islamic judicial system, the Christian legal apparatus, and the hazy interface between them. *Mudéjares* skillfully used and abused written evidence, avenues of appeal, bribery, and coercion to obtain favorable results in their legal travails – sometimes against Christian parties and for the good of their own communities, but often against fellow Muslims, or in direct prejudice to the interests of their own *aljamas*. At times, Muslims themselves found

125 Like the office of *qāḍī*, that of the *faqīh* was transformed by Christian rule. In some locales the term *alfaquí* designated an official post, at others, it was a vague and informal designation. See G. Wiegers, *Islamic Literature*, pp. 82–84.

126 See, for example, S. Abboud Haggar, "Conflicto de jurisdicción," and B. Catlos, *The Victors and the Vanquished*, p. 377.

127 As Nirenberg points out, this was not always a successful ploy, especially for Muslim women accused of sex crimes. See D. Nirenberg, *Communities*, p. 139, n. 44.

128 Ibn Jubayr, *Travels*, p. 369.

themselves at odds with the precepts of the *sharīʿa*, and in such circumstances Christian law and authority provided a route of escape. For example, in 1416, when Acsa (ʿĀʾisha), the wife of Mahoma Matarran, was convicted of adultery with a Christian, a crime for which "she deserved to be flogged, and stoned to death according to the law [*çunya*] of the Muslims," her husband and father sought a pardon from Carlos III of Navarre which they purchased for a hefty 170 *florines* – offense to God's law and family honor notwithstanding.[129] On the other hand, over the centuries Christian officials and institutions doggedly whittled away at *mudéjar* jurisdictions both as a consequence of their larger political agendas and to take a greater share in the revenue they generated.[130] Yet, despite all of the circumstances acting to undermine the efficacy and integrity of Islamic law, royal privileges from across the peninsula reiterate, through the fifteenth century, the jurisdiction of the *sunna Saracenorum* over inter-*mudéjar* disputes and offenses against the *sharīʿa*.[131]

## Mudéjar *law, written and unwritten*

Prior to the Romance redactions of *mudéjar* law codes that were produced in fourteenth-century Valencia and Castile-León, there are few indications of the particular powers that Muslim magistrates in Iberia were able to wield. Two fourteenth-century royal charters from the Crown of Aragon, however, provide a clue. In 1356, the *aljama* of Ricla (along with twenty other nearby communities), received a privilege from Pere the Ceremonious of Aragon confirming *mudéjar* jurisdiction over crimes including slander, assault, wounding, and homicide, as well as establishing the penalty for women who became pregnant "through fornication," and limiting the king's rights in terms of intestate Muslims, and establishing the *corvée* or labor services that *mudéjares* were liable for.[132] A year earlier, the elected officials (*adelantats*) of the community at Lleida had been granted the right to "correct, condemn and punish, according to the *çuna* and their law, assaults, slanders, follies and other ill acts, that are subject to civil penalty," reserving only those crimes punishable by

[129] M. García-Arenal and B. Leroy, *Moros y judíos en Navarra*, p. 108 {xxx}.

[130] That said, Christian officials also aggressively intruded on the rights and jurisdictions of other Christian officials. See, for example, the careers of Bartholomew Thomasii and Egidius Tarin in B. Catlos, *The Victors and the Vanquished*, pp. 373–76 and 377–80. In 1360, the Aragonese Queen Elionor de Sicilia brought Domingo Llull, the Bailiff of Elche, to book for having been financially abusing the town's Muslim *aljama*; see K. Boswell, *The Royal Treasure*, pp. 504–06 (and cf: pp. 507–08).

[131] For a late example see M. J. Brito de Almeida Costa and E. Borges Nunes, *Ordenações afonsinas*, vol. II, pp. 532–35 {II:CI}.

[132] E. Lourie, "An Unknown Charter."

"penalty of blood" for the Crown.[133] In other words, *mudéjar* magistrates were largely limited to imposing fines in civil or minor criminal offenses, although in some locales they could also mandate non-disfiguring corporal punishment, which is to say, the lash (*açots*).[134]

It was around this time or in the succeeding decades that two digests of *mudéjar* law were produced: one, an untitled work written in Catalan and originating in Valencia (the so-called *El llibre de la çuna e xara*), and the other, produced in Castile, and known as *Los leyes de los Moros*.[135] Both of these works were written by Muslim authors, and apparently intended for a Christian readership – likely those officials who by the late Middle Ages were taking an increasingly active role in overseeing Islamic judicial proceedings or adjudicating appeals against sentences given by *mudéjar* magistrates.

Each of these works is clearly based on a Mālikī legal foundation and acknowledges the legitimacy of the other three orthodox *madhāhib*, but neither could be confused with a legal manual produced within the *dār al-Islām*.[136] The focus of the Valencian digest is on religious observance, inheritance law, sexual morality (particularly regarding women and female adultery), crimes such as murder, wounding, and slander, and procedural issues relating to giving testimony. The Castilian work covers these general themes as well, although it is less specific regarding religious observation, and dwells in more detail on law relating to marriage and dower (*alçidaque*), as well as on commercial transactions and laws relating to slave-holding. In each of the codes certain crimes are to be punished by flogging, stoning, or unspecified capital punishment. In Valencia, slander merited eighty lashes, a husband who secretly converted to Christianity and had sex with his Muslim wife was to be obliged to stone her, and those guilty of homosexual sex ("the … crime against nature") were to be killed.[137] The Castilian work, for its part, specifies that apostasy from Islam should be punished by decapitation.[138] Each of the codes is fundamentally correct in its description of Islamic belief and ritual, including

[133] J. Mutgé i Vives, *L'aljama sarraïna*, pp. 309–11 {134}.

[134] As in, for example, the Vall d'Aiora (Valencia); see M. T. Ferrer i Mallol, "La carta de població," p. 92 {21}. In 1379 Hucey Corayet received his annual salary of 50 *solidi* for serving as the Count of Denia's "sergeant-at-arms (*saig*) and for flogging Muslims." See J. Argente Vidal, "Un libro de cuentas," 313.

[135] For an overview and typology of the surviving legal treatises, see A. Carmona González, "Textos jurídicos-religiosos islámicos."

[136] M. Á. Ladero Quesada, "Las relaciones," p. 41. In fact, the Castilian *leyes* are a partial and re-edited translation of the ninth-century Mālikī digest, *Al-Tafrīʿ* (c.f. above, p. 323). See S. Abboud-Haggar, "*Las Leyes moros.*"

[137] C. Barceló Torres, *Un tratado catalán*, pp. 6 {XVI}, 8 {XXXI}, and 23 {LXXXVI}.

[138] P. de Gayangos, *Las leyes de los moros*, pp. 142–43 {179}.

the ʾ*adhān* (transcribed accurately in the Valencian collections, but significantly expanded upon), marriage law, ritual ablutions, the Five Pillars, and so on. There are signs, however of Christian influence, such as the permitting of the use of torture on suspects, and indications of a reaction to Christian encroachment, such as the maxim that decisions made according to the *çuna* could not be subject to appeal.

Given their content, and the fact that in each there are provisions that clearly go against Christian law (not the least the provision that converts to Christianity should be executed, and the lengthy and detailed rules regarding Muslims' ownership of non-Muslim slaves), it is clear that these were not practical manuals of law. Rather, as L. P. Harvey concluded, they likely served as orientational texts for Christian authorities so they might understand Islamic law in cases where Christian parties (and, therefore, Christian magistrates) were involved, or when Christian judges were charged with evaluating the deliberations of *fuqahāʾ*.[139] As such, they provided an opportunity for their authors – learned *mudéjares* – to engage in what was at once a rhetorical exercise and an attempt to influence the way that Islamic law was understood by Christian authorities. The culmination of this trend can be seen ʿĪsā b. Jābir's *Brevario sunni*, produced in 1462 at the request of Juan de Segovia. This digest is even more religiously oriented and idealistically Islamic than those earlier compendiums, and cannot have possibly reflected the way that Islamic law was actually practiced among *mudéjar* communities in Castile.[140]

In sum, Islamic law in the Latin West was as ill defined and imprecise as Christian law. Not only was it subject to the same limitations in terms of enforcement and consistency, it faced the additional challenge of being constantly undermined by the existence of a divergent and more authoritative legal order – the Christian one – to which it was forced to conform. That said, *mudéjar* magistrates certainly functioned in a judicial role: they administered fines and light corporal punishment, and in grave matters, turned offending parties over to the royal authorities.[141] The law remained, after all, an important instrument for maintaining communal discipline and community cohesion for a minority community – hence, the emphasis such codes placed on inheritance rules, sexual conduct, and slander. Moreover, the exercise of the law provided an important source of income for Muslim communities and their officers, who were generally entitled to a share of the fines they levied (typically, one quarter to one third).

139 L. P. Harvey, *Islamic Spain*, pp. 74–76. 140 See p. 195, above.

141 Seen in this light, *mudéjar* law functioned in a manner analogous to Canon Law, with many of the same limitations.

However, the dissonance between the ideal of Islamic legal administration and the reality as it was practiced had two consequences. First, there are indications that *mudéjares* sometimes bypassed the magistrates that had been officially appointed by Christian authorities, and turned to popular religious figures to arbitrate their disputes.[142] This was undoubtedly the case across the Latin Mediterranean and is attested to in sources from the Holy Land, Sicily, and Iberia. The second consequence was that informal punishments and community pressure, not to mention extra-judicial violence, came to be seen as much more effective approaches for enforcing public morality. We can assume that those who offended or upset the public order in Muslim communities – particularly smaller communities – would be subject to informal ostracization, but by the fourteenth century *mudéjar* administrative and judicial officials began formally to employ embargoes of community religious services against Muslim subjects who defied their authority and the will of their *aljamas*.

This can be most readily seen in the tax disputes that wracked Aragonese *aljamas* from the thirteenth through the fifteenth centuries. Typically, a Muslim family would obtain by royal favor or through some seigniorial relationship an exemption (*franquitas*) from contributing to *aljama* taxes, and subsequently attempt to parlay that limited privilege into a heritable right to a total tax exemption valid *in perpetuam*. The result was legal battles and feuds that often lasted generations and stretched over centuries.[143] The struggles fractured communities into (literally) warring factions, and almost inevitably ended in an impasse, which by default favored those claiming *franquitas*. It was only when evaders were prohibited by their fellow Muslims from attending the mosque, being buried in the Islamic cemetery, and enjoying the benefits of the community of Muslims, that they accepted the verdicts of their communities and began to contribute.[144] Indeed, the Valencian *çuna* treatise cites such embargos as a matter of law; but in many cases, it was the informal power of consensus that had the greatest coercive authority over Muslims.[145]

Nor were Muslim communities and their officials powerless against the Christian sovereigns and lords who ruled over them. Unlike Islamic law, with its scripturally established concept of the protected minority community (*dhimma*), the status of Muslims under Christian rule was by and large a

[142] See B. Catlos, *The Victors and the Vanquished*, pp. 156–57, and "The de Reys," p. 215.

[143] See, for example, B. Catlos, *The Victors and the Vanquished*, "Case Study 1: Fiscal and Confessional Identity, The Galips, Templar Vassals in Zaragoza (1179–1390)," pp. 329–38, and B. Catlos, "The de Reys."

[144] See M. T. Ferrer i Mallol, "Francos pero excluidos," and B. Catlos, "The de Reys," pp. 214–15.

[145] C. Barceló Torres, *Un tratado catalán*, p. 34 {134}.

function of the will of kings. Therefore, the specific privileges and rights that each community enjoyed were seen essentially as contracts (*conveniençes*) between rulers and *aljamas*. When a new king came to power – which was frequently an occasion of vulnerability for the monarchy – or when kings faced political threats, whether external or internal, Muslim communities could either claw back privileges that they had held previously and lost, or obtain broader rights than they had ever enjoyed. The privilege the *aljamas* of Ricla and its environs leveraged from Pere the Ceremonious in 1356 represented a reinstatement of rights they had been granted in 1210 by Pere the Catholic; likewise, the Ceremonious's concession to the Muslims of Lleida in 1355 amounted to a restoration of constitutions that had been established by Jaume II in 1293.[146] It was not magnanimity that prompted Pere to expand the jurisdiction of Islamic law in these communities but, rather, uncertainty and desperation as the war with Castile turned against him. It was the sort of opportunity that *mudéjar* judicial and fiscal officials were keen to exploit, both for their own good and that of their communities.

## Judicial and fiscal administration

Moreover, so that the said Muslims may be better maintained within their rights and not be subject to any oppression or aggravation, I establish by right and command that their officials should be Muslims appointed from among the inhabitants of their *aljama*, and they should appoint those to the *aljama* who are clearly at my service, and who will act in their favor and preserve them. And moreover, the *aljama* may remove them and appoint others in their place. (Fernando IV of Castile and León (1295–1312), privilege granted to the Muslims of Murcia, 1305[147])

Many of the same principles and limitations that characterized *fiqh* and its relationship to Christian legal jurisdictions in subject Muslim societies contributed to the character of their administrative culture and institutions. Indeed, the two are often difficult to separate. As the foregoing chapters show, and Fernando IV's decree of 1305 reflects, Christian rulers had a strong interest in conceding to Muslim communities the greatest autonomy possible; their aim was to maximize their economic and political exploitation of these communities, and to keep them complacent, docile, loyal, and productive. As was the case with the law, it was these practical concerns that led to the emergence of an approach to the administration of ethno-religious minorities that resembled *dhimma*, rather than a conscious or deliberate imitation or adaptation of the Islamic approach. Across the breadth of the Latin Mediterranean, Christian conquest had been incremental and

[146] See p. 176. [147] A. Echevarría Arsuaga, "De cadí a alcalde mayor (I)," 147.

piecemeal. Almost without exception, Muslim territory came under Christian control town by town, and, as a result, the administrative organization and political status of these communities varied as widely as the individual circumstances of their submission. When one surveys the panorama of Islamic minorities in Latin Christendom, one is confronted with a dizzying and ever-shifting array of officials, institutions, and competencies, and communities whose capacity for self-determination oscillated according to changing political, social, and economic circumstances. Nevertheless, general patterns can be discerned among the multiplicity of arrangements that were employed to govern subject Muslims across Latin Christendom, although it is for Iberia that we have an immense preponderance of documentation.

### *The new order*

Across the Latin-occupied territories, the conquests effectively removed the military–political elite from subject Muslim societies. However frequently Muslim subjects might serve their new lords under arms, they effectively lost this aspect of communal autonomy. What remained to them was the judicial and fiscal administration intended to maintain the peace, and the flow of revenue. Thus, Muslims in Iberia were constituted into semi-autonomous local communities (e.g. *aljamas*, *comunas*) under the leadership of officers and officials who were either elected by the local Muslim communities (or the oligarchies that dominated them) or appointed by Christian kings. Pre-conquest Islamic administration had typically been characterized by a split between secular/military authority, represented by the *al-qāʾid*, or "commander," and civil/religious authority, personified in the *al-qāḍī*. With the establishment of Christian rule, the former was rendered obsolete and the latter – designated variously as the *alcaydus*, *alcaide*, *alcadi*, *alcalde*, *alfaquí*, *alaminus* (from *al-amīn*), *alguazir* (from *al-wazīr*), or *caualchén* (from *ṣāḥib al-ḥukm* "master of justice"), to list but a few permutations – came to function as the head of the local community and its magistrate.[148]

This reflected a process that was already underway in many locales as a consequence of the deterioration of Islamic political power.[149] Further, just as the *qāḍī* had been assisted by elected auxiliaries known as *al-umanāʾ* (sing: *al-amīn*, "trustworthy"), under Christian rule the *alcaydus* was often assisted by elected *adelantados* (also *vereadores*, *procuradores*, *repartidores*), or by a royally appointed *alaminus* – officials in charge of assessing and

[148] In the Crusader kingdom of Jerusalem, the term used was *rays* (see p. 148).
[149] See above, p. 41.

collecting tribute. In some *aljamas* the *alfaquí* (from *faqīh*, or "jurisprudent") or *alfaquíes* functioned as advisors or auxiliaries to the *alcaydus*, and were either popularly acclaimed or appointed by Christian authorities.[150] Most *aljamas* also had a designated notary (e.g. *scriptor*), and many had an official religious official (e.g. the *alhomadar*, or the *sabasala*, from *ṣāḥib al-ṣalāh*, "master of prayer" – meaning an *imām* and/or *mu'adhdhan*), each of whom would have been appointed or ratified by the royal court or the local seigniorial authority. In the Crown of Aragon, major *aljamas* tended to have all of these functionaries, and exercised authority over the hamlets in their hinterland (sometimes mirroring pre-conquest administrative divisions), while smaller *aljamas* might have had only some of these officials, or even none. Some *aljamas* had additional officers, such as market supervisors, sergeants, and other specialized positions. In others, particularly in the kingdom of Valencia, the local elders (*shuyūkh*) were at times given a formal role in government, or general assemblies were held annually (as at Xàtiva), or on an *ad hoc* basis (as in many *aljamas* in the Jalón and upper Ebro valleys of Aragon and Navarre).

Generally, however, at least in the Crown of Aragon, the Islamic principle of unipersonality was maintained; there would be one supreme judicial authority in each *aljama* who answered to the royal court. The appointment mechanism of these officials varied from locale to locale and over time; sometimes communities were able to elect their own officials, at other times they were appointed without consultation and even over the strenuous objections of communities. Archival documentation abounds in the Crown of Aragon, and we know the names and can trace the careers of scores of minor officials in the thirteenth and fourteenth centuries, and sketch out the administrative framework of dozens of *aljamas*. Even here, however, the power of the magistrate was contingent on Christian authority; often disputes that should have fallen under his jurisdiction were instead entrusted to Christian authorities or *mudéjar* popular juries.[151] What is revealed, thus, is a variety of institutional arrangements and local privileges that makes it all but impossible to generalize. The situation in the other kingdoms is even less clear, although it appears that in this respect, Navarre resembled Aragon. On the other hand, some large *aljamas* in Castile, such as Ávila, had multiple *alcaydi*, each associated with his own mosque. In Portugal, it is not until the late fourteenth century that any sort

[150] In Valencia, the *alfaquí* was appointed by the Bailiff-General of the kingdom. M. Febrer Romaguera, "Tribunales," p. 6[illegible]. A sense of the various permutations and combinations of *mudéjar* administrative offices can be gained by surveying the major monographs on Muslim minorities in the various kingdoms. For Portugal, see M. F. Lopes de Barros, *Tempos e espaços*, pp. 347–85.

[151] See for example, A. Macho y Ortega, "Condición social," pp. 212–13 {1}.

of formal administrative structure can be discerned from the extant documents or that the names of individual officials appear in the records with any regularity. The resemblance of the titles and attributes of *mudéjar* officials to Islamic precedents should not be misinterpreted as indicating continuity, at least, after the first generation or two. These offices were "Christian institutions," predicated on non-Muslim principles of administration and justice. Hence the concern of many foreign *muftūn* that it was simply not possible to live as a Muslim under Infidel rule, because the entire apparatus of law was illegitimate under such regimes, which by their nature embodied *ʿadawa*, or "hostility to the Law."[152]

The *aljama* ("local community"; *comuna* in Portugal) – not to be confused with the *morería*, or "Muslim neighborhood" – was the corporate manifestation of the Islamic community of a given locale. It was the unit by which taxes were assessed, and it defined the limits of the jurisdiction of *mudéjar* officials, and acted as the framework for monopolies and licenses (such as *ḥalāl* butcher shops, public baths, mills, market stalls, inns, and ovens) that provided further revenue to the royal fisc. It was the body by which the kings transmitted their will to their Muslim subjects, and the collective that represented and defended Muslims' interests against royal, seigniorial, and ecclesiastical authorities, Christian municipalities, Jewish individuals and *aljamas*, and other neighboring Muslim *aljamas*.[153] The *aljama* defended Muslims' interests, whether by negotiating new privileges or obtaining tax relief from the Crown, or by protecting them against corrupt and abusive royal and municipal officials, litigious Jewish creditors, and popular Christian violence. Not all Muslims belonged to an *aljama* – some communities were too small to be constituted and some locales had no more than a handful of families.[154] Nor did the *aljama* necessarily include all local Muslims; some were engaged in direct tenant or seigniorial relationships with noblemen or ecclesiastical foundations.[155] This fact

[152] The tenth-century *mufti* al-Qabīsī of Ifrīqiya raised this objection in relation to Muslims living in Sub-Saharan Africa; his argument was later deployed by those who resisted Norman rule. See M. Brett, "Muslim Justice," esp. pp. 325–37, also pp. 63ff. and 314ff.

[153] See B. Catlos, *The Victors and the Vanquished*, pp. 126–28.

[154] For example, in 1314 there was apparently a single craftsman and his family ("saracenis alforris," meaning perhaps "free but unincorporated into an *aljama*") in Girona (Catalunya), a town that never had a native Muslim community. Local Christian officials petitioned for him to be excused from contributing to local taxes on the grounds of his poverty and good character. See ACA, CRD Jaume II no. 4947 (July 27, 1314); thanks to Jaume Riera for this reference. Similarly, some towns in northern Portugal, like Guimarães, had small, unconstituted communities of *mouros*. See M. F. Lopes de Barros, *Tempos e espaços*, p. 117.

[155] See B. Catlos, *The Victors and the Vanquished*, pp. 125–28.

complicated the *aljama*'s role as a tributary institution, given that the array of royal taxes to which these communities were subject tended to be imposed as a lump sum. The ambiguity of some Muslims' role in and obligations towards their own communities regularly gave rise to tensions, violence, and factionalism. These dynamics were mirrored in Jewish and Christian communities, where similar struggles played out between Jews who claimed *franquitas* and their *aljamas*, and Christian *universitates* (municipalities) and their members who claimed the status of *infanzón* – the broad, lower nobility, whose rights and privileges also included certain tax exemptions.

In Islam, taxation, particularly the *zakāt*, is a religious obligation laid out in the Qur'ān, *ḥadīth*, and *fiqh*, and therefore any change to the tax regime of Muslim communities touches the essence of Islamic identity. Hence, in the initial period of Christian conquest, tax regimes tended to be left intact and in the hands of *mudéjar* community leaders. Sometimes, Muslims rationalized new Christian-instituted taxes by characterizing them as a "*jizya*" that they, as "*dhimmīs*" of the Christians, were now required to pay.[156] Even as the decades passed and Christian fiscal regimes developed and expanded, some Islamic-era taxes were simply Christianized.[157] In the lands of Castile, in particular, there is considerable evidence of this type of institutional diffusion.[158] However, it would be wrong to characterize this as "continuity"; over time, the basis of the assessment, collection, and administration of these "Islamic" taxes was transformed, and subject Muslims were liable for an array of royal, seigniorial, and municipal taxes, some of which may have represented the transfer of tribute the community would have paid under Islamic rule, while others represented completely alien innovations.[159] Christian peasants, for their part, were subject to taxes and obligations that *mudéjares*

[156] See p. 32. For example, the fifteenth-century *mudéjar* traveller and memoirist Ibn al-Ṣabbāh described his fellows as living "under the *dhimma*" of the Christians." See F. Franco Sánchez, "Los mudéjares," 383. The same rationale was made in Sicily; see J. Johns, "The Boys From Mezzoiuso"; cf. above, pp. 25 and 32.

[157] See below, p. 400. Although evidence is rare, particularly prior to the mid-thirteenth century, it may have been the case that Islamic taxation was also adapted by Christian lords in the Frankish east. See P. C. Sidelko, "Muslim Taxation."

[158] See S. Abboud Haggar, "Precedentes andalusíes."

[159] In the Crown of Aragon, for example, *mudéjares*, like their Christian and Jewish co-subjects, regularly paid *peyta* ("tribute") as well as *cena* ("hospitality tax"), *exercitum* ("military service tax"), *monetaticus* ("minting tax"), as well as an array of extra-ordinary levies. Moreover, because taxation regimes were negotiated locally at the time of surrender, they were not uniform even within the same kingdom. The Muslims of Tudela, for example, were never liable for the *azofra*, and the other Navarrese royal *aljamas* eventually managed to escape this obligation. See A. Ozaki, "El régimen tributario," p. 467.

were not, and therefore one cannot conclude that overall Muslims were necessarily taxed at a heavier rate than Christians.[160]

Although it was justified variously on the basis of protecting Christian society from Muslim contamination, protecting *mudéjares* from Christian violence, and preventing inappropriate social interaction, the establishment of *morerías*, or "Muslim neighborhoods," was a measure undertaken to a great extent to supervise taxation of *mudéjar* communities – to ensure that Muslims did not escape their fiscal obligations to king or *aljama* or engage in activities in violation of Christian or Islamic law or conscience. Hence, it was gradually required that all Muslims of a given locale live within the precincts of a distinct neighborhood, and prohibited that Christians live in the same. However, as with the sumptuary laws and the prohibitions of the *ʾadhān*, although this legislation was promulgated as early as the time of the conquest in some areas, it was not enforced with any consistency.

In many of the larger towns of the Crown of Aragon, officials were regularly complaining of Christians' purchasing property or settling in *morerías*, and yet in the late fourteenth century, a town as substantial as Tarazona could still be without a separate Muslim quarter.[161] According to the *Ordenaçoes Afonsinas*, domestic segregation did not become law until the early 1400s and was not generalized until the reign of Afonso V in the middle of the century.[162] On the other hand, in Burgos it was reported that Jews and Muslims were moving out into Christian areas of the city because their own quarters were full.[163] In any event, sometimes it was the *mudéjares* (who had much more to fear from socio-religious contamination than Christians) who wanted to construct *morerías*, and Christians who resisted their efforts.[164] Living in such close quarters could blur the lines separating the communities, whether living or dead; in Lleida, for example, the *mudéjar* and Christian cemeteries were so close that some of the less sophisticated Christian faithful apparently

160 See B. Catlos, *The Victors and the Vanquished*, p. 197, contra E. Lourie, "Anatomy of Ambivalence," p. 16.

161 M. L. Ledesma Rubio, "Marginación y violència," p. 205. This despite the fact that in 1361 Pere the Ceremonious ordered a walled *morería* to be constructed for the exclusive use of Muslims. See J. Boswell, *The Royal Treasure*, pp. 469–70.

162 See Afonso, *Ordenações afonsinas*, vol. II, p. 535 {II: CII: "Que os mouros vivem em Mourarias aparades dos Christaãos"}.

163 L. Torres Balbás, *Algunos Aspectos*, p. 27.

164 The Muslims of Teruel requested and received a privilege to construct a walled *morería* in 1275, but faced with resistance by local Christian authorities, petitioned the King to enforce it. The project was held up for twelve years. See B. Catlos, *The Victors and the Vanquished*, p. 302.

ended up unintentionally praying for the salvation of the occupants of Muslim graves![165]

*Mudéjar* fiscal instability was aggravated by the fact that as Christian society became more complex, and as its institutions matured towards the mid thirteenth century, *aljamas* suffered a loss of autonomy. The consensual aspects of *aljama* government were eroded, as kings sought to control ever more tightly the revenue they generated, and as Christian municipalities worked to encroach on the competencies (and revenue streams) of *mudéjar* officials.[166] There was a general trend for the power within *aljamas* to fall into the hands of an artisanal elite: cliques and families whose industrial and craft activities (such as soap-making, cloth manufacture, carpentry, or construction) provided them with the capital and connections required to obtain official positions.[167] By the late thirteenth century these posts had been converted into little more than tax-farming arrangements, to be rented from the monarchy with the aim of maximizing one's profit and influence in the community by collecting commissions on judicial fines and by the exercise of both soft and hard power. Sometimes administrative posts were simply bought and sold.[168] Official positions in a given locale tended to become concentrated in the hands of single individuals, who would simultaneously hold multiple offices, and pass these down to their children and grandchildren. Of course, there had been dynasties of jurists and petty officials in the Islamic era, but in the absence of the checks and balances inherent in a society ruled by a Muslim prince and bound by a common commitment to Islamic ideals, this dynamic had a particularly corrupting effect.[169] Occasionally, *aljamas* complained that illiterates or otherwise unqualified individuals had been

165 J. Mutgé i Vives, "La aljama sarracena," p. 104. If this was indeed the case and this does not represent some sort of fabrication on the part of Christians looking to relocate the Muslim cemetery, it raises interesting questions regarding the character and style of local Christian and *mudéjar* grave markings and burial customs.

166 See, for example, the struggle on the part of the Crown to maintain control over local Muslim courts in Cocentaina and Alcoi (Valencia), in I. O'Connor, "The Mudejars and the Local Courts," esp. pp. 338–55.

167 *Aljama* functionaries often used Romance surnames derived from the Arabic words relating to trades, such *al-najjār* ("carpenter"), which appears as "Anajar" or "Atnajar." See for example, B. Catlos, *The Victors and the Vanquished*, pp. 214–21, and J. Argente Vidal, "Un libro de cuentas," p. 293.

168 In 1314 the position of *alaminus* was "sold" (*fue vendido*) to Salim, the carpenter, by Miguel de Boyl, bailiff of Teruel. The sale was overturned based on the *aljama*'s privileges. See ACA, ARP, MR, v. 1688, ff. 122r. From the point of view of Christian lords, *mudéjar* magistrates effectively "rented *aljamas*" (i.e. the right to exercise justice and collect revenue), as in a fourteenth-century seigneurial account book. See J. Argente Vidal, "Un libro de cuentas," pp. 295 and 296.

169 This practice was extremely widespread. See, for example, M. L. Ávila, "Cargos hereditarios." To be sure, this sort of medieval *enchufismo* was practiced also in Islamic Spain.

appointed as magistrates or officials.[170] The power of these petty, spurious aristocracies that took control of many *aljamas* was entrenched by the right officials were typically granted to an exemption (*franquitas*) from royal taxation – a privilege that could be passed down in perpetuity to an ever-broadening pool of descendants. Such largesse cost the king nothing, given that it did not reduce his total entitlement from the community, but did drive a wedge of self-interest between *mudéjar* officials and their constituents, and set the scene for bitter feuding and factionalism, linked to competition for these lucrative posts.[171] Petitions by disgruntled *mudéjar* communities, who periodically sent delegations to complain of the scandalous abuses and tyranny of their *aljama* officials, were largely disregarded by the royal court, at least until such a time as the tax flow was interrupted. At that point, the kings did not hesitate to depose unsatisfactory officials swiftly and appoint replacements.[172]

In the Crown of Aragon – where the most abundant documentation has survived – it can be observed that the cycle of appointment, oppression, and decadence typically lasted an Ibn-Khaldunian three generations.[173] On the one hand, this indicates that *aljamas* may have been subject to frequent misgovernment, but on the other it reflects communities that had a broad base of prosperous families engaging in what might be described as an "healthy" competition for power that helped to counter decadence and stagnation. Moreover, it shows that ordinary *mudéjares* were not powerless in shaping their own government. Sustained complaints to the royal court, lobbying of local Christian powers, and the withholding of taxes could rid the *aljamas* of their most abusive, corrupt, and incompetent rulers. Corrupt Muslim officials were not infrequently brought to

Just prior to the Christian conquest the underqualified *qāḍī* of Calatayud apparently succeeded in passing his appointment down to his equally unqualified son. See R. El Hour, "The Andalusian Qāḍī," pp. 70–71.

170 See, for example, B. Catlos, *The Victors and the Vanquished*, p. 156. Certainly this happened under Islamic rule as well. See R. El Hour, "The Andalusian Qāḍī," pp. 74–77. The great twelfth-century Andalusī jurist Abū 'l-Walīd b. Rushd (the grandfather of the famous philosopher "Averroës") complained of the appointment magistrates and *muftūn* who were incompetent and corrupt.

171 This can be observed across the Crown of Aragon, Castile, and Portugal. See for example, M. F. Lopes Barros, *Tempos e espaços*, p. 383, and B. Catlos, *The Victors and the Vanquished*, pp. 136–38.

172 The case of Abraham Abengentor, *çaualquem* of Huesca in the late thirteenth century is exemplary; see B. Catlos, *The Victors and the Vanquished*, pp. 357–65. This dynamic in which local Muslim officials entrenched themselves and their families, began to commit fiscal and judicial abuses, provoked the complaints of their communities, and were finally replaced, can be observed across the Iberian kingdoms from the thirteenth through the fifteenth centuries. In other instances, however, popularly deposed magistrates were reinstated by kings. See, for example, *ibid.*, p. 161.

173 See, for example, the case study in B. Catlos, "Privilegio y poder."

trial, at times with the collaboration of local Christians.[174] Failing bringing abusive officials to justice, more violent measures could be resorted to. In 1415, the Muslims of the Serra d'Eslida paid a fine for having sent the "*alcadí* of the lord-king" packing ("put him on the road") at the instigation of a "wise *mudéjar* woman" ("çabia mora").[175] Similar incidents occurred in Castile, also, as in 1492, when the Muslims of Ágreda ran "maestre Amete," their *alcalde de moros*, out of town, and in 1476 in Ávila, when dissatisfied Muslims and Jews first endeavored unsuccessfully to bribe the Christian *corrigedor* ("governor") into action, they subsequently threatened to abandon the city.[176]

Smaller and more isolated communities and those of less consequence to the royal treasury may have escaped some of these ill effects of Christian rule, but in larger centers it is clear that the integrity of *aljama* officials in Islamic terms had eroded considerably, if not completely. That said, communal factionalism and administrative corruption was a near-universal characteristic of *mudéjar* life, and whereas at times it was Christian rule that encouraged such decadence, it was often the monarchy or other Christian institutions that offered ordinary Muslims their only defense.[177] When the violent and corrupt de Abdella family who ruled over a terrorized *aljama* of Daroca was finally deposed in the late 1200s, it was the Bailiff of Aragon who brought them and their accomplices to trial. Among their crimes were murder and assault, as well as property and financial crimes. As *alaminus*, Mahomet de Abdella, under cover of a purported royal order, had been enslaving and selling married Muslim women who had been accused of adultery, without regard to due process or trial.[178]

As discussed in chapter 5, the crises of the mid fourteenth century provoked dramatic changes in both *mudéjar* and Christian societies and institutions, and the way that they interacted. Warfare, plague, social upheaval, and economic reconfigurations across the peninsula prompted the disappearance or decline of many *aljamas* and led to the foundation of new ones. In Castile and Portugal there was a clear will on the part of the monarchies to centralize *mudéjar* administration, and to establish a formal

174 Examples abound from the late thirteenth century forward. For a detailed case study, see E. Marín Padilla, "Investigación sobre la conducta."

175 C. Barceló Torres, "Mujeres, campesinas," pp. 217.

176 See E. Cantera Montenegro, "Las comunidades mudéjares," pp. 160–62, and S. de Tapia Sánchez, "Los mudéjares de la Extremadura," p. 121. Subject Muslims in the Crusader Levant also used the threat of emigration as a lever; see E. Sivan, "Réfugiés syro-palestiniens."

177 Kings (and queens) intervened frequently to reprimand or restrain predatory Christian officials, noblemen, and even members of their own families; see, for example, J. Boswell, *The Royal Treasure*, pp. 504–05.

178 See B. Catlos, *The Victors and the Vanquished*, pp. 353–54.

hierarchy of *mudéjar* authority wherein Islamic magistrates (or at least those in royal *aljamas*) might answer to a local or regional *alcalde mayor*, who himself was under the *Alcalde Mayor de las Aljamas de Moros de Castilla*.[179] It was really only in Castile that this effort seems to have obtained any success, and even there it was tenuous, at best.[180] In Navarre and the Crown of Aragon, all but the smallest *aljamas* remained autocephalous, their officials answering not to a higher Islamic authority but to the royal administration. In Aragon, the *alcaydus Saracenorum* of the capital, Zaragoza, might presume on occasion to wield power over the lesser *alcaydi* of the kingdom, but in fact his only advantage was in terms of prestige – appeals against the decisions of local judges went directly to the king, and it was the king or his agents who ratified or appointed local magistrates.[181] In some areas, for example the hinterland around Lleida, the town's Islamic magistrates were endowed with some authority over village *alcaydi*, but it is not clear what this meant in real terms. Likewise, in Valencia, the *alcaydus Saracenorum* embodied some sort of kingdom-wide authority, but it is not clear, if it was much more than an honorific in legal terms.[182] In any event, in Aragon and Castile, seigniors and Military Orders appointed their own *alcaydi* and *alcaldes mayor de moros*, who functioned independent of the royal hierarchy.[183]

The decentralized nature of the *mudéjar* administration in the Crown of Aragon was undoubtedly advantageous for Muslim communities. Jewish administration in virtually all of the Iberian kingdoms was centralized, but in each kingdom Jewish society tended to be dominated by a small, ultra-influential financial and administrative elite, whose value to the various monarchies helped to sustain the position of Jewish society as a whole in each kingdom. It put Jews here in a position of privilege, in a sense (at least relative to the position of Jews in other Latin realms), but made them more vulnerable. With rare exceptions, *mudéjar* society lacked such an elite – its value to the kings and other Christian authorities lay in the productive

[179] See G. Wiegers, *Islamic Literature*, pp. 84–88. [180] See above, p. 193.

[181] See B. Catlos, *The Victors and the Vanquished*, p. 383. In the Vall d'Aiora (Valencia), for example, *mudéjares* could appeal a sentence passed down by their local *alcadi*, to any royally appointed Islamic magistrate in the kingdom. See M. T. Ferrer i Mallol, "La carta de població," p. 91 {22}.

[182] See above, p. 431.

[183] For example, in Castile, the Order of Santiago had their own "alcalde mayor de las aljamas de los moros de la Orden de Santiago," whereas in Aragon, Martí I, while still an *infant*, decades before he came to the throne, appointed his own *alcadi Sarracenorum*, who had jurisdiction over his various estates in Aragon, Catalonia, and Valencia. See M. García-Arenal, "Dos documentos," p. 168, n. 2; and B. Catlos, "'Entre eulx pluiseurs Sarrazins . . .'." Each hamlet of any size in the County of Denia had an independent *alamín*. See J. Argente Vidal, "Un libro de cuentas."

capacity of the broad lower ranks, who were themselves engaged in a wide range of economic relationships with many Christian individuals, corporations, and collectives. In the case of *mudéjares*, the autonomy of local communities allowed them to adapt better to local circumstances and to independently negotiate more advantageous arrangements with both local and royal authorities. This was a likely contributing factor to the comparative success of Aragonese, Navarrese, and Catalan *aljamas* in preserving their wealth, status, and cultural independence, as when compared to those of Portugal and Castile.

### *Beyond the urban environment and the Iberian Peninsula*

The last two centuries of *mudéjar* history also saw a trend towards the seigniorialization of Muslim communities across much of the peninsula. Although the kings had generally managed to limit the number of Muslim urban communities under the control of lay lords, many rural and village *aljamas* existed under seigniorial control. Indeed, in all of the kingdoms except for Navarre, the Military Orders ruled over numerous Muslim subjects and hamlets, particularly in late conquered regions (for example, southern Valencia, the Extremadura, and Algarve) for which there were insufficient numbers of Christian noblemen and settlers to colonize. In the Ebro and Jalón valleys, monasteries (notably the Cistercian foundations of Veruela, Rueda, and Poblet) also had many *mudéjar* vassals and tenants. At times Muslim communities or individuals exercised their right to pledge themselves to noblemen or ecclesiastical orders, either in order to gain a protector more engaged than a distant and distracted royal *curia*, or to obtain better conditions or privileges.[184] At other times, when threatened by local lords or municipalities, they pledged themselves formally to the kings. From the late fourteenth century onwards as royal legislation took an ideological turn, and urban environments became increasingly polarized and fraught, more and more *mudéjares* sought refuge in seigniorial lands, where complicit lords regularly and readily cast a blind eye towards Muslims' (and Moriscos') religious and cultural expressions as long as they remained loyal and productive subjects.[185]

It would be wrong to equate this process of seigniorialization with "feudalization" – free subject Muslims in Iberia were not serfs; indeed, their link with royal authority protected them from the sorts of abuses to

[184] Some *aljamas* in Aragon and Navarre clearly enjoyed greater autonomy under ecclesiastical lordship. See M. García-Arenal, "Documentos árabes," p. 32.

[185] See, for example, M. Monjo i Gallego, "Sarraïns sota el domini," pp. 113–14; and pp. 286–87, above.

which Christian commoners were sometimes subject (such as the infamous *mals usos* or "evil customs" of Catalonia). Generally, speaking, the process of encastellation (a better term than the nebulous and distorting "feudalization"), which was one of the salient characteristics of socio-administrative transformation in high medieval Europe, occurred in Iberia on only a limited scale, and had a varying impact on free Muslims.[186] *Mudéjares* were vassals and tenants of noblemen and Orders, but however much the latter might encroach on their liberties and rights, they remained free, capable of owning their own property and unencumbered as both legal and physical persons by land-holding arrangements. Moreover, through the thirteenth century, they were largely free to leave. That said, many Muslims did not "own" (i.e. could not alienate) the land they worked, but held it either through *conplantatio* or *exaricus* (sharecropping) relationships – the latter representing a Christian adaptation of the Islamic *shirka*.[187]

As Christian-style seigniorial emphyteusis (in which peasants exercised usufruct, or *dominium utile*, over their lands) became increasingly current, truly private land ownership, which Islamic law recognized, would have declined. Moreover, progressive legal restrictions on Muslims' right to move and to change lords would have effectively tied some Muslims to their lands. Even so, apart from slaves, there did not exist a "class" of "Muslim serfs" or *exarici* – many Muslims, including *mudéjar* officials and religious figures, combined urban activities with rural ones, engaged in various types of land-tenure agreements (ownership, sharecropping and renting) simultaneously, and even invested and speculated in land. This was true also in Norman Sicily and, we may assume, in the Crusader Levant.[188] In some lordships in Iberia, Muslims were obliged to perform limited labor and transport services (e.g. *azofra*, *çofra*, *azemila*), but this was as much an adaptation of Islamic-era obligations (*al-ṣufra*), as the imposition of a foreign and novel *corvée*.[189] On the other hand, Muslim

186 Glick examines the impact of encastellation on subject Muslim communities and synthesizes the work of Spanish landscape archeologists in *From Muslim Fortress to Christian Castle*.

187 See B. Catlos, *The Victors and the Vanquished*, pp. 181–88. T. W. Barton's exhaustive local study, "Muslims in Christian Countrysides," shows how the post-conquest institution of *exaricus* in Catalonia and Aragon was highly diversified. This is hardly surprising, and is consistent with virtually all of the institutions of *mudéjar* society. However, this does not undermine the argument for adaptation and institutional diffusion (which, among his other misreadings, he mischaracterizes Catlos as presenting as "continuity").

188 For Sicily, see, for example, J. Johns, *Arabic Administration*, p. 315.

189 See, for example, E. Guinot Rodríguez, "'Sofras' y prestaciones personales." Kings, too, called upon their Muslim subjects (as well as Christians and Jews) to perform occasional, extraordinary services of labor or craft, but usually compensated them with payment. The widespread opinion among historians of Valencia that *al-ṣufra* was a tax that originated with the Almohads is discredited by the fact that it is mentioned in the mid

(and Christian) peasants across Latin Christendom were no doubt liable for a whole array of minor dues of the type that surface rarely, if at all, in documentation.[190]

Because they were not subject to royal record-keeping, we know much less about rural, seigniorial *aljamas*. Clearly, they were organized on slightly different lines, but the principles of institutional life and the legal regime that they lived under were similar.[191] For example, when the *aljama* of Cervera (now "del Maestre") in Valencia offered the Order of the Hospital their submission in 1233, the conditions agreed included: the payment of the tribute, taxes and *azofra*, religious, administrative, and judicial autonomy for the Muslims, the right to trade freely, and social and domicile segregation (evidently at the *mudéjares*' request).[192] In the Catalan Barony of Aitona, where the Montcada family ruled over several hamlets inhabited in whole or in part by *mudéjares*, the basic structure of *aljama* organization seems to have been comparable, although far simpler than on larger royal *aljamas* [193] In any event, the distinction between seigniorial and royal *aljamas* does not correspond to a rural/urban dichotomy.[194] In the fifteenth century the *comuna* of Loulé was Portugal's most productive Muslim community in terms of tax generation, yet its economy centered on food production. Despite being a royal *comuna*, its organization had the sort of imprecision, consensual elements, and the blurring of communal boundaries in administration typical of highly interdependent agricultural economies.[195]

Rural lands clearly underwent a tremendous transformation as a consequence of the Christian conquest and, clearly, as power structures, economic and fiscal regimes, markets and commercial networks, and the cultural priorities of the ruling class changed with the establishment of the Christian order, the entire structure of the countryside would have been altered. The highly efficient pre-conquest irrigation systems, responsible

twelfth century and in areas (such as Navarre) that were never under Almohad rule. See, for example, A. Ozaki, "El régimen tributario," pp. 467–70. In any event, this represents yet another case of institutional diffusion from Andalusī to Christian administration.

190 See, for example, J. Argente Vidal, "Un libro de cuentas," pp. 291–93.

191 For example, a passing reference discloses that Jucef filo Çalema de Rey, who would found a local bourgeois dynasty in Huesca, began his career as his lord Blasco de Maça's bailiff in Monflorite, a hamlet of perhaps a dozen homesteads. See B. Catlos, "The De Reys," pp. 200–02. There must have been scores like him who have passed anonymously out of history.

192 C. Barceló Torres, *Un tratado catalán*, pp. 39–41 {CLII–CLVIII}.

193 M. Monjo i Gallego, "Sarraïns sota el domini."

194 See also M. García-Arenal, "Dos documentos," E. Marín Padilla, "Los moros de Calatorao (I)," and "Los moros de Calatorao (II)"; also, the studies relating to the Muslims of the Sierra de Moncayo under the jurisdiction of the Monastery of Veruela (see below, p. 423, n. 4).

195 See M. F. Lopes de Barros, "Las élites mudéjares."

for the tremendous output of Andalusī market-gardens emerged out of the segmentary, agnatic kinship systems typical of both Arabia and Maghrib; with the introduction of new fiscal regimes which privileged cereal production, with the growing importance of transhumance, and with the disruption of traditional kinship dynamics, in many areas these systems were fractured, undermined, or obliterated.[196] Similarly, the *ḥiṣn-qarya* administrative-settlement pattern that characterized the Andalusī countryside disappeared; it was incompatible with the municipal–seigniorial organizational structure that the Christians brought.[197] Finally, although only traces emerge in the formal documentation, it is clear that the rural population underwent a process of reorganization and redistribution. In many areas *mudéjares* or their settlements disappeared, while other hamlets remained or became homogenously Muslim, and still others emerged as centers of mixed population. At times such changes came about as a result of direct and deliberate seigniorial intervention, even the wholesale expulsion or transfer of Muslim inhabitants. In 1332, for example, the Abbot of Poblet received permission from Alfons III to expel the Muslims of Quart de Poblet (Valencia), as a response to the latters' resistance to the illegal *azofras* the monastery had been imposing on them.[198] At others times, Christian lords and municipalities actively recruited Muslim settlers. Finally, to a large extent, this tendency seems to have resulted from an organic process, in which Muslims became concentrated in certain villages, either out of convenience or opportunity, or for mutual protection. Similarly, the transformation of Muslim agricultural practice under the

196 See, for example, J. Torró i Abad, "Field and Canal Building," and J. Bolòs, "Changes and Survival." Historians who study the Christian conquest in terms of its impact on rural structures of settlement and irrigation, and who use archaeology, are much more prone to view it in "catastrophic" terms. See, for example, P. Sénac, "Poblamiento," p. 401, and the comments of B. Catlos in *The Victors and the Vanquished*, pp. 118–20.

197 See, generally, P. Sénac, "Poblamiento," and "De *ḥiṣn* musulmán," C. Laliena Corbera, "Expansión territorial," and J. Torró i Abad, *El naixement d'una colònia*. In the 1980s, the effect of the Christian conquest in the Iberian Levant was contested by historians who perceived of the Christian conquest as "rupture" and those whose position was characterized as "continuist." Much of the debate was the result of the distinctive methodologies and sources favored by its most visible protagonists: Pierre Guichard and Fr. Robert I. Burns. See, for example, P. Guichard, "Quelques remarques," and R. I. Burns, "Christian–Muslim Conflict," pp. 17–20. J. Brufal Sucarrat, "Rural Muslim Lleida," provides an overview and critique of various models of Andalusī rural organization and how they have been applied and misapplied in the peninsula. Referring to post-Islamic Sicily, Molinari notes that it is historians (like Bresc, in her example, but also Sénac and Barceló i Perelló) who focus on rural settlement who tend to perceive of the Christian conquest in terms of cataclysm and rupture. See A. Molinari, "The Effects of the Norman Conquest," p. 259.

198 S. Romeu Alfaro, *Carta de poblament*.

colonial regime was at times the result of lords' policies (either to the benefit of or detriment of *mudéjares* vis-à-vis their Christian neighbors), and at times the natural consequence of the changing market conditions and tributary structures in this evolving economic environment. However, to brand such changes as "catastrophic" or portray them in genocidal terms not only represents an exaggeration but a narrow and idealized conception of what comprises an "Islamic society." Cultures and societies (or, rather, their constituent collectives and individuals) are constantly adapting to changing conditions; it is the nature of history.

Similar processes can be construed as having taken place in the two regions of Latin Christendom where subject Muslims are usually imagined as having lived under something approaching a "feudal" regime – Frankish Palestine and Norman Sicily, although it is perhaps only in the latter where this qualification makes any sense. Whereas the powerful feudal nobility of the Crusader Levant could hardly have been restrained by the weak royal authority of the kingdom of Jerusalem, the realities of the ethno-religiously and juridically complex, and (relatively) commercially oriented economy in which they found themselves, and the tremendous organizational inertia (or "path dependence") of the order they inherited, would have seriously mitigated their will and capacity to transform the countryside. Evidently, there were movements of peasants, and a tendency towards the ethno-religious Balkanization of the countryside, but the Frankish aristocracy's swift adoption to a town-based, rentier approach to rural resource management hardly encouraged the establishment of "feudal"-type arrangements of labor exploitation. Unfortunately, there are virtually no extant sources for the administrative structure of subject Muslim communities in twelfth-century Palestine; nevertheless, one may assume that – whether officially sanctioned or not – traditional judicial and tributary-fiscal structures served as the basis for whatever arrangements functioned in the Frankish-dominated countryside. The net situation was probably similar in Hungary. Here, detailed evidence of the fiscal and administrative character of subject Muslim society is non-existent; however, a sort of autonomy comparable to that of twelfth-century Iberia or Jerusalem can be construed from the fact that Muslims figure so fleetingly in medieval Hungarian legislation that they lived for the most part in separate enclaves given the relative underdevelopment of contemporary Christian administrative institutions.

In Norman Sicily and southern Italy, Muslim administration in the larger cities undoubtedly functioned in a manner analogous to that of the Iberian *aljamas*, as did that of their ultimate refuge, Lucera. In the large Muslim enclaves of the twelfth century, such as western Sicily – where Norman control was even more tenuous, and colonization superficial or non-existent – Muslim autonomy would have been even greater. Indeed, the uprisings and insurgencies of Sicilian Muslims in the last decades of that century were very likely undertaken, at least in part, because of increasing infringement on Islamic institutions as a consequence of Christian settlement and institutional development. On the other hand, Sicily was also the locus of a deliberate and intensive process of seigniorialization of Muslim subjects.[199] In the 1170s and 1180s, William II granted over 1200 square kilometers of land in northwestern Sicily to Santa Maria Nuova in Monreale. In addition to collaborating in the construction of the stunning and immense Arabo-Norman cathedral-abbey church, Muslims here comprised much of the monastery's rural population base. Indeed, it was largely as a consequence of the archbishop-abbots' abuse of seigniorial privileges, and in particular the imposition of labor dues, that the Muslims of Monreale rose up in a series of rebellions that lasted from the 1180s until their expulsion under Frederick II.[200] In Sicily, both the excessively repressive regime of Monreale and the extreme independence of the western enclaves inspired disobedience and revolt among subject Muslims. In other words, minority communities appear to have been most stable when fiscal and administrative intervention was neither too heavy nor too light. Too much interference could drive Muslims to revolt in desperation, while too little might inspire them to rebel out of optimism. In any event, it is clear that the legal and administrative structures of *mudéjar* communities cannot be analyzed in isolation; they must be considered in the light of the larger systems in which they functioned and the other communities alongside which they lived.

### *Muslim and non-Muslim administration*

Difficult as it may have been to disentangle Islamic and Christian legal jurisdictions in the areas of Latin Christendom where Muslims lived, the situation as regards administrative institutions and structures was even more complex. Muslim communities and their officials did not operate as independent entities or in isolation, but were engaged in relationships of dependency and interdependency with Christian and Jewish institutions and officials. These were encouraged by the imprecise, varied, and mutating nature of the administrative institutions and official posts in each of the communities. Again, if only because of the tremendous quantity of

[199] This is described above in chapter 3, pp. 117ff.
[200] See J. Johns, *Arabic Administration*, pp. 165–66, for the *jarīda* of Monreale.

surviving documentation from the Crown of Aragon, it is here that these relationships come most clearly to light, at least for the period prior to the fifteenth century. The great majority of Muslim *aljamas* existed in settlements that also had Christian municipalities and Jewish communities, formally incorporated as *universitates* and *aljamas*, respectively. The structure of each of these was analogous, although the municipalities had more extensive jurisdictions – including, for example, policing and other institutions that involved the use of coercive force, and market supervision (such as the control of weights and measures); and they were directly represented in the *cortes*. Christian municipalities functioned in a manner analogous to seigniors: they responded directly to the monarchs, and enjoyed certain privileges and bore certain responsibilities (including the obligation to field troops to defend the realm). Moreover, they could be just as independent-minded and capricious as noblemen: in Aragon and Valencia, many major towns, including the royal capitals Zaragoza and Valencia, rose up against the kings in the *Uniones* of the thirteenth and fourteenth centuries. Jewish *aljamas* were in a similar position to Muslim communities, the chief difference being that Jewish communities tended to be far wealthier *per capita* and generate far more revenue (at least, direct revenue, in the form of taxes and forced loans) than Muslim *aljamas*. This fact tended to give them a certain edge over *mudéjares*, at least in terms of leverage with the monarchy.

Broadly speaking, Christian official jurisdictions that directly affected Muslim communities included both royal, seigniorial, and municipal officials and functionaries. In the various kingdoms royal officials exercised juridical and fiscal competency over *mudéjar* communities; thus, the royal *merini* (singular: *merinus/merino*) in Castile and the Crown of Aragon collected rents and exercised legal powers. Other officials, for example, the Royal Bailiff (*baiulus/batlle*, etc.) in the Crown of Aragon, collected fines due to the kings, while royal magistrates (e.g. *adelantati*, *justiciae*), supervised Muslim magistrates, directly intervened in their cases, or heard appeals against their sentences. In addition, any number of royal functionaries and informally commissioned agents intervened regularly and on an *ad hoc* basis to collect taxes, rents, license fees, extraordinary tributes, and forced loans from *aljamas* or individual Muslims. *Mudéjares* who lived on seigniorial lands or who were vassals or tenants of noblemen or orders were faced, in addition, with a parallel array of noble proxies and subordinates. Finally, for those Muslims who lived in settlements formally constituted as towns and hamlets – which was undoubtedly the majority in medieval Iberia – Christian municipal officers, whether local magistrates (e.g. *alcaldes*, *justiciae*, *zalmedinas*, etc.), bailiffs, sergeants-at-arms (e.g. *sayones*), market officials (e.g. *mustaçafs*, *zabalzoques*), jailers, and any number of other functionaries each exercised some power and influence, whether direct or not, over the Muslim subjects or their officials. In other words, far from the ideal of communal separation, *mudéjar* jurisdictions never existed in isolation.

In fact, the nature of the relationships between Christian officials and Muslim communities is quite complex. Needless to say, there was inevitably an exploitative element, but this was present also in relationships between these officials and their Christian charges, as well as between *mudéjar* authorities and their constituents. This was (if not is) simply the nature of administrative institutions, wherein the individuals who bear authority frequently rationalize away whatever scruples they may have and see their official capacity as an opportunity to maximize personal gain. As a general rule, Christian officials may have regarded Muslim subjects as more vulnerable and easier prey than Christian peasants, but there is no evidence that *mudéjares* were the victims of a generalized and systematic oppression on the part of Christian officials (although this happened locally, at times). The nature of these relationships was shaped by the particular circumstances of the communities and the agendas of the individuals involved – the archival evidence does not support the contention that Christian (or Muslim) functionaries were primarily motivated by ideological concerns or prejudices. But evidence of official corruption abounds, and Christian, Muslim, and Jewish functionaries were as ready to abuse members of their own religious community as they were others.[201]

Thus, whereas *mudéjar* complaints regarding the infringements and oppressions wrought by Christian functionaries are certainly common, instances where the latter positioned themselves as protectors and patrons of the subject Muslims also abound. To look only at the Crown of Aragon in the late thirteenth and early fourteenth centuries one finds Military Orders using their Muslim subjects to attack Christian townsmen, protecting them against hostile local *mudéjares*, and regulating and profiting from organized Muslim prostitution. One finds local Muslim and Christian officials collaborating against factions within their own constituents or resisting neighboring towns and even royal representatives.[202] More than once, the kings of the Crown of

[201] See, for example, the individuals described in "Case Study 6: The Good, the Bad and the Indifferent: Christian Officials in the Ebro Region," in B. Catlos, *The Victors and the Vanquished*, pp. 366–72.

[202] The Aragonese town of Daroca provides the best-documented case of this dynamic, but it can be observed throughout the peninsula. See, for example, B. Catlos, *The Victors and the Vanquished*, pp. 339–46, and B. Catlos, "Dos musulmanas." For Huesca, see B. Catlos, "The de Reys," pp. 212–13.

Aragon felt obliged to caution the Christians and Muslims of Daroca for becoming embroiled in each other's factions; in Huesca, *mudéjares* actively collaborated in a minor noble rebellion in the 1490s.[203] Not only are such episodes common in the Crown of Aragon, but once comparable documentation for the other Christian kingdoms begins to appear from the later fourteenth century onwards, similar relationships of interdependency are revealed.[204]

This dynamic is particularly clear in the case of seigniors and their Muslim vassals, and especially from the mid fourteenth century forward, as more and more *mudéjares* attempted to flee the towns and royal lands for the seclusion and security of more homogenous and isolated rural enclaves. Aside from their role as seigniorial authorities and landowners, the nobility became economically embroiled with *mudéjares* through the purchase of *censales* (tax annuities), lending, and co-proprietorship. Seigniors, therefore, took an active interest in these communities' continuing prosperity.[205] These included ecclesiastical lords as well; monasteries' and Military Orders' support of their Muslim tenants and vassals is well documented. From the late fourteenth century, lords (including kings when they were functioning in seigniorial mode) took an increasing interest in the minutiae of *mudéjar* judicial administration, including intervening in specific cases to ensure that justice or their own interests were upheld. Local Muslim religious and judicial authorities developed a symbiotic relationship with seigniors, in which the two parties reinforced each other's authority.[206] Hence, in the early 1300s, a figure such as Martín de Azlor, Bishop of Huesca, would complain to the King on behalf of local Muslims that the *aljama*'s Islamic magistrate should be deposed for not properly applying the *sunna*![207] And just as the kingdom-wide *mudéjar* elite prospered thanks to personal ties of interest and affinity with the kings, local elites on seigniorial lands became the clients of aristocratic lords.

Such were the bonds of confidence that developed that these Muslims were sometimes endowed with competences and authorities beyond their

[203] See E. Lourie, "Anatomy of Ambivalence," pp. 46–47.

[204] See, for example, C. Conde Solares, "Social Continuity," p. 322, and F. Segura Urra, "Mudéjares navarros," p. 240.

[205] See the documents in F. Macho y Ortega, "Condición social," for example, pp. 214–19 {2–11, 7bis, 8bis, 11bis, 12bis, 13, 16, 18 and 20}.

[206] See A. Echevarría Arsuaga, "'Vassal and Friend'"; M. Meyerson, "Slavery and the Social Order," pp. 163 and 166–68; also above, p. 277.

[207] See B. Catlos, "Privilegio y poder," pp. 179–80 {7}.

communities. Hence, the corrupt *alamín* of Aranda, Mahoma de Ovecar, became so close to the aristocratic Ximenes de Urrea family that he was appointed as one of the *procuradores* of their heir.[208] The fortune of the Belvís family was not only tied to the royal house of Aragon, but also to the Luna line – and in particular, the long-reigning anti-Pope, Benedict XIV.[209] In the early fifteenth century, the master carpenter Lope de Barbicano of Navarre served as *procurador* for Christians and was a squire to King Juan (Joan II of Aragon).[210] In 1500, the affairs and properties of the Order of Calatrava in Plasencia were in the care of a Muslim majordomo, Zulema, although when the Order's higher-ups got wind of this, they ordered his immediate dismissal.[211] In Valencia, the interdependence of factions within the *mudéjar* elite and the fractured and feuding Christian aristocracy was particularly close and volatile.[212] The Christian aristocracy was not motivated either by sympathy or disdain for *mudéjares* or Islamic law, but rather by self-interest, tempered by the sense of pastoral responsibility, and even paternalistic affection, that sometimes characterized seigniorial culture.[213]

In sum, while on the one hand, the intrusion of Christian seigniors, officials, and jurisdictions undermined the institutional integrity of Islamic society in Latin lands, it established relationships of interdependence that helped to sustain and protect subject Muslims and *mudéjar* society (and enrich individual Muslims), regardless of whether these relationships were exploitative or symbiotic in nature, as well as serving as a powerful medium for Muslim acculturation and socio-economic integration.[214] The supposed jurisdiction of Islamic law notwithstanding, Christian authorities

208 E. Marín Padilla, "Investigación sobre la conducta," p. 278. Previously, Mahoma had parlayed his service as *procurador* (legal agent) of Anton Ferriol of Zaragoza into an appointment as *alamín* of Calatorao. See E. Marín Padilla, "Los moros de Calatorao (I)," pp. 298–99. As noted above, the de Rey family of Huesca owed their ascent to an ancestor's influence with the nobleman Blasco de Maza (see above, n. 191).

209 See F. J. García Marco, "El Papa Luna."

210 C. Conde Solares, "Social Continuity," p. 317. In 1387 he was appointed "Royal Master of Works of the castle of Tudela and the *merindad* of the Ribera." See A. Ozaki, "Regimen tributario," p. 452.

211 I. Montes Romero-Camacho, "Las comunidades mudéjares," p. 447, n. 361.

212 See, for example, M. Ruzafa, "Élites valencianas."

213 This pastoral/paternalistic sentiment is most clearly manifested in Christian seigniors' sponsorship of and participation in *mudéjar* and Morisco popular festivities.

214 In the hinterland of Denia, for example, the lord's wife regularly purchased cloth produced by local Muslim women, and *mudéjares* were lent money by the Count to purchase livestock, and rented his seigniorial mills and ran them (one may presume) at a profit, not to mention earning salaries as seigniorial functionaries. See below, p. 501, n. 303, and J. Argente Vidal, "Un libro de cuentas," pp. 290, 296, 313, and 316.

regularly intervened to grant pardons for offences committed, in exchange for cash.[215]

The relationship between *mudéjar* and the Jewish communities and their officials was somewhat more fraught. Muslims and Jews were both considered dependent, "minor" communities whose members did not enjoy full participation in Christian society or instutions.[216] As such, neither enjoyed a formal or structural advantage over the other. However, in practice the Jewish community enjoyed certain advantages. Unlike *mudéjar* society, Jewish communities in the Iberian kingdoms included narrow, highly educated, and financially engaged élites whose wealth rivaled that of all but the highest strata of Christian aristocracy.[217] Members of this elite enjoyed power and privilege disproportionate to their ideal position in Christian society – they hobnobbed with royalty, were specifically exempted from sumptuary laws and the visible insignia of Jewish identity, and engaged in enterprises both within their own kingdoms and across the Mediterranean. The kings and the aristocracy called on them as financiers, physicians, advisors, diplomats (especially to the Islamic world), translators (of both Hebrew and Arabic), and tax collectors. It is in this latter function that they encountered *mudéjar* communities in an official capacity. Indeed, until the *Privilegium generale* of 1283 – the Aragonese "Magna Carta," which prohibited *inter alia*, Jews from serving as royal functionaries – Jews (which is to say a handful of powerful magnate families) had traditionally dominated the highest offices of the realm. These functionaries, like Muça de Portella, who served as Bailiff-General of the kingdom of Aragon in the 1270s, exercised tremendous formal and informal power over the Christians, Muslims, and Jews of the realm.[218]

This Jewish elite, whose wealth and usefulness to the Crown were what helped sustain Jewish autonomy and privileges in the face of papal prohibitions, were scarcely less principled than their Christian or Muslim counterparts. However, *mudéjares* were particularly grated by their influence. This was not the fruit of some medieval "anti-Semitism"; rather, it was seen as insult added to injury. Muslims could justify their subjugation to Christians based on the latters' right of conquest, but to be lorded over

215 This is well documented in the case of royal authorities, but even seigniors engaged in this sort of revenue generation. See, for example, J. Argente Vidal, "Un libro de cuentas," pp. 299–302, where Muslims are recorded paying to avoid floggings they had been sentenced to by *mudéjar* magistrates.

216 Jews were subject to the same limitations in these regards as Muslims; see above, pp. 353 and 363.

217 See, for example, Y. T. Assis, *The Golden Age of Aragonese Jewry*; and D. Romano, "Cortesanos judíos," and *Judíos al servicio*.

218 For Muça, see D. Romano, *Judíos al servicio*, pp. 17–56, 179–92, and 201–07; and M.Á Motis Dolader, "Mosé (Muça) de Portella."

by Jewish *dhimmiyyūn* who had not gained that right was all the more offensive. Hence, several surrender treaties specify that Muslims should not be subject to Jewish officials, and as early as the 1090s, the Muslims of Valencia complained when El Cid appointed a Jewish *wazīr* to represent his interests in the city.[219] Such sentiments were further inflamed by widespread Jewish ownership of Muslim slaves, and the use of bonded Muslim women as concubines by Jews. However, there was also a practical side to this. Until the mid fourteenth century Jews dominated the credit sphere, and were very active in tax-farming; hence, the Jewish officials who were wringing tribute from *mudéjar* communities were in league (or seen as being in league) with the creditors to whom many Muslims communities and individuals were chronically indebted.[220] Moreover, in cases of dispute, the influence of highly placed Jews leveraged privileges which rendered Jews all but immune from *mudéjar* jurisdiction in civil suits, and acted to bring the authority of the royal court firmly on the side of Jewish creditors when such disputes went to trial.[221]

The cycle of taxation and debt galvanized local Muslim communities to resist the efforts of Jewish creditors to collect their debts by means both legal and illicit, while encouraging collaboration between *mudéjar aljamas* and local Christian communities who found themselves in the same position. The identity of Jews as the common enemy, however, was incidental; Jewish and Muslim communities also joined forces when their agendas coincided.[222] When Christian and Muslim communities shared a common goal of resisting outside pressure – most notably royal demands for tribute – they frequently joined forces to resist, at times together with Jewish *aljamas*, even to the point of violence. Moreover, Jewish and Muslim communities sometimes found themselves acting in solidarity as common victims of popular Christian violence and institutional abuse, as when their places of worship and burial were desecrated, and as common targets of coercive evangelization. *Mudéjares* – charged as their relations with Jews may have been – did not collude in Christian

219 R. Fletcher, *The Quest for El Cid*, p. 118.

220 By way of illustration, in the late fifteenth century over sixty individuals of the tiny Muslim *aljama* of Brea (Aragon) owed sums totaling in excess of 14,000 *solidos* to a single Jewish creditor, Caçón Namías of Zaragoza. See E. Marín Padilla, "Antecedentes," pp. 562–64.

221 Scanning the chancery records, it is easy to get the impression that *mudéjares* were chronically delinquent debtors and that Jewish lenders needed extra legal protections; however, Jewish creditors could be equally unscrupulous and abusive – seizing collateral unlawfully, or failing to return goods posted as bond. See for example, J. Regné, *History of the Jews*, p. 173 {962}. For *mudéjar* debt evasion, see B. Catlos, *The Victors and the Vanquished*, pp. 202–09.

222 See, for example, J. Torné Cubells, "Plet dels sarraïns i jueus."

popular religious violence. Indeed, in the Crown of Aragon, Muslim–Jewish communal posturing tended to play out in the formally choreographed context of public ceremonial, notably the funeral processions that were held in the towns across the realm following the death of the monarch, and at other public observances marking royal coronations, births, and so on. Here, violence occasionally broke out between Jews and *mudéjares* as each community's leaders jockeyed for the prestige of being next in line after the Christians in the parade.[223] Such shows of one-upmanship were less exercises aimed at staking a claim against each other than at reaffirming their importance before their own constituents and the town's Christian officials and community.

For their part, Muslims in the Iberian Peninsula reacted to the infringement of Christian institutions and jurisdictions and the undermining of their own law and authority not by rejecting or resisting "on Islamic terms," but by adapting to, and attempting to subvert the very apparatus of oppression. Both as communities and individuals, *mudéjares* quickly became adept at manipulating the ambiguities of both *mudéjar* and Christian jurisdictions, playing rival Christian authorities off against each other, preserving, deploying, and even forging documentary evidence, concocting false precedents, bribing and threatening rivals and officials, launching interminable and often unjustifiable legal appeals, resisting the threats posed by duly constituted but essentially weak royal and municipal functionaries, and even taking up arms. However much their resistance at a cultural and religious level might imply marking the difference between themselves and the larger society in which they lived, on a corporate and institutional level the effect of their resistance was to integrate them further into Christian society, its institutions, and its networks of patronage and protection. This, in turn, drove the acculturation of *mudéjares* – particularly townsfolk, and mostly (although far from exclusively) the men, who tended to take a broader and more active role in public life. By the end of the thirteenth century those who had been living under Christian rule since the eleventh and twelfth centuries had become, in many ways, indistinguishable in terms of speech, dress, and

[223] See J. Riera i Sans, "La precedencia entre judíos y moros"; M. L. Ledesma Rubio, "Marginación y violència," pp. 208–10; and S. de Tapia Sánchez, "Los mudéjares de la Extremadura," p. 113. Several episodes were reported in the 1390s, a time when Jewish communities were fighting for recognition in the wake of the pogroms of 1391, and when there would have been a succession of royal funerals. Between 1388 and 1394 alone, five of the children borne by Queen Violant de Bar (r. 1387–96) died, followed by her husband, Joan I, in 1396. Muslims also participated in royal funeral processions and public acts of mourning in Sicily, Castile, and the kingdom of Jerusalem. See H. Mayer, "Latins, Muslims and Greeks," p. 180.

outwardly manifested daily habits from their Christian countrymen. Once again, the communities of Southern Italy and Sicily and the Frankish East present a counterpoint to the example of Christian Iberia, although in each region we have far fewer sources for institutional and administrative structures, and in each case the history of the subject Muslims came to an abrupt and early end. Setting aside the highly regulated urban centers of the East, Palermo, Lucera, and the seigniorial estates of Sicily, a lack of institutional integration and convergence, together with the persistence of a high degree of autonomy and communal self-sufficiency, would have mitigated both the distorting effects of Latin domination and the corresponding acculturation of subject Muslims in both Sicily and the Crusader principalities.

On the other hand, Christian institutions were not established in a void. For the most part, the Latin conquests, the bulk of which were complete before 1300, can be characterized as a process by which a rather crude warrior people who practiced near-subsistence agriculture colonized rather more sophisticated, urbanized, market-oriented, and technologically advanced societies.[224] These Islamic societies had their own elaborate and sophisticated institutions, whereas, prior to the late thirteenth century, Latinate institutional structures and social organization were primitive and inchoate. This situation provided circumstances conducive to institutional diffusion and the adaptation of aspects of Islamicate administrative organization by Latin Christians. This was manifested in a range of contexts. Some territorial configurations persisted after the conquest, such as the Castilian *alfoz* (from *al-huz*). Certain administrative offices were adapted by Christians either in name or function: from the municipal magistrate, or *zalmedina* (from the Arabic *ṣāḥib al-madīna*, "commander of the city"), and market supervisor, and the *mustaçaf* or *zabalzoque* (from *al-muhtasib*, "public morality officer," and *ṣāḥib al-sūq*, "market master"), to the *Justicia de Aragón*, a magistrate-ombudsman whose competencies may represent an emulation of the Islamic *maẓālim* court.[225] In agriculture, not only was the Islamic *shārik* ("sharecropper") transformed into the Latin *exaricus*, but irrigation regimes and land distribution patterns sometimes persisted, as evidenced by the *Tribunal de las*

[224] That said, this contrast should not be exaggerated, as does Bentley, when he describes the "Castilians, who led the drive to conquer and Christianize Iberia," as "a people of peasants and shepherds . . . unsophisticated and rude . . . using their faith as an ideological weapon," and includes them in his chapter on "Nomadic expansion." See J. Bentley, *Old World Encounters*, p. 150.

[225] See P. Chalmeta Gendrón, *El zoco medieval*, and "El almotacén"; T. F. Glick, "Muhtasib and Mustasaf"; J. Ribera Tarragó, *Orígenes del Justicia de Aragón*; and A. Giménez Soler, "El justicia de Aragón."

*Aguas* in Valencia, which survives to this day and continues to employ Islamicate standards of evidence and procedural rules. Informally, frequent recourse was made in land disputes to local *shuyūkh* and elders, who might recall where boundaries lay and how things were done "in the time of the Muslims."[226] This was to be expected in times and places where Christian settlement was sparse, written records were few, and where the new lords of the land quickly learned that they intervened in their Muslim peasants' practices at peril to their profit.

But while such institutional diffusion may have eased the transition from Muslim to Christian rule for some *mudéjares*, it should not be mistaken for crystallization, nor should its impact on Latin organization be exaggerated. In many areas, Islamicate institutions and rural organization were simply eradicated. In others, change was slow but dramatic. Christian society was based on different types of social relations and classes, mechanisms of patronage, fiscal principles, agricultural systems, and market forces, than those of Muslim society, and together these factors inevitably transformed Islamic institutions in both theory and function, if not in name. In many areas highly tuned and productive Muslim irrigation systems were destroyed, either because Christian systems better suited to the needs of Latin administration and economy were installed, or because the complex and particular social systems which sustained them could not survive in a Latin-dominated environment.[227] Finally, by the late 1200s, the colonizers had developed their own institutions – the municipality, the parish, confraternities, and convents – which had the capacity and were driven by the will to organize society on Latin, Christian terms. Thereafter, the dynamic of contact between subjected Muslims and their Christian lords and neighbors would be more clearly confrontational.[228] At bottom, however, institutions and corporations function in the world of *realpolitik*, or they do not survive; hence, even in an age of direct and explicit ideological confrontation and antipathy, political and institutional compromise between Christians and Muslims remained not only possible, but normal.

[226] See B. Catlos, *The Victors and the Vanquished*, pp. 44 and 275–76. For the water-court, see E. Guinot Rodríguez, "Historia del Tribunal," and E. Guinot Rodríguez and J. Romero, "El Tribunal de les Aigües." Muslim elders were still called on in the fifteenth century to verify land boundaries, long after memory of the Muslim era was forgotten. See, for example, J. Carranza Larroso, "Els Costums De Flix," p. 69.

[227] See J. Torró Abad, "Field and Canal Building," and E. Guinot Rodríguez, *Feudalismo en expansion*, chapter 2, "La concreción del modo de producción feudal en el norte país valenciano: análisis de las cartas pueblas," pp. 31–85.

[228] The differences between Aragonese conquest and colonization in the twelfth-century Ebro and the thirteenth-century *Sharq al-Andalus* demonstrate the difference the development of these institutions entailed. See B. Catlos, "The Ebro Valley and Valencia."

## *Realpolitik* and religious identity

To the very noble and honoured Abū ʿAbd Allāh ibn Nāṣr, by the grace of God, King of Granada, from Us, lord Alfonso, by that same grace, King of Aragon, of Mallorca, of Valencia, and Count of Barcelona. Know that since for Our part We desire You such great good fortune as to a friend who We love greatly and from the heart, We sent You the other day, two knights of Muḥammad b. al-ʿĀdil, so that You might convey to Us that what You may know of the movement of the fleet of Abojacob Abū Yaʿqūb Yūsuf, King of Morocco . . . (Alfonso III of Aragón, letter to Muḥammad II al-Faqīh of Granada, August 16, 1290[229])

This spirit of institutional accommodation in the face of chauvinistic ideological rhetoric is most evident in the relations between Latin powers and Muslim principalities in the Middle Ages – foreign powers that, by dint of their ruling over lands that were once "Christian," were qualified as legitimate military targets unanimously by Canon Lawyers from the twelfth century on. Thus, it was generic war against Islam, rather than the specific goal of the restoration of a Christian Jerusalem, that became the focus of Crusading ideology. Hence, from 1179 the papacy began to advocate for the cessation of trade with the *dār al-Islām*.This began with orders for an embargo on strategic materials, including iron, arms, timber, and other material for war, but was soon expanded to include foodstuffs (also a strategic commodity). Under Clement III (1187–91) a total trade ban was mandated – a decree that would be incorporated formally into Canon Law in Gregory IX's *Decretals* in 1234 (and would remain in place until 1918, when the legislation of the *Liber extra* was annulled).[230]

Nevertheless, the same Clement had also begun to license exemptions to the embargo, and laid the foundations for a policy wherein trade with the Muslim world would be licit, but only through the port of Alexandria. Over the course of the following centuries the papacy would issue hundreds of exemptions to the embargo to specific towns, traders, or principalities, with conditions that varied in scope in terms of duration and commodities. Clearly, an embargo could not be enforced effectively, and there was little will to do so, even on the part of the Curia; like the larger Crusading movement, the embargo became another tool of papal

[229] ACA, C., reg., 73, f. 87r–v (August 16, 1290). For Muḥammad b. al-ʿĀdil, see p. 246, above.

[230] For the history of papal embargos, see J. Trenchs Odena, "'De Alexandrinis'"; S. Menache, "Papal Attempts"; and S. K. Stantchev, "Embargo." Calls for the rigorous application of the embargo multiplied among reactionary clerics and polemicists after the fall of Acre in 1291. See, for example, "On How to Defeat the Saracens," p. 35, in G. Constable, *et al. William of Adam*, p. 35. William was, in fact, the most sophisticated of these ideologues; he recommended striking militarily at the port of the Indian Ocean to undermine the Egyptian economy. *Ibid.*, p. 9.

authority, and constituted another means of enforcing communal discipline within Latin Christendom. That said, by the thirteenth century, the trade embargo was being echoed in the royal and municipal law codes of the Iberian Peninsula, where there was a very strong and immediate interest in preventing the flow of strategic commodities to neighboring Islamic lands (as well as, it must be said, to enemy Christian kingdoms). In times of tension and warfare, or when it suited political agendas, these embargos were certainly enforced, and the archival register records occasional prosecutions of merchants and confiscations of contraband from the late 1200s on.[231] At other times, even at the height of Crusade, they were ignored.[232]

Yet trade between Latin Christendom and the Islamic world increased through the later Middle Ages, both on a local level and on a regional or "international" scale. In 1184, at the height of the Crusade era in the Latin East, the pilgrim Ibn Jubayr marveled at the sight of Latin caravans departing Damascus, even as enslaved Franks were being led captive into the city.[233] Moreover, the papacy was hardly consistent; for example, Alexander IV (1254–61) ordered the crusading Bishop of Tarragona to desist from attacking Muslim Tunis on account of the Curia's trading interests.[234] Over the following centuries this commerce only intensified. Indeed, it was trade between the Christian West and the Islamic world that was the prime factor behind the transformation of the economy of Latin Europe, and drove economic, cultural, and political developments. Latin merchant colonies were established in the major Muslim port cities, as well as major inland centers, and commodities and products from the Islamic world became increasingly available and sought after by the wealthier classes of Christendom. The major trading powers, notably Genoa, Venice, and the Crown of Aragon, aggressively pursued trade privileges and monopolies, through a combination of diplomacy and coercion, both for purely commercial ends and as a consequence of the strategic imperative to deny advantage to their Christian rivals in the contest to dominate the Mediterranean and access African and Asian trade termini.

The consular activity and treaties that emerged in the context of commercial relations between Muslim and Christian principalities cannot be

231 For the complex relationship of commerce and Crusade, see G. Christ, *Trading Conflicts*, chapter 2, "Crusade and Levant Trade," pp. 113–20.
232 At the very time Louis IX was on Crusade against Tunis, Jaume I of Aragon authorized a *mudéjar* of Valencia to buy a shop there, and to take as his partners any Muslim or Christian he chose. See C.-E. Dufourcq, "Chrétiens et Musulmanes," p. 221.
233 Ibn Jubayr, *Travels*, p. 313.
234 See R. I. Burns, "Christian–Muslim Confrontation," p. 82.

separated from an even longer tradition of political and military alliances and diplomatic relations between powers on opposite sides of the confessional divide. It originated in the early years of Latin–Islamic contact in eighth- to tenth-century Iberia – a time when alliances were cemented by intermarriage among Islamic and Christian royal and noble families.[235] The fall of the Umayyad Caliphate initiated a period of dynastic disentanglement but intensifying competition amongst the Christian principalities and among the *taifa* kingdoms, thus setting the stage for military alliances between rulers of different faiths against their co-religionists. Religious difference notwithstanding, the language of the letters and treaties was not only formally cordial – peppered with declarations of "friendship" and "love," but also specifically conceded the legitimacy of each party's authority. If Alfons III of Aragon was King "by grace of God," he recognized that Muḥammad II of Granada was King "by that same grace."[236]

The surprisingly equanimous and convivial attitude of these treaties is not a reflection of Iberian peculiarities, but of the necessities of *realpolitik* and the affinities of members of a princely class, that in certain contexts overrode confessional difference. All across the Mediterranean, as Latins engaged with Muslim powers, diplomatic apparatuses were developed. In Sicily, the resulting alliances served as a prelude to the Norman conquest, whereas in the Levant, "normal" relations between the Latin rulers, the Fāṭimids, and the petty princes of Syria were established within the first generation.[237] At times the resulting agreements were clearly tributary in nature – as was the case with Castile's patronage of the *taifa* kingdoms – but even these alliances implied mutual obligations and demonstrate an element of reciprocity, specifically in the field of mutual defense. The situation was little different in the central Mediterranean, where the d'Hauteville dynasty's alliances with the Fāṭimids and Zīrids provided the Normans with the opportunity to expand against Byzantium and hold off their Latin rivals on the mainland. In the Latin East, the interdependence between Muslim and Christian principalities (including the Military Orders, who pursued independent foreign policies) was even clearer. Indeed, the survival of the kingdom of Jerusalem depended on the maintenance of a succession of peace treaties with Damascus, just as the fortunes of the *taifa* kingdoms

[235] Both the later Umayyad Caliphates and their ʿĀmirid usupers married Christian consorts of both noble and slave origin, but the practice was also not uncommon among the regional aristocracy of the borderlands. See S. Barton, "Marriage across Frontiers," and J. Vernet Ginés, "El valle del Ebro como nexo," p. 267.
[236] Catlos, "Mahomet Abenadalill," pp. 287–8; also p. 254 above.
[237] See pp. 95 and 140.

rested on the precarious balance of hostilities between the various Christian and Muslim rulers of Iberia and North Africa.

The pacts and treaties that were made between Christian and Muslim powers covered a range of contingencies and contexts.[238] Alliances for mutual defense (or at least, the cessation of aggression) were common, and frequently these were contingent on the payment of tribute or the cessation of other privileges. Sometimes, as in the twelfth-century Orontes Valley and the Golan, or in thirteenth-century Pantelleria, zones of condominium or tribute-sharing were established.[239] The exchange of captives and the return of illegally plundered goods and abducted subjects was frequently regulated. In Iberia official redeemers (*exeas*, *alfaqueques*) were employed. In the fourteenth century, Castile and the kingdom of Granada developed elaborate protocols for the apprehension and punishment of cross-border raiders, including the establishment of special frontier magistrates, *alcaldes entre moros y cristianos* ("magistrates [for disputes] among Muslims and Christians"), who were supported by *fieles de rastro* – professional trackers. Guarantees of protection for diplomats and merchants were a common feature. Freedom of circulation was sometimes guaranteed, while at other times merchants were restricted to specific towns, neighborhoods, or compounds. Standard tariffs and duties were established, as were protocols for the resolution of disputes.

Terms were set by formally empowered envoys, by *ad hoc* representatives such as merchants, and sometimes by the rulers themselves, or members of their inner circles. When bilingual agents were not available, a translator – a *dragoman* (from the Arabic, *tarjumān*), or *scriptor Arabicum* – was employed. Some Latin rulers, such as Reginald of Sidon, and Raymond III of Tripoli, were apparently well-enough versed in Arabic to carry out their own negotiations directly.[240] A rather high proficiency of formal Arabic and Latin was required to draft treaties and letters, however, and this disqualified both the majority of subject Muslims and the many Christians who had conversational proficiency in Arabic. Thus, in late medieval Iberia, educated Jews were frequently used as official translators and envoys to Muslim lands, although occasionally *mudéjares* were employed, as were foreign Muslim subjects who were

[238] See, for example, L. de Mas-Latrie, *Traités de paix et de commerce*; M. Alarcón y Santón and R. García de Linares, *Los documentos árabes diplomáticos*; A. S. Atiya, *Egypt and Aragon*; M. Martin, "The Venetian–Seljuk Treaty"; P. Holt, *Early Mamluk Diplomacy*; M. T. Ferrer i Mallol, "Les relacions"; and R. Salicrú i Lluch, "La diplomacia y las embajadas."

[239] See H. Bresc, "Pantelleria," p. 106.

[240] H. Dajani-Shakeel, "Diplomatic Relations," p. 211.

attached to Christian courts (like Muḥammad b. al-ʿĀdil, in the excerpt above).[241]

Treaties and agreements of these types varied in duration from several months to periods of five or ten years or even longer (sometimes with a provision for renewal). In other instances the term was unspecified. The operating principle was that these were personal agreements concluded between rulers, who were responsible for the compliance of their subjects. As such, they were taken very seriously, not only because the prestige and authority of rulers rested on their capacity to ensure the compliance of their subordinates, but because in the absence of formal institutions of "international law," the self-regulation of treaties provided the only medium for guaranteeing the sort of stable political environment that all players regarded as being in their interest. Hence, there was a strong impetus for rulers to adhere to treaties even when they had the power to break them or when they no longer seemed in their interests. Conversely, the abrogation of a treaty could provide a pretext for attack. Thus, the stage for the fall of the Kingdom of Jerusalem in 1187 was set first by Renaud de Châtillon's brazen violation of the treaty with Salāḥ al-Dīn, and subsequently by the latter's successful baiting of the Templars. A peace prevented the ʾAyyūbid sultan from invading the kingdom, so he went on maneuvers in the zone around Tiberias – as he was entitled to – thereby provoking the Knights into attacking him, and breaking the kingdom's treaty. On the other side of the Mediterranean, from the late thirteenth century onwards, the dense diplomatic correspondence between the Crown of Aragon, Granada, and Morocco is peppered with arrangements for the repatriation of Muslim subjects who were protected by truce, but had been abducted by Christian privateers and raiders on both land and sea.[242]

Aside from reflecting the same pragmatic approach on the part of Latin princes to foreign Muslims as was displayed to their Islamic subjects, the atmosphere of regional political stability and the mutual concession of legitimacy between Muslim and Christian rulers that emerged out of this diplomacy provided the medium by which subject Muslim communities maintained the economic, cultural, and political ties that were crucial to their survival and prosperity. Within this framework, *mudéjares* could undertake pilgrimage or embark on commercial missions to Islamic

[241] For the role of Jews see, for example, D. Romano, "Judíos escribanos."

[242] This is a constant theme in the diplomatic documentation between the Crown of Aragon, Granada and Marīnid Morocco; see À. Masià i de Ros, *Jaume II: Aragó, Granada, i Marroc.*

lands, where they established networks of contacts and collaborators.[243] The wealthiest and most successful *mudéjar* families were precisely those who managed to move in both worlds. High-status foreign Muslims, including diplomats, soldiers, and officials, circulated in Latin territory, where they would have inevitably developed relationships with subject Muslims. There are indications that they occasionally intervened in or influenced the internal affairs of Muslim *aljamas*, as when "Abucaquere," the "alguazire" of Murcia, arranged the appointment of a Muça "filius de Maruham" to be appointed *alfaquinus* of Borja in 1274, or when the Granadan envoy "Bulhabbes" obtained a royal pardon for Haçan, the son of the *mudéjar* notary in Teruel, who had been convicted of murder.[244] Finally, from the fourteenth century onwards, foreign Muslim rulers used their influence with Christian kings to enshrine protections for subject Muslims in peace treaties, or to exert diplomatic pressure in order to dissuade Latin regimes from oppressing them by the threat of retaliation against subject Christians in Islamic lands.[245] In sum, despite the theoretical legal, administrative, and institutional separation of subject Muslim communities and the Christian societies within which they existed, the two populations were profoundly enmeshed. The depth of this interdependence becomes dramatically clear when one turns to the informal, quotidian reality of *mudéjar* society – the subject of this book's final chapter.

[243] See above, p. 184. [244] See B. Catlos, *The Victors and the Vanquished*, p. 286.
[245] See above, pp. 214 and 218.

# 10 Deed

## The economic, social, and cultural life of the Muslims of Latin Christendom

While the ideologies that informed Christian–Muslim relations were by nature chauvinistic and oppositional, and the legal and administrative institutions that formally defined Latin-dominated society were predicated on the subjugation and segregation of the subject Muslim community, the reality of daily life in Latin Christendom was one in which Muslims and Christians were engaged in a diverse range of interdependent relationships – at times symbiotic, at times exploitative – that often blurred, or even erased the boundaries that were intended to divide them. Nor was either community homogenous. Islamicate society under Latin rule was divided in terms of class, ethnicity, gender, ideology, vocation, and regional identities, and thus engaged with its correspondingly diverse Christian host societies across a broad spectrum. Hence, the final chapter of this study turns to the mechanics of quotidian existence, as it relates to the internal characteristics of subject Muslim society, and Muslims' relations with the Christians and Jews amongst whom they lived.

Sources for daily life vary dramatically from region to region. For the Muslims of Hungary and the Crusader principalities, we have little, apart from some meager literary material. For Sicily considerably more survives, including tax and land records. For the Iberian Peninsula we have little documentation prior to the late fourteenth century, with the exception of the Crown of Aragon and, to a lesser extent, Navarre. Indeed, for the Crown there is a tremendous abundance of material going back to the eleventh century, including detailed chancery and legal material, land transfer and tenure records, notarial registers, court documents, as well as other material preserved in municipal, seigniorial, and ecclesiastical archives. For Castile and Portugal there is no comparable amount or variety of documentation prior to the fifteenth century. In any case, the overwhelming bulk of the evidence is filtered through Christian institutions and media; it is not until the late fifteenth century and the twilight of Latinate Muslim society that we begin to have access to a significant body of textual evidence produced by *mudéjares* and Moriscos.

## Subject Muslims and the economy of Latin Christendom

In all of the Kingdoms of Spain, that of Aragón has the most Muslims, because they are very diligent in the cultivation of the land. The nobles receive a very high tribute from them, which consists of one quarter of their harvests, not to mention other exactions. Hence, the provenance of that Spanish saying, "He who has no Muslims, has no money." (Hieronymus Münzer, *Itinerarium* (1495)[1])

The long-standing stereotype of the subject Muslim is that of a poor farmer, largely dispossessed, socially isolated, and living at the mercy of exploitative Christian lords, relegated to the poorest lands, despised for his religion and suffering under the arbitrary exactions of his seignior. As the preceding chapters have made clear, such a generalization is clearly a distortion. Nevertheless, agriculture and husbandry did indeed comprise the largest sector of the medieval economy, and just as the overwhelming majority of Christians in the Latin West were engaged in food production, the same was true for subject Muslims. Most were peasants who were poor, or at least not rich, and most must have smarted at least occasionally under the authority of the classes who ruled over them. That said, the economic role of the *mudéjares* was far more complex than is often assumed; they were also active in commerce, educated professions, skilled trades, and craft industries. Both as individuals and societies they showed the capacity to engage with the Christian economy effectively and creatively and to respond to shifting limitations and opportunities.[2]

### *Muslim subjects in the larger economy*

The need for manpower in the agricultural sector and in certain key industries, such as silk-making in fifteenth-century Granada, was at bottom the reason why Muslim minorities existed in Latin Christendom. Such was the case at the time of the conquests that established Muslims as Latin subjects in Iberia, the Latin East, and Sicily, as well as in the wake of the crises of the mid fourteenth century. In each of these regions there were significant zones and settlements which remained exclusively or nearly exclusively under Muslim cultivation, including the north of the kingdom

1 "The Journey," in H. Münzer, *Viaje por España*, p. 123. Münzer was a physician and Humanist from Nürnberg.

2 There is no monograph dedicated to the economic history of subject Muslims. Reference should be made to the general works cited at the beginning of each chapter; detailed studies can be found in the proceedings of the triennial *Simposio Internacional de Mudéjarismo* (see *Actas* in the Bibliography).

of Jerusalem, the Biqāʿ and Orontes valleys, and the Lebano-Syrian coast, western and central Sicily, significant areas of the kingdoms of Aragon and Valencia, and enclaves in Navarre, Portugal, and Castilian lands, not to mention – much later – the Kingdom of Granada. In other zones, Muslims lived alongside Christian and Jewish settlers, often initially as a numerical majority.

In each of these scenarios, Muslims generated revenue both in the form of seigniorial and royal rents, tributes and taxes, labor services, administrative fees and licenses, and judicial fines, while producing agricultural and industrial output, performing services, and supporting a secondary economy of distribution and resale, as well as generating demand for a range of products and services, and supplying important materials, as well as finished or partially finished goods. Their precise contribution is difficult to assess, and the comparative analyses of Christian and Jewish versus *mudéjar* tax receipts that historians occasionally produce in an effort to quantify their relative economic value cannot be trusted, given the primitive and imprecise nature of contemporary financial records, and the fact that so much of the economic benefit yielded by Muslim (and non-Muslim) producers was indirect, in kind, or otherwise impossible to effectively measure and compare. In the end, the value of *mudéjar* production is probably best indicated by the survival of Muslim communities and the recruitment of Muslim settlers. When the benefits they generated were outweighed by their perceived potential for unrest or the moral censure accrued by accommodating Christian lords, or when Christian settlers were available on better terms, Muslim farmers were often pushed out of prime lands or expelled altogether. Over the course of nearly six centuries, this happened relatively rarely, but when it occurred on a large scale the effects could be devastating, both for the deportees and the economies of the regions they had departed. In any event, the motivations behind such policies can hardly be understood simply as "religious." Both the expulsions in the aftermath of the revolts of Andalucía in the 1260s and the transportation of rebellious Sicilians in the previous decades were a response to the threat posed by Muslim unrest. The dissolution of the colony at Lucera and the expulsion of Spain's Moriscos were possible because the populations in question were no longer a source of sufficient revenue or political advantage to the powers that were. The decline in the need for Muslim labor cannot be separated from the decline of subject Muslim societies.

Inevitably, the Islamic agricultural economy was dramatically transformed by Christian dominion, whether primarily by displacements, as in the Latin East, which was occupied for only a brief period, or by profound systematic change, as in Sicily and Iberia.[3] Except for rare enclaves that remained homogeneously Muslim, Christian (and Jewish), colonization inevitably followed the conquests. Economic and structural inertia, the pace of settlement, and differing agricultural strategies, meant that – in zones where Muslims remained – Christians tended either to settle in lands adjacent but separate from those worked by Muslims, or acquired parcels within Muslim field systems. In any event, in those regions where Muslims were not simply expelled, change may have been slow to apprehend in the first generations.[4] The gradual character of Christian colonization is reflected in the frequent evocation that land, water, or pasturing rights be observed "as they were in the times of the Muslims," and for *mudéjar* elders to be called on as witnesses in boundary disputes involving other locales. This occurred even when the conquest was distant memory. Thus, in 1291 a boundary dispute between Ágreda and Bocayren was ordered to be resolved by the "counsel of trustworthy male elders," including both Christians and Muslims, nearly two centuries after the end of Muslim rule in the area.[5]

### *Agriculture and the rural landscape*

Whereas in many areas the Islamic countryside was rapidly transformed, in others Christians evidently adapted to the agricultural practices of their Muslim neighbors. Indeed, there was a strong disincentive to disrupting traditional practices; Christian lords quickly learned this led to a decline in returns.[6] Change, however, was inevitable, given the transformation of markets and distribution systems under Christian rule, the establishment of fiscal regimes which privileged certain crops (notably dry-cultivated cereal) over "traditional" *mudéjar* irrigated horticulture, the predatory pressure of advantaged Christian settlers, and the Church, which as a matter of general policy, sought the displacement of Muslim tenants.[7]

As a consequence, the decline of traditional Islamic irrigation and production systems, tremendously productive and highly sophisticated as they may have been, was something of a foregone conclusion. It is

[3] See the discussion in chapter 9, p. 402, above.

[4] For two contrasting scenarios, compare the situation in the Sierra de Moncayo (Aragon), where the Monastery of Veruela gradually transformed the Muslim land grid, and the area in and around Lleida, where change was much more abrupt. This may be related to a prevalence of irrigated horticulture in the former, and large-estate cereal farming in the latter. See Á. González Palencia, "Notas sobre el régimen"; S. Teixeira, "El dominio del Monasterio de Veruela"; J. Vispe Martínez, "La fundación"; and J. Bolòs, "Changes and Survival."

[5] See B. Catlos, *The Victors and the Vanquished*, pp. 272–77; cf. above, p. 413.

[6] T. F. Glick, From *Muslim Fortress to Christian Castle*, p. 159. [7] See above, pp. 376ff.

doubtful, however, that this represented a catastrophe in socio-cultural terms, as some historians have characterized it. In the end, the purpose of an agricultural system is to sustain a population, and *mudejares*' ready transition to foreign systems of land tenure and production ensured their survival as a community. Their ability to adapt can thus be seen, rather, as a success, and as an indicator of the robust character of *mudéjar* society. In any event, in Iberia, where structured and cooperative "manorial"-type farming was not common, individual farmers, whether Christian or Muslim, tended to maintain a high degree of autonomy and independence in terms both of what they chose to produce and how. Regions such as central and western Sicily, with its great monastic estates, where the liberties of farmers were curtailed by seigniorial powers, tended to decline in prosperity and became *focii* of Muslim resistance. In any event, the stereotype of the sophisticated and vulnerable market gardens of Islamic horticulturalists being overrun by the flocks of Christian herders – a stock image in many a textbook – simply does not hold. The documentation of the great herders' associations, the Castilian *Mesta*, and the Aragonese *Casa de los ganaderos* – are all but absent of mentions of conflicts with Muslims, but replete with reports of clashes with Christian municipalities and seigniors. In Iberia, the transition to a more pastoral economy did not begin until the late thirteenth century, and the conflicts and tensions that it generated did not play out along confessional lines. Many Muslims were herders as well as farmers; individual *mudéjares* are attested to as owners of hundreds of head of livestock, and in the fifteenth-century kingdom of Valencia, for example, Muslims seem to have owned as much livestock proportionate to population as did Christians.[8]

Indeed, Arabo-Islamic practices not only survived, but transformed the Latin rural economy. While the impact of this "green revolution" may have been overstated, a whole range of high-value crops, including rice, sugar, and mulberries (for silk) – not to mention agronomical theories and techniques – were incorporated into Latin Christendom as a consequence of the conquests.[9] But while this may have had a transformative effect on European culinary habits, its effect on subject Islamic communities was less clear, given that the cultivation of these crops did not remain the preserve of Muslims. In fact, the crucial aspect of agricultural activity vis-à-vis the persistence and character of *mudéjar* society was the resulting

[8] M. Meyerson, *The Muslims of Valencia*, pp. 125–26; for Navarre, see A. Ozaki, "El régimen tributario," p. 480; for Aragon, see E. Pascua, "Round and about Water," esp. pp. 308–9. Local population charters, such as that granted by the Hospital to La Aldea (Tarragona) in 1258, include broad pasturing rights for Muslims, with their "cows, horses, asses, sheep and goats." See J. M. Font Rius, *Cartas de población*, vol. I, p. 445 {303}.

[9] See A. Watson, *Agricultural Innovation*.

integration and assimilation of Muslims in Christian chains of production and structures of power. From the late fourteenth century onwards, seigniors became the strongest supporters of rural Muslim and crypto-Muslim communities because of the ties of mutual interest that bound them.

However, even well prior to this – as early as the twelfth century – individual lords, cathedral chapters, monasteries, and convents of Military Orders all advocated for and defended their Muslim subjects and tenants against the encroachments both of Christian powers and their own *aljamas*. In thirteenth-century Alcañiz, the Order of Calatrava used Muslim men-at-arms in their feuding with the townsfolk; in the 1200s the Order of Santiago employed *mudéjar* archers against the forces of Rodrigo Jiménez de Rada, the Archbishop of Toledo. Across the peninsula, the Templars and Hospitalers resolutely defended the rights of their *mudéjar* "brothers" against local Muslim communities.[10] In these cases, and others, however, the problematic nature of discussing subject Muslims generically as "farmers" or "peasants" becomes evident; the sources reveal that it was very typical for *mudéjares*, whether as individuals or families, to be engaged in an array of economic activities that crossed the rural/urban and agriculture/craft divides. In the medieval Islamicate Mediterranean, the distinction between town and country was seldom clearly drawn.

### *Craft and industry*

As with agriculture, *mudéjares*' engagement with craft and artisanal activities represented a combination of skills and trades that were rooted in the Islamic era, along with adaptations and innovations relating to the Latin world. Naturally, in independent Islamic society every trade had been represented, and most, undoubtedly, continued to be practiced by Muslims in the era of Christian rule. However, in the twelfth and thirteenth centuries Muslims came to dominate certain vocations, a trend that continued into the sixteenth century in Iberia. As in Sicily, Muslims were active in building trades, including brick-working, carpentry, stucco and plastering, and engineering, and at times they exercised a near monopoly in such sectors. The churches of Aragon and Castile built in the twelfth and thirteenth centuries were built largely by Muslim manpower and adorned with *mudéjar* decorative techniques: notably, distinctive and elaborate patterns of brickwork and ceramic.[11] Although this

[10] See, for example, B. Catlos, *The Victors and the Vanquished*, pp. 280–81, and M. García-Arenal, "Dos documentos," p. 167, and "Documentos árabes," pp. 37–38.

[11] For the two waves of transmission of this style to Ifrīqiya, see J. Peña, "Los moriscos aragoneses en el exilio," and "La arquitectura andalusí-zagrí en Tunicia," pp. 130 and

fashion had largely run its course by the late thirteenth century, Muslim builders continued to dominate the sector, constructing and decorating buildings in "Christian styles."[12] The stunning polychrome ceiling of the cathedral of Teruel is a clear example of the adaptation of non-Muslim styles by *mudéjar* workers – its hundreds of panels feature both geometric designs and hundreds of caricatures of monsters, animals, and the stock personalities of medieval society: pictorial representations of people and animals painted by *mudéjar* artists, notwithstanding the problematic nature of representative art in Islam.[13] Likewise, the elaborate cabinet-work *artesonado* ceilings, which became a hallmark of aristocratic style from the fourteenth century, were constructed almost exclusively by Muslims. From this time onwards in Aragon, a distinctive *mudéjar* civic architecture – one that featured indigenous rather than "Moorish" stylings – came to dominate the high-end "secular" market, including palaces made for ecclesiastical officers, and was used for renovations and additions to collegiate churches and cathedrals (particularly, the massive lanterns that were constructed in the fifteenth and sixteenth centuries).[14]

Hence, in the late fourteenth century the exiled anti-Pope Benedict XIII, or "Papa Luna," employed Muslim artisans and architects on projects at Penyiscola (Valencia) as well as on his Aragonese lands.[15] In Sicily, the Normans' stunningly decorated *capella palatina* was only one of an array of renovated and refurbished formerly Islamic monumental buildings and installations which comprised their rambling palace complex. These, together with dazzlingly brilliant churches and monasteries (such as Monreale and Cefalú), bear the clear mark of Muslim (and Byzanto-Orthodox) craftsmen. As early as the thirteenth century, Muslim master builders served the count-kings of Barcelona, and in the fourteenth they were outfitting "Moorish style" palaces for the Castilian kings. Wealthy Jews patronized the same craftsmen; the lavish synagogue ("del Tránsito") commissioned in Toledo by Pedro the Cruel's treasurer, Samuel ha-Levi,

131–33, in J. L. Corral Lafuente, *et al.*, *La cultura islámica.* So crucial and common was this *mudéjar* role that one of Alfonso X's *Cantigas* recounts how the Virgin miraculously aided the master builder Ali find material to construct the Church of Santa Maria in the port of Cádiz "even though he was a Muslim." See M. García-Arenal, "Los moros en las Cantigas," p. 137.

[12] An exhaustive list of *mudéjar* and Morisco architects and the projects they worked on can be found in J. Martínez Verón, and J. Yneva Laborda, *Arquitectos en Aragón.*

[13] See E. Rabanque, *et al.*, *El artesonado*, pp. 90, 153, for one of these cartoons, one that depicts the artists themselves at work.

[14] See J. L. Corral Lafuente and J. Peña, "Aragón mudéjar (ss. XIV–XV)," and "Aragón en el Renacimiento," pp. 59–94 and 95–128, in J. L. Corral Lafuente, *et al.*, *La cultura islámica.*

[15] See F. J. García Marco, "El Papa Luna," and J. Peña Gonzalvo, "Mahoma Ramí."

is unmistakably Naṣrid in style – from the lobed windows to the Qur'ānic inscriptions in Arabic that ring its walls. The nearby Almohad-styled synagogue, (now) Santa María la Blanca, was likely built a century earlier by another treasurer, Joseph ben Meir ben Shoshan.[16] Through all of this, Muslim master builders continued to direct the construction of churches in Castile.[17] In Navarre, Muslim craftsmen and builders occupied positions of influence and importance within royal circles – including the post of chief architect – and were in charge of the construction and maintenance of castles, palaces, and fortifications.[18]

The tax rolls and censuses of fifteenth-century Castilian, Navarrese, and Aragonese *aljamas* confirm the continuing domination of Muslims in building and decorating trades and a range of crafts.[19] Nor did Muslim labor provide a "budget option": these craftsmen were valued for their specific skills and paid well – no less than Christians – in both cash and privileges.[20] For example, when Carlos II of Navarre wanted to establish a cloth industry in his kingdom, he dispatched his master carpenter Zalema Zaragozano, a Muslim, on two missions to Zaragoza (in 1365 and 1372) in order to recruit dyers and study the construction of textile mills. He rode on horse in the company of Ponce de Eslava, the royal *Recibidor* of the Ribera, and the two feasted on venison and wine in the course of their missions. The cost for travel alone was 14,000 *denarii*. We may assume the endeavor was successful, as in 1387 Zalema was appointed "Master-general for all carpentry projects in all of the kingdom." There is no reason, however, to presume the mills constructed under Zalema's supervision were particularly "mudéjar" in style, or of "Islamic" origin.[21] By contrast, there is no indication that Islamicate architectural projects were sponsored by the Latin elite in the Crusader lands of the East.[22] This eschewal is likely rooted in the fact that the propensity to adapt foreign style and genre is related to political and cultural self-assurance; hence, in zones where Christian dominance was more tenuous and the atmosphere

16 See J. Dodds, "Mudéjar Tradition."

17 At times, they simply oversaw Christian builders, as at Uclés in the mid fourteenth century. See M. García-Arenal, "Dos documentos," p. 168.

18 See p. 186, above; C. Conde Solares, "Social Continuity," p. 315; and A. Malalana Ureña and I. Muñoz Cascante, "Mudéjares," p. 528. Zalema Alpuliente was appointed "Master of Works of the Castles of the Ribera."

19 See, for example, the many local studies published in the proceedings of *Simposio Internacional de Mudéjarismo*.

20 For example, when Abrafim Bellido, royal master of works at Valencia, was fired in 1298, his replacement, a Christian, was paid the same rate. See B. Catlos, *The Victors and the Vanquished*, p. 196.

21 F. Serrano Larráyoz and M. Boroiz Lazcano, "Viajeros navarros," p. 370 and 374; and A. Ozaki, "Régimen tributario," p. 452.

22 See A. Boas, "Archaeological Sources."

was more confrontational, such as Palestine, Valencia, or the Guadalquivir, *mudéjar*-type styles were too provocative to be adapted by an insecure Christian colonial population, but this does not mean the Muslims were squeezed out of the sector as workers.

Subject Muslims were also active in a wide range of specialist crafts and industries, particularly the production of luxury textiles, ceramics, and leather. Silk came to the Latin west largely via the Islamic world, a clear site of transmission being the royal *ṭirāz*, or silk works, of Palermo, which was responsible for the famous coronation cape of Roger II. Muslim silversmiths, who presumably had the technical finesse to produce fine filigree, were also highly sought after.[23] In Navarre, *mudéjar* goldsmiths were appointed to the royal court.[24] References to master silk weavers and tailors appear in thirteenth- and fourteenth-century documentation, as when Jaume I awarded Hameth Abenhali Auanalaçat, his "tailor for silk and other special material," a lifetime exemption from royal taxes as a boon.[25] *Mudéjar* tailors and shoemakers, tent-makers and leather workers also served lesser clients, in both Muslim and Latin markets. This was true also in Sicily and Italy, where subject Muslims specialized in iron and silverwork, as well as leather work, carpentry, and construction.[26] These trades, however, and other Muslim-dominated vocations, like soap-making and ceramic manufacture, depended on techniques that could be appropriated or imitated over time, and therefore were subject to mounting Christian competition.[27] On the other hand, *mudéjares* remained entrenched in trades such as iron-working and weapons-making.[28] While the clattering of Muslim smiths irritated intolerant parish priests, the kings depended on being able to command a free *mudéjar* labor force to produce the crossbows, bolts, and other ordnance upon which their military increasingly depended.

In each of these sectors subject Muslims faced the challenges of preserving their proprietary knowledge in the face of deliberate attempts by

[23] In 1287 two enslaved Menorcans, one a silversmith and one a metalworker, were freed and allowed to settle in Barcelona with their families. See B. Catlos, *The Victors and the Vanquished*, p. 195.

[24] C. Condes Solares, "Social Continuity," pp. 318–19.

[25] B. Catlos, *The Victors and the Vanquished*, p. 195.

[26] J. A. Taylor, "Lucera Sarracenorum," p. 117.

[27] See, for example, B. Catlos, *The Victors and the Vanquished*, p. 196, n. 85. Reorientation did not necessarily imply decline. In Sicily, in the aftermath of the Christian conquest, Italy rather than Ifrīqiya became the chief market for Muslim potters and they continued to dominate the sector. See A. Molinari, "The Effects of the Norman Conquest," p. 261.

[28] In Navarre, *mudéjares* were valued for their expertise in artillery since the thirteenth century, and many Muslim smiths in Tudela produced weapons. See above p. 187; M. García-Arenal, "Vidas ejemplares," p. 459; and A. Ozaki, "El régimen tributario," p. 445.

Christian craftsmen to appropriate their techniques, while servicing a new and transforming market. The resistance of subject Muslims to conversion, the continuing use of Arabic within the community, and the family-oriented nature of business and trade ventures, all helped stave off encroachment. On the other hand, access to skilled Muslim slaves and the coercive capacity of Christians worked against it.[29] Hence, by the end of the Middle Ages, Muslims had gradually lost their dominance of a number of crafts, including silk, paper, and ceramics, as Christians developed parallel industries.

In the interim, however, free Muslims and slaves both benefited from their special skills. The former were able to obtain lucrative local monopolies, whereas the latter were able at times to negotiate their manumission or more favorable terms of bondage. However, the most fundamental way in which the practice of crafts influenced the status of subject Muslims was as a force of integration in the broader economy. Both craft and technical activities put *mudéjares* in the middle of Christian networks of supply and consumption, by consuming raw materials produced by Christians and providing goods and services to them. If the Muslim *aljama* of Huesca was a major producer of crossbow bolts in the late thirteenth century, its craftsmen must have depended on and supported Christian suppliers of raw materials (wood, cord, charcoal, and so on) as well as a network of Christian clients and distributors.[30] In 1309 there were no fewer than nineteen *mudéjar* carpenter shops, twenty-three smiths, twenty-six shoemakers, fourteen *esparteros* (straw-weavers), and six barbers in Tudela alone; clearly, these were serving the Christian market and not merely producing goods for the local *aljama*.[31]

Formal business partnerships between Christians and *mudéjares*, both *ad hoc* and long-term, were also very common. The benefit prosperous *mudéjar* artisans brought to local economies would not have been lost on those Christian officials charged with assessing and collecting tribute. Nor were these professions and crafts confined to urban centres; *mudéjar* potters, smiths, and carpenters were scattered throughout the hamlets and villages as well.[32] In sum, the broader the range of activities practiced, the broader their networks of economic interdependence with Christians. This interdependence, in turn, brought Muslims into direct, symbiotic relationships, and helped to establish common agendas with Christian individuals, collectives, and institutions, and thereby mitigated organically against the marginalization

29 See, for example, p. 270, above.

30 See, for example, B. Catlos, *The Victors and the Vanquished*, p. 196. For networks of *mudéjar* butchers and their Christian suppliers, see J. Apirici Martí, "Tolerar y convivir."

31 A. Ozaki, "El régimen tributario," p. 445.

32 See M. I. Álvaro Zamora, "El trabajo en los alfares mudéjares," for a study of rural and urban networks of production and distribution.

of subject Muslim communities. It is no surprise that it was the Kingdom of Valencia, where Christians competed against Muslims in all of these industries, that was a rare scene of chronic urban anti-*mudéjar* popular violence.[33]

Muslim involvement in commerce fulfilled an analogous function, and while subject Muslims may not have been involved in "international" commerce to the degree or scale that Christian and Jews were, their religious identity and language proficiency gave them an advantage in trade with the Islamic world.[34] Hence, subject Muslims were heavily involved in trade between Norman Sicily and Ifrīqiya in the twelfth century, as well as between Iberia and the Maghrib from the fourteenth century onwards. It was less common for them to engage in trade with Latin lands, except as investors or partners with Christians. As noted above, *mudéjares* were also involved in trade between and within the Iberian kingdoms; occasional reports of Muslim merchants being robbed or abducted by noblemen are indicative of a broader circulation between and within these lands.[35] Larger towns, like Zaragoza and Huesca, had a *funduq* specifically appointed for Muslim traders.[36] On the lowest level, Muslim producers carried their goods to local and regional markets, where they maintained stalls or stores, and itinerant *mudéjar* craftsmen (tinkers, carpenters, bee-keepers, and so on), followed their own circuits.[37] Thus, *mudéjar* commercial activities provided another source of wealth and of interconnection with Christian society, whereas – as in the case of the foreign Muslims discussed above – these native merchants, along with the ubiquitous *mudéjar* muleteers, helped to maintain the cultural cohesion and integrity of Islamicate

[33] Palermo and rural Sicily also saw popular uprisings against Muslims in the late twelfth century; it is not clear that economic competition was at the root of this in the island's capital, but it seems to have been an important factor in the countryside.

[34] See p. 222, above.

[35] This was the case also in Italy. In 1296, for example, Adrahamem and Achemet, two merchants of Lucera, complained they had been waylaid on a journey from Salerno. See P. Egidi, *Codice diplomatico*, p. 68 {185}.

[36] O. R. Constable, *Housing the Stranger*, pp. 168–69; and B. Catlos, *The Victors and the Vanquished*, p. 200.

[37] See, for example, the list of stallholders and vendors in Zaragoza (*c.* 1300) listed in M. Bofarull y Sartorio, *El registro del merino*, pp. 16–24. Around 1300, the Muslim market of the city boasted eighty shops and one hundred twenty stalls, many of which were operated by Muslims from surrounding towns, some as far afield as Monzón and Tudela. Likewise, Muslim itinerant carpenters and tinkers plied the hamlets and villages of Castile and Aragon. See, for example, M. L. Ledesma Rubio, *Vidas mudéjares*, "El Ollero Loco," pp. 9–31. For beekeepers, see J. Argente Vidal, "Un libro de cuentas," p. 292. Craftsmen came from longer distances also. When the anti-Pope Benedict XIII wanted to have a piece of furniture made to store his liturgical books in Zaragoza, he contracted two Muslim master carpenters from Andalucía. See P. Galido y Romeo, "Un mueble cristiano mudéjar," pp. 371–78.

society under Christian rule. It was precisely the same class of educated Muslim burghers who engaged in trade and that formed the educated and pious elite of their communities.[38]

### *Medicine and prestige professions*

With formal education under the purview of the Church in the Latin West, Muslims (like Jews and women) were technically excluded from some of the higher professions, notably medicine. From the thirteenth century, local and royal legislation in many areas specifically limited or forbade the practice of medicine by Muslims, either absolutely or on Christian patients.[39] For example, the Council of Jaffa (1251) included such a provision, and broad prohibitions against Muslim men and women practicing medicine on Christians were promulgated in Valencia and elsewhere in the peninsula in the 1320s and 1330s.[40] In the fourteenth century the formalization and regularization of medical certification also marginalized Muslim practitioners. Certification was often in the hands of Church authorities or royal inspectors who discriminated against them. However, demand made such measures unenforceable, and in the face of widespread defiance by both patients and physicians, it was better to regulate Muslim physicians than pretend they were not practicing. Thus, by the late 1300s medical examination boards in some realms, like the Crown of Aragon, included provisions for Muslims to be certified (and in some cases to be included on examination committees).[41] Nevertheless, few physicians went through this process. In Valencia, for example, of the multitude of *mudéjar* practitioners who were operating, only a handful were licensed.[42] This was a general problem; hence, in 1400 Martí I ordered an audit of the credentials of all of the physicians in his realms, whatever their faith.[43] In any event, this was not strictly speaking a

[38] Many, if not most of those individuals who became *mudéjar* magistrates were first (and perhaps, foremost) merchants or craftsmen. For example, in the 1280s, both before and after he served as *alcaydus* of Lleida, Çalema Alitili was the king of Aragon's master engineer.

[39] For the problems associated with medical practice in an ethno-religiously diverse environment, see, for example, L. García Ballester, *Medicine in a Multicultural Society*, and É. Lepicard, "Medical Licencing and Practice."

[40] J. Prawer, *The History of the Jews*, p. 108; M. H. Green, "Conversing with the Minority," p. 111; I. O'Connor de los Angeles, "Muslim Mudéjar Women," p. 66; L. García Ballester, *Historia social de la medicina*, p. 43; and L. Torres Balbás, *Algunos aspectos*, p. 71.

[41] J. Prawer, *The History of the Jews*, pp. 107 and 109; L. García Ballester, *Historia social de la medicina*, p. 47; and A. Blasco Martínez, "Médicos y pacientes," p. 159.

[42] L. García Ballester, *Historia social de la medicina*, pp. 44–45.

[43] A. Blasco Martínez, "Médicos y pacientes," p. 159.

religious issue, it was also a matter of professional competition – Morisco physicians were subject to the same hostilities, including concerted campaigns by university medical faculties.[44]

As it was, the legal prohibitions rang rather hollow, not only because Muslims, both men and women, continued to practice medicine, but because they often served royal households and members of the higher clergy, and were sought after by municipalities.[45] While the "Oriental" physicians that, according to William of Tyre, the kings of Jerusalem preferred over Latins may have included Christians, Muslims, and Jews, the Norman kings – at least William II – certainly preferred Muslims, as claimed by Ibn Jubayr, and corroborated by the illustration of the King's death in Petrus de Ebolo's *Liber ad honorem Augusti*.[46] The situation was even more pronounced in Iberia. In 1342, when Pere the Ceremonious needed an eye surgeon, the best he could find was a Muslim slave in Vilafranca del Penedès; and when his son and heir, Joan, suffered an accident in 1387, he summoned a Muslim doctor from Valencia.[47] Muslim and Jewish physicians were noted serving the Cistercian nuns at the royal monastery of Las Huelgas (outside Burgos) in the late fourteenth century, and receiving a license to bear arms in recognition.[48] In 1394 Carlos III of Navarre granted a lifetime tax exemption to Mahoma Almonahar of Tudela and his family, after the latter cured the royal falconer of a "grave and dangerous illness."[49] Half a century later Muza Alcortobí served as physician to King Joan II of Navarre, Queen Blanca II, and also the ill-fated heir-apparent, Carlos de Viana.[50] In Castile, the Xarafí family of Alcalá started as physicians for the Archbishop of Toledo, eventually serving as the official medics of Alfonso XI; Abraham Xarafí parlayed this into political influence and an appointment as *Alcalde Mayor* of the *mudéjares* of the realms of Castile.[51] In 1484 a master physician named

44 Eventually, the position was developed that held that any cure effected by a Morisco physician can only have resulted from a pact with the Devil. L. García Ballester, "The Minority of Morisco Physicians," pp. 210–13.

45 M. McVaugh, *Medicine Before the Plague*, p. 106; and L. García Ballester, *Historia social de la medicina*, pp. 43–44.

46 J. Prawer, *The History of the Jews*, p. 107; Ibn Jubayr, *Travels*, p. 341; and the illustrations in T. Kölzer, *et al.*, *Liber ad honorem*, p. 43 (f. 97r).

47 M. McVaugh, *Medicine before the Plague*, p. 161; and L. García Ballester, *Historia social de la medicina*, p. 54.

48 L. Torres Balbás, *Algunos aspectos*, p. 28.

49 M. García-Arenal and B. Leroy, *Moros y judíos en Navarra*, p. 104 {XXVI}.

50 C. Condes Solares, "Social Continuity," 317 and 319; and A. Ozaki, "El régimen tributario," 458.

51 A. Blasco Martínez, "Médicos y pacientes," p. 165; also p. 194 above.

Hamete offered to treat *pro bono* those convalescing in the monasteries of Burgos, but was instead allotted an annual stipend of 2,000 *maravedís* by the municipality.[52]

The status and esteem that Arabo-Islamic medical science enjoyed among Christians were reflected in the adaptation of eastern texts – not the least the *Qānūn fi'l-ṭibb* ("Canon of Medicine") of Ibn Sīnā (Avicenna), which remained central to medical education in Europe beyond the seventeenth century.[53] Latin savants eagerly absorbed this learning. Arnau de Vilanova – whose formal attitude to Islam was confidently antagonistic – read medical treatises in Arabic and Hebrew, and used this knowledge to reform the famous medical school at Montpellier.[54] A similar process of transmission and *translatio* went on at other centers of medical knowledge, like Salerno, with the presence of educated Muslim slaves serving as a catalyst.[55] Higher Islamic medicine did not disappear under Latin rule in Iberia. There was a functioning medical *madrasa* in Zaragoza in the fourteenth century, and Paterna remained an important center; through the late fifteenth century new Arabo-Islamic medical texts continued to arrive from the *dār al-Islām*.[56] Even in the absence of formal education, techniques were passed on orally, and the lively *mudéjar* medical culture is reflected in the original treatises subject Muslims composed.[57] Thus, for example, a figure like Muḥammad al-Shafra (d. 1360), a *mudéjar* of Crevillent, composed an important practical manual on "wounds and tumors" in the 1340s.[58] Even if Muslims were prohibited from practicing on Christians, the *mudéjar* population provided enough patients to sustain a tradition.

The use of Muslim physicians and medical knowledge is hardly surprising; medicine could be a matter of life or death and, as a consequence,

[52] L. Torres Balbás, *Algunos aspectos*, p. 28. Hamete may have seen this as a means of reinforcing good will towards the Muslims, but even so, both his offer and the gesture of the town council were impressive.

[53] The work of translators of Arabic texts, beginning with Constantinus Africanus, transformed medicine in Latin Christendom. See above, p. 337, and F. Newton, "Arabic Medicine." In the late 1200s Arnau de Vilanova was also a major contributor. See L. García Ballester, "Las influencias de la medicina islámica."

[54] L. García Ballester, *Historia social de la medicina*, pp. 17ff.

[55] M. Green, "Conversing with the Minority," p. 107.

[56] L. García Ballester, *Historia social de la medicina*, pp. 68–70 and 72. In the *taifa* period Zaragoza had been an important center of science and Islamic culture and literature. See, for example, J. Vernet Ginés, "El valle del Ebro."

[57] L. García Ballester, *Historia social de la medicina*, p. 133; and M. Á. Ladero Quesada, "Las relaciones," p. 40.

[58] L. García Ballester, *Historia social de la medicina*, p. 121. The renowned author came from a line of Alicantine physicians. Although he emigrated to the Maghrib and retired to Granada, his fame was such that to "know more than al-Shafra" remains a popular local saying to this day. See F. Franco Sánchez and M. Sol Cabello, *Muhammad aš-Šafra*, p. 13.

people were not likely to chose a physician on the basis of religious affiliation when their own survival was at stake. They would choose what worked, and Islamic medical science was clearly regarded as superior to Latin medicine, at least until the later Middle Ages.[59] Hence, although Cardinal Cisneros had prohibited Christians from using Muslim midwives, when he himself fell ill, he was attended by a Morisca practitioner.[60] As late as 1600 the anti-Morisco polemicist, Jaime Bleda, could not help but praise New Christian physicians.[61] *Mudéjares* – including women – were sometimes called in when Christian doctors failed, or as consultants in inquests.[62] Alfons III of Aragon depended on Olmocat, his "Muslim surgeon from Valencia," and after she died in 1346, he granted her children a tax exemption in recognition of her skill.[63] When a Jewish woman of Teruel died of suspected poisoning in 1294, Jaume II ordered a forensic inquest to be carried out by three doctors: a Christian, a Muslim, and a Jew.[64]

Moreover, Muslims were particularly highly regarded in certain fields of specialization, including surgery and obstetrics.[65] In both Navarre and Castile, Muslim midwives served the royal families in the fourteenth and fifteenth centuries, including Haxa of Segovia, who served as obstetrician to Blanca II of Navarre while the latter was Queen of Castile (1440–53).[66] The popularity of female practitioners led some authorities, like the municipality of Burgos in 1494, to grant formal licenses to them.[67] Indeed, such was Muslims' reputation for healing that *mudéjar* barbers (who did minor surgery), *curanderos*, and *curanderas* – who could escape the formal legal prohibitions placed on physicians – were broadly popular even after 1500.[68] In Zaragoza, the Peix family served as *curanderos* to the

[59] That said, Muslims sometimes turned to Christian *curanderos*, as did members of the Xama family – silk manufacturers and merchants in fifteenth-century Zaragoza. See J. Abella Samitier, "Una familia de mudéjares," p. 209. Usāma b. Munqidh was horrified by Frankish surgical techniques and medical ethics, but was forced to recognize the efficacy of their herbal cures. See *The Book of Contemplation*, pp. 145–56 and 150.

[60] G. López de la Plaza, "Las mujeres moriscas," p. 315, and M. Green, "Conversing with the Minority," p. 111.

[61] L. García Ballester, *Historia social de la medicina*, p. 55; Bleda was the author of the polemical *Defensio fidei* ("Defense of the Faith"), and of an inculpatory "history" of the Muslims of Spain, as well as an energetic lobbyist for the expulsion. See G. Magnier, *Pedro de Valencia*, p. 30.

[62] C. Barceló Torres, "Mujeres, campesinas," p. 212.

[63] M. Green, "Conversing with the Minority," p. 111.

[64] ACA C., reg. 97, f. 257r (January 29, 1294).

[65] M. Green, "Conversing with the Minority," p. 111.

[66] See *ibid.*, pp. 111–12, and J.-P. Molénat, "Privilégiées ou poursuives," for *doña* ("Lady") Haxa, her mother, *doña* Fatima, and other Muslim royal midwives.

[67] C. Barceló Torres, "Mujeres, campesinas," p. 212.

[68] A. Blasco Martínez, "Médicos y pacientes," p. 167; and L. García Ballester, *Historia social de la medicina*, pp. 120ff.

local Franciscans, who continued to use them even after Mahoma Peix (a carpenter by day) had been charged with malpractice in 1340.[69]

But the distinction between medicine, magic, and religion was not so clear. The anonymous late fifteenth-century treatise, "The Miscellany of Solomon," and the contemporary writings of a *faqīh-curandero* from Madrid, reveal an approach to medicine blending astrology, incantation, recipes, and prayer.[70] In the novel *Lo spill*, Jaume Roig portrays a Christian woman going to a Valencian *faqīh* for medical help – Islamic learning and literacy were inevitably associated with the Muslim faith.[71] Indeed, magic and medicine converged particularly strongly in matters such as lactation and fertility.[72] Thus, the role of religious authorities, and the use of talismans, astrology, magic squares, incantations, and prayers blurred the lines between medicine, proselytism, and witchcraft in the eyes of suspicious Christians, and led Muslims and Moriscos sometimes to be accused of poisoning or brought before the Inquisition.[73] Moreover, the notion that infidels could enjoy a special prestige and knowledge, and be trusted even by kings and queens in matters of life and death, represented an inversion of the established order. Hence, figures like Eiximenis and Ferrer railed against Christians who consulted Muslim physicians. On the other hand, there was much in Islamic learned medicine that resonated with (and influenced) Christian practices, including the Galenic and Aristotelian scientific underpinnings, the theory of humors, the idea of the micro- and macrocosm, and the role of astrology. Hence, even as anti-*mudéjar* and anti-Morisco popular sentiment increased in the sixteenth century, the use of Muslims as medics continued.[74]

Other higher status professions or vocations that brought individual Muslims into contact with the upper levels of Christian society included warriors and grooms (the latter also practiced veterinary medicine). In the fourteenth century, Muslims served royalty and the aristocracy as grooms in both Aragon and Castile; the influence at court they gained as

69 A. Blasco Martínez, "Médicos y pacientes," pp. 163–64.

70 See J. Albarracín Navarro, "Actividades de un faqih mudéjar," and, with J. Ruíz Martinez, "Medicina, farmacopea y màgia."

71 C. Barceló Torres, "Mujeres, campesinas," p. 213.

72 This is reflected in the books of popular magic that circulated among Moriscos. See Y. Cardaillac-Hermosilla, "Les Livrets," pp. 53–56.

73 M. McVaugh, *Medicine before the Plague*, pp. 158, 162 and 187; L. García Ballester, *Historia social de la medicina*, pp. 127, 138–89 and 158; C. Barceló Torres, "Mujeres, campesinas," p. 213; A. Labarta, "La mujer morisca," p. 226; J. Maiso González, "Rito y medicina," pp. 158–89; and A. Blasco Martínez, "Médicos y pacientes," p. 156. Contrary to the case of the Christian authorities, magic was not understood by Moriscos as necessarily diabolical or inherently evil. See Y. Cardaillac-Hermosilla, "Les Livrets," p. 50.

74 L. García Ballester, *Historia social de la medicina*, pp. 53 and 121.

a consequence served to establish their families in positions of prosperity and power.[75] *Mudéjar* soldiers were used widely in Sicily and in the Crown of Aragon, alongside foreign Muslim mercenaries. These included both irregular levies – except in the Latin East, military service was one of the tributes Muslims were typically liable for – and professionals.[76] Frederick II was notorious for having a Muslim *praetorian* guard, as had the kings of Aragon and Castile in the fourteenth and fifteenth centuries, whereas the kings of Navarre appointed *mudéjares* as their artillery masters.[77] In late fifteenth-century Portugal, local Muslim officials served as *cavaleiros*, just as their Christian homologues did.[78] In Iberia, Muslims were prized for their skill with the crossbow, and abundant references to the surname or denomination "Crossbowman" (*Ballestarius*) indicate that many were in permanent or frequent royal service.[79]

In a Christian culture that lauded violence as a virtue and as a signal of masculinity and virility, the opportunity or obligation to fight under arms granted considerable prestige.[80] For example, in 1392 Joan I of Aragon settled a long-standing dispute between the Muslims and Jews of Huesca regarding who would have priority in municipal processions in favor of the *mudéjares* on the grounds that they risked their lives for the Crown by serving in the military.[81] Occasionally, individual *mudéjares* distinguished themselves. In the 1360s Mahoma Ballestarius, the scion of a family of royal builders from Zaragoza, served as knight in the service of Pere the Ceremonious and his Queen, Elionor de Sicilia. In return he received a spate of privileges that set him apart from his own community and made him, in effect, an "honorary" Christian: these included tax exemptions, as

75 Serving as royal groom was a pathway to wealth and influence for *mudéjar* families, for example the Bellvíses in the Crown of Aragon, the Xarafís in Castile, and the Madexas in Navarre. See pp. 194ff above, and A. Ozaki, "El régimen tributario," p. 457. Serving as royal master builder was another privileged career path; as it proved for the Bellidos in the Crown of Aragon, and the Alpelmís and others in Navarre. See pp. 184 and 194, above.

76 For the Latin East, see above, p. 244. For Sicily, see A. Metcalfe, *The Muslims of Medieval Italy*, p. 143; for the Crown of Aragon, see B. Catlos, *The Victors and the Vanquished*, pp. 262–72, and J. Boswell, *The Royal Treasure*, pp. 171–93; and for Portugal, F. Soyer, *The Persecution*, pp. 55–57. Some local Muslim communities negotiated exemptions from the obligation; see, for example, M. T. Ferrer i Mallol, "La carta de població," p. 91 {14}.

77 C. Maier, "Crusade and Rhetoric," p. 344; see pp. 187 and 197, above.

78 M. F. Lopes de Barros, *Tempos e espaços*, pp. 379–81.

79 In 1287 the enslaved Menorcan, Abdalla Auanalaçat, was granted his freedom by Alfons III of Aragon and allowed to settle in Valencia because he was a crossbowman. See B. Catlos, *The Victors and Vanquished*, p. 195.

80 See, for example, R. I. Burns, "Los mudéjares de la Valencia," pp. 23 and 31 {4}; B. Catlos, *The Victors and the Vanquished*, p. 263. In 1328 Hamet el Ballestro was one of two *sindichs* who negotiated the terms of submission of the Vall d'Aiora (Valencia) to Alfons the Benign. See M. T. Ferrer i Mallol, "La carta de població."

81 M. L. Ledesma Rubio, "Marginación y violència," p. 209; see p. 411, above.

well as the right to be exempt from the jurisdiction of Islamic law and *mudéjar* magistrates.[82]

Norman Sicily was exceptional in terms of the breadth and sophistication of the subject Muslim elite. Thanks to the particularly tenuous circumstances surrounding the establishment of the dynasty, and the Arabophile inclinations of the rulers, much of the structure of cultural patronage survived the Christian conquest. As a result, at least through the mid twelfth century the kingdom not only preserved its Muslim cultural and professional elite, but continued to attract Muslim scholars and literary figures from the Islamic world. And yet, whereas it was evidently a point of diffusion for Arabic literary styles, Palermo did not become a major center for the transmission and translation of Arabo-Islamic science. And whereas the relative continuity of the Muslim elite here may have contributed to the confidence of Sicilian *mudéjares*, it may have ultimately contributed to the early demise of their community, given that the influence of the Muslim and crypto-Islamic elite was perceived of as a threat by the Lombard colonists.[83]

### *Low-status professions*

Muslims were also amply represented in what are typically regarded as the lowest-status professions, including prostitutes, singers, musicians, dancers, porters, and muleteers. None of these was the exclusive province of subject Muslims – Christians practiced all of these vocations – although *mudéjares* did come to be associated specifically with them. Nor were these professions necessarily as "low" as they are sometimes portrayed. The carrying trade, for example, helped to keep disparate *mudéjar* and Morisco communities of the Extremadura, Castile, and Aragon connected and current, as Muslim muleteers plied the highways and trails that crisscrossed the peninsula.[84] Mobility in itself represents a sort of freedom, and profession travelers accrued valuable knowledge, together with the power to act as couriers and intermediaries. Music and performance, however, were particularly potent and ubiquitous media of contact.

Muslim and Morisco musicians, acrobats, dancers, and singers were popular at both noble and more humble entertainments and festivities, and were common fixtures at weddings and other celebrations,

[82] When the *aljama* of Zaragoza, attempted to trample these privileges, Queen Elinor intervened on his behalf. See J. Boswell, *The Royal Treasure*, pp. 43, 132, 185, 124–25, and 381.

[83] See, pp. 110ff. above.

[84] F. J. García Marco, *Comunidades mudéjares*, p. 193.

particularly women.[85] This trend continued through the Morisco period, when they came to be associated particularly with these performances.[86] From at least the mid thirteenth century *mudéjar* and slave musicians were featured at royal and noble courts in Navarre, Castile, and Aragon, and were incorporated permanently into royal households. At times the kings set out in search of a particular type of player, or even famous individuals.[87] When Martí I was organizing an event in March 1409 he dispatched his royal baliff, to

> order and make to come to Us, Nesma, the dancer, and her husband, and another Muslim who knows acrobatics [*sapia voltejar*], and some who know how to dance the "Cavallet" and the "Camadair." And if they do not want to come of their own accord, We order you to make them come by force . . .[88]

In 1474 Muslims (and Jews) took part in the ceremonies marking the death of Enrique IV at the Cathedral of Ávila, and at the proclamation of Isabel I as Queen, performing dances with swords and other feats.[89] Muslim musicians also played in churches, particularly during night vigils, which prompted the Council of Valladolid to ban such performances in 1322. This prohibition was no more efficacious, however, than embargos on Muslim physicians, and the practice continued. It is ironic that in the 1300s *mudéjar* musicians became fixtures in the same raucous Corpus Christi processions that Muslims were supposedly obliged by municipal and royal law to hide from.[90]

Some of these musicians (the women at any rate), undoubtedly did sex work on the side (or, perhaps, sang and danced on the side!). Indeed, the two documents from the late thirteenth century that confirmed the right of the Templars of Tortosa to collect fees from the *Saracenae cantatrices*

85 See, for example, J. Aparici Martin, "Juglares mudéjares."
86 A famous color depiction of four Granadan Moriscos playing various instruments together with a female dancer appeared in Christoph Weidetz's travelogue, published in 1529. See *Authentic Everyday Dress*, plates LXXXIX and XC (and the back cover for a color reproduction). See, generally, R. Salicrú i Lluch, "Crossing Boundaries," pp. 42–44.
87 See D. F. Reynolds, "Music," pp. 242–44.
88 D. Gironai Llagostera, *Itinerari del rei en Martí*, p. 229 {23}.
89 *Ibid.*, p. 41. In contrast with Aragon, the joint participation of Muslims and Jews does not seem to have produced violent confrontations between the two groups.
90 L. Torres Balbás, *Algunos aspectos*, p. 72. In 1498 the townsfolk of Epila hired Mahoma el Marruequo to dance and play the tambourine for a period of one year at "Easter, every Sunday, the feast of Saint Mary, the Apostles and whatever other holidays ordered by the Church and observed by the town," including everyday "between Christmas and Saint Julian." He was to have Fridays off, even if they were holidays (although he would need to make them up), and he was free to work on the side at any Christian, Jewish, or Muslim weddings. See F. Macho y Ortega, "Condición social," pp. 308–09 {96}. Muslims and Jews were particularly important in the Corpus Christi pageants celebrated in Murcia in the 1400s; see below, p. 482.

("female Muslim singers") and the *Saracenae meretrices* ("female Muslim prostitutes") of the city, clearly refer to the same group – an interesting example of the emergence of common agenda between this order of chaste Paladins and these adulterous Infidels.[91] There was certainly no shortage of Christian prostitutes, but Muslim women were disproportionately represented in the trade, particularly in those Iberian kingdoms where women convicted of adultery or other capital crimes were seized by the king and set to work in royal brothels (typically with the willing consent of their own community leaders).[92] It may be that Christians derived some particular salacious delight from expressing their domination of Islam through having sex with Muslim women (and the reverse for Muslim men and Christian women), but this is not a phenomenon that needs to be over-analyzed. As a group, men are widely acknowledged as not being particularly distinguishing regarding the objects of their physical desire, particularly in the heat of the moment.

In any event, Muslim practitioners of the lower trades, like those of the high professions – and perhaps analogous to popular "Colored" musicians and performers in the US during the era of Segregation – both contributed to the validation of Islamic culture among the Christian elite, and came to form part of socio-economic networks which aligned their interests with those of Christian parties. In the early 1300s the frustrated royal bailiff of Aragón, Rodrigo Gil Tarín, reported that Amir[a], a Muslim woman of Torellas he was trying to arrest for prostitution, was being hidden from him by the Christian townsfolk.[93] Some of these individuals, for instance the physicians, barbers, and *curanderas*, parlayed patronage into power and wealth. In the 1430s a trumpet player from Tudela, Alí el Castellano, who normally played for the nobleman Martín de Lacarra, received a series of bonuses from Carlos III, and came to serve as the official liaison between the Muslim farmers of southern Navarre and the local nobility.[94]

[91] See B. Catlos, *The Victors and the Vanquished*, p. 311, nn. 220 and 221. In 1356 in order to help finance the upkeep of their monastery Pere the Ceremonious granted the monks of Rueda in Aragon the right for three years to enslave any Muslim woman from the surrounding area found to be having sex with a Christian. Shortly after, however, he was forced to rescind the privilege because the monks themselves had taken it upon themselves to have sex with *mudejar* women in order to then seize them as slaves. See M. T. Ferrer i Mallol, *El sarraïns*, pp. 26–27.

[92] In 1432, for example, a municipal ordinance of Zaragoza forbade prostitutes and concubines "of whatever status, law or condition" from walking about uncovered or sitting in church amongst "good women." See M. del C. García Herrero, "Prostitución y amancebamiento," p. 305.

[93] ACA, ARP, MR, v. 1688, f. 124v.

[94] C. Conde Solares, "Social Continuity," p. 314.

### *Diversity and integration*

In sum, the viability and continuity of Muslim subject communities was rooted essentially in their economic role and capacity. In the first place it was their economic and strategic value to the Christian conquerors which was the sole reason these populations were not expelled, and it was their continuing value as tributaries, laborers, and participants in the Christian economy that was evidently a necessary (but not sufficient) condition for their ongoing survival. The ruminations of the decretalists on the toleration of peaceful subject Muslims represented either *post hoc* rationalizations or intellectual exercises that were effectively unrelated to the formulation or enactment of policy. The continuing value of the subject communities and the degree of their integration in the Christian economy was a function of their integration into larger networks, and depended on their capacity to exploit economic niches and create wealth both for themselves and for their Christian collaborators (and exploiters). Those Muslim communities that were most successful at this – those of the kingdoms of Aragón, Castile, Navarre, and Valencia – were those that survived the longest.

Each of these communities was characterized by economic diversity, both at the group and individual level. Here, *mudéjares* participated in a wide range of activities with a diverse array of Christian parties, and the most prosperous *mudéjares* amongst them were those individuals and families who were engaged in a variety of concerns simultaneously. The wealthiest subject Muslims might practice a trade or craft, obtain an administrative appointment, own rural land and/or sharecrop, own urban real estate either for speculation or for income stream, own livestock, engage in tax-farming, and lend money at interest, or some combination of these. It was not uncommon for *mudéjares* to be able to generate considerable capital for investment (and as insurance against judicial fines, extraordinary royal exactions, tributes or obligatory "gifts").

Moreover, when *mudéjares* in Iberia needed money, they could generally get it, thanks to a highly developed credit market. Although Jews did not monopolize the financial sector, they were by far the most common lenders, and through this medium became directly embroiled in the experience of subject Muslim communities. The archival registers of the Iberian kingdoms abound with lawsuits between Jewish creditors and allegedly recalcitrant and delinquent Muslim debtors, both individuals and communities.[95] While it would tempting to interpret a tendency of

[95] See above, p. 355.

Muslims to default on loans *prima facie* as evidence of *mudéjar* poverty, one must remember that (recent history aside) bankers seldom lend to poor people and debtors often claim insolvency. Rather, this dynamic is symptomatic of a co-dependency that developed between Jewish creditors and Muslim debtors, wherein each negotiated his or her position based on respective advantages. Powerful Jewish creditors could make up for projected losses by lending at illegally high rates, and could count on their influence with royal authorities to help ensure repayment. *Mudéjares*, for their part, were conscious of their capacity to resist repayment through litigation or simply by ignoring their obligations to their creditors and defying the agents of the Crown. And while these credit disputes were bitterly fought, such struggles were carried out almost exclusively through the courts; there is little evidence of Jewish–Muslim credit conflicts being expressed violently in communal or "religious" terms. As often as not, the creditors were not locals, and as a result the conflicts were perceived of as conflicts of locals versus outsiders, rather than as Muslims against Jews.[96] This perception helped to engender solidarity at a local level, not only with Muslim communities, but also with local Christians (and occasionally, local Jews). Less commonly, Muslims were also creditors, lending money to both *mudéjares* and Christians, these lenders sometimes found themselves facing the same challenges vis-à-vis collection as Jewish lenders, but had fewer resources to marshal in their own defense.[97]

However, maintaining viable niches and networks of independence in the shifting economic and demographic environment of Latin Christian kingdoms over the passing of centuries was no easy prospect. The Spain of 1550 was far different from the Iberia of 1350 or 1050: Christian culture and institutions had matured, new kingdoms had replaced fledgling principalities, the economic orientation of the peninsula had been transformed, and the political players, demographic elements, and balances of power in the region had gone through several mutations. *Mudéjar* communities were therefore under frequent threat of economic decline, through the loss of competivity and encroachment. At times Muslims were the victims of deliberate economic displacement, most notably in the kingdom of Valencia, where Christian farmers and artisans deprived *mudéjares* of the best lands, or launched concerted attacks against them. Just as frequently, however, encroachment was passive, or the result of

[96] See B. Catlos, *The Victors and the Vanquished*, pp. 206–09.

[97] There is abundant documentation relating to Muslims engaging in lending on both large and small scales across the peninsula, from the thirteenth to the fifteenth centuries. See, for example, J. Carrasco Pérez, "Los Mudéjares de Navarra," p. 94, and E. Marín Padilla, "Los moros de Calatorao (II)," pp. 184–85.

accident. When subject Muslim societies became less internally diverse or focused too tightly on certain activities or sectors, they became more vulnerable to shifting market conditions. Population decline and institutional corruption could contribute also – by undermining the total economic and tributary output of a community and its capacity to defend its members' interests in the face of competition or abuse. Moreover, as a subject Muslim economy became less diverse, the diversity of relationships between Christians and Muslims decreased, *mudéjares* came to regarded by fewer Christians as necessary or beneficial, and the community as a whole became more vulnerable. Such a progression can be observed also in the case of Iberian Jews, who in the fourteenth century gradually lost economic diversity and weight, until it was only the influence of a narrow class of financiers and administrators who were able to "lobby" for their communities' survival. The decline of the Jews in Iberia coincided with their decline in diversity, whereas the establishment of a thriving Jewish community in contemporary Sicily occurred precisely as Jews became integrated in various sectors of the southern Italian economy. Indeed, Meyerson's study of the Jews of Sagunt (Morvedre) in Valencia shows how even in the late fifteenth century a local Jewish community could regain ethno-cultural security by successfully re-establishing economic integration and interdependence with local Christians on new terms.[98]

The Christianization of the economy was a more subtle threat, as can be seen in the growing influence of guilds and confraternities from the fourteenth century on. These were at bottom vocational collectives, but their ideals and ceremonies were framed on religious terms and they were organized along parochial lines, and thereby came to be associated ever more closely with Christian worship and ritual. By the early fourteenth century controversies were erupting, such as when Muslim guild members objected to having to contribute to defray the cost of Christian ceremonies, or for candles to be placed in churches.[99] Such tensions represent one of the consequences of the progressive sacralization of the Christian economy – a development which cut both ways; by excluding them from formal institutions, Christian authorities' capacity to control *mudéjar* professionals declined. Frustrated with the negligence of the architect they had commissioned to rebuild their bell tower, the canons of the cathedral of Tarazona promulgated an act of formal "excommunication" against Alí Darocano in 1479. But Alí was a Muslim; he would have

[98] See M. D. Meyerson, *A Jewish Renaissance.*
[99] D. Nirenberg, *Communities*, p. 39, and B. Catlos, *The Victors and the Vanquished*, p. 249.

shrugged off this religious gesture as absolutely irrelevant – but less so, perhaps, the chapter's decision to grant him no further commissions.[100]

Nevertheless, in the late fifteenth century there was at least one mixed confraternity: that of San Eloy and San Antón, in Segovia. This guild represented Christian and Muslim smiths and grooms, under the protection of these two patrons. The formal language of their protocols was Christian ("in the name of God the Father, and Son, and Holy Spirit, who are three persons and the One True God"), but ambiguous enough that Muslims might be able to rationalize swearing to them (that is, if the "and" before "the One True God" is taken as disjunctive, rather than conjunctive). In any event, the obligations and rights of its members were equal (although Muslims were exempted from paying for missal candles).[101] The members ate and drank together (including wine) and attended each other's weddings and funerals. This, however, was not the rule, and by this time in most locales it would have been impossible for Muslims to participate in these organizations, and therefore to enjoy the economic benefits, protections, and advocacy that they provided. On the contrary, Christian trade confraternities would be drawn to lobby actively against Muslim competitors. One exception should be noted: early in the sixteenth century there was an all-Muslim confraternity of construction workers in Zaragoza, dominated by the Galí dynasty of master builders and carpenters. Judging by their commissions, which included castles, palaces, homes, and churches around the Kingdom of Aragon, the guild must have been a success, but this seems to have been a unique case – perhaps an adaptation or experiment that came too late in the chronology of *mudéjar* history to be adopted as a model.[102]

The problem of guild membership vis-à-vis *mudéjares* was symptomatic of a general dynamic in which social networks and economic networks overlapped and informed each other, and as result came to take on a religious dimension. Torró proposes the paradigm of "separate reproduction" – a process by which canonical prohibitions on intermarriage led inevitably to the emergence of "biologically" separate ethno-religious communities, and this inevitably led to the alignment of economic agendas with

[100] Alí took no chances, however; after the decree he quickly sold his property in the city, packed up his things and moved to Navarre. J. M. Sanz Artibucilla, "Alarifes moros aragoneses," pp. 69–71.

[101] L. Gómez García, "Los mudéjares menestrals segovianos," pp. 36–37. If the "and" is read disjunctively, this oath could be recited also by Muslims, in that they would only be swearing in the name of the "One True God."

[102] C. Gómez Urdáñez, *Arquitectura civil*, vol. II, p. 149.

ethno-religious identity.[103] As a result, over time subject Muslims came to be perceived as economic as well as religious competitors, and the rhetoric of difference and discrimination originating in these two poles energized each other; hence, the economic condition of subject Muslims cannot be considered without taking into account also their social interactions, both with Christians and each other.

### Muslim and Latin society

> . . . as a consequence of the evil habits and vices and sins that are tolerated in this city, and especially the socializing that Christians engage in with Muslims and Jews, by which great harm and evil and abominable sins occur, and since neither Muslims nor Jews could be distinguished as Muslims, Jews or Christians, they ought to be visibly marked off, since it is well known that Jews and Muslim have been having their way with Christian women to such a degree that many Christians thought that they had children by their women that were theirs, but that were [*in fact*] Muslims and Jews . . . (Ferran d'Antequera, King of Aragon, letter regarding Zaragoza (January 30, 1414)[104])

Read uncritically, the ideological and legal texts relating to Muslim and Christian interaction give the impression of two homogenous and separate societies coexisting in an uneasy state of separation, and until recently, historians largely accepted these presumptions. Indeed, the historiography of subject Muslims, particularly in Iberia, has tended to be framed in terms of a monolithic "Muslim community," with little reference to contemporary people and events in neighboring Christian and Jewish communities. However, Muslim societies and communities were far from homogenous or unified, and many of the most bitter conflicts that subject Muslims experienced played out within their own communities. Moreover, Muslims' social interaction and embroilment with Christian and Jews was a crucial factor in their historical experience, in terms of both the limitations and opportunities these presented. *Mudéjar* integration into Christian society provided opportunities for subject Muslims, both as individuals and as communities, but it was not a situation that either Christian or *mudéjar* authorities looked on with approval.

[103] J. Torró i Abad, "Peasants like the Others?" This tendency towards separation of family lines and a corresponding divergence of agendas was aggravated by the absence in Christian society of integrating mechanisms, like that of *mawla* (conversion/clientage), in Islam. Meyerson posits *mawla* as one of the key factors determining Islamic societies' capacity for converting and integrating out-group members, and notes the absence of a comparable institution in medieval Christian society. M. D. Meyerson, "Conquest, Kinship, and Conversion."

[104] M. J. Roy Marín, "Aportación al estudio del delito sexual," p. 199, n. 24.

*Arabo-Islamic identities*

In exploring the internal life of subject Muslim communities we are severely limited by the sources at our disposal, which are overwhelmingly Christian in provenance and voice, and tend to address Muslim affairs only as they directly intersect with Christian interests and agendas. Hence, the evidence we have of ethno-cultural diversity, competition, and tensions within these *mudéjar* populations appears only in specific contexts. Traditionally, the internal dynamics of early Arabo-Islamic history have been mapped out with an emphasis on tribal identity, and supposed conflicts between rival confederations (notably, the northern, Qaysī, and the southern, Yamanī). Recent research has discredited the uncritical acceptance of this paradigm, and at any rate, by the mid eleventh century the Muslim *umma* was certainly not defined in any real sense by tribal identity or genealogy.[105]

Certainly, in Iberia there was a long history of antagonism between Arab-identifying indigenous Andalusīs and "Berber" North Africans – an antipathy that was rooted in generic disdain for native Maghribīs that dated back to the eighth century. This became particularly intense in the final decades of the Caliphate of Córdoba, as North African immigrants, notably, warriors, came to dominate the political scene and displace native elites. Christian observers became aware of these tensions over the course of the following century, when the indigenous Muslim resistance to North African rule, specifically the Almoravids and Almohads, came to be expressed in ethno-religious terms.[106]

In Islamic Sicily and during the period of Norman pacification, there were surely tensions between and within indigenous and Ifrīqiyan Muslim clans and factions, but by the early decades of the twelfth century, Christian domination seems to have pushed this dynamic into the background. We may presume that there were similar tensions at work among the subject Muslim communities of the Crusader Levant, where native Arabs were in competition with powerful newcomers, including Turks and Kurds, but we lack explicit evidence for such conflicts existing among subject Muslims. In any event, none of these groups was itself monolithic; the primary mode of group-identification and vector of decision-making was the family, or extended family, rather than tribal or ethno-religious affiliation writ large. Hence, any number of other considerations could override whatever solidarity of purpose might emerge out of shared

[105] For a critique of the tribal interpretation of the early history of the Islamic West, see A. Ṭāha, *The Muslim Conquest*.

[106] See P. Guichard, *Structures sociales*, p. 479; cf. B. Catlos, *The Victors and the Vanquished*, p. 47. See p. 53, above.

communal identity. In the twilight era of the *taifa* kings in Al-Andalus, Berber, Andalusī, and Christian factions allied with each other and against co-religionists with consistent indifference to religious solidarity, as happened also in contemporary Sicily, Ifrīqiya, and Palestine.

In Iberia, the question of Berber settlement and integration and the persistence of tribal culture and "Oriental family" structures – tribal and segmentary, endogamous and agnatic – that some historians have come to characterize as essential to Islamic societies, has been the subject of considerable scholarly controversy.[107] Much effort has been expended in establishing that there was significant Berber settlement over much of al-Andalus, extending from the time of the conquest even into the *taifa* period. This is reflected not only in literary-historical sources, but in toponymy, and the arrangement and distribution of irrigation systems and settlements.[108] Irrigation and settlement patterns have also been linked to tribal, segmentary social structures, in that both the physical and administrative organization of these systems has been seen to reflect, and reinforce, these social patterns.[109] These are seen to have developed within the framework of the "tributary-mercantile" society of al-Andalus – which was characterized by the absence of a seigniorial class and land-based aristocracy or economic elite, and in which producers interacted directly – or, rather, by the medium of a town or city – with a "state" that provided services in exchange for taxes. Although evidence for the earlier period is often scant, the persistence of these structures in Naṣrid Granada as late as the fifteenth century supports the contention that they characterized much or most of al-Andalus prior to the Christian conquests of the twelfth and thirteenth centuries.[110] And, although less work has been done on these areas, indications suggest that Islamic Sicily and Palestine were similar.

Tracing the effect of the Latin conquest on these social structures, however, is more problematic, given that Christians took virtually no interest in the internal workings of subject Muslim society prior to the late thirteenth century. Surveys of land-exchange documents featuring Muslim landowners and tenants from across Iberia from the twelfth

[107] This runs through the scholarship of Guichard and Miquel Barceló, particularly the latter's work in uncovering the organization of Andalusi irrigation systems (see, for example, M. Barceló i Perelló, *et al.*, *The Design of Irrigation Systems*). However, it is not clear that these structures persisted after the conquest, especially in urban environments. See the discussion in B. Catlos, *The Victors and the Vanquished*, pp. 41–44, and in T. F. Glick, *From Muslim Fortress to Christian Castle*, pp. 56–58.

[108] See T. F. Glick, *From Muslim Fortress to Christian Castle*, pp. 29–36.

[109] See the excellent summary in C. Trillo San José, "A Social Analysis of Irrigation," pp. 164–72.

[110] See above, p. 291, n. 33

century onwards do not reveal evidence of lateral succession in family inheritance (i.e. the lead position in a broad family group being passed to the eldest male member, rather than from father to son, as one might expect in an extended, agnatic family), of extended family groups as owners of property (e.g. the "*Banū* so-and-so"), or other hallmarks of the "Oriental" family. Rather, landed property is consistently described as being owned either by individuals (male or female), by married couples (with little indication of polygamy), or occasionally by a parent and several children. The same holds in urban environments, where the families who dominated local *mudéjar* offices practiced primogeniture, endeavoring to pass down all of their appointments, as a package, to a single son.

This may be simply a question of context; it is possible that traditional Arabo-Islamic family arrangements were invoked or observed in specific circumstances, such as the preferred choice of a spouse, or in other contexts that would not appear in Christian documentation. But the internal struggles of Muslim *aljamas* of the thirteenth to fifteenth centuries, which are abundantly documented, fail to yield evidence of these types of family structures even among the *mudéjar* elite, and there is no indication that power struggles and factions within *aljamas* corresponded to "clans" (let alone "tribes"), as historians might presume they should.[111] A more likely case is that – to the extent that "traditional" Arabo-Islamic family structures survived to the era of conquest – they faded out shortly after, for the simple reason that they were no longer appropriate to the conditions of subject Muslim society, much as modern immigrants tend to abandon traditional social conventions and configurations within a generation or two of immigration, without necessarily "losing their culture," or ceasing to appreciate and advocate (and occasionally invoke) the values that had been associated with those practices. That said, such customs may have been maintained at least affectatiously, particularly among the *mudéjar* elite, who continued to use the Arabic language and employ Arabo-Islamic naming conventions (including tribal-identifying *nisab*) in certain contexts into the sixteenth century.[112] As late as 1509 in Navarre, *mudéjar* notaries

[111] The fact that in factional struggles within *aljamas* relations between families sometimes shifted quite rapidly, and alliances formed and dissolved frequently, shows that these were not larger factional/tribal rivalries. See, for example, "Case Study 3. Litigation and Competition within the Muslim Community: The Abdellas of Daroca (1280–1310)," pp. 347–56, in B. Catlos, *The Victors and the Vanquished*; and B. Catlos, "Privilegio y poder."

[112] See, for example, J. Bosch Vilá, "Los documentos árabes y hebreos," and "Los documentos árabes"; C. Barceló Torres and A. Labarta, "Fondos documentales árabes," and *Archivos moriscos*; A. Labarta, "La aljama de musulmanes"; and M. J. Viguera Molins, "Les mudejars et leurs documents," p. 160. The *nisba* (plural: *nisab* ) is that element in the formal Arabic name that acts as an adjective for tribal affiliation, geographic origin, or occupation.

continued to draft contracts in Arabic alongside the Romance version, maintaining Islamicate notarial conventions such as the "bismillah," and the *hijra* calendar, and in which the local *alcaydus*, Yayel Cortobí, referred to himself as "*al-faqīh*, *al-qāḍī*, Yaḥya al-Qurṭubī."[113]

### *Language and identity*

The survival of Arabic among *mudéjares* has been the subject of some debate. Until recently, established wisdom declared that it had disappeared both as a written and a spoken language in Aragon and Navarre by the late fourteenth century, persisting somewhat longer in Valencia, and – naturally – much later in Granada. To a significant degree these arguments were based on the absence of Arabic or mention of Arabic in surviving documentation. This, however, is a function of genre and of institutional interest. Only those rare Arabic-language documents that Christian institutions had a stake in preserving would survive. Hence, Arabic land-transfer documents do occasionally turn up in cathedral and municipal archives – some from the fifteenth and sixteenth centuries.[114]

Moreover, education in Arabic was sustained not only by those formal Islamic educational institutions that survived, including the *madrasa* at Zaragoza, and others, possibly at Lucera, Segovia, and Murcia, but by the informal schools run out of mosques in both town and countryside across the Iberian Peninsula.[115] Such was the vitality of the rural literary culture that a library of nearly sixty manuscript books was discovered in a small town in Aragon in the sixteenth century.[116] The continuing circulation of Arabic texts among *mudéjares* in the late Middle Ages confirms this, as does the recent discovery of numbers of quotidian and religious documents produced by *mudéjares* throughout the period, in Arabic or in *aljamiado*, Romance vernaculars, or all three.[117] In this light, the fulminations of the Valencian *ʿālim*, Ibn ʾAmīra, against the loss of Arabic in the conquered territories, reads as ideologically driven, rhetorical hyperbole, rather than a reflection of socio-cultural reality.[118]

Language is not a zero-sum-game, and in many (if not most) societies multilingualism is normal; and children who grow up in bilingual

[113] See M. García-Arenal, "Un nuevo documento," p. 459, for the Arabic.
[114] See, for example, J. Bosch Vilá, "Los documentos árabes."
[115] I. O'Connor de los Angelos, "Muslim Mudéjar Women," p. 64; J. A. Taylor, "*Lucera Sarracenorum*," p. 54; G. Wiegers, *Islamic Literature*, pp. 78 and 79; and P. van Koningsveld, "Andalusian-Arabic Manuscripts," pp. 8, 9, and 14.
[116] See A. Labarta and J. Carlos Escribano, "Las bibliotecas."
[117] See C. Barceló and A. Labarta, *Archivos moriscos*; and C. López-Morillas, "'Trilingual' Marginal Notes."
[118] See p. 320, above.

environments naturally develop native proficiency in more than one language, and do not necessarily identify each language as proprietary to a specific group.[119] Therefore, there is no reason to conclude that *mudéjares*' broad facility in Romance vernaculars indicated a loss or decline of Arabic as a spoken language. A critical mass of Arabic speakers, together with informal education in the household (particularly through the medium of women), would have been sufficient to sustain it. Moreover, there is strong tacit evidence to support this notion, in that there are no indications that *mudéjares* from different regions had any difficulty communicating with each other or with foreign Muslims, whether these were rare visiting dignitaries or ubiquitous slaves. Nor does language seem to have been a barrier to *mudéjares* who traveled to or traded in the *dār al-Islām*, or traveled there to consult with *muftūn* or other religious authorities.[120] The Hungarian *bashkir* Yāqūt al-Rūmī encountered in thirteenth-century Aleppo evidently spoke Arabic, as did the *mudéjares* of Valencia in the early 1500s – at least according to a Venetian merchant who traveled the kingdom and observed, "In the kingdom of Valencia, there are innumerable Muslims ... and they all speak Arabic [*moresche*], except some who know how to speak Spanish."[121]

There is also overwhelming evidence for subject Muslims' cultural and linguistic integration into Latin society, and there is little evidence that *mudéjares* had any difficulty communicating with Christian commoners or officials. As the body of documentary evidence broadens from the late thirteenth century, even humble Muslims, men and women, can be found deposing in court documents in Romance, without the benefit of a translator.[122] Late medieval Valencia represents something of an exception. Here more *mudéjares*, especially women, claimed to be speakers only of *Algarabía* (Arabic), and required translators when they went before the courts or inquisition.[123] Though this may be indicative of a lack of facility, perhaps relating to Muslim women's comparative social isolation, it might

[119] Such linguistic ambiguities can be observed not only in medieval Iberia, but in Sicily, where an Arabic language liturgy was in use by the mid twelfth century, and multilingual funerary markers were used even by non-elite persons. See J. Johns, "The Greek Church," pp. 140 and 142.

[120] See above, pp. 317 and 328.

[121] See above, p. 228; M. T. Ferrer i Mallol, "La frontera meridional," pp. 1580–81.

[122] See, for example, the trial transcripts in B. Catlos, "Dos musulmanas pleitean," and "Tyranny and the Mundane." In the latter case, two foreign Muslim slaves were interrogated in Arabic by local *mudéjares* and local Christians, whereas the local *mudéjares* deposed in Romance.

[123] See the discussion in E. Císcar Pallarés, "'Algaravia'". He estimates that only 2–3 percent of Valencian *mudéjares* did not speak Valencian Romance (*Algemía*; from the Arabic *'ajam* for "foreign," or "barbaric"), but notes that some 50 percent of women taken before the inquisition required interpreters (see p. 141).

rather have been a canny and effective strategy of resistance and defense, given that inquisitorial tactics often turned on the precise meanings of specific terms, and, therefore, did not translate well.[124] On the other hand, this might represent a decline in the use of Romance by Muslims here – either a symptom of growing cultural distance, or a deliberate turning away from the language of their oppressors. In either case, linguistic estrangement here would have served to aggravate the cultural and social disaffection that broadly characterized Christian–Muslim relations in this kingdom

Overall, however, the clear capacity of Muslims to "pass" as Christians when they were not distinguished by particular clothing or hairstyles attests to their native-level facility with these local vernaculars. Indeed, just as many Christians spoke Arabic (whether a few words or very well), not all subject Muslims would have been raised speaking or reading the language of the Qur'ān – although, broadly speaking, most – except for the poorest or those in the most marginalized or peripheral communities – would have likely had some proficiency. Members of the commercial and artisanal class, and in particular, those who occupied official positions in *aljamas*, or were in the service of seigniors, ecclesiastical institutions, or the Crown, would not only have spoken one or more Christian vernaculars, either as a native language, or as an acquisition, but often some Latin, as well.[125] Many – not only exceptional figures such as the scholar 'Īsā b. Jābir – were also literate in Latin and local languages. For members of the "middle classes" this literacy may have been rudimentary, but it was certainly functional.[126] Subject Muslims straddled cultures, employing different languages and even different personal names in different contexts and for different audiences.[127] They lived in a world circumscribed by Latinate institutions and marked by the Christian solar calendar,

124 See, for example, B. Ehlers, "Violence and Religious Identity," p. 116.

125 This was clearly the case in the Iberian Peninsula, and all but certainly in Sicily. Even Muslims in Lucera in the 1290s and 1300s received letters in Latin, whether "Abdalassis, Our faithful knight," or the humble merchants who sought redress after having been robbed on the way back from Salerno. See P. Egidi, *Codice Diplomatico*, pp. 80 {211} and 68 {165}, respectively.

126 This is clear from *mudéjar* families' conservation of and recourse to royal privileges in Latin that they received, safeguarded, and duly trotted out in court when necessary. See also C. Conde Solares, "Social Continuity," p. 317.

127 See, for example, M. García-Arenal and B. Leroy, *Moros y judíos en Navarra*, p. 59. The use of parallel names can be seen even among immigrant communities today, where in North America, for example, it is not uncommon for newcomers to Anglicize their names or adopt pseudonyms for public use. That said, in Castile in the fourteenth century, Alfonso XI had prohibited *mudéjares* by law from bearing Christian names, at least officially. See M. García-Arenal, "Dos documentos," p. 170. In twelfth-century Sicily, converts to Christianity at times simply continued to use Islamicate names. See J. Johns, "The Greek Church," p. 150.

the feasts and saints' days of which provided the temporal framework for business contracts, fiscal administration, and the agricultural cycle.[128] For all this, they were hardly unique; Jews too, but also Christians, moved in multilingual, multicultural environments – individuals of all ethno-religious orientations deployed multiple regional vernaculars and communal languages, and dabbled in each others' cultural affectations with an ease and facility that is characteristic of diverse societies the world over.

### *The feminine ideal*

Even something as fundamental as the status and role of women in subject Muslim society raises questions as to the persistence of supposedly "Islamic" cultural values in the period after the Christian conquest, and particularly after two centuries of Latin domination, when in the 1400s processes of institutional and informal integration and acculturation were intensifying among the remaining subject Muslim communities. In principle, Islamic marriage and inheritance laws remained in effect, including the rules revolving around the dower (*mahr*, or *ṣadāq*) and divorce. At the same time, Muslim women from across the socio-economic spectrum figure as independent property owners in Latin documentation in both Iberia and Sicily.[129] They have independent business interests, and represent themselves in court, in cases against both Christians and fellow Muslims – including their own husbands.[130] Such litigiousness is not at all inconsistent with the situation in Muslim-ruled societies, where women's property rights were grounded in Scripture and enshrined in law; but under Latin rule, there can be little doubt that the existence of a parallel and more powerful Christian legal order provided opportunities for *mudéjar* women to pursue their own agendas more robustly than previously. Like *mudéjar* men, they could choose jurisdictions and judicial venues that better favored their own circumstances, and engage in appeals or seek recourse according to legal principles that ran contrary to the *sharīʿa*.

Polygamy, like slavery, continued to be practiced among *mudéjares*, but – as among Jews in Christian Iberia – it fell into desuetude. This was not because it was forbidden, but because it was likely no longer considered a

128 This was true even in the era of Islamic rule, when the Christian solar calendar was used alongside the Muslim lunar calendar, which was less appropriate for marking the seasons because of the moveable character of its months. See, for example, C. Pellat, *Le calendrier de Cordoue*.

129 For example, the registers of Monreale in Sicily list Muslim women as heads of families. See H. Bercher, *et al.*, "Une abbaye latine," p. 533.

130 See "Gendering the *Mudéjar*," below, pp. 497–508.

model for behavior, and perhaps because it no longer yielded advantages, in terms either of expanding the prosperity and influence of the family unit – particularly in the "urban" milieu in which most of these Muslims moved – or in terms of sexual advantage to the male, given the widespread practice of concubinage, and easy access to prostitutes.[131] Through the fourteenth and fifteenth centuries occasional inter-Muslim disputes centered on the rights of a second or first wife, but evidence of these is rare and confined generally to the more prosperous members of these communities. References to third or fourth wives are exceedingly rare, even among the wealthiest Muslims. Nevertheless, the late medieval legal texts produced by *mudéjares* show a considerable emphasis on a "conservative" approach to matters relating to gender, including marriage and polygamy, inheritance, sexual morality, and the dangers of female gossip.[132] However, it is clear that these manuals represent idealizations rather than being indicative of actual judicial practice, and thus, their emphasis on normative female behavior may have been a reflection of the anxieties associated with the changing status and increasing independence of women as a consequence of Latin domination, and the undermining of the fabric of "traditional" Islamic society and of Islamic law.

### *Social class in subject Muslim society*

Nor do these legal texts or the other literature produced emphasize distinctions of class or wealth among Muslims living under Latin rule, but it is clear from the Christian documentation that their societies were stratified, and that Muslims of different social rank and wealth experienced Christian domination differently. Unlike Latin Christendom, Islamic society was theoretically egalitarian and did not formally distinguish social classes. Nevertheless, a broad distinction between the *khāṣṣa* ("aristocracy") and *umma* ("the people," or "masses") was recognized, and continued to inform *mudéjar* society in some sense, if only internally and in limited contexts. Across the Mediterranean, with the exception of Norman Ifrīqiya, the Christian conquest precipitated a complete, or near-complete departure of the political and religious elite; in the vacuum

131 Even in al-Andalus polygamy does not seem to have been practiced widely except among the upper classes. See M. Marín, *Mujeres en al-Andalus*, pp. 442–52. In 1379 Mahomat Alamçarofi of Murla (Valencia) paid off a debt of 65 *sous* owed by Mochdia, a prostitute from Algar, perhaps out of piety or charity, but more likely in return for service to be rendered. See J. Vidal Argente, "Un libro de cuentas," p. 300.

132 See, for example the clauses relating to polygamy in C. Barceló Torres, *Un tratado catalán*, e.g., pp. 15 {56}, 15 {54}, 15 {57}, 16 {59}, as well as 16ff.

that was created a new elite emerged, but one that was necessarily less advantaged and less sophisticated than the previous.[133] Hence, under Latin rule, both the identity and the conception of who comprised the *khāṣṣa* changed. In the *dār al-Islām* it referred to those who were close to the court, including members of the upper administration and bureaucracy, governors and commanders, and the religious and economic elite. With the disappearance of a "secular" elite as a consequence of the Christian conquest, and the unchallenged, if diluted authority of the religious class that remained, the *mudéjar ʿulamāʾ* appears to have appropriated the term to refer to themselves.[134]

While under Latin rule, there certainly were Muslims who were close to the court and influential in Christian institutions of power, these were not conceived of as an elite on Islamicate terms – they were a colonial elite, whose prestige within the *mudéjar* community was limited, based as it was on ties of patronage with illegitimate and foreign, Infidel oppressors. This characterized the subject Muslim experience across Latin Christendom (with the exception of the Crusader Levant), but is most evident in the case of Navarre. Here, in particular, many *mudéjar* craftsmen developed exceptionally close personal and economic ties to the royal household and held a range of positions in the kingdom's administration.[135] For many, this translated into official appointments in local Muslim administrations, including offices with a religio-judicial dimension, such as the *alcaydus*, but none enjoyed a power or prestige equivalent to the pre-conquest *khāṣṣa*. At the lower end of the scale, a distinct rural peasantry, the *fallāḥīn*, had emerged in the Islamic eastern Mediterranean, especially as a consequence of the entrenchment of *iqṭāʿ*.[136] This existence of this semi-disenfranchised class likely facilitated the transition to the Frankish feudal regime in Crusader Syria and Palestine. In contrast to the *dār al-Islām*, in Latin lands, four broad socio-economic categories of free Muslims can be distinguished: an upper or "international" elite, a regional elite or "patriciate," the free Muslim population that comprised the overwhelming bulk of *mudéjar* society, and slaves.

[133] This phenomenon was undoubtedly most acute in the Latin East, but is most obvious (thanks to the sources at our disposal) in Latin Iberia. It occurred also in Sicily, although Norman patronage of the Islamicate high culture mitigated the process here. See A. Metcalfe, *The Muslims of Medieval Italy*, pp. 123–34.

[134] See, for example, L. G. Jones, "The Boundaries of Sin," p. 411.

[135] C. Condes Solares, "Social Continuity," p. 314.

[136] *Iqṭāʿ* was a Turco-Muslim administrative institution originally established to support the military elite in Egypt and Syria-Palestine. It is sometimes misrepresented as a "feudal" institution.

*The "international" elite*

At the top of this hierarchy was the extremely reduced group that comprised a supra-regional, or "international" elite. Many of these were not natives but sojourners in Latin lands – high-status, educated, and wealthy Muslims who located either temporarily or permanently in Christian territory. Leaving aside the autonomous client warlords of the Iberian frontier of the likes of Muḥammad b. Mardanīsh, the most prestigious among these were political hostages, such as the Naṣrid princes who were obliged to settle in Castile, exiles, like Sayf al-Dawla, the dispossessed heir of Hūdid Zaragoza, or the Almohad princes who settled in Valencia in the late thirteenth century and served the count-kings of Barcelona as soldiers, and the Granadans who served in the Castilian *guardia morisca*.[137] The "noblemen," or grandees, among the subject Muslims who served Christian rulers in Sicily, families like the Banū Ḥammūd, or their analogues in Hungary and Lithuania, might also fall into this category.[138] Next in status were the diplomats and mercenaries, whose affairs led them to cultivate both personal and business relationships with members of the Latin elite – individuals such as the memoirist Usāma b. Munqidh, the Granadan and Moroccan mercenaries, and professional *mudéjar* warriors who peopled the courts and ranged across the countryside of Castile and the Crown of Aragon from the late thirteenth to the mid fifteenth centuries. Some Muslim physicians, intellectuals, and educated "professionals" also fall into this category; including well-known figures such as the geographer al-Idrīsī, as well as a plethora of lesser-known or historically anonymous individuals. Finally, the Muslim merchants, both Latin subjects and foreigners, who traded between the Christian kingdoms, or back and forth across the confessional frontier, from the Latin East to Portugal, fall into this category.

This elite was almost certainly far more numerous than the available evidence indicates; the nature of their participation in Christian society, compounded by the unease associated with cross-confessional rapprochement (which could be taken as a reflection of Christians' lack of faith or resolve), did not necessarily lend itself to representation in higher literature, or acknowledgement in institutionally oriented historical sources. And yet, this was a group that interacted on quite intimate terms with the Latin elite; whether they were physicians or fellow soldiers, they could find themselves in a position where the fate of powerful Christians hung in their hands. Shared vocation and class has a way of effacing

[137] See, above, pp. 33, 70, and 197.
[138] J. Johns, *Arabic Administration*, pp. 234ff for the Ḥammūdids.

ethno-religious differences, and this becomes particularly obvious in the highest echelons, where Crusaders could fight alongside infidels as easily as a "born-again" American president in the twenty-first century could stroll hand-in-hand through his rose garden with the "fundamentalist" Wahhābī prince who was his ally. Seven centuries earlier in the royal palace at Barcelona, a Granadan prince took a formal vow of hereditary vassalship to a Christian king with as little compunction. Membership in the upper classes took Muslims (and Jews) out of the context of their religious identity; hence, they were typically granted privileges that exempted them from the requirement to wear special clothing to mark themselves off as non-Christians. Muslim knights and mercenaries received gifts of rich cloth, shoes, expensive tack, and falcons, not as enticements to service, but as parting tokens of esteem. Moreover, it is clear they participated in court ceremonies – ritual that was, as a matter of course, steeped in Christian imagery.[139] How members of this elite viewed and interacted with lower-status subject Muslims is a difficult question to answer. In certain contexts they must have certainly felt an affinity based on their ethno-religious identity, and there is evidence that they used their influence to advocate the rights of subject Muslims, as the Andalusī traveler Abū Ḥāmid al-Gharnāṭī claimed to have done in Hungary.

That said, at other times these individuals' self-perception as members of a privileged aristocracy may have led them to look at Muslim commoners with indifference or disdain. The archival record is not only thin, but ambiguous. What can we presume regarding such attitudes when we read of a Granadan mercenary who received permission to marry a *mudéjar* woman from Zaragoza?[140] Was it a case of true romance, or legitimized *raptus*? And what does this indicate, if anything, about the attitude of this warrior or his brothers-in-arms towards the subject Muslim population? In any event, this group – particularly, the native Muslims among them – would have played an important role in maintaining the subject Muslim communities connected with the larger *dār al-Islām*, and helped to sustain *mudéjar* cultural confidence by presenting examples of an Islamic military elite whose prestige was recognized and validated even by Christians.

The exception was, again, Norman Sicily, where thanks to the proclivities of the d'Hauteville monarchs and the delicate balance of power on the island and in the central Mediterranean, much of the apparatus of

139 See B. Catlos, "A Muslim Mercenary," pp. 287–90; also p. 246, above. Falconry was one of several media for socialization and acculturation that arose out of the common vocational orientation of the Christian and Muslim aristocracy. Both Alfonso X and Frederick II produced books on the subject; see, for example, A. Metcalfe, *The Muslims*, p. 243.

140 See B. Catlos, "A Muslim Mercenary," p. 293, n. 135.

Islamic high culture was not only maintained but deliberately adopted, at least superficially. Here, Muslims and crypto-Muslims openly exercised power in the heart of the palace, and held some of the most powerful positions in the kingdom, including those of chamberlain and admiral. Such integration was no mere affectation or shallow Islamophilia – under Roger II Fāṭimid chancery practices were deliberately adopted, and through the reign of William II, the court at Palermo was peopled by Muslim intellectuals, poets, and "scientists." According to Ibn Jubayr, the King used Muslim cooks and servants, and consulted Muslim physicians and astrologers.[141]

Remarkably, even an Islamic religious and political elite seems to have survived here, not only in Palermo, but in also in western Sicily, which remained a predominantly Muslim and semi-autonomous enclave; there, local grandees attempted to carry out independent diplomatic initiatives, and conspired actively for the restoration of Islamic rule. This situation, which persisted for a full century, strengthened Islamic society in Norman Sicily, but may have also contributed to its rapid decline in the late 1200s. On the one hand, an inordinately powerful and independent Muslim and crypto-Muslim minority would have been seen as a threat by Latin colonizers, and on the other, it would have inspired a confidence and defiance within the minority that would have provoked further reaction. In any event, influential as the Muslim elite may have been in Sicily, they evidently had little power (and, perhaps, little will) to protect common Muslims living under the authority of Christian lords from abuse, including the many Muslim tenants of the cathedral-abbey of Monreale. In the post-exile period, when the remaining Muslims had been relocated to mainland Lucera, the social structure of the colony resembled those of local *mudéjar* communities in contemporary Iberia – a subject community shorn of its religio-cultural elite.

### *The regional upper class*

More numerous and ultimately more important in quotidian Muslim affairs was the local elite – a group Robert I. Burns described, when writing of thirteenth-century Valencia, as the *mudéjar* "urban patriciate."[142] Even in Castile, the only Latin kingdom that actively pursued a coherent policy of centralizing *mudéjar* administration, subject Muslim communities remained effectively independent, and power within the

141 Ibn Jubayr, *Travels*, p. 341.
142 Burns coined the term in reference to the wealthy class of post-conquest Valencian *mudéjares*. See R. I. Burns, *Islam under the Crusaders*, pp. 406ff.

communities remained locally entrenched. In the broadest sense, the "urban patriciate" included those Muslim families who were able to secure and retain official appointments within the Christian-dominated *mudéjar* officiate – often against the consent and will of their constituents. As discussed in the previous chapter, these families typically enjoyed a fortune based on craft industry or high-status professions, which provided them with the necessary capital to purchase royal or seigniorial monopolies and appointments.[143] By accruing tax privileges and preferential treatment, and cultivating relationships with Christian authorities, they set themselves apart from their own communities – a fact reflected in their propensity to exploit their co-religionists.[144]

From the perspective of the Latin power structure, their role was to ensure the peace and acquiescence of their communities and the flow of tribute; in real terms, this translated into domination of the fiscal and judicial administration of the *aljamas*. This put them in a situation of conflict of interest, given that Islamic justice and taxation should ideally operate according to Islamic criteria and for the benefit of the community. They functioned in a role analogous to that of modern indigenous colonial elites.[145] It is a reflection of the power and confidence of these families, however, that they commonly engaged in wanton abuse of their own communities, and regularly and openly defied both Christian law and Christian – even royal – authorities. Not a few were called up on the capital charge of having sex with Christian women, but they were inevitably successful at purchasing a royal pardon in such cases, even when they were caught *in flagrante*.[146] On the one hand, this swaggering self-confidence increased the potential for corruption and abuse, but on the other, it meant that these families could act as fierce and determined defenders of communal rights, when they perceived of these as being congruent with their own interests. Even the most corrupt *aljama* officials vehemently defended the jurisdiction of *mudéjar* official institutions, the integrity of Muslim cemeteries and places of worship, local grazing rights, and Muslim tax treaties, and battled against their communities' creditors, whether these encroachments were carried out by Christians, Jews, or neighboring Muslim communities.[147]

143 See above, p. 396. 144 This was equally true of Jewish and Christian local elites.

145 See B. Catlos, "Mudéjar Communities and their Rulers."

146 See, for example, the case of Mahomet, *alaminus* of Borja, caught in the act in 1284, and Mafoma Abenferre, scion of the ruling family of *mudéjar* Lleida, one of several of the town's Muslims ("alguns moros," "nonnulli Saraceni") who was said to be enjoying carnal affairs with Christian women in 1380. See B. Catlos, *The Victors and the Vanquished*, p. 369, and J. Mutgé i Vives, *L'aljama sarraïna*, pp. 361–3 {181–83}.

147 For examples, see "Case Study #4: Administrative Corruption and Royal Complicity: Abrahim Abengentor, *Çavalquen* of Huesca (1260–1304)," and "Case Study #5:

The most successful of these families diversified economically and extended their contacts in Christian society, serving as liaisons for, or becoming tenants or vassals of, ecclesiastical foundations, including military and monastic orders, monasteries (particularly royal monasteries), magnates, and even the royal household; and they cultivated mutually beneficial relations with their homologues within the local Christian municipality.[148] Nevertheless, with the exception of a handful of families, such as the Bellidos and Bellvíses in thirteenth- and fourteenth- to fifteenth-century Aragon, or the Alpelmís and Aludalís in Navarre, and a number of families in fifteenth-century Castile, including the Bellvíses and Xarafís, these elites remained resolutely local in character, and their influence seldom extended beyond the boundaries of the municipality where their *aljama* was located.[149]

In fact, this "urban patriciate" did not comprise a distinct class, *per se*. Rather, it represented the most historically visible portion of broad and fluctuating "upper middle class," made up of Muslim landowners, merchants, professional soldiers, and religious figures. Indeed, the "urban patriciate" did not necessarily represent the wealthiest Muslim families in any given locale. Occasional and usually oblique but unequivocal references in Christian documentation betray the existence of Muslim individuals and families who had considerable wealth at their disposal, in the form of agricultural lands, urban property, livestock, merchandise, moveable goods, and cash; or who enjoyed close connections with the upper echelons of Latin Christian society, and yet who did not participate actively in the colonial institutional structure.[150] This was the larger pool from which the "patriciate" families emerged (and dissolved back into as their power waned).

Such individuals (usually men, but occasionally independent women) tend to surface in tax rolls when they were occasionally forced to make extraordinary "gifts" to the royal fisc; in notarial records, where their business interests are revealed; in criminal cases, whether as victims or culprits; and in cases where they came into conflict with Jewish creditors, Christian officials, and institutions, or their own *aljama* officials. It is only because her home was robbed by a band of her fellow townsfolk in the

Overlapping Agendas: The Career of Mahomet, *Alaminus* of Borja (1276–1302)," in B. Catlos, *The Victors and the Vanquished*, pp. 357–66 and 366–72; and J. Mutgé i Vives, "Els Bimferre."

148 Çalema Alitili, for example (see p. 431, n. 38, above), is attested to as *alcaydus*, master engineer, property owner, and livestock owner; these likely represent only part of his economic activities and interests.

149 See above, pp. 194.

150 See for example, M. F. Lopes de Barros, *Tempos e espaços*, p. 110, for Portugal, and J. Carrasco Pérez, "Los Mudéjares de Navarra," p. 97, for Navarre.

1290s that we learn of Villeta, a wealthy *mudéjar* woman of Ricla, who apparently had a sentimental relationship with a Christian knight. An investigation into the murder of Mahomet de Rey in 1357 (by two fellow Muslims) reveals that this Aragonese tailor traveled with an inventory worth 1,200 *solidi*.[151] A single trial record reveals the wealth of Sultana, who sued her husband Saydo, of Vilafranca, for a dower of 1,500 *solidi* in 1300. Another document recounts the case of the Portuguese smuggler, Shuayb Xoay, caught crossing the Castilian frontier with 300 head of livestock in tow in 1468, and who was assessed a fine of 1,000 *reales* in consequence.[152] These random and serendipitous documentary survivals indicate the existence of a wealthy class of *mudéjares* that was much more numerous than previously assumed.

It was in this stratum that whatever remained of an independent, pious Islamic elite can be found: the teachers and tutors at "underground" *madrasas*; the unofficial *muftūn*, to whom *mudéjares* occasionally turned to resolve legal disputes, much to the ire of officially appointed *alcaydi*; and the *mudéjar* and Morisco *ᶜulamāʾ*, who were so instrumental in maintaining Islamic culture and identity, particularly in the late fifteenth to early seventeenth centuries.[153] But more importantly, perhaps, the members of this "upper middle class" contributed to the economic diversity and the economic weight that sustained ethno-religious diversity, and they too were engaged in formal and informal relationships of economic and political interdependence and social interaction with a broad range of Christian constituencies – a major factor militating against ethno-religious balkanization.[154]

Although the sources are frustratingly reticent, they hint at the existence of some sort of analog to the "patriciate" group in the Latin principalities of the Levant, Hungary, and the northeast. By virtue of the communal organization of taxation and justice in these lands, the existence of individuals or families who could act as liaison between the dominant group and the minorities was inevitable, and it is also clear that these would be drawn from among the most prosperous elements of these societies, and would, in turn, accrue privileges and influence as a consequence. The

151 B. Catlos, *The Victors and the Vanquished*, pp. 220–21, and "The de Reys (1220–1501)," pp. 207–8.

152 For Saydo, see ACA, Processes en Quart, 1301J (December 14, 1300). It is remarkable that Shuayb could came up with such a substantial amount of cash. See M. F. Lopes de Barros, *Tempos e espaços*, p. 526.

153 In some cases, these *madrassas* and mosques were quite literally underground, as was the case with subterranean *masjid* attested to in the 1560s in Ain Cabdon, Valencia. L. García Ballester, *Historia social de la medicina*, p. 149.

154 Many local studies bear out this hypothesis. See, for example, F. J. García Marco, "El trabajo de los mudéjares."

enigmatic Muslim minters, as well as the merchants and the cavalrymen of Hungary and Lithuania, must have played such a role, whereas in Palestine, "headmen," such as the prosperous individual encountered by Ibn Jubayr on the way to Acre, together with Muslim urban professionals and tradesmen, likely fell into this set. As with the upper elite, the exceptional environments would have been the kingdoms of Valencia and Murcia (prior to the "Saracen wars" of the 1270s), and Norman-dominated western Sicily and Ifrīqiya in the eleventh-century. Here, Islamic society persisted – overlain by only the thinnest veneer of Christian domination. Hence, individuals and families such as the Banū Hudayr of Crevillent, al-Azrāq of Vall d'Alcalà, or Sicily's Abū 'l-Ḍaw' Sirāj could imagine themselves to be potentates in a functioning Islamic society, only temporarily suffering under Infidel tribute.

### *Diversity and survival*

In Iberia, *mudéjares* who worked in positions of familiarity and trust within the highest circles of the aristocracy were able to leverage privileges and official appointments for themselves and their family members, but it is not clear – as was the case with Jews – that they used these to reinforce the autonomy and privileges of *mudéjar* society as a whole. This was not because Muslims were subject universally to a special and specific disdain by Christians. It may be true, for example, that unlike Christians, *mudéjares* almost never appear in royal chancery records with the honorary prefix "*don*" (from *dominus*, and corresponding roughly to "mister") before their names, but this is a consequence of the conventions of official decrees. High- and mid-status *mudéjares* frequently are qualified as "*don*" in correspondence, trial records, and other documentation (even, rarely, in less formal communications coming from the royal court).[155] It is symptomatic, perhaps, of *mudéjar* confidence and diversity that the wealthiest members of this society saw it neither in their power nor purview to become advocates for Islamic society in general. It was apparently not until the age of forced conversion at the turn of the sixteenth century that the *mudéjar*-cum-Morisco elite began to perceive the need to express solidarity on Islamic terms. On the other hand, in contrast to the more cohesive and uniform Jewish society in much of Christian Iberia, *mudéjares* seem to have been spared the agonizing intra-communal struggles that characterized the Jewish elite, or the plague of the *malsines* – the traitorous informers

[155] High-status *mudéjar* women, rare as they may have been, were also referred to as "Lady" (i.e.: *doña* ); see above, n. 66.

whose activities fractured Jewish communities and undermined the power of their leadership.[156]

Of course, the most numerous sector of subject Muslim population in each of these regions would have been the silent majority of commoners – all but invisible to historians – who, like their Christian counterparts, survived primarily by agriculture and labored under a range of conditions. In the Crusader East, the lot of the common *fallāḥīn* was already quite difficult under the Fāṭimid and Saljūq regimes. In Sicily, Muslim peasants' transformation into seigniorial villeins signaled a reduction in status, wealth, and opportunity – one that for many, turned out to be too oppressive to endure. In the Iberian peninsula, the situation of the common Muslim seems to have been generally brighter; it was here that the rule of law functioned most clearly in their favor, and that communal advocacy was most effective. On the whole, their situation was probably no worse than that of many Christian peasants. In some areas, *mudéjar* peasants were subject to particularly oppressive conditions, and were mistreated by lords and neighbors whose predatory tendencies were unrestrained by any sense of religious solidarity, but – slaves aside – even those Iberian Muslims who lived under the most arbitrary and abusive rule were never subjected to the institutionalized servility that the Christian *remença* peasants of upland Catalonia suffered.[157]

In any event, the Muslim "peasant class" was diverse too, and would have included not only landless tenant farmers, but also a significant population of petty merchants, and semi-skilled, low-status craftsmen: the roving tinkers and carpenters, itinerant merchants, millers, boatmen, and muleteers who crop up serendipitously now and again in the official documentation of the time. Many lived unobtrusively, unincorporated into any formal Muslim community or *aljama*, and simply formed part of what was regarded by Christians and Muslims alike as the normal society of the time. Most of these would have lived their lives largely unaffected by larger historical currents; for them, Infidel domination may have meant little, as long as they felt secure in person and property, and were allowed to follow, undoubtedly only discretely at times, the observances they associated with their faith.

The diversity of socio-economic position and status within subject Muslim communities, and the upward and downward social mobility

[156] See, for example, E. Lourie, "Mafiosi and Malsines," and A. Blasco Martínez, "Los malsines." It is possible that *mudéjar* jurists' obsession with women's "slander" represents an analog to the problem of informants in Jewish society.

[157] For the *mals usos*, or "evil customs," under which disenfranchised *remençna* peasants in upland Catalonia labored, see P. H. Freedman, *The Origins of Peasant Servitude*, pp. 79–83.

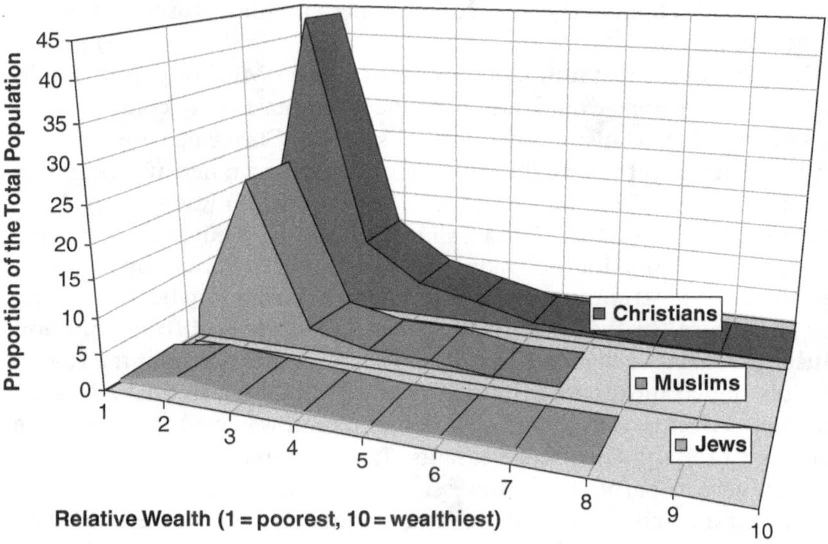


Figure 1 Communal and individual wealth

that can be observed, were important factors in maintaining the vigor and viability of these communities both economically and culturally. For whereas, taken as a totality, it may be true that these Muslim populations were poorer than the Christian and Jewish populations alongside whom they lived, by virtue of their diversity, there would have been significant numbers of Muslims who were better off as individuals than the overwhelming majority of the Christian population (see figure 1, above). It was in those regions where the Muslim socio-economic strata remained broad and fluid that these communities tended to survive. Moreover, this diversity provided opportunities for a range of contacts and affinities to form between members of different social strata who happened to belong to distinct ethno-religious communities, and this acted to mitigate conflict and competition across confessional lines.

Indeed, the history of the Muslim minorities of Latin Christendom is not generally one of competition – *mudéjares* were in no position to defend themselves when the interests of Christian society as a whole or significant factions within it perceived them as a threat to their spiritual or material welfare, nor could the will of monarchs alone preserve Muslim minorities in the face of broad resistance. Frederick II's Arabophilia could not sustain the subject Muslim community of southern Italy in the thirteenth century, nor could the beneficent apathy of the Trastámara kings of Aragon or the Árpád dynasty of Hungary towards their subject Muslims save these from the progressive erosion of their status. By the same token, neither Jaume the Conqueror of Aragon nor his successor Pere the Great could rid themselves of what they saw as their ungrateful and rebellious *mudéjar* subjects, wish as they might; their Muslims were simply too important to too many elements within Valencian society to dispense with.

In other words, these Muslim societies did not survive in the face of Christian competition, but rather because they did *not* compete with Christians. The concentration of Muslims in later medieval Castile in certain key professions – specifically, certain building and decorative trades – was reflective of this situation. Muslims may have come to dominate these professions in part because they enjoyed some sort of technical advantage or special knowledge, but it would have also been because those professions were seen as preferable precisely because they did not face substantial Christian competition. In turn, Muslim domination of these low-margin trades would have discouraged Christians from breaking into them. It was a self-reinforcing dynamic. Likewise, those Christian lords who defended their *mudéjar* subjects, or turned a blind eye to their Moriscos' open apostasy, did so for the most part because they did not have access to Christian tenants and vassals to replace them, or who would prove such docile subjects. On the other hand, when Christians and Muslims competed for the same resources and positions – whether as farmers or artisans – this competition tended to be expressed as communal rivalry. This could lead both to popular violence and to seigniorial oppression, as can by observed in the fourteenth-century kingdom of Valencia and fifteenth-century Andalucía, respectively.[158]

On the other hand, tension and competition played out fiercely and constantly within *mudéjar* communities, as rival elite families jockeyed for influence in local *aljamas* or within kingdom-wide bureaucracies, and as lower-status Muslims competed locally for the same niches – *ḥalāl* butchers' monopolies, market stalls, building contracts, and licenses for practicing crafts and trades. Vidal de Canellas's declaration in his 1247 compilation of Aragonese royal law that the fine for killing a Jew or Muslim was set at one thousand *sueldos* "because there is so much disdain for them, that if the fine were not higher than that for [killing a Christian], the Christians would kill them off like animals" was the fantasy of a bigoted cleric and little more.[159] Christian–Muslim relations were not characterized by widespread popular or official violence aimed against Muslims in particular – when it did take place, it was linked to specific,

[158] See, for example, J. Torró i Abad, "De bona guerra," and "Jérusalem ou Valence?"
[159] G. Tilander, *Vidal Mayor*, vol. II, p. 510 {IX: 22.2}.

and usually local, circumstances, and religious identity was only one among many mundane factors contributing to these episodes.[160]

In any case, quite a considerable amount of violence was normal in these societies; disputes, whether between individuals or collectives, were often settled at the point of a sword, capital punishment was common, brutal, and public. Members of the interminably restive nobility and (in Iberia) municipal militias struck at each other's and at the kings' subjects and vassals with all but total impunity, both as a tactic in their internecine struggles, and out of pure opportunism and the lure of plunder. Slavery and non-consensual sex were both institutionalized. Muslims were not necessarily the preferred victims of such violence, but they were undoubtedly more exposed to it, by virtue of their secondary legal and social status and the perception, on the part of the Christians, of their vulnerability.

On the one hand, it is impressive, for example, that in the fourteenth-century Crown of Aragon there are so many records of Muslim travelers suing for their freedom after they had been arbitrarily imprisoned by local or seigniorial authorities; but on the other, these cases reveal how uncertain it could be for Muslims to travel even if they carried royal *guidatica* ("safe conducts").[161] There are also many references to cases of abduction, when free Muslims were kidnapped and sold on the slave market in distant towns or kingdoms; sometimes the perpetrators of these crimes were fellow *mudéjares*.[162] And whereas both Christian and Muslim peasants were targeted by warring lords and roving bands of mercenaries, Muslims were undoubtedly more likely to be killed or abducted in such actions. Finally, Muslim women were particularly vulnerable to sexual violence, both because of their secondary status, and because of the delicate situation of *mudéjar* women who wished to lodge accusations of sexual assault against men, whether Muslim or Christian.[163] A conviction would be extremely difficult to obtain, whether according to Muslim or Christian standards of evidence, and the mere process would likely

[160] See the discussion of Muslim–Jewish violence in B. Catlos, *The Victors and the Vanquished*, p. 207.

[161] See R. I. Burns, "The *Guidaticum* Safe-Conduct."

[162] See, above, chapter 6, p. 271, n. 190.

[163] That said, *mudéjar* women did indeed launch suits against their attackers; for example, see M. F. Lopes de Barros, *Tempos e espaços*, p. 594. In 1361 the Hospitaler commander near Lleida complained of the Christian d'Alos family that had been abusing local Muslims. It was claimed that one Arnald d'Alos, having been rebuffed by a local Muslim girl, took a ladder and entered her bedroom by night where he raped her, after which she had to be sent off to marry in another village. See J. Boswell, *The Royal Treasure*, p. 424–25. Such documents, however, cannot always be taken at face value; this might have been a cover-up for a tryst.

taint the victim as an adulteress.[164] As Lourie put it, *mudéjar* women were subject to a "double vulnerability" – first as Muslims, and second, as women.[165]

On the other hand, Muslims and Christians defended their communities against incursions and encroachments by neighboring locales and mounted raids on rival communities of Muslims and Christians, both together and separately. In the Crown of Aragon, for example, all subjects, regardless of faith, were obliged by law to respond to the general alarm and defend their communities – and they did. At times, when raiders carried off their Muslim neighbors, Christian townsmen abandoned them to their fate, but at others, they ransomed them or sued for their release. Not only did Muslims participate in municipal militias, *mudéjares* who were vassals of noblemen and Military Orders also took part in organized violence against their lords' enemies, whether these were rival seigniors, or local Christian and Muslim subjects. Factional and family struggles were as common in local Muslim and Christian communities and this encouraged collaborative violence across ethno-religious lines, as parties on each side of the religious divide sought to attack or undermine rival co-religionists. Muslims were not only victims of the aristocratic *bandositats* or feuds that plunged the kingdom of Valencia into chaos in the late fourteenth and early fifteenth centuries, but also participants, as a consequence of their ties of patronage to Christian families, and the opportunities such disorder presented.[166] In general, subject Muslims do not seem to have been any less prone to committing violent crimes than Christian subjects; moreover, there is little evidence that they felt any constraint in responding to or initiating violence against Christians – their secondary status notwithstanding.[167]

[164] The legal requirement in Islamic law for there to be four living witnesses to the act of penetration sets a rather high bar of evidence in cases of both fornication and rape. This might discourage women from reporting coerced sex because to do so would be to admit the act and, in doing so impugn oneself in the absence of the four witnesses required to establish that it was nonconsensual.

[165] See E. Lourie, "Anatomy of Ambivalence," pp. 69–72; and "Confessions of a Muslim Prostitute," in O. R. Constabale, *Medieval Iberia*, p. 340–42.

[166] See, for example, ACA, C., reg. 2339, ff. 9v (May 9, 1403), 12v (May 28, 1403), 13r (May 26, 1403), 13r (May 26, 1043), 14v (May 10, 1403), 18r–v (July 10, 1403), 18v–19r (July 12, 1403), 19v–20r (July 19, 1403), 20r (July 19, 1403). See also M. Benítez Bolorinos, "La familia Corella"; B. Ehlers, "Violence and Religious Identity," p. 109; A. Ferrer Taberner, "Bandosidades rurales mudéjares"; N. Ruzafa Garcia, "Élites valencianas," p.178; and S. Ponsoda López de Atalaya and J. L. Soler Milla, "Violencia nobiliaria," p. 326.

[167] See, for example, F. Segura Urra, "Los mudéjares navarros," p. 248ff. Alexander de Telese relates that in 1132 Muslim workers who had been sent by Roger II to supervise the construction of fortifications in Bari apparently killed a local nobleman. The Christian laborers who were working under them went on strike in response. See

Crimes of opportunity were also common and were committed unhindered by any sense of communal solidarity – indeed, it is generally easier to bilk one's fellows than outsiders. Muslims, operating singly or in bands, on their own or with Christian accomplices, carried out thefts, murders, abductions, home invasions, forgery, extortion, graft, and smuggling, with both Christians and Muslims as their victims. Both the propensity to work around the Christian-dominated judicial system and the prevalence of the frequency of family feuds contributed to the crime rate among subject Muslims.[168] Centuries before conquest of Granada and the politicized "banditry" of the Muslim resistance, Muslim highwaymen led notorious careers, preying on whomever they could, sometimes in cahoots with Christian villains.[169] Muslims were implicated in Jewish counterfeiting rings. *Mudéjares*, including women, participated in gangs that abducted and sold free Muslim men, women, and children.[170] And even Christians sometimes suffered as a result of "Muslim vulnerability" – unscrupulous Muslim and Christian villains were known to abduct young Christian boys, circumcise them, and sell them off as slaves – indeed, in 1293 a complaint was brought against Alvaro Lupi, Commander of the Order of at Alcañiz, for refusing to restore such a boy to his rightful faith and family even once the truth had been made known.[171]

## *Integration and separation*

The relationship of Christian and subject Muslim (and Jewish) society was complex and polyvalent, and generalizations can be made only with great care. At the most informal, local, and personal level, Muslims, Jews, and Christians were capable of collaborating closely, sometimes for the local good, and at other times, to perpetrate specific ills. They were also just as capable of turning against each other, both as communities and

G. Loud, *Roger II*, p. 90. Alfons III of Aragon pardoned a *mudéjar* crossbowman in his service, Ali Mariner, after the latter killed a knight of the English King, Edward I (1272–1307). See B. Catlos, *The Victors and Vanquished*, p. 263.

168 See for example, B. Ehlers, "Violence and Religious Identity," pp. 106–07. This may have been true of Christians and Jews as well, but non-Christians would have been especially untrusting of the Christian-dominated judicial culture.

169 In the late 1200s the *mudéjar* bandit "Garcia el Moro" had a gang of Christian and Muslim confederates. See B. Catlos, *The Victors and Vanquished*, p. 314. In the early 1600s the Dick Turpin-esque Maghribi highwayman Miquel Abaix operated with the support of the Morisco populace. See B. Ehlers, "Violence and Religious Identity," pp. 111–12 and 116.

170 See, for example, E. Lourie, "Anatomy of Ambivalence," pp. 69–70; I. O'Connor de los Angeles, "Muslim Mudéjar Women," p. 60; F. Segura Urra, "Los mudéjares navarros"; B. Catlos, *The Victors and the Vanquished*, "Christians and Muslims as Partners in Crime," pp. 277–79; "Justice served"; and "The de Reys."

171 B. Catlos, "Four kidnappings," pp. 175–76 {1 and 2}.

individuals. The controversies associated with royal taxation provide an illustration of this range of response. When royal tribute was levied on local Christian and Muslim communities separately, as was usually the case, they can be found collaborating in resisting royal tax collectors. However, when these communities were assessed jointly, it was more common for them to turn on each other in an effort to push a greater share of the obligation on the other community. The bitter, drawn-out, and frequently violent controversies that resulted from some *mudéjares* claims to *franquitas*, or exemptions from communal taxes, that characterized *aljamas* across Iberia, corresponded to parallel struggles within Jewish *aljamas* and Christian *universitates*. Likewise, the desire to shirk contractual obligations to Jewish lenders, or resist their sometimes predatory practices, also drove local Christian and Muslim communities to collaborate.[172]

Certainly, the cumulative effects of "reproductive separation," the sacralization of political institutions and economic structures, the propensity for episodes of mundane competition to be expressed in religious terms, together with occasional incidents of religiously framed violence, contributed to the mutual estrangement of Muslim and Christian subjects and the polarization of their communities. Yet this was mitigated to an extent by the affinities borne out of living in a common locale and being subjects of the same king, of economic interdependency, shared vocation, and class solidarities, and the obligation of mutual defense against external threats, all of which cut across communal lines. In the Latin West, as in the Islamic world, personal identity was informed not only by religious affiliation (*umma*) but also by loyalty to homeland (*waṭan*) and locale. Correspondingly, communal political resistance on the part of Muslims to Christian domination was also situational.[173]

There is no evidence for resistance in Hungary, and in the Crusader East it took on subtle forms. Although religiously informed opposition was intense in Ifrīqiya during the brief Norman occupation, it was not until the 1170s that engagement in political struggle characterized subject Muslim society in Sicily; but even then, except in rare cases (such as that of Muḥammad b. ʿAbbād) it tended to play out within the framework of Christian domination and struggles among powerful Christian factions (i.e. by *mudéjares* giving support to those Christian parties they viewed as favoring their interests).[174] In Iberia, Islamic consciousness and solidarity were expressed politically in specific moments and locales, such as the

[172] For example, B. Catlos, *The Victors and the Vanquished*, pp. 272–77.
[173] For example, a tract written in Sicily in 1194 called on all Sicilians, Muslim and Christians to join forces against the German invaders. See G. Loud, *The Latin Church*, p. 519.
[174] See p. 123, above.

uprisings in the south in the late thirteenth century; it was not until the first decade of the 1500s and the forced conversion of the *mudéjares* that this sentiment became generalized. Even then, it varied markedly in degree and expression across the peninsula – from the revolts of the Alpujarras and the Serra d'Espadà, to the armed resistance of the bandits of post-conquest Granada and Valencia, to the religious subversion of Aragonese and Castilian crypto-Muslim Moriscos, to the quiet acquiescence of *mudéjares* in Catalonia and Navarre.[175] In other words, despite the best efforts of legists and ideologues, the lines between ethno-religious communities remained permeable and situational, and individuals conceived of themselves and interacted with others in a whole range of contexts, often directly defying the religious categories that were supposedly essential to their identity.

## Social relations and cultural identity

Concerning baths, it is said: indeed, men may go to the public baths on Tuesday, on Thursday, and on Saturday, as according to the law-code. Similarly, women may go on Monday, and on Wednesday, to the same aforesaid baths. Jews and Muslims may go on Friday, and not on any other day under any circumstances . . . [but] if a Jew or Muslim should bathe on any day except Friday, whoever is bathing there, is to be fined thirty *solidi* . . . should it be proven. (*Fuero of Teruel* (late twelfth century)[176])

For Muslims, Jews, and Christians, the public bath represented a common tradition, one of the customs that formed part of the vague but potent cultural substratum of the Mediterranean, and which included both secular attitudes and mores (for example, shared notions of honor, valor, and female sexuality), common intellectual traditions (notably, Helleno-Persian science and philosophy) and parallel religious practices (such as pilgrimage and mystical asceticism). This Mediterranean *habitus* provided the basis for the particularly intimate and profound interaction characteristic of ethno-religious diversity here; but as each religious culture manifested this common culture through the narrow filter of a particular ideology, it served to reinforce difference as much as similarity.[177] Hence, social interactions here that crossed communal lines had a fraught character, and public bathing particularly so. In the baths insignia of rank and of religious identity were stripped away along with clothing, and communal bathing invited an unguarded intimacy and vulnerability that was

[175] See pp. 217, 225, and 296.
[176] J. Caruana Gómez de Barreda, *El fuero latino de Teruel*, pp. 232–33 [291].
[177] See below, p. 509.

potentially dangerous and subversive.[178] In addition, washing had a ritual dimension for Muslims and Jews, while for Latin Christians it touched the sexophobic vein that ran through clerical thought and culture.[179] Moreover, each of these ethno-religious cultures associated religious outsiders – both their beliefs and their bodies – with uncleanliness in some sense; therefore both corporal and social contact ran the risk of polluting the body and contaminating the community.[180]

*Public baths*

Thus, communal bathing was regulated in Latin lands, with an aim of segregating the sexes and the faiths.[181] The rules, however, were not consistent, and the laws varied from region to region, town to town, and even bath to bath. Whereas in Portugal and northern Castile non-Christians tended to be absolutely prohibited from using Christian baths, in much of the central and northern peninsula Muslims and Jews were limited to certain days, while in some areas, including parts of southern Catalonia, there were no restrictions on the books.[182] Even when there were, however, as at Teruel, the prescribed punishment for violation was a substantial but hardly catastrophic fine.[183] In 1280 the Bishop of Lleida ruled at a local synod that Christians who dared bathe with Muslims were to be excommunicated.[184] In any event, however, conviction would have depended on a complaint being lodged, and sufficient and willing witnesses appearing. Thus, we may assume that there may have been a great deal of proscribed fraternization alongside the many other illicit, immoral activities that were practiced widely in Iberian public baths, prohibitions notwithstanding.[185] Because religious segregation in baths

178 Although male Jews and Muslims practiced circumcision, this was not likely to be noticed given that normally one's genitals were only uncovered within the confines of a private bathing stall.

179 See above, p. 328.

180 See the discussion in M. F. Lopes de Barros, *Tempos e espaços*, pp. 18–198, "O corpo como fronteira"; c.f. above, p. 139.

181 See J. Powers, "Frontier Municipal Baths"; M. F. Lopes de Barros, "Body, Baths and Cloth."

182 The *Costums* of Tortosa state explicitly that the municipal baths are open to all with no mention of segregated days or times. Here, the income generated from the baths was to go to the repair of the city walls. See J. Massipi Fonollosa, *Costums*, p. 13 {1.1.15}.

183 For the Crown of Aragon, see B. Catlos, *The Victors and the Vanquished*, p. 297.

184 J. Mutgé i Vives, "La aljama sarracena," p. 106.

185 See J. Powers, "Frontier Municipal Baths," pp. 663–67. In 1319 when Jaume II repeated an ordinance passed only two years earlier forbidding Christian prostitutes from fraternizing with Muslim in taverns, he added a clause banning pimps, procurers and prostitutes from bathhouses. See *Aureum opus*, p. 168 {LIVV–LXIR}.

was aimed primarily at men, cross-cultural socializing would have been particularly common and intimate among women of different religions who used the baths together, depilating, sharing cosmetic techniques, and consulting each other on matters of feminine health and the female social condition. Such sororization was evidently common practice from Frankish Jerusalem to Sicily and Iberia, where late medieval literature depicts women sheltering themselves temporarily from a male-dominated world at the baths: dancing, singing, and eating – very much in the Arabo-Islamic tradition.[186] Moreover, Muslim women appear as the owners of private bathing establishments, some of which, like that of "Doña Xanci" in fourteenth-century Madrid, were quite prosperous.[187]

In any event, Muslims (and Jews) continued to build and use their own baths. The reasons for this were multiple. Most would have undoubtedly preferred to have segregated facilities for their own comfort and personal and communal protection. Moreover, there were issues of ritual and spiritual "cleanliness." And, finally, bathhouses and their licenses represented sources of revenue for both investors and seigniors.[188] As a consequence, there was an incentive both to construct and maintain multiple bathhouses in some locales and to keep them separated both for socio-religious reasons and in order to guarantee a customer base and prevent real competition. In sum, the rules that regulated communal bathing reflect the essence of medieval *convivencia* – the necessity of maintaining boundaries in an environment of plurality that demanded interaction and compromise, and in which priorities and policy tended to be set by economic as well as religious concerns.[189] As it was, by the late fifteenth century, bathing seems to have fallen progressively out of fashion among the Christians of the peninsula, and it was viewed with increasing suspicion as a non-Christian and morally suspect custom.[190]

The bathhouse represented only the highest order of the broad quotidian interaction that characterized all of these societies. Christians, Muslims, and Jews (and, in Hungary, pagans) also encountered each other in the street, in markets, as a consequence of the existence of utility monopolies

186 See, for example, S. Menache, "When Jesus Met Mohammad," p. 77; Ibn Jubayr, *Travels*, pp. 320–21; and L. Torres Balbás, *Algunos aspectos*, p. 56.

187 L. Torres Balbás, *Algunos aspectos*, p. 53.

188 *Ibid.*, p. 63. The bath run by the *mudéjar* "Doña Xanci" must have been lucrative, given the high rate of rent she could afford to pay.

189 At Cuenca, for example (the *fuero* of which does not mention Muslims in connection with bathing), a statute noted that if a Jew or Christian was at the baths on a day other than those mandated he did so at his own risk. If in such circumstances an argument gave rise to killing or injury, no charges could be laid. See J. F. Powers, *The Code of Cuenca*, p. 49 {32}.

190 Thanks to Remie Constable for this, and the references to the *Fuero* of Cuenca and *Costum* of Tortosa, above.

(such as royal-licensed or seigniorially-held ovens and mills) that they were all obliged to patronize; in civic gatherings and assemblies, including council meetings and civil defense levies (whether militias or in the context of the hue and cry), and in non-religiously exclusive festivities (such as royal weddings and funerary celebrations), not to mention the various institutional and economic contexts (noted in this chapter and the previous) in which Muslims and Christians were brought together. In some regions, including Norman Ifrīqiya, much of Crusader Palestine, and certain zones in Christian Iberia, where most Muslims lived in tightly self-contained and self-sufficient communities that interfaced with Latins only for the purpose of rendering tribute, such social contact may have been minimal, but even in these regions there were significant elements within subject Muslim society – at the very least the administrative "hinge" groups described previously – whose contact with Christian society ran across a wide gamut of situations.

### *The body religious, the body social*

Interaction in these various contexts was facilitated by the fact that, generally, in each region, within a generation or so of the conquest, a process of acculturation got under way in which subject Muslims became fluent to some degree in local Christian vernaculars as well as in Latin. Except in the most closed and reactionary of subject Muslim communities, a broad multilingualism was clearly the norm, and many Latin Christians evidently had at least a functional verbal proficiency in Arabic, limited as this may have been to the context of the market, their profession, or communicating with recently arrived slaves. In the Iberian Peninsula subject Muslims soon also began to dress in Latin fashions (at least in some situations, and when they chose to do so), even in the face of royal and municipal requirements that they wear distinguishing clothes.[191] Moreover, they adopted "Christian" mores and affectations, at least superficially, and probably situationally; and began to "perform" as Latins in public contexts.[192] In Iberia, where the *mudéjar* population was overwhelmingly indigenous of origin, in many cases there would have been no visible cues to distinguish Muslims from their Christian neighbors; and at any rate, the process of conversion, slow as it may have been, would have undermined any visible association of physical characteristics with

[191] See p. 201, above.

[192] The "performance" by subject Muslims of their religious and cultural identity is analogous to that proposed for gender in J. Butler, *Gender Trouble*; see especially chapter 4: "Bodily Inscriptions, Performative Subversions," pp. 163–92.

communal identity. The outward distinctiveness of Christians and Muslims was further undermined by the profound engagement of the Christians of Iberia with Islamicate culture, in terms of dress, language, and quotidian culture.[193] The case in Sicily was perhaps even more dramatic; here the shared styles and habits of Muslims, converts, and Arabized Christians, together with the Normans' intense attraction to fashion, made it very difficult to tell them apart.[194]

But whereas an image of happy cosmopolitanism may appeal to the sensibilities of twenty-first century Anglo-European academia, and the blurring of ethno-religious boundaries would have provided subject Muslims with a greater range of opportunities, there would have been many Christians and Muslims, particularly among the religio-cultural elite, who would have found this situation threatening and dangerous, no less than is the case today. In environments that were characterized by an aggressive and entrenched sense of Christian–Muslim confrontation, such as Crusader Palestine, the kingdom of Valencia, or post-1492 Spain, such casual acculturation would have been slowed or even reversed. Hence, both documentary and iconographic evidence indicates that Moriscos dressed in particular fashions that set them apart from their Christian co-subjects, whereas this does not seem to have been the case with their *mudéjar* ancestors in the previous century. Significantly, prior to 1492 *mudéjares* are typically found resisting the obligation to wear distinctive clothing, whereas afterwards they protested the prohibition against wearing it.[195]

The element of perceived threat embodied by subject Muslims would have increased in the context of activities that had an explicitly religious dimension, were physically intimate, or that were unrestrained or libidinous in nature, and that, therefore, undermined the formal barriers that separated the communities.[196] There is abundant documentation ranging from legal texts to notarial documents and trial records showing that it was common for Muslims and Christians in Iberia to drink together in taverns, to gamble, and to use prostitutes (both Christian and Muslim) together, despite the fact that these were all considered crimes against municipal, royal, Islamic, and Canon Law. There is no reason not to suspect this was the case also in Sicily, Hungary, and urban Palestine. It was not until the fourteenth century that authorities began to show an explicit concern for Muslim men having sex with Christian prostitutes,

193 See D. Wacks, "Reconquest Colonialism," p. 92.
194 A. Metcalfe, *The Muslims of Medieval Italy*, pp. 239 and 225.
195 See below, p. 496.
196 This is very much the thrust of "Systematic Violence, Power, Sex and Religion," the second part of D. Nirenberg, *Communities of Violence*.

but this emerged as one of the few scenarios of miscegenation that was punished consistently.[197]

There is less direct evidence for Christian and Muslim attendance at out-group weddings and other religious ceremonies (such as baptisms), or for the exchange of gifts among members of different religious communities; many law codes forbade such practices.[198] Indeed, the participation of converts to Christianity in the festivities and rituals of Muslim and Jewish communities was a source of much anxiety, not the least because of the suspicions of apostasy it engendered.[199] At times, such prohibitions – like that against the use of Christian nursemaids by Jews (and, implicitly, Muslims) – may have been hypothetical in nature, or recycled from older law codes, but we can be all but certain that fraternization of this type was not uncommon, particularly as a consequence of conversion to Christianity. As the case of the Moriscos shows, religious converts did not generally want to abandon their cultural practices and social customs. In the preceding centuries, individual conversions created family units (fraught as these may have been) whose membership straddled the religious divide.

The most complex and ideologically charged scenarios that Muslims and Christians engaged in together were those relating to the body and which were physically intimate, and it is these transactions that provoked the greatest anxieties. By their nature they required that individuals think of themselves in terms of their religious identity, and therefore demanded

197 In Daroca in 1311, Ali de Matalón was convicted and burned at the stake for having had sex with a Christian woman; later it was revealed that she was a virgin and that the charges were false. See M.T. Ferrer i Mallol, *Els sarraïns*, pp. 31–33. In Valencia in 1312, Jaume II prescribed a punishment of twenty lashes for Christian prostitutes and Muslim men who were found to be cavorting and drinking together in taverns. If local lords turned a blind eye, they were to be prosecuted. See *Aureum Opus*, p. 166 {LIIIV/LVI}. Sex in such a case was already considered a capital crime, but was considerably harder to prove. In 1304, a Christian prostitute sued a Christian and his *mudéjar* friend, whom he had helped pass off as Christian so as to have sex with her. By suing them she probably hoped to avoid prosecution herself. See ACA, Processes en Quart, 1304–1305; ed. in A. Domingo i Grabiel, "La veu de sarraïns," pp. 18–22. There is a report of a Christian prostitute being burned at the stake as punishment for having sex with a Muslim in fourteenth-century Navarre after only one such transgression. See F. Segura Urra, "Los mudéjares navarros," p. 251; also, C. Conde Solares, "Social continuity," p. 326. In fifteenth-century Aragon, transgressive Muslims, Christian prostitutes, and their panderers were subject to exemplary punishment; see M. Gómez de Valenzuela, "Esclavos moros," p. 120.

198 D. Reynolds, "Music," p. 244. It was particularly common for converts to attend social occasions of their erstwhile co-religionists – a matter of great concern to Christian authorities. See M. T. Ferrer i Mallol, *El sarraïns*, pp. 11–12.

199 See, for example, the case of the formerly Jewish *conversa* who fell under suspicion for having attended, danced, and eaten at a Muslim wedding in fifteenth-century Castile. See E. Cantera Montenegro, "Las comunidades mudéjares," p. 164.

the deliberate manifestation of Christian social rank over Muslims. Similarly, it would have seemed incongruous and offensive for Infidels to be invested with the power of life and death over Christians and to develop relationships, such as that of physician–patient, wherein they exercised power and influence over the rulers of Christian society and the Church. However, it must be said that issues of professional competition were certainly also a factor behind the prohibitions against Muslims and Jews from practicing medicine on Christians.

In terms of the problem of physical intimacy undermining communal hierarchy, domestic slaves provide an illuminating analogy to that of physicians. Muslim and (nominally) converted slaves were used as domestic servants through most of the Latin Mediterranean. They bathed and dressed their masters and mistresses, prepared and served their foods, and were privy to the most intimate (not to say embarrassing and illicit) secrets of the household.[200] Many were engaged in sentimental or sexual relationships with their owners, whether consensual, indirectly coerced, or physically forced. And yet, this was not generally viewed as problematic, except perhaps by some legists and clerics, because the master–slave relationship permitted few ambiguities regarding the authority and power of the Christian party and the submission and powerlessness of the Muslim.

### *Love and sex*

It was sexual relations between free Muslims and Christians that represented the most threatening scenario in the diverse societies of the Latin Mediterranean because it was regarded as having the most clearly subversive potential and struck to the heart of people's intuitive sense of communal and family identity.[201] The notion that Muslims and Christians might have intimate physical relationships was seen as threatening by religious ideologues and lay-folk in both societies, particularly when the scenario involved an out-group male having relations with an in-group female.[202] This was rooted both in the widespread if unacknowledged sense that women – who were regarded legally inferior to men in each tradition – continued to be thought of on an instinctual level as community property. Therefore, the "loss" of women to outsiders constituted an affront to the honor and virility of the in-group. Moreover, such dalliances were seen

[200] See p. 266, above. Note also O. R. Constable's observations in "Chess and Courtly Culture," p. 346.

[201] See, generally, D. Nirenberg, *Communities of Violence*, chapter 5, "Sex and Violence between Majority and Minority," pp. 127–65.

[202] See, for example, Eudes de Châteauroux's paranoid fantasies of Muslim sexual predation, in C. T. Maier, "Crusade and Rhetoric," pp. 372–73.

as culturally and religiously subversive, and all the more so should they produce issue. Sexual and sentimental relations could be something of a slippery slope to conversion. Thus, those who considered themselves authorities in both Muslim and Christian society would have been keen to eliminate miscegenation and even social relations between their own and Infidel members of the opposite sex. Hence, the increasing obsession with the idea of the sexually predatory Muslim in late medieval Castilian law, and the terrible punishments prescribed by municipal law codes for inter-communal adultery: death at the stake in Teruel, and drawing and quartering in Tortosa, for example.[203]

On the other hand, this situation was characterized by asymmetries – men who engaged in such dalliances were not necessarily subject to condemnation. In fact, both for *mudéjares* and Latins, the seduction or sexual possession of an out-group woman could be seen as empowering and reaffirming. For Christian men, sex with Muslim women could serve to reinforce their sense of social domination, whereas for subject Muslim men it could be seen as an act in defiance of their subordination, as communal resistance, or, merely – especially in the case of the *mudéjar* patriciate – a badge of social prestige and success, of having "arrived."[204]

Indeed, the majority of judicial prosecutions of Muslim men in such cases involved members of the *mudéjar* elite. As it was, they were virtually never condemned to death as the law dictated, but nearly always absolved after having made a payment to the Crown.[205] In Navarre, the first execution for such a crime is not recorded until as late as 1367.[206] The preponderance of documentation relating to the *mudéjar* elite, however, does not necessarily imply that it was only, or even primarily, members of this group who had sex with Christians. Muslim commoners were also called up on such charges; however, it was more likely for wealthy *mudéjares* to leave a paper trail, given that they had the capacity to fight in court and to buy their way out of a conviction. Poorer Muslims may

203 For Tortosa and Teruel, see B. Catlos, *The Victors and the Vanquished*, p. 308. The penalty for Christian–Christian adultery was also death. For Castilian law, and in particular the allegations in the *Sentencia Arbitral de Medina del Campo* that Muslims were seducing both virgins and married Christian women, see I. Montes Romero-Camacho, "Las comunidades mudéjares," pp. 407–08.

204 For Christian–Muslim miscegenation, see D. Nirenberg, *Communities of Violence*, pp. 138–56.

205 See, for example, M. F. Lopes de Barros, "Body, Baths and Cloth," p. 7; and I. O'Connor de los Angeles, "Mudejars Helping," p. 102. Refer also to the table in B. Catlos, *The Victors and the Vanquished*, pp. 308–9. See also n. 146, above. On the other hand, capital punishment was applied with rigor to those guilty of *sodomitia* and zoophilia, in both Navarre and the Crown of Aragon.

206 The convict was stoned to death. F. Segura Urra, "Los mudéjares navarros," p. 251.

have been prosecuted with less frequency, either because there was less to gain from prosecution in terms of fines, or because they may have been dealt with by informal or extra-judicial methods.[207]

As it was, convicting a *mudéjar* of having sex with a Christian was no easy matter. For example a privilege of 1446 granted to the *aljama* of Alfajarín specified that two witnesses to the act were necessary, and one had to be a Muslim.[208] In 1360, two Muslims of nearby Zaragoza had charges of having sex with two Christian women dismissed because of certain "fraudulent" irregularities in the investigation (and after they had paid a heavy fine of 1,800 *solidi*).[209] In Portugal and Navarre, by contrast, anxiety regarding such liaisons, and correspondingly the resulting penalties, seem to have been lower. In 1294, a Muslim of Ablitas who had been cohabiting with a Christian woman was fined a mere thirty *solidi*, whereas the standard fine for inter-communal sexual relations in fourteenth-century Navarre was only sixty.[210] In Portugal, where there are many reports of such crimes, a clear distinction was made between prostitutes and non-prostitutes. In the latter case, a fine – often quite substantial – was imposed, but in the former, Muslims acted with near impunity. When in 1465, a Muslim from Lisbon who was visiting Evora was caught in a Christian woman's bed, he claimed he had wound up there because he couldn't find his way home in the dark through the unfamiliar *mouraria*. Another *mouro*, who was convicted of pandering Christian women, was given only a year of internal exile (a sentence that was later commuted to a fine).[211]

Similarly, whereas in Valencia and Aragon Muslim magistrates worked hand-in-glove with royal authorities to convict and enslave *mudéjar* women who violated sexual laws (a process by which moral authority and discipline were maintained and a considerable amount of revenue generated), in Portugal and Navarre, in the absence of prostitution having been institutionalized as a judicial punishment, an entirely different situation developed. In these kingdoms adulterous Muslim women were much more likely to be forgiven by their families, even when they had sex with Christians. In 1486 Fotes Carota of Santarém was forgiven by her husband for just such a crime, and was let off with a fine.[212] In Tudela, Haitziti, a wife of one of the powerful Alpelmí clan (who held the office of

[207] *Mudéjares* employed these methods also, as when in 1344 a group of Muslims stripped and beat a Jew they found using the services of a Muslim brothel. D. Nirenberg, "Love between Muslim and Jew," p. 137.

[208] J. Boswell, *The Royal Treasure*, p. 369. [209] *Ibid.*, pp. 455–56.

[210] F. Segura Urra, "Los mudéjares navarros," p. 251; M. F. Lopes de Barros, "Body, Baths and Cloth," p. 7.

[211] M. F. Lopes de Barros, *Tempos e espaços*, pp. 590–92.

[212] M. F. Lopes de Barros, "Body, Baths and Cloth," p. 7.

*alfaquí*), was sentenced to only a 100-*florin* fine.[213] Even when the local Islamic magistrate prescribed death by stoning to adulteresses, their families might intervene and secure their absolution in the royal court.[214] Christian jurisdiction also intruded in cases of inter-Muslim sexual violence, either through the mechanism of royal intervention, as in the above cases, or when the prosecution of such crimes was carried out under the authority of Christian magistrates and according to their protocols.

However, if there is one human characteristic that does not need to be over-explained or over-analyzed it is our desire for sex; for that matter, nor does our penchant for variety, nor the tantalizingly seductive appeal of the illicit. Together with the ethno-religious diversity and quotidian interaction that characterized these Latin societies in the Middle Ages, these factors made for an environment in which sexual encounters and sentimental relationships between members of different religious groups would have occurred with some frequency. This is not to suggest that this was some Irving Berlinish world of randy *convivencia*, in which "ev'rybody [was] doin' it" with glib indifference to religious identity, but hints of seductions, elopements, and un-canonical marriages surface regularly in the documentation and are a fixture of contemporary literature.[215] But if oblique references to inter-religious marriages occur in legal texts and royal decrees in both the Crusader Levant and Christian Iberia, these likely refer to marriages between Muslims in which one partner has converted to Christianity but the couple has not divorced (as would be required by both Christian and Islamic law).[216] There are rare, but tantalizing suggestions in the sources that inter-communal marriages (even those involving Christian women and Muslim men) were sometimes tolerated, but it is unlikely that these are indicative of widespread

213 Her husband, Jayel, had to pay a fine of thirty-two and a half *libras* for beating to death her unfortunate paramour, Farach Arondí. This seems to have been part of an ongoing family feud; earlier that year Muça Rondí had been fined for wounding Çayt and Jayel Alpelmí with a sword, a condemnation he had escaped due to his (somewhat contradictory) claim of poverty coupled with a payment of fifteen *libras* to the king's treasury. See M. García-Arenal and B. Leroy, *Moros y judíos en Navarra*, pp. 90–92 {XIX}.

214 In 1382 Carlos III saved Axa of Ablitas from a death sentence at the request of her husband and father, in exchange for a relatively light fine of 110 *florines*. See M. García-Arenal and B. Leroy, *Moros y judíos en Navarra*, p. 108 {XXX}. When Pere IV made similar interventions this was met by protests from local communities (or their judicial authorities); see M. J. Fuente Pérez, *Velos y desvelos*, pp. 261ff, especially p. 265.

215 Romances like *Floire et Blancheflor* and *Aucassin et Nicolette* center on the impossible affair between a noble Christian and a converted Infidel – a device derived from the Arabo-Islamic tradition. See M. Kahf, *Western Representations*, pp. 46–47.

216 See, for example, M. Nader, "Urban Muslims," p. 260. For the Christian position on such marriages, see R. J. Zorgati, *Pluralism in the Middle Ages*, pp. 113–28.

practice.[217] Prior to the eleventh century, Christian noblemen in Iberia willingly gave their daughters in marriage to more powerful Muslim princes. But after this point, the shift in the balance of power in the northern Mediterranean towards the Latins together with the elaboration of Canon Law meant that Christians had a clearer and narrower idea of what constituted a legitimate marriage, and would no longer countenance out-group marriages, even to secure political advantage.

Hence the perceived need to maintain social boundaries through the mandate of clothes or hairstyles that put the wearers' religious affiliation on clear and public view, the urge for residential and social quarantine and self-segregation, and the maintenance and public display of social customs, dietary, or culinary preferences, and other practices that marked group members off from others. Enforcement, however, was uneven, and the penalties imposed on violators hardly constituted a deterrence.[218] In 1366 Pedro I of Portugal forbade Christian women from entering the kingdom's *judiarias* and *mourarias* on the allegations made by "men of credible character [that] Christian women, single and widows and even some married ones" were having sex in the ghettos with non-Christian men. In Lisbon's *mouraria* Christian women could only travel on specific streets and in the company of Christian men – under penalty of death according to the statute. In Evora, in 1469 a Christian widow was allowed to sell oil in the Jewish and Muslim neighborhoods – an exception granted on account of her advanced (i.e. post-sexual) age and good character.[219]

When barriers to opportunity and interaction disappear, or when subordinated minority groups cannot be readily identified by sight, anxieties increase. Hence, the hysteria that gripped certain circles of white America in the 1970s as African-Americans gained access to unsegregated universities in large numbers – a fear that unsupervised, privileged young white women would take African-American lovers and having "tried Black, never go back" (as the crude, racist saying went), or the preoccupation in Israel over the last three decades regarding the ability of Arab Israeli men to visibly "pass," and to use this advantage intentionally and deceptively to seduce and embark on sexual adventures with young Jewish

217 See, for example, the case of "Ona," a Christian girl who was abducted by the Muslims of Calatorao in 1282, and not only married a *mudéjar*, but converted to Islam. See B. Catlos, *The Victors and the Vanquished*, p. 311. The case of Mascharose, who is described in 1270 as a Christian and the mother of Çaat de Tevicino is somewhat more puzzling; perhaps she was a convert to Christianity, however, her name is somewhat unusual for this to be the case. See R. I. Burns, "Los mudéjares de Valencia," pp. 22 and 30 {2}.

218 In 1379 Alí Almale of Beniarjó (kingdom of Valencia) was assessed a fine of a mere fifteen *sous* for not sporting the *garceta*, or soup-bowl haircut *mudéjares* were obliged by law to wear. See J. Argente Vidal, "Un libro de cuentas," p. 303.

219 M. F. Lopes de Barros, "Body, Baths and Cloth," p. 8.

women.[220] And certainly, examples of such deliberate deception can be found, not only in the Israeli criminal courts of the twenty-first century, but in the statutes and court records of Christian Iberia from the thirteenth century onwards.[221] Prior to the forced conversions of the 1500s, in Christian Iberia, it was minority men who tended to have their clothing and visible appearance regulated, and not minority women – it was men, and their potential penetration of the female body physical and the Christian body religious that were seen as a threat. In the age of the Moriscos, on the other hand, women's continuing use of traditional Islamicate clothes, in particular the veil, was perceived as a threat to the Christian order.

### *The practice of religion*

Of course, the public practice of non-Christian religion was clearly problematic and would have demanded regulation in the Latin world, all the more so in the case of Islam, given the emphasis placed on public ritual and communal worship. The calling of the *ʾadhān*, regular communal ablution and prayer, the fasting and feasting of Ramaḍān, the sacrifices of the *ʿĪd al-aḍḥā*ʾ, and the departure for the *ḥājj*, as well as the various non-canonical and heterodox popular religious rituals revolving around local pilgrimage, Sufi practices, the commemoration of the birthday of the Prophet and the "saints," not to mention dancing and singing at weddings and circumcisions, were all noisy and public manifestations of Islam as a religion and a social phenomenon. Therefore, it is only to be expected that Christian authorities would have a direct interest in suppressing the public aspects of Islamic worship. The existence of a vibrant and dynamic Islamic religious culture would be perceived as a threat to Christians not only because it might encourage curiosity and apostasy,

220 See, for example, J. Cook, "Israeli Drive to Prevent Jewish Girls Dating Arabs," *The National* (Abu Dhabi), September 25, 2009; and S. Frenkel, "Vigilantes Patrol for Jewish Women Dating Arab Men," *National Public Radio*, October 12, 2009. In the early 1990s the Israeli media made much of the economic advantages enjoyed by young Arab-Israeli men as a consequence of not being required (or allowed) the compulsory three-year military service, and fretted about these same young men's supposed habit of seducing young Jewish women.

221 The *Costums de Tortosa*, for example, exempted Christian women from penalty in cases in which they had been seduced by a Muslim disguised as a Christian, which was held to be the functional equivalent of rape. J. Massip, *Costums de Tortosa*, p. 415 {9.2.7}. In a case that resonates remarkably with the legal culture of the Crown of Aragon, an Arab-Israeli was convicted for having had sex with a Jewish woman under pretense of being a Jew. The judgement read, "The court is obliged to protect the public interest from sophisticated, smooth-tongued criminals who can deceive innocent victims at an unbearable price – the *sanctity of their bodies and souls*" (My emphasis). See T. Zarchin, "Arab Man Who Posed as Jew to Seduce Woman Convicted of Rape," *Haaretz*, May 4, 2012.

but because it would violate and upset the religio-cultural hierarchy, embolden and give confidence to Muslims, and blur the notion that they were a subject, Infidel people.

However, there were virtually no comprehensive measures taken against the public display of Islam until the mid thirteenth century, with the exception of Hungary, where legislation was enacted (although not necessarily enforced) aimed at limiting Islamic worship from the twelfth century onwards. Through the thirteenth century, the call of the *muʿadhdhīn* echoed through the Latin Mediterranean, from the Guadalquivir across to the exilic enclave of Lucera, and numerous privileges were granted across Western Christendom specifically confirming this right, even in the face of legislation to the contrary. In Castile, Alfonso X outlawed public displays of faith in the lands of Castile, but clearly they continued.[222] In Aragon, a king like Jaume I may have preferred not to be personally woken by the call from the minaret, but he and his successors did not suppress it as a matter of policy. Indeed, licenses for the *ʾadhān* to be called or signaled by trumpet and for the celebration of the *ʿĪd* continued to be granted in the following centuries, occasional locale-specific prohibitions notwithstanding. Even after the Council of Vienne (1311–12) forbade both the call to prayer and the noisy festivities held in the course of pious visitations (*ziyārāt*) to local sites of pilgrimage, Clement V complained to Jaume II of Aragon that these activities were continuing.[223]

At the turn of the fourteenth century, when the papacy, municipalities, and kings began to legislate in this regard, measures were adopted capriciously, and often on an *ad hoc* basis, and were enforced only fitfully. In 1318, for example, Jaume II ordered his bailiff to pursue and detain the Muslim inhabitants who he was given to understand were continuing to "proclaim the *çabaçala* and the abominable name of Muhammad out loud."[224] He made calling the *ʾadhān* a capital offense, but soon backtracked, whereas during the War of the Two Peters, Pere the Ceremonious included privileges for the call to prayer among the incentives he granted to Muslim *aljamas* to buy their loyalty.[225]

Licenses for religious functionaries represented a source of income for the Aragonese crown and lords, while seigniors who were interested in keeping their Muslim vassals content and quiet were happy to turn a blind eye. This can be seen most clearly in the case of Martí I, who as King of

[222] The seventh *Partida* reads, "Muslims shall not have mosques in Christian towns, or make their sacrifices publicly in the presence of men." See Alfonso X, *Las Siete Partidas*, vol. v, p. 1438 {vii:xxv:1}.
[223] See above, p. 438; and O. R. Constable, "Regulating Religious Noise," pp. 70–74.
[224] J. A. Taylor, "Lucera Sarracenorum," p. 124; *Aureum Opus*, p. 193 {lxviir/cxii}.
[225] O. R. Constable, "Regulating Religious Noise," pp. 78–79.

Aragon at the turn of the fifteenth century, railed against the persistence of rituals condemned at Vienne, but as a lord granted permission to the Muslim tenants of his own estates to conduct these same observances. The call to prayer was not outlawed in Portugal until the *cortes* of Coimbra (1390), while in Huesca, deep in the Aragonese heartland, the Archbishops of Zaragoza did not succeed in having the minarets ordered demolished until 1477.[226] Nevertheless, in the countryside of Aragon and Valencia, and particularly on seigniorial lands, the call of the *mu'adhdhin* could be heard even after 1525 and the edicts of conversion, thanks to the indifference or sympathy of Christian seigniors, the indignation of the Inquisition notwithstanding.[227]

Muslim policies towards public celebrations and pilgrimages were equally ambiguous. Condemned by many orthodox *fuqahā'*, but defended by figures of the magnitude of Abū Ḥāmid al-Ghazālī (d. 1111), the practice of visiting the tombs of prophets, Companions of the Prophet, popular religious figures (*awliyā'*, "saints"), *shuyūkh, shuhadā'* (singular: *shahīd*, "martyr"), and even holy springs and rocks, has deep roots in popular Islam, and was further encouraged with the emergence of Sufism from the tenth century on.[228] In thirteenth-century Ceuta the *mawlid*, or celebration of the Prophet's birthday, was established deliberately as a means of strengthening Islamic identity in the face of Castilian irredentism and providing competition for Christian celebrations, which Muslims were participating in. Soon the custom spread through the Islamic West, including the subject communities of Iberia.[229] Across the Latin Mediterranean the landscape was peppered by sites holy to Muslims, not only in Palestine and Syria, but in Sicily and Iberia. Shrines in Sicily, including a cluster of tombs of "ascetic and pious Muslims" at Solanto Castle, between Cefalú and Palermo, attracted visitors from the *dār al-Islām*.[230] In Iberia, major shrines near Zaragoza (a site where two Companions of the Prophet were said to be buried), at Santa Maria de la Rápita in Catalonia, at Atzeneta (in the Vall de Guadalest) in Valencia, and in the south, at Rota and Granada – as well as countless other sites – were the loci of exuberant celebrations, even into the sixteenth century.[231] These cannot have been exceptional. Sufis and wandering

[226] M. F. Lopes de Barros, *Tempos e espaços*, p. 198; and Á. Conte Cazcarro, *La aljama de Moros*, p. 477. On the other hand, Charles II of Naples instituted the restrictions called for at Vienne nine years *before* the council took place. See p. 127, above.

[227] See also, p. 200, above.

[228] See W. Diem and M. Schüller, *The Living and the Dead*, chapter 1, "'Approach the Dead, Greet them, and Pray for them' The visitation of tombs and cemeteries," pp. 11–44.

[229] *Mudéjares* are attested celebrating it in 1515; the custom may have been spread as result of the Granadan diaspora, or earlier, by the medium of slaves or merchants. See M. García-Arenal, "*Shurafā*," pp. 170–71.

[230] Ibn Jubary, *Travels*, p. 345. [231] See p. 184, above.

ascetics –normally under the radar of our sources – are attested to in thirteenth-century Catalonia by Ramon Llull, and in sixteenth-century Castile by foreign travelers.[232] And while Latin authorities expressed indignant outrage at these activities, they could not have continued over the centuries without tacit approval. Indeed, Pere the Ceremonious not only allowed the pilgrimages to Atzeneta to continue, but ordered the local lord to stop charging *mudéjar* pilgrims admission.[233]

Curiously, popular religious festivals and observances were one of the contexts in which Christians, Muslims, and Jews either set aside or choreographed their formal religious differences.[234] In times of great crisis – famine, plague, or drought – Christians, Muslims, and Jews took part together in supplicatory rituals.[235] Christians certainly attended mosques and synagogues on occasion. Muslims worshiped at the shrine at ʿAyn al-Baqr, outside Acre, and attended the so-called Miracle of the Holy Fire in Jerusalem, despite the Islamic disinclination to recognize miracles – and that miracle in particular.[236] Popular religious festivals also attracted *mudéjares* (in addition to those who were performing as musicians in them), and likely Jews, who participated occasionally in church celebrations and pageants.[237] Indeed, in 1322 the Council of Valladolid complained of the practice.[238] Nevertheless, the practice continued. The Corpus Christi pageants in late fifteenth-century Murcia provide an interesting illustration. These events, which were as much civic as religious in character, involved the local Muslim and Jewish communities both as paid performers and – apparently – willing participants. Into the 1480s Muslims and Jews were allowed to wear their traditional clothes without penalty, and decorated their houses as did their Christian neighbors. As the war with Granada intensified, however, and Christian victory appeared more assured, the atmosphere soured. Minority performers had to be drafted, unpaid, to perform, and their communities' subject status

[232] O. R. Constable, "Regulating Religious Noise," pp. 82–88.
[233] See above, p. 200. In 1400 Martí prohibited the pilgrimage, but in the 1500s the local lord was still permitting it. See M. T. Ferrer i Mallol, *Els sarraïns*, p. 97, and above, p. 286.
[234] See O. Limor, "Sharing Sacred Space," pp. 219–20; M. García Arenal, "A Catholic Muslim Prophet," p. 268.
[235] See O. Limor, "Sharing Sacred Space," pp. 221–22.
[236] See B. Kedar, "Convergences," p. 90; see p. 157.
[237] See, for example, the *rabbi* in fourteenth-century Aragon who was investigated for having kicked over a cross while dancing on an altar during a church service, in E. Lourie, "Cultic Dancing and Courtly Love," pp. 151–82.
[238] M. J. Fuente Pérez, "Christian, Muslim and Jewish Women," p. 328.

was emphasized in what had become volatile and occasionally violent celebrations of Christian triumphalism.[239]

The shared repertoire of Prophets (including Jesus and John the Baptist for Christians and Muslims), saints, and Biblical/Qur'ānic and folk figures (such as al-Khiḍr/St. George/Elias), Alexander the Great (Dhu'l-Qarnayn/al-Iskandar), and Mary (Maryam, the only woman mentioned by name in the Qur'ān), together with the common substrata of Mediterranean folk belief, mythology, and tradition, provided a framework for popular religious observance that functioned in spite of, or that could accommodate, formal religious divisions, and would have exercised considerable appeal to those marginalized by structured religious observance – particularly women and the mystically inclined.[240] Common sacred spaces, such as springs, groves, and hillocks, were the site of shared or parallel worship, including well-known sites like the tombs of the Patriarchs at Hebron, and more local shrines, like the sacred cave outside Tyre.[241] The *mudéjar* pilgrimage site at Santa Maria de la Rápita was a church, while in Murcia, Muslim tradition imagined St. Ginés de la Jara, a locally venerated Christian saint, to be a kinsman of the Prophet.[242] This is not, however, a case of Muslim adopting a Christian tradition, rather "St. Ginés," who is said to have come from the "land of the Muslims," was likely a Christian appropriation of a local Muslim holy man – a phenomenon that undoubtedly occurred across Iberia and Sicily. On the other hand, Franks were known to make pilgrimages into the *dār al-Islām*, for example, to the shrine of "Our Lady of Saydnaya" outside Damascus.[243]

As it is, Islam is well suited to survive under Infidel domination; every believer can be thought of as constituting his or her own community, no mandatory quorum is required for prayer, there is no magically ordained priesthood, no indispensible sacraments, and it is not dependent on an institutionalized hierarchy of authority. Under extreme duress, *taqiyya* ("dissimulation") provides a final defense against apostasy. In other words, the aspects of Islam that were gradually regulated and suppressed within Latin Christendom were not essential to it; they represented only the surface of the religion. With the exception of those slaves who were shipped to the Latin hinterland and whose religious identity atrophied under the combined effect of coercion and isolation, and prior to the era of the Moriscos, Islam persevered, and remained dynamic, if increasingly

239 It should be noted, this shift coincided with the progressive loss of Muslims' and Jews' economic power in the city. See T. Devaney, "An 'Amiable Enmity'," chapter 6, "Murcia and the Body of Christ Triumphant," pp. 318–73.

240 See p. 321, above. 241 See p. 157, above.

242 J. Torres Fuentes, "El Monasterio de San Ginés," pp. 45–49.

243 B. Hamilton, "Our Lady of Saidnaya."

discrete, in Christian lands. The continued development of *mudéjar* and Morisco "theology" and the concerted resistance of the shadowy *ᶜulamāʾ* of late medieval and early modern Iberia bear this out. Muslims and crypto-Muslims continued to make the *ḥājj*, to absorb ideas and texts originating in the *dār al-Islām*, and to adapt and translate them as they developed indigenous strategies for solidarity and resistance. Sacred and secular literary output in *aljamiado* is only the most visible manifestation of this dynamic.[244] Other forms of resistance included self-ghettoization and flight – not necessarily to the Islamic world, but to the homogenous rural enclaves that became magnets for Muslim settlement in Iberia from the fifteenth century onwards, and the rigorous application of Islamic moral law, particularly as it applied to women, and related to miscegenation and sexuality – the porous boundary of the ethno-religious community.

However, it is clear that many "ordinary believers," whether Muslim, Christian, or Jew, did not see religious identity as necessarily exclusive, or as a zero-sum-game; many partook or participated in two, or even three confessional traditions, participating in various religious identities, according to environment, circumstance, and opportunity. This is common to religiously plural environments, from the contemporary Ottoman Balkans to modern South Asia, where individuals see the ability to draw on a broad repertoire of rites, rituals, and resources as natural and advantageous.[245] Glimpses of this are revealed occasionally, as in Ibn Jubayr's account of Sicily, in the chancery and notarial archives of Navarre and the Crown of Aragon, and in the records of the Inquisition in Iberia. Indeed, the establishment of the Inquisition – an institution dedicated to the affirmation and reinforcement of rigid and formal socio-religious boundaries – in Castile in the 1480s, and its spread to neighboring kingdoms, reveals a fluid and ambiguous approach to religious identity that must have been characteristic also of the preceding centuries and not merely of an age of forced conversion. Two *procesos* ("legal inquisitions") from the Crown of Aragon in the 1480s, that of the Valencian "public woman," Ursula/Fāṭima, and the other of the Aragonese adolescent, Mahoma Joffre/Joan de Granada, show how individuals either manipulated the religious divide or simply did not clearly understand it.[246] In 1609 a Portuguese *converso* would go so far as to declare to the Holy Office

[244] A concrete example of this can be seen in the *aljamiado* religious manual found at Ocaña, and studied in I. Hofman Vannus, "Historias religiosas."

[245] See H. T. Norris, *Islam in the Balkans*, p. 17.

[246] See M. L. Ledesma Rubio, *Vidas mudéjares*, "La conversa Úrsula, de nuevo Fátima," pp. 57–62, and "Juan de Granada, el Moro de Alfajarín," pp. 63–103.

in defense against charges of crypto-Judaism and apostasy, that he was, in effect, both a Jew and a Christian.[247] For most, religion was a question of performance as much as conscience.

### *Language and culture*

Nor could religion be easily disentangled from what we in our post-Enlightenment age would characterize as "secular" culture. In the strictly religious sense – the sense of doctrine and ritual – *conversos* and crypto-Muslims may have been "commuters," as in Thomas F. Glick's words, but they, and their only slightly less peripatetic ancestors had long been borrowing from the religiously infused cultures of their confessional rivals, as well as participating in broader, collective popular and learned traditions.[248] These traditions, based on common folk/religious and literary/intellectual origins (Abrahamic and Helleno-Persian, respectively), and coalescing as a consequence of the particular geographic and socio-economic characteristics of the Mediterranean basin, imbued the various ethno-religious communities with a "mutual intelligibility" that was both nourished and facilitated by polyvalent currents of acculturation and appropriation.[249] For subject Muslim communities in Latin Christendom, this enabled a certain level of informal socio-cultural integration, helped to mitigate cultural crystallization, and provided the basis for trajectories of cultural development that were profoundly entangled with that of their Latin Christian host societies. Because many cultural activities were not explicitly associated with religious affiliation, the stakes were lower, inclusion was less problematic, and it was not as necessary for the majority to demonstrate its subjugation of the minority communities explicitly.

Contrary to what one may presume based on European ideas of community, in which national identity has been conflated with ethnic identity and has been posited on the notion that each ethno-national community has a proprietary language, in fact, human society across the globe and across history has been characterized by a broad and functional multilingualism. In the medieval Latin world, it was common for Christians, Muslims, and Jews to speak and understand (with varying facility) each other's vernacular and literary languages, and the languages of their own

247 See the case studied in F. Soyer, "'It is not possible.'"

248 T. F. Glick, "On Converso and Marrano Ethnicity," p. 74.

249 This picture of Mediterranean culture emerges out of P. Horden and N. Purcell's characterization of environmental and economic connectivity and interdependence as proposed in their *The Corrupting Sea*. The "mutual intelligibility" that characterizes pre-modern Mediterranean culture across confessional divisions is a consequence of this (cf. p. 468, above).

co-religionists who haled from different geographical regions. Leaving aside clerics and intellectuals, whose multilingualism enabled the tremendous process of the translation of Arabic-language works of philosophy and science to Latin, there is abundant evidence, both direct and inferred, to suggest that across the Latin world, many subject Muslims spoke local Christian vernaculars (to the extent that these should be qualified as "Christian"!) and read, or even spoke, some Latin. For their part, many Jews, and a not insignificant number of Christians, had proficiency in Arabic, ranging from rudimentary and context-specific, up to literary competence.

This was true of men and women across virtually the entire socio-economic spectrum, and is reflected in anecdotal episodes in chronicles and letters, in court records and chancery documents, and in contemporary literature. This was not by any means universal, and there were certainly many monolingual individuals – there is also considerable comparable evidence of an inability for people to understand each other, and the need for translators and interpreters. We must not assume, as some historians have implied, that the use of Romance vernaculars by *mudéjares* necessarily indicates the disappearance of Arabic as a language. Languages are deployed according to content, context, and audience, and there are many levels of proficiency. Hence, when in 1363 Pere the Ceremonious dispatched an order to Lleida in search of a Muslim "who can read and translate written Arabic," this was not an indication – as J. Boswell believed – that *mudéjares* "in the north rapidly lost whatever Arabic they knew in the fourteenth century."[250] What this meant was that that he could not find any Muslims who were willing to admit to a high enough proficiency in the formal and stylized Arabic of international diplomacy to act as his translator.[251]

Indeed, for minorities the preservation of language could function as a strategy for maintaining autonomy. As long as Arabic remained the internal administrative language of *mudéjar* communities, the capacity of Christian functionaries to intrude on these communities' internal affairs or usurp the competence of *aljama* officials would have been dramatically reduced. Conservation of a minority language provides a means by which the subaltern can maintain a certain independence in the face of oppression and marginalization.[252] The maintenance of a distinct language – particularly one as different and difficult to access as Arabic

[250] J. Boswell, *The Royal Treasure*, pp. 381–82.

[251] This is one of the reasons why Jews were so often used as official translators of Arabic – many educated Jews in Iberia through the thirteenth century were extremely well versed in formal, classical, literary Arabic.

[252] Many of the strategies of furtive and structural resistance surveyed in J. C. Scott's *Weapons of the Weak* have analogies in the experience of subject Muslim communities.

would have been for most Christian Romance speakers – served to maintain the community's defensive boundaries, facilitate "argument as resistance" by limiting the majority authorities' access to information, and act as a pole for socio-cultural solidarity.[253] It would also serve as a means for maintaining the political cachet and economic advantage of the "*mudéjar* patriciate" by preserving their role as indispensable intermediaries between Christian lords and Muslim subjects. Nevertheless, on the balance, language acted to unite rather than separate subject Muslims from their Christian and Jewish neighbors, while providing them with a buffer against Christian authority. Moreover, it was one of the few arenas of interaction in which the minority could exercise some choice as regards the terms of engagement.

Linguistic boundaries are no less fluid than ethno-cultural boundaries, and across Latin Christendom creoles, pidgins, and *linguae francae* coalesced and dissolved again as speakers of various European vernaculars, Arabic, and Hebrew rubbed up against each other and intermingled.[254] Some of these hybrids, like the Catalano-Aragonese of the lower Ebro, are manifest as literary languages only in the scraps of first-person legal testimony that have survived the ages, whereas others persevered, like the Siculo-Arabic dialect that survives as Maltese. If, as J. Wansborough suggests, "the polyglot phenomenon is . . . an index to the process and rate of cultural symbiosis," then this is evidence of significant interaction.[255] Moreover, it corresponds to other evidence – the counter-examples of the Latin East and Hungary, which were characterized respectively by the isolation and assimilation of Muslim minorities, and where linguistic and literary borrowings from Arabic were minimal. In Sicily, on the other hand, and in Iberia, the impact of Arabic on linguistic development was tremendous; Spanish has some 4,000 loan words, and even Catalan and Valencian – languages we often contrast with Castilian for their lack of Arabization – have hundreds. Clearly, vocabulary can be transferred from language to language independently of living human beings, through literary transmission; but the types of words adapted by Romance speakers in Iberia and Sicily from Arabic refer to a great extent to quotidian matters, and are not likely to have been transmitted textually. As such

[253] J. Boswell, *The Royal Treasure*, pp. 233ff.

[254] A concrete and canonizable *lingua franca* presents something of a Questing Beast for certain literary scholars. There is virtually no evidence for it, nor was there any linguistic need for it. The best study of the phenomenon to date is J. Wansbrough, *Lingua Franca in the Mediterranean*. For issues regarding language and communication between Muslims and Christians in the Western Mediterranean, see R. Salicrú i Lluch, "Más allá del negociación," especially pp. 420ff.

[255] J. Wansbrough, "Diplomatica Siciliana," p. 16.

they constitute further, suggestive evidence for the broad and informal cultural engagement – and a shared conceptual repertoire – among subject Muslims and Christians.

*Literary resonance*

Whereas the impact of Arabo-Islamic thought and literature on European Christian science and philosophy is well established, the unifying power of language can be seen further in the impact that Arabo-Islamic literary and oral traditions had on the popular literature of Latin Christendom, in the dissemination and appropriation both of literary forms and themes, within the context both of courtly, aristocratic literature and that of the lower strata.[256] The epicenters of these developments were in lands where there were substantially socio-economically integrated subject Muslim populations, and in those parts of the Latin hinterland that had political–patrimonial connections with the Mediterranean. Indeed, it was this evidence of this process of linguistic and literary development that prompted Americo Castro to propose the paradigm of *convivencia* ("living together") to characterize Muslim–Christian–Jewish relations and ethnogenesis in Iberia.[257] Subsequent scholarship has demonstrated that this process was not exclusively "Spanish," but characterized developments also in Sicily and reverberated across southern Latin Europe.

The crucial role of Hispano-Arabic literary culture in the emergence of troubadour and courtly love genres in Provence has been established, and there are strong suggestions that similar influences emanated from the royal Arabic language literary salon of Norman Sicily.[258] With Arabic as the medium, Persian and South Asian tales, including those of the *Kalīla wa-dimna*, *Sendibar* (or "The Seven Sages"), elements of the Alexander Legend, and the tales that would make up the "Thousand and One Nights," came to the Latin West.[259] Much of the translation of literature was indirect, and can be seen in the adaptation of genre and textual form. Hence, the widespread appropriation of the *maqāmāt*, or "frame-tale," the

[256] See pp. 346ff.

[257] See p. 310, n. 2, above. Castro's thesis, developed as means of understanding the development of Spanish culture, was soon taken to represent a reflection of social relations among the various religious communities. The term *convivencia* was first coined by Ramón Menéndez-Pidal, but popularized by Castro and his followers.

[258] See, generally, J. Abu-Haidar, *Hispano-Arabic Literature*; R. Boase, "Arab Influences on European Love-Poetry"; T. J. Gorton, "Arabic Influence on the Troubadours"; K. Mallette, "Translating Sicily"; M. R. Menocal, *The Arabic Role*, and "Arab Influences on European Love-Poetry"; and D. Wacks, "Reconquest Colonialism."

[259] See, for example, K. Mallette, "The Twice-Written Text"; S. Kinoshita, "Translatio/N"; and D. Wacks, *Framing Iberia*, especially chapter 3, "The Cultural Context of the Translation of *Calila e Dimna*," pp. 86–128.

picaresque, and the influence exerted by Arabo-Islamic literature on figures such as Jaume Roig, the Archpriest of Hita, Dante, and Boccacio.[260] Occasionally, direct translations were commissioned and carried out, as when Alfonso X of Castile ordered translations of the *Kalīla* and Ibn Fātik's *Mukhtār al-ḥikam.*[261]

Early Old French and Provençal romances, like *Floire et Blancheflor* and *Aucassin et Nicolette* – tales of star-cross'd love and Muslim–Christian miscegenation – not only had their origin in the Arabo-Islamic narrative tradition, but were comprehensible because of the plural, slave-owning societies which their Latin audience lived in or were aware of.[262] The imprint of popular Arabo-Islamic literature is also strong in *chansons de geste/cantares de gesta*, the Castilian *romancero* (folk ballads), and the *mester de clerecía* genre – all of which originated in the oral tradition of the common peoples, Christian, Muslim, and Jewish, of the Latin Mediterranean. It can be seen in Don Juan Manuel's fourteenth-century "Tales of the Conde Lucanor" (*Libro de los enxiemplos del Conde Lucanor et de Patronio*; 1335) – an early "bestseller" in Castilian, and a work that for D. Wacks is emblematic of the tensions between conquest and acculturation.[263]

But a more profound resonance can be seen in the spread of Arabo-Islamic poetic genres to the Latin West, particularly the *zajal* and *muwashshaḥ* – Andalusī vernacular styles that, said or sung, became fixtures of the Romance tradition. Indeed, *muwashshaḥ* verses in Arabic, including those composed by Muslims and Jews, ended with a *kharja*, a rhyming couplet not infrequently composed partly or wholly in Romance vernacular.[264] This was part of a transformation of European lyric and music that came about as a consequence of exposure to and adaptation

260 See J. T. Monroe, "Arabic Literary Elements (I)" and "Arabic Literary Elements (II)"; D. Wacks, *Framing Iberia*, and "Reading Jaume Roig's *Spill*"; and J. Abu-Haidar, "'Maqāmāt' Literature." Centuries later, a similar influence was exercised on the Christian folk literature of southeastern Europe as a consequence of Ottoman hegemony. See J. S. Miletich, "Muslim Oral Epic."

261 D. Wacks, "Reconquest Colonialism," p. 89; L. P. Harvey, "The Alfonsine School of Translators," p. 113. The *Mukhtār al-ḥikam wa-maḥāsin al-kalim* ("Choice wise sayings and fine statements") was an eleventh-century work of wisdom literature written in Fāṭimid Egypt. It was translated in Castile as *Bocados d'oro* ("Mouthfuls of gold"), and later in a number of European languages, usually as *Liber philosophorum moralium antiquorum* ("The Book of the Dictates of the Ancient Philosophers").

262 Cf. Arnald d'Alos, above, p. 465, n. 164.

263 D. Wacks, "Reconquest Colonialism," pp. 88 and 94. Indeed, the book does not present individual Muslims in a particularly favorable light, but rather, morally skewed and unscrupulous. See *ibid.*, pp. 95–96.,

264 O. Zwartjes, *Love Songs from al-Andalus*; J. T. Monroe, "*Zajal* and *muwashshaḥa*"; and G. Schoeler, "Muwashshaḥ" in *Encyclopaedia of Islam, Second Edition*.

of Arabo-Islamic instruments, genres, and styles, particularly but not exclusively through the medium of Christian Iberia. Direct historical evidence of musical influence for an age in which musical notation was in its infancy is elusive, but innovative scholarship and careful inference has left no doubt that this was a profoundly transformative process for the Latin West and saw the introduction of almost every stringed instrument, most wind instruments, and new percussion instruments from the Islamic world.[265] Nor was the influence unidirectional; the *kharjas* were evidently inspired by the voices of Christian slave girls in Andalusī courts, and Romance traditions were adapted by Muslims as they made this the language of their own *aljamiado* literature, and as Muslims made Castilian an "Islamic" literary language.[266] The case of music and literature shows that "transmission" is not the best paradigm to describe the process of cultural innovation that took place in Latin lands that had significant free or enslaved Muslim populations. Rather, it was a process of synthesis, a consequence of an environment in which Muslims, Christians, and Jews followed their own traditions, while drawing freely on and contributing to each other's, both deliberately and unconsciously. These were processes that were not restricted to aristocratic and literary elites, but in which all of society was broadly engaged.[267]

### *Song and dance*

As was the case with language and literature, there were several vectors of transmission for Arabo-Islamic music, song, and poetry. The Latin aristocracy were important protagonists in this process, particularly the royals, magnates, and bishops across Iberia and in Sicily, who from the twelfth century onwards deliberately fostered cosmopolitan court cultures. These included the d'Hauteville dynasty, Frederick II, Alfons II ("the Troubador") of Aragon, and Alfonso X of Castile, to name only

[265] In addition to the works cited above in n. 259, see M. R. Menocal, *Shards of Love*, and *The Arabic Role*; K. Mallette, *Kingdom of Sicily*; and C. Robinson, *In Praise of Song*. For music, see E. Gutwirth, "Music, Identity and the Inquisition"; D. F. Reynolds, "Music in Medieval Iberia"; and A. Shiloah, *Music in the World of Islam*, pp. 77–83. For art, see J. Dodds, *et al.*, *The Arts of Intimacy*, and V. Mann, *et al.*, *Convivencia*. S. K. Jayyusi, *The Legacy of Muslim Spain*, contains a number of relevant chapters; including J. Dodds, "The Mudéjar Tradition," O. Grabar, "Two Paradoxes," L. López-Baralt "The Legacy of Islam," D. Waines, "The Culinary Culture," and O. Wright, "Music in Muslim Spain." For an overview, see T. F. Glick, *Islamic and Christian Spain*, chapter 9: "Cultural Process in Medieval Spain," pp. 337–71.

[266] See O. Zwartjes, "The Andalusi Kharjas," p. 12; M. Á. Vázquez, "Poesía morisca."

[267] Again, Wacks provides an overview of acculturation in influence in "Reconquest Colonialism."

a few. Indeed, Muslim performers were a fixture in virtually every royal court of the Iberian Peninsula in the thirteenth and fourteenth centuries.[268] Foreign lords who visited or had links with the Latin Mediterranean acted as vectors for the dissemination of these styles into the Latin hinterland. For example, Guillem VIII of Aquitaine (1058–86), whose son, Guillem IX (1086–1126), is traditionally credited as the first troubadour, not only took part in the Norman-led campaign against Barbastro, but brought back a considerable number of slaves, notably women, to his court at Poitiers. Muslim slaves – men and women – purchased, brought back as booty, or sent as gifts to popes, kings, and clergy, and put to work as musicians, dancers, and singers, would have reinforced and further disseminated Arabo-Islamic styles. Finally, in those lands where there were subject Muslim populations, local Christians would have been acculturated both as a consequence of exposure to Muslim popular festivities (as Ibn Jubayr observed), and through the medium of converts.[269] Dance seems to have followed a similar pattern; in 1429 the Archbishop of Lisbon complained at a party in Valladolid that the episcopal robes he was wearing were too tight for him to dance the *zambra* – the same dance that was a subject of scandal for Isabella of Portugal in 1532 and of a spirited defense by Francisco Núñez Muley in 1567.[270] The popularity of Muslim and Morisco entertainers, whether free subjects or slaves, is widely attested across the Latin Mediterranean.

The reasons why Infidel cultural affectations would be taken up with such gusto by such a broad constituency of Christian society are manifold. First and foremost, Arabo-Islamic music and lyric were, simply put, far more sophisticated and entertaining than the indigenous traditions of homogenous and isolated Latin Europe; moreover, by the eleventh century Islamic culture had become synonymous in the Latin imagination with chic and refinement. Employing exotic performers who were masters of fashionable and foreign styles would be seen as an adornment to a court, a sign of the power and finesse of the master of the household – not unlike the menageries of rare animals that were common fixtures of fourteenth- and fifteenth-century royal courts.[271] There was undoubtedly also a "colonial" or "Maurophilic" element; to have Muslim performers represented an affirmation of Christian domination and mastery over

268 D. F. Reynolds, "Music in Medieval Iberia," p. 243.

269 See A. Metcalfe and J. Birk, "Ibn Jubayr's Account," p. 240.

270 D. Reynolds, "Music in Medieval Iberia," pp. 244–45. The *zambra* derives from the Arabic *samra*, or *samar*, and refers not to a particular dance, but a nocturnal entertainment session, including dance, music and poetry. See A. Shiloah, *Music in the World of Islam*, pp. 77–78. See also pp. 284 and 289.

271 See p. 346, above.

Islamic culture and peoples – and this would have exercised an appeal both to the Latin aristocracy and the common classes. For subject Muslim communities, the "entertainment industry" may have provided economic opportunity and a certain degree of cultural validation, but did not necessarily lead to an amelioration of formal status. Muslim singers and dancers, no matter how talented, remained "Saracens" and Infidels. To draw a recent analogy, the great popularity of certain performers of color with white American audiences in the mid twentieth century did little to change the status – legal or conceptual – of African-Americans, although it did transform white American music.[272] In the world of Latin Christendom, this sort of patronage and acculturation was a feature even in those societies characterized by a high index of ethno-religious conflict and subordination of Muslims, such as the kingdom of Valencia or Crusader Jerusalem, where Fulcher of Chartres famously observed in the early twelfth century, "We are all Orientals now . . ."[273]

### *Fashion and adornment*

Similarly complex processes of transmission, adoption, acculturation, and synthesis characterized the influence of Arabo-Islamic material, craftsmanship, and industry on the Latin West, including both luxury and everyday implements. At the upper of end of the scale, members of the Latin Christian elite adopted materials (notaby silk) and styles of dress from the Islamic world, or appropriated, or received as gifts, luxury objects, such as silk brocade, ivory boxes, glass vessels, and so on, at times fundamentally transforming their function and use. A glass oil lamp could become a decanter, a silk robe a mantle for a *santo* or the chasuble of an archbishop, or an ivory casket a reliquary.[274] Through the entire Middle Ages, *mudéjar* silk producers and tailors, as well as cordwainers, retained a significant (if gradually diminishing) role in the high-end apparel sector. "Islamic" styles of ceramics and domestic wares circulated on both the local and regional scale in the Latin West, at times manufactured by *mudéjar* craftsmen and at times by Christians. In late medieval Iberia,

[272] See E. Lourie's comments in "Cultic Dancing," pp. 156–57. [273] See p. 142.

[274] Such appropriation is normal. The meaning of art and objects lies with the observer; it changes with the cultural context of the audience and user. Nevertheless, certain motifs, styles, and modes resonated across time, space, and community, thanks in part to the shared traditions Latin and Arabo-Islamic culture, particularly in the Mediterranean. Gift-giving and plunder, the use of *spolia* and the potential to re-use and reinterpret objects contributed to this. See, for example, G. T. Beech, "The 'Eleanor Vase'"; E. Hoffman, "Pathways of Portability"; D. Jacoby, "Silk Economies," pp. 204–05; and O. Grabar, "The Shared Culture of Objects." For Tordesillas, see P. J. Lavado Paradinas, "El palacio mudéjar de Astudillo."

low-status itinerant craftsmen – carpenters, tinkers, potters – followed regional circuits, serving Christian, Muslim, and Jewish clientele. It was at the lowest levels of cultural complexity – that which is most elusive to the historian – that members of the different religious communities interacted most easily. The degree to which Muslims, Christians, and Jews in Latin lands felt compelled to articulate formally the boundaries between their communities is indicative of the tremendous amount they held in common and to which their daily experience was unmarked by religious difference. C. Robinson's observations regarding architectural and artistic influence at the Clarissan convent at Tordesillas in Castile apply across the whole gamut of cultural contact, and not only in Iberia (as she notes here), but wherever in the Latin Mediterranean there were significant communities of free Muslims:

> this group of motifs is one whose coalescence was generated not by the appropriation of a category of motifs, or of an aesthetic by one tradition from another entirely separate from it, but by the participation of specific groups from among the practitioners of all three traditions (namely, those attached to the Castilian court) in the creation of a devotional language, literature, practice, and visual tradition which is both specifically Iberian and strikingly different from those prevalent at contemporary moments elsewhere in Europe and the Islamic world.[275]

The whole matter of clothing reflects this complex process of multilateral diffusion and the problems and tensions that it generated. For Muslims and Christians, although certain items or styles of dress, notably the custom of covering Muslim women's hair or faces, or Muslim men's eschewal of gold and silk, were rooted in widely accepted religious interpretation, there were few clear canonical mandates in this regard, other than general enjoinments to modesty. In other words, there were few *a priori* barriers to the adaptation of out-group styles of dress. Hence, members of the Christian and Muslim elites freely borrowed each others' fashions, whether as a consequence of common vocation – as was the case, for example, with Christian and Muslim knights and soldiers, who dressed and armed themselves with "foreign" equipment – or in self-conscious and deliberate communal cross-dressing, as in the flamboyant Maurophilia of the d'Hauteville kings and the royalty of late medieval Castile, or the subversive, Latinizing conformity of the *mudéjar* patriciate.

References to acculturation in terms of costume among humbler classes are frequent also, from the Muslim Bashkurts of Hungary to Fulcher's Frankish "Orientals," and the Arabized women Ibn Jubayr observed in Sicily. In Iberia the situation was at least as fluid and complex. Apparently,

275 C. Robinson, "Mudéjar Revisited," pp. 52–53.

the use of the *ḥijāb* ("veil") and the practice of head-covering was common even in late fifteenth-century Granada, but varied both by region and over time in the rest of the peninsula. Evidence from late medieval Portugal indicates that *Mouros* dressed like Christians, as had been the case for *mudéjar* men and women in most of the Crown of Aragon and Navarre since at least the thirteenth century. There are suggestions that this was the case also in late medieval Castile, especially for indigenous *mudéjares* (as opposed to Granadan exiles and émigres).[276] If the famous sixteenth-century illustrations by Cristoph Weidtiz in 1529 are any guide, it may be that Moriscos wore distinctive costumes, but these did not necessarily resemble "traditional Islamic" dress, and may have represented recent innovations – adopted, perhaps, in reaction to the marginalization of New Christians.[277]

In any event, there were likely differences between town and country. In the rural environment, idiosyncratic and particular styles – "traditional" or not – which corresponded to local ethno-religious identities may have persevered longer, especially in isolated or homogenous enclaves. In town and city, Muslims – both men and women – may have been more likely to conform to Latin-Christian fashions, except for those places and times where they felt marginalized on the basis of religion or culturally threatened. In these latter cases, reverting to ethno-religiously particular costume could serve as a strategy for reinforcing communal identity and solidarity. In any event, clothes can be easily changed, and the same individuals would have likely tailored their dress and appearance to the contexts and environments they were moving in and audiences they were performing for at any given moment. In matters of dress, as in language and literature, there is no inherent conflict between innovation and conservatism; the same individuals can practice both simultaneously. The problem with dress lay in the potential for this type of borrowing to undermine the confessional boundaries that helped to ensure social stability and mitigate inter-communal competition and violence. Miscegenation, apostasy, and subversion of the recognized socio-religious hierarchy were real consequences of the broad tendency for Christians and Muslims to dress alike, a phenomenon widely attested to in late medieval juridical and chancery records, and one against which the sumptuary laws and calls for segregation which emanated from both minority and majority community leaders must be understood.

[276] M. F. Lopes de Barros, "Body, Baths and Cloth," pp. 10–11.

[277] See C. Weiditz, *Authentic Everyday Dress of the Renaissance*, plates LXXIX–LXXXVIII. Other near-contemporary illustrators, such as Hogenberg and Heldt, are less dependable. See J. N. Hillgarth, *The Mirror of Spain*, pp. 248–49.

*Tastes and appetites*

If the appropriation of clothing styles was a visible manifestation of the broad dynamic of reciprocal acculturation that characterized Muslim–Christian(–Jewish) interaction in the Latin Christian lands that had subject Muslim populations, a more visceral matrix of acculturation and synthesis was undoubtedly the kitchen. Whether the impact of the Islamic expansion can accurately be characterized as a "green revolution," the impact of the introduction of new crops, spices, and food preparation techniques from the Islamic world to the Latin world is undeniable.[278] As with music and dance, this process did not leave much of a textual record – accounts of style mavens, like the ninth-century polymath, epicure, and fashion guru, Ziryāb, who transformed "the look" and the tastes of the emiral court in Córdoba and those of its Christian client kings, are rare. However, a survey of the cuisine of the Iberian Peninsula and of Sicily today leaves little doubt of this process, the absence of direct evidence in late medieval European cookbooks notwithstanding.[279] Muslims and Christians would have consumed many of the same prepared foods, whether purchased *prêt-a-porter* in market stalls, or cooked at home by the Muslim domestic servants and slaves who were so common in Christian households, palaces, and convents. Indeed, as Ibn Jubayr and Usāma b. Munqidh observed in Sicily and the Frankish Levant, high-status Christians sought out Muslim cooks and cuisine for their own tables.[280] This was not a situation the moral arbiters of Latin Christendom were entirely comfortable with.[281]

And whereas certain foods, such as wine and pork, and certain slaughter and preparation techniques (e.g. *ḥalāl*), carried a ritual significance or were subject to canonical restrictions for Muslims, this was hardly a bar to consumption – then, as today – except, perhaps, openly.[282] Quite the contrary; issues arising as a consequence of Muslims, Christians and Jews drinking and gambling together in taverns appear not only in the often formulaic law codes of medieval Iberia, but in actual trial and inquisition

278 The standard work on the impact of Arabic agriculture is A. Watson, *Agricultural Innovation*.

279 See H. Bresc and G. Bresci-Bautier, *Palerme*, p. 64; and, generally, D. Waines, "The Culinary Culture." The impact of Arabo-Islamic cuisine on the Latin lands of the Mediterranean is broad and obvious, ranging from the introduction of new ingredients, to preparation styles, to the order of courses. This is not necessarily reflected in medieval Latin cookbooks, which as a genre represent only a small part of what Christians ate or prepared. See C. Nadeau, "Contributions of Medieval Food Manuals."

280 See Ibn Jubayr, *Travels*, p. 341; Ibn Munqidh, *The Book of Contemplation*, pp. 153–54.

281 See D. M. Freidenreich, "Sharing Meals With Non-Christians."

282 For the problem relating to food, see D. M. Freidenreich, *Foreigners and Their Food*.

records, and are confirmed in archival sources.[283] Such fraternization put subject Muslims in situations of unguarded intimacy and candor, if not libidinous recklessness, with Christians, who – the camaraderie of cups notwithstanding – remained their social and juridical superiors. A wrong word, a lost temper, a lustful advance, or furtive glance, any of these had the possibility of converting a neutral and good-natured social gathering into a violent communally informed conflict. Moreover, for the formal and informal custodians of Islamic faith and culture, this sort of intimacy appeared profoundly threatening, particularly when it encouraged Muslims to disregard fundamental moral principles, including sobriety and sexual continence. Hence, an anonymous thirteenth-century *mudéjar* sermonary (from either Zaragoza or Huesca), puts considerable emphasis on the relationship of food to sin and virtue; indeed, first and most important of "principles of reprehensible character" the anonymous imam lists is "sinful food" – the epitome of individual desire.[284]

Food was not merely what one ate: it was both a symbol and constituent of what one was, in a physical, metaphysical, and communal sense.[285] In al-Andalus on the eve of the Christian conquest the *ʿālim*, al- Ṭurṭūshī (d. 1126), complained that the lure of specially prepared sweets was tempting Muslims into participating in Christian holidays like Epiphany, Holy Thursday, and St. John's Day.[286] In this spirit, a late fifteenth-century *mudéjar* didactic treatise intended for women records a parable in which a *mudéjar* woman recounts with shame how, by fault of her brother's drinking, she became the mother of her own son's son. It ends with the despairing warning, "Avoid wine, [ye] servants of God, for it is forbidden, and will lead you to Hell."[287]

Likewise, conflicts revolving around the obligation of local Muslims to purchase meat *only* from *ḥalāl* butchers, and for these to sell *only* to local Muslims are also frequent. In substantial towns there was generally at least one butcher-shop serving each of the three religious communities, although in villages and hamlets, Jews and *mudéjares* might share the same facility.[288] At

283 See, for example, M. T. Ferrer i Mallol, *El sarraïns*, pp. 12–13.
284 L. G. Jones, "The Boundaries of Sin," pp. 464, 471, and 474–75.
285 See, for example, C. Fischler, "Food, Self and Identity."
286 L. G. Jones, "The Boundaries of Sin," pp. 475–76.
287 I. Hofmann Vannus, "Espejo de mujeres mudéjares," pp. 10–11. The woman in question was raped by her brother on account of his drunkenness, and she became pregnant. When the child was born in secret, she laid him out to die of exposure so as to preserve her reputation. But the boy lived, and growing up, made a fortune in far-off lands. Returning home, Oedipus-like, he unwittingly married his own mother (although she was aware, but dared not protest), and she bore him a son.
288 See, for example, A. Ozaki, "El régimen tributario," p. 456. Of course, the fact that there was one abattoir does not necessarily mean that there was not more than one butcher using the facility.

times Muslim butchers were reprimanded for selling to Christians, but it was typically Jewish butchers who were caught up in these controversies. Given that many Muslims were prepared to regard *kasher* slaughter protocols as meeting the standards of *ḥalāl*, *mudéjares* would buy at a discounted price cuts of meat prohibited to Jews that Jewish butchers would otherwise discard. The violation of these rules offended Christian authorities not so much on religious grounds, but because butcher-shops operated as seigniorial, royal, or municipal monopolies, and the rights and profits of the license holders (and the officials who earned commissions on those licenses) had to be defended. For Muslim authorities, the stakes would obviously have been higher; permitting Muslims to buy meat anywhere but the official *majzir* constituted a threat to the solidarity and integrity of the community and – by extension – the faith.

This strikes at the heart of the problem of inter-communal acculturation in the diverse societies of Latin Christendom – "the religious" was virtually impossible to disentangle from the banal, the social, the economic, and the institutional, and the interests and agendas inherent in these. Socio-cultural interaction and appropriation were constant and multidirectional, but – particularly in more formal contexts – could never be entirely separated from communal identity and the differentiation and hierarchization that this presumed and entailed. At the same time, it was impossible to disconnect and disentangle Christian, Muslim, and Jewish culture and society, both because individuals and corporations engaged with each other in ways that ran across the formal division of religious community, and as a consequence the potent relationships of power that bound them to each other. Thus, in some sense, it was those groups in society that operated furthest out of the institutional sphere who had the greatest opportunity to engage with and affect Latin society and culture and, simultaneously, were best positioned to isolate and protect their distinct communal identity. Hence, the penultimate section of this chapter looks at the position of women in *mudéjar* communities, and of *mudéjar* women in the larger Christian-dominated societies in which they lived.

## *Gendering the* mudéjar

With the Muslims of the morería of Zaragoza having gathered in the old mosque ... the said lieutenant held counsel on the dispute between Jahiel Albalentí and his wife, regarding the *peyta* that was owed last Saint John's day in the month of June just passed, since the said Jahiel and his wife were and are husband and wife, and are not separated, and in the *aljama* it is customary that the husband pay for his wife, it was ordered that the said Jahiel pay for the entire month of March just past all of the *peyta* which they owed to *don* Ramon de Navalles, collector of the said *peyta*; but on that said day past, because it was said that the said wife of the said Jahiel was no longer living with him, that from here on forward the said Mariem would be held to pay for the goods that were found in her possession in the said *peyta* . . . (Ximeno de Alburuela, notary, transcript of a hearing of a tax dispute (1400–21)[289])

As many historians have recognized, subject Muslim women were in a doubly disadvantaged position due to both their gender and their religious identity: "doubly marginalized," suffering from a "double vulnerability," and bearing a "double burden."[290] Moreover, they have been further disregarded by historians, both as a consequence of how contemporaries shaped the historical record and of scholars' presumptions regarding the role of women in Islamic societies.[291] Nevertheless, *mudéjar* women's position within their own society was hardly worse than that of their Christian and Jewish sisters, as the natural misogyny of masculine culture trumped even considerations of ethnicity and religion. For the fifteenth-century moralist and physician Jaume Roig, all women "of whatever state, color, age, religion, nation, or condition, big and bigger, small and smaller, young and old, ugly and beautiful, sick and healthy, Christian, Jewish, and Muslim, black and dark, blonde and white, right-handed and one-armed, hump-backed, talkative and mute, free and enslaved" were members of the same defective fellowship as a consequence of their sex.[292]

### *Women on top*

And yet, subject Muslim women were neither voiceless nor powerless. In fact, despite the vulnerabilities they were subject to, they played particular and important roles both as regards integration and acculturation with Christian society and safeguarding Islamic culture and identity, precisely by virtue of their gender. Indeed, the laws in medieval Islam that circumscribed the roles and rights of Muslim women, afforded

289 F. Macho y Ortega, "Condición social," pp. 212–13 {1}.

290 See E. Lourie, "Anatomy of Ambivalence," pp. 69–72; I. O'Connor de los Angeles, "Muslim Mudéjar Women," p. 56; and M. Green, "Conversing with the Minority." For *mudéjar* and minority women, see E. Baumgarten, "'A Separate People'?"; M. E. Perry, "Between Muslim and Christian Worlds"; I. Hofman Vannus, "Mujeres mudéjares en la España medieval"; C. Villanueva Muerte, "Las mujeres mudéjares en Aragón". For the status of women in al-Andalus and the Islamic world, see L. Ahmed, *Women and Gender in Islam*; G. R. E. Hambly, *Women in the Medieval Islamic World*; G. López de la Plaza, *Al-Andalus: mujeres, sociedad y religión*; M. Marín, "Las mujeres en al-Andalus," and *Mujeres en al-Andalus*; Y. Rapoport, *Marriage, Money and Divorce*; M. Shatzmiller, *Her Day in Court*; J. E. Tucker, *Women, Family, and Gender*; and M. J. Viguera, *La mujer en al-Andalus*.

291 C. Barceló Torres, "Mujeres, campesinas," p. 211, and M. Green, "Conversing with the Minority."

292 See J. Roig, *The Mirror*, p. 277 {412–33}.

protection of person, property, and status, and a scope for independent action that contemporary Christian women did not enjoy. Muslim women had a right to inherit, received a dower on marriage (usually in trust, but that they could redeem in case of widowhood or divorce), and had the right to own and manage their own property and defend themselves and their interests in court. Moreover, Islamic law served to undermine "traditional" roles for women and models of gender relations that limited female autonomy.[293] And if Islamic law, on the other hand, limited women's capacity to act independently in the public sphere, the overriding authority of Christian law counteracted this for *mudéjares*, and opened up further opportunities for women's legal and economic independence.[294] Hence, women such as Mariem, the wife of Jahiel Albalentí, could use their subordinate status as a spouse to their own advantage – in her case to temporarily evade paying taxes after separating from her husband.[295] The possibility of appealing to Christian jurisdictions made obtaining and enforcing their rights in divorce easier, and allowed women even to legally resist attempts to marry them against their own consent.[296] On the other hand, their status under Christian law meant that Muslim women also bore the full legal obligations of a subject of the king.

Although absence of documentation does not permit generalizations regarding the situation of *mudéjar* women in the Frankish East, Sicily, or Hungary, it can be shown that across the Iberian Peninsula from the thirteenth century forward Muslim women exercised their legal prerogatives independently and aggressively, petitioning their lords and sovereigns,

293 Both Christian law and Islamic law worked against endogamous and agnatic ("Oriental," in Guichard's parlance) models of kinship and marriage. See J. Coope, "Marriage, Kinship, and Islamic Law." Indeed, there is virtually no evidence for these sorts of family structures in Latin lands after the thirteenth century (which is to say, the Iberian Peninsula); see above, p. 446. These marriage strategies seem to have persisted in the kingdom of Granada, and in the 1540s the Church actively sought to repress them. See G. López de la Plaza, "Las mujeres moriscas," p. 316. However, this itself is not necessarily indicative of continuity; "Oriental" marriages may have been revived as a reaction to Christian conquest and a means of resisting acculturation and absorption. See also E. Martínez Gonzalez, "Matrimonio y divorcio islámicos"; al-Qayrawānī, *Risala*; M. I. Fierro Bello, "La mujer y el trabajo."

294 I. O'Connor de los Angeles, "Muslim Mudéjar Women," p. 55. For *mudéjar* women's capacity to act independently in the legal sphere, and to work, in spite of the declarations of jurists, see C. de la Puente, "Juridical Sources," and M. F. Lopes de Barros, "Body, Baths and Cloth," pp. 12, respectively. See also n. 301, below.

295 See above, p. 498.

296 See, for example, ACA, C., reg. 2063, f. 186v (February 3, 1364). Here the Countess (and future Queen) Maria de Luna ordered her *mudéjar* subject, Almorag, to desist from his efforts to marry off his daughter "Exemci" against her will, ordering expressly that the girl be married to no man without her consent (and only to another of the Countess's Muslim vassals). See also Axa Granada's divorce suit against her husband Yayel Cortoví in Tudela in 1509 (see p. 379, n. 112).

suing Christian, Jewish, and Muslim men, including their own husbands, and defending their rights and privileges in court.[297] They abandoned their husbands, obtained divorces and remarried, changed residence independently, and received permission to emigrate and to travel – even to undertake the *ḥājj*. Both in the peninsula and in Sicily, they figure regularly in land title, transfer, and tax documents, both as co-proprietors and full owners of farmland and urban properties from the eleventh century onwards.[298] The fact that subject Muslim women were also prepared to violate the law, and to commit crimes both against fellow Muslims, Christians, and Jews, reflects a remarkable degree of confidence and integration.[299]

*Mudéjar* women also participated broadly in the economies of the Latin kingdoms; at least in the Iberian Peninsula, where subject Muslim communities persevered long enough to produce the types of records that attest to this.[300] From Portugal to Catalonia, Muslim women owned properties and operated businesses – including bathhouses, smithies, and a wide range of craft enterprises – they borrowed and lent money, and bought and sold properties both for their own use and for speculation.[301] They were active in agriculture and oleoculture as owners, producers, and millers, as well as workers. Women worked in the building and decorative trades that were so important to the *mudéjar* economy, notably

[297] See, for example, the case of a *mudéjar* woman in early fourteenth-century Daroca who took on the men of the corrupt *aljama* regime when they tried to deprive her of her blacksmith's license, in M. de C. García Herrero, "Doña Xemçi de Taher." In 1346 Mariem d'Alcadi sued to prevent her ex-husband Hamet Alquir, a merchant from Zaragoza, from sailing east, on the grounds he had appropriated her dower. See M. T. Ferrer i Mallol, *El sarraïns*, p. 156.

[298] See, for example, G. López de la Plaza, "Propiedades femeninas;" M. F. Lopes de Barros, "A mulher muçulmana," pp. 108–09. This is borne out by monastic, municipal, and ecclesiastical land records from the twelfth century onwards. See the sources surveyed in B. Catlos, *The Victors and the Vanquished*, pp. 100–18, and, for Sicily, J. Johns, *Arabic Administration*, pp. 316–18.

[299] In Navarre, Muslim men and women were committing (or at least getting caught for) petty property crimes (*hurtos*) at the same rate. F. Segura Urra, "Los mudéjares navarros," p. 249.

[300] Refer, for example, to the tables in the appendices of C. Villanueva Muerte, "Las mujeres mudéjares," pp. 532–76, and J. Carrasco Pérez, "Los Mudéjares de Navarra," pp. 101–7. Aside from women who formally owned and operated businesses, many were engaged in usufacture or putting-out, particularly in the silk industry and olive culture. A. Labarta, "La mujer morisca," p. 230. In Almería women owned 3.4 percent of the olive trees, 8.5 percent of other trees, and 5.8 percent of market gardens, vines, and mulberry and fig plantations, 8 percent of homes, and 24 percent of the watermills, according to the *repartimiento* of 1489–90. See G. López de la Plaza, "Propiedades femeninas," 212. For the broad economic role of *mudéjar* women, see C. Barceló Torres, "Mujeres, campesinas," p. 214; M. E. Díez Jorge, "Relaciones de género," and *Mujeres* y *arquitectura.*

[301] For example, for Portugal, see, M. J. da Silva Leal, *Livro do almoxarifado*, pp. 35 and 45; for Aragon, see M. García-Arenal, "Documentos árabes," pp. 57–58 {III}, 60–61 {VI}, and E. Marín Padilla, "Los moros de Calatorao (I)," 260.

as preparers of stucco and plaster, but also as general manual laborers, and worked in both ceramic and textile production, both from home and outside. Muslim women were particularly common in, even dominating, certain low-status sectors, such as prostitution, entertainment, and wet-nursing, but also highly regarded and well-compensated fields such as midwifery and "traditional medicine," where both their gender and their Arabo-Islamic cultural background provided them with a cachet and an advantage over non-Muslim and male competitors.[302] Women were also very active in low-yield economic activities; the types of *zofras*, or labor dues, *mudéjar* women were obliged to render their lords, reveals their role as cleaners, producers of cloth, and domestic items through usufacture, and in raising small animals, such as chickens.[303]

In the economic sphere, Muslim women frequently related to men and non-Muslims in contexts in which their own gender and religious identity clearly became secondary to the nature of the exchange. In exceptional cases, through inheritance and the active accumulation of wealth, *mudéjar* women became both rich and independent, and consequently were able to exercise informal political influence within their own communities.[304] Not all subject Muslim women were created (or created themselves) equal – social class, kinship networks, religious knowledge, and prestige, were all factors that contributed to individual women's status and power, and could put them at a relative advantage in many contexts not only to other Muslim women, but even Christians, and even Christian men.[305]

302 See pp. 434 and 439, above.

303 C. Barceló Torres, "Mujeres, campesinas," p. 215. In the County of Denia, Muslim women produced cloth and clothing for the "senyora marquesa" on an ongoing basis; given that they were paid for this (it was not a tax or labor dues) and it was produced at the Countess's request, we can assume it was used by the lady and her court. See J. Argente Vidal, "Un libro de cuentas," pp. 314–15 and 317.

304 For women's financial independence, see K. A. Miller, *Guardians of Islam*, pp. 98–99; also, C. Díaz de Rábago Hernández, "Mujeres mudéjares." Women's wealth is not always measurable in terms that emerge clearly in the documentation. For example, jewelry and silk clothes constituted an important reserve of capital for many women, and one that was not encumbered legally or by male supervision the way that landed property was. See M. F. Lopes de Barros, *Tempos e espaços*, p. 197. For an illustration of the wealth-in-kind some Muslim women owned, see the impressive inventory of Montesina Pérez, a Morisca exiled to Lorca after the War of the Alpujarras in 1570, in M. Arcas Campoy, "Inventario de bienes."

305 Like religious identity, gender cannot be considered in isolation; *mudéjar* women's potential and experience was shaped not only by their sex and their communal affiliation, but by social class, material wealth, ethno-physiognomy, kinship networks, religio-cultural prestige, and participation in relationships of clientage-patronage with powerful figures within Christian and Muslim society. See, for example, R. Deguilhem and M. Marin, "Introduction"; B. C. Aswad, "Women, Class, and Power"; J. Coope, "Marriage, Kinship, and Islamic Law." For an example of "soft power," and women's participation in male political networks, see B. Catlos, "Justice Served."

This would have been most clear and common in Sicily (prior to the voluntary exoduses and the forced transportations of the late twelfth and early thirteenth centuries) and Granada, both of which retained a broad, wealthy upper class of subject Muslims. Hence, in 1190, when a certain Zaynab was taken captive by "Christians" (*al-Rūm*), presumably in the course of a voyage, she was able to dispatch her agent to Palermo to sell one of her properties in order to raise a ransom.[306] Even so, the overwhelming majority of *mudéjar* women found themselves at the bottom of the social hierarchy of Latin Christian societies – not unlike disadvantaged African-American women in the twentieth-century United States. Overall, they had fewer opportunities, were more vulnerable, and more isolated than either Muslim men or Christian women, and for most, their worlds – social, economic, and cultural – were centered on the home and its close environs. The female condition, with all of the formal and conceptual limitations it entailed, was both obvious and inescapable.

### *Women on the margins*

Women's secondary status is most evident in the legal and didactic texts that were produced by *mudéjares* in the fourteenth and fifteenth centuries, which focused on the subordinate role of women and the need for them to contain themselves, in terms of sexual activity, public activities, and speech.[307] This was consonant with a broader conception of the place of women in society that was common to all three religio-cultural groups.[308] Hence the notion – universal among contemporaries – that since women were subordinate to masculine authority, violation of their intimacy or suggestion of sexual incontinence (perceived or real) was seen as a threat to the fabric of their family and community and the prestige of the men who were in formal positions of power. Hence, the tendency of *mudéjar fuqahāʾ* to work together with Christian authorities to punish rigorously moral offenses committed by women, and the double-standard regarding outward appearance – whereby *mudéjar* men objected to and resisted

[306] J. Johns, *Arabic Administration*, p. 323.

[307] See M.-M. Rivera Garretas, "La construcción de lo femenino." *Mudéjar* law codes showed a serious concern with the issue of defamation, particularly as practiced by women, likely because of the incendiary nature women's accusations could have in violent, male-dominated societies characterized by a strong sense of honor (as was the case with *both* Latin Christian and *mudéjar* society). Such laws were not dead letters, as records of prosecutions attest. See, for example, C. Barceló Torres, "Mujeres, campesinas," p. 216.

[308] I. Hofmann Vannus, "Espejo de mujeres mudéjares."

sumptuary laws that marked them off as Muslims, but supported regulations that marked their women off in the same way.[309]

There was certainly a tendency to commodify women, and to treat them, if not as chattel, then certainly as objects or assets that could be put to the service of extending or reinforcing economic and social networks through marriage.[310] Most seriously, the propensity to see women as sex objects, coupled with the power disadvantages that *mudéjar* women were subject to, made them particularly vulnerable to sexual abuse and violence, whether this was institutionalized in the form of judicial slavery and forced prostitution, or informal, taking the form of sexual assault or non-violent coercion.[311] Muslims were certainly over-represented among prostitutes, proportionate to the population.[312] In some cases this may have represented a conscious choice on the part of the women concerned – however risky and unsavory, it could represent a path towards a personal autonomy and self-determination of sorts, particularly for women who had already fallen afoul of the moral guardians of their communities.[313] Contemporary Christian literature, which must have in some sense reflected and reinforced social values and standards of behavior, also objectified Muslim women, and even encouraged sexual aggression and predation against them.[314] But religious difference was hardly a prerequisite for sexual exploitation; just as unscrupulous or desperate Muslim women and men committed acts of violence and crimes against female and minor *mudéjares*, so they coerced or otherwise violated them sexually.[315] Neverthelesss, Muslim women did not necessarily consent to serving as the passive victims of sexual or physical violence; just as in the case in the economic sphere, women *mudéjares* – even single women – can be found aggressively and publicly litigating both against members of their

309 See p. 277, above. It is interesting that this collaboration seems to have been most clear in the kingdom of Valencia and in Granada – contested regions, where communal tensions ran high, and where the *mudéjar* men who held positions of authority felt insecure. When the Moriscos of Valencia and Granada called on the Ottomans to rescue them from Christian domination, one of the aspects of the oppression they complained of was that Muslim women were obliged to uncover their faces in public. See G. López de la Plaza, "Las mujeres moriscas," p. 308.

310 See, for example, M. Ruzafa García, "El matrimonio."

311 One must recall that women of all faiths were vulnerable to sexual and physical violence. See, for example, M. de C. García Herrero, "Violencia sexual."

312 For the popular generic identification of Muslim women as prostitutes, see above, p. 343, n. 123.

313 See M. de C. García Herrero, "Prostitución y amancebamiento," and M. Meyerson, "Prostitution of Muslim Women."

314 See p. 331, above. Christian literature at times encouraged the sexual predation against Muslim women; see L. Mirrer, *Women, Jews, and Muslims*, p. 51.

315 See C. Barceló Torres, "Mujeres, campesinas," p. 217, for the case of a Muslim minstrel attempting to put a *mudéjar* girl to work as a prostitute.

own community and against non-Muslims in such cases, Islamicate ideals of feminine restraint and passivity notwithstanding.[316]

As a consequence of their gender, subject Muslim women likely enjoyed a far broader and more intimate spectrum of contact and interaction with Christians and Jews than their male counterparts did. The factors that contributed to this are manifold, but a shared sense of vulnerability and marginalization, the common sense of the challenges of child-raising, and the empathy that emerges as a consequence of facing the same medical risks, social stigmas, and physiological rhythms associated with reproduction may have been a factor. Most women, whatever their religious identity, lived their lives in domestic environments that were broadly similar. At the same time their public activities, centered as they tended to be on a common "feminised topography" shaped by the market, the bathhouse, and the well, provided a medium for frequent and unguarded contact and interaction with women from outside their own community.[317] Gender, like vocation and class, served as a "cross-cutting circle" – an affiliation out of which would have emerged informal and mutating communities of women as well as long-term personal friendships that ran across communal boundaries.[318]

### *The world of women*

Most remarkably – at least in terms of cultural power – Muslim women seem to have enjoyed greater status in these relationships across Latin Christendom, with the probable exception of the kingdom of Hungary. From the kingdom of Jerusalem to Sicily and to Portugal, it is Christian women who actively turn to their *mudéjar* counterparts for models of

[316] For example, in 1295, Hale, a woman from Cocentaina, denounced a Christian for raping her daughter, Muhdia, and demanded he be punished according to the *Furs*. Single Muslim women also took people to court, as in the case of Fotox, a woman of the same town, who pursued Musse, a Jew, for having thrown a rock at her in the street. See I. O'Connor de los Angeles, "Muslim Mudéjar Women," pp. 62–63.

[317] See M. Green, "Conversing with the Minority," pp. 106–10, for informal networks of interfaith women. For "feminised topography," see C. Newman Goldy, "A Thirteenth-Century Anglo-Jewish Woman," p. 144, and P. Skinner, "Spatial Relations: Mapping Interfaith Interaction through Topography and Material culture," cited in M. Green, "Conversing with the Minority," p. 109, n. 10.

[318] If Jaume Roig's attitude was at all representative (see above, p. 499) Green's contention that women of all faiths were bound by their common inferiority vis-à-vis masculine culture is undoubtedly correct. See M. Green, "Conversing with the Minority," p. 117, and E. Baumgarten, "'A Separate People'?" p. 216. For women, then, gender comprised a "cross-cutting circle" that served as a framework for solidarity. See G. Simmel, *Conflict*; and P. Blau and J. E. Schwartz, *Cross-Cutting Circles*. Elusive as it is by nature, there is documentary evidence of interfaith female friendships. See, for example, M. J. Fuente Pérez, "Christian, Muslim and Jewish Women," pp. 325–26.

dress, beauty, hygiene, and feminine medical advice and attention, and not the reverse.[319] This is hardly surprising, given the greater sophistication and variety of expression of Islamicate culture in these various fields.[320] Such acculturation was encouraged by women's observance of and participation in each other's public and private celebrations, including religious processions and festivities, weddings, and parties. Here, special foods were prepared, games were played, poetry and stories recited, and songs sung and dances danced.[321] In these contexts, as performers, patrons, and participants, Arabophone Jewish women must have certainly provided one of the bridges or conduits for acculturation, but it is clear from the documentation that *mudéjar* women shared the same broad multilingualism as subject Muslim men and could communicate directly even with monolingual Christians.[322] The widespread use of foreign Muslim slaves would have encouraged bilingualism – of at least a basic functional sort – among Christian women as well.[323] Moreover, the use of Muslim domestic slaves by Christians and the integration of these into the home environment – not infrequently as household managers – would have constituted a powerful vector of low-level acculturation. This must have carried the influence of Islamicate culture far beyond those lands where there were free subject Muslim communities, and into zones that were, in formal terms, homogenously Christian.[324] In sum, it is clear that that Muslim women had a far greater impact on Christian society that Christian women had on *mudéjares*.

This imbalance is the root of the anxieties that these sororal relationships provoked among masculine authorities. Clerics like Jacques de Vitry, the reactionary Bishop of Acre, thundered against those who adopted Eastern habits, preachers like Vicent Ferrer warned against the Muslim contagion, and moralists like Francesc Eiximenis specifically instructed young girls

319 See, for example, p. 491, n. 270, and p. 501, n. 305, above.

320 See M. Green, "Conversing with the Minority," p. 106; C. Barceló Torres, "Mujeres, campesinas," p. 21; A. Metcalfe, *Muslims of Medieval Italy*, pp. 226ff; and C. Caballero-Navas, "The Care of Women's Health."

321 See, for example, M. J. Fuente Pérez, "Christian, Muslim and Jewish Women," p. 328; and C. Carrete Parrondo and M. F. García Casar, *El tribunal*, p. 157.

322 See, for example, E. Gutwirth, "A Song and Dance."

323 M. Green, "Conversing with the Minority," p. 112.

324 *Ibid.* Citing Balard and Stuard's studies, Green notes that from the thirteenth to the fifteenth centuries, the percentage of slaves who were women in Genoa rose from 62.9 percent to 85.5 percent, and that most of these would be domestics under the control of and interacting with Christian women – an undoubtedly powerful motor for acculturation and influence. (That said, not all of these women were Muslims, particularly in the later centuries.) See M. Balard, "La femme-esclave," and S. M. Stuard, "Ancillary Evidence."

against socializing with Muslims and Jews.[325] From the thirteenth century onwards warnings had been issued against employing Muslim wet-nurses, even those who were slaves or nominally converted to Christianity – a practice common all along the northern shore of the Latin Mediterranean.[326] As the fifteenth century ended and the mass conversions of the Iberian Peninsula blurred the ethno-social barriers between Muslims and Christians, this practice became even more widespread and dangerous, providing a means by which crypto-Muslim *conversas* could infiltrate Christian homes.[327] The amulets, incantations, and prayers that formed part of Muslim and Morisca midwives' and *curanderas*' toolkits were increasingly perceived as diabolical or heretical, and not the manifestations of an erroneous but legitimate religion.[328] Nevertheless, as was the case with wet-nurses, neither formal legislation nor pressure from religious authorities curbed their employment, even among the Christian elite. Finally, broad prohibitions were passed against socializing with Christians and the holding of Islamicate festivals – laws that were aimed specifically at Muslim and Morisco women.[329]

To a certain extent, such Christian fears were justified: Muslim women were, in many ways, the true guardians of Islam and Islamicate culture among the subject communities of Latin Christendom. It was women who raised children, who prepared food, and organized festivities, and who provided basic moral, social, religious, and language instruction to young *mudéjares* and Moriscos – fundamentals of that unwritten, quotidian culture that underpinned subject Muslim identity and fomented communal cohesion.[330] It was largely women who shaped and carried the rites and rituals that marked the distinct phases of one's passage through life: birth, marriage, and death. In defiance of the law, they taught their children to pray and perform the *ṣalāt*, and washed the dead – even circumcised boys.[331]

[325] See F. Eiximenis, *Lo libre de les dones*, p. 31.

[326] See R. L. Winer, "Conscripting the Breast."

[327] M. J. Fuente Pérez, "Christian, Muslim and Jewish Women," p. 327.

[328] A. Labarta, "La mujer morisca," p. 226. This is reflected in Valencian legislation of 1329, and in the persecution of *curanderas* as witches. See I. O'Connor de los Angeles, "Muslim Mudéjar Women," p. 66, and F. Segura Urra, *Fazer justícia*, pp. 378–79.

[329] For prohibitions against Muslim women acting as mid-wives and socializing with Christians issued in 1498 in Granada, see G. López de la Plaza, "Las mujeres moriscas," pp. 315ff.

[330] See A. Labarta, "La mujer morisca," p. 227; and C. Barceló Torres, "Mujeres, campesinas," p. 216. This is analogous to the role played by Christian women in ninth-century al-Andalus, as revealed in the episode of the "voluntary martyrs" of Córdoba. See J. Coope, *The Martyrs of Córdoba*.

[331] A. Labarta, "La mujer morisca," p. 229. In pre-conquest al-Andalus, there had been renowned women poets, scholars of *hadīth*, and calligraphers. See M. L. Ávila, "Mujeres 'sabias.'" For midwives performing circumcisions, see L. García Ballester, "The Minority of Morisco Physicians," p. 216.

Moreover, women's religious and scientific knowledge was sophisticated and respected. Both those who served the Christian aristocracy and their own communities as midwives, were powerful figures, and even in the male-dominated world of Islamic jurisprudence there were women, like Nuzay Calderán and the "*mora* of Úbeda," who gained considerable renown.[332] For each of these exceptional figures who made it into the historical record, there must have been scores more, operating on a local level, who did not.

After 1500 and the suppression of Islam in the Iberian Peninsula, the role of women as resisters of Christian religious aggression became even clearer.[333] They conspired to hide religious and literary texts from the authorities (in contrast to their acquiescent menfolk) – acts that were all the more striking considering that many of these women would have been illiterate and unable to relate directly to the books they so passionately defended.[334] For them, persisting in their folk customs and rituals became an explicit and deliberate strategy of defiance.[335] Hence, in the sixteenth century Christian authorities focused sharply on suppressing Morisco women's traditional practices. Thus, in the context of this legislation, for the Moriscas of Granada and Valencia, like many Muslim women in twenty-first century France and Quebec, covering the face became an act of liberation and independence.

And, indeed, it was in Valencia (in contrast to less confrontational and contested environments like Old Castile, Aragon, and Navarre) where female resistance was most deeply entrenched. There were no Morisco nuns in Valencia.[336] In sixteenth-century court and inquisition processes held in the kingdom, fully half of the women who were interrogated could not, or claimed they could not, speak *Algemía* (i.e. Romance vernacular). And there were a considerable number of women who did go to trial: over five hundred, or 27 percent of the total accused between 1566 and 1620 – a striking number, given the cloistered isolation from Christian

[332] See p. 397, above; also J.-P. Molénat, "Privilégiées ou poursuives," and C. Barceló Torres, "Mujeres, campesinas," p. 217.

[333] The fact that the Inquisition often focused on women shows that the clerical authorities were aware of the religious prestige that Morisco women carried. See, for example, the persecution of the women of the Compañero family, in L. F. Bernabé Pons, "On Morisco Networks," p. 131; and, generally, J. Fournel-Guérin, "Un famille morisque."

[334] See R. E. Surtz, "Morisco Women."

[335] In sixteenth-century Granada women continued to maintain Islamicate social customs including wearing the veil, applying henna to the hands, and conducting traditional cultural rituals at weddings and baptisms. A. Labarta, "La mujer morisca," p. 225; and G. López de la Plaza, "Las mujeres moriscas," pp. 308 and 311.

[336] A. Labarta, "La mujer morisca," p. 221.

society and authority that many of these chose or were obliged to live in.[337] The capacity of these women, many little more than children, to face interrogation and duel with inquisitors, is impressive.[338] When Esperança Ratal of Benimodo (Valencia), the fourteen-year-old wife of Bartolomé Gazi, appeared before the Inquisitor Pedro de Carete in 1574 and was asked if she wanted to be a Muslim or a Christian from that time forward, she answered "that which the God and his lordship commands."[339]

## Cultural identity, religious difference, and social relations

And Johannes Siscar, farmer, inhabitant of the town of Fuentes, recently converted, an ex-Hagarene, was questioned under oath ... Asked if he knew that the said Fatima had been Christian, he responded and said, "yes."

And how did he know it?

He knew it by rumor and by her own admission, that she herself told him. And that she went by the name "Ursula."

And the said Fatima told him that she [became] Christian in the place called Belchite, because a Muslim threatened her, and he was called Audella de Figuera and he was married to the said Fatima ...

And a party called Amet, a Muslim, told the deponent that when [Fatima] was in his power she had converted to Christianity in Valencia.

And, moreover, he knows that a little bit after Saint John's day one year past, she had married a Muslim named Yuciron de Letux in Oserra ... (Inquisition regarding Ursula/Fatima, a "public woman" from Vall d'Almonacid, Valencia (June 10, 1484)[340])

Reading the formal documents and historical sources of the medieval Latin West, ethno-religious identity appears concrete, primordial, inescapable, and almost immutable. Scanning the law codes, contracts, and chronicles of Latin Christendom, when Muslims or Jews appear, they are all but inevitably labeled as such – as if reminders and confirmations of their subordinate status, of their difference, and of their exclusion from normative society, were constant. And indeed, the societies of the Middle Ages were openly and confidently chauvinistic in terms of religious community. The formal regulations and institutions of Latin Christendom (and the Islamic world) including those relating to law, administration,

337 The inquisition in Valencia tried 525 women, or 27 percent of the total trials in the period 156–1620. See A. Labarta, "La mujer morisca," pp. 221 and 224; R. E. Surtz, "Morisco Women," p. 421.
338 See, for example, B. Vincent, "Et quelques voix de plus," pp. 141–42.
339 *Ibid.*, p. 145.
340 M. L. Ledesma Rubio, *Vidas mudéjares*, pp. 61–62. For more on Fatima, see C. Villanueva Muerte, "Las mujeres mudéjares," pp. 515–19.

fiscal regimen, personal morality, social interaction, and conscience, were all predicated on the legitimacy and validity of a narrow range of religious ideals and interpretations. These were explicitly and deliberately hierarchical societies, wherein religious out-groups – to the extent they were accommodated – were held to be of secondary status, and subject to the authority of the dominant "majority." It was an arrangement that resonated with the ideals and expectations of all involved, both minorities and members of the community that wielded political/military power. It was a world in which the prerogatives of the group were seen as paramount, and in which loyalty and constancy, even to an illegitimate religious ideology or community, were considered signs of honor and virtue.

On the other hand, as the present chapter has shown, Latin Christian society was also an arena for social and economic interaction that crossed communal lines, and the locus of powerful and multivalent currents of acculturation. For all that separated them, Muslims and Christians (and Jews), spoke the same languages, held many of the same social values, ate many of the same foods, and even shared much by the way of folk tradition, religious belief, and theological orientation. Their cultures and actions were characterized by a "mutual intelligibility" that emerged from the broad socio-cultural *habitus* – originating with common sources, but refracted distinctly through the specific traditions of each ethno-religious culture – within which Christians, Muslims, and Jews all lived their lives and pursued their agendas, whether individual or communal.[341] Even as they worked to maintain their particular religio-cultural identities, they borrowed freely from each other's traditions, did business with each other, and socialized with each other, however askance Christian authorities or those of their own communities might regard this. It took until 1368 for Carlos II to ban the Jews and Muslims of Navarre from gambling at the *tafurería* of Tudela, the only legal casino in his kingdom, and probably then to little effect.[342] Their ready ability to communicate linguistically, intuitively and culturally, at once stimulated the collaboration and interdependence of Christians, Muslims, and Jews, and presented dangers. Close relations could be volatile, and in many circumstances provoked or demanded the need for Christians to reinforce the formal hierarchy of communities by exhibiting their generic superiority or actively marginalizing the minorities.

The point at which simple *human* collaboration became *communal* engagement varied according to time, locale, and circumstance; however,

[341] Here, I refer to Bourdieu's sense of *habitus*, see, for example, P. Bourdieu, *Distinction*, and Z. Navarro, "In Search."

[342] F. Segura Urra, "Los mudéjares navarros," p. 254.

a general pattern emerges that reflects both the ease with which individuals of different ethno-religious communities could engage with each other and the conflicted nature that often tended to characterize such exchanges. The degree to which a type of transaction relates to the religious practice might be termed "ritual content." Some transactions by their nature are mundane, and do not demand actors or agents to conceive of themselves in religious terms. For example, were a Muslim to purchase an article of clothing or some other innocuous commodity from a party who happened to be Christian (or vice versa), this would not necessarily provoke the parties to consider their own or the other's religious identity. This would have been true for many quotidian exchanges, which would have been carried out unproblematized by issues of communal hierarchy. More formal or complex economic exchanges – the taking of a loan, the purchase of landed property, the establishment of a relationship of tenancy or vassalship, however, would have demanded the parties consider their religious identity, if for no other reason than it would have figured in any contract that was signed, or whatever other legal choreography was required, and would have determined to a degree the respective rights or obligations of each.

Activities such as the exercise of justice and the payment of taxes embodied an even greater formality, and a commensurately greater degree of ritual content. When one went to court against a member of a different religious community, the choice of jurisdiction, the value of one's testimony, the standards of evidence, and process and procedure, all brought each party's ethno-religious identity towards the foreground. Court was never a neutral space in this regard. And as the individuals involved were forced to think of themselves as "Muslims" or "Christians," they were obliged to act like Muslims or Christians – to take on a role and adopt a position that reflected their communal status, whether or not this reflected their personal inclination.

Moreover, the formal communal hierarchy needed to be acknowledged to the degree that ethno-religious identity was evoked and recognized as relevant to the transaction in question. This, in turn, demanded that the majority or dominant-group party exhibit his or her superiority over the out-group party, and that the minority party acquiesce in recognition of his or her own subjugation. In other words, the greater the ritual content inherent in a specific transaction, the greater the gulf between the two parties' ideological regimes, and the greater the ritual incompatibility of the two parties in this particular context. And the greater the ritual incompatibility, the more the Christian party was obliged or invited to exercise the privilege of superiority by exercising the rights and advantages due to the members of the superior caste.

Hence, transactions that for both parties embodied the highest degree of ritual content became impossible to carry out except within the framework of the explicit subjugation of the minority party. To engage in such transactions outside of the framework of domination was to challenge the established order and the privilege of the majority, and would invite visceral and violent reaction. For example, consensual inter-communal sexual relations were extremely problematic in this society, and inter-communal marriage became functionally impossible. Apostasy or out-group religious conversion carried an even greater ritual component and hence represented an even greater taboo. Therefore, when such transactions did take place, they happened illicitly, and this demanded a reaction on the part of communal authorities, unless they were prepared to turn a blind eye. Such a reaction might come in the form of formal prosecution (however little the institutions of power may have been pre-occupied with such matters), an informal or popular show of authority, or perhaps, violence.

By way of illustration, transactions of different types can be mapped out on a graph that indicates the amount of ritual content embodied in each. This yields the ritual differential or incompatibility inherent in the transaction, and indicates the degree to which Christian domination would need to be expressed as a consequence. In Figure 2 (below), an activity such as "farming" (e.g. in which a Muslim rents a field from a Christian, or vice-

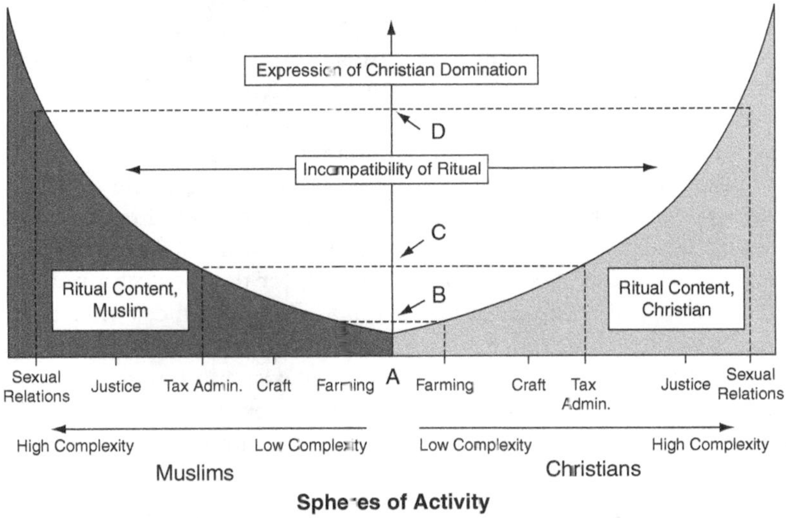


Figure 2 Ritual divergence and expression of domination

versa), has a low ritual differential (B) and, therefore, does not demand an explicit expression of Christian superiority (B–D). Tax administration (e.g. the integration of a *mudéjar* community in a Christian fiscal framework) carries considerably more ideological baggage, and therefore reflects a greater incompatibility (C) and a commensurately more explicit and formal expression of Christian domination (C–A) and *mudéjares*' acknowledgement of their own subordination. Finally, the wide differential (D) that characterizes sexual relations between members of different faiths demands a most firm and rigid reiteration of the communal hierarchy (D–A).

Naturally, while the foregoing diagram illustrates a basic operating principle of inter-communal relations, it is a rather drastic simplification. A number of factors contributed to both the degree of ritual incompatibility and the expression of domination/subordination. For example, transactions were not necessarily symmetrical in terms of ritual content. Buying meat carried far more ideological import for a Muslim than for a Christian. Hence, for a Muslim to purchase food from a Christian butcher might not elicit an expression of Christian domination, but it would almost certainly provoke a sense of Islamic subordination. The time and place of transactions also mattered. If an exchange took place on a Friday or Sunday, the ideological stake for either party might vary; so too, for transactions that took place in a church or at mosque. The general ideological climate of the specific time or locale in which a transaction was carried out was also important; what might be regarded as innocuous exchange in one environment might be perceived as provocative in another, where audience expectations (whether on the part of Christians, Muslims, or both) varied, or where minority groups or those who interacted with them were perceived or presented as bearing a stigma. An atmosphere of fear of violence or of attack (whether by local Christians or foreign Muslims), or a situation of entrenched economic competition, might heighten sensitivities and provoke a more acute expression of domination or subordination than a given transaction might elicit within the context of a more stable environment. In any event, it is clear that the overwhelming bulk of daily transactions that Christians and Muslims engaged in with each other were those of the lower scale of complexity and were for the most part unproblematic in terms of ethno-religious identity. This dynamic, rather than a deliberate or conscious sense of "tolerance," was what permitted these communal groups, Muslim and Christian, to coexist and interact as constituents of a larger society. It was also what provoked the failure of the Morisco experiment. The forced conversion of Spain's Muslims raised sensibilities to such a degree that virtually every transaction came to be perceived in communal terms. Integration was impossible, and interaction was fraught.

Nevertheless, one should not necessarily confuse acculturation and interaction with affection or affinity; as Glick has astutely pointed out, conflict can serve as a catalyst for acculturation. The predations of the Latin aristocracy and Italian traders and the polemical impulse of a chauvinistic Christian clergy were some of the most powerful engines that drove the adaptation and appropriation of Islamic culture, science, and technology in "the West." Nor should we mistake an affinity for the accouterments of a foreign culture as a validation of its principles. Fulchers of Chartres' Orientalized Frankish knights (see p. 142, above) were the medieval equivalent of the male youth of Islamic south Asia wearing baseball caps and blue jeans; they are drawn to the power and the prosperity such items signify in their imagination, but by wearing them they are not necessarily signaling an aspiration to be Americans or engage with American values in any profound sense. Nor do the Hip-Hop fashion and "ghetto" affectations of the white suburban youth of the USA reflect a personal affinity or empathy for their African-American fellow citizens whose aesthetic they happily commodify and appropriate. On the other hand, nor is an apparent lack of acculturation or adaptation necessarily symptomatic of tension, animosity, or disengagement between ethno-religious communities. Indeed, indifference to out-groups may be interpreted as the most significant indicator of confidence, self-assurance, and social stability.

In the end, it was the symbiotic and informal character of so much of Muslim–Christian relations in the Latin West that provided for the persistence and prosperity of subject Muslim communities. And the most stable and secure *mudéjar* societies were characterized by the most diverse array of relationships of interdependence.[343] If contemporary research is any indicator, it appears that the type of quotidian social contact and economic and institutional integration discussed in this chapter encouraged Christians to adopt more positive attitudes towards their Muslim neighbors. The anxiety provoked by out-group contact decreased with familiarity and the bar of "expression of domination" was, thereby, pushed downwards.[344] Moreover, networks tend to be self-reinforcing; they become more stable and valuable the broader and more entrenched they become. In sum, interaction on the human level was what held together Christian and Muslim societies and sustained ethno-religious diversity in medieval Latin Christendom. It functioned both as a necessary and sufficient cause for the survival of subject Muslim communities there.

We must remember that the history of the Muslim communities of Latin Christendom is also one of individual human beings, and is therefore

[343] See below, pp. 524ff.
[344] See, for example, P. Hutchison and H. E. S. Rosenthal, "Prejudice Against Muslims."

characterized by all of the complexity, inconsistency, and self-contradiction that this entails. As primary and concrete as religious identity may have been, for "ordinary" people going about their daily business it remained fluid and situational, and comprised only one of many vectors of self-identification they might conjure up or be carried away by in any given circumstance. These people were Muslims or Christians, but they were also members of a profession, a social class, an age group, and a gender, subjects of a lord, inhabitants of a locale, associates of a parish or a mosque, of a confraternity, an *aljama*, or a municipality, subjects of a king, speakers of a vernacular, adherents of a particular approach to spirituality, and of a particular vision of society, and so on. These various vectors of self--realization crossed communal lines and engendered solidarity among members of distinct ethno-religious affiliations. Moreover, not only did individuals participate in many of these modes of identity simultaneously, they often recognized this, and – as was the case with Fāṭima/Ursula – were prepared to move between them as it suited their needs, whether in pursuit of long-term agendas or in response to immediate necessity or opportunity.

We must ask then, what makes a sectarian episode? How can we presume that the reports of Christians perpetrating acts of violence against Muslims or Jews, or Muslims against Jews or Christians that appear with regularity in the documentary record relate to events that have anything but the most passing connection to religious identity, even if the actors themselves present them this way? What are we to make of a the trial in 1364 of two Christians and eight Muslims for the murder of two Jews near Lleida?[345] There are no easy answers. Often the identities of the victims and perpetrators were incidental, or the events themselves were sparked by tensions or conflicts that had absolutely nothing to do with religious belief or identity, but were rooted in long-standing economic, legal, or personal disputes in which the opposing parties only happened to be members of different ethno-religious communities.[346] As the psychologist R. D. Laing observed, "the person who moves through different pluralities in a pluralistic society functions in different modes, even simultaneously."[347]

345 The incident, which took place in the hamlet of Ajabut, involved the local bailiff, another Christian, and eight Muslim inhabitants; the three victims are unnamed. J. Boswell, *The Royal Treasure*, p. 431.

346 See, for example. B. Catlos, *The Victors and the Vanquished*, pp. 207 and 319.

347 R. D. Laing, *The Politics of the Family*, p. 12

# Postscript: *Convivencia*, intolerance . . . or "questions badly put"?

> Above all, let us maintain, because it is like a guardian and is alone able to illuminate the over-dense history of an age pregnant with several centuries of struggle and conflict, let us maintain the great principle of discrimination. There is religion and there are churches, the domain of ecclesiastical and political organization on the one hand, the domain of the internal life and spiritual freedom on the other . . . What is happening . . . is that all the drama which constitutes the true greatness of the history. . . is being shut out – that drama, which for thousands of consciences tormented with scruples and divided between contrary obligations, set the need for social discipline against the free aspirations of individual conscience.
>
> Lucien Febvre, *Une question mal posée?* (1929)[1]

This is not the book I imagined I would write several years ago when I proposed the project to Cambridge University Press. Already confident that I knew a fair bit about subject Muslims in Latin Christian society, I imagined that I could knock off a general survey fairly easily and so complete my first post-tenure monograph in good time. The Devil, however, is in the details – particularly when it comes to the history of the *mudéjares*. The more I read, the less I found I knew, and the more I realized that virtually every apparently safe generalization I had planned to make needed to be tempered, qualified, and contextualized, if not simply rejected. (And, even so, I am well aware that my fellow *mudéjarists* will be able to marshal legions of counter-examples to the general picture I have set forth here.) This is a consequence not only of the great variety of *mudéjar* experience, which spanned centuries, continents, and a dozen regional cultures, but of the tremendous and uneven array of sources (each with its own perspectives, biases, problems, and opportunities) at our disposal – sources that when read side-by-side may at first (or even second) blush, appear to present varying or contradictory evidence. As a consequence, the scholar of the history of the *mudéjares* is forced to go beyond the obvious, to dig deeper, to discard presumptions, and to

[1] L. Febvre, "The Origins of the French Reformation: A Badly-Put Question?," pp. 87–88.

stumble through alien methodological ground that is unfamiliar and perhaps even suspicious. There are no easy answers, but one must begin, as Febvre belabored, with the right questions.

We tend to think of history as something that can be expressed in some sort of narrative form; but we expect narratives to have a clear structure on which they hang – whether it be the experiences of a political elite or dynasty (as in the histories of kings), or the evolution of unifying institutions or common cultural practices. These are notably lacking in the history of the subject Muslims of Latin Christendom, except on the most local level, and even there they are elusive. Moreover, this is a history of a "people" (or "peoples") that was so diverse that in many contexts they cannot be approached as anything but particular manifestations of only the vaguest unity. This may be frustrating, but it is also liberating. Freed of the tyranny of an established meta-narrative, one can explore a history more complex and subtle, more open to alternative interpretations and perspectives, and one that is not so heavily burdened by expectations and preconceptions. It also invites one to adopt a multi-dimensional methodology – one that does not attempt to hammer the evidence of so many diverse sources into a unified whole, but rather that follows each down their particular pathways, divergent or even incompatible as these may seem. Febvre may have been talking about the French Reformation when he evoked the tremendous gulf between the world of the ideologues and the strivings of the peasants, burghers, and noblemen, who each in the pursuit of their own agendas transformed the world they lived in, but he might well have been talking about the multi-confessional societies of the medieval Latin Mediterranean.

Given all of this, and considering the complexity and variety of the historical experience of subject Muslims of Latin Christendom, if all that I have done in the preceding pages is provide a survey in the most general terms, an approximation of their experience and their place in the history of Europe and the West, then I will consider this endeavor to have been worth the effort. To return to my Foreword: this is not a history of heroes, of grandiose monuments, of grand triumphs, or ringing victories, but of peoples who were conquered and colonized by force, who were maintained apart, whose role in the development of the larger societies in which they lived was inevitably secondary, and whose ultimate destiny was absorption, exile, and extinction. Nevertheless, theirs is an important story (or stories) and deserves to be told, even imperfectly, but as much as possible on its own terms, and not subject to the retroactive colonization of an uncritical and self-absorbed academy. In sum, the call that Febvre made eighty-seven years ago vis-à-vis the study of the century of the French Reformation, is a fitting sentiment for our study today of the centuries of the multi-confessional, Mediterranean Middle Ages: "We must not swerve from a comprehensive study of that century that was so full of consequences. No single generation of historians will be able to complete it. All the more reason to concentrate our efforts and not to waste them in sterile repetition."[2]

## A distant, shattered mirror

Christians in the eleventh century were not paranoid fanatics. Muslims really were gunning for them. While Muslims can be peaceful, Islam was born in war and grew the same way. From the time of Mohammed, the means of Muslim expansion was always the sword ... in traditional Islam, Christian and Jewish states must be destroyed and their lands conquered ... From the safe distance of many centuries, it is easy enough to scowl in disgust at the Crusades ... Whether we admire the Crusaders or not, it is a fact that the world we know today would not exist without their efforts. The ancient faith of Christianity, with its respect for women and antipathy toward slavery, not only survived but flourished. Without the Crusades, it might well have followed Zoroastrianism, another of Islam's rivals, into extinction. (Thomas Madden, "The Real History of the Crusades" (April 2002)[3])

The distance of time may make some uncomfortable subjects easier to address, but that is evidently not the case with Muslim–Christian relations in the Middle Ages. The events of 9/11, the long history of Western colonization and subjugation of North Africa and the Muslim Near East, Zionism and the Palestinian "problem," the war in Iraq (and the apparently impending war in Iran), "jihadism," al-Qaeda, programs of Christian mission and Western "modernization," academic and popular "Orientalism," notions of papal infallibility, and of European superiority, not to mention plain old nativism, self-righteous religious prejudice, racism, and chauvinism, or the often equally visceral reactions against all of these, whether nostalgic or deliberately corrective, make it difficult even for scholars to take a detached view of the history of the era of the Christian–Muslim conflict and Latin irredentism. But the resulting debates disguise what are, perhaps, more fundamental intellectual divergences. Some of us are Platonic in temperament, and believe in the ultimate reality, extemporality, and creative force of historical "forms": "Christianity," "Islam," "Europe," and "the East." Others, more Aristotelian by inclination, deny that these are anything but categories – convenient, artificial, and *a posteriori*. Most of us, whatever our personal beliefs, allow our moral and political values to intrude on and misshape our analysis, either consciously, in the service of what we imagine is a greater good, or as unexamined certainties, even when

[2] *Ibid.*, p. 88. [3] T. Madden, "The Real History of the Crusades."

they run counter not only to what we know is true, but what is manifestly evident.

Thus, some historians produce exculpatory rationalizations of conquest, massacre, and oppression, grounding these variably in claims of self-defense, moral superiority, or notions of the inevitability of "civilizational" conflict, while others evoke nostalgic visions of an enlightened age of innocence, *convivencia*, and inter-communal, boundary-bending "love." Or not. "Muslims *can* be peaceful." Indeed. Presumably, as with the subject Muslims of this book, what they require is a healthy dose of a more rigorous sort of Christian "love" – "tough love," as it were, which it is presumably "the White Man's burden" to dispense. In the end, these countervailing idealizations of the past do not move us towards a new synthesis, but lead to ever-more determined retrenchments of positions that the spokespersons of each camp regard as *a priori*. As such, scholars who fall into this trap – the trap of projecting their own morality on the peoples of the past – run the danger of becoming sophists, and of revealing far more about themselves than about the people they set out to study. To a certain extent such distortions are inevitable – a consequence of the nature of the historical discipline and the challenge in reconciling evidence which, by its character as much as its content, appears to be contradictory. What we all have in common is that we run the danger of shutting out the drama of history – the drama that lies between the hermetically sealed declarations of contemporary ideologues, and the mundane yet powerful choices that reflect the strivings of ordinary people grappling with the tension between the aspirations instilled in them and the limitations they faced.

Because of the nature and number of sources at our disposal, the historiographical problem is all the more acute and obvious when the subject of study is the Muslim minorities of Latin Christendom. This is a people (or peoples) who produced almost no literature that has survived – with the exception of the Moriscos, the final, localized, and particular manifestation of subject Muslim society in Latin Christendom. And this is evidence that can only be "read backwards" or applied to other regions with the greatest of care, and which itself lay buried, sometimes quite literally, for the most part until our own time. Moreover, these works reflect the preoccupations and agendas of a very narrow and specific literary set, and are so burdened with the formality of genre, and the expectations of their authors and audience, that their wider interpretation becomes problematic. The *mudéjar* scarcely exists in the first person in either Arabic, Latin, or Romance texts, except as exile, object, or the accused, and even then almost only through the medium of Christian scribes and the filter of Christian institutions. Like the subject Muslim of the third person, he or she is discernable only through multiple layers of mediation, intervention, conservation, and editorial manipulation, not to mention the random and unpredictable role of fate and circumstance. Thus, we have been left only with a small fraction of the historical record, while the rest has succumbed to the effects of flood, fire, war, revolution, or indifference. Add to this the fact that modern historians, editors, and archivists have edited, selected, abridged, translated, and interpreted the surviving evidence through their own particular political, cultural, national, ethno-religious, and gender lenses, and the picture is rendered even less clear.

Given such a yawning gulf between ourselves and these people whom we study, to talk of the feelings and aspirations of people so remote is very risky, and the temptation to regard every incident and episode that involves a Christian and a Muslim as a "Christian–Muslim" encounter is to presume much. A Christian may attack a Muslim or vice versa for any number of reasons, many of which will have no relation to religious identity. In most cases, terse reports of incidents with little context or detail, we can have no idea of the motives or tensions that lay behind them. It is only when one analyzes a great deal of evidence and over a long period of time that conclusions of this type can be drawn, even tentatively.

In sum, there exists a tremendous range of evidence, all of it compelling in its own way, but almost all of it ambiguous, and subject to multiple readings and interpretations. It is as if in seeking to understand the past of this distant, vanished people, we reach out to pluck up the slivers of a shattered mirror, and in regarding each, see some distorted fraction of ourselves, which we carefully arrange with others into what seems to us to be a coherent representation of the past. Shards of love, and shards of hate . . . of hope, of fear, and pride . . . of shame. The pursuit of empirical proof, of evidence, becomes an exercise that is at once obligatory, yet futile. It may be, indeed, that History must be grounded in some sense of objective fact, but how can our evidence be read objectively when we can so easily make of it what we will, and when our conclusions so obviously reflect our own agendas and anachronistic preoccupations, no matter how well intentioned? History exhibits a "quantum effect" similar, if less obvious, to that of anthropology, in that the mere act of observing, and the presence of the observer, shapes the evidence as she perceives it. The mere act of framing a question, whether "badly put" or not, determines to a great extent the answer one will arrive at.

Perhaps, then, rather than striving for a two-dimensional realism, neatly verisimilar but inevitably incomplete, we should seek as historians to be ever-conscious of the limitations of our methodologies and disciplines, and thereby avoid producing a caricature while laboring to paint a portrait. Or perhaps, even better, we should embrace a multi-dimensional approach to such a history, not only balancing the meta-narrative with local histories, mentalities with practica, and ideologies with policy, but admitting the possibility of simultaneous yet divergent historical "truths," arising not only out of our own subjectivity but out of those of the people who we are studying. We should not expect the people of the past to be any more coherent, consistent, or comprehensible than those of today. Better, then, perhaps, for the historian to abandon the impossible futility of realism and embrace a cubist approach, and to approach historical reality (such as it can be apprehended) deliberately and consciously through a variety of perspectives – to strive to be a Picasso, rather than a Courbet.

## Diversity, equilibrium, and *conveniencia*

And they should be righteously admonished [for protecting] those Muslims on account of these seven evils that [the Muslims] were inflicting on Christians: some they robbed, others they led into captivity, others they wounded, others they mutilated, others they frightened with swords, others they converted to their sect and implored them to deny the law of Christ, and nourished many in this to a great degree, and they carried off the wives of Christians and deflowered virgins, joining to them in unhappy concubinage ... This Lucera was captured and its walls destroyed by this admonishment ... but, O woe!, nevertheless there remained only Muslims there, and these under [the king's] protection ... Those Muslims should have been all thrown out from the land just as an accursed thing, so that none would remain, but some [Christians], captive to the desire of gold and silver and precious cloths, protected them, on the grounds of the benefit the king could derive from them, should they remain in his land ... (Eudes de Châteauroux, *Sermo de rebellion Sarracenorum Lucherie in Apulia* (1268–69)[4])

In preaching the Crusade against Lucera – an isolated and vulnerable island of a few thousand Muslims living within a sea of Christians – the Cardinal-Bishop of Frascati evoked the Israelites' destruction of Jericho, and their subsequent punishment by God on the grounds that – in defiance of His will (which was to exterminate the inhabitants) – Achan, of the tribe of Judah, had spared "Rahab the harlot" and her family, having coveted "a goodly Babylonish garment, and two hundred shekels of silver, and a wedge of gold of fifty shekels weight." In order to appease his angry God, Joshua had Achan and his entire family and all their livestock stoned to death and then burnt (Joshua 6–7). Some millennia later and a continent away, Charles of Anjou spared the Lucerans destruction after his defeat of Manfred in 1266 on the condition they destroy their town walls

4 "Sermon on the Rebellion of the Muslims of Lucera in Apulia," in C. Maier, "Crusade and Rhetoric," pp. 380–81 {Sermon 2, lines 58–76}.

and hand over the deposed King's treasure that they were holding. But in 1268 they rose up in support of the last Hohenstaufen pretender, Conradín. Thus, Eudes's message was clear – if Charles, the Angevin king, whom the Cardinal styled as Joshua, were to behave like the Hohenstaufen Achans he had overthrown, he would bring God's wrath down on his people as a consequence of his greed.[5]

Eudes was a verteran of the culture wars. Cistercian abbot, Chancellor of the University of Paris, Dean of the College of Cardinals, and comrade on Crusade of Louis IX, he not only served as prosecutor at the trial of the Talmud in Paris in 1240, but defied Innocent IV's order in 1242 to return to the Jews any copies that had escaped the flames – all in the name of the greater Good.[6] For Eudes, the Talmud was "the most important reason why the Jews remain obstinate in their perfidy," and for Eudes, the existence of a free Muslim colony within Christendom represented an inexcusable perversion, whatever immediate, worldly good it might seem to serve.[7] No less than modern intellectual ideologues and partisan historians, he was prepared to twist the truth or lie in the service of what he regarded as a greater truth. And, in fact, his attitude reflected a sentiment remarkably close to that of rigorous Muslim jurists when they regarded subject Muslim societies; for them worldly comfort and prosperity were no excuse for willingly remaining under the rule of Infidel princes.[8] Or, as a thirteenth-century Aragonese *mudéjar* preacher put it, "love of this world and longing to remain in it [is] the summit of all sin," before warning:

> God Almighty said, "whoever was yearning after the life in this world, we shall make it fast and easy for him in it and [give him] whatever he desires. Then we shall prepare for him a dark, reprehensible, gloomy Inferno. And whoever sought after the hereafter and strove for it with great effort, he is a true believer. They shall have their efforts gratified."[9]

Both Eudes de Châteauroux and the unsympathetic *muftūn* of the *dār al-Islām* expressed the essence of the paradox that was the foundation of the experience of the Muslim communities of Latin Christendom. They should not have existed. Neither Latin Christianity nor Islam was ideologically inclined to countenance the existence of a Muslim community living willingly and freely under Christian rule. Such communities persevered, however, and often throve – in those areas that they did – because on the one hand, they were perceived of as valuable, or an "asset" to Christian

[5] For the revolt and the aftermath, see pp. 125ff., above.
[6] S. Grayzel, and K. Stow, *The Church and the Jews*, p. 9.
[7] See Eudes's letters in J. R. Marcus, *The Jew in the Medieval World*, pp. 146–49.
[8] P. S. van Koningsveld and G. Wiegers, "The Islamic Statute," p. 30.
[9] L. G. Jones, "The Boundaries of Sin," pp. 479 and 490.

society or at least its rulers, and because the Muslims themselves felt that life under the Infidel, dangerous and compromising as it might be, provided a more desirable or viable option than emigration. This was not a consequence of a predisposition towards "tolerance," or because of a culture of *convivencia*, but rather, as a result of *conveniencia*. It was a "Principle of Convenience" that operated to establish the Muslim communities as semi-autonomous, legitimate entities within Latin society at the time of their conquest.[10] Bilateral negotiations in which the Latin potential for violence weighed against the need for a productive and complacent Muslim population, rather than ideological priorities, established the fact, and determined the terms of their subjugation. These laid the foundation for the development of Muslim societies that engaged creatively and dynamically with the Christian majorities alongside whom they lived, and that adapted to changing conditions, and continued to evolve institutionally, culturally, and economically. To think of these *mudéjar* societies as decadent or degenerated versions of some ideal "Islamic society," or to analyze their constituents strictly in terms of their religious identity, is to begin by asking "questions badly put." The Latin conquests did not herald the end of Islamic society and culture in Christian lands, it marked the era of the development of a whole series of new Islamic societies.[11] Some endured only briefly, some lasted centuries, but their fate was hardly sealed by the mere fact that they had come under the authority of Christian princes.

## *Conveniencia*, or "the principle of convenience"

Indeed, it is only in the rarest of instances can we see something resembling ideology operating as the root of policies towards Muslims in the Latin Mediterranean. The prohibitions of Canon Lawyers and secular jurists and the fulminations of preachers and missionaries seem to have existed almost within their own sealed world, following their own logic, and with little impact on the social and political practices of princes and their subjects. The "persecuting society" appears for the most part to be little more than a political posture or an intellectual conceit. Of

[10] The "Convenience Principle" or *conveniencia*, is a paradigm for ethno-religious relations I have been developing for some time, and which will be the subject of a coming monograph, *Paradoxes of Plurality: Ethno-Religious Diversity and the Medieval Mediterranean*. See, for example, B. Catlos, "'Accursed, Superior Men,'" "¿'Conflicte entre culturas'?," "Contexto social y 'conveniencia,'" "Mudéjar Ethnogenesis," in *The Victors and the Vanquished*, pp. 390–408, and the forthcoming *Paradoxes of Plurality*.

[11] See the discussion of "Mudéjar Ethnogenesis," in B. Catlos, *The Victors and the Vanquished*, pp. 390–93.

course, that is not quite the case. Ideology and law provided a structure for conceiving of the place of Muslims in Latin society, and whether or not their dictates were acted upon consistently, they provided a conceptual framework of marginalization, exclusion, and violence that could be invoked instinctively or deployed deliberately by institutions, collectives, and individuals in times of spiritual anxiety, social stress, or political and economic competition.[12] Christianity and Islam – scriptural, redemptory, revealed religions, that regard themselves not only as universal but unique in their veracity and validity – cannot contemplate the notion of religious equality. Legitimizing diversity demanded the establishment of a hierarchy and the subjugation and marginalization of minority out-groups.[13]

But, whereas the religious elites of Muslim and Christian society were all but unanimously chauvinistic, and hostile to the notion of diversity (at least when they were expressing themselves dogmatically, or in terms of their faith), ordinary people (including members of these same elites, when they were not thinking or expressing themselves on ideological terms) could be quite indifferent to the religious identity of their neighbors and fellow subjects. As proposed in the conclusion of chapter 10, the way that people conceived of themselves and of members of religious out-groups depended on various factors, including the nature of the transaction they were engaged in, the attitude and expectations of their audience of peers, and the advantage they felt they might derive from expressing themselves in terms of religious identity and difference.[14] Hence, within the environment of broader society and the context of

[12] Although the generalities on which his analysis is based have not weathered well in view of the last quarter-century of research, Halperin's reflections on the relationship between pragmatism and ideology still have merit. See C. Halperin, "The Ideology of Silence," pp. 464–66.

[13] Islam did indeed develop an institutionalized approach to legitimizing diversity in *dhimma* or the "pact of protection." But *dhimma* was not about equality, it was about the subjugation of certain well-intentioned but erroneous religions. It provided certain basic "constitutional guarantees" but little more; moreover, "humiliation" came to be seen as a key component in the status of non-Muslim minorities. In any event, conditions for *dhimmiyyūn* varied as broadly as conditions for Muslims in the Latin West, who did not enjoy any similar scripturally enshrined rights. At times *dhimmiyyūn* were allowed to participate as near-equals in Islamic societies, even exceeding the role they were limited to under *dhimma*, yet at other times they were subject to brutal and gratuitous oppression and the arbitrary abrogation of their "protection." As was the case in Latin Christendom, dogma and religious "law" came second to mundane factors and pragmatic concerns in shaping the actual experience of religious minorities. The terms "minority" and "majority" as used in this study do not correspond to the relative size or proportion of populations, but rather to groups' roles in society. In Latin Christian society Christians were the "majority" group even when they were outnumbered by non-Latin Christians, because it was they who formally exercised power and held authority in these societies.

[14] See above, pp. 508ff.

quotidian interaction we find a spectrum of relations between Muslims and Christians running from intimate affection and camaraderie, to acculturation and imitation, to rejection and contempt, to the violence of blind fury, and everything in between – often at the same time. Muslims and Christians did business together, entertained and educated each other, created works of art for each other, fought side-by-side against their co-religionists, celebrated together, prayed side-by-side, had sex with each other (consensually or not) and even, evidently, fell in love. They also killed each other, stole from each other, marginalized, abused, oppressed, and expelled each other, or simply ignored each other. Theirs was a charged and volatile sort of intimacy; "love," perhaps, but in a most visceral sense – of the sweating, mounting, possessing type. Through all of this, subject Muslims were certainly the more disadvantaged and vulnerable party, but they were neither passive, nor powerless, and on a societal level there was certainly an element of consent.

The glue that held Muslim and Christian society was interest – the self-interest of Christians and of Muslims, and the mutual interest generated by an interdependence that emerged as a consequence of the broad range of economic and political relationships that they engaged in, whether by circumstance, by choice, or by force, and that benefited either the constituent members and collectives of one group or both. This is not to say that Christian–Muslim relations were simply shaped by a conscious utilitarianism on the part of the majority society – although this was clearly a factor at certain times and places. The minorities survived also as a consequence of stimulus response: those who derived benefit, security, or income from Muslims, or whose prosperity depended on the stability of *mudéjar* society, were less likely to embark on policies that would debilitate or undermine the function of that society. On the other hand, in the absence of such links of mutual interest (or even in the absence of the *perception* of such links), or where and when there was a sense, whether deluded or not, that attacking or marginalizing Muslims would yield benefits (whether short-term profit, or long-term salvation), there was relatively little to restrain Christian individuals and institutions from taking a predatory approach to subject Muslims. Hence, we find kings, bishops, lords, or municipalities upholding or expanding the rights of subject Muslims in some cases, and oppressing, or allowing them to be oppressed in others.

And it was precisely in the realm of the institution and the collective that the bonds of interest that held together Christian and Muslim society were most clearly perceived and maintained. The treaties, *convenienças*, *pletesías*, *fueros*, and privileges that established and secured the place of subject Muslims in Latin society were negotiated as personal contracts between rulers and institutions and local *mudéjar* communities and their elites. Pragmatically motivated, the conditions they established often bore little relation to either the principles of law or the dictates of the Church, and often ran counter to popular Christian sentiment. They provided a medium-term stability: their durability often did not extend beyond the lifetimes of the authorities who signed them, their efficacy was only as clear as the power of the institutions that underwrote them, and they tended to be renegotiated either with each succeeding generation, or as the relative bargaining position of each of the parties changed.

Hence, it was those Muslim minority societies that were larger and most diverse that tended to be more stable and survive longer, as a consequence of the breadth and variety of their links with their Christian "host" societies. The *mudéjares* of the Iberian kingdoms outlasted and out-performed their analogues in Palestine, Sicily, and Hungary in part because the former were numerically large, but most crucially because they occupied a variety of niches in the Christian-dominated socio-economic environment. Their survival did not depend merely on the good will of kings; in fact, in the Crown of Aragon and Castile they were able to outlive it. In Hungary, where subject Muslims were few and played a rather narrow and non-exclusive role, and in Sicily, where they were in direct competition with Christians as merchants and farmers, they quickly disappeared.

Some historians have expressed surprise at how little *mudéjares* contributed to the royal fisc relative to their numbers in comparison to Jewish minorities in many of these kingdoms; however, royal taxation represents only one measure of worth and only one vector of utility. Muslim minorities may have been worth less to kings than Jews in strictly fiscal terms, but they tended to be worth more to Christian society as a whole. Hence, with the brief exception of Portugal and Hungary, Muslim minorities tended to outlast Jewish ones. On the other hand, the situation was reversed in Sicily, where Jews came to fill niches in commerce and trade that Christians did not; here, the Jewish minority consolidated in the fourteenth century, after the Muslims had been expelled.

### *Physics of scale and registers of expression*

Once medieval society is understood as a complex system, the apparent paradoxes and inconsistencies of pluralism fade. Complex systems consist of components that correspond to distinct orders of magnitude, each of which has particular characteristics and is governed by different rules of behavior. In the present case, the macro-, meso-, and micro- correspond to different modes of self-identification. The macro-, or "ecumenian," scale relates to formal, dogmatic-informed religious identity ("thought," in Part 2); it is the mode in which people imagined themselves as "Christians" or "Muslims" – rigidly defined and mutually exclusive groups, each of which claimed a monopoly on religious truth and political legitimacy, and the object of which was spiritual salvation and earthly peace.[15] It was characterized by confrontation, competition, and a rigid approach to worldly affairs, but one that was largely restricted to the abstract, and had relatively little direct impact on policy. Its approach to diversity was conservative but stable; it was opposed to diversity except in the context of formal hierarchy.[16]

The micro- or "local" scale corresponds to individuals and informal collectives – those that apprehend their goals in terms of the immediate, and act in a manner that may or may not reflect their ecumenian affiliation. It is the sphere of syncretism, of intermarriage and cross-communal friendship and solidarity, as well as of unorganized communal violence and intuitive and ill-defined, but powerful, currents of anxiety and reaction.[17] It is the locale, the family, the personal bond – although sometimes tense – between neighbor, co-religionist, patron and client, or lord and vassal. This is the realm of action, or "deed." The micro-level is volatile, and its approach to diversity is ambiguous; its actors have little capacity to affect the broader environment of Muslim–Christian relations except in rare moments of spontaneous solidarity – uprisings, pogroms, and rebellions.

In the middle, the meso-, or "corporate" stratum is that of the formal collective, of the "firm" – conscious of, informed by, but not necessarily influenced by ecumenian ideology on a practical level. It is the stratum of law, regulation, and institution – "word." Corporations and institutions, whether lay or ecclesiastical, must by their nature adopt a pragmatic approach to policy, based on the attainment of concrete, mid-range, apparently achievable goals, and giving the greatest priority to those that relate to their own survival as an institution. These institutions' approach to ethno-religious identity – both their own and that of rivals – is

15 I coin the term "ecumenian" in reference to the limiting nature of such universalist ideologies (to distinguish it from "ecumenical," which has connotations of accommodation).

16 This is not to propose a false equivalency between the Christian, Jewish, and Islamic positions on the legitimacy of out-group religions. Islam, certainly, had a more broadly inclusive notion of the "People of the Book" (*ahl al-kitāb*), which provided a legitimate but subordinate status (*dhimma*) to adherents of the scriptural, Abrahamic religions. However, interpretation of what this meant varied according to place and time – in some instances "People of the Book" were subject to harsh oppression, at others *dhimma* was extended even to pagans (e.g. in South Asia). In any event, in the final analysis, with few exceptions Muslims held that Islam was the unique path to salvation.

17 Here is where one encounters the organic *convivencia* described in S. B. Schwartz, *All Can be Saved*.

functionally ambivalent, and it is these institutions that played the greatest role as actors in shaping the material circumstances, socio-economic potential, and physical experience of religious minorities.

Each of the three modes has a corresponding register of expression or rhetoric relating to communal identity and ethno-religious diversity. The ecumenian mode is moralizing, and expresses itself dogmatically and rigidly, through the language of doctrine, principle, eternal truth, and opposition to compromise. The corporate mode of expression is formal – articulated in terms of obligations to patrons and dependants, and agreements among free actors, of law in practice. It is the language of business and negotiation, and readily sets aside the ideal in the name of the functional. Finally, the individual mode relates fundamentally to the self and its aims, and is essentially neutral, expressing itself in terms of feelings, needs, and appetites. The three modes may be thought of as analogous to Freud's super-ego, ego, and id – formal identity, the functional self, and libidinous, emotive appetite. Any given individual participates in each of these modes of identity simultaneously, evoking each in specific circumstances.

Hence, for example, the Templars might be an organization of individuals sworn to defend Christianity and Christendom and to battle the Infidel (the ecumenian mode), while on a local level a commander and his troop might protect and provide for their Muslim vassals, or conclude alliances with Islamic powers (the corporate mode). Finally, as individuals, knights might form friendships with Muslim warriors and noblemen or patronize or participate in the folk and religious festivals of their *mudéjar* subjects (the individual mode). "Papa Luna," who ruled as Pope Benedict XIII, had analogously complex relations with non-Christians. He was a dedicated and aggressive proselytyzer of Jews, an owner of Muslim slaves, and a patron of Muslim artists and artisans. Benedict sponsored the Disputation of Tortosa of 1413–14 – a determined attack on the Jewish communities of the peninsula – employed Muslim slaves for hard labor on his various construction projects, and yet was a great aficionado of *mudéjar* style, contracting Muslim architects and carpenters to build and furnish his palaces and churches.[18] Similarly, a king like Jaume I of Aragon may have been a Crusader, but as king, allow his Muslim vassals liberties prohibited by the Church, and personally refer to individual Muslims as friends or, in one case, an "angel." On the other hand, a Christian farmer or townsman might live his entire life living alongside subject Muslims, befriending them as individuals and enjoying the solidarity of purpose and

[18] See H. Maccoby, *Judaism on Trial*, pp. 82–94; R. Salicrú i Lluch, "Benedicto XIII," especially pp. 702–5 and 709; M. Gómez de Valenzuela, "Esclavos moros," pp. 123–24.

goals of neighbors; nevertheless, a shift in economic conditions, the transgression of a sexual boundary, or an unrelated act of violence or a spark of religious fervor might provoke him to assess his surroundings in dogmatic terms, and suddenly turn against his erstwhile fellows for the mere fact that they happened to be Muslim.

Overall, the ecumenian mode was remarkably consistent. Through the centuries ideology evolved and formal approaches to Islam and Muslims may have rigidified as they were increasingly formalized, but, as was the case with Judaism and Christianity, the encounter between these two religions and their reactions to each other shaped each of them, not only through rejection, but appropriation of both ideas and rituals. Moreover, it is difficult to see a correlation between the experience of *mudéjares* across Latin Christendom and the evolving attitudes of theologians and canon legists. In some areas the public display of Islam was banned prior to Vienne, in other regions it outlived it by centuries. Whether Muḥammad was thought of in Paris or Rome as an idolator, a pseudo-Prophet, or a sphere of hammered metal, had little impact on the life of a subject Muslim, whether she was in Portugal, Hungary, or the Holy Land. Rather, it was the interplay between the three modes of identity and expression, and particularly the overlapping and intersecting agendas of corporate actors that shaped the history of subject Muslim communities.

### *Generalities and particularisms*

The importance of local circumstances in shaping minority–majority relations accounts for the tremendous variety of experience of each regional and local subject Muslim community. The Crown of Aragon and Navarre had the most durable, stable, and prosperous subject Muslim societies because these minority communities were the most diverse in Latin Christendom, in terms of their political and economic interdependence with Christian collectives and institutions. In Aragon, in particular, the minority was not only large, but varied – consisting of tenants, farmers, and craftsmen who were engaged in a broad gamut of relationships with a whole range of Christian collectives and institutions. In Valencia the minority was both relatively and absolutely more numerous, but to the point that many Christians considered the subject Muslims a threat. Moreover, economic integration here did not effectively mitigate this anxiety because Christians competed with *mudéjares* both for land and in industry – a circumstance that only further encouraged communal antipathy. The situation in Sicily was analogous to that of Valencia, but without the advantage of large numbers there was little to deter Christian authorities from turning to transportation and exile to solve the problem of the increasingly marginalized and restless domestic *sarraceni*. In the Holy Land – another similar scenario – it was precisely the Frankish noblity's need for peasantry that prevented them from taking this drastic step. In Ifrīqiya, a militantly resistent Muslim minority was accommodated because the Norman rulers simply had no choice; emptying the cities and countryside would have destroyed the local economy and rendered the region a liability for its Latin overlords. Thus, for a minority, size could be an advantage, but the case of Navarre, where in the late Middle Ages Muslims were quite secure and confident, but comprised less than 3 percent of the population (as compared to Jews' nearly 8 percent), shows that size was not a necessary factor for maintaining stability. It was the fact that *mudéjares* in Navarre accounted for over 5 percent of royal rents and dominated a whole range of key crafts that ensured their status and security.[19] The Muslim population of Portugal may have been comparable to that of Navarre in terms of relative size, but here, the *mouros*' failure to make themselves indispensable as a community – to dominate a critical niche – meant that they could eventually be disposed of without leaving a clear trace even of their expulsion. Hungary, another region where the disappearance of the Muslims left no historical trace, combined the least favorable characteristics of each scenario – it had a tiny Muslim population, whose only clear role in the kingdom, a military one, was being filled over time more effectively by foreign Christian and pagan settlers. Within each of these regions, however, the conditions of local Muslim communities varied tremendously as a consequence of the particular relations they had, not only with their respective sovereigns, but with the local Christian collectives and institutions alongside and under whom they lived. Local experience could easily run counter to the regional narrative.

Localized as the history of these communities may have been, a certain chronological progression or arc of experience can be discerned. In the great period of Latin conquest, from the mid eleventh to the mid twelfth centuries, subject Muslim communities were largely left to the their own devices once the trauma of the conquest had been overcome. Latin institutions were primitive, there was little interest on the part of the Church in converting Muslims or interfering with Islamic practice, and generally speaking the communities were fiscally and judicially autonomous, and were ascribed broad rights of self-determination as well as individual legal safeguards.

[19] M. R. García Arancón, "Marco jurídico," pp. 464–65.

From the mid thirteenth to mid fourteenth centuries, as Christian legal and administrative institutions matured, as towns developed, and the monarchy and nobility vied for political advantage, Muslim communities were brought increasingly under the control of Christian secular and religious law. This was a period of subjugation. Increasing economic integration and interdependence demanded that earlier rights and liberties be rescinded, and the situation of subject Muslims regularized as they were brought under Christian control. The loss of autonomy and these first explicit expressions of Christian authority provoked rebellions and resistance, and with the exception of those of the mainland of the Iberian Peninsula, the various communities were expelled or absorbed.

After a second period of instability and upheaval coinciding with the Black Death, the great economic and demographic adjustments, and the wars of the late 1300s, another phase of relative stability – a colonial period – ensued. On the one hand the administrative and economic integration of Muslim communities continued. Indeed, Christian powers in some kingdoms began to vie for control of what was now seen as a valuable resource. Whether as a consequence of Christian diversification, changing economic structures, or "reproductive separation," competition between Christian and Muslim individuals and collectives increased in many areas. Christians began to think of themselves more in terms of their Christianity, thanks to the establishment and entrenchment of sacraments, the development of the parish as a framework for local communities, and the spread of religiously colored guilds and vocational confraternities.

Officially, *mudéjar* autonomy continued to decline, but unofficially, Muslim communities began to express a non-institutional independence. As collaborationist *mudéjar* colonial native elites lost prestige within their own communities, alternative, clandestine religious elites emerged. As Muslims' cultural distance with the Christians closed through the appropriation of language, mores, and beliefs, Muslims' frustration at their own exclusion increased. In the regions characterized by such tensions, distinct *mudéjar* folk customs and an explicit Islamic identity were cultivated as a reaction to the growing religious polarization of Christian society and the marginalization of Muslims within it. In areas where interdependence between Christians and Muslims narrowed and declined, *mudéjares* were radicalized – they turned back to the *dār al-Islām* for religious guidance and political support, even as religious acculturation with Christians intensified. These processes would have been stimulated by the ingress and integration of Muslim slaves from the Maghrib in *mudéjar* communities. On the other hand, as established *mudéjar* religious and administrative institutions failed, a greater field of opportunity may have opened up for women, who came in some ways to serve as the bulwark of Islamic and crypto-Muslim culture and identity. As a consequence of these divergences, by the end of the fifteenth century Portugal's Muslims had been expelled, and Valencia's were increasingly taking refuge in seigniorial lands to escape popular Christian violence and increasingly restrictive royal policy.

### *Of black swans and black sheep*

It was the policy turns of the early sixteenth century: the forced conversion of the *mudéjares* of Granada, Castile, the Crown of Aragon, and Navarre, that represented an uncharacteristic, unexpected, and inconsistent turn of events – a "black swan" in the words of economist Nassim Taleb.[20] The Church's position on Islam had not changed, aside from an increasingly rancorous trend among certain theologians, bishops, and would-be evangelizers who were frustrated by Muslims' failure to recognize Christianity as the True Faith, and the Islamic world's unsettling resurgence in the form of the Ottomans. Forced conversion was still regarded as inappropriate, and peace-abiding Muslims were still considered legitimate subjects of Latin princes. But the *mudéjares* had shown themselves to be rebels, and the Moriscos, apostates in the eyes of Christian authorities. Hence, again, it was the corporate stratum that most affected the fate of the subject Muslim communities, and specifically, the royal court and certain powerful ecclesiastical lobbies and municipal collectives.

The first mass conversions – those that took place in Granada from 1499 to 1502 under Ferran the Catholic – were not, strictly speaking, forced. Muslims were given a choice, at least formally, to convert or depart. By 1526, however, and the final stages of the process of conversion of the *mudéjares*, such pretenses had been dropped. The remaining communities had been drawn into the framework of a new kingdom, Spain, under the rule of a new dynasty, and it would be the *Deus ex machina* of Hapsburg ascendency that would put an end to what remained of Islamic society in the Latin West (with the exception of the *Lipqa* in the far northeast). The force of the new ruling family's will was perhaps somewhat less of a factor in bringing about this conclusion than the pure chance that all of the Spanish kingdoms would fall under their rule. Hence, viable or not, stable or not, complacent or not, the Muslim communities of the Crown of Aragon and Navarre had the same policies and laws applied to them as had been developed specifically for the Crown of Castile.

The protests and resistance of certain Latin Christian corporations, namely some of the Military Orders, a few dioceses, and many landed aristocrats, were not sufficient to displace this royal determination. The

[20] See N. Taleb, *The Black Swan.*

extent to which the expulsions might have crippled the rural economies of Aragon and Valencia was of little concern to the monarchy – the insistence of these kingdoms' aristocracies in upholding their traditional rights and privileges had been a sharp thorn in the Hapsburg throne, and in any event, the center of the economy of Spain under the rule of the imperial dynasty had shifted towards Sevilla, the Netherlands, and the Americas.

Not surprisingly, the transformation in name from Muslim to Christian did little to affect the situation of these former *mudéjares* whose judicial, personal, and religious situation seems to have remained overwhelmingly unchanged. The next step, expulsion – also undertaken as a meso-level policy – was no black swan; the fate of the Moriscos was carefully weighed and debated at length before a decision was taken to exile them *en masse*. Again, there was no precedent or justification for this on the ideological level – these were Christians, after all, at least in name; to send them to the land of the Infidel would be to imperil not only their bodies but their souls, and not only their souls but those of their offspring. But the demands of the corporation trumped both the spirit of law and the principles of faith, and the few advocates that the Moriscos found among Old Christian society and New Christian administrators were too weak to prevent an expulsion that had come to be seen in royal circles as both inevitable and desirable.

And so, with an Eliotic whimper, the first age of *Sarracenus Europeus*, the European Muslim, ended. Or almost, given that in the northeast, subject Muslim communities – the Tatars – persisted and even throve, notwithstanding the cultural, ideological, and institutional changes that had transformed Europe. For them the conditions of Convenience still held. Similarly, as early modern Christian powers expanded as imperial powers into the Islamic world beyond European shores, they continued to offer their new Muslim subjects the basic menu of rights and obligations that their predecessors had five centuries earlier.[21] Of course, the Tatars, *mudéjares*, and Moriscos were not merely Muslims. They were not two-dimensional entities, who defined themselves solely in terms of their religious identity. As discussed in chapter 10, they were internally varied as groups: by regional identity, class, vocation, locale, gender, ethnic origin, and legal status. As individuals, in much of their daily lives, within the rhythms of quotidian existence, they must have often set aside the fact that they were Muslims, disregarded that they were different, and forgotten that they occupied a formal place in the ideological hierarchy below

[21] See, for example, the surrender documents of Jerba (1520) and Gabès (1541 and 1551) in M. de Epalza Ferre, "Quelques épisodes," pp. 86–91.

even the most humble of Christians, regardless of their own personal wealth and prosperity. But while this may have characterized much of their daily experience, religious identity could never be forgotten or dispensed with. Every contract and legal document they were involved in characterized them as *sarecena* or *moro*, if only to make explicit the particular limitations, rights, and mandates they were subject to under law. It was obvious when it came to paying taxes, going to court, making friends, taking baths, buying food, and later, traveling, changing residence, wearing clothes, and bearing arms. They were reminded of it at least two days a week (Friday and Sunday) and on many holidays throughout the year.

Contrary to what various historians have proposed, the situation of the subject Muslims of Latin Christendom was not that of the Blacks of the Old South, or the pre-civil rights North, of the colonized and oppressed indigenous peoples of the Americas, or of the modern, near-stateless Palestinians. They were not regarded as less than human, they were not victims of genocide, nor systematically deprived of their rights or property (although this occurred episodically). Notions of "race" as a pseudo-scientific concept had only begun to coalesce in the very last phase of these communities' existence. Nevertheless, if a modern analogy must be drawn, perhaps their situation could be compared to the "Latinos" in the USA, the continental-born "Arabs" of modern France, or the "Israeli-Arabs" of the Jewish state. That is to say, they were subject to more subtle and slightly less absolute forces of marginalization and discrimination. These were different times, of course, and the *mudejares* expected neither equality nor fraternity, and only a certain type of liberty – the liberty to live apart under their own laws. Their submission to Christian authority and law, grating as it may have been, would have corresponded largely to their expectations as Muslim *dhimmiyyūn* in the *dār al-ḥarb*.

But rather than look for facile comparisons, it may be more useful to contemplate briefly just how little or much has changed for Muslim minorities in the Christian world of today, particularly, the avowedly and formally secular lands of Western Europe and the Anglo-American world. Stereotypes of Muslim violence, primitivism, "filthiness," and sexual excess are widely held in many countries (and actively promoted by both bigoted politicians and the yellow media), as is the notion that Muslims are invading or infiltrating whatever it is that is identified according to the imprecise notion of "Western civilization." Hence, deranged reactionaries, like Anders Breivik, responsible for a massacre at a Norwegian Labor Party youth gathering, perpetrate acts of violence against innocent third parties, and even allegedly "respectable" politicians and pundits speak openly about a "Muslim threat," or an "Arab problem," in manner in which it would be unthinkable to characterize other groups. Issues regarding law and legal rights continue to pose problems to both Muslim and Christians even in these self-declared secular societies. In the USA, for example, the citizens of states like Oklahoma (where fewer than 1 percent of the population is Muslim) field ballots intending to amend their constitutions to prohibit "sharia law" (however little idea they may have of Islam or its legal tradition). The French and the Quebecois move to ban the headscarf and the veil, and other countries consider outlawing "Islamic" feminine facial and body coverings. Muslims, for their part, lobby for the recognition of "personal law," and against the local sale of alcohol, work to establish "Islamic banking" as part of the accepted services offered by financial institutions, or engage in furtive polygamy, forced marriage, or female ablation. Some religious Muslims fear the encroachment of "polytheism" in their communities in the shape of even the superficial celebration of popular Christian (or formerly Christian) holidays like Christmas, the exposure to noxious "Western media," or popular mores – in particular unrestrained or ambiguous sexuality – on their children. A tiny minority, comparable to the Christian extremists on the other side – Mahmoud Abouhalima, the 1993 World Trade Center bomber, and his ilk – come to imagine that what they are engaged in is a war for the survival of their faith against modern "Crusaders."

The chief difference, perhaps, between those medieval European societies and the Anglo-European West of today is that the latter is officially and ostensibly secular, and has made a virtue of individual rights over communal integrity and security. But while religion has become a matter of conscience and choice rather than birth and community, and only one legal system and set of standards is held to apply to all, this has made the practice of religion for minorities no less problematic than before, and has made the influence of the majority both more overpowering and more insidious. In post-Morisco Europe, as much as in the Latin Christendom of the *mudéjares*, the Islamic community cannot function according to the principles that are held as ideals; but for that matter, neither can Christian ones – even if today's secular society represents only the latest manifestation of European Christian culture.

*Convivencia* has its price – a tab that, as Claudio Sánchez Albornoz cannily pointed out, it is the minorities who must pick up – and a price that is evidently, at times, considered too high to be worth paying.[22] As Antonio Moreno, an Aragonese *mudéjar* who lived outside Madrid in the

[22] As he put it, "Medieval Hispano-Christian tolerance? Yes; but tolerance on the part of the minorities, not of the [Hispano-Christian] people, [who were] driven by passion and inflamed by holy war." C. Sánchez Albornoz, *España: un enigma histórico*, vol. I, p. 299.

early sixteenth century, recited in what his interrogators of the Holy Office labeled a "Moorish Romance":

They said we have to go
    and take ourselves from here;

we must get on our way –
    towards that land so dear,
where gold and fine silver
    cover hills both far and near.
And since they fight us all the way,
    let us all be for there bound,
where there are many Muslims,
    and where all Good is found.
They say they must proclaim
    that we must all retreat,
that they do it for good reason,
    not merely to mistreat;
and they will give us passage
    in a sturdy sea-bound boat,
and we will not be abandoned
    to danger as we float.
They let us sell our goods,
    and our burden thus relieve,
though if we gain something,
    then something we must leave:

We may lose all we have,
    but to our Law we cleave.[23]

[23] Freely adapted from M. F. Gómez Vozmediano, *Mudéjares y moriscos*, pp. 38–39.

# Glossary

The following list is not intended to be exhaustive, but rather to provide a quick guide to some of the more common foreign terms found in the text. Obscure and less frequently used terms can be found in the index and are generally defined the first time that they appear in the text.

*ʾadhān* (Arabic) the Islamic "call to prayer"; issued five times daily

*albaranum* (Latin) a receipt showing that the one-fifth duty had been paid on a slave

*Alcalde Mayor* (Castilian) senior *mudéjar* magistrate in Castile

*alcadi* (Latin, Romance) *mudéjar* magistrate

*alcaydus* (Latin, Romance) *mudéjar* magistrate

*ʿālim* (Arabic; see *ʿulamāʾ*) a member of the intellectual and/or religious elite

*aljama* (Latin, Castilian) the institutional incorporation of a local *mudéjar* community (in Portugueuse: *comuna*)

*aljamiado* (Castilian) Romance or Castilian written with Arabic characters

*amān* (Arabic) a truce, or pact

*amīr* (Arabic) a prince, or potentate

al-Andalus (Arabic) the Arabic name for the Iberian Peninsula, particularly Muslim-ruled Iberia

Andalusī (Arabic) a native or inhabitant of al-Andalus

*Banū* (Arabic; singular: *ibn*) "sons of"; used to denote a tribe or clan

*baptizatus* (Latin; French: *batié*) a convert to Christianity, usually a former Muslim

*bilghriyyūn* (Arabic) "pilgrims"; the Arabic name for Crusaders

*Cantigas* (*Las Cantigas de Santa María*) an illustrated anthology of Marian parables in verse, written in Galician, compiled in the late thirteenth century and ascribed to King Alfonso X of Castile

*carta-puebla* (Castilian, Latin) a local population charter granted by a king or lord

*cavalquem* (Latin, Romance) *mudéjar* magistrate

*comuna* (Portuguese) see *aljama*

*dār al-ʿahd* (Arabic) "the abode of Truce"; non-Muslim lands in peaceful diplomatic relations with the world of Islam
*dār al-ḥarb* (Arabic) "the abode of War"; non-Muslim lands
*dār al-Islām* (Arabic) "the abode of Islam"; that portion of the world under Islamic political authority
*dhimma* (Arabic) the "Pact of Protection" that defined the subjugation of non-Muslim subjects (*dhimmiyyūn*; singular *dhimmī*) in the *dār al-Islām*
*dinar* (Arabic; plural: *danānīr*) an Arabo-Islamic unit of money derived from the Roman *denarius*
*dīwān* (Arabic; plural: *dawāwīn*) an account book, ledger, or bureaucratic department
*exaricus* (Latin) a sharecropper, derived from the Arabic *al-shārik*
*fallāḥ* (Arabic; plural: *fallāḥīn*) a Muslim peasant, in Islamic Egypt and Syria
*faqīh* (Arabic; plural: *fuqahāʾ*) an Islamic jurisprudent
*fatwa* (Arabic; plural: *fatāwā*) a *responsum*; a jurist's assessment of a hypothetical legal case
*fiqh* (Arabic) Islamic jurisprudence
*franquitas* (Latin) an exemption from (usually royal) taxes
*fuero* (Castilian; Latin: *forum*, Catalan: *fur*) a law, or legal code
*guidaticum* (Latin) an official safe-conduct
*ḥadīth* (Arabic) a "tradition" of the Prophet, a Companion, or other venerable figure in Islam; one of the sources of Islamic law
*ḥājib* (Arabic) "chamberlain," the official designation preferred by *taifa* kings
*ḥajj* (Arabic) the pilgrimage to Mecca, ideally undertaken at least once during the lifetime of a believer
*ḥallāl* (Arabic) adhering to Islamic requirements for standards of food preparation and consumption
ibn (Arabic) "son of"
al-Ifranj (Arabic) "Franks," and Arabic term for Latin Christians
*imām* (Arabic) a prayer-leader; an official or *ad hoc* individual who leads Muslims in prayer
*iqṭāʿ* (Arabic) in the Islamic Eastern Mediterranean, a system by which the military elite was supported by tax-farming
*al-jizya* (Arabic) the poll tax paid by a *dhimmī*
*judería* (Castilian; Catalan: *call*) in Spain, a neighborhood set aside for Jews
*khāṣṣa* (Arabic) the upper class or aristocracy in Islamicate society
*khuṭba* (Arabic) an exhortation, or a sermon

*madhhab* (Arabic; plural *madhāhib*) a school of interpretation of Islamic Law, of which four were recognized in orthodox medieval Islam: Ḥanafī, Shāfiʿī, Ḥanbalī, and Mālikī

Maghribī (Arabic) of, or pertaining to the Islamic West, specifically, northwest Africa

Mālikī (Arabic) founded in the eighth century by Mālik b. Anas, the dominant school of Sunnī jurisprudence in al-Andalus and the Maghrib

*masjid al-jāmiʿa* (Arabic) congregational mosque, where the entire local Muslim community ought to gather for noon prayers on Fridays

Melkite Byzantine (Greek) Orthodox

*morería* (Castilian: Portuguese: *moureria*) in Spain, a neighborhood set aside for Muslims

Morisco (Romance) a *mudéjar* or descendent of a *mudéjar* of the Iberian peninsula forced to convert to Christianity

*moro* (Romance; Latin: *maurus*, Portuguese: *mouro*) a Muslim; free Muslim subjects were referred to specifically as *moros de paz, moros del palio*, or *moros forro*

Mozarab (Arabic; from *mustʿarab*) an Arabized Christian of Andalusī origin

*muʾadhdhin* (Arabic) the individual who calls the Islamic faithful to prayer by chanting the *ʾadhan*; a muezzin

*mudéjar* (Castilian; Arabic: *mudajjan*): a free Muslim subject of Castile-León, the Crown of Aragon, and Navarre; also used generically

*mufti* (Arabic; plural: *muftūn*) a jurist, either officially appointed or otherwise, who issues *fatāwā* (see *fatwa*)

*mujāhid* (Arabic) someone engaged in *jihād*, particularly military struggle in the name of Islam

*muwallad* (Arabic; plural: *muwalladūn*) in al-Andalus a Christian convert/client or a descendant thereof

*nisba* (Arabic; plural *nāsib*) in Arabic names, a relation name referring to one's town or place of origin, tribe, or occupation

*parias* (Latin) tribute rendered to Christian princes by the *taifa* kings of al-Andalus

*qāḍī* (Arabic; plural: *quwwād*) an Islamic magistrate

*qāʾid* (Arabic) a military governor or military commander

*raʾīs* (Arabic) an imprecise term referring to a chief, leader or headman

Ramaḍān (Arabic) the Islamic holy month, characterized by fasting and abstention during daylight hours; it concludes with the feast of *ʿĪd al-Fiṭr*

*repartimiento* (Castilian; Catalan: *repartiment*) "allocation"; books of allocations (*libros de repartimientos/ llibres de repartiment*) were compiled by the authorities of Castile and the Crown of Aragon in the wake of conquests of Muslim territory as inventories and records of the sharing out of spoils

al-Rūm (Arabic) the Arabic term for "Romans," used to refer to Byzantines, or Christians in general

*ṣalāt* (Arabic) the highly choreographed formal Islamic prayer, to be performed five times daily

*saracenus*/ *sarracenus* (Latin; Romance/Catalan: *sarray, sarrayn*) Muslim

*servus camere* (Latin) "servant/slave of the [royal] chamber," a designation applied in some locales to subject Muslims and Jews

al-Shām, Bilād (Arabic) the region comprising Syria and Palestine

*sharīʿa* (Catalan: *xara*; Latin/Romance: *sunna*) Islamic prophetic law and religion, and (in the Romance variants) the Latin-Christian understanding thereof

*shārik* (Arabic) see *exaricus*

*shaykh* (Arabic; plural *shuyūkh*) an elder, by assumption wise through experience

*solidus* (Latin; Castilian: *sueldo*; Catalan: *sou*) a unit of currency in Latin Christendom, derived from the Roman antecedent

*sufra* (Arabic) a labor obligation or tax in kind of Almohad origin

*ṣulṭān* (Arabic) political/military authority, or the bearer thereof

*sunna* (Arabic) the "tradition" of the Prophet, the Companions, or other fundamental figures of Islam, one of the bases of Islamic law

Sunnī (Arabic) "orthodox" Islam, recognizing the validity of the *sunna*, and used in opposition to Shīʿī Islam

*tahrif* (Arabic) the conviction that Jesus's teachings could not be in conflict with Islam, and that therefore the Christian Gospels represent a corruption of the original message

*taifa* (Castilian; from Arabic *ṭāʾifa*) referring to a "faction" or "party," specifically, the petty successor states of the Caliphate of Cordoba

*taqiyya* (Arabic) "prudence"; concealment of Islamic faith

*tarjumān* (Arabic; Romance: *dragoman*) a translator

Turcopole the Turkic-style cavalry employed by the Frankish principalities of the East

*ʿulamāʾ* (Arabic: singular: *ʿālim*) the Islamic intellectual/religious elite

*umma* (Arabic) a people, the Islamic community in its broadest sense

*ʿushr* (Arabic) the "tenth"; one of the canonical taxes in Islam

*wazīr* (Arabic; plural: *wuzarāʾ*) chief minister

*zakat* (Arabic) the "alms tax"; one of the canonical taxes in Islam

# Bibliography

The following list includes only a portion of those works that were consulted in the course of this study and is restricted for the most part to those cited. Much has been left out, including important primary sources, books, and articles, but a complete list would simply be impractically long. Given the nature of this book, I have preferred to cite primary source translations in English, where available, or in other modern European languages; sources in Arabic are cited only when translations are not available, or when the original text is specifically referred to.

## PRIMARY SOURCES


Abboud Haggar, Soha, "Al-Tafrīʿ de Ibn al-Ǧallāb: edición, estudio lingüístico y glosario del manuscrito aljamiado número XXXIII de la Biblioteca de la Junta y su confrontación con el original árabe." Doctoral thesis (Madrid: Universidad Complutense de Madrid, Humanidades, 1997).

Abū Ḥāmid al-Garnāṭi and Ingrid Bejarano, *Al-muʿrib ʿan baʿd ʿayāʾib al-Magrib = (elogio de algunas maravillas del Magrib)* (Madrid: CSIC, 1991).

Ademari Chabannensis, "Chronicle (on Roger of Tosny)," in E. van Houts (ed.), *The Normans in European History* (Manchester University Press, 2000), p. 51.

*Chronicon*, P. Bourgain (ed.), (Turnhout: Brepols, 1999).

Afonso, King of Portugal, *Ordenações afonsinas*, 5 vols. (Lisbon: Fundação Calouste Gulbenkian, 1984). Reprint of *Ordenaçoens do Senhor Rey D. Affonso V* (Coimbra: Real Imprensa da Universidade, 1792).

Alarcón y Santón, Maximilliano and Ramón García de Linares, *Los documentos árabes diplomáticos del archivo de la corona de Aragón* (Madrid: E. Maestre, 1940).

Alfonso X, King of Castile and León, *Espéculo. Texto jurídico atribuido al rey de Castilla don Alfonso X, el Sabio*, Robert A. MacDonald (ed.), (Madison, WI: The Hispanic Seminary of Medieval Studies, 1990).

*Libro del axedrez, dados et tablas* (Madrid: Vicent García, 1987).

*Las siete partidas*, S. P. Scott and R.I. Burns (eds. and trans.), 5 vols., (Philadelphia: University of Pennsylvania Press, 2001).

Algora Hernando, Jesús Ignacio and Felicísimo Arranz Sacristán, *Fuero de Calatayud* (Zaragoza: Institución "Fernando el Católico", 1982).

Amari, Michele, *et al.*, *Biblioteca arabo-sicula. Ossia raccolta di testi arabiciche che toccano la geografia, la storia, le biografie e la bibliografia della Sicilia*, 2 vols. (Palermo: Accademia nazionale di scienze, lettere e arti, 1987 [1857]).

Amatus de Montecasino, *The History of the Normans by Amatus of Montecasino.* Prescott N. Dunbar and G. A. Loud (trans.), (Woodbridge, Suffolk: Boydell Press, 2004).

Ibn ʾAmīra al-Mahzūmī, *Kitāb taʾrīḫ Mayūrqa. Cronica arabe de la conquista de Mallorca*, M. Ben Ma'mar, N. Roser Nebot (eds. and trans.), (Palma: Universitat de les Illes Balears, 2009).

Anonymous and Master Roger, *Gesta Hungarorum*, Simon Kezai, László Veszprémy, Frank Schaer, and Jenő Szűcs (eds. and trans.), (Budapest: Central European University Press, 2010).

Ibn al-ʿArabī. *The Sufis of Andalusia. The Ruh Alquds and Al-Durrat Al-Fakhirah of Ibn ʿArabi*, R. W. J. Austin (trans.), (Berkeley: Allen & Unwin, 1977).

Arberry, A.J. (trans.), *Kings and Beggars: the Five Chapters of Saʿdī's Gulistān. Translated into English with Introduction and Notes* (London: Luzac & Co., 1945).

*Moorish Poetry: A Translation of the Pennants. An Anthology Compiled in 1243 by the Andalusian Ibn Saʿīd* (Cambridge University Press, 1953).

Arcas Campoy, Maria, "Inventario de buenes de una morisca granadina emigrado a Lorca (Murcia)," *al-Masāq* 4 (1991), 35–49.

Argente Vidal, Javier, "Un libre de cuentas de las morerías del condado de Denia (1379)," *Bolletín de la Sociedad Castellonense de Cultura* 62 (1988), 285–329.

Asbridge, Thomas S. and Susan B. Edgington (trans.), *Walter the Chancellor's The Antiochene Wars* (Aldershot: Ashgate, 1999).

Atiya, Aziz Suryal (ed.), *Egypt and Aragon. Embassies and Diplomatic Correspondence Between 1300 and 1330* AD (Nendeln: Kraus, 1966 [1938]).

*Aureum opus regalium privilegiorum civitatis et regni Valentie*, Luis Lanya and María Desamparados Cabanes Pecourt (eds.), (Valencia: Anubar, 1972).

Bacharach, Bernard S. and David S. Bachrach (trans.), *The Gesta Tancredi of Ralph of Caen. A History of the Normans on the First Crusade* (Aldershot: Ashgate, 2005).

de Baena, Juan Alfonso, *El cancionero de Juan Alfonso de Baena*, Pedro José Pidal (ed.), (Leipzig: F.A. Brockhaus, 1860).

Bak, János M., György Bónis, James Ross Sweeney, and Andor Czismaia (eds. and trans.), *The Laws of the Medieval Kingdom of Hungary*, vol. I, "1000–1301" (Bakersfield: C. Schlacks, 1989).

Barceló Torres, Carme, *Un tratado catalán medieval de derecho islámico. El llibre de la çuna e xara dels moros* (Universidad de Córdoba, 1989).

Barceló Torres, Carme, and Ana Labarta (eds.), *Archivos moriscos: textos árabes de la minoría islámica valenciana, 1401–1608* (Universitat de València, 2009).

Barrero García, Ana María, *El fuero de Teruel. Su historia, proceso de formación y reconstrucción crítica de sus fuentes* (Teruel: Instituto de Estudios Turolenses, 1979).

Simon Barton and Richard A. Fletcher (eds. and trans.), *The World of El Cid. Chronicles of the Spanish Reconquest. Selected Sources Translated and Annotated* (Manchester University Press, 2000).

Ibn Baṭṭūṭa, Muḥammad, *The Travels of ibn Baṭṭūṭa,* AD *1325–1354*, H. A. R. Gibb (ed. and trans.), (Cambridge: Hakluyt Society, 1962).

Bleda, Jaime, *Corónica de los moros de España. Diudida en ocho libros* (Valencia: Felipe Mey, 1618).

de Bofarull y Mascaró, Pascual, *Repartimientos de los reinos de Mallorca, Valencia y Cerdeña, publicados de real orden* (Barcelona: Imprenta del Archivo, 1856).

de Bofarull y Mascaró, *et al.* (eds.), *Colección de documentos inéditos de la Corona de Aragón*, 42 vols. (Barcelona: José Eusebio Montfort, 1847–1973).

Bofarull y Sartorio, Manuel, *El registro del merino de Zaragoza, El caballero Gil Tarin, 1291–1312* (Zaragoza: Hospicio Provincial, 1889).

Bonet, Honoré, *Medieval Muslims, Christians, and Jews in Dialogue. The Apparicion Maistre Jehan de Meun of Honorat Bovet. A Critical Edition With English Translation*, Michael G. Hanly (ed. and trans.), (Tempe, AZ: Arizona Center for Medieval and Renaissance Studies, 2005).

Bosch Vilá, Jacinto, "Los documentos árabes y hebreos de Aragón y Navarra," *Estudios de edad media en la Corona de Aragón* 5 (1952), 407–16.

"Los documentos árabes del archivo de la Catedral de Huesca," *Revista del Instituto de Estudios Islàmicos en Madrid* 5 (1957), 1–48.

Brito de Almeida Costa, Mário Júlio, and Eduardo Borges Nunes (eds.), *Ordenações afonsinas*, 2nd edn., 5 vols. (Lisboa: Fundação Calouste Gulbenkian, 1998).

Brundage, James A., *The Crusades. A Documentary Survey* (Milwaukee, WI: Marquette University Press, 1962).

Burns, Robert Ignatius (ed.), *Diplomatarium of the Crusader Kingdom of Valencia*, 4 vols. (Princeton University Press, 1985–2007).

Cabanes Pecourt, Maria Desamparados (ed.), *Crónica latina de los reyes de Castilla* (Zaragoza: Anubar, 1985).

Cabanes Pecourt, Maria Desamparados and Ramón Ferrer Navarro (eds.), *Llibre del repartiment del Regne de València*, 3 vols. (Zaragoza: Anubar, 1979).

Caffaro, *De captione Almerie et Tortosue*, Antonio Ubieto Arteta (ed.), (Valencia: Facsímil, 1973).

Canellas López, Angel, *Colección diplomática del concejo de Zaragoza* (Universidad de Zaragoza, 1972).

Carranza Larroso, Josefina, "Els Costums De Flix," *Miscel·lània del Centre d'Estudis Comarcal de la Ribera d'Ebre* 10 (1995), 63–83.

Carrete Parrondo, Carlos and María Fuencisla García Casar (eds.), *El tribunal de la inquisición de Sigüenza, 1492–1505* (Universidad Pontificia de Salamanca, 1997).

Caruana Gómez de Barreda, Jaime (ed.), *El fuero latino de Teruel* (Teruel: Instituto de Estudios Turolenses, 1974).

Casassas Canals, Xavier (ed.), *Los siete alhaicales y otras plegarias aljamiadas de mudéjares y moriscos* (Almuzara: Almuzara Estudios SA, 2007).

Castro, Américo and Federico de Onîs (eds.), *Fueros leoneses de Zamora, Salamanca, Ledesma y Alba de Tormes* (Madrid: Centro de Estudios Históricos, 1916).

Catlos, Brian A. (ed.), "Fuero General de Navarra" [AGN: Archivos generales C3] in F. Waltman (ed.), *Textos y concordancias electrónicos del 'Fuero General de Navarra'* CD-ROM (Madison Hispanic Seminary of Medieval Studies, 1999).

Charlo Brea, Luis (ed.), *Crónica latina de los reyes de Castilla* (Universidad de Cádiz, 1984).

Cipollone, Giulio, "From Intolerance to Tolerance. The Humanitarian Way, 1187–1216," in Michael Gervers and James M. Powell (eds.), *Tolerance and Intolerance*, pp. 28–40.
Colón, Germa and Arcadi Garcia i Sanz (eds.), *Furs de València*, 8 vols. (Barcelona: Barcino, 1970).
Constable, Giles *et al.* (eds.), *William of Adam. How to Defeat the Saracens* (Washington, DC: Dumbarton Oaks Research Library, 2012).
Constable, O. Remie (ed.), *Medieval Iberia: Readings From Christian, Muslim, and Jewish Sources* (Philadelphia: University of Pennsylvania Press, 1997).
*Consuetudines Dertosae* (Tarragona, Diputación Provincial, 1972 [1539]).
Cowans, Jon. *Early Modern Spain: A Documentary History* (Philadelphia: University of Pennsylvania Press, 2003).
Crawford, Paul (ed. and trans.), *The "Templar of Tyre." Part* III *of the "Deeds of the Cypriots"* (Aldershot: Ashgate, 2003).
David, Charles Wendell, (ed.), *The Conquest of Lisbon. De expugnatione lyxbonensi* (New York: Columbia University Press, 2001).
*Decretales D. Gregorii Papae IX· suae integritati una cum glossis restitutae: ad exemplar Romanum diligenter recognitae* (Lyon: P. Rousselet, 1613).
Desclot, Bernat, *Chronicle of the Reign of King Pedro III of Aragon* AD *1276–1285*, F.L. Critchlow (trans.), (Princeton University Press, 1928).
"Llibre del rei en Pere," in F. Soldevila (ed.), *Les quatre grans cròniques* (Barcelona: Selecta, 1971).
Donizone di Canossa, *Vita Mathildis celeberrimae principis Italiae carmina scripta a Donizone presbytero qui in arce canusina vixit*, L. Simeoni *et al.* (eds.), (Bologna: Zanichelli, 1930).
Eadmer, *The Life of St. Anselm, Archbishop of Canterbury*, R.W. Southern (ed.), (London: T. Nelson, 1962).
Edbury, Peter W. (ed. and trans.), *The Conquest of Jerusalem and the Third Crusade* (Aldershot: Ashgate, 1998).
*John of Ibelin and the Kingdom of Jerusalem* (Rochester: Boydell Press, 1997).
Egidi, Pietro (ed.), *Codice diplomatico dei Saraceni di Lucera [dall' anno 1285 al 1343]* (Naples: L. Pierro, 1917).
Eiximenis, Francesc, *Lo libre de les dones*, Frank Naccarato (ed.), (Barcelona: Curial Edicions Catalanes, 1981).
de Epalza Ferre, Míkel (Miguel), "Dos textos moriscos bilingües (árabe y castellano) de viajes a Oriente (1395 y 1407–1412)," *Hesperis–Tamuda* 20–21 (1982–83), 25–112.
Fagnan, Edmond (ed. and trans.), *Ibn el-Athir, Annales du Maghreb et d'Espagne* (Algiers: A. Jourdan, 1901).
Falcandus, Hugo, *The History of the Tyrants of Sicily by "Hugo Falcandus," 1154–69*, G.A. Loud and Thomas Wiedermann (trans.), (Manchester University Press, 1998).
Febrer Romaguera, Manuel Vicente (ed.), *Cartas pueblas de las morerías valencianas y documentación complementaria*, vol. I, "1234–1372," (Zaragoza: Facsímil, 1991).
Flores, Alexandre M. and António J. Nabais (eds.), *Os forais de Palmela* (Câmara Municipal de Palmela, 1992).

Font y Ríus, José María (Font i Rius, Josep Maria) (ed.), *Cartas de población y franquicía de Cataluña*, 2 vols. (Barcelona: CSIC, 1969).

"La carta de seguridad de Ramon Berenguer IV a las morerías de Ascó y Ribera del Ebro (siglo XII)," in *Homenaje a Don José Maria Lacarra* (Pamplona: Institución Príncipe de Viana, 1977), pp. 261–83.

Font y Ríus, José María (ed.), *Documents jurídics de la història de Catalunya* (Barcelona: Generalitat de Catalunya, 1992).

*Fori Aragonum von Codex von Huesca (1247) bis zu Reform Philipps II (1547), nach der Ausgabe Zaragoza 1476/1477* (Liechtenstein: Topos Verlag, 1979).

Gabrieli, Francesco (ed. and trans.), *Arab Historians of the Crusades* (Berkeley: University of California Press, 1969).

García-Arenal, Mercedes, *Los Moriscos* (Madrid: Editora Nacional, 1975).

Garcia Edo, Vicente (ed.), *Suna e xara. La ley de los mudéjares valencianos, siglos XIII–XV* (Castellón de la Plana: Universidad Jaume I, 2009).

García Gallo, Alfonso, "Los fueros de Toledo," *Anuario de historia de derecho español* 45 (1975), 341–488.

García y García, Antonius (ed.), *Constitutiones concilii quarti lateranensis una cum commentariis glossatorum* (Biblioteca Apostolica Vaticana, 1981).

García y García, Luis (ed.), *Una embajada de los Reyes católicos a Egipto, según la "Legatio Babylonica" y el "Opus epistolarum" de Pedro Mártir de Anglería. Traducción, prólogo y notas de Luis García y García* (Valladolid: CSIC, 1947).

García de Linares, R., "Escrituras árabes pertenecientes al archivo de ntra. sra. del Pilar de Zaragoza," in Eduardo Saavedra (ed.), *Homenaje á D. Francisco Codera en su jubilación del profesorado. Estudios de erudición oriental con una introducción de D. Eduardo Saavedra* (Zaragoza: Maríano Escar, 1904), pp. 171–97.

García López, Aurelio, "Moriscos andalusíes en Pastrana. Las quejas de una minoría marginada de Moriscos, con noticias sobre su paralelismo en el Reino de Granada," *Sharq al-Andalus* 12 (1995), 163–77.

de Gayangos, Pascual (ed.), *Las leyes de los moros* (Madrid: Real Academia de la Historia, 1853).

al-Gharnāṭī, Abū Ḥāmid, *Abu Hamid el Granadino y su relacion de viaje por tierras eurasiáticas*, César E. Dubler (ed. and trans.), (Madrid: Maestre, 1953).

Gibb, H.A.R., (ed. and trans.), *The Damascus Chronicle of the Crusades* (London: Luzac, 1932).

Giménez Soler, Andrés, "La Corona de Aragón y Granada," *Boletín de la Real Academia de Buenas Letras de Barcelona* 3 (1905), 101–33.

Girona i Llagostera, Daniel, *Itinerari del rei en Martí (1396–1410)* (Barcelona: 1916).

González, Julio, *Repartimiento de Sevilla: estudio y edición* (Sevilla: Colegio Oficial de Aparejadores y Arquitectos Técnicos de Sevilla, 1993 [1951]).

Gorosch, Max, *El fuero de Teruel* (Stockholm: Almqvist & Wiksells Boktryckeri AB., 1950).

Grayzel, Solomon and Kenneth R. Stow, *The Church and the Jews in the XIIIth Century* 2 vols. (New York: Jewish Theological Seminary in America, 1989).

Guerrero Lovillo, José (ed.), *Las Cántigas. Estudio arqueológico de sus miniaturas* (Madrid: Instituto Diego Velázquez, 1949).

Guillaume de Pouillem, *La geste de Robert Guiscard*, Marguerite Mathieu and Henri Grégoire (eds. and trans.), (Palermo: Pio X, 1961).

al-Hajarī, Aḥmād b. Qāsim, *Kitāb nāṣir al-dīn ʻalā ʼl-qawm al-kāfirīn [The Supporter of Religion Against the Infidels]*, P. S. van Koningsveld, Qasim al-Samarrai, and Gerard A. Wiegers (eds.), (Madrid: Consejo Superior de Investigaciones Científicas, 1997).

Hamilton, Rita and Janet Perry (trans.), *The Poem of the Cid* (London: Penguin, 1975).

Hatem, Anouar, *Les poèmes épiques des Croisades: genèse-historicité-localisation. Essai sur l'activité littéraire dans les colonies franques de Syrie au moyen âge* (Paris: P. Geuthner, 1932).

Herculano, Alexandre and Joaquim José da Silva Mendes Leal (eds.), *Portugaliae monumenta historica: a saeculo octavo post Christum usque ad quintumdecimum.* (Lisbon: Typis Academicis, 1856–1936).

Hermosilla Llisterri, María José, "Una traducción aljamiada de Corán 38, 34–36 y su original árabe," *Anaquel de Estudios Árabes* 3 (1992), 47–52.

Hernández Segura, Amparo (ed.), *Crónica de la población de Ávila* (Zaragoza: Anubar, 1966).

al-Himyarī, Muhammad b. ᶜAbd al-Munᶜim, *La péninsule ibérique au moyen-âge d'après le Kitâb ar-rawd al-mi'târ fî habar al-akbâr d'ibn 'Abd al-Mun'im al-Himyarî* [Al-Rawd al-miʻtàr]. É. Lévi-Provençal (ed. and trans.), (Leiden: Brill, 1938).

Holt, P. M. (ed.), *Early Mamluk Diplomacy, 1260–1290. Treaties of Baybars and Qalāwūn with Christian Rulers* (Leiden: Brill, 1995).

al-Idrīsī, Muḥammad, *Géographie d'Édrisi traduite de l'Arabe en Français d'après deux manuscrits de la Bibliothèque du Roi et accompagnée de notes.* P. Amédée Jaubert (ed. and trans.), 2 vols. (Paris: L'Imprimerie Royale, 1836).

Jaubert, Pierre (ed. and trans.), *Géographie d'Édrisi traduite de l'arabe en français d'après deux manuscrits de la Bibliothèque du roi et accompagnée de notes*, 2 vols. (Paris: L'imprimerie Royale, 1836–40).

Jaume I, *The Book of Deeds of James I of Aragon. A Translation of the Medieval Catalan Llibre dels fets*, Damian J. Smith and Helena Buffery (trans.), (Aldershot: Ashgate, 2003).

*El Llibre dels Fets de Jaume el Conqueridor*, Robert Vinas (ed.), (Barcelona: Moll, 2008).

Juan Manuel, *El Conde Lucanor. A Collection of Mediaeval Spanish Stories*, John England (trans.), (Warminster: Aris and Phillips, 1987).

Ibn Jubayr, Muḥammad, *The Travels of Ibn Jubayr. Being the Chronicles of a Mediaeval Spanish Moor Concerning His Journey to the Egypt of Saladin, the Holy Cities of Arabia, Baghdad the City of the Caliphs, the Latin Kingdom of Jerusalem, and the Norman Kingdom of Sicily*, Ronald J.C. Broadhurst (trans.), (London: J. Cape, 1952).

Kagay, Donald J., *The Usatges of Barcelona. The Fundamental Law of Catalonia* (Philadelphia: University of Pennsylvania Press, 1994).

al-Kardabūs, Ibn, *Historia de Al-Andalus (kitāb al-Iktifāʼ)*, Felipe Maillo Salgado (ed. and trans.), (Madrid: Ediciones Akal, 1986).

Ibn Khaldūn, ʿAbd al- Raḥmān b. Muḥammad, *Histoire des Berbères et des dynasties musulmanes de l'Afrique septentrionale*, Baron de Slane and Paul Casanova (eds. and trans.), 5 vols. (Paris: P. Geuthner, 1925–56).

*The Muqaddimah. An Introduction to History*, F. Rosenthal (trans.), 3 vols. (London: Routledge & Kegan Paul, 1958).

Kölzer, Theo, Marlis Stähli, and Gereon Becht-Jördens (eds.), *Liber ad honorem Augusti sive de rebus Siculis. Codex 120 II der Burgerbibliothek Bern. Eine Bilderchronik der Stauferzeit* (Sigmaringen: J. Thorbecke, 1994).

Krey, August Charles (ed. and trans.), *The First Crusade. The Accounts of Eye-witnesses and Participants* (Princeton University Press, 1921).

Lacarra, José María (ed.), *Documentos para el estudio de la reconquista y repoblación del valle del Ebro*, 2 vols. (Zaragoza: Anubar, 1982).

Lagardère, Vincent (ed. and trans..), *Histoire et société en Occident musulman au Moyen Age: analyse du Miʿ Yār d'al-Wanšarīsī* (Madrid: CSIC, 1995).

Ledesma Rubio, Maria L. (ed.), *Cartas de población del reino de Aragón en los siglos medievales* (Zaragoza: Institución Fernando el Católico, 1991).

Llull, Ramon, *Doctor Illuminatus. A Ramon Llull Reader*, Anthony Bonner (ed. and trans.), (Princeton University Press, 1993).

*Ramon Llull. A Contemporary Life*, Anthony Bonner (ed. and trans.), (Barcelona: Tamesis, 2010).

López Baralt, Luce, *Un káma sútra español* (Madrid: Siruela, 1992).

Loud, Gordon A. (trans.), *The Deeds of Robert Guiscard* (Leeds Medieval History Texts in Translation Website, University of Leeds, 2002).

Loud, Gordon A. (ed. and trans.), *Roger II and the Creation of the Kingdom of Sicily* (Manchester University Press, 2012).

Lyons, Ursula *et al.*, *Ayyubids, Mamlukes and Crusaders: Selections from the "Tarikh al-Duwal wa'l-Muluk" of Ibn al-Furat* (Cambridge: Heffer, 1971).

Maillo Salgado, Felipe, *Vocabulario de historia árabe e islámica* (Madrid: Akal, 1986).

Malaterra, Goffredo, *The Deeds of Count Roger of Calabria and Sicily and of His Brother Duke Robert Guiscard*, Kenneth Baxter Wolf (trans.), (Ann Arbor: University of Michigan Press, 2005).

Mandeville, John, *The Travels of Sir John Mandeville*, Charles W. Moseley (ed.), (New York: Penguin, 1995).

al-Maqqarī, Aḥmad b. Muḥammad, *The History of the Mohammedan Dynasties in Spain*, Pascual Gayangos (ed. and trans.), 2 vols. (London: Routledge, 2002 [1840–43]).

Marcus, Jacob Rader (ed.), *The Jew in the Medieval World. A Source Book: 315–1791* (New York: Atheneum, 1973).

Martin, M. E., "The Venetian-Seljuk Treaty of 1220," *English Historical Review* 95 (1980), 321–30.

Martín Palma, María Teresa (ed.), *Los repartimientos de Vélez-Málaga. Primer repartimiento* (Universidad de Granada, 2005).

Masià i de Ros, Àngels. *Jaume II: Aragó, Granada i Marroc. Aportació documental* (Barcelona: CSIC, 1989).

de Mas-Latrie, Louis (ed. and trans.), *Traités de paix et de commerce et documents divers concernant les relations des Chrétiens avec les Arabes de l'Afrique septentrionale au moyen-âge* (Paris: H. Plon, 1866).

Massip i Fonollosa, Josep (ed.), *Costums de Tortosa* (Barcelona: Fundació Noguera, 1996).

Mayer, Hans Eberhard and Jean Richard, *Die Urkunden der lateinischen Könige von Jerusalem = Diplomata regum latinorum Hierosolymitanorum*, 4 vols. (Hannover: Hahnsche Buchhandlung, 2010).

Mehren, August Ferdinand van (ed.), *Manuel de la Cosmographie du Moyen Âge. Traduit de l'Arabe "Nokhbet ed-dahr fi 'adjaibil-birr wal-bah'r"* (Amsterdam: Meridian, 1964).

Menéndez Pidal, Ramón (ed.), *Primera crónica general de España* (Madrid: Gredos, 1977).

Metcalfe, Alex and Joshua Birk (trans.), "Ibn Jubayr's Account of Messina and Palermo (1184–85)," in Katherine Ludwig Jansen, Joanna H. Drell, and Frances Andrews (eds.), *Medieval Italy: Texts in Translation* (Philadelphia: University of Pennsylvania Press, 2009), pp. 234–41.

Mickūnaitė, Giedrė (ed. and trans.), "Ruler, Protector and Fairy Prince: The Everlasting Deeds of Grand Duke Vytautas as Related by the Lithuanian Tatars and Karaites," in Gerhard Jaritz and Michael Richter (eds.), *Oral History of the Middle Ages. The Spoken Word in Context* (Budapest: Central European University, 2001).

Mills, Kenneth, William B. Taylor, and Sandra Lauderdale Graham, *Colonial Latin America: A Documentary History* (Wilmington, DE: Scholarly Resources, 2002).

Molho, Mauricio (ed.), *El Fuero de Jaca* (Zaragoza: Instituto de Estudios Pirenaicos, 1964).

Monroe, James T. (ed. and trans.), *Hispano-Arabic Poetry. A Student Anthology* (Berkeley: University of California Press, 1974).

Morales Gómez, Juan José, and Manuel José Pedraza García (eds.), *Fueros de Borja y Zaragoza* (Zaragoza: Anubar, 1986).

Muñoz y Romero, Tomás, *Colección de fueros municipales y cartas pueblas de las [sic] reinos de Castilla, León, Corona de Aragón y Navarra* (Valladolid: Lex Nova, 1977).

Munqidh, Usāma b., *The Book of Contemplation. Islam and the Crusades*, Paul Cobb (ed. and trans.), (New York: Penguin, 2008).

Muntaner, Ramón, *Chronicle*, Lady Goodenough (trans.), (Cambridge: In Parentheses, 2000).

Münzer, Hieronymus. *Viaje por España y Portugal, 1494–1495*, Julio López Toro (ed. and trans.), (Madrid: Almenara, 1951).

Narváez Córdova, María Teresa (ed.), *Tratado [Tafsira]* (Madrid: Trotta, 2003).

Navarrete, Martín Fernández *et al.* (eds.), *Colección de documentos inéditos para la historia de España*, 110 vols. (Madrid: 1861–).

Noble, Thomas F. X. (ed. and trans.), *Charlemagne and Louis the Pious: The Lives by Einhard, Notker, Ermoldus, Thegan, and the Astronomer* (University Park: Pennsylvania State University Press, 2009).

di Novara, Filippo, *Le Livre de Forme de Plait*, Peter W. Edbury (ed. and trans.), (Nicosia: Cyprus Research Centre, 2009).

Núñez Muley, Francisco, *A Memorandum for the President of the Royal Audiencia and Chancery Court of the City and Kingdom of Granada*, Vincent Barletta (trans.), (University of Chicago Press, 2007).

Olivo, Jorge del, *Los moriscos de Calatayod y de la comunidad de Calatayud, 1526–1610* (Teruel: Centro de Estudios Mudéjares, 2008).

Pellat, Charles (ed. and trans.), *Le calendrier de Cordoue* (Leiden: Brill, 1961).

Pérez Martín, Antonio, *Los fueros de Aragón: la compilación de Huesca. Edición critica del texto official latino* (Zaragoza: El Justicia de Aragón, 2010).

Peters, Edward (ed. and trans.), *The First Crusade. The Chronicle of Fulcher of Chartres and Other Source Material* (Philadelphia: University of Pennsylvania Press, 1998).

Pons Guri, Josep Maria, "Constitutions conciliars tarraconensia," *Analecta sacra Tarraconensi*, 47 and 48 (1974), 65–128 and 241–363.

Pons i Marquès, Joan (ed.), *Cartulari de Poblet. Edició del manuscrit de Tarragona* (Barcelona: Institut d'Estudis Catalans, 1938).

Porres Martín-Cleto, Julio (ed. and trans.), *Historia de Ṭulayṭula (711–1085)* (Toledo: Instituto Provincial de Investigaciones y Estudios Toledanos, 1985).

Powell, James M. (ed. and trans.), *The Liber Augustalis. Or, Constitutions of Melfi, Promulgated by the Emperor Frederick II for the Kingdom of Sicily in 1231* (Syracuse University Press, 1971).

Powers, James F. (ed. and trans.), *The Code of Cuenca. Municipal Law on the Twelfth-Century Castilian Frontier* (Philadelphia: University of Pennsylvania Press, 2000).

al-Qayrawānī, Ibn Abī Zayd, *Risala ou traité abrégé de droit malékite et morale musulmane*, Eduoard Fagnan (trans.), (Paris: P. Geunther, 1914).

*Recueil des historiens des croisades*, 16 vols. (Paris: Imprimerie Nationale, 1841–81).

Regné, Jean (ed.), *History of the Jews in Aragon. Regesta and Documents 1213–1327* (Jerusalem: Magnes Press, 1978).

Reinaud, Joseph Toussaint (ed. and trans.), *Géographie d'Aboulféda. Texte arabe publié d'après les manuscrits de Paris et de Leyde*, 2 vols. (Paris: Imprimerie Royal, 1848–83).

Richards, D. S. (ed. and trans.), *The Chronicle of Ibn al-Athīr for the Crusading Period From al-Kāmil fī'l-Ta'rīkh. Part 3, The Years 589–629/1193–1231. The Ayyūbids After Saladin and the Mongol Menace* (Aldershot: Ashgate, 2006).

*The Rare and Excellent History of Saladin, or, al-Nawādir al-Sultaniyya wa'l-Mahasin al-Yusufiyya* (Aldershot: Ashgate, 2002).

Robinson, James Harvey (ed.), *Readings in European History. A Collection of Extracts from the Sources Chosen with the Purpose of Illustrating the Progress of Culture in Western Europe Since the German Invasions* (Boston: Ginn and Company, 1906).

Roig, Jaume, *The Mirror of Jaume Roig: An Edition and an English Translation of Ms. Vat. Lat. 4806*, Maria Celeste Delgado-Librero (ed. and trans.), (Tempe: Arizona Center for Medieval and Renaissance Studies, 2010).

Romeu Alfaro, Sylvia (ed.), *Carta de poblament: Quart de Poblet* (Quart de Poblet: Ajuntament de Quart de Poblet, 1987).

de Rozière, Eugène (ed.), *Cartulaire de l'Église du Saint Sépulcre de Jérusalem. Publié d'après les manuscrits du Vatican* (Paris: Imprimerie Nationale, 1849).
Ruíz Lagos, Manuel (ed.), *Moriscos. De los romances del gozo al exilio* (Seville: Guadalmena, 2001), p. 269.
Ibn Sab'īn, 'Abd al-Ḥaqq b. Ibrāhīm and Luisa María Arvide Cambra, *Las cuestiones sicilianas* (Granada: Universitario, 2010).
Salvador Martínez, H. (ed.), *Alfonso X, the Learned. A Biography* (Leiden: Brill, 2010).
Sánchez Belda, Luis (ed.), *Chronica de Adefonsi Imperatoris* (Madrid: CSIC, 1950).
Santamaría, Alvaro (ed.), *Ejecutoria del Reino de Mallorca 1230–1343* (Palma: Ajuntament, 1990).
Sarasa Sánchez, Esteban (ed.), *El privilegio general de Aragón* (Zaragoza: Cortes de Aragón, 1984.
Schroeder, Henry Joseph (ed.), *Disciplinary Decrees of the General Councils. Text, Translation and Commentary* (St. Louis, MO: B. Herder, 1937).
Silva Leal, Maria José da (ed.), *Livro do almoxarifado de Silves. Século XV* (Silves: Câmara Municipal de Silves, 1984).
Smith, Colin (ed. and trans.), *Poema de mio Cid* (Madrid: Catedra, 1988).
Soldevila, Ferran (ed.), *Les quatre grans cròniques* (Barcelona: Selecta, 1971).
Sourdel-Thomine, Janine (ed. and trans.), *Guide des lieux de pèlegrinage* (Damas: Institut Français de Damas, 1957).
*Suma de fueros de las ciudades de Santa Maria de Albarrazin, y de Teruel* (Valencia: J. Costilla, 1531).
Sweetenham, Robert and Carol (eds. and trans.), *Robert the Monk's History of the First Crusade. Historia Iherosolimitana* (Aldershot: Ashgate, 2005).
Talmon-Heller, Daniela, "*The Cited Tales of the Wondrous Doings of the Shaykhs of the Holy Land* by Ḍiyā' al-Dīn Abū 'Abd Allāh Muḥammad b. 'Abd al-Wāḥid Al-Maqdisī (596/1173–643/1245). Text, Translation and Commentary," *Crusades* 2 (2002), 111–54.
Tibi, Amin T. (trans.), 'Abd Allāh, *The Tibyān: Memoirs of 'Abd Allāh B. Buluggīn, Last Zīrid Amīr of Granada*, Amin T. Tibi (trans.), (Leiden: Brill, 1986).
Tilander, Gunnar (ed.), *Los fueros de Aragón* (Lund: C. W. K. Gleerup, 1937).
*Vidal Mayor. Traducción aragonesa de la obra de "In excelsis dei thesauris" de Vidal de Canellas*, 3 vols. (Lund: Håkan Ohlssons Boktryckeri, 1956).
Torres Fontes, Juan (ed.), *Repartimiento de la huerta y campo de Murcia en el siglo* XIII (Murcia: CISC, 1971).
*Repartimiento de Murcia, edición preparada por Juan Torres Fontes* (Madrid: CSIC, 1960).
Ubieto Arteta, Antonio (ed.), *Crónicas anónimas de Sahagún* (Zaragoza: Facsímil, 1987).
de Vitry, Jacques, *Exempla. Or, Illustrative Stories From the Sermones Vulgares of Jacques De Vitry*, Thomas Frederick Crane (ed. and trans.) (New York: B. Franklin, 1971).
Waltman, Franklin M. (ed.), *Textos y concordancias del fuero general de Navarra* (Madison, WI: Hispanic Seminary of Medieval Studies, 1999).
Weiditz, Christoph, *Authentic Everyday Dress of the Renaissance: All 154 Plates From the "Trachtenbuch"* (New York: Dover, 1994).

Wilkinson, John (ed. and trans.), *Jerusalem Pilgrimages, 1099–1185* (London: Hakluyt Society, 1988).

William of Tyre, *A History of Deeds Done Beyond the Sea*, Emily Babcock and August Krey (trans.), 2 vols. (New York: Columbia University Press, 1943).

Wolf, Kenneth Baxter (ed. and trans.), *Conquerors and Chroniclers of Early Medieval Spain*, 2nd edn. (Liverpool University Press, 1999).

Zacour, Norman P. (ed. and trans.), *Jews and Saracens in the Consilia of Oldradus de Ponte* (Toronto: Pontifical Institute of Mediaeval Studies, 1990).

SECONDARY SOURCES

Abboud Haggar, Soha, "Al-Ǧihād, según el manuscrito aljamiado al-Tafrīʿ de Ibn al-Ǧallāb," *Sharq al-Andalus* 12 (1995), 325–38.

"Conflicto de jurisdicción en un pleito entre mudéjares: Ágreda 1501 (Documentos)," *Cuadernos de historia del derecho* 6 (1999), 415–34.

"Diffusión del tratado jurídico de al-Tafrîʿ de Ibn al-Gallâb en el Occidente musulmán," *Aragón en la Edad Media* 14–15 (1991), 1–18.

"Ibn al-Ǧazarī en la literatura aljamiado-morisca a través de los manuscritos J-LII Y T-232," *Anaquel de estudios árabes* 14 (2003), 21–29.

"*Las Leyes moros* son el libro de *al-Tafrīʿ*," *Cuadernos de historia del derecho* 4 (1997), 163–201.

"Leyes musulmanes y fiscalidad mudéjar," in *Finanzas y fiscalidad municipal. V Congreso de Estudios Medievales* (Ávila: Fundación Sánchez-Albornoz, 1997), pp.166–205.

"Una muestra de transmisión de asuntos religiosos del oriente al occidente mudéjar en el s.XV," *Identidad andalusa* (December 10, 2010) [http://identidadandaluza.wordpress.com/2010/12/10/].

"Precedentes andalusíes en la fiscalidad de las comunidades mudéjares," *En la España medieval* 31 (2008), 475–512.

Abdel-Rahim, A. "Al-Moriscos Settlement in Egypt through the Religious Court Documents of The Ottoman Age," in M. de Epalza (ed.), *L'expulsió dels moriscos*, pp. 158–63.

Abella Samitier, Juan, "Una familia de mudéjares aragoneses en el tránsito de la Edad Media a la Moderna: los Xama de Zaragoza," *En la España medieval* 28 (2005), 197–212.

Abou el Fadl, Khaled, "Islamic Law and Muslim Minorities. The Juristic Discourse on Muslim Minorities from the Second/Eighth to the Eleventh/Seventeenth Centuries," *Islamic Law and Society* 1 (1994), 141–87.

Abu-Haidar, Jareer, *Hispano-Arabic Literature and the Early Provençal Lyrics*, (Richmond, Surrey: Curzon, 2001).

""Maqāmāt" Literature and the Picaresque Novel," *Journal of Arabic Literature* 5 (1974), 1–10.

Abulafia, David, "The End of Muslim Sicily," in J. M. Powell (ed.), *Muslims Under Latin Rule*, pp. 103–33.

*Frederick II. A Medieval Emperor* (London: Allen Lane, 1988).

"The Italian Other. Greeks, Muslims and Jews," in *Italy in the Central Middle Ages. 1000–1300* (Oxford University Press, 2004), pp. 217–36.

"The Norman Kingdom of Africa and the Norman Expeditions to Majorca and the Muslim Mediterranean," *Anglo-Norman Studies* 7 (1985), 26–49.
"Sugar in Spain," *European Review* 16 (2008), 191–210.
*The Two Italies. Economic Relations Between the Norman Kingdom of Sicily and the Northern Communes* (Cambridge University Press, 1977).
*The Western Mediterranean Kingdoms, 1200–1500: The Struggle for Dominion* (New York: Longman, 1997).
Acien Almansa, Manuel, *Entre el feudalismo y el Islam: 'Umar Ibn Ḥafṣūn en los historiadores, en las fuentes y en la historia* (Universidad de Jaén, 1994).
Acosta Montoro, José, *Aben Humeya. Rey De Los Moriscos* (Almería: Instituto de Estudios Almerienses, 1988).
*Actas del* I *Simposio Internacional de Mudejarismo (1975)* (Teruel–Madrid: CSIC, 1981).
*Actas del* II *Simposio Internacional de Mudejarismo. Arte (1981)* (Teruel: Instituto de Estudios Turolenses, 1982).
*Actas del* III *Simposio Internacional de Mudejarismo (1984)*. (Teruel: Instituto de Estudios Turolenses, 1986).
*Actas del* IV *Simposio Internacional de Mudejarismo. Economía (1987)* (Teruel: Instituto de Estudios Turolenses, 1990).
*Actas del* V *Simposio Internacional de Mudejarismo (1990)* (Teruel: Instituto de Estudios Turolenses, 1991).
*Actas del* VI *Simposio Internacional de Mudejarismo (1993)* (Teruel: Instituto de Estudios Turolenses, 1995).
*Actas del* VII *Simposio Internacional de Mudejarismo (1996)* (Teruel: Instituto de Estudios Turolenses, 1997).
*Actas del* VIII *Simposio Internacional de Mudejarismo (2002) De mudéjares a moriscos: Una conversión forzada* (Teruel: Instituto de Estudios Turolenses, 1999).
*Actas del* IX *Simposio Internacional de Mudejarismo: Mudéjares y moriscos. Cambios sociales y culturales*, 2 vols. (Teruel: Instituto de Estudios Turolenses, 2004).
*Actas del* X *Simposio Internacional de Mudejarismo (2005)* (Teruel: IET, 2008).
Aguilera, Manuel Barrios and Bernard Vincent (eds.), *Granada 1492–1992: Del Reino de Granada al futuro del mundo mediterráneo* (Universidad de Granada, 1995).
Ahmed, Leila, *Women and Gender in Islam: Historical Roots of a Modern Debate* (New Haven: Yale University Press, 1992).
Aillet, Cyrille, *Les Mozarabes: christianisme, islamisation et arabisation en Péninsule Ibérique (*IX*e*–XII*e* siècle)* (Madrid: Casa de Velázquez, 2010).
Akasoy, Anna, "Ibn Sab'īn's Sicilian Questions: The Text, Its Sources, and Their Historical Context," *al-Qanṭara* 29 (2008), 115–46.
Akbari, Suzanne Conklin, *Idols in the East: European Representations of Islam and the Orient, 1100–1450* (Ithaca, NY: Cornell University Press, 2009).
Albarracín Navarro, Joaquina, "Actividades de un faqih mudéjar," in *Actas VI Simposio Internacional de Mudejarismo*, pp. 437–44.
Albarracín Navarro, Joaquina and Juan Ruíz Martínez, *Medicina, farmacopea y magia en el "Misceláneo de Salomón": texto árabe, traducción, glosas aljamiadas, estudio y glosario* (Universidad de Granada, 1987).

Alcover, José María, *Diccionari català-valencià-balear*, 10 vols. (Palma de Mallorca: Moll, 1930–69).

Alemany, José, "Milicias cristianas al servicio de los sultanes musulmanes del Almagreb," in Eduardo Saavedra (ed.), *Homenaje a D. Francisco Codera* (Zaragoza: M. Escar, 1904), pp. 133–69.

Allaire, Gloria, "Noble Saracen or Muslim Enemy? The Changing Image of the Saracen in Late Medieval Italian Literature," in D. Blanks and M. Frassetto (eds.), *Western Views of Islam*, pp. 173–84.

Almagro Gorbea, Antonio, "El Alcázar de Sevilla. Un palacio musulmán para un rey cristiano," in J. I. Ruíz de la Peña and M. Á. Ladero Quesada (eds.), *Cristianos y musulmanes en la península Ibérica*, pp. 331–36.

Alonso Acero, Beatriz, *Sultanes de berbería en tierras de la cristianidad* (Barcelona: Bellaterra DL, 2006).

Altisent, Agustín, "Conversión de un Sarraceno aragonés (1449)," *Al-Andalus* 31 (1966), 373–76.

Alvarez, Lourdes María, "Prophecies of Apocalypse in Sixteenth-Century Morisco Writings and the Wondrous Tale of Tamīm al-Dārī," *Medieval Encounters*, 13 (2007), 566–601.

Álvaro Zamora, María Isabel, "El trabajo en los alfares mudéjares aragoneses. Aportación documental acerca de su obra, controles de su producción y formas de comercialización y venta," *Cuadernos de historia Jerónimo Zurita* 65–66 (1992), 97–138.

Amari, Michele, "Questions philosophiques addressées aux savants musulmans par l'Empereur Frédéric II," *Journal asiatique* ser. 5–1 (1853), 240–74.

*Storia dei Musulmani di Sicilia. Seconda edizione modificata e accresciuta dall'autore*, 3 vols. (Catania: Romeo Prampolini editore, 1933).

Ames, Christine Caldwell, *Righteous Persecution. Inquisition, Dominicans, and Christianity in the Middle Ages* (Philadelphia: University of Pennsylvania Press, 2009).

Anaya Hernández, Luis Alberto, "The Canary Moriscos: A Different Reality," in K. Ingram (ed.), *The Conversos and Moriscos in Late Medieval Spain*, vol. I, pp. 35–50.

Anderson, Benedict, *Imagined Communities. Reflections on the Origin and Growth of Nationalism* (London: Verso, 1983).

Aparici Martin, Joaquin, "Juglares mudéjares en Vila-Real durante el siglo XV," in *Actas del* X *Simposio Internacional de Mudejarismo*, pp. 579–92.

"Tolerar y convivir: carnicerías musulmanas en tierras de Castelló," in *Actas del* VIII *Simposio Internacional de Mudejarismo*, pp. 315–32.

Ara Otín, Vicente, *Lupercio Latrás. Bandolero del rey* (Zaragoza: Ara, 2003).

Armstrong, Karen, *Muhammad. A Biography of the Prophet* (San Francisco: Harper, 2001).

Arnold, T.W., *The Preaching of Islam* (London: Luzac, 1935).

Asbridge, Thomas S., *The Creation of the Principality of Antioch, 1098–1130* (Woodbridge: Boydell Press, 2000).

"The 'Crusader' Community at Antioch. The Impact of Interaction with Islam and Byzantium," *Transactions of the Royal Historical Society* 6 (1999), 305–25.

"The Jabal as-Summaq and the Principality of Antioch," in J. Phillips (ed.), *The First Crusade: Origins and Impact* (Manchester University Press, 1997), pp. 142–52.

"Knowing the Enemy. Latin Relations with Islam at the Time of the First Crusade," in N. Housley (ed.), *Knighthood of Christ* (Aldershot: Ashgate, 2007), pp. 17–25.

Asín Palacios, Miguel, "La polémica anti–cristiana de Mohamed el Caisi," *Revue hispanique* 59 (1909), 339–61.

Assis, Yom Tov, *The Golden Age of Aragonese Jewry. Community and Society in the Crown of Aragon, 1213–1327* (London: Vallentine Mitchell, 1997).

Aswad, B. C., "Women, Class, and Power: Examples From the Hatay, Turkey," in Lois Beck and Nikki R. Keddie (eds.), *Women in the Muslim World* (Cambridge, MA: Harvard University Press, 1978), pp. 473–81.

Atiya, Aziz Suryal, *Crusade, Commerce and Culture* (New York: John Wiley and Sons, 1966).

Ávila, María Luisa, "Cargos hereditarios en la administración judicial y religiosa de al-Andalus," in *Saber religioso y poder político en el Islam: Actas del Simposio Internacional (Granada, 15–18 de octubre de 1991)* (Madrid: Agencia Española de Cooperación Internacional, 1994), pp. 27–37.

"Mujeres 'sabias' en al-Andalus," in M. J. Viguera Molins (ed.), *La mujer en al-Andalus*, pp. 139–184.

de Ayala Martínez, Carlos, "Fernando I y la sacralización de la Reconquista," *Anales de la Universidad de Alicante. Historia Medieval* 17 (2011), 67–115.

*Las órdenes militares hispánicas en la Edad Media (siglos* XII–XV*)* (Madrid: Marcial Pons, 2007).

Aziz, Ahmad, *A History of Islamic Sicily* (Edinburgh University Press, 1962).

Babinger, Franz, "Bajezid Osman (Calixtus Ottomanus)," *La nouvelle Clio* 3 (1951), 349–88.

*Mehmed the Conqueror and His Time* (Princeton University Press, 1992).

Backman, Clifford R., *The Decline and Fall of Medieval Sicily. Politics, Religion, and Economy in the Reign of Frederick III, 1296–1337* (Cambridge University Press, 2002).

Balard, Michel, "La femme-esclave à Gênes à la fin du moyen âge," in Michel Rouche and Jean Heuclin (eds.), *La femme au moyen-âge. Colloque international* (Maubeuge: Centre de Recherches sur le Haut Moyen Âge, 1990), pp. 299–313.

Balard, Michel *et al.*, *Dei gesta per Francos. Études sur les croisades dédiées à Jean Richard. Crusade Studies in Honour of Jean Richard* (Aldershot: Ashgate, 2001).

Baldwin, M. W., "The Latin States under Balwin III and Amalric I (1143–1174)," in Setton Kenneth Meyer (ed.), *A History of the Crusades*, vol. I, pp. 528–62.

Barber, Malcolm, "Lepers, Jews and Moslems: The Plot to Overthrow Christendom in 1321," *History* 66 (1981), 1–17.

"The Pastoureaux of 1320," *Journal of Ecclesiastical History* 32 (1981), 143–66.

Barbero, Alessandro, *Il mito angioino nella cultura italiana e provenzale fra duecento e trecento* (Turin: Deputazione Subalpina di Storia Patria, 1983).

Barbour, Neville, "The Relations of King Sancho VII of Navarre – with the Almohads," *Revue de l'Occident musulmane et de la Méditeranée* 4 (1967), 9–21.

"Two Christian Embassies to the Almohad Sultan Muhammad Al-Nasir at Seville in 1211," in *Actas, Primer Congreso de Estudios Arabes e Islamicos, Córdoba, 1962* (Madrid: Comité Permanente del Congreso de Estudios Àrabes e Islamicos, 1964), pp. 189–214.

Barceló i Perelló, Miquel, Helena Kirchner, *et al.*, *The Design of Irrigation Systems in al-Andalus* (Bellaterra: Universitat Autònoma de Barcelona, 1998).

Barceló i Perelló, Miquel, "'...Per sarraïns a preïcar' o l'art de predicar a audiències captives," *Estudi general. Revista de l'Estudi de Lletres* 9 (1989), 117–32.

Barceló Torres, Carmen, "Mujeres, campesinas, mudéjares," in M. J. Viguera Molins (ed.), *La mujer en al-Andalus*, pp. 211–17.

Barceló Torres, Carmen and Ana Labarta, "Fondos documentales árabes de la minoría musulmana en tierras valencians," *Sharq al-Andalus* 4 (1987), 101–7.

Barkaï, Ron, *Cristianos y Musulmanes en la España medieval (el enemigo en el espejo)* (Madrid: Rialp, 1991).

"Une invocation musulmane au nom de Jésus et de Marie," *Revue de l'histoire des religions* 200 (1993), 257–68.

Barletta, Vincent, *Covert Gestures. Crypto-Islamic Literature as Cultural Practice in Early Modern Spain* (Minneapolis: University of Minnesota Press, 2005).

Barrios Aguilera, Manuel, *Granada morisca, la convivencia negada. Historia y textos* (Albolote: Comares, 2002).

Bartlett, Robert, *The Making of Europe. Conquest, Colonization and Cultural Change, 950–1350* (London: Penguin, 1994).

Barton, Simon, "Marriage across Frontiers: Sexual Mixing, Power and Identity in Medieval Iberia," *Journal of Medieval Iberian Studies* 3 (2011), 1–25.

"Traitors of Faith? Christians Mercenaries in al-Andalus and the Magreb, c. 1100–1300," in R. Collins and A. Goodman (eds.), *Medieval Spain*, pp. 23–45.

Barton, Thomas W., "Muslims in Christian Countrysides: Reassessing Exaricus Tenures in Eastern Iberia," *Medieval Encounters* 17 (2011), 233–320.

Basáñez Villaluenga, María Blanca, *La aljama sarracena de Huesca en el siglo* XIV (Barcelona: CSIC, 1989).

Baumgarten, Elisheva, "'A Separate People'? Some Directions for Comparative Research on Medieval Women," *Journal of Medieval History* 34 (2008), 212–28.

Beech, George T., *The Brief Eminence and Doomed Fall of Islamic Saragossa: A Great Center of Jewish and Arabic Learning in the Iberian Peninsula During the* 11*th* *Century* (Zaragoza: Instituto de Estudios Islámicos y del Oriente Próximo, 2008).

"The 'Eleanor Vase': Witness to Christian–Muslim Collaboration in Early Twelfth-Century Spain," *Medieval Life* 3 (1995), 12–16.

"A Norman-Italian Adventurer in the East. Richard of Salerno 1097–1112," *Anglo-Norman Studies* 15 (1993), 25–40.

Bejarano Robles, Francisco, "El Repartimiento de Málaga. Introducción a su estudio," *Al-andalus* 31 (1966), 1–46.

Bejczy, István, "*Tolerantia*: A Medieval Concept," *Journal of the History of Ideas* 58 (1997), 365–84.

Belkhodja, K., "Roger II en Ifriqiya," *Africa (Tunis)* 1 (1969), 111–18.

Ben-Ami, Aharon, *Social Change in a Hostile Environment. The Crusaders' Kingdom of Jerusalem* (Princeton University Press, 1969).

Benítez Bolorinos, Manuel, "La familia Corella: 1457, un caso de bandolerismo nobiliario," *Anales de la Universidad de Alicante. Historia Medieval* 14 (2003), 53–68.

Bensch, Stephen, "From Prizes of War to Domestic Merchandise: The Changing Face of Slavery in Catalonia and Aragon, 1000–1300," *Viator* 25 (1994), 63–93.

Bentley, J.H., *Old World Encounters. Cross-Cultural Contacts and Exchanges in Pre-Modern Times* (New York: Oxford University Press, 1993).

Béraud-Villars, Jean, *Les Touareg au pays du Cid. Les invasions almoravides en Espagne aux* XI*e et* XII*e siècles* (Paris: Plon, 1946).

Bercher, Henri, Annie Courteaux, and Jean Mouton, "Une abbaye latine dans la société musulmane: Monreale au XIIe siècle." *Annales. Économies, sociétés, civilisations* 34 (1979), 525–47.

Berend, Nora, *At the Gate of Christendom. Jews, Muslims, and "Pagans" in Medieval Hungary, c. 1000–c. 1300* (Cambridge University Press, 2001).

"Medieval Patterns of Social Exclusion and Integration: the Regulation of non-Christian Clothing in Thirteenth-Century Hungary," *Revue Mabillon*, n.s. 8 (1997), 155–76.

Bernabé Pons, Luis F., "Las emigraciones moriscas al Mágreb: balance bibliográfico y perspectivas," in Ana I. Planet and Fernando Ramos (eds.), *Relaciones hispano-marroquíes: Una vecindad en construcción* (Guadarrama: Ediciones del Oriente y del Mediterráneo, 2005), pp. 63–100.

"Una fama sin biografía. El Mancebo de Arévalo," in A. Echevarría Arsuaga (ed.), *Biografías mudéjares*, pp. 517–48.

*Los moriscos. Conflicto, expulsión y diáspora* (Madrid: Catarata, 2009).

"Notas sobre la cohesión de la comunidad morisca más allá de su expulsión de España," *al-Qanṭara* 29 (2008), 307–32.

"On Morisco Networks and Collectives," in K. Ingram (ed.), *The Conversos and Moriscos in Late Medieval Spain*, vol. II, pp. 121–34.

Berthier, Annie, "Nouveaux documents sur les crypto-musulmans en France au XVIIIe siècle: le cas d'un marchand bordelaise," in *Actes du* IV *Simposium International d'Études Morisques sur Métiers, Vie Religieuse et Problematiques d'Histoire* (Zaghouan: Ceromdi, 1990), 25–34.

Bertran i Roigé, Prim, "Conflictes socials a Cervera, segons el llibre del batlle Antoni de Cabrera (1357–1357)," *Miscel·lània cerverina* 6 (1989), 53–70.

Biarnes i Biarnes, Carmel, "Tres motius d'expulsió dels moriscos d'Ascó : la conservació de la sunna, els enfrontaments amb els de flix i els deutes de la vila d'Ascó," in *L'expulsiò del moriscos: Conseqüències en el món islàmic i el món cristià: Congrés internacional, Sant Carles de la Ràpita, 5–9 de desembre de 1990* (Barcelona: Generalitat de Catalunya, 1994), pp. 235–40.

Birk, Joshua, "From Borderlands to Borderlines. Narrating the Past of Twelfth-Century Sicily," in James Peter Helfers (ed.), *Multicultural Europe and Cultural Exchange in the Middle Ages and Renaissance* (Turnhout: Brepols, 2005), pp. 9–31.

"Sicilian Counterpoint: Power and Pluralism in Norman Sicily," PhD dissertation: History (University of California Santa Barbara, 2006).

Bisaha, Nancy, *Creating East and West. Renaissance Humanists and Ottoman Turks* (Philadelphia: University of Pennsylvania Press, 2004).

""New Barbarian" or Worthy Adversary? Humanist Constructs of the Ottoman Turks," in D. Blanks and M. Frassetto (eds.), *Western Views of Islam*, pp. 185–206.

Bishko, Charles Julian, "The Castilian as Plainsman. The Medieval Ranching Frontier in La Mancha and Extremadura," in Archibald F. McGann and Thomas F. Lewis (eds.), *The New World Looks at its History* (Austin: University of Texas Press, 1963), pp. 47–63.

"The Spanish and Portuguese Reconquest, 1095–1492," in Harry W. Hazard (ed.), *A History of the Crusades, Vol. 3. The Fourteenth and Fifteenth Centuries* (University of Wisconsin Press, 1975), pp. 396–456.

Bishop, Adam M., "Criminal Law and the Development of the Assizes of the Crusader Kingdom of Jerusalem in the Twelfth Century," PhD thesis (University of Toronto, 2011).

Bisson, Thomas N., *The Medieval Crown of Aragon. A Short History* (Oxford: Clarendon, 1986).

Blackmore, Josiah, "Imagining the Moor in Medieval Portugal," *diacritics* 36 (2006), 27–43.

Blanks, David R., "Western Views of Islam in the Pre-Modern Period: A Brief History of Past Approaches," in D. Blanks and M. Frassetto, *Western Views of Islam*, pp. 11–44.

Blanks, David R. and Michael Frassetto (eds.), *Western Views of Islam in Medieval and Early Modern Europe: Perception of Other* (New York: St. Martin's Press, 1999).

Blasco Martínez, Asunción, "Los malsines del Reino de Aragón: una aproximación," in *Proceedings of the Eleventh World Congress of Jewish Studies, Division B, Volume 1, The History of the Jewish people. 1, From the Second Temple Period to Modern Times* (Jerusalem: World Union of Jewish Studies, 1994), pp. 83–90.

"Medicos y pacientes de las tres religiones (Zaragoza siglo XIV y comienzos del XV)," *Aragón en la Edad Media* 12 (1995), 153–82.

Blau, Peter and Joseph E. Schwartz, *Crosscutting Circles. Testing a Macrostructural Theory of Intergroup Relations* (Orlando, FL: Academic Press, 1984).

Blumenthal, Debra, *Enemies and Familiars. Slavery and Mastery in Fifteenth-Century Valencia* (Ithaca, NY: Cornell University Press, 2009).

Blumenthal, Uta-Renate, *The Investiture Controversy: Church and Monarchy From the Ninth to the Twelfth Century* (Philadelphia: University of Pennsylvania Press, 1988).

Boas, Adrian J., "Archaeological Sources for the History of Palestine. The Frankish Period. A Unique Medieval Society Emerges," *Near Eastern Archaeology* 61 (1998), 138–73.

*Crusader Archaeology. The Material Culture of the Latin East* (London: Routledge, 1999).

Boase, Roger, "Arabic Influences on European Love-Poetry," in S. Jayyusi (ed.), *The Legacy of Muslim Spain*, pp. 457–82.

"Autobiography of a Muslim Courtier. Anselm Turmeda (*c.* 1353–*c.* 1430)," *al-Māsāq* 9 (1996–7), 45–98

Bogelin, Michael, "Between Rumor and Resistance," in K. Ingram (ed.), *Conversos and Moriscos*, vol. I, pp. 211–42.

Boissellier, Stéphane, "Une tolérance chrétienne dans l'historiographie portugaise de la Reconquête (XIIe–XIIe siècles)?" in Guy Saupin (ed.), *La tolérance. Colloque international de Nantes (mai 1998). Quatrième centenaire de l'édit de Nantes* (Presses Universitaires de Rennes, 1999), pp. 371–83.

Bollo-Panadero, María Dolores "Heretics and Infidels: The Cantigas de Santa María as Ideological Instrument of Cultural Codification," *Romance Quarterly* 55 (2008), 163–74.

Boloix Gallardo, Bárbara, *De la taifa de Arjona al Reino Nazarí de Granada (1232–1246): en torno a los orígenes de un estado y de una dinastía* (Jaén: Instituto de Estudios Giennenses, 2005).

Bolòs, Jordi, "Changes and Survival: The Territory of Lleida (Catalonia) after the Twelfth-Century Conquest," *Journal of Medieval History* 27 (2001), 313–29.

Boswell, John, *The Royal Treasure. Muslim Communities Under the Crown of Aragon in the Fourteenth Century* (New Haven, CT: Yale University Press, 1977).

Bourdieu, Pierre, *Distinction: A Social Critique of the Judgement of Taste* (London, Routledge, 1984).

Boyle, John A., "Rashīd al-Dīn and the Franks," *Central Asiatic Journal* 14 (1970), 62–67.

Bresc, Henri, "Féodalité coloniale en terre d'Islam. La Sicilie (1070–1240)," in *Structures féodales et féodalisme dans l'Occident méditerranéen (Xe-XIIIe siècles)* (École Française de Rome, 1980), pp. 631–47.

"Frédéric II et l'Islam," in A.-M. Héricher Flambard (ed.), *Frédéric II, 1194–1250, et l'héritage normand de Sicile: Actes [du] colloque de Cerisy-La-Salle, 25–28 septembre 1997* (Caen: Presses Universitaires de Caen, 2001), pp. 79–92.

"Mudejars des pays de la Couronne d'Aragón et Sarrasins de la Sicile normande: Le probleme de l'acculturation," in *Jaime I y su época*. X *Congreso de Historia de la Corona de Aragón* (Zaragoza: CSIC, 1975), pp. 51–60.

"Pantelleria entre l'Islam et la Chrétienté," *Cahiers de Tunisie* 19 (1971), 105–27.

"Le Royaume normand d'Afrique et l'Archevêché de Mahdiyya," in *Les relations des pays d'Islam avec le monde latin du milieu du* Xe *siècle au milieu du* XIIIe *siècle. Articles réunis par Françoise Micheau* (Paris: Éditions Jacques, 2000), pp. 264–83.

Bresc, Henri and Geneviève Bresc-Bautier, *Palerme 1070–1492. Mosaïque de peuples, nation rebelle: la naissance violente de l'identité sicilienne* (Paris: Autrement, 1993).

Brett, Michael, "The Armies of Ifriqia, 1052–1160," in *Guerre et paix dans l'histoire du Maghreb.* VIe *Congrès d'Histoire et de Civilisation du Maghreb, décembre 1993. Cahiers de Tunisie* (Tunis: Université de Tunis, 1997), pp. 107–250.

"The City-State in Medieval Ifriqiya: the Case of Tripoli," *Cahiers de Tunisie* 34 (1986) 69–94.

"Ifriqiya as a Market for Saharan Trade from the Tenth to the Twelfth Century," *Journal of African History* 10 (1969), 347–64.

"Muslim Justice Under Infidel Rule. The Normans in Ifriqiya, 517–555H/ 1123–1160AD," *Cahiers de Tunisie*, 43 (1995), 1–26.

Britt, Karen C. "Roger II of Sicily: Rex, Basileus, and Khalif? Identity, Politics, and Propaganda in the Cappella Palatina," *Mediaeval Studies* 16 (2007), 21–45.

Brodman, James W., *Ransoming Captives in Crusader Spain. The Order of Merced on the Christian–Islamic Frontier* (Philadelphia: University of Pennsylvania Press, 1986).

Brown, Gordon S., *The Norman Conquest of Southern Italy and Sicily* (Jefferson, MI: McFarland, 2003).

Bruce, Travis, "The Politics of Violence and Trade: Denia and Pisa in the Eleventh Century," *Journal of Medieval History* 32 (2006), 127–42.

Brufal Sucarrat, Jesús, "Rural Muslim Lleida: Marginality or Integration?" *Early Medieval Europe* 19 (2011), 436–50.

Brunschvig, Robert, *La Berberie orientale sous les Hafsides des origines à la fin du XV siècle*, 2 vols. (Paris: Adrien-Maisonneuve, 1940).

Bulliet, Richard W., *Conversion to Islam in the Medieval Period: An Essay in Quantitative History* (Cambridge, MA: Harvard University Press, 1979).

de Bunes Ibarra, Miguel Angel *et al.*, *The Invention of Glory. Afonso V and the Pastrana Tapestries* (Manchester, VT: Hudson Hills Press, 2011).

Burman, Thomas E., "Cambridge University Library MS Mm. v. 26 and the History of the Study of the Qur'ān in Medieval and Early Modern Europe," in T. E. Burman, Mark D. Meyerson, and Leah Shopkow (eds.), *Religion, Text, and Society in Medieval Spain and Northern Europe: Essays in Honor of J.N. Hillgarth* (Toronto: Pontifical Institute of Mediaeval Studies, 2002), pp. 335–63.

*Reading the Qur'ān in Latin Christendom, 1140–1560* (Philadelphia: University of Pennsylvania Press, 2007).

*Religious Polemic and the Intellectual History of the Mozarabs, c. 1050–1200* (Leiden: Brill, 1994).

Burnett, Charles, "Antioch as a Link Between Arabic and Latin Culture in the Twelfth and Thirteenth Centuries," in A. Tihon, I. Draelants, and B. van den Abeele (eds.), *Occident et Proche-Orient: contactes scientifiques au temps des croisades* (Louvain-la-Neuve, 2000), pp. 1–19.

"The Coherence of the Arabic–Latin Translation Program in Toledo in the Twelfth Century," *Science in Context* 14 (2012), 313–31.

"A Group of Latin-Arabic Translators Working in Northern Spain in the Mid-12th Century," *Journal of the Royal Asiatic Society* (1977), 62–108.

"The Second Revelation of Arabic Philosophy and Science," in Charles Burnett and Anna Contadini (eds.), *Islam and the Italian Renaissance* (London: Warburg Institute, 1999), pp. 185–98.

"The Translating Activity in Medieval Spain," in S. Jayyusi (ed.), *The Legacy of Muslim Spain*, pp. 1036–58.

"The Transmission of Arabic Astronomy via Antioch and Pisa in the Second Quarter of the Twelfth Century," in J. P. Hogendijk and A. I. Sabra (eds.), *The Enterprise of Science in Islam. New Perspectives* (Cambridge, MA: MIT Press, 2003), 23–51.

Burns, Robert I., "Almohad Prince and Mudejar Convert: New Documentation on Abū Zayd," in Donald J. Snow and Joseph T. Kagay (eds.), *Medieval*

*Iberia: Essays on the History and Literature of Medieval Spain* (New York: Peter Lang, 1997), pp. 171–88.

"Christian–Muslim Confrontation: The Thirteenth Century Dream of Conversion," in *Muslims, Christians and Jews in the Crusader Kingdom of Valencia* (Cambridge University Press, 1984), pp. 80–107.

*The Crusader Kingdom of Valencia. Reconstruction of a Thirteenth-Century Frontier* (Cambridge, MA: Harvard University Press, 1967).

"The Daughter of Abū Zayd, Last Almohad ruler of Valencia. The Family and Christian Seigniory of Alda Ferrándis 1236–1300," *Viator* 24 (1993), 143–87.

"The *Guidaticum* Safe-Conduct in Medieval Arago-Catalonia. A Mini-Institution for Muslims, Christians and Jews," *Medieval Encounters* 1 (1995), 51–113.

*Islam under the Crusaders. Colonial Survival in the Thirteenth-Century Kingdom of Valencia* (Princeton University Press, 1973).

"Mudéjar Parallel Societies. Anglophone Historiography and Spanish Context, 1975–2000," in Mark D. Meyerson and Edward D. English (eds.), *Christians, Muslims and Jews in Medieval and Early Modern Spain* (University of Notre Dame Press, 2000), pp. 91–124.

"Los mudéjares de la Valencia de las cruzadas: un capitulo olvidado de la historia islámica," *Sharq al-Andalus* 1 (1984), 15–34.

"Muslim–Christian Conflict and Contact: Mudéjar Methodology," in *Muslims, Christians, and Jews in the Crusader Kingdom of Valencia. Societies in Symbiosis* (Cambridge University Press, 1984), pp. 1–51.

"Muslims in the Thirteenth-Century Realms of Aragon. Interaction and Reaction," in J. M. Powell (ed.), *Muslims Under Latin Rule*, pp. 57–102.

*Society and Documentation in Crusader Valencia* (Princeton University Press, 1985).

*The Worlds of Alfonso the Learned and James the Conqueror. Intellect & Force in the Middle Ages* (Princeton University Press, 1985).

Burns, Robert I. and P. Chevedden, *Negotiating Cultures. Bilingual Surrender Treaties in Muslim–Crusader Spain under James the Conqueror* (Leiden: Brill, 1999).

Bū Sharab, Ahmad, *Os pseudo-mouriscos de Portugal no séc. XVI: estudo de uma especificidade a partir das fontes inquisitoriais*, Maria Filomena Lopes de Barros (trans.), (Lisbon: Hugin, 2004).

Butler, Alban, Paul Burns, and David Hugh Farmer (eds.), *Butler's Lives of the Saints. April* (Tunbridge Wells: Burns & Oates Liturgical Press, 1999).

Butler, Judith, *Gender Trouble: Feminism and the Subversion of Identity* (New York: Routledge, 1990).

Caballero–Navas, Carmen, "The Care of Women's Health and Beauty: An Experience Shared By Medieval Jewish and Christian Women," *Journal of Medieval History* 34 (2008), 146–63.

Cabanelas Rodríguz, Darío, *Juan de Segovia y el problema islámico* (Universidad de Madrid, 1952).

Cabrillana, Nicolás, *Santiago Matamoros: historia e imagen* (Málaga: Diputación de Málaga, 1999).

Cabzuelo Pliego, José Vicente, "Cristiano de Alá, renegardo de Cristo. El caso de Abdalla, fill d'En Domingo Vallés, un valenciano al servicio del Islam," *Sharq al-Andalus* 13 (1996), 27–46.

Cahen, Claude, "Notes sur l'histoire des croisades et de l'Orient latin: le régime rural syrien au temps de la domination franques," *Bulletin de la Faculté des Lettres de l'Université de Strasbourg* 29 (1950/1), 286–310.

*La Syrie du nord à l'époque des croisades et la principauté franque d'Antioche* (Paris: P. Geuthner, 1940).

Calero Secall, M. Isabel, "Rulers and Qadis. Their Relationship During the Nasrid Kingdom," *Islamic Law and Society* 7 (2000), 235–55.

Cantera Montenegro, Enrique, "El apartamiento de judíos y mudéjares en las diócesis de Osma y Sigüenza a fines del siglo XV," *Anuario de estudios medievales* 17 (1987), 501–10.

"Las comunidades mudéjares de las diócesis de Osma y Sigüenza a fines de la Edad Media," *Revista de la Facultad de Geografía y Historia* 4 (1989), 137–73.

Cardaillac, Denise, "«Alcayçi Et Le Moine De Lerida», Ou Comment Affirmer Une Identité Islamique En Milieu Chrétien," in *Actes du* II *Symposium International du C.I.E.M. sur Religion, Identité, et Sources Documentaires sur les Morisques Andalous* (Tunis: ISD, 1984), vol. I, pp. 129–37.

Cardaillac, Louis, "Un aspecto de las relaciones entre Moriscos y Cristianos: polémica y taqiyya," in *Actas del Coloquio Internacional sobre literatura aljamiada y morisca* (Madrid: Gredos, 1978), pp. 107–22.

*Moriscos y cristianos. Un enfrentamiento polémico, 1492–1640* (Madrid: Fondo de Cultura Economica, 1979).

"A propósito del paso de los Moriscos por Languedoc," in M. B. Aguilera and B. Vincent (eds.), *Granada 1492–1992*, pp. 133–40.

Cardaillac, Louis and José Luís Arántegui (eds.), *Toledo, siglos* XII–XIII*: musulmanes, cristianos y judíos: la sabiduría y la tolerància* (Madrid: Alianza, 1992).

Cardaillac-Hermosilla, Yvette, "Les livrets aljamiados de magie: une littérature populaire à l'usage des familles," in A. Temimi (ed.), *Actes du* VII^e^ *Symposium International*, pp. 49–71.

Cardini, Franco, *Europe and Islam* (Oxford: Blackwell, 2001).

Carmona González, Alfonso, "Textos jurídicos-religiosos islámicos de las épocas mudéjar y morisca," *Areas: Revista internacional de ciencias sociales* 14 (1992), 13–26.

Carrasco Pérez, Juan, "Los Mudéjares de Navarra en la segunda mitad del siglo XIV (1352–1408). Economía y sociedad," *Príncipe de Viana* 47, anejo 2 (1986), 75–107.

Carrasco Urgioti, María Soledad, *El problema morisco en Aragón en al comienzo de reinado de Felipe II (estudio y apéndices documentales)* (Chapel Hill: University of North Carolina, 1969).

Casasnovas, Miquel-Ángel, *História de Menorca* (Mallorca: Moll, 2005).

Castro, Américo, *España en su historia. Cristianos, moros y judíos* (Buenos Aires: Losada, 1948).

Catlos, Brian A., "'Accursed, Superior Men': Ethno-religious Minorities and Politics in the Medieval Mediterranean," *Comparative Studies in Society and History* 56 (2014): 844–69.

"The de Reys (1220–1501). The Evolution of a 'Middle-Class' Muslim Family in Christian Aragon," *Viator* 40 (2009), 197–219.

"Dos musulmanas pleitean contra un oficial de su aljama, en un proceso concluido en Daroca, el 10 de noviembre de 1300," in *Actas del* XI *Simposio Internacional de Mudéjarismo*, pp. 619–32.

"The Ebro Valley and Valencia. Mudéjar Experiences Related, Distinct," *Revista d'història medieval* 12 (2002), 293–305.

"'Entre eulx plusieurs Sarrazins...': Jueus i musulmans al regne de Martí I," in M. T. Ferrer i Mallol (ed.), *Actas: Martí l'Humà, el darrer rei de la dinastia de Barcelona (1396–1410), L'interregne i el compromis de Casp* (Barcelona: Institut d'Estudis Catalans, forthcoming), pp. 313–39.

"Esclavo o ciudadano: fronteras de clase en la Corona de Aragón, s. XIII," in M. T. Ferrer i Mallol and J. Mutgé Vives (eds.), *De l'esclavitud a la llibertat*, pp. 151–66.

"Four Kidnappings in s. XIII Aragon: Christian Children as Victims of Christian–Muslim Domination," *Scripta Mediterranea* 19/20 (1998), 165–80.

"A Genealogy of Marginalization? Non-Christians in the Royal Law of the Kingdom of Valencia, 1238–1525" (forthcoming).

"Justice Served or Justice Subverted? Two Muslim Women Sue a Local Mudéjar Official in Thirteenth-Century Aragon," *Anuario de Estudios Medievales* 39 (2009), 177–202.

"Mahomet Abenadalill. A Muslim Mercenary in the Service of the Kings of Aragon (1290–1291)," in H. J. Hames (ed.), *Jews, Muslims and Christians*, pp. 257–302.

"Mudéjar Communities and their Rulers: A 'Colonial Elite' in the Medieval Crown of Aragon," *Mélanges de L'École Française de Rome* 124 (2012) 495–509.

*Paradoxes of Plurality: Ethnic and Religious Diversity in the Medieval Mediterranean and Beyond* (New York: Basic Books, forthcoming).

"Privilegio y poder en el Aragón mudéjar. El auge y declive del çaualaquem Çalema," in A. Echevarría Arsuaga (ed.), *Biografías mudéjares*, pp. 133–82.

"Secundum suam zunam. Muslims and the Law in the Aragonese 'Reconquest,'" *Mediterranean Studies* 7 (1999), 13–26.

"Tyranny and the Mundane: Bureaucracy and (In)Justice in 14th-Century Aragon as Glimpsed through the Slave Trade and the Exercise of Law (Daroca, 1318)," in Josefina Mutgé i Vives *et al.* (eds.), *La Corona cotalanoaragonesa, L'Islam i el món mediterrani. Estudis d'història medieval en homenatge a la Professora Maria Teresa Ferrer i Mallol* (Barcelona: Consejo Superior de Investigaciones Cientificas, 2013), pp. 149–55.

*The Victors and the Vanquished. Christians and Muslims of Catalonia and Aragon, 1050–1300* (Cambridge University Press, 2004).

"Who was Philip of Mahdia and Why Did He Have to Die? Confessional Identity and Political Power in the Twelfth-Century Mediterranean," *Mediterranean Chronicle* 1 (2011), 73–102.

Chalandon, Ferdinand, *Histoire de la domination normande en Italie et en Sicile*, 2 vols. (New York: B. Franklin, 1960).

Chalmeta Gendrón, Pedro, "El almotacén a través de los 'llibre del Mustaçaf'," *Aragón en la eded media* 20 (2008), 203–23.

*El zoco medieval. Contribución a la historia del mercado* (Almeria: Fundación Ibn Tufayl de Estudios Árabes, 2010).

Chazan, Robert, *The Jews of Medieval Western Christendom 1000–1500* (Cambridge University Press, 2006).

Chevedden, Paul E., "A Crusade from the First. The Norman Conquest of Islamic Sicily, 1060–1091," *al-Māsāq* 22 (2010), 191–225.

"The Islamic View and the Christian View of the Crusades. A New Synthesis," *History* 93 (2008), 181–200.

"The View of the Crusades from Rome and Damascus: The Geo-Strategic and Historical Perspectives of Pope Urban II and ʿAlī ibn Ṭāhir al-Sulamī," *Oriens* 39 (2011), 257–329.

Chiarelli, Leonard Charles, "The Ibadiyah in Muslim Sicily," *Al-ʿUsur al-Wusta* 16 (April 2004), 11–17.

"Sicily During the Fatimid Age," PhD Dissertation, History (Salt Lake City: University of Utah, 1986).

Childers, William, "An Extensive Network of Morisco Merchants Active Circa 1590," in Kevin Ingram (ed.), *The Conversos and Moriscos*, vol. II. 135–60.

Christ, Georg, *Trading Conflicts: Venetian Merchants and Mamluk Officials in Late Medieval Alexandria* (Leiden: Brill, 2012).

Ciggaar, Krijnie N., "Adaptation to Oriental Life by Rulers in and Around Antioch. Examples and Exempla," in K. Ciggaar *et al.*, *East and West*, pp. 261–82.

Ciggaar, Krijnie N., M. Metcalfe, and H. Teule (eds.), *East and West in the Crusader States. Context, Contacts, Confrontations. Acta of the Congress Held at Hernen Castle in September 2000* (Leuven: Uitgeverij Peeters, 2003).

Cipollone, Giulio (ed.), *La liberazione dei "captivi" tra Cristianità e Islam: oltre la crociata e il ğihād: tolleranza e servizio umanitario* (Archivio Segreto Vaticano, 2000).

Císcar Pallarés, Eugenio, "'Algaravía' y 'Algemía.' Precisiones sobre la lengua de los Moriscos en el Reino de Valencia," *al-Qanṭara* 15 (1994), 131–59.

Clément, François, "Reverter et son fils, deux officiers catalans au service des sultans de Marrakech," *Medieval Encounters* 9 (2003), 79–106.

Cobb, Paul M., *Usama ibn Munqidh. Warrior-poet of the Age of Crusades* (Oxford: Oneworld, 2005).

Cohen, Mark R., "What was the Pact of ʾUmar? A literary-historical study," *Jerusalem Studies in Arabic and Islam* 23 (1999), 100–57.

Cole, Penny J., "'O God, the Heathen have Come into your Inheritance' (Ps. 78.1): the Theme of Religious Pollution in Crusade Documents, 1095–1188," in M. Shatzmiller (ed.), *Crusaders and Muslims*, pp. 84–111.

*The Preaching of the Crusades to the Holy Land, 1095–1270* (Cambridge, MA: Medieval Academy of America, 1991).

Coleman, David, *Creating Christian Granada. Society & Religious Culture in an Old-World Frontier City, 1492–1600* (Ithaca, NY: Cornell University Press, 2003).

Collantes de Terán Sánchez, Antonio, "La aljama mudéjar de Sevilla," *al-Andalus* 43 (1978), 143–62.

Collins, Roger and Anthony Goodman (eds.), *Medieval Spain: Culture, Conflict, and Coexistence. Studies in Honour of Angus MacKay* (New York: Palgrave Macmillan, 2002).

Conde Solares, Carlos, "Social Continuity and Religious Coexistence. The Muslim Community of Tudela in Navarre before the Expulsion of 1516," *Continuity and Change* 26 (2011), 309–31.

Constable, Giles, "The Historiography of the Crusades," in Angeliki E. Mottahedeh and Roy Parviz Laiou (eds.), *The Crusades from the Perspective of Byzantium and the Muslim World* (Washington DC: Dumbarton Oaks, 2001), pp. 1–22.

Constable, Olivia Remie, "Chess and Courtly Culture in Medieval Castile. The Libro de Ajedrez of Alfonso X, el Sabio," *Speculum* 82 (2007), 301–47.

"Cross-Cultural Contracts: Sales of Land Between Christians and Muslims in 12th-Century Palermo," *Studia Islamica* 85 (1997), 67–84.

*Housing the Stranger in the Mediterranean World. Lodging, Trade, and Travel in Late Antiquity and the Middle Ages* (Cambridge University Press, 2003).

"Regulating Religious Noise The Council of Vienne, the Mosque Call and Muslim Pilgrimage in the Late Medieval Mediterranean World," *Medieval Encounters* 16 (2010), 64–95.

*Trade and Traders in Muslim Spain. The Commercial Realignment of the Iberian Peninsula, 900–1500* (Cambridge University Press, 1994).

Conte Cazcarro, Ánchel, *La aljama de moros de Huesca* (Huesca: Instituto de Estudios Altaragoneses, 1992).

"La decadència de la aristocracía morisca: el caso de los Çafar de Huesca," *Sharq al-Andalus* 14–15 (1997–98), 177–99.

"La inquisición y los moros de la ciudad de Huesca," in *Don Antonio Durán Guidol Homenaje* (Huesca: Instituto de Estudios Altoaragoneses, 1995), pp. 213–27.

"La morería de Huesca," in *Actas del* VI *Simposio Internacional de Mudejarismo*, pp. 613–18.

Coope, Jessica, "Marriage, Kinship, and Islamic Law in al-Andalus: Reflections on Pierre Guichard's al-Ándalus," *al-Masāq* 20 (2008), 161–77.

*The Martyrs of Córdoba. Community and Family Conflict in an Age of Mass Conversion* (Lincoln: University of Nebraska Press, 1995).

Corcos, David, "The Nature of the Almohad Rulers' Treatment of the Jews," *Journal of Medieval Iberian Studies* 2 (2010), 259–85.

Corral Lafuente, José Luis, "El proceso de represión contra los mudéjares aragoneses," *Aragón en la Edad Media* 14–15 (1999), 341–56.

Corral Lafuente, José Luis, Javier Gonzalvo Peña, and C. Echeverría Bressel (eds.), *La cultura islámica en Aragón* (Zaragoza: Diputación Provincial, 1986).

Cortés López, José Luís, *Los moriscos y sus esclavos negros* (Madrid: Darek Nyumba, 1993).

Cortés Peña, Antonio Luis, "Mudéjares y moriscos granadinos, una visión dialéctica tolerància-intolerància," in M. B. Aguilera and B. Vincent (eds.), *Granada 1492–1992*, pp. 97–113.

Coureas, N., "Christian and Muslim Captives on Lusignan Cyprus. Redemption or Retention?," in G. Cipollone (ed.), *La liberazione dei "captivi,"* pp. 525–31.

Courtois, Charles, "Gregoire VII et l'Afrique du Nord: remarques sur les communautés chrétiennes d'Afrique du Nord au XIe siècle," *Revue historique* 195 (1945), 97–122 and 193–226.

Cruz Hernández, Miguel, "Islamic Thought in the Iberian Peninsula," in S. Jayyusi (ed.), *The Legacy of Muslim Spain*, pp. 777–803.

Csaba, Ahmad Okvath, "The Way Leading to the Translation of the Glorious Qur'ān into Hungarian. A Short Historical and Bibliographical Survey of the Attempts Made by Hungarians," *Journal of Qurānic Research and Studies* 2 (2007), 5–28.

Cutler, Allan, "Who Was the Monk of France and When Did he Write?" *Al-Andalus* 28 (1963), 149–69.

Daftary, Farhad, *The Isma'ilis: Their History and Doctrines* (Cambridge University Press, 1990).

Daiber, Hans, "Islamic Roots of Knowledge in Europe," in C. Marcinkowski (ed.), *The Islamic World and the West*, pp. 63–84.

Dajani-Shakeel, Hadia, "Diplomatic Relations between Muslim and Frankish Rulers 1097–1153 A.D.," in M. Shatzmiller (ed.), *Crusaders and Muslims*, pp. 190–215.

"Jihād in Twelfth-Century Arabic Poetry: A Moral and Religious Force to Counter the Crusades," *Muslim World* 66 (1976), 96–113.

"Natives and Franks in Palestine. Perceptions and Interaction," in Michael Gervers and Ramzi Jibran Bikhazi (eds.), *Conversion and Continuity*, pp. 161–84.

"Some Aspects of Muslim-Frankish Christian Relations in the Shām Region in the Twelfth-Century," in Yvonne Yazbeck Haddad, and Wadī' Zaydān Ḥaddād (eds.), *Christian-Muslim Encounters* (Gainesville: University of Florida Press, 1995), pp. 193–209.

Dalli, Charles, "Contriving Coexistence. Muslims and Christians in the Unmaking of Norman Sicily," *Religion and Philosophy* 4 (2009), 30–43.

Daniel, Norman, *Heroes and Saracens. An Interpretation of the Chansons de Geste* (Edinburgh University Press, 1984).

*Islam and the West. The Making of an Image* (Edinburgh: Longman, 1960).

Danylenko, Andrii, "On the Language of Early Lithuanian Tatars, or Have Lithuanian Tatars Ever Written in Ukrainian?" *The Slavonic and East European Review* 84 (2006), 201–36.

Davis, Natalie Zemon, *Trickster Travels. A Sixteenth-Century Muslim Between Worlds* (New York: Hill and Wang, 2006).

Davis-Secord, Sarah, "Muslims in Norman Sicily. The Evidence of Imam al-Mazari's Fatwas," *Mediaeval Studies* 16 (2007), 46–66.

Deguilhem, Randi and Manuela Marín, "Introduction: Visibility, Agency and the Consciousness of Women's Actions: To What Extent?" in R. Deguilhem and M. Marín (eds.), *Writing the Feminine*, pp. xv–xxvi.

Deguilhem, Randi and Manuela Marín (eds.), *Writing the Feminine. Women in Arab Sources* (London: I. B. Taurus, 2002).

Devaney, Thomas C., "An 'Amiable Enmity': Frontier Spectacle and Intercultural Relations in Castile and Cyprus," PhD Dissertation (History: Brown University, 2011)

Díaz Borrás, Andrés, *El miedo al mediterráneo: la caridad popular valenciana y la redención de cautivos bajo el poder musulmán, 1323–1539* (Barcelona: CSIC, 2001).

Díaz de Rábago Hernández, Carmen, "Mujeres mudéjares en operaciones económicas durante el siglo XV valenciano: el papel de la dote islámica," in *Actas del* VII *Simposio Internacional de Mudejarismo*, pp. 55–64.

Diem, Werner and Marco Schüller, *The Living and the Dead in Islam: Studies in Arabic Epitaphs* (Wiesbaden: Harrassowitz, 2004).

Díez Jorge, María Elena, *Mujeres y arquitectura: mudéjares y cristianas en la construcción* (Universidad de Granada, 2011).

"Relaciones de género en las artesanas mudéjares y las artesanas moriscas," in *Actas del* VIII *Simposio Internacional de Mudejarismo*, pp. 771–82.

Dodds, Jerrilynn D., "The Mudéjar Tradition in Architecture," in S. Jayyusi (ed.), *The Legacy of Muslim Spain*, pp. 592–98.

"Mudéjar Tradition and the Synagogues of Medieval Spain: Cultural Identity and Cultural Hegemony," in Vivian B. Mann *et al.* (eds.), *Convivencia*, pp. 113–132.

Dodds, Jerrilynn D., Maria Rosa Menocal, and Abigail Krasner Balbale, *The Arts of Intimacy: Christians, Jews, and Muslims in the Making of Castilian Culture* (New Haven, CT: Yale University Press, 2008).

Domingo i Grabiel, Anna, "La veu de sarraïns i sarraïnes de la Corona d'Aragó a la documentació cristiana del segle XIV," *Sharq al-Andalus* 12 (1995), 11–22.

Domínguez Ortiz, Antonio, and Bernard Vincent, *Historia de los moriscos: vida y tragedia de una minoría* (Madrid: Revista de Occidente, 1978).

Domínguez Sánchez, Santiago, "Cristianos y musulmanes en la península Ibérica: la guerra, la frontera y la convivencia. Una visión a través de las «bulas» del siglo XIII," in J. I. Ruíz de la Peña, Juan Ignacio, and M. Á. Ladero Quesada (eds.), *Cristianos y musulmanes en la peninsula Ibérica*, pp. 451–73.

Donner, Fred McGraw, *Muhammad and the Believers: At the Origins of Islam* (Cambridge, MA: Belknap Press of Harvard University Press, 2010).

Doubleday, Simon *et al.* (eds.), (Special Edition: Las Navas de Tolosa), *Journal of Medieval Iberian Studies* 4(1) (2012).

Drory, Joseph, "Ḥanbalīs of the Nablus Region in the Eleventh and Twelfth Centuries," *Asian and African Studies* 22 (1988), 93–112.

"Some Observations during a Visit to Palestine by Ibn Al-Arabi of Seville in 1092–1095," *Crusades* 3 (2004), 101–24.

Dufourcq, Charles-Emmanuel, "Chrétiens et Musulmanes durant les derniers siècles du Moyen Âge," *Anuario de estudios medievales* 10 (1980), 207–25.

Dulin-Mallory, Nina, "Seven trewe bataylis for Jesus Sake: The Long-Suffering Saracen Palomides," in D. Blanks and M. Frassetto (eds.), *Western Views of Islam*, pp. 165–72.

Dunbabin, Jean, *The French in the Kingdom of Sicily, 1266–1305* (Cambridge University Press, 2011).

Dunlop, D. M., "A Christian Mission to Muslim Spain in the Eleventh Century," *Al-Andalus* 17 (1952), 259–310.

Dunn, Ross E., *The Adventures of Ibn Battuta, a Muslim Traveler of the 14th Century* (Berkeley: University of California Press, 1986).

Echevarría Arsuaga, Ana, "Las aljamas mudéjares castellanas en siglo XV: redes de poder y conflictos internos," *Espacio, tiempo y forma* III 14 (2001), 93–112.

"De cadí a alcalde mayor. La élite judicial mudéjar en el siglo XV (I)," *al-Qanṭara* 24 (2003), 139–68.

"De cadí a alcalde mayor. La élite judicial mudéjar en el siglo XV (II)," *al-Qanṭara* 24 (2003), 273–90.

"Los Caro de Ávila, Una familia de alfaquíes y comerciantes mudéjares," in A. Echevarría Arsuaga (ed.), *Biografías mudéjares*, pp. 203–32.

"Catalina of Lancaster, the Castilian Monarchy and Coexistence," in R. Collins and A. Goodman (eds.), *Medieval Spain*, pp. 79–122.

"Conversión y ascenso social en la Castilla del siglo XV: los casos de Farax de Belvis y García de Jaén," in *Actas del* VIII *Simposio Internacional de Mudejarismo*, pp. 555–67.

"Esclavos musulmanes en los hospitales de cautivos de la orden militar de Santiago (siglos XII y XIII)," *al-Qanṭara* 27 (2007), 465–88.

*The Fortress of Faith: The Attitude Towards Muslims in Fifteenth-Century Spain* (Leiden: Brill, 1999).

*Knights on the Frontier: The Moorish Guard of the Kings of Castile (1410–1467)* (Leiden: Brill, 2009).

"La 'mayoría' mudéjar en León y Castilla: legislación real y distribución de la población (siglos XI–XIII)," *En la España medieval* 29 (2006), 7–30.

"Los mudéjares de los reinos de Castilla y Portugal," *Revista d'història medieval* 12 (2002), 31–46.

"'Vassal and Friend.' Strategies of Mudejar Submission and Resistance to Christian Power in Castile," in H. Hames (ed.), *Jews, Muslims and Christians*, pp. 183–96.

Echevarría Arsuaga, Ana (ed.), *Biografías mudéjares, o la experiencia de ser minoría: Biografías islámicas en la España cristiana* (Madrid: CSIC, 2009).

Edbury, P. W., *The Kingdom of Cyprus and the Crusades, 1191–1374* (Cambridge University Press, 1991).

Eddé, Anne-Marie, "Francs et Musulmanes de Syrie au début du XIIe siècle d'après l'historien Ibn Abi Tayyi'," in Benjamin Z. Kedar, Jonathan Riley-Smith, and Michel Balard (eds.), *Dei gesta per Francos: Études sur les Croisades dédiées à Jean Richard/Crusade Studies in Honour of Jean Richard* (Aldershot: Ashgate, 2001), pp. 159–69.

Eddé, Anne-Marie and Françoise Micheau, *L'Orient au temps des Croisades* (Paris: Flammarion, 2002).

Edgington, Susan, "Antioch: Medieval City of Culture," in K. Ciggaar *et al.* (eds.), *East and West*, pp. 247–60.

Ehlers, Benjamin, "Violence and Religious Identity in Early Modern Valencia," in Kevin Ingram (ed.), *The Conversos and Moriscos*, pp. 103–20.

El Hour, Rachid, "The Andalusian Qāḍī in the Almoravid Period: Political and Judicial Authority," *Studia Islamica* 90 (2000), 67–83.

Elisséeff, Nikita, "The Reaction of Syrian Muslims after the Foundation of the First Latin Kingdom of Jerusalem," in M. Shatzmiller (ed.), *Crusaders and Muslims*, pp. 162–72.

Ellenblum, Roni, *Frankish Rural Settlement in the Latin Kingdom of Jerusalem* (Cambridge University Press, 1998).

Elliot, J. H., *Imperial Spain 1469–1716* (London: Penguin, 1963).

Elukin, Jonathan M., *Living Together, Living Apart: Rethinking Jewish–Christian Relations in the Middle Ages* (Princeton University Press, 2007).

*Encyclopaedia of Islam, Second Edition*, P. Bearman, Th. Bianguis, C. E. Bosworth, E. van Donzel, and W. P. Heinrichs (eds.), (Leiden: Brill, 2012), online.

de Epalza Ferre, Míkel (Miguel), "El Cid y los musulmanes, el sistema de parias-pagas, la colaboración de Aben Galbón, el título de Cid-León, la posadita fortificada de Alcocer," in *El Cid En El Valle De Jalon* (Zaragoza: IPF, 1991), pp. 103–21.

*Jésus otage: Juifs, Chrétiens et Musulmans en Espagne*, VI$^{e}$–XVII$^{e}$ *siècles* (Paris: Cerf, 1987).

"Los Moriscos frente a la Inquisición, en su versión islámica del cristianismo," in Joaquín Pérez Villanueva, Bartolomé Escandell Bonet, and Ángel Alcalá (eds.), *Historia de la Inquisición en España y América* (Madrid: Centro de Estudios Inquisitoriales, 2000), pp. 737–70.

"Notes pour une histoire des polémiques anti-chrétiennes dans l'Occident musulman," *Arabica* 18 (1971), 99–106.

"Quelques épisodes des relations historiques entre l'Espagne et l'île de Jerba," in *Actes du Colloque sur l'histoire de Jerba, avril 1982* (Tunis: Ministère des affaires culturelles, 1986), pp. 85–91.

"Sidi Bulgayz, protector de los moriscos exiliados en Túnez (s. XVII). Nuevos documentos traducidos y estudiados," *Sharq al-Andalus* 16–17 (1999), 141–72.

de Epalza Ferre, Míkel (Miguel) (ed.), *L'Expulsió dels moriscos: conseqüències en el món islàmic i el món cristià: 380è aniversari de l'expulsió dels moriscos, Congrés international, Sant Carles de la Ràpita, 5–9 de desembre de 1990* (Barcelona: Generalitat de Catalunya, 1994).

de Epalza Ferre, Mikel (Miguel) and Bernabé Pons, Luis F., "Bibliografía de mudéjares y moriscos, I," *Sharq al-Andalus* 12 (1995), 631–55.

"Bibliografía de mudéjares y moriscos, II," *Sharq al-Andalus* 13 (1996), 273–309.

"Bibliografía de mudéjares y moriscos, III," *Sharq al-Andalus* 14–15 (1996), 473–510.

Eph'al, I. "'Ishmael' and 'Arab(s)': A Transformation of Ethnological Terms," *Journal of Near Eastern Studies* 35 (1976), 225–35.

Epstein, Steven, *Purity Lost: Transgressing Boundaries in the Eastern Mediterranean, 1000–1400* (Baltimore, MD: Johns Hopkins University Press, 2007).

*Speaking of Slavery: Color, Ethnicity, and Human Bondage in Italy* (Ithaca, NY: Cornell University Press, 2001).

Erdmann, Carl, *The Origin of the Idea of Crusade* (Princeton University Press, 1977).

Espinar Moreno, Manuel, "Abelcoçen aben Cohbe se convierte al cristianismo como Diego de Mendoza. El alguacilazgo de Purchena en manos de esta familia desde octubre del 1500 hasta 1568," *Roel* 7–8 (1986), 83–114.

Esteban Abad, Rafael, *Estudio histórico-político sobre la ciudad y comunidad de Daroca* (Teruel: Instituto de Estudios Turolenses, 1959).

d'Eszlary, Charles, "Les musulmans hongrois au Moyen Âge (VIIe–XIVe siècles)," *Revue de l'Institut des Belles Lettres Arabes* 19 (1956), 375–86.

Fanjul, Serafín, *La quimera de al-Andalus* (Madrid: Siglo Veintiuno, 2004).

Faroqhi, Suraiya, *The Ottoman Empire and the World around It* (London: I.B. Taurus, 2000).

Febrer Romaguera, Manuel Vicente, *Les aljames mudéjars valencianes en el segle* XV (Universitat de València, 2006).

"Los Bellvís: una dinastía mudéjar de Alcadíes Generales de Valencia, Aragón y principado de Cataluña," in *Actas del* III *Simposio Internacional de Mudejarismo*, pp. 277–90.

"Derecho común, fueros y estatuto islámico de los mudéjares de los señores aragoneses: el caso de las alhóndigas y de la ordenanza de D. Pedro Fernández de Híjar para prohibir el juego de dados a sus vasallos moros (1297)," *Aragón en la Edad Media* 20 (2008), 301–19.

"Los tribunales de los alcadies moros en las aljamas mudéjares valencianas," *Anuario de estudios medievales* 22 (1992), 45–77.

Febvre, Lucien, "The Origins of the French Reformation: A Badly-Put Question?," in Peter Burke (ed.), *A New Kind of History: From the Writings of Febvre* (New York: Harper & Row, 1973), pp. 44–107.

Fernández, Manuel F., and Rafael M. García Pérez, *En los márgenes de la ciudad de Dios: Moriscos en Sevilla* (Universidad de Valencia, 2009).

Ferreiro, A., "The Seige of Barbastro, (1064–1065): A Reassessment," *Journal of Medieval History* 9 (1983), 129–44.

Ferrer i Mallol, Maria Teresa, "L'alfaqui Mahomat Alhaig i la lluita de poder a la moreria d'Elx (1448–1457)," *Revista d'història medieval* 12 (2002), 185–241.

"L'aljama islàmica de Tortosa a la baixa Edat Mitjana," *Recerca* 7 (2003), 179–230.

*Les aljames sarraïnes de la governació d'Oriola en el segle* XIV (Barcelona: CSIC, 1988).

"La capitulación de Borja en 1122," *Aragón en la Edad Media* 10–11 (1993), 269–79.

"La carta de població dels Sarraïns de la Vall d'Aiora (1328)," *Sharq al-Andalus* 3 (1986), 81–94.

"L'emigració dels Sarraïns residents a Catalunya, a Aragó i al Païs Valencià durant l'Edat Mitjana," in M. de Epalza Ferre (ed.), *L'expulsió dels moriscos*, pp. 19–26.

*Entre la paz y la guerra. La Corona Catalano–aragonesa y Castilla en la Baja Edad Media* (Barcelona: CSIC, 2005).

"Évolution du statut de la minorité islamique dans les pays de la couronne catalano-aragonaise au XIV siècle," in Michel Balard et Alain Ducellier (eds.), *Le partage du monde, échanges et colonisation dans la Méditerranée médiévale* (Paris: Publications de la Sorbonne, 1998), pp. 439–452.

"Francos pero excluidos de la mezquita y del cementerio: los Bellito y los Galip de la morería de Zaragoza," in María del Val González de la Peña (ed.), *Estudios en memoria del Profesor Dr. Carlos Sáez. Homenaje* (Alcalá de Henares: Universidad de Alcalá, 2007), pp. 341–52.

*La frontera amb l'Islam en el segle XIV. Cristians i Sarraïns al País Valencià* (Barcelona: CSIC, 1988).

"Frontera, convivencia y proselitismo entre Moros y Cristianos en los textos de Eiximenis y San Vicente Ferrer," in José María Rábanos Soto (ed.), *Pensamiento medieval hispano: homenaje a Horacio Santiago-Otero* (Madrid: CSIC, 1998), pp. 1579–600.

"La frontera meridional valenciana durant la guerra amb Castella dita dels Dos Peres," in *Pere el Cerimoniós i la seva època* (Barcelona: CSIC, 1989), pp. 245–357.

"La incursió de l'exèrcit de Granada de 1304 pel regne de València i l'atac a Cocentaina," *Alberri* 15 (2002), 55–150.

"La moreria de Xàtiva (segles XIV–XV)," in *Xàtiva, els Borja: una projecció europea* (Xàtiva: Museu de l'Almodí, 1985), pp. 189–200.

"The Muslim *Aljama* of Tortosa in the Late Middle Ages: Notes on Its Organisation," *Scripta Mediterranea* 19/20 (1998), 143–164.

*Organització i defensa d'un territori fronterer: la governació d'Oriola en el segle* XIV (Barcelona: CSIC, 1990).

"La organización militar en Cataluña en la Edad Media," *Revista de historia militar* [Extra] (2001), 119–221.

"Les phénomènes migratoires parmi les Musulmans soumis à la Couronne Catalano–aragonaise pendant le Moyen Âge," in Michel Balard and Alain Ducellier (eds.), *Migrations et diasporas méditerranéennes (*XI–XVI *siècles) (Toulouse-Conques, 14–17 octobre 1999)* (Paris: Publications de la Sorbonne, 2002), pp. 259–81.

"Un procés per homicidi entre sarraïns de l'Horta d'Alacant (1315)," *Sharq al-Andalus* 7 (1990), 135–50.

"Els redemptors de captius: mostolafs, eixees o alfaquecs (segles XII–XIII)," *Medievalia* 9 (1990), 85–106.

"Les relacions entre Catalunya, Granada i el Magrib medieval," in *L'Islam i Catalunya* (Barcelona: Institut Català de la Mediterrània, 1998), pp. 251–59.

*Els sarraïns de la corona catalano-aragonesa en el segle* XIV (Barcelona: CSIC, 1985).

"La tinença a costum d'Espanya en els castells de la frontera meridional valenciana," *Miscel·lània de textos medievals* 4 (1988), 1–102.

Ferrer i Mallol, María Teresa Vives and Josefina Mutgé (eds.), *De l'esclavitud a la llibertat: Esclaus i lliberts a l'edat mitjana: Actes del col·loqui internacional celebrat a Barcelona, del 27 al 29 de maig de 1999* (Barcelona: CSIC, 2000).

Ferrer Taberner, Andrés, "Bandosidades rurales mudéjares en las montañas valencianas: el caso de los vasallos del señorío de Serra," in *Actas del* VIII *Simposio Internacional de Mudejarismo*, pp. 261–274.

Fierro Bello, María Isabel, "Alfonso X 'The Wise': The Last Almohad Caliph?" *Mediterranean Encounters* 15 (2009), 175–98.

"Christian Success and Muslim Fear in Andalusi Writings during the Almoravid and Almohad Periods," in Uri Rubin and David J. Wasserstein (eds.), *Dhimmis and Others: Jews and Christians and the World of Classical Islam* (Winona Lake, IN: Eisenbrauns, 1997), pp. 155–78.

"La emigración en el Islam: conceptos antiguos, nuevos problemas," *Awrāq* 12 (1991), pp. 11–41.

"La mujer y el trabajo en el Corán y el hadiz," in M. J. Viguera (ed.), *La mujer en al-Andalus*, pp. 35–51.
"The *Qāḍī* as Ruler," in *Saber religioso y poder político en el Islam: Actas del Simposio Internacional (Granada, 15–18 de octubre de 1991)* (Madrid: Agencia Española de Cooperación Internacional, 1994), pp. 71–116.
Finkel, Caroline, *Osman's Dream: The Story of the Ottoman Empire, 1300–1923* (New York: Basic Books, 2006).
Firestone, Reuven, *Jihād: The Origin of Holy War in Islam* (New York: Oxford University Press, 1999).
Fischler, Claude, "Food, Self and Identity," *Social Science Information* 27 (1980), 275–292.
Fletcher, Richard A., *The Quest for El Cid* (New York: Knopf, 1990).
*St. James's Catapult. The Life and Times of Diego Gelmírez of Santiago de Compostela* (New York: Clarendon, 1984).
Flores Arroyuelo, Francisco José, *Los últimos Moriscos: (Valle de Ricote, 1614)* (Barcelona: PPU, 1993).
Folda, Jaroslav, *Crusader Art in the Holy Land, 1098–1187* (Cambridge University Press, 1995).
Font y Ríus, José María (Font i Rius, Josep Maria), "Notas sobre algunas cartas pueblas de la región oriental aragonésa," *Anuario de historia del derecho español*, 41 (1971), 699–766.
Forey, Alan J. *The Templars in the "Corona de Aragón"* (Oxford University Press, 1973).
Fournel-Guérin, Jacqueline, "Un famille morisque de Saragosse: les Compañero," *al-Awrāq* 4 (1981), 179–84.
Franco Sánchez, Francisco, "Los mudéjares, según la riḥla de Ibn aṣ-Ṣabbāh (m. después 895/1490)," *Sharq al-Andalus* 12 (1995), 375–91.
*Muhammad aš-Šafra: el médico y su época* (Universidad de Alicante, 1990).
"El reino nazarí de Granada según un viajero mudéjar almeriense: Ibn as-Sabbah (m. después 895/1490)," *Sharq al-Andalus* 13 (1996), 203–24.
Franco Sánchez, Francisco and María Sol Cabello, *Muhammad aš-Šafra: el médico y su época* (Universidad de Alicante, 1990).
Frassetto, Michael, "The Image of the Saracen as Heretic in the Sermons of Ademar de Chabannes," in D. Blanks and M. Frassetto (eds.), *Western Views of Islam*, pp. 83–96.
Freedman, Paul H., *The Origins of Peasant Servitude in Medieval Catalonia* (Cambridge University Press, 1991).
Freely, John, *Jem Sultan: The Adventures of a Captive Turkish Prince in Renaissance Europe* (London: HarperCollins, 2004).
Freidenreich, David M., *Foreigners and Their Food: Constructing Otherness in Jewish, Christian, and Islamic Law* (Berkeley: University of California Press, 2011).
"Muslims in Canon Law, ca. 650–1000," in David Thomas *et al.* (eds.), *Christian–Muslim Relations: A Bibliographic History* (Leiden: Brill, 2009), vol. I, pp. 83–98.
"Muslims in Western Canon Law, 1000–1500," in David Thomas *et al.* (eds.), *Christian–Muslim Relations: A Bibliographic History* (Leiden: Brill, 2011), vol. II, pp. 41–68.

"Sharing Meals with Non-Christians in Canon Law Commentaries, ca. 1160–1260: A Case Study in Legal Development," *Medieval Encounters* 14 (2008), 41–77.

Friedman, Yvonne, *Encounter between Enemies: Captivity and Ransom in the Latin Kingdom of Jerusalem* (Leiden: Brill, 2002).

"Women in Captivity and Their Ransom During the Crusader Period," in S. Menache *et al.* (eds.), *Cross Cultural Convergences*, pp. 75–87.

Fromherz, Allen James, *The Almohads: The Rise of an Islamic Empire* (London: I.B. Tauris, 2010).

*Ibn Khaldun: Life and Times* (Edinburgh: Edinburgh University Press, 2010).

Fuchs, Barbara, *Exotic Nation: Maurophilia and the Construction of Early Modern Spain* (Philadelphia: University of Pennsylvania Press, 2009).

Fuente Pérez, María Jesús, "Christian, Muslim and Jewish Women in Late Medieval Iberia," *Mediterranean Encounters* 15 (2009), 319–33.

*Velos y desvelos: cristianas, musulmanas y judías en la España medieval* (Madrid: Esfera de los Libros, 2006).

Gabrielli, Francesco, "Frederick II and Moslem Culture," *East and West* 9 (1958), 53–61.

Galán Sánchez, Ángel, "El dinero del rey y la «ley de la comunidad». Pacto político y contrato fiscal en el Reino de Granada tras la conquista", in F. Foronda (ed.), *Avant le contrat social. Le contrat politique dans l'Occident médiéval (XIII^e–XV^e siècle)* (Paris, Sorbonne, 2011), pp. 653–86.

"*Fuqahā'* y musulmanes vencidos en el Reino de Granada (1485–1520)," in A. Echevarría Arsuaga (ed.), *Biografías mudéjares*, pp. 329–83.

*Los mudéjares del reino de Granada* (Universidad de Granada, 1991).

"The Muslim Population of the Christian Kingdom of Granada: Urban Oligarchies and Rural Communities," in M. Asenjo González and A. M. Rodrigues (eds.), *Oligarchy and Patronage in Spanish and Portuguese Late Medieval Urban Society* (Turnhout: Brepols, 2009), pp. 71–90.

*Una sociedad en transición. Los granadinos de mudéjares a moriscos* (Universidad de Granada, 2010).

"Turcos y Moriscos en la rebelión de las Alpujarras," in *La organización militar en los siglos* XV *y* XVI. *Actas de las* II *Jornadas de Historia Militar* (Málaga: Consejería Cultura Junta Andalucía, 1993), pp. 129–36.

Galido y Romeo, Pascual, "La bellas artes en Zaragoza (siglo XVI). Estudios históricos," *Memorias de la Facultad de Filosofía y Letras* 1 (1922–23), 369–472.

"Un mueble cristiano mudéjar. El facistol del Papa Luna," *Memorias de la Facultad de Filosofía y Letras* 1 (1922–23), 371–78.

Gallego y Burín, Antonio and Sandovol Alfonso Gámir, *Los moriscos del Reino de Granada, según el Sínodo de Guadix de 1554* (Universidad de Granada, 1968).

Galloway, J. H., "The Mediterranean Sugar Industry," *Geographical Review* 67 (1977), 177–94.

García Arancón, María Raquel, "Marco jurídico y proyección social de las minorías navarras: judíos y mudéjares (siglos XII–XIV)," *Iura vasconiae* 4 (2007), 459–516.

"Martin Sánchez, un andalusí converso en Navarra (c. 1230-c. 1263)," *Anaquel de estudios árabes* 3 (1992), 217–22.

"Los mudéjares de Navarra ante la fiscalidad eclesiástica," *Príncipe de Viana* 72 (2011), 387–407.

"Origen y azares de un moro converso en Navarra (siglo XIII)," *Príncipe de Viana* 42 (1981), 691–95.

García-Arenal, Mercedes, "La aljama de los moros de Cuenca en el siglo XV," *Historia, instituciones, documentos* 4 (1977), 35–47.

"Los Andalusíes en el ejército sa'dī: un intento de golpe de estado contra Aḥmad al-Manṣūr al-Ḏahabī (1578)," *al-Qanṭara* 5 (1984), 169–202.

"A Catholic Muslim Prophet. Agustín de Ribera, 'The Boy Who Saw Angels,'" *Common Knowledge* 18 (2012), 267–91.

"Documentos árabes de Tudela y Tarazona," *al-Qanṭara* 3 (1982), 27–72.

"Dos documentos sobre los Moros de Uclés en 1501," *Al-Andalus* 42 (1977), 167–81.

*Inquisición y Moriscos: los procesos del tribunal de Cuenca* (Madrid: Siglo Veintiuno, 1978).

*Messianism and Puritanical Reform: Mahdīs of the Muslim West* (Leiden: Brill, 2006).

"Los moros de Tudela (Navarra) en torno a los años de la conversión (1515)," in *Les Morisques et leurs temps* (Paris: Centre National de la Recherche Scientifique, 1983), pp. 73–102.

"Los moros en las Cantigas de Alfonso X El Sabio," *al-Qanṭara* 6 (1985), 133–51.

"Un nuevo documento árabe de Tudela, año de 1509," *al-Qanṭara* 5 (1984), 455–62.

"Religious Dissent and Minorities: The Morisco Age," *Journal of Modern History* 81 (2009): 888–920.

"*Shurafā* in the Last Years of al-Andalus and in the Morisco Period. Laylat Al-Mawlid and Geneaoligies of the Prophet Muḥammad," in Kazuo Morimoto (ed.), *Sayyids and Sharifs in Muslim Societies. The Living Links to the Prophet* (London: Routledge, 2012), pp. 161–84.

"Vidas ejemplares: Sa'īd ibn Faraŷ al-Dugālī, (m. 987/ 1579), un granadino en Marruecos," in M. García-Arenal and M. J. Viguera (eds.), *Relaciones de la Península ibérica*, pp. 453–85.

García-Arenal, Mercedes and Ana Labarta, "Algunos fragmentos aljamiados del proceso inquisitorial contra Yuçe de la Vaçía, alfaquí de la villa de Molina (1495)," *Nueva revista de filologia hispanica* 30 (1981), 127–42.

García-Arenal, Mercedes and Béatrice Leroy, *Moros y judios en Navarra en la Baja Edad Media* (Madrid: Hiperion, 1984).

García-Arenal, Mercedes and F. Rodríguez Mediano, "Mèdico, traductor, inventor: Miguel de Luna, cristiano arábigo de Granada," *Chronica nova* 32 (2006), 187–231.

*Un oriente español: los moriscos y el Sacromonte en tiempos de Contrarreforma* (Madrid: Marcial Pons Historia, 2010).

García-Arenal, Mercedes and María Jesús Viguera (eds.), *Relaciones de la Península Ibérica con el Magreb, siglos* XIII–XVI*: Actas del coloquio (Madrid, 17–18 Diciembre 1987)* (Madrid: CSIC, 1988).

García-Arenal, Mercedes and Gerard A. Wiegers (eds.) *Los Moriscos: expulsión y diáspora: una perspectiva internacional* (Universitat de València, 2013).

García Ballester, Luis, *Historia social de la medicina en la España de los siglos* XIII *al* XVI (Madrid: Akal, 1976).

"Las influencias de la medicina islámica en la obra mèdica de Arnau de Vilanova," *Estudi general* 9 (1989), 79–95.

"A Marginal Learned Medical World: Jewish, Muslim and Christian Medical Practitioners and the Use of Arabic Sources in Late Medieval Spain," in L. García Ballester, Roger French, Jon Arrizabalaga, and Andrew Cunningham (eds.), *Practical Medicine From Salerno to the Black Death* (Cambridge University Press, 1993), pp. 353–94.

*Medicine in a Multicultural Society: Christian, Jewish and Muslim Practitioners in the Spanish Kingdoms, 1220–1610* (Aldershot: Ashgate, 2001).

"The Minority of Morisco Physicians in the Spain of the 16th Century and Their Conflicts in a Dominant Christian Society," *Sudhoffs Archiv* 60–3 (1976), 209–34.

García Gallo, Alfonso, "Los fueros de Toledo," *Anuario de historia de derecho español* 45 (1975), 341–488.

García García, Bernardo José, "La cuestión morisca y la restauración de la milicia (1595–1614)," in M. de Epalza (ed.), *L'Expulsió dels moriscos*, pp. 46–50.

García Herrero, María del Carmen, "Doña Xemçi de Taher y la venta de hierro en Daroca (1311–1314)," *Aragón en la Edad Media* 20 (2008), 361–71.

"Prostitución y amancebamiento en Zaragoza a fines de la Edad Media," *En la España medieval* 12 (1989), 305–22.

"Violencia sexual en Huesca a finales de la Edad Media," *Revista de historia Jerónimo Zurita* 74 (2000) 109–26.

García Marco, Francisco Javier, *Comunidades mudéjares de la comarca de Calatayud en el siglo* XV (Calatayud: CSIC, 1993).

"El Papa Luna y los mudéjares de Aragón," in VI *Centenario del Papa Luna: Jornadas de estudio, Calatayud–Illueca, 1994* (Calatayud: Centro de Estudios Bilbilitanos, 1996), pp. 95–112.

"El trabajo de los mudéjares de Daroca (Zaragoza) en la segunda mitad del siglo XV. Evidencias en favor de la hipótesis de la complementariedad de las economías cristiana y mudéjar en el Aragón medieval," in *Actas del* VI *Simposio Internacional de Mudejarismo*, pp. 167–86.

García Mercadal, José, *Viajes de extranjeros por España y Portugal* (Madrid: Aguilar, 1952).

Garrad, K., "La Inquisición y los moriscos granadinos, 1526–1580," *Bulletin hispanique* 67 (1965), 63–77.

Gautron, Yannick, "Assassins, Druze et Nosayris d'après les sources occidentales médiévales," in Louis Pouzet and Louis Boisset (eds.), *Chrétiens et Musulmans au temps des Croisades: entre l'affrontement et la rencontre* (Beirut: Presses de l'Université Saint-Joseph, 2007), pp. 31–62.

Gazulla, Faustino D., "Las compañías de zenetes en el Reino de Aragón (1284–1291)," *Boletín de la Real Academia de la Historia* 90 (1927), 174–96.

Geary, Patrick J., "Ethnic Identity as a Situational Construct in the Early Middle Ages," *Medieval Perspectives* 3 (1988), 1–17.

*The Myth of Nations: The Medieval Origins of Europe* (Princeton University Press, 2002).

Gelfer-Jørgensen, Mirjam and Caroline Henriksen, *Medieval Islamic Symbolism and the Paintings in the Cefalú Cathedral* (Leiden: Brill, 1986).

Gervers, Michael and Ramzi Jibran Bikhazi (eds.), *Conversion and Continuity: Indigenous Christian Communities in Islamic Lands Eighth to Eighteenth Centuries* (Toronto: Pontifical Institute of Mediaeval Studies, 1990).

Gervers, Michael and James M. Powell (eds.), *Tolerance and Intolerance: Social Conflict in the Age of the Crusades* (Syracuse University Press, 2001).

Gibbon, Edward, *The Decline and Fall of the Roman Empire*, 6 vols. (London and New York: Peter Fenelon Collier & Sons, 1901 [1796]).

Gilbert, Claire, "Language Liquidity in Empire: A Mediterranean Question," paper presented at the Fall Workshop of the Mediterranean Seminar/ University of California Mediterranean Studies Multi-Campus Research Project (October 29, 2011, University of California Los Angeles).

Gilchrist, John T., "The Papacy and the War Against the Saracens, 795–1216," *International History Review* 10 (1988), 174–97.

Gilles, Henri, "Législation et doctrine canoniques sur les Sarrasins," in E. Privat (ed.), *Cahiers de Fanjeux. Islam et Chrétiens du Midi (*XII–XIV *s.)* (Toulouse: Centre d'Études Historiques de Fanjeux, 1983), pp. 195–213.

Giménez Soler, Andrés, "La Corona de Aragón y Granada," *Boletin de la Real Academia de Buenas Letras de Barcelona* 3 (1905), 101–33.

"El justicia de Aragón ¿Es de origen musulman?" *Revista de archivos, bibliotecas y museos* (1901), 1–24 [repr.: Madrid: M. Tello, 1901].

Giordano, Christian, "Interdependent Diversities: Self-Representations, Historical Regions, and Global Challenges in Europe," in C. Marcinkowski (ed.), *The Islamic World and the West*, pp. 41–62.

Glick, Thomas F., *From Muslim Fortress to Christian Castle. Social and Cultural Change in Medieval Spain* (Manchester University Press, 1995).

*Islamic and Christian Spain in the Early Middle Ages*. Rev. edn. (Leiden: Brill, 2005 [1979]).

"Muhtasib and Mustasaf: A Case-Study of Institutional Diffusion," *Viator* 2 (1971), 59–81.

"On Converso and Marrano Ethnicity," in B. Gampel (ed.), *Crisis and Creativity in the Sephardic World, 1391–1648* (New York: Columbia University Press, 1997), pp. 59–76.

"Sharing Science: Jews, Muslims, and Practical Science in the Medieval Islamic World," in Joseph Montville (ed.), *History as Prelude: Muslims and Jews in the Medieval Mediterranean* (Lanham, MD: Lexington Books, 2011), pp. 27–54.

"«Thin Hegemony» and Consensual Communities in the Medieval Crown of Aragon," in Miquel Barceló, *et al.* (eds.), *El fuedalisme comptat i debatut. Formació i expansió del feudalisme català* (Universitat de València, 2003), pp. 523–38.

Glick, Thomas F. and Oriol Pi-Sunyer, "Acculturation as an Explanatory Concept in Spanish History," *Comparative Studies in Society and History* 2 (1969), 136–54.

Goldenberg, David M., *The Curse of Ham: Race and Slavery in Early Judaism, Christianity, and Islam* (Princeton University Press, 2004).
Goldstein, Bernard R., "Astronomy as a 'Neutral Zone': Interreligious Cooperation in Medieval Spain," *Medieval Encounters* 15 (2009), 159–74.
Gómez García, Luz, "Los mudéjares menestrals segovianos," *Sharq al-Andalus* 14–15 (1997–98), 35–45.
Gómez Renau, Mar, "La aljama de Valladolid: nuevas aportacions," *Anaquel de estudios árabes* 15 (2004), 141–64.
Gómez Urdáñez, Carmen, *Arquitectura civil en Zaragoza en el siglo* XVI, 3 vols. (Ayuntamiento de Zaragoza, 1987–88).
"El Morisco, la doncella y el fraile. Un cuadro de la práctica de la construcción en Zaragoza en 1605," *Artigrama* 15 (2000), 313–43.
Gómez de Valenzuela, Manuel, "Esclavos moros en Aragón (ss. XI al XVI)," *Argensola* 102 (1989), 115–32.
Gómez Vozmediano, Miguel Fernando, *Mudéjares y moriscos en el campo de Calatrava* (Ciudad Real: Diputación Provincial, 2000).
González Cavero, Ignacio, "Una revisión de la figura de Ibn Mardanish. Su alianza con el Reino de Castilla y la oposición a los Almohades," *Miscelánea medieval murciana* 31 (2007), 95–110.
González Jiménez, Manuel, "El fracaso de la convivencia de moros y judíos en Andalucía (ss. XIII–XV)," in Eufemio Sanz Lorenzo (ed.), *Proyección histórica de España: en sus tres culturas – Castilla y León, América y el Mediterráneo*, 2 vols. (Valladolid: Junta de Castilla y León, 1993), vol. I, pp. 125–49.
*La repoblación de la zona de Sevilla durante el siglo* XIV (Sevilla: Secretariado de Publicaciones, 1993).
González Palencia, Ángel, *Los Mozárabes de Toledo en los siglos* XII *y* XIII (Madrid: Instituto de Valencia de Don Juan, 1926).
"Notas sobre el régimen de riegos en la région de Veruela en los siglos XII y XIII," *Al-Andalus* 10 (1945), 79–88.
González Paz, "Sarracenos, moros, mudéjares y moriscos en la Galicia medieval," *Cuadernos de estudios gallegos* 51 (2004), 281–312.
Goodrich, P. H., "Saracens and Islamic Alterity in Malory's 'Le Morte Darthur'," *Arthuriana* 16 (2006), 10–28.
Gorton, T. J., "Arabic Influence on the Troubadours: Documents and Directions," *Journal of Arabic Literature* 5 (1974), 11–16.
Gouguenheim, Sylvain, *Aristote au Mont-Saint-Michel: les racines grecques de l'Europe chrétienne* (Paris: Seuil, 2008).
Grabar, Oleg, "The Shared Culture of Objects," in Henry Maguire (ed.), *Byzantine Court Culture From 829 to 1204* (Washington, DC: Dumbarton Oaks Research Library and Collection, 1998), pp. 115–129.
"Two Paradoxes in the Islamic Art of the Iberian Peninsula," in S. Jayyusi (ed.), *The Legacy of Muslim Spain*, pp. 583–91.
Granara, William, "Ibn Hawqal in Sicily," *Alif: Journal of Comparative Poetics* (1983), 94–99.
de la Granja, Fernando, "Condena de Boabdil por los alfaquíes de Granada," *Al-Andalus* 36 (1971), 145–76.

"Una polémica religiosa en Murcia en tiempos de Alfonso el Sabio," *Al-Andalus* 31 (1966), 47–72.

Green, Monica H., "Conversing With the Minority: Relations Among Christian, Jewish, and Muslim Women in the High Middle Ages," *Journal of Medieval History* 34 (2008), 105–18.

Greif, Avner, "Contract Enforceablity and Economic Institutions in Early Trade: The Maghribi Traders' Coalition," *American Economic Review* 83 (1993), 525–48.

Guemara, Raoudha, "La libération et le rachat des captifs. Une lecture musulmane," in Giulio Cipollone (ed.), *La liberazione dei "captivi"*, pp. 333–34.

Guichard, Pierre, *Les musulmans de Valence et la Reconquête (XI$^{e}$–XIII$^{e}$ siècles)*, 2 vols. (Damascus: Institut Français de Damas, 1990).

"Quelques remarques à propos de l'oeuvre de R. I. Burns," *Revista d'Història Medieval* 1 (1990), 217–24.

"Le Šarq al-Andalus, l'Orient et el Maghrib aux XIIe et XIIIE siècles: Reflection sur l'évolution politique de l'Espagne musulmane," in M. García-Arenal and M. J. Viguera (eds.), *Relaciones de la Península ibérica*, pp. 1–20.

"Un seigneur musulman dans l'Espagne chrétienne: le «ra'is» de Crevillente (1243–1318)," *Mélanges de la Casa de Velázquez* 9 (1973), 283–334.

*Structures sociales "orientales" et "occidentales" dans l'Espagne musulmane* (Paris: Mouton, 1977).

Guillén Diop, Fabiana, "Esclavage et métissages a Barcelone entre 1385 et 1445: une overture phénotypique contrôlée?" Paper presented at "Recherches francophones sur les traites, les esclavages et leurs productions sociales et culturelles" (Paris: June 2006).

Guinot Rodríguez, Enrique, *Feudalismo en expansión en el norte valenciano: antecedentes y desarrollo del Señorío de la Orden de Montesa, siglos XIII y XIV* (Castelló: Diputación, 1986).

"Historia del Tribunal de las Aguas de Valencia", in E. Guinot and M. Martínez (eds.), *El consejo de hombres buenos de la Huerta de Murcia y el Tribunal de las Aguas de la Vega de Valencia* (Murcia: Dirección General de Patrimonio, Gobierno de Murcia, 2005), pp. 35–40 and 62–79.

"'Sofras' y prestaciones personales en los mudéjares valencianos," in *Actas del VI Simposio Internacional de Mudejarismo*, pp. 329–56.

Guinot Rodríguez, Enrique and J. Romero, "El Tribunal de les Aigües de l'Horta de València: continuïtat institucional i canvi social", in *Derecho, historia y universidades. Estudios dedicados a Mariano Peset* (Universitat de València, 2007), vol. I, pp. 755–69.

Guinot Rodríguez, Enrique and J. Torró Abad, *Repartiments a la Corona d'Aragó* (Universitat de València, 2007).

Gutwirth, Eleazar, "Music, Identity and the Inquisition in Fifteenth-Century Spain," *Early Music History* 17 (1998), 161–81.

"A Song and Dance: Transcultural Practices of Daily Life in Medieval Spain," in H. Hames (ed.), *Jews, Muslims and Christians*, pp. 207–28.

Haensch S., R. Bianucci, M. Signoli, M. Rajerison, M. Schultz, *et al.*, "Distinct Clones of Yersinia Pestis Caused the Black Death," *PLoS Pathogens* 6 (10) (2010): e1001134, doi:10.1371/journal.ppat.1001134

Halavais, Mary Hoyt, *Like Wheat to the Miller. Community, Convivencia, and the Construction of Morisco Identity in Sixteenth-Century Aragon* (New York: Columbia University Press, 2002).
Haliczer, Stephen, *Inquisition and Society in the Kingdom of Valencia, 1478–1834* (Berkeley: University of California Press: 1990).
Halperin, Charles J., "The Ideology of Silence: Prejudice and Pragmatism on the Medieval Religious Frontier," *Comparative Studies in Society and History* 26 (1984), 442–66.
Hambly, Gavin R. G., *Women in the Medieval Islamic World* (New York: Palgrave Macmillan, 1998).
Hamdani, Abbas, "An Islamic Background to the Voyages of Discovery," in S. K. Jayyusi (ed.) *The Legacy of Muslim Spain*, pp. 273–306.
Hames, Harvey J., *The Art of Conversion: Christianity and Kabbalah in the Thirteenth Century* (Leiden: Brill, 2000).
"From Calabria Cometh the Law, and the Word of the Lord From Sicily: The Holy Land in the Thought of Joachin of Fiore and Abraham Abulafia," *Mediterranean Historical Review* 20 (2005), 187–99.
"A Jew amongst Christians and Muslims: Introspection in Solomon Ibn Adret's Response to Ibn Hazm," *Mediterranean Historical Review* 25 (2010), 203–19.
*Like Angels on Jacob's Ladder: Abraham Abulafia, the Franciscans and Joachimism* (Albany: State University of New York Press, 2007).
"A Seal Within a Seal: The Imprint of Sufism in Abraham Abulafia's Teachings," *Medieval Encounters* 2 (1996), 153–72.
Hames, Harvey J. (ed.), *Jews, Muslims and Christians in and Around the Crown of Aragon. Essays in Honour of Professor Elena Lourie* (Leiden: Brill, 2003).
Hamilton, Bernard. "Our Lady of Saidnaya: An Orthodox Shrine Revered by Muslims and Knights Templars at the Time of the Crusades," in R.N. Swanson (ed.), *The Holy Land, Holy Lands and Christian History* (Woodbridge, Suffolk: Bodywell, 2000), pp. 207–215.
Hankins, James, *Humanism and Platonism in the Italian Renaissance* (Rome: Edizioni di storia e letteratura, 2003).
Hansen, Craig L. "Manuel I Comnenus and the "God of Muhammad": A Study in Byzantine Ecclesiastical Politics," in J. Tolan (ed.), *Medieval Christian Perceptions*, pp. 55–84.
Harari, Yuval. "The Military Role of the Frankish Turcopoles: A Reassessment," *Mediterranean Historical Review* 12 (1997), 75–116.
Harris, A. Katie, *From Muslim to Christian Granada: Inventing a City's Past in Early Modern Spain* (Baltimore: Johns Hopkins University Press, 2007).
Harrison, Alwyn, "Behind the Curve: Bulliet and Conversion to Islam in Al-Andalus Revisited," *al-Masāq* 24 (2012), 35–51.
Harvey, L. P., "The Alfonsine School of Translators: Translations from Arabic into Castilian Produced under the Patronage of Alfonso the Wise of Castile (1221–1252–1284)," *The Journal of the Royal Asiatic Society of Great Britain and Ireland* 1 (1977), 109–17.
*Ibn Battuta* (London: I.B. Tauris, 2007).
*Islamic Spain, 1250 to 1500* (University of Chicago Press, 1990).

"El Mancebo de Arévalo and his Treatises on Islamic Faith and Practice," *Journal of Islamic Studies* 10 (1999), 249–76.

"The Morisco Who Was Muley Zaidan's Spanish Interpreter," *Miscelânea de estudios árabes y hebraicos* 8 (1959), 67–97.

"The Moriscos and the Hajj," *Bulletin* (British Society for Middle Eastern Studies) 14 (1987), 11–24.

*Muslims in Spain, 1500 to 1614* (University of Chicago Press, 2004).

"Una referencia explícita a la legalidad de la práctica de la Taqīya por los Moriscos," *Sharq Al-Andalus* 12 (1995), 561–63.

"Yuse Banegas: un moro noble en Granada bajo los Reyes Católicos," *Al-Andalus* 21 (1956), 297–302.

Harvey, Richard, *Raymundus Martini and the Pugio Fidei: The Life and Work of a Medieval Controversialist* (University College London, 1991).

Hendrickson, Jocelyn N., "The Islamic Obligation to Emigrate: Al-Wansharīsī's *Asnā al-matājir* Reconsidered," PhD Dissertation: Religion (Emory University, QA, 2009).

Heng, Geraldine, "The Romance of England," in Jeffrey Jerome Cohen (ed.), *The Postcolonial Middle Ages* (New York: St. Martin's Press, 2000), pp. 135–72.

Herde, P., "Christians and Saracens at the Time of the Crusades: Some Comments of Contemporary Medieval Canonists," *Studia graciana* 12 (1967), 361–76.

Hernando, Josep, "De nuevo sobre la obra antiislámica atruibida a Ramón Martí, Dominico catalàn del siglo XIII," *Sharq al-Andalus* 8 (1991), 97–108.

Herrero Soto, Omayra, "La arenga de Tariq b. Ziyad: un ejemplo de creación retórica en la historiografía árabe," *Talia Dixit* 5 (2010), 45–74.

Hillenbrand, Carole, *The Crusades: Islamic Perspectives* (New York: Routledge, 2000).

Hillgarth, J. N., *The Mirror of Spain, 1500–1700: The Formation of a Myth* (Ann Arbor: University of Michigan Press, 2000).

*The Spanish Kingdoms, 1250–1516*, 2 vols. (Oxford: Clarendon Press, 1976).

Hinojosa, Eduardo, "Mezquinos y exáricos, datos para la historia de la servidumbre en Navarra y Aragón," in Eduardo Saavedra (ed.), *Homenaje a Don Francesco Codera en su jubilación del profesorado. Estudios de erudición oriental* (Zaragoza: Mariano Escar, 1904), pp. 523–31.

Hinojosa Montalvo, José, "Cristianos contra musulmanes: la situación de los mudéjares," in José-Luis Martín and José Ignacio de la Iglesia Duarte (eds.), *Conflictos sociales, políticos e intelectuales en la España de los siglos* XIV *y* XV/XIV *Semana de Estudios Medievales, Nájera, del 4 al 8 de agosto de 2003* (Logroño: Instituto de Estudios Riojanos, 2004), pp. 335–92.

*La morería de Elche en la Edad Media* (Teruel: Instituto de Estudios Turolenses, 1994).

*Los mudéjares: la voz del Islam en la España cristiana*, 2 vols. (Teruel: Instituto de Estudios Turolenses, 2002).

"Las relaciones entre Elche y Granada (ss. XIV–XV). De Ridwan a la guerra de Granada," *Sharq al-Andalus* 13 (1996), 47–61.

Hitchcock, Richard, *Mozarabs in Medieval and Early Modern Spain: Identities and Influences* (Aldershot: Ashgate, 2008).

Hodgson, Marshall G. S., *The Venture of Islam. Conscience and History in a World Civilization*. 3 vols. (University of Chicago Press, 1974).

Hoffman, Eva, "Pathways of Portability: Islamic and Christian Interchange from the Tenth to the Twelfth Century," in Eva Hoffman (ed.), *Late Antique and Medieval Art of the Mediterranean World* (Oxford: Blackwell, 2007), pp. 317–47.

Hofman Vannus, Iris, "Espejo de mujeres mudéjares: Ideales de mujer reflejados en el manuscrito mudéjar de Ocaña," *Encuentro / Liqā'*, 416 (December 2006), 1–15.

"La figura de Jesús en el manuscrito mudéjar-morisco de Ocaña," *Encuentro* Serie D: 396 (2005), 1–11.

"Historias religiosas musulmanas en el manuscrito mudéjar-morisco de Ocaña: edición y estudio," PhD Dissertation (Departamento de Estudios Árabes e Islámicos: Universidad Complutense de Madrid, 2004).

"El manuscrito mudéjar-morisco de Ocaña," *Anaquel de estudios árabes* 14 (2003), 119–28.

"Mujeres mudéjares en la España medieval," *Hesperia culturas del Mediterráneo* 4 (2006), 279–90.

Holt, P. M., *The Age of the Crusades: The Near East From the Eleventh Century to 1517* (New York: Longman, 1986).

Horden, Peregrine and Nicholas Purcell, *The Corrupting Sea: A Study of Mediterranean History* (Malden: Blackwell, 2000).

Houben, Hubert, "Religious Toleration in the South Italian Peninsula During the Norman and Staufen Periods," in G. A. Loud and A. Metcalfe (eds.), *The Society of Norman Italy*, pp. 319–40.

*Roger II of Sicily: A Ruler Between East and West* (Cambridge University Press, 2002).

Huici Miranda, Ambrosio, *Historia política del imperio almohade*, 2 vols. (Tetuan: Marroquí, 1956).

Hutchison, Paul and Rosenthal, Harriet E. S., "Prejudice Against Muslims: Anxiety as a Mediator Between Intergroup Contact and Attitudes, Perceived Group Variability and Behavioural Intentions," *Ethnic and Racial Studies* 34 (2011), 40–61.

Hysell, Jesse, "*Pacem Portantes Advenerint*: Ambivalent Images of Muslims in the Chronicles of Norman Italy," *al-Masāq* 24 (2012), 139–56.

Idris, Hady Roger, *La Berbérie orientale sous les Zirides*, X^e^–XII^e^ *siècles*, 2 vols. (Paris: Adrien-Maisonneuve, 1959).

Inalcik, Fatih, "A Case Study in Renaissance Diplomacy: The Agreement Between Innocent VIII and Bayezid II on Djem Sultan," *Journal of Turkish Studies* 3 (1979), 209–230.

Ingram, Kevin (ed.), *The Conversos and Moriscos in Late Medieval Spain and Beyond*, 2 vols. (Leiden: Brill, 2009–12).

Iogna-Prat, Dominique, "The Creation of a Christian Armory Against Islam," in Constance H. Berman (ed.), *Medieval Religion: New Approaches* (New York: Routledge, 2005), pp. 325–46.

*Order & Exclusion: Cluny and Christendom Face Heresy, Judaism, and Islam (1000–1150)* (Ithaca, NY: Cornell University Press, 2002).

Jacoby, David, "Silk Economies and Cross-Cultural Artistic Interaction: Byzantium, the Muslim World, and the Christian West," *Dumbarton Oaks Papers* 58 (2004), 197–241.

Jamil, Nadia and Jeremy Johns, "An Original Arabic Document From Crusader Antioch (1213 AD)," in D. S. Richards, and Chase F. Robinson (eds.), *Texts, Documents, and Artefacts: Islamic Studies in Honour of D.S. Richards* (Leiden: Brill, 2003), pp. 157–90.

Jamison, Evelyn M., *Admiral Eugenius of Sicily, His Life and Work, and the Authorship of the Epistola ad Petrum, and the Historia Hugonis Falcandi Siculi* (Oxford University Press, 1957).

Janer, Florencio, *Condición social de los moriscos de España* (Barcelona: Alta Fulla, 1987).

Jayyusi, Salma Khadra (ed.), *The Legacy of Muslim Spain* (Leiden: E.J. Brill, 1992).

Jehel, Georges, "Jews and Muslims in Medieval Genoa: From the Twelfth to Fourteenth Centuries," *Mediterranean Historical Review* 10 (1995), 120–32.

Johns, Jeremy, *Arabic Administration in Norman Sicily: The Royal Dīwān* (Cambridge University Press, 2002).

"Arabic Sources for Sicily," *Proceedings of the British Academy* 132 (2007), 341–60.

"The Boys From Mezzoiuso: Muslim Jizya-Payers in Christian Sicily," in A. Jones, Robert G. Hoyland, and Philip F. Kennedy (eds.), *Islamic Reflections, Arabic Musings: Studies in Honour of Professor Alan Jones* (Cambridge: Gibb Memorial Trust, 2004), pp. 243–55.

"The Greek Church and the Conversion of Muslims in Norman Sicily?" *Byzantinische Forschungen* 21 (1995), 133–57.

"*Malik Ifrīqiya*: The Norman Kingdom of Africa and the Fāṭimids," *Libyan Studies* 18 (1993), 89–101.

Johns, Jeremy and Alex Metcalfe, "The Mystery At Chùrchero: Conspiracy or Incompetence in Twelfth-Century Sicily?" *Bulletin of the School of Oriental and African Studies* 62 (1999), 226–59.

Johnson, Carina L., *Cultural Hierarchy in Sixteenth-Century Europe: The Ottomans and Mexicans* (Cambridge University Press, 2011).

Jones, Linda Gale, "The Boundaries of Sin and Communal Identity: Muslim and Christian Preaching and the Transmission of Cultural Identity in Medieval Iberia and Maghreb (12th to 15th Centuries)," PhD dissertation: Religious Studies (University of California Santa Barbara, 2004).

"Retratos de la emigración: la (re)conquista y la emigración de los ulemas a Granada, según *al-Iḥāṭa* de Ibn al-Jaṭīb," in A. Echevarría Arsuaga (ed.), *Biografías mudéjares*, pp. 21–59.

Jotischky, Andrew, "The Mendicants as Missionaries and Travellers in the Near East in the Thirteenth and Fourteenth Centuries," in Rosamund Allen (ed.), *Eastward Bound: Travel and Travellers, 1050–1550* (Manchester University Press, 2004), pp. 88–106.

Jubb, Margaret A., "Enemies in the Holy War but Brothers in Chivalry: The Crusaders' View of Their Saracen Opponents," in Hans van Dijk and Willem Noomen (eds.), *Aspects de l'épopée romane: mentalités - idéologies – intertextualités* (Groningen: Forsten, 1995), pp. 251–59.

*The Legend of Saladin in Western Literature and Historiography* (Lewiston, NY: Edwin Mellen Press, 2000).

Kafadar, Cemal, "A Death in Venice (1575): Anatolian Merchants Trading in the Serenissima," *Journal of Turkish Studies* 10 (1986), 191–218.

Kagan, Richard L. and Abigail Dyer, *Inquisitorial Inquiries: Brief Lives of Secret Jews and Other Heretics* (Baltimore, MD: Johns Hopkins University Press, 2004).

Kagay, Donald J., "The Treason of Center and Periphery: The Uncertain Contest of Government and Individual in the Medieval Crown of Aragon," *Mediterranean Studies* 12 (2003), 17–36.

Kahf, Mohja, *Western Representations of the Muslim Woman: From Termagant to Odalisque* (Austin: University of Texas Press, 1999).

Kamen, Henry, "The Mediterranean and the Expulsion of Spanish Jews in 1492," *Past & Present* 119 (1988), 30–55.

*Spain, 1469–1714: A Society of Conflict*, 3rd edn. (New York: Longman, 2005).

Kedar, Benjamin Z., "Convergences of Oriental Christian, Muslim, and Frankish Worshippers: The Case of Saydnaya," in Yitzhak Hen (ed.), *De Sion exibit lex et verbum domini de Hierusalem: Essays on Medieval Law, Liturgy and Literature in Honour of Amnon Linder* (Turnhout: Brepols, 2001), pp. 59–69.

*Crusade and Mission. European Approaches Toward the Muslims* (Princeton University Press, 1984).

"Ecclesiastical Legislation in the Kingdom of Jerusalem: The Statutes of Jaffa (1253) and Acre (1254)," in R. C. Smail and Peter W. Edbury (eds.), *Crusade and Settlement. Papers Read At the First Conference of the Society for the Study of the Crusades and the Latin East, Cardiff, September 1983* (University College Cardiff Press, 1985), pp. 225–30.

"*De Iudeis et Sarracenis.* On the Categorization of Muslims in Medieval Canon Law," in *Studia in honorem emenentissimi cardinalis Alphonsi M. Stickler* (Rome: LAS, 1992), pp. 207–13.

"The Massacre of 15 July 1099 in the Historiography of the Crusades," *Crusades* 3 (2004), 15–75.

"Multidirectional Conversion in the Frankish Levant," in James Muldoon (ed.), *Varieties of Religious Conversion in the Middle Ages* (Gainesville: University Press of Florida, 1997), pp. 190–99.

"Muslim Conversion in Canon Law," in Stephan Kuttner and Kenneth Pennington (eds.), *Proceedings of the Sixth International Congress of Medieval Canon Law. Berkeley California, 28 July – 2 August 1980* (Vatican: Biblioteca Apostolica, 1985), pp. 321–32.

"On the Origins of the Earliest Laws of Frankish Jerusalem: The Canons of Nablus, 1120," *Speculum* 74 (1999), 310–35.

"The Subjected Muslims of the Frankish Levant," in Thomas Madden (ed.), *The Crusades: The Essential Readings* (Malden: Blackwell, 2002) pp. 233–64.

Kedar, Benjamin Z. and Muḥammad Al-Ḥajjūj, "Muslim Villagers of the Frankish Kingdom of Jerusalem. Some Demographic and Onomastic Data," in Raoul Curiel and Rika Gyselen (eds.), *Itinéraires d'Orient. Hommages à Claude Cahen* (Leuven: Peeters, 1994), pp. 145–56.

Keene, Derek, Nagy Balázs, and Katalin Szende (eds.), *Segregation, Integration, Assimilation: Religious and Ethnic Groups in the Medieval Towns of Central and Eastern Europe* (Burlington: Ashgate, 2009).

Kennedy, Hugh, *Muslim Spain and Portugal: A Political History of Al-Andalus* (London and New York: Longman, 1996).

Kinoshita, Sharon. "The Politics of Courtly Love: La prise d'Orange and the Conversion of the Saracen Queen," *Romantic Review* 86 (1995), 265–87.

"Translatio/N, Empire, and the Worlding of Medieval Literature: The Travels of *Kalila Wa Dimna*," *Postcolonial Studies* 11 (2008), 371–85.

Kitzinger, Ernst, "On the Portrait of Roger II in the Mortorana in Palermo," *Proporzioni* 3 (1950), 30–35.

Klein, Elka, *Jews, Christian Society, and Royal Power in Medieval Barcelona* (Ann Arbor: University of Michigan, 2006).

Kopanski, Ataullah Bogdan, "Muslim Communities of the European North-Eastern Frontier: Islam in the Former Polish-Lithuanian Commonwealth," in C. Marcinkowski (ed.), *The Islamic World and the West*, pp. 85–108.

Kostick, Conor, *The Social Structure of the First Crusade* (Leiden: Brill, 2008).

Kosto, Adam, "Hostages during the First Century of the Crusades," *Medieval Encounters* 9 (2003), 3–31.

Krey, A. C., "William of Tyre: The Making of an Historian in the Middle Ages," *Speculum* 16 (1941), 149–66.

Kroemer, James, "Vanquish the Haughty and Spare the Subjected: A Study of Bernard of Clairvaux's Position on Muslims and Jews," *Medieval Encounters* 18 (2012), 55–92.

Labarta, Ana, "La aljama de musulmanes de Calatorao nombra procurador (documento árabe de 1451)," *al-Qanṭara* 9 (1988), 511–17.

"La mujer morisca: sus actividades," in M. J. Viguera (ed.), *La mujer en al-Andalus*, pp. 219–31.

Labarta, Ana and J. Carlos Escribano, "Las bibliotecas de dos alfaquíes borjanos," *Anaquel de estudiós árabes* 11 (2000), 355–67.

Lacam, Jean, *Les Sarrazins dans le haut moyen-âge français. (Histoire et archéologie)* (Paris: Maisonneuve, 1965).

Lacarra, José María, "Dos tratados de paz y alianza entre Sancho el de Peñalén y Moctádir de Zaragoza (1069 y 1073)," in *Homenaje a Johannes Vincke para el 11 de mayo, 1962*, 2 vols. (Madrid: Consejo Superior de Investigaciones Científicas, 1962), vol. I, pp. 121–34.

"La reconquista y repoblación del Valle del Ebro." in J. M. Lacarra (ed.), *La reconquista española y la repoblación del pais* (Zaragoza: Instituto de Estudios Pirenaicos, 1951), pp. 39–84 and 207–22.

Lacarra Ducay, María del Carmen, *Arte mudéjar en Aragón, León, Castilla, Extremadura y Andalucía* (Zaragoza: Institución "Fernando El Católico", 2006).

Ladero Quesada, Miguel Ángel, *La formacion medieval de España: territorios, regiones, reinos* (Madrid: Alianza, 2004).

"Los mudéjares de Castilla en la Baja Edad Media," *Historia, instituciones, documentos* 5 (1978), 257–304.

"Los mudéjares de Castilla en la Baja Edad Media," in *Actas del* I *Simposio Internacional de Mudejarismo*, pp. 349–90.

*Los mudéjares de Castilla en tiempos de Isabel I* (Valladolid: Instituto "Isabel la Católica" de Historia Eclesiástica, 1969).

"Las relaciones con los musulmanes en la Baja Edad Media: Rechazo, coexistencia, proselitismo," in J. I. Ruíz de la Peña and M. Á. Ladero Quesada (eds.), *Cristianos y musulmanes*, pp. 15–65.

Lagardère, Vincent, *Les Almoravides jusqu'au règne de Yūsuf B. Tāšfin (1039–1106)* (Paris: Harmattan, 1989).

*Les Almoravides. Le djihâd andalou (1106–1143)* (Paris: Harmattan, 1998).

Laing, R. D., *The Politics of the Family* (London: Tavistock Publications, 1969).

Laliena Corbera, Carlos, "Expansión territorial, ruptura social y desarollo de la sociedad feudal en el valle del ebro, 1080–1120," in Carlos Laliena and Juan F. Utrilla (eds.), *De Toledo a Huesca. Sociedades medievales en transición a finales del siglo XI (1080–1100)* (Zaragoza: CSIC, 1998), pp. 199–228.

"Guerra santa y conquista feudal en el noroeste de la península a mediados del siglo XI: Barbastro, 1064," in J. I. Ruíz de la Peña and M. Á. Ladero Quesada, *Cristianos y Musulmanes*, pp. 187–218.

Laliena Corbera, Carlos and Philippe Sénac, *Musulmans et Chrétiens dans le Haut Moyen Âge: aux origines de la reconquête aragonaise* (Paris: Minerve, 1991).

Lalinde Abadía, Jesús, *Los fueros de Aragón* (Zaragoza: Librería General, 1976).

Lapiedra Gutiérrez, Eva, "Christian Participation in Almohad Armies and Personal Guard," *Journal of Medieval Iberian Studies* 2 (2010), 235–50.

"Giraldo Sem Pavor, Alfonso Henríquez y los Almohades," in Fernando Esteban Díaz (ed.), *Batalyús: El reino taifa de Badajoz: estudios* (Madrid: Letrúmero, 1996), pp. 147–58.

"Los reyes taifas como dhimmíes y su posible repurcusión en la terminología referida a los Cristianos en las fuentes árabes," in *Bataliús II. Nuevos estudios sobre el reino taifa* (Madrid: Letrúmero, 1999), pp. 49–60.

Latham, J. D., "Mustafa de Cardenas et l'apport des "Morisques" à la société tunisienne du XVii° siècle," in Slimane-Mostafa Zbiss, Abdel-Hakim Gafsi, Mohiedine Boughanmi, and Míkel de Epalza (eds.), *Études sur les Morisques andalous* (Tunis: Institut National d'Art et d'Archéologie, 1983), pp. 157–78.

Launay, Marcel, "Tolérance et dialogue inter-religieux: une problématique," in Guy Saupin *et al.* (eds.), *La tolérance: Colloque International de Nantes, Mai 1998: Quatrième centenaire de l'Édit de Nantes* (Presses Universitaires de Rennes, 1999), pp. 351–61.

Lavado Paradinas, Pedro José, "El palacio mudéjar de Astudillo," in María Valentina Calleja González (ed.), *Actas del* II *Congreso de Historia de Palencia, 27, 28 y 29 de abril de 1989* (Diputación Provincial de Palencia, 1990), pp. 579–604.

Lay, Stephen, *The Reconquest Kings of Portugal: Political and Cultural Reorientation on the Medieval Frontier* (New York: Palgrave Macmillan, 2009).

Lea, Henry Charles, *The Moriscos of Spain* (Philidelphia: Lea Brothers, 1901).

Ledesma Rubio, María Luisa, *Estudios sobre los mudéjares en Aragón* (Teruel: Instituto de Estudios Turolenses, 1996).

"Marginación y violencia. Aportación al estudio de los mudéjares aragoneses," *Aragón en la Edad Media* 9 (1991), 203–24.

*Los mudéjares de Aragón* (Zaragoza: Anubar, 1979).
*Vidas mudéjares: Aspectos sociales de una minoría religiosa en Aragón* (Zaragoza: Mira Editores, 1994).
Lepicard, Étienne, "Medical Licencing and Practice in Medicine in Medieval Spain: A Model of Interfaith Relationships," in L. Ballester García, and S. Kottek (eds.), *Medicine and Medical Ethics in Medieval and Early Modern Spain: An Intercultural Approach* (Jerusalem: Magnes Press, 1996), pp. 50–60.
Lev, Yaacov, "Prisoners of War During the Fatimid-Ayyubid Wars With the Crusaders," in Michael Gervers and James M. Powell (eds.), *Tolerance and Intolerance*, pp. 11–27.
Lévi-Provençal, Évariste, "Alphonse VI et le prise de Tolède (1085)," *Hésperis* 12 (1931), 33–49.
Levy, Thomas Evan, *The Archaeology of Society in the Holy Land* (London: Leicester University Press, 1998).
Lewis, Bernard, *The Assassins: A Radical Sect in Islam* (London: Al Saqi, 1985).
*Islam, From the Prophet Muhammad to the Capture of Constantinople* (New York: Harper & Row, 1974).
*The Muslim Discovery of Europe* (New York: W.W. Norton, 1982).
*Race and Color in Islam* (New York: Harper & Row, 1971).
*Race and Slavery in the Middle East: An Historical Enquiry* (New York: Oxford University Press, 1990).
*What Went Wrong?: The Clash Between Islam and Modernity in the Middle East* (New York: Perennial, 2003).
Lewis, Bernard and Buntzie Ellis Churchill, *Islam: The Religion and the People* (Indianapolis, IN: Wharton Press, 2009).
Limor, Ora, "Sharing Sacred Space: Holy Places in Jerusalem Between Christianity, Judaism and Islam," in Iris Shagrir *et al.* (eds.), *In Laudem Hierosolymitani*, pp. 219–232.
Linehan, Peter, *Spain, 1157–1300: A Partible Inheritance* (Malden: Blackwell, 2008).
Lisón Hernández, Luis, "Mito y realidad de la expulsión de los mudéjares murcianos del Valle de Ricote," *AREAS: Revista internacional de ciencias sociales* 14 (1992), 141–70.
Liss, Peggy K., *Isabel the Queen: Life and Times* (New York: Oxford University Press, 1992).
Lomas Cortés, Manuel, *La expulsión de los Moriscos del Reino de Aragón. Política y administración de una deportación (1609–1611)* (Teruel: Centro de Estudios Mudéjares, 2008).
Lomax, Derek, "Frederick II, his Saracens, and the Papacy," in J. Tolan (ed.), *Medieval Christian Perceptions*, pp. 175–98.
*The Reconquest of Spain* (New York: Longman, 1978).
Lopes de Barros, Maria Filomena, "Body, Baths and Cloth: Muslim and Christian Perception in Medieval Portugal," *Portuguese Studies* 21 (2005), 1–12.
*A comuna muçulmana de Lisboa, sécs.* XIV *e* XV (Lisbon: Hugin, 1998).
"Las élites mudéjares del reino portugués," in A. Echevarría Arsuaga (ed.), *Biografías mudéjares*, pp. 101–32.

"Foral dos Mouros forros de Lisboa, Almada, Palmela e Alcácer," in Alexandre M. Flores, and António Maia Nabais (eds.), *Os forais de Palmela* (Palmela: Câmara Municipal de Palmela, 1992).

"A mulher muçulmana no Portugal medieval," *Clio* 16/17 (2007), 105–17.

*Tempos e espaços de mouros. A minoria muçulmana no reino Português (séculos* XII *a* XV*)* (Lisbon: Fundação Calouste Gulbenkian, 2008).

López Anguita, Gracia and Amina González Costa, *Historia del sufismo en al-Andalus: maestros sufíes de al-Andalus y el Magreb* (Cordoba: Almuzara, 2009).

López-Baralt, Luce, "The Legacy of Islam in Spanish Literature," in S. Jayyusi (ed.), *The Legacy of Muslim Spain*, pp. 505–44.

*La literatura secreta de los últimos musulmanes de España* (Madrid: Trotta, 2009).

López Coca de Castaner, José Enrique, "Granada y el Magreb: La emigración andalusí," in M. García-Arenal and M. J. Viguera (eds.), *Relaciones de la Península Ibérica*, pp. 409–52.

"The Making of Isabel of Solis," in R. Collins and A. Goodman (eds.), *Medieval Spain*, pp. 225–241.

"Mamelucos, otomanos y caída del reino de Granada," *En la España Medieval* 28 (2005), 229–58.

"La migración mudéjar al reino de Granada en tiempo de los Reyes Católicos," *En la España medieval* 26 (2003), 203–26.

"Los mudéjares valencianos y el reino nazarí de Granada. Propuestas para una investigación," *En la España medieval* 2 (1985), 643–66.

López Elum, Pedro, "Apresamiento y venta de moros cautivos en 1441 por acaptar sin licencia," *Al-Andalus* 34 (1969), 329–79.

López Martínez, Celestino, *Mudéjares y moriscos sevillanos* (Sevilla: Renacimiento, 1994 [1935]).

López-Morillas, Consuelo, "El Corán romanceado: la traducción contenida en el manuscrito T235," *Sharq al-Andalus* 16–17 (1999), 263–84.

*Textos aljamiados sobre la vida de Mahoma: el profeta de los Moriscos* (Madrid: CSIC, 1994).

""Trilingual" Marginal Notes (Arabic, Aljamiado and Spanish) in a Morisco Manuscript From Toledo," *American Oriental Society* 103 (1983), 495–503.

López Pérez, María Dolores, *La Corona de Aragón y el Magreb en el siglo* XIV, *1331–1410* (Barcelona: CSIC, 1995).

"Las repercusiones económicas de la Guerra de los Dos Pedros en las aljamas musulmanas aragonesas: el caso de Escatrón y Alborge," in *Actas del* VII *Simposio Internacional de Mudejarismo*, pp. 211–28.

López de la Plaza, Gloria, *Al-Andalus: mujeres, sociedad y religión* (Universidad de Málaga, 1992).

"Las mujeres moriscas granadinas en el discurso político y religioso de la Castilla del siglo XVI (1492–1567)," *En la España medieval* 16 (1993), 307–20.

"Propiedades femeninas en el alfoz de Almería: Mujeres musulmanas en el Libro del Repartimiento," in *Almería entre culturas, siglos* XIII *al* XVI*: Actas del Coloquio, Almería 19, 20 y 21 de abril de 1990. Almería)* (Almería: Instituto de Estudios Almerienses, 1990), pp. 211–24.

Loud, G. A., *The Age of Robert Guiscard: Southern Italy and the Norman Conquest* (New York: Longman, 2000).

*The Latin Church in Norman Italy* (Cambridge University Press, 2007).

Loud, G. A. and Alex Metcalfe (eds.), *The Society of Norman Italy* (Leiden: Brill, 2002).

Lourie, Elena, "Anatomy of Ambivalence. Muslims under the Crown of Aragon in the Late Thirteenth Century," in *Crusade and Colonisation*, Essay VII.

*Crusade and Colonisation: Muslims, Christians, and Jews in Medieval Aragon* (Aldershot: Variorum, 1990).

"Cultic Dancing and Courtly Love: Jews and Popular Culture in Fourteenth-Century Aragon and Valencia," in in S. Menache *et al.* (eds.), *Cross Cultural Convergences*, pp. 151–82.

"Free Moslems in the Balaerics under Christian Rule in the Thirteenth Century," *Speculum* 45 (1970), 624–49. [Repr. in *Crusade and Colonisation*, Essay VI.]

"A Jewish Mercenary in the Service of the King of Aragon," *Revue des études juives* 137 (1978), 367–73. [Repr. in *Crusade and Colonisation*, Essay VIII.]

"Mafiosi and Malsines: Violence, Fear and Faction in the Jewish Aljamas of Valencia in the 14th Century," in C. Carrete Parrondo (ed.), *Actas del* III *Congreso Internacional Encuentro de las Tres Culturas: Toledo, 15–17 octubre 1984* (Ayuntamiento de Toledo, 1988), pp. 69–102. [Repr. in Elena Lourie, *Crusade and Colonisation*, Essay XII.]

"A Society Organized for War: Medieval Spain," *Past and Present* 35 (1966), 54–76. [Repr. in *Crusade and Colonisation*, Essay I.]

"An Unknown Charter Given by King Peter II 'the Catholic' in 1210 to Mudejars in the Jalón and Jiloca Valleys," in *Actas del* VII *Simposio Internacional de Mudejarismo*, pp. 113–22.

"The Will of Alfonso I 'El Batallador' King of Aragon and Navarre: A Reassessment," *Speculum* 50 (1975), 635–51. [Repr. in *Crusader Colonization*, Essay III.]

"The Will of Alfonso I 'El Batallador' King of Aragon and Navarre: A Reply to Dr. Forey," *Durham University Journal* 71/72 (1984–85), 165–72.

Lowe, Kate, "Black Africans' Religious and Cultural Assimiliation to, or Appropriation of Catholicism in Italy, 1470–1520," *Renaissance and Reformation* n.s. 31 (2008), 67–86.

Lower, Michael, "A Black Slave on the Run in Thirteenth-Century England," *Nottingham Medieval Studies* 51 (2007), 111–19.

"Negotiating Interfaith Relations in Eastern Europe: Pope Gregory IX, Bela IV of Hungary and the Latin Empire," *Essays in Medieval Studies* 21 (2004), 49–62.

Luchitskaya, Svetlana, "Muslims in Christian Imagery of the Thirteenth Century: The Visual Code of Otherness," *al-Masāq* 12 (2000), 37–67.

Luttrell, Anthony, "Malta nel periodo normanno," in *Atti del Congresso Internazionale di Studi sulla Sicilia Normanna (Palermo, 4–8th December, 1972)* (Palermo: Università di Palermo, 1973), pp. 467–76.

"Slavery at Rhodes, 1306–1440," *Bulletin de l'Institut Historique Belge de Rome* 46–47 (1976), 81–100.

Maccoby, Hyam, *Judaism on Trial: Jewish–Christian Disputations in the Middle Ages* (London: Associated University Presses, 1982).

MacEvitt, Christopher Hatch, *The Crusades and the Christian World of the East: Rough Tolerance* (Philadelphia: University of Pennsylvania Press, 2008).
Macho y Ortega, Francisco, "Condición social de los mudéjares aragoneses," *Memorias de la Facultad de Filosofía y Letras* (1923), 138–319.
MacKay, Angus and M'hammad Benaboud, "Alfonso VI of León and Castile, 'al-Imbraṭūr dhū'l-Millatayn'," *Bulletin of Hispanic Studies* 56 (1979), 95–102.
"Yet Again Alfonso VI, 'The Emperor, Lord of [The Adherents Of] the Two Faiths, the Most Excellent Ruler': A Rejoinder to Norman Roth," *Bulletin of Hispanic Studies* 61 (1984), 171–82.
Madden, Thomas, "The Real History of the Crusades," *Crisis Magazine* (April 1 2002; online).
Madgearu, Alexandru, and Gordon Martin, *The Wars of the Balkan Peninsula: Their Medieval Origins*, revd. edn. (Lanham, MD: Scarecrow Press, 2008).
Madurell Marimón, Josep María, "Un convenio entre Judíos y Sarracenos (1474)," *Sefarad* 38 (1978), 143–46.
Magnier, Grace, "The Controversy About the Baptised Children of the Moriscos at the Time of the Expulsion," in Abdeljelil Temimi (ed.), *Actes du VII$^{e}$ Symposium International*, pp. 194–217.
"Millenarian Prophecy and the Mythification of Philip III at the Time of the Expulsion of the Moriscos," *Sharq Al-Andalus* 16–17 (1999), 187–209.
*Pedro de Valencia and the Catholic Apologists of the Expulsion of the Moriscos: Visions of Christianity and Kingship* (Leiden: Brill, 2010).
Maier, Christoph T., "Crusade and Rhetoric Against the Muslim Colony of Lucera: Eudes of Châteauroux's *Sermones De Rebellione Sarracenorum Lucherie in Apulia*," *Journal of Medieval History* 21 (1995), 343–85.
Maiso González, Jesús, "Rito y medicina en los sanadores moriscos," *Sharq al-Andalus* 8 (1991), 153–63.
Malalana Ureña, Antonio and Itziar Muñoz Cascante, "Mudéjares de la merindad de la Ribera y bailía de Tudela en los ejércitos de Carlos II de Navarre," *Principe de Viana* 49, Anejo 3 (1988), 525–31.
Mallette, Karla, *Kingdom of Sicily, 1100–1250: A Literary History* (Pittsburgh: University of Pennsylvania Press, 2005).
"Translating Sicily," *Medieval Encounters* 9 (2003), 140–63.
"The Twice-Written Text: Historians, Literary Historians, and the Medieval Mediterranean," paper presented at "Alternative Teleologies: The Mediterranean and the Modern World(s)," a conference held at the University of California, January, 16 and 17 2008, under the sponsorship of the Mediterranean Seminar.
Mann, Vivian B., Thomas F. Glick, and Jerrilynn Dodds (eds.), *Convivencia: Jews, Muslims, and Christians in Medieval Spain* (New York: George Braziller, 1992).
Marcinkowski, Christoph (ed.), *The Islamic World and the West: Managing Religious and Cultural Identities in the Age of Globalisation* (Zurich: Lit, 2009).
Marín, Manuela, "Biographical Dictionaries and Social History of al-Andalus: Trade and Scholarship," *Scripta Mediterranea* 19–20 (1998–99), 239–57.
"Des migrations forcées: les 'Ulema d'al-Andalus face à la conquête chrétienne," in Mohammed Hammam (ed.), *L'Occident musulman et l'Occident chrétien au moyen âge* (Rabat: Faculté des Lettres, 1995), pp. 43–60.

*Mujeres en al-Ándalus* (Madrid: CSIC, 2000).
"Las mujeres en al-Andalus: fuentes e historiografia," in Celia del Moral (ed.), *Árabes, Judías y Cristianas: Mujeres en la europa medieval* (Universidad de Granada 1993), pp. 35–52.
Marín Padilla, Encarnación, "Antecedentes y resultados de una sentencia arbitral (siglo XV)," *Anuario de estudios medievales* 14 (1984), 555–80.
"Investigación sobre la conducta del *alamin* de Aranda, Mahoma de Ovecar en 1489," *al-Qanṭara* 14 (1993), 275–92.
"Los moros de Calatorao, lugar aragonés de señorío en los siglos XIV y XV (I)," *al-Qanṭara* 9 (1988), 249–96.
"Los moros de Calatorao, lugar aragonés de señorío en los siglos XIV y XV (II)," *al-Qanṭara* 10 (1989), 175–214.
"Notas sobre la relación de Moros de la aljama de Zaragoza y conversos de su comunidad (siglo XV)," *al-Qanṭara* 24 (2003), 169–78.
Markowski, Mark, "*Crucesignatus*: Its Origins and Early Usage," *Journal of Medieval History* 10 (1984), 157–65.
Marlow, Louise, "A Thirteenth-Century Scholar in the Eastern Mediterranean: Sirāj al-Dīn Urmavī, Jurist, Logician, Diplomat," *al-Masāq* 22 (2010), 315–24.
Márquez Villanueva, Francisco, *El problema morisco: desde otras laderas* (Madrid: Libertarias, 1991).
Martínez Gonzalez, Esther, "Matrimonio y divorcio islámicos," in Eufemio Sanz Lorenzo (ed.), *Proyección histórica de España: En sus tres culturas – Castilla y León, América y el Mediterráneo* (Valladolid: Junta de Castilla y León, 1993), vol. III, pp. 125–130.
Martínez Verón, Jesús and José Yneva Laborda, *Arquitectos en Aragón: Diccionario histórico*, 5 vols. (Zaragoza: CISC, 2000–01).
Marzal Palacios, Francisco Javier, "Solidaridad islámico, negocio cristiano: la liberación de esclavos musulmanes por mudéjares en la Valencia de inicios del Cuatrocientos," in G. Cipollone (ed.), *La liberazione dei "captivi,"* pp. 777–87.
Masonen, Pekka, "Leo Africanus: The Man with Many Names," *Al-Andalus Magreb. Estudios árabes e islámicos* 8–9 (2000), 115–44.
Matar, N. I., *In the Lands of the Christians: Arab Travel Writing in the Seventeenth Century* (New York: Routledge, 2003).
Matthew, Donald, *The Norman Kingdom of Sicily* (Cambridge University Press, 1992).
Mayer, Hans Eberhart, *The Crusades* (London: Oxford University Press, 1972).
"Latins, Muslims and Greeks in the Latin Kingdom of Jerusalem," *History* 63 (1978), 175–92.
McVaugh, Michael R., "Constantine the African," in C. C. Gillispie (ed.), *Dictionary of Scientific Biography* (New York: Charles Scribner's Sons, 1970), vol. III, pp. 393–95.
*Medicine Before the Plague: Practitioners and Their Patients in the Crown of Aragon, 1285–1345* (Cambridge University Press, 1993).
Menache, Sophia, "Papal Attempts At a Commercial Boycott of the Muslims in the Crusader Period," *Journal of Ecclesiastical History* 63 (2012), 236–59.

"When Jesus Met Mohammed in the Holy Land: Attitudes Toward the "Other" in the Crusader Kingdom," *Medieval Encounters* 15 (2009), 66–85.

Menache, Sophia, Sylvia Schein, and Michael Goodich (eds.), *Cross Cultural Convergences in the Crusader Period: Essays Presented to Aryeh Grabois on His Sixtieth Birthday* (New York: Peter Lang, 1995).

Mendes Drumond Braga, Isabel M., *Mouriscos e Cristãos no Portugal quinhentista: duas culturas e duas concepções religiosas em choque* (Lisboa: Hugin, 1999).

"Os mouriscos perante a Inquisição de Évora," *Eborensia* 7 (1994), 43–76.

"Relaçoes familiares e parafamiliares dos mouriscos portugueses," *Historia y genealogía* 2 (2012), 201–13.

Menéndez Pidal, Ramón, *La España del Cid*, 2 vols. (Madrid: Plutarco, 1929).

*Poema de Yuçuf: materiales para su estudio* (Universidad de Granada, 1952).

Menéndez Pidal, Ramón and Emilio García Gomez, "El conde mozárabe Sisnando Davídez y la política de Alfonso VI con los taifas," *Al-Andalus* 22 (1947), 27–41.

Menjot, Denis, "Les mudéjares du Royaume de Murcie," *Revue du monde musulman et de la Méditerranée* 63–64 (1992), 165–78.

Menocal, Maria Rosa, "Arab Influences on European Love-Poetry," in S. Jayyusi (ed.), *The Legacy of Muslim Spain*, pp. 457–83.

*The Arabic Role in Medieval Literary History: A Forgotten Heritage* (Philadelphia: University of Pennsylvania Press, 2004).

*The Ornament of the World: How Muslims, Jews, and Christians Created a Culture of Tolerance in Medieval Spain* (Boston: Little Brown, 2002).

*Shards of Love: Exile and the Origins of the Lyric* (Durham, NC: Duke University Press, 1994).

Meri, Josef W., *The Cult of Saints Among Muslims and Jews in Medieval Syria* (New York: Oxford University Press, 2002).

Metcalfe, Alex, *Muslims and Christians in Norman Sicily: Arabic Speakers and the End of Islam* (New York: Routledge, 2003).

*The Muslims of Medieval Italy* (Edinburgh University Press, 2009).

"The Muslims of Sicily Under Christian Rule," in in G. A. Loud and A. Metcalfe (eds.), *The Society of Norman Italy*, pp. 289–318.

Meyerson, Mark D., "Conquest, Kinship, and Conversion: Comparative Perspectives on Muslim–Christian Relations in the Medieval Mediterranean," paper presented at the 124th American Historical Association Annual Meeting (January 9, 2010, San Diego, CA).

*A Jewish Renaissance in Fifteenth-Century Spain* (Princeton University Press, 2004).

*Jews in an Iberian Frontier Kingdom: Society, Economy, and Politics in Morvedre, 1248–1391* (Leiden: Brill, 2004).

*The Muslims of Valencia in the Age of Fernando and Isabel: Between Coexistence and Crusade* (Berkeley: University of California Press, 1991).

"Prostitution of Muslim Women in the Kingdom of Valencia: Religious and Sexual Discrimination in a Medieval Plural Society," in Marilyn Joyce Segal Chiat and Kathryn Reyerson (eds.), *The Medieval Mediterranean: Cross-Cultural Contacts* (St. Cloud, MN: North Star Press, 1988), pp. 87–96.

"Slavery and the Social Order: Mudejars and Christians in the Kingdom of Valencia," *Medieval Encounters* 1 (1995), 144–73.
"Slaves and Solidarity: Mudejars and Foreign Muslim Captives in the Kingdom of Valencia," *Medieval Encounters* 2 (1996), 286–343.
"The Survival of a Muslim Minority in the Christian Kingdom of Valencia (Fifteenth-Sixteenth Centuries)," in Michael Gervers and Ramzi Bikhazi (eds.), *Conversion and Continuity*, pp. 365–80.
"The War Against Islam and the Muslims at Home: The Mudejar Predicament in the Kingdom of Valecnia During the Reign of Fernando "El Católico"," *Sharq al-Andalus* 3 (1986), 103–13.
de Miguel Rodríguez, Juan Carlos, *La comunidad mudéjar de Madrid: un modelo de análisis de aljamas mudéjares castellanas* (Madrid: Asociación Cultural Al-Mudayna, 1989).
Miletich, John S., "Muslim Oral Epic and Medieval Epic," *The Modern Language Review* 83 (1988), 911–24.
Millás Vallicrosa, José María and T. Carreras y Artau, *Nuevas aportaciones para el estudio de la transmisión de la ciencia a Europa a través de España* (Barcelona: Escuela de la Casa Provincial de Caridad, 1943).
Miller, Kathryn A., *Guardians of Islam: Religious Authority and Muslim Communities of Late Medieval Spain* (New York: Columbia University Press, 2008).
"Muslim Minorities and the Obligation to Emigrate to Muslim Territory: Two Fatwas From Fifteenth-Century Granada," *Islamic Law and Society* 7 (2000), 256–77.
Mirrer, Louise, *Women, Jews, and Muslims in the Texts of Reconquest Castile* (Ann Arbor: University of Michigan Press, 1996).
Molénat, Jean-Pierre, "*Alcaldes* et *alcaldes mayores de moros* de Castille au XVe siècle," in François Gál (ed.), *Regards sur al-Andalus (VIII$^{e}$–XV$^{e}$ siècle)* (Madrid: Casa de Velázquez, 2006), pp. 147–68.
*Campagnes et monts de Tolède du XIIe au XVe siècle* (Madrid: Casa de Velázquez, 1997).
"The Failed Encounter Between Ibn Khaldun and Pedro I of Castile," in *Ibn Khaldun. The Mediterranean in the 14th Century. Rise and Fall of Empires* (Seville: Fundación José Manuel Lara, 2006).
"Une famille d'élite mudejare de la couronne de Castile: les Xaraff de Tolède et d'Alcalá de Henares," in Abdeljelil Temimi (ed.), *Mélanges Louis Cardaillac* (Zaghovan: Fondation Temimi pour la Recherche Scientifique et l'Information, 1995).
"Hornachos fin XVE–début XVIe siècles," *En la España medieval* 31 (2008), 161–176.
"Mudéjars et mozarabes à Tolède du XIIe au XVe s.," *Revue du monde musulman et de la Méditerranée* 63 (1992), 143–53.
"Privilégiées ou poursuives: quatre sages – femmes musulmanes dans la Castille du XVe siècle," in Cristina de la Puente (ed.), *Identidades marginales* (Madrid: CSIC, 2003), pp. 413–30.
Molina Molina, Angel Luis and María del Carmen Veas Arteseros, "Situación de los mudéjares en el Reino de Murcia (siglos XIII–XV)," *Areas: Revista internacional de ciencias sociales* 14 (1992), 91–106.

Molinari, Alessandra, "The Effects of the Norman Conquest on Islamic Sicily (11th–13th Centuries)," in R.-P. Gayraud (ed.), *Colloque International d'Archéologie Islamique, IFAO, Le Caire. 1993* (Cairo: Institut Français d'Archéologie Orientale, 1993), pp. 259–76.

Møller Jensen, Janus, "Peregrinatio sive expeditio. Why the First Crusade Was Not a Pilgrimage," *al-Masāq* 15 (2003), 119–37.

Monjo i Gallego, Marta, "Sarraïns sota el domini de la família Montcada: les aljames de la Baronia d'Aitona al segle XV," *Anuario de estudios medievales* 34 (2004), 99–124.

*Sarraïns sota el domini feudal. La Baronia d'Aitona al segle* XV (Lleida: Ajuntament d'Alguire, 2004).

Monroe, James T., "Arabic Literary Elements in *El libro de buen amor* (I)," *al-Qanṭara* 32 (2011), 27–70.

"Arabic Literary Elements in *El libro de buen amor* (II)," *al-Qanṭara* 32 (2011), 307–32.

"A Curious Morisco Appeal to the Ottoman Empire," *al-Andalus* 21 (1966), 281–303.

"*Zajal* and *muwashshaḥa*,' in S. Jayyusi (ed.), *The legacy of Muslim Spain*, pp. 398–419.

Montes Romero-Camacho, Isabel, "Las comunidades mudéjares en la Corona de Castilla durante el siglo XV," in *Actas del* VIII *Simposio Internacional de Mudéjarismo*, pp. 367–480.

"Judíos y mudéjares," *Medievalismo* 13/14 (2004), 241–74.

Montes Romero-Camacho, Isabel and Manuel González Jiménez, "Los mudéjares andaluces (siglos XIII–XV): aproximación al estado de la cuestión y propuesta de un modelo teórico," *Revista d'història medieval* 12 (2001), 47–77.

Moore, Robert Ian, *The Formation of a Persecuting Society: Power and Deviance in Western Europe, 950–1250*, 2nd edn. (Oxford: Basil Blackwell, 2007).

"Heresy, Repression, and Social Change in the Age of the Gregorian Reform," in Scott L. Waugh and Peter D. Diehl (eds.), *Christendom and Its Discontents: Exclusion, Persecution, and Rebellion, 1000–1500* (Cambridge University Press, 1996), pp. 19–46.

Moran Cruz, Jo Ann H., "Popular Attitudes Toward Islam in Medieval Europe," in D. Blanks and M. Frassetto (eds.), *Western Views of Islam*, pp. 55–82.

Morray, D. W., *An Ayyubid Notable and His World: Ibn al-'Adīm and Aleppo as Portrayed in His Biographical Dictionary of People Associated with the City* (Leiden: Brill, 1994).

Motis Dolader, Miguel Ángel, "Mosé (Muça) de Portella, judío de Tarazona, baile del rey," in María Teresa Ainaga Andrés and Jesús Criado Mainar (eds.), *La comarca de Tarazona y el Moncayo* (Zaragoza: Diputación General de Aragón, 2004), pp. 245–52.

Mott, Lawrence V., *Sea Power in the Medieval Mediterranean: The Catalan–Aragonese Fleet in the War of the Sicilian Vespers* (Gainesville: University Press of Florida, 2003).

Muldoon, James, *Popes, Lawyers and Infidels* (Philadelphia: University of Pennsylvania Press, 1979).

"Tolerance and Intolerance in the Medieval Canon Lawyers" in Michael Gerves and James Muldoon (eds.), *Tolerance and Intolerance: Social Conflict in the Age of the Crusades* (Syracus University Press, 2001), pp. 117–123.

Muñoz Sebastià, Joan-Hilari, "Actitud dels Moriscos de La Ribera davant el decret d'expulsió: El cas dels Guasquí de Benissanet," *Miscel·lània del Centre d'Estudis Comarcal de la Ribera d'Ebre* 13 (1999), 143–47.

"Procés contra Llorenc Casals, Rector de Benissanet, defensor dels Moriscos (1587)," *Miscel·lània del Centre d'Estudis Comarcal de la Ribera d'Ebre* 12 (1998): 19–24.

Munsuri Rosado, María Nieves, and Francisco Javier Marzal Palacios, "Los esclavos sarracenos entre el Islam y el Cristianismo: el caso de Bernat Sans," in *Actas del* VIII *Simposio Internacional de Mudejarismo*, pp. 303–14.

Murray, Alan V., "Ethnic Identity in the Crusader States: The Frankish Race and the Settlement of Outremer," in Lesley Johnson, Alan V. Murray, and Simon Forde (eds.), *Concepts of National Identity in the Middle Ages* (University of Leeds, 1995), pp. 59–73.

Murray, Alan V. (ed.), *From Clermont to Jerusalem: The Crusades and Crusader Societies, 1095–1500: Selected Proceedings of the International Medieval Congress, University of Leeds, 10–13 July 1995* (Turnhout: Brepols, 1998).

Mutgé i Vives, Josefina, "La aljama sarracena de Lleida cristiana: noticias y conclusions," in *Actas del* VII *Simposio Internacional de Mudejarismo*, pp. 111–18.

*L'aljama sarraïna de Lleida a l'Edat Mitjana* (Barcelona: CSIC, 1992).

"Els Bimferre," in Manuel Acién Almansa (ed.), *L'Islam i Catalunya* (Barcelona: Lunwerg, 1998), pp. 291–95.

Nadeau, Carolyn A., "Contributions of Medieval Food Manuals to Spain's Culinary Heritage," *Cincinnati Romance Review* 33 (2012), 59–77.

Nader, Marwan, "Urban Muslims, Latin Laws, and Legal Institutions in the Kingdom of Jerusalem," *Medieval Encounters* 13 (2007), 243–70.

Nagy, Balázs, "The Towns of Medieval Hungary in the Reports of Contemporary Travellers," in Derek Keene, *et al.* (eds.), *Segregation, Integration, Assimilation*, pp. 169–78.

Navarro, Zander, "In Search of Cultural Intepretation of Power: The Contribution of Pierre Bourdieu," *IDS Bulletin* 37(6) (2006), 11–22.

Nederman, Cary J., "Introduction: Discourses and Contexts of Tolerance in Medieval Europe," in John Christian Laursen and Cary J. Nederman (eds.), *Beyond the Persecuting Society: Religious Toleration Before the Enlightenment* (Philadelphia: University of Pennsylvania Press, 1998), pp. 13–24.

*World of Difference. European Discourses of Tolerance, c. 1100–1500* (Philadelphia: University of Pennsylvania Press, 2000).

Newman Goldy, Charlotte, "A Thirteenth-Century Anglo-Jewish Woman Crossing Boundaries: Visible and Invisible," *Journal of Medieval History* 34 (2008), 130–45.

Newton, Francis, "Arabic Medicine and Other Arabic Cultural Influences in Southern Italy At the Time of Constantinus Africanus (saec. XI22)," in Florence Eliza Glaze and Brian K. Nance (eds.), *Between Text and Patient. The Medical Enterprise in Medieval and Early Modern Europe* (Florence: Sismel, 2011), pp. 25–55.

Nietzsche, Friedrich, *On the Genealogy of Morals*, W. Kaufmann and R. J. Hollingdale (trans.), (London: Vintage, 1969).

Nirenberg, David, *Communities of Violence. Persecution of Minorities in the Middle Ages* (Princeton University Press, 1996).

"The Current State of Mudejar Studies," *Journal of Medieval History* 24 (1998), 381–89.

"Love Between Muslim and Jew in Medieval Spain: A Triangular Affair," in H. Hames (ed.), *Jews, Muslims and Christians*, pp. 127–56.

"Muslim–Jewish Relations in the Fourteenth-Century Crown of Aragon," *Viator* 24 (1993), 249–68.

Norris, Harry T., *Islam in the Balkans: Religion and Society Between Europe and the Arab World* (London: Hurst, 1994).

*Islam in the Baltic: Europe's Early Muslim Community* (London: Tauris Academic Studies, 2009).

Novikoff, Alex A., "Between Tolerance and Intolerance in Medieval Spain: An Historiographic Enigma," *Medieval Encounters* 11 (2005), 7–36.

O'Brien, Peter, *European Perceptions of Islam and America from Saladin to George W. Bush: Europe's Fragile Ego Uncovered* (New York: Palgrave Macmillan, 2009).

O'Callaghan, Joseph F., *The Gibraltar Crusade: Castile and the Battle for the Strait* (Philadelphia: University of Pennsylvania Press, 2011).

*History of Medieval Spain* (Ithaca, NY: Cornell University Press, 1975).

"Mudejars of Castile and Portugal in the Twelfth and Thirteenth Centuries," in J. Powell, (ed.), *Muslims Under Latin Rule*, pp. 87–106.

*Reconquest and Crusade in Medieval Spain* (Philadelphia: University of Pennsylvania Press, 2003).

O'Connor, Isabel de los Angeles, *A Forgotten Community: The Mudejar Aljama of Xàtiva, 1240–1327* (Leiden: Brill, 2003).

"Mudejars Helping Other Mudejars in the Kingdom of Valencia," *al-Masāq* 17 (2006), 99–107.

"The Mudejars and the Local Courts: Justice in Action," *Journal of Islamic Studies* 16 (2005), 332–56.

"Muslim Mudejar Women in Thirteenth-Century Spain: Dispelling the Stereotypes," *Journal of Muslim Minority Affairs* 27 (2007), 55–70.

Olstein, Diego Adrián, *La era mozárabe: los mozárabes de Toledo (siglos* XII *y* XIII*) en la historiografía, las fuentes y la historia* (Universidad de Salamanca, 2006).

Oman, Giovanni, "Vestiges arabes en Sardaigne," *Revue de l'Occident Musulman* 8 (1970): 175–84.

Ozaki, Akio A., "El régimen tributario y la vida económica de los mudéjares en Navarra," *Principe de Viana* 47 (1986), 437–83.

Pardo Molero, Juan Francisco, "'*Per salvar la sua ley*.' Historia del levantamiento, juicio y castigo de la villa de Benguacil contra Carlos V (1525–1526)," *Sharq al-Andalus* 14–15 (1997–98), 113–54.

Pareja Pareja, Francisco Ángel, "Los matrimonios mixtos: una estrategia usada por el poder en el proceso de aculturación cristiana," *Qurtuba. Estudios andalusíes* 2 (1997), 163–73.

Parpal y Marquès, Cosme, *La conquesta de Menorca, el 1287, per Alfons el Liberal* (Barcelona: R. Dalmau, 1964).

Pascua, Esther, "Round and about Water: Christians and Muslims in the Ebro Valley in the Fourteenth Century," in Simon Barton and Peter Linehan (eds.), *Cross, Crescent and Conversion. Studies on Medieval Spain and Christendom in Memory of Richard Fletcher* (Leiden: Brill, 2008), pp. 293–311.

Peinado Santaella, Rafael Gerardo, *Los inicios de la resistencia musulmana en el Reino de Granada, 1490–1515* (Granada: Fundación el Legado Andalusí, 2011).

Peña Gonzalvo, Javier, "Mahoma Ramí, arquitecto de Benedicto XIII," in VI *Centenario del Papa Luna: jornadas de estudio, Calatayud–Illueca, 1994* (Calatayud: Centro de Estudios Bilbilitanos, 1996), pp. 299–316.

Perceval Verde, José-María, "Asco y asquerosidad del morisco según los apologistas cristianos del Siglo de Oro," *La Torre* 4 (1990), 21–47.

*Todos son uno: arquetipos, xenofobia y racismo: la imagen del morisco en la monarquía española durante los siglos* XVI *y* XVII (Almería: Instituto de Estudios Almerienses, 1997).

Pérez Ordóñez, Alejandro, "Viejas mezquitas, nuevas iglesias. Materializaciones formales de la implantación del cristianismo en la sierra de Cádiz tras la conquista castellana (1485–1500)," in *Jornadas de historia "abadía, iglesias y fronteras" (Alcalá La Real, 2004)* (Diputación Provincial de Jaén, 2005), pp. 633–42.

Perry, Mary Elizabeth, "Between Muslim and Christian Worlds: Moriscas and Identity in Early Modern Spain," *Muslim World* 95 (2005), 177–98.

*The Handless Maiden: Moriscos and the Politics of Religion in Early Modern Spain* (Princeton University Press, 2005).

Pescador del Hoyo, María del Carmen, "Alí Dordux, un personaje controvertido," *Anuario de estudios medievales* 17 (1978), 491–500.

Petrovics, István, "Foreign Ethnic Groups in the Towns of Southern Hungary in the Middle Ages," in Derek Keene *et al.* (eds.), *Segregation, Integration, Assimilation*, pp. 67–88.

Phillips, Jonathan and Martin Hoch, *The Second Crusade: Scope and Consequences* (Manchester University Press, 2001).

Pick, Lucy K., *Conflict and Coexistence: Archbishop Rodrigo and the Muslims and Jews of Medieval Spain* (Ann Arbor: University of Michigan, 2004).

"What Did Rodrigo Jiménez de Rada Know about Islam?" *Anuario de historia de la Iglesia* 20 (2011), 221–35.

Pirenne, Henri, *Mohammed and Charlemagne* (London: Allen & Unwin, 1958 [1937]).

Plazolles Guillén, Fabienne, "Trayectorias sociales de los libertos musulmanes y negroafricanos en la Barclona tardomedieval," in M. T. Ferrer i Mallol and J. Mutgé Vives (eds.), *De l'esclavitud a la llibertat*, pp. 617–40.

Ponsoda López de Atalaya, Santiago, "Migracions mudèjars i disputes senyorials al sud València a les darreries de l'Edat Mitjana," *Anales de la Universidad de Alicante. Historia medieval* 17 (2011), 469–82.

Ponsoda López de Atalaya and Juan Leonardo Soler Milla, "Violencia nobiliaria en el sur del Reino de Valencia a finales de la Edad Media," *Anales de la Universidad de Alicante. Historia medieval* 16 (2009–10), 319–47.

Pop, Ioan-Aurel, "The Religious Situation in the Medieval Kingdom of Hungary," in Celia Hawkesworth, Muriel Heppell, and H. T. Norris (eds.),

*Religious Quest and National Identity in the Balkans* (New York: Palgrave, 2001), pp. 78–90.

Powell, James M., "Frederick II and the Rebellion of the Muslims of Sicily, 1200–1224," in Dil Atatürk Kültür and Tarih Yüksek Kurumu (eds.), *Uluslararasi Hacli Seferleri Sempozyumu* (Ankara: Türk Tarih Kurumu Basımevi, 1999), pp. 13–22.

Powell, James M. (ed.), *Muslims Under Latin Rule, 1100–1300* (Princeton University Press, 1990).

Powers, James F., "Frontier Municipal Baths and Social Interaction in Thirteenth-Century Spain," *American Historical Review* 84 (1979), 649–70.

*A Society Organized for War: the Iberian Municipal Militias in the Central Middle Ages, 1000–1284* (Berkeley: University of California Press, 1987).

Prawer, Joshua, *The Crusaders' Kingdom; European Colonialism in the Middle Ages* (New York: Praeger, 1972).

*The History of the Jews in the Latin Kingdom of Jerusalem* (New York: Oxford University Press, 1988).

*The Latin Kingdom of Jerusalem: European Colonialism in the Middle Ages* (London: Weidenfeld and Nicolson, 1973).

"Social Classes in the Latin Kingdom: The Minorities," in Norman P. Zacour and Harry W. Hazard (eds.), *A History of the Crusades, Vol. 5. The Impact of the Crusades on the Near East* (Madison: University of Wisconsin Press, 1969), pp. 59–115.

Pringle, Denys, *Fortification and Settlement in Crusader Palestine* (Aldershot: Ashgate, 2000).

*Secular Buildings in the Crusader Kingdom of Jerusalem: An Archaeological Gazetteer* (Cambridge University Press, 1997).

de la Puente, Cristina, "Juridical Sources for the Study of Women: Limitations of the Female's Capacity to Act According to Maliki Law," in R. Deguilhem and M. Marín (eds.), *Writing the Feminine*, pp. 95–110.

"Vivre et mourir pour Dieu, oeuvre et héritage d'Abû `Ali al-Sadafî (m. 514/ 1120)," *Studia islamica* 88 (1988), 77–102.

Puig Montada, Josep, "Francesc Eiximenis y la tradición antimusulmana peninsular," in José María Rábanos Soto (ed.), *Pensamiento medieval hispano: Homenaje a Horacio Santiago-Otero* (Madrid: CSIC, 1998), pp. 1551–57.

Qamber, Rukhsana, "Inquisition Proceedings Against Muslims in 16th Century Latin America," *Islamic Studies* 45 (2006), 21–57.

Quinn, Frederick, *The Sum of All Heresies: The Image of Islam in Western Thought* (New York: Oxford University Press, 2008).

Rabanaque, Emilio, Angel Novella, Santiago Sebastian, and Joaquín Yarza, *El artesonado de la Catedral de Teruel* (Zaragoza: Ibercaja, 1993).

Ramos y Loscertales, José María, "Recopilación de fueros de Aragón," *Anuario de historia del derecho español* 2 (1925), 491–523.

Rapoport, Yossef, *Marriage, Money and Divorce in Medieval Islamic Society* (Cambridge University Press, 2005).

Ratcliffe, Marjorie, "Judíos y musulmanes en la jurisprudència medieval española," *Revista canadiense de estudios hispánicos* 9 (1985), 423–438.

Ray, Jonathan, "Beyond Tolerance and Persecution: Our Approach to Medieval Convivencia," *Jewish Social Studies* 11 (2005), 1–18.

*The Sephardic Frontier: The Reconquista and the Jewish Community in Medieval Iberia* (Ithaca, NY: Cornell Universtic Press, 2006).

Razūq, Muhammad, "Observaciones sobre la presencia de los moriscos en Marruecos," in M. de Epalza (ed.), *L'expulsió dels moriscos*, pp. 384–87.

Reilly, Bernard F., *The Contest of Christian and Muslim Spain: 1031–1157* (Oxford: Basil Blackwell, 1992).

*The Kingdom of León-Castilla under King Alfonso VI, 1065–1109* (Princeton University Press, 1988).

*The Kingdom of León-Castilla under King Alfonso VII, 1126–1157* (Princeton University Press, 1998).

*The Kingdom of León-Castilla under Queen Urraca, 1109–1126* (Princeton University Press, 1982).

Remensnyder, Amy G., "Beyond Muslim and Christian: The Moriscos' Marian Scriptures," *Journal of Medieval and Early Modern Studies* 41 (2011), 545–76.

Reyes Pacios Lozano, A., "Bibliografía de arte mudéjar. Addenda (1992–1995)," *Sharq Al-Andalus* 12 (1995), 613–30.

"Bibliografía de arte mudéjar. Addenda (1995–1996)," *Sharq Al-Andalus* (1996), 267–71.

Reynolds, Dwight F., "Music in Medieval Iberia: Contact, Influence and Hybridization," *Mediterranean Encounters* 15 (2009), 236–55.

Ribera Tarragó, Julián, *Orígenes del Justicia de Aragón* (Zaragoza: Comas Hermanos, 1897).

Richard, Jean, *The Crusades, c. 1071–c. 1291* (Cambridge University Press, 1999).

"Frankish Power in the Eastern Mediterranean," *Mediterranean Historical Review* 2 (1987), 168–87.

"Huon de Tabarié: la naissance d'une figure épique," in René Louis (ed.), *La chanson de geste et le mythe carolingien. Mélanges R. Louis* (Saint-Père-sous-Vézelay: Musée Archéologique Régional, 1982), pp. 1073–78.

"La seigneurie franque en Syrie et à Chypre: modèle oriental ou modèle occidental?" in *117e Congrès national des sociétés savantes, Clermont-Ferrand, 1992. Histoire medieval* (Paris: CTHS, 1994), pp. 155–66.

"Les Turcopoles au service des royaumes de Jérusalem et de chypre: Musulmans converts ou Chrétiens orientaux?" *Revue des études islamiques* 54 (1988), 259–70.

Riera i Sans, Jaume, *Fam i fe* (Barcelona: Pages, 2004).

"Penjat pels peus," in F. Sabaté i Curell and Claud Denjean (eds.), *Cristianos y Judíos en contacto en la Edad Media: polémica, conversión, dinero y convivencia* (Lleida: Milenio, 2009), pp. 605–22.

*Els poders públics i les sinagogues, segles* XIII–XV (Girona: Ajuntament, 2006).

"La precedencia entre judíos y moros en el reino de Aragón," in Elena Romero (ed.), *Judaísmo hispano. Estudios en memoria de José Luis Lacave Riaño* (Madrid: CSIC, 2002), pp. 549–60.

Riley-Smith, Jonathan, *The Crusades: A History* (New Haven: Yale University Press, 2005).

*The Crusades: A Short History* (London: Athlone, 1987).

"Crusading as an Act of Love," *History* 65 (1980), 177–92.

Riley-Smith, Jonathan, and Louise Riley-Smith, *The Crusades, Idea and Reality, 1095–1274* (London: E. Arnold, 1981).

Rivera Garretas, María-Milagros, "La construcción de lo femenino entre musulmanes, judíos y cristianos (al-Andalus y reinos cristianos, siglos XI–XIII)," *Acta historica et archaeologica mediaevalia* 16–17 (1995), 167–79.

Robinson, Cynthia, *Imag(in)ing Passions: Christ, the Virgin, Images and Devotion in a Multi-Confessional Castile, 14–15th c.* (University Park: Pennsylvania State University Press, 2011).

*In Praise of Song: The Making of Courtly Culture in Al-Andalus and Provence, 1005–1134 A.D.* (Leiden Brill, 2002).

"Mudéjar Revisited: A Prologoména to the Reconstruction of Perception, Devotion, and Experience at the Mudéjar Convent of Clarisas, Tordesillas, Spain (Fourteenth Century A.D.)," *Anthropology and Aesthetics* 43 (2003), 51–77.

"Trees of Love, Trees of Knowledge: Toward the Definition of a Cross-Confessional Current in Late Medieval Iberian Spirituality," *Mediterranean Encounters* 12 (2006), 388–435.

Robinson, Cynthia and Leyla Rouhi (eds.), *Under the Influence: Questioning the Comparative in Medieval Castile* (Leiden: Brill, 2005).

Rodríguez, Jarbel, "Conversion Anxieties in the Crown of Aragon in the Later Middle Ages," *al-Masāq* 22 (2010), 315–24.

Rodríguez Llopis, Miguel, *Alfonso X: aportaciones de un rey castellano a la construcción de Europa* (Región de Murcia, Consejería de Cultura y Educatión, 1997).

Rogers, R., *Latin Siege Warfare in the Twelfth Century* (New York: Oxford University Press, 1992).

Roldán Castro, Fátima, *Niebla musulmana (siglos* VIII–XIII*)* (Diputacion Provincial de Huelva, 1993).

Romano, Davíd, "Cortesanos judíos en la Corona de Aragón," *Destierros aragoneses* 1 (1988), 25–37.

*Judíos al servicio de Pedro el Grande de Aragón (1276–1285)* (Universidad de Barcelona, 1983).

"Judíos escribanos y turjamanes de árabe en la Corona de Aragón (reinados de Jaime I a Jaime II)," *Sefarad* 38 (1978), 71–105.

Romero Sáiz, Miguel, *Mudéjares y Moriscos en Castilla-La Mancha: aproximación a su estudio* (Piedrabuena: Llanura, 2007).

Rosselló Bordoy, Guillermo, *L'Islam a Les Illes Balears* (Palma: Daedalus, 1968).

Rota, Giorgio, *Under Two Lions: On the Knowledge of Persia in the Republic of Venice (Ca. 1450–1797)* (Vienna: Akademie der Wissenschaften, 2009).

Rouighi, Ramzi, *The Making of a Mediterranean Emirate* (Philadelphia: University of Pennsylvania Press, 2011).

Roy Marín, María José, "Aportación al estudio del delito sexual: el caso de los moros de Zaragoza en el siglo XIV," in *Actas del VII Simposio Internacional de Mudejarismo*, pp. 195–210.

Rubenstein, Jay, *Armies of Heaven. The First Crusade and the Quest for Apocalypse* (New York: Basic Books, 2011).

"Cannibals and Crusaders," *French Historical Studies* 31 (2008), 525–52.

Rubiera Mata, María Jesús, "La família morisca de la Muley-Fez, príncipes meriníes e infantes de Granada," *Sharq al-Andalus* 13 (1996), 159–67.

"Un insolito caso de conversas musulmanas al Cristianismo: la princesas toledanas del siglo XI", in Angela Fernández Muñoz (ed.), *Las mujeres en el Cristianismo medieval: imágenes teóricas y cauces de actuación religiosa* (Madrid: Asociación Cultural Al-Mudayna, 1989).

Ruíz, Teolfilo, "Trading with the 'Other': Economic Exchanges between Muslims, Jews, and Christians in Late Medieval Northern Castile," in R. Collins and A. Goodman (eds.), *Medieval Spain*, pp. 63–78.

Ruiz Lagos, Manuel, *Moriscos: de los romances del gozo al exilio* (Sevilla: Guadalmena, 2001).

Ruiz de la Peña, Juan Ignacio, and Miguel Angel Ladero Quesada *et al.* (eds.), *Cristianos y musulmanes en la península Ibérica: la guerra, la frontera, la convivencia:* XI *Congreso de Estudios Medievales* (Ávila: Fundación Sánchez Albornoz, 2009).

Runciman, Sir Steven, *A History of the Crusades*, 3 vols. (Cambridge University Press, 1957).

Rustow, Marina, *Heresy and the Politics of Community: The Jews of the Fatimid Caliphate* (Ithaca: Cornell University Press, 2008).

Ruzafa García, Manuel, "Alí Xupió, senyor de la moreria de València," in Rafael Narbona, *et al.* (eds.), *L'univers dels prohoms* (Valencia: Elieu Climent, 1995), pp. 137–74.

"Élites valencianas y minorías sociales: la élite mudéjar y sus actividades (1370–1500)," *Revista d'historia medieval* 12 (2001–2), 163–90.

"Façen-se cristians los Moros o muyren!" *Revista d'història medieval* 1 (1990), 87–110.

"La familia Xupió en la morería de Valencia (1360–1465)," in Ana Echevarría Arsuaga (ed.), *Biografías mudéjares*, pp. 233–90.

"El matrimonio en la familia mudéjar valenciana," *Sharq al-Andalus* 9 (1992), 165–76.

"Els orígens d'una família de mercaders mudèjars en el segle XV: Çaat Ripoll (1381–1422)," *Afers: Fulls de recerca i pensament* 7 (1988), 169–88.

"Las relacions de frontera entre Valencia y el Islam en el cuatrocientos," in José Rodríguez Molina and Francisco Toro Ceballos (eds.), III *Estudios de frontera. Actividad y vida en la frontera* (Jaen: Diputación, 2000), pp. 659–79.

Sabaté i Curull, Flocel, "La pena de muerte en la Cataluña bajomedieval," *Clio & Crímen: Revista del Centro de Historia del Crimen de Durango* 4 (2007), 117–276.

Said, Edward W., *Orientalism* (New York: Vintage Books, 1994).

Saliba, George, *Islamic Science and the Making of the European Renaissance* (Cambridge: MIT Press, 2007).

Salicrú i Lluch, Roser, "Benedicto XIII y los Musulmanes. Aspectos de una dualidad," in *Iglesias y fronteras. V Jornadas en la Abadía – Alcalá La Real. Homenaje al profesor José Rodríguez Molina* (Diputación Provincial de Jaén, 2005), pp. 699–711.

"Crossing Boundaries in Late Medieval Mediterranean Iberia: Historical Glimpses of Christian-Islamic Intercultural Dialogue," *International Journal of Euro-Mediterranean Studies* 1 (2008), 33–51.

"La diplomacia y las embajadas como expresión de los contactos interculturales entre Cristianos y Musulmanes en el Mediterráneo occidental durante la baja Edad Media," *Estudios de historia de España* 9 (2007), 77–106.

"L'esclau com a inversió? Aprofitament, assalariament i rendibilitat del treball esclau en l'entorn català tardomedieval," *Recerques* 52–53 (2006), 49–85.

*Esclaus i proprietaris d'esclaus a la Catalunya del segle* XV (Barcelona: CSIC, 1998).

"Fugues, camuflatge i treball esclau a l'entorn del castell de Tortosa i de les terres de l'Ebre en el primer terá del segle XV," *Acta historica archaeologica medievalia* 25 (2003), 423–43.

"La implantació de la Guarda d'Esclaus i el manifest de 1421 a la vegueria de Cervera," *Miscel·lània cerveriana* 12 (1998), 35–56.

"Intérpretes y diplomáticos. Mudéjares mediadores y representantes de los poderes cristianos en la Corona de Aragón," in A. Echevarría Arsuaga (ed.), *Biografías mudéjares*, pp. 471–96.

"Más allá de la mediación de la palabra: negociación con los infieles y mediación cultural en la Baja Edad Media," in *Negociar en la Edad Media: Actas del coloquio celebrado en Barcelona los días 14, 15 y 16 de octubre de 2004 = Négocier au Moyen Âge: Actes du colloque tenu à Barcelone du 14 au 16 octobre 2004* (Barcelona: CSIC, 2005), pp. 409–39.

"Mudéjares y cristianos en el comercio con Berbería: quejas sobre favoritismo fiscal y acusaciones de colaboracionismo mudéjar, una reacción cristiana a la defensiva," in *Actas del* VIII *Simposio Internacional de Mudejarismo*, pp. 283–301.

"Sarraïns desaveïnats d'Elx a mitjan segle XV (1449) segons llur propi testimoni: dificultats econòmiques i conflictivitat interna de la moreria," *Sharq al-Andalus* 12 (1995), 23–66.

"Slaves in the Professional and Family Life of Craftsmen in the Late Middle Ages," in Simonetta Cavaciocchi (ed.), *La famiglia nell'economia europea secoli* XIII–XVIII / *The Economic Role of the Family in the European Economy from the 13th to the 18th Centuries* (Florence: Firenze University Press, 2009), pp. 325–42.

*El Sultanat de Granada i la Corona d'Aragó, 1410–1458* (Barcelona: CSIC, 1998).

Salvador Martínez, H., *Alfonso X, the Learned: A Biography*, Odile Cisneros (trans.), (Leiden: Brill, 2010).

Samarrai, Alauddin, "Arabs and Latins in the Middle Ages: Enemies, Partners, and Scholars," in D. Blanks and M. Frassetto (eds.), *Western Views of Islam*, pp. 137–46.

Sánchez-Albornoz, Claudio, *España: un enigma histórico* (Buenos Aires: Sudamericana, 1956).

Sánchez Martínez, Manuel, "Aspectos del cautiverio musulmán en los países de la Corona de Aragón (primer tercio del s. XIV), a través de tres procesos," *Acta historica et archaeologica mediaevalia* 22 (2001), 373–96.

Santonja, Pedro, "Arnau de Vilanova (A. de Villeneuve) et la pensée islamique," *Annales du Midi* 196 (1991), 421–39.

Sanz Artibucilla, José María, "Alarifes moros aragoneses," *al-Andalus* 3 (1935), 63–89.

Sarnelli Cerqua, Clelia, "Il morisco ispano-marrochino al-Hagari (XVI–XVII sec.): a Saint-Jean-De-Luz e a Parigi (I)," in Antonino Pellitteri and Umberto Rizzitano (eds.), *Azhàr: Studi Arabo-Islamici in Memoria Di Umberto Rizzitano: (1913–1980)* (Palermo: Facoltà di Lettere e Filosofia, 1995), pp. 195–204.

Saxton, Alexander Plaisted, *The Indispensable Enemy: Labor and the Anti-Chinese Movement in California* (Berkeley: University of California, 1971).

Schenk, David P., *The Myth of Guillaume: Poetic Consciousness in the Guillaume d'Orange Cycle* (Birmingham: Summa Publications, 1988).

Schramm, Matthias, "Frederick II of Hohenstaufen and Arabic Science," *Science in Context* 14 (2012), 313–31.

Schwartz, Stuart B., *All Can be Saved: Religious Tolerance and Salvation in the Iberian Atlantic World* (New Haven: Yale University Press, 2008).

Schwinges, Rainer Christoph, "William of Tyre, the Muslim Enemy and the Problem of Tolerance," in Michael Gervers and James M. Powell (eds.), *Tolerance and Intolerance*, pp. 124–32.

Scott, J. C., *Weapons of the Weak* (New Haven: Yale University Press, 1987).

Segura Urra, Félix, *Fazer justicia: fuero, poder político y delito en Navarra (siglos* XIII–XIV*)* (Pamplona: Gobierno de Navarra, 2005).

"Los mudéjares navarros y la justicia regia: cuestiones penales y peculiaridades delictivas en el siglo XIV," *Anaquel de estudios árabes* 14 (2003), 239–58.

"Víctimas y agresoras: la mujer ante la justicia en Navarra durante la primera mitad del siglo XIV," in *Grupos sociales en la historia de Navarra, relaciones y derechos: Actas del* V *Congreso de Historia de Navarra, Pamplona, septiembre de 2002*, 2 vols. (Pamplona: Eunate, 2002), vol. I, pp. 145–65.

Sénac, Philippe, "De *ḥiṣn* musulmán au *castrum* chrétien," in Carlos Laliena Corbera and Juan F. Utrilla (eds.), *De Toledo a Huesca. Sociedades medievales en transición a finales del siglo* XI *(1080–1100)* (Zaragoza: CSIC, 1998), pp. 113–30.

*L'Image de l'autre. L'Occident médiéval face a l'Islam* (Paris: Flammarion, 1983).

"Poblamiento, hábitats rurales y sociedad en la marca superior de al-Andalus," *Aragón en la Edad Media* 9 (1991), 389–402.

Serrano, Delfina, "Dos fetuas sobre la expulsión de Mozárabes al Magreb en 1126," *Anaquel de estudios árabes* 2 (1991), 163–82.

Serrano Larráyoz, Fernando and M. Boroiz Lazcano, "Viajeros navarros por Aragón: dos cuentas de viajes a Zaragoza durante la segunda mitad del siglo XIV (1364 y1372)," in Eloísa Ramírez Vaquero and Roser Salicrú i Lluch (eds.), *Cataluña y Navarra en la Baja Edad Media* (Pamplona: Universidad Pública de Navarra, 2010), pp. 365–401.

Setton, Kenneth Meyer (ed.), *A History of the Crusades*. 2nd edn., 6 vols. (Madison: University of Wisconsin Press, 1969).

Shagrir, Iris, Roni Ellenblum, J. Riley-Smith, and B. Z. Kedar (eds.), *In Laudem Hierosolymitani: Studies in Crusades and Medieval Culture in Honour of Benjamin Z. Kedar* (Aldershot: Ashgate, 2007).

Shahîd, Irfan, *Rome and the Arabs: A Prolegomenon to the Study of Byzantium and the Arabs* (Washington, DC: Dumbarton Oaks Research Library, 1984).

Shatzmiller, Maya (ed.), *Crusaders and Muslims in Twelfth-Century Syria* (Leiden: Brill, 1993).

*Her Day in Court: Women's Property Rights in Fifteenth-Century Granada* (Cambridge, MA: Harvard University Press, 2007).

"Marīnids (Banū Marīn)," in P. Bearman, Th. Bianquis, C. E. Bosworth, E. van Donzel, and W. P. Heinrichs (eds.), *Encyclopaedia of Islam, Second Edition* (Leiden: Brill, 2012), online.

Shiloah, Amnon, *Music in the World of Islam: A Socio-Cultural Study* (Detroit: Wayne State University Press, 1995).

Sidelko, Paul L., "The Acquisition of the Landed Estates of the Hospitallers in the Latin East, 1099–1291," PhD Dissertation: History (University of Toronto, 1998).

"Muslim Taxation Under Crusader Rule," in Michael Gervers and James M. Powell (eds.), *Tolerance and Intolerance*, pp. 65–74.

Silleras-Fernández, Núria, "Failed Expectations and Desire: Widowhood and Sexuality in Late Medieval Iberia," *Viator* 42 (2011), 353–70.

"Nigra sum sed formosa: Black Slaves and Exotica in the Court of a Fourteenth-Century Aragonese Queen," *Medieval Encounters* 13 (2007), 546–65.

Silva Conceição, Vinícius, "Mouros, judeus e o espaço urbano português nas Ordenações Afonsinas (século XV)," *Noctua* 4 (2011), 5–8.

Simmel, Georg, *Conflict: the Web of Group Affiliations* (New York: Free Press, 1964).

de Simone, Adalgisa, "Ruggero II e l'Africa islamica," in Giosuè Musca (ed.), *Il Mezzogiorno normanno-svevo e le Crociat: Atti delle Quattordicesime Giornate Normanno-Sveve, Bari, 17–20 ottobre 2000* (Bari: Edizioni Dedalo, 2002), pp. 95–130.

Sivan, Emmanuel, "Réfugiés syro-palestiniens au temps des Croisades," *Revue des études islamiques* 35 (1967), 135–47.

Skinner, Patricia, "Spatial Relations: Mapping Interfaith Interaction through Topography and Material Culture," paper presented at the 40th International Congress on Medieval Studies, May 5–8, 2005.

Smail, R. C., *The Crusaders in Syria and the Holy Land* (London: Thames and Hudson, 1973).

Smarandache, Bogdan, "The Franks and the Nizārī Ismāʿīlīs in the Early Crusade Period," *al-Masāq* 24 (2012), 221–39.

Soifer, Maya, "Beyond Convivencia: Critical Reflections on the Historiography of Interfaith Relations in Christian Spain," *Journal of Medieval Iberian Studies* 1 (2009), 19–35.

Soler Milla, Juan Leonardo, "Comercio musulmán versus comercio cristiano: la actividad de los mercaderes mudéjares y la producción de las aljamas sarracenas. Valencia, primera mitad del siglo XIV," *Revista de historia medieval* 14 (2003–06), 229–47.

"Relaciones comerciales entre Valencia y el Norte de África en la primera mitad del siglo XIV," *Miscelánea medieval murciana* 27–28 (2003), 125–57.

Soria Mesa, Enrique, "De la conquista a la asimilación: la integración de la aristocracia nazarí en la oligarquía granadina, siglos XV–XVII," *Areas: Revista internacional de ciencias sociales* 14 (1992), 49–64.

"Los moriscos que se quedaron. La permanencia de la población de origen islámico en la españa moderna: Reino de Granada, siglos XVII–XVIII," *Vínculos de historia* 1 (2012), 205–30.

Soyer, François, "The Expulsion of the Muslims From Portugal (1496–1497)," *al-Masāq* 20 (2008), 161–177.

"'It is Not Possible to be Both a Jew and a Christian': Converso Religious Identity and the Inquisitorial Trial of Custodio Nunes (1604–5)," *Mediterranean Historical Review* 26 (2011), 81–97.

"Muslim Freedmen in León, Castile and Portugal (1100–1300)," *al-Masāq* 18 (2006), 129–43.

"Muslim Slaves and Freedmen in Medieval Portugal," *al-Qanṭara* 27 (2007), 489–516.

*The Persecution of the Jews and Muslims of Portugal: King Manuel I and the End of Religious Tolerance (1496–7)* (Leiden: Brill, 2007).

Sroka, Stanislaw, "Methods of Constructing Angevin Rule in Hungary in the Light of the Most Recent Research," *Quaestiones medii aevi novae* 1 (1996), 77–90.

Stalls, Clay, *Possessing the Land. Aragon's Expansion Into Islam's Ebro Frontier Under Alfonso the Battler, 1104–1134* (Leiden: Brill, 1995).

Stantchev, Stefan K., "Embargo: The Origins of an Idea and the Implications of a Policy in Europe and the Mediterranean, ca. 1100 – ca. 1500," PhD Dissertation: History (University of Michigan, 2009).

Stanton, Charles D., *Norman Naval Operations in the Mediterranean* (Woodbridge: Boydell Press, 2011).

"Roger de Hauteville, Emir of Sicily," *Mediterranean Historical Review* 25 (2010), 113–32.

Stearns, Justin K., *Infectious Ideas: Contagion in Premodern Islamic and Christian Thought in the Western Mediterranean* (Baltimore, MD: Johns Hopkins University Press, 2011).

Stewart, Devin, "The Identity of 'the *Muftī* of Oran,' Abū l-'Abbās Aḥmad b. Abī Jum'ah al-Maghrāwī al-Wahrānī (d. 971/1511)," *al-Qanṭara* 27 (2006), 265–301.

Strickland, Debra Higgs, *Saracens, Demons, & Jews: Making Monsters in Medieval Art* (Princeton University Press, 2003).

Stuard, Susan Mosher, "Ancillary Evidence on the Decline of Medieval Slavery," *Past and Present* 149 (1995), 3–32.

Surtz, Ronald E., "Morisco Women, Written Texts, and the Valencia Inquisition," *The Sixteenth Century Journal* 32 (2001), 421–33.

Székely, György, "Les contacts entre Hongrois et Musulmans aux XIe–XIIe siècles," in Gyula Káldy-Nagy (ed.), *The Muslim East. Studies in Honour of Julius Germanus* (Budapest: Loránd Eoetvoes, 1974), pp. 53–74.

Szolnoki, László, Ferenc Gyulai, and László Daróczi-Szabó, "A Hajdúböszörmény Téglagyár 2. lelőhelyen 2011-ben végzett megelőző régészeti feltárások eredményei," *Magyar Régészeti és Művészettörténeti Társulat* (Society of Hungarian Archaeology and Art History) 14–15.05.2012 [http://mrmt.blog.hu/].

Szpiech, Ryan, "The Convivencia Wars: Decoding Historiography's Polemic with Philology," in Suzanne Conklin Akabari and Karla Mallette (eds.), *A Sea of Languages: Rethinking the Arabic Role in Medieval Literary History* (University of Toronto, www.utpublishing.com/A-sea-of-Languages-Rethinking-the-Arabic-role-in-Medieval-Literary-History.html 2013).

Ṭāha, Abdulwāḥid Dhanūn, *The Muslim Conquest and Settlement of North Africa and Spain* (London: Routledge, 1989).
Takayama, Hiroshi, *The Administration of the Norman Kingdom of Sicily* (Leiden: Brill, 1993).
"The Admininstration of Roger I," in Guglielmo de Giovanni (ed.), *Ruggero I Gran Conte di Sicilia 1101–2001* (Troina: Laboratorio per l'arte, la cultura, l'ambiente, 2007), pp. 124–40.
"Amiratus in the Norman Kingdom of Sicily – a Leading Office of Arabic Origin in the Royal Administration," in *Forschungen Zur Reichs-, Papst- Und Landesgeschichte, Herausgegeben Von K. Borchardt & E. Bunz* (Stuttgart: Anton Hiersemann, 1993), pp. 133–44.
"Central Power and Multi-Cultural Elements at the Norman Court of Sicily," *Mediterranean Studies* 12 (2004), 1–16.
"The Financial and Administrative Organization of the Norman Kingdom of Sicily," *Viator* 16 (1985), 129–58.
"The Great Administrative Officials of the Norman Kingdom of Sicily," *Papers of the British School at Rome* 58 (1990), 317–55.
"Religious Tolerance in Norman Sicily? The Case of Muslims," in E. Cuozzo, V. Deroche, A. Peters-Custot, and V. Prigent (eds.), *Puer Apuliae. Melanges offerts à Jean-Marie Martin* (Paris: Centre de recherche d'Histoire et Civilization de Byzance 2009), pp. 451–64.
Taleb, Nassim, *The Black Swan: The Impact of the Highly Improbable* (New York: Random House, 2007).
Talmon-Heller, Daniela, "Arabic Sources on Muslim Villagers Under Frankish Rule," in A. Murray (ed.), *From Clermont to Jerusalem*, pp. 103–17.
"Islamic Preaching in Syria During the Counter-Crusade (Twelfth–Thirteenth Centuries)," in Iris Shagrir, *et al.* (eds.), *In Laudem Hierosolymitani*, pp. 61–75.
"Muslim Martyrdom and Quest for Martyrdom in the Crusading Period," *al-Masāq* 14 (2002), 131–39.
"The Shaykh and the Community: Popular Hanbalite Islam in the 12th–13th Century Jabal Nablus and Jabal Qasyun," *Studia Islamica* 79 (1994), 103–20.
Talmon-Heller, Daniela and Benjamin Z. Kedar, "Did Muslim Survivors of the 1099 Massacre of Jerusalem Settle in Damascus? The True Origins of the Al-Āliiyya Suburb," *al-Masāq* 17 (2005), 165–69.
de Tapia Sánchez, Serafín, *La comunidad morisca de Ávila* (Universidad de Salamanca, 1991).
"Los Moriscos de Castilla la Vieja ¿Una identidad en proceso de disolución?" *Sharq al-Andalus* 12 (1995), 179–95.
"Los mudéjares de la Extremadura castellano-leonesa: notas sobre una minoría dócil (1085–1502)," *Studia historica. Historia medieval* 7 (1989), 95–124.
Tarayre, Michel, "L'image de Mahomet et de l'Islam dans une grande encyclopédie du Moyen Âge, le *Speculum historiale* de Vincent de Beauvais," *Le Moyen Âge* 109 (2003), 313–43.
Taylor, Julie Anne, "Lucera Sarracenorum: A Muslim Colony in Medieval Christian Europe," *Nottingham Medieval Studies* 43 (1999), 110–25.
*Muslims in Medieval Italy: The Colony At Lucera* (Lanham, MD: Lexington Books, 2003).

Teixeira, Simonne, "El dominio del Monasterio de Veruela: la gestión de un espacio agrario andalusí," PhD Dissertation (Universitat Autònoma de Barcelona, 1995).
Temimi, Abdeljelil (ed.), *Actes du* VII*e Symposium International des Études Morisques sur: Famille morisque, femmes et enfants* (Zaghouan: FoundationTemimi, 1997).
"Une lettre des morisques de Granade au Sultan Suleiman al-Kanuni en 1541," *Revue d'histoire maghrebine* 3 (1975), 101–15.
"Lettre du Sultan ottoman Ahmad 1er au Doge de Venise en 1614 au sujet des morisques," *Revue d'histoire maghrebine* 7–8 (1977), 259–61.
"La politique ottomane face à l'implantation et à l'insertion des Morisques en Anatolie," in M. de Epalza (ed.), *L'expulsió dels moriscos*, pp. 164–70.
Testas, Abdelaziz, "Models of Cultural Exclusion and Civilizational Clashes: A Comparison Between Huntingdon and Siddiqui," *Islam and Christian–Muslim Relations* 14 (2003), 175–89.
Theotokis, Georgios, "The Norman Invasion of Sicily, 1061–1072: Numbers and Military Tactics," *War in History* 7 (2010), 381–402.
Tibi, Amin, "Ibn Bassām al-Shantarīnī and his Anthology *Al-Dhakhīra*," *Journal of Islamic Studies* 10 (1999), 313–16.
Tolan, John Victor, *Petrus Alfonsi and His Medieval Readers* (Gainesville: University Press of Florida, 1993).
"'Saracen Philosophers Secretly Deride Islam'," *Medieval Encounters* 8 (2002), 184–208.
*Saracens: Islam in the Medieval European Imagination* (New York: Columbia University Press, 2002).
Tolan, John Victor (ed.), *Medieval Christian Perceptions of Islam: A Book of Essays* (New York: Garland, 1996).
Tolan, John Victor, Gilles Veinstein, and Henry Laurens, *Europe and the Islamic World: A History* (Princeton University Press, 2013).
Tolmacheva, Marina, "The Medieval Arabic Geographers and the Beginnings of Modern Orientalism," *International Journal of Middle East Studies* 27 (1995), 141–56.
Torné Cubells, Josep, "Plet dels sarraïns i jueus de Móra contra els cristians de la població, 1421–1422," *Miscel·lània del Centre d'Estudis Comarcal de la Ribera d'Ebre* 20 (2010), 227–40.
Torres Balbás, Leopoldo, *Algunos aspectos del mudejarismo urbano medieval* (Madrid: Maestre, 1954).
Torres Delgado, Cristóbal, "El Mediterráneo nazarí. Diplomacia y pirateria, siglos XIII–XIV," *Anuario de estudios medievales* 10 (1980), 227–36.
Torres Fontes, Juan, "El alcalde mayor de las aljamas de Moros en Castilla," *Anuario de historia de derecho español* 32 (1962), 131–82.
"La hermanidad de Moros y Cristianos para el rescate de cautivos," in *Actas del* I *Simposio Internacional de Mudejarismo*, pp. 499–507.
"El Monasterio de San Ginés de la Jara en la Edad Media," *Murgetana* 25 (1965), 39–90.
Torró i Abad, Josep, "*De bona guerra.* El ambiguo estatuto del cautivo musulmán en los países de la Corona de Aragón (siglos XII–XIII)," in María Isabel Fierro, Rafael Mayor Barroso, and Francisco García Fitz (eds.), *El cuerpo derrotado:*

*como trataban musulmanes y cristianos a los enemigos vencidos (Península Ibérica, ss. VIII–XIII)* (Madrid: CSIC, 2008) pp. 435–83.

"Field and Canal Building after the Conquest: Modifications to the Cultivated Ecosystem in the Kingdom of Valencia, ca. 1250–ca. 1350," in Brian A. Catlos (ed.), *Worlds of History and Economics. Essays in Honour of Andrew M. Watson* (Universitat de València, 2009), pp. 77–108.

"Jérusalem ou Valence: la prèmiere colone d'Occident," *Annales. Histoire, Science Sociales* 5 (2000), 983–1008.

*El naixement d'una colònia. Dominació i resistència a la frontera valenciana (1238–1276)* (Universitat de València, 1999).

"Peasants like the Others? Christian vs. Muslim Farmers in the 'Latin' Kingdom of Valencia," [unpublished paper, by courtesy of the author].

"Pour en finir avec la 'Reconquête.' L'occupation chrétienne d'al-Andalus, la soumission et la disparition des populations musulmanes (XIIe–XIIIe siècle)," *Cahiers d'histoire* 78 (2000), 79–97.

"Vivir como cristianos y pagar como moros. Genealogía medieval de la servidumbre morisca en el Reino de Valencia," *Revista de historia moderna* 27 (2009), 11–40.

Trenchs Odena, José, "'De Alexandrinis' (El comercio prohibido con los musulmanes y el Papado de Aviñón durante la primera mitad del siglo XIV)," *Anuario de estudios medievales* 10 (1980), 237–318.

Trillo San José, Carmen, "A Social Analysis of Irrigation in al-Andalus: Nazari Granada (13th–15th Centuries)," *Journal of Medieval History* 31 (2005), 163–83.

Tritton, A. S., *The Caliphs and Their Non-Muslim Subjects. A Critical Study of the Covenant of 'Umar* (London: F. Cass, 1970).

Tronzo, William, *The Cultures of His Kingdom: Roger II and the Cappella Palatina in Palermo* (Princeton University Press, 1997).

Tucker, Judith E., *Women, Family, and Gender in Islamic Law* (Cambridge University Press, 2008).

Tyerman, Christopher, *God's War: A New History of the Crusades* (London: Allen Lane, 2006).

*The Invention of the Crusades* (Houndmills: Macmillan Press, 1998).

Usunáriz, Jesús María, "Entre dos expulsiones: Musulmanes y Moriscos en Navarra (1516–1610)," *al-Qanṭara* 33 (2012), 45–81.

Valérian, Dominique, "Ifrîqiyan Muslim Merchants in the Mediterranean at the End of the Middle Ages," *Mediterranean Historical Review* 14 (1999), 47–66.

van Koningsveld, Pieter Sjoerd, "Andalusian-Arabic Manuscripts from Christian Spain: A Comparative, Intercultural Approach," *Israel Oriental Studies* 12 (1992), 75–110.

and Gerard Wiegers, "An Appeal of the Moriscos to the Mamluk Sultan and Its Counterpart to the Ottoman Court: Textual Analysis, Context, and Wider Historical Background," *al-Qanṭara* 20 (1999), 161–89.

"The Islamic Statute of the Mudejars in the Light of a New Source," *al-Qanṭara* 17 (1996): 19–58.

"The Polemical Works of Muhammad al-Qaysī (fl. 1309) and their Circulation in Arabic and Aljamiado among the Mudejars in the Fourteenth Century," *al-Qanṭara* 15 (1994): 163–199

Vásáry, István, "Western Sources on the Early Towns of the Middle Volga Region," *Acta Orientalia Academia Scientiarum Hungaricae* 55 (2002), 263–68.

Vázquez, Miguel Ángel, "Poesía morisca (o de cómo el español se convirtió en lengua literaria del Islam)," *Hispanic Review* 75 (2007), 219–42.

Velázquez Basanta, Fernando Nicolás, "Ibn 'Amīra, Abū l-Muṭarrif," in Jorge Lirola Delgado and José Miguel Puerta Vílchez (eds.), *Biblioteca de al-Andalus*, vol II: *De Ibn Adhà a Ibn Busrà* (Almería: Fundación Ibn Tufayl de Estudios Árabes, 2009), pp. 107–15.

Verlinden, Charles, "Aspects quantitatifs de l'esclavage méditerranéen au bas Moyen Âge," *Anuario de estudios medievales* 10 (1980), 769–89.

"L'esclavage agricole en Crète vénetienne," *Bulletin de l'Institut Historique Belge de Rome* 53–54 (1983–84), 156–64.

*L'esclavage dans l'Europe médiévale*, 2 vols. (Bruges: De Tempel, 1955).

"L'esclavage dans la péninsule Ibérique au XIVe siècle," *Anuario de estudios medievales* 7 (1970/1971), 577–91.

"Esclavage noir en France méridionale et courants de traite en Afrique," *Annales du Midi* 78 (1966), 335–43.

"Esclaves fugitifs et assurances en Catalogne (XIVe–XVe siècles)," *Annales du Midi* 62 (1950), 301–28.

"Les esclaves musulmans du Midi de la France," *Cahiers de Fanjeaux. Islam et chrétiens du Midi (*XII–XIV *s.)* 18 (1983), 215–34.

Vernet Ginés, Juan, *La cultura hispanoárabe en Oriente y Occidente* (Madrid: Ariel, 1978).

"La exégesis musulamana tradicional en los Coranes aljamiados," in *Actas del Coloquio Internacional sobre literatura aljamiada y morisca* (Madrid: Gredos, 1978), pp. 123–44.

*Lo que Europa debe al Islam de España* (Barcelona: El Acantilado, 1999).

"Le tafsir au service de la polémique antimusulmane," *Studia islamica* 32 (1970), 305–09.

"Un texto árabe de la corte de Alfonso X el Sabio," *al-Andalus* 43 (1978), 405–21.

"El valle del Ebro como nexo entre Oriente y Occidente," *Boletín de la Real Academia de Buenas Letras de Barcelona* 22 (1950), 249–86.

Vicéns Sáiz, Belén, "Swearing by God: Muslim Oath-Taking in Late Medieval Christian Iberia," unpublished paper, cited with the permission of the author.

Viera, David J., "The Treatment of the Jew and the Moor in the Catalan Works of Francesc Eiximenis," *Revista canadiense de estudios hispánicos* 9 (1985), 203–12.

Viguera Molins, María Jesús, *Aragón musulmán* (Zaragoza: Mira Editores, 1988).

"Dos nuevos documentos árabes de Aragón (Jarque y Morés, 1492)," *Aragón en la Edad Media* 4 (1991), 235–61.

"Les mudejars et leurs documents écrits en arabe," *Revue du monde musulman et de la Méditerranée* 63/64 (1992), 156–63.

(ed.) *La mujer en al-Andalus: reflejos históricos de su actividad y categorías sociales* (Universidad Autónoma de Madrid, 1989).

*El Reino Nazari de Granada (1232–1492)* (Madrid: Espasa Calpe, 2000).

Viguera Molins, María Jesús, Ramón Menéndez Pidal, and José María Jover Zamora, *El reino Nazarí de Granada (1232–1492). Sociedad, vida y cultura. Vols.* VIII–IV *of Ramón Menéndez Pida and José Maria Jover Zamora Historia de España Menéndez Pidal* (Madrid: Caple, 2000).

Viktus, Daniel J., "Early Modern Orientalism: Representations of Islam in Sixteenth- and Seventeenth-Century Europe," in D. Blanks and M. Frassetto, *Western Views of Islam*, pp. 207–30.

Villanueva Muerte, Concepción, "Las mujeres mudéjares en Aragón. Balance y perspectivas de estudio," in *Actas del* X *Simposio Internacional de Mudejarismo*, pp. 513–78.

Vincent, Bernard, "La famille morisque," *Historia, instituciones, documentos* 5 (1978), 469–83.

"Et quelques voix de plus: de Francisco Núñez Muley à Fatima Ratal," *Sharq al-Andalus* 12 (1995), 131–45.

Vincent, Bernard and Antonio Luis Cortés Peña, *El río morisco* (Universidad de Zaragoza, 2006).

Vispe Martínez, Joaquín, "La fundación del monasterio cisterciense de Veruela y la constitución de su dominio monástico (1146–1177)," *Cistercium* 36 (1984), 279–388.

Vose, Robin, *Dominicans, Muslims, and Jews in the Medieval Crown of Aragon* (Cambridge University Press, 2009).

Wacks, David A., *Framing Iberia: Maqāmāt and Frametale Narratives in Medieval Spain* (Leiden: Brill, 2007).

"Reading Jaume Roig's *Spill* and the *Libro de Buen Amor* in the Iberian Maqāma Tradition," *Bulletin of Spanish Studies* 83–5 (2006), 597–616.

"Reconquest Colonialism and Andalusī Narrative Practice in the Conde Lucanor," *diacritics* 36 (2006), 87–103.

Waines, David, "The Culinary Culture of al-Andalus," in S. Jayyusi (ed.), *The Legacy of Muslim Spain*, pp. 725–40.

Wansbrough, John, "Diplomatica Siciliana," *Bulletin of the School of Oriental and African Studies* 47 (1984), 10–21.

*Lingua Franca in the Mediterranean* (Richmond, Surrey: Curzon, 1996).

"A Mamluk Ambassador to Venice in 913/1507," *Bulletin of the School of Oriental and African Studies* 26 (1963), 503–30.

Wasserstein, David, *The Rise and Fall of the Party-Kings: Politics and Society in Islamic Spain 1002–1086* (Princeton University Press, 1985).

Watson, Andrew M., *Agricultural Innovation in the Early Islamic World* (Cambridge University Press, 1983).

Watt, Montgomery W., *The Influence of Islam on Medieval Europe* (Edinburgh University Press, 1972).

Wiegers, Gerard A., "Bibliographical Elements in Arabic and Spanish Anti-Christian and Anti-Jewish Mudéjar Writings," in A. Echevarría Arsuaga (ed.), *Biografías mudéjares*, pp. 497–515.

"El contenido de los textos árabes de los plomos: *El Libro de los misterios enormes (Kitāb al-asrār al-ʿazīma)* como polémico islámica anticristiana y antijudía," in *Nuevas aportaciones al conocimiento y estudio del Sacro Monte. VI centenario fundacional (1610–2010)*, (Granada: Fundación Euroarabe, 2011), pp. 197–214.

"'Isà b. Yabir and the Origins of Aljamiado Literature," *al-Qanṭara* 11 (1990), 155–91.
"Islam in Spain during the Early Sixteenth Century: The Views of the Four Chief Judges in Cairo (Introduction, Translation, and Arabic Text)," in Ed de Moor, Otto Zwartjes, and G. J. H. van Gelder (eds.), *Poetry, Politics, and Polemics. Cultural Transfer Between the Iberian Peninsula and North Africa* (Amsterdam: Rodopi, 1996), pp. 133–52.
*Islamic Literature in Spanish and Aljamiado: Yça of Segovia (fl. 1450), His Antecendents and Successors* (Leiden: Brill, 1994).
"Jean de Roquetaillade's Prophecies Among the Muslim Minorities of Medieval and Early Modern Christian Spain: An Islamic Version of the *Vademecum in Tribulatione*," in *The Transmission and Dynamics of Textual Sources in Islam. Essays in Honour of Harald Motzki* (Leiden: Brill, 2011), pp. 229–47.
"Language and Identity. Pluralism and the Use of Non-Muslim Languages in the Islamic West," in Jan Platvoet and Karel van der Toorn (eds.), *Pluralism and Identity. Studies in Ritual Behaviour* (Lieden: Brill, 1995), pp. 303–36.
"Managing Disaster: Networks of the Moriscos During the Process of the Expulsion From the Iberian Peninsula Around 1609," *Journal of Medieval Religious Cultures* 36 (2010), 141–68.
"Moriscos and Arabic Studies in Europe," *al-Qanṭara* 31 (2010), 587–610.
"Mudejar Biographies Contained in Arabic and Aljamiado texts," in A. Echevarría Arsuaga (ed.), *Biografías mudéjares*, pp. 497–516.
"The Persistence of Mudejar Islam? Alonso De Luna (Muhammad Abū 'l-ʿĀsī), the *Lead Books*, and the *Gospel of Barnabas*," *Mediterranean Encounters* 12 (2006), 498–518.
Winer, Rebecca Lynn, "Conscripting the Breast: Lactation, Slavery and Salvation in the Realms of Aragon and Kingdom of Majorca, c. 1250–1300," *Journal of Medieval History* 34 (2008), 164–84.
*Women, Wealth, and Community in Perpignan, c. 1250–1300: Christians, Jews, and Enslaved Muslims in a Medieval Mediterranean Town* (Aldershot: Ashgate, 2006).
Wolf, Kenneth Baxter, "*Convivencia* in Medieval Spain: A Brief History of an Idea," *Religion Compass* 3 (2008), 72–85.
Wright, Elizabeth R., "Narrating the Ineffable Lepanto: The Austrias Carmen of Joannes Latinus (Juan Latino)," *Hispanic Review* 77 (2009), 71–92.
Wright, Owen, "Music in Islamic Spain," in S. Jayyusi (ed.), *The Legacy of Muslim Spain*, pp. 555–82.
Yassine Bahri, Raja, "L'organisation interne de l' al-jamaä," in *Actes du* V *e centenaire de la chute de Grenade, 1492–1992* (Zaghouan: CEROMDI, 1993), pp. 141–61.
Zabálburu, Francisco de, *et al.*, *Collección de documentos inéditos para la historia de España*, vol. XI (Madrid: Imprenta de viuda de Calero, 1842).
Zabalo Zabalegui, Javier, *La administración del reino de Navarra en el siglo* XIV (Pamplona: Universidad de Navarra, 1973).
Zagorin, Perez, *How the Idea of Religious Toleration Came to the West* (Princeton University Press, 2003).
Zaid, Rhona, "The Muslim/Mudejar in the Cantigas of Alfonso X, El Sabio," *Sharq al-Andalus* 4 (1987), 145–52.

Zeitler, Barbara, "'Urbs Felix Dotata Populo Trilingui': Some Thoughts About a Funerary Memorial From Twelfth-Century Palermo," *Medieval Encounters* 2 (1996), 114–39.

Zilio-Grandi, Ida, "Le opere di controvèrsia islamo-cristiana nella formazione di una letteratura filosofica araba", in C. d'Ancona (ed.), *Storia della filosofia nell'Islam medievale* (Turin: Einaudi, 2005), vol. I, pp. 101–36.

Zorgati, Ragnhild Johnsrud, *Pluralism in the Middle Ages: Hybrid Identities, Conversion, and Mixed Marriages in Medieval Iberia* (New York: Routledge, 2012).

Zuccato, Marco, "Gerbert of Aurillac and a Tenth-Century Jewish Channel for the Transmission of Arabic Science to the West," *Speculum* 80 (2005), 742–63.

Zuñiga López, Ramón, "Un morisco, peregrino en La Meca en el siglo XVI," *Historia* 16 (1992), 99–104.

Zuwiyya, David D., "A Typological Approach to Aljamiado-Morisco Literature," *Qurtuba: Estudios andalusíes* 5 (2001), 187–212.

Zwartjes, Otto, "The Andalusi Kharjas: A Courtly Counterpoint to Popular Tradition?" *Scripta Mediterranea* 19–20 (1998), 45–54.

*Love Songs from al-Andalus: History, Structure, and Meaning of the Kharja* (Leiden: Brill, 1997).

# Index